SECOND EUROPEAN EDITION

MACROECONOMICS

SECOND EUROPEAN EDITION

MACROECONOMICS

N. GREGORY MANKIW

Harvard University

MARK P. TAYLOR

University of Warwick

Worth Publishers
A Macmillan Higher Education Company

Senior Vice President, Editorial and Production: Catherine Woods
Associate Publisher: Steven Rigolosi
Development Editor: Helen Bugler
Marketing Manager: Thomas Digiano
Marketing Assistant: Tess Sanders
Media Editor: Lukia Kliossis
Assistant Editor: Mary Walsh
Director of Print and Digital Development: Tracey Kuehn
Art Director: Babs Reingold
Cover and Interior Designer: Kevin Kall
Photo Editor: Brenda Harris
Production Manager: Barbara Anne Seixas
Composition: MPS Ltd.
Printing and Binding: LSC Communications

Cover Art: © Humbak/Alamy

ISBN-13: 978-1-4641-4177-5
ISBN-10: 1-4641-4177-0

Fourth printing

Worth Publishers
41 Madison Avenue
New York, NY 10010
www.worthpublishers.com
www.palgrave.com/home/index.asp

Palgrave Macmillan
Houndmills, Basingstoke
Hampshire RG21 6XS, England
www.palgrave.com/home/index.asp

about the authors

N. Gregory Mankiw is Professor of Economics at Harvard University, based in Cambridge, Massachusetts, USA. He began his study of economics at Princeton University, where he received an AB in 1980. After earning a PhD in economics from the Massachusetts Institute of Technology, he began teaching at Harvard in 1985 and was promoted to full professor in 1987. Today, he regularly teaches both undergraduate and graduate courses in macroeconomics.

Professor Mankiw is a regular participant in academic and policy debates. His research ranges across macroeconomics and includes work on price adjustment, consumer behaviour, financial markets, monetary and fiscal policy and economic growth. In addition to his duties at Harvard, he has been a research associate of the National Bureau of Economic Research, a member of the Brookings Panel on Economic Activity, and an advisor to the Federal Reserve Bank of Boston and the Congressional Budget Office. From 2003 to 2005 he was chairman of the US President's Council of Economic Advisors.

Professor Mankiw lives in Wellesley, Massachusetts, USA, with his wife Deborah; children Catherine, Nicholas and Peter; and their border terrier Tobin.

Mark P. Taylor is Dean of Warwick Business School and Professor of Finance at the University of Warwick, UK. He obtained his first degree in philosophy, politics and economics from Oxford University. He then worked as a foreign exchange dealer in London for two years, while simultaneously studying part-time for a master's degree in economics at London University, from where he also holds a doctorate in economics.

Professor Taylor has taught economics at various universities (including Warwick, Oxford, Marseille and New York). He also worked for several years as a Senior Economist at the International Monetary Fund and, before that, as an Economist at the Bank of England. His work has been published extensively in scholarly journals, such as the *Journal of Political Economy,* the *European Economic Review* and the *Economic Journal,* and he is today one of the most highly cited economists in the world in economic research. In addition, Professor Taylor has acted as an advisor to the International Monetary Fund, the World Bank, the Bank of England, the European Commission and to senior members of the UK government. He is a Research Fellow of the Centre for Economic Policy Research, Director of the UK Economic and Social Research Council's Research Programme in Macroeconomics and Chair of the ESRC's Money, Macro and Finance Research Group.

To Deborah and Anita

Those branches of politics, or of the laws of social life, on which there exists a collection of facts sufficiently sifted and methodized to form the beginning of a science should be taught *ex professo*. Among the chief of these is Political Economy, the sources and conditions of wealth and material prosperity for aggregate bodies of human beings. . . .

The same persons who cry down Logic will generally warn you against Political Economy. It is unfeeling, they will tell you. It recognises unpleasant facts. For my part, the most unfeeling thing I know of is the law of gravitation: it breaks the neck of the best and most amiable person without scruple, if he forgets for a single moment to give heed to it. The winds and waves too are very unfeeling. Would you advise those who go to sea to deny the winds and waves — or to make use of them, and find the means of guarding against their dangers? My advice to you is to study the great writers on Political Economy, and hold firmly by whatever in them you find true; and depend upon it that if you are not selfish or hardhearted already, Political Economy will not make you so.

John Stuart Mill, 1867

brief contents

Preface xxiv
Companion Website Resources xxxiv

part 1
Introduction 1

Chapter 1 The Science of Macroeconomics 3
Chapter 2 The Data of Macroeconomics 23

part 2
Classical Theory: The Economy in the Long Run 59

Chapter 3 National Income: Where It Comes From and Where It Goes 61
Chapter 4 The Monetary System: What It Is and How It Works 97
Chapter 5 Inflation: Its Causes, Effects and Social Costs 121
Chapter 6 The Open Economy 153
Chapter 7 Unemployment 201

part 3
Growth Theory: The Economy in the Very Long Run 231

Chapter 8 Economic Growth I: Capital Accumulation and Population Growth 233
Chapter 9 Economic Growth II: Technology, Empirics and Policy 265

part 4
Business Cycle Theory: The Economy in the Short Run 301

Chapter 10 Introduction to Economic Fluctuations 303

Chapter 11 Aggregate Demand I: Building the *IS-LM* Model 331
Chapter 12 Aggregate Demand II: Applying the *IS-LM* Model 359
Chapter 13 The Open Economy Revisited: The Mundell–Fleming Model and the Exchange-Rate Regime 393
Chapter 14 Aggregate Supply and the Short-Run Trade-Off between Inflation and Unemployment 437

part 5
Macroeconomic Policy Debates 469

Chapter 15 Stabilization Policy 471
Chapter 16 Government Debt 499
Chapter 17 Common Currency Areas and European Economic and Monetary Union 533

part 6
More on the Microeconomics behind Macroeconomics 565

Chapter 18 Consumption 567
Chapter 19 Investment 601
Chapter 20 The Financial System: Opportunities and Dangers 623

Epilogue What We Know, What We Don't 647

Glossary 657
Index 669

contents

Preface   xxiv

Companion Website Resources   xxxiv

part 1 Introduction   1

Chapter 1 The Science of Macroeconomics   3

1-1   What Macroeconomists Study   3

▶ CASE STUDY *Inflation and Unemployment: Some European Comparisons*   6

▶ CASE STUDY *The Historical Performance of the UK Economy*   9

1-2   How Economists Think   12

Theory as Model Building   12

▶ FYI *Using Functions to Express Relationships among Variables*   16

A Multitude of Models   16

Prices: Flexible versus Sticky   17

▶ FYI *Nobel Macroeconomists*   18

Microeconomic Thinking and Macroeconomic Models   19

1-3   How This Book Proceeds   20

Chapter 2 The Data of Macroeconomics   23

2-1   Measuring the Value of Economic Activity:
Gross Domestic Product   24

Income, Expenditure and the Circular Flow   24

▶ FYI *Stocks and Flows*   26

Rules for Computing GDP   26

▶ CASE STUDY *The Size of the Black Economy: Some International Estimates*   30

Real GDP versus Nominal GDP   31

The GDP Deflator   32

Chained-Volume Measures of Real GDP   32

▶ FYI *Two Arithmetic Tricks for Working with Percentage Changes*   33

The Components of Expenditure and the National Income Accounts   34

▶ FYI *What Is Investment?*   37

▶ CASE STUDY *GDP and Its Components*   37

Other Measures of Income   42

▶ CASE STUDY *Real GDP per Person across the European Union*   42

Seasonal Adjustment   44

2-2   Measuring the Cost of Living: The Consumer Price Index   45

The Price of a Basket of Goods   45

The CPI versus the GDP Deflator   46

Does the CPI Overstate Inflation? 47

▶ CASE STUDY *The Consumer Price Index and the Retail Price Index: A Study of European Harmony* 48

2-3 **Measuring Joblessness: The Unemployment Rate** 52

▶ CASE STUDY *Trends in Labour-Force Participation in the UK* 54

2-4 **Conclusion: From Economic Statistics to Economic Models** 56

part 2 Classical Theory: The Economy in the Long Run 59

Chapter 3 National Income: Where It Comes From and Where It Goes 61

3-1 **What Determines the Total Production of Goods and Services?** 63

The Factors of Production 63

The Production Function 63

The Supply of Goods and Services 64

3-2 **How Is National Income Distributed to the Factors of Production?** 65

Factor Prices 65

The Decisions Facing the Competitive Firm 65

The Firm's Demand for Factors 67

The Division of National Income 70

▶ CASE STUDY *The Black Death and Factor Prices* 72

The Cobb–Douglas Production Function 72

▶ FYI *The Growing Gap between Rich and Poor in the US* 75

▶ CASE STUDY *UK Labour Productivity as the Key Determinant of Real Wages* 76

3-3 **What Determines the Demand for Goods and Services?** 77

Consumption 77

Investment 79

▶ FYI *The Many Different Interest Rates* 80

Government Purchases 81

▶ CASE STUDY *Consumption, Investment and Government Purchases in European Countries* 81

3-4 **What Brings the Supply and Demand for Goods and Services into Equilibrium?** 83

Equilibrium in the Market for Goods and Services: The Supply and Demand for the Economy's Output 83

Equilibrium in the Financial Markets: The Supply and Demand for Loanable Funds 84

Changes in Saving: The Effects of Fiscal Policy 86

▶ FYI *The Financial System: Markets, Intermediaries, and the Crisis of 2008–2009* 87

▶ CASE STUDY *Wars and Interest Rates in the United Kingdom, 1730–1920* *88*

Changes in Investment Demand 90

3-5 Conclusion 92

Chapter 4 The Monetary System: What It Is and How It Works 97

4-1 What Is Money? 98

The Functions of Money 98

The Types of Money 99

▶ CASE STUDY *Cigarette Money* *99*

How Fiat Money Evolves 100

▶ CASE STUDY *Money and Social Conventions on the Island of Yap* *100*

How the Quantity of Money Is Controlled 101

▶ FYI *How Do Credit Cards Fit into the Monetary System?* *102*

How the Quantity of Money Is Measured 102

4-2 The Role of Banks in the Monetary System 105

100 Per Cent Reserve Banking 105

Fractional Reserve Banking 106

Bank Capital, Leverage and Capital Requirements 108

4-3 How Central Banks Influence the Money Supply 109

A Model of the Money Supply 109

The Three Instruments of Monetary Policy 111

▶ CASE STUDY *Quantitative Easing and the Exploding Monetary Base in the US* *113*

Problems in Controlling the Money Supply 115

▶ CASE STUDY *US Bank Failures, the Money Supply and the Great Depression* *116*

4-4 Conclusion 117

Chapter 5 Inflation: Its Causes, Effects and Social Costs 121

5-1 The Quantity Theory of Money 122

Transactions and the Quantity Equation 123

From Transactions to Income 124

The Money Demand Function and the Quantity Equation 124

The Assumption of Constant Velocity 125

Money, Prices and Inflation 126

▶ CASE STUDY *Inflation and Money Growth* *126*

5-2 Seigniorage: The Revenue from Printing Money 128

▶ CASE STUDY *The Inflation Tax and Money Growth on the Island of Yap* *129*

5-3 Inflation and Interest Rates 130

Two Interest Rates: Real and Nominal 130

The Fisher Effect 130

▶ CASE STUDY *Inflation and Nominal Interest Rates* *131*

Two Real Interest Rates: *Ex Ante* and *Ex Post*   132

▶ CASE STUDY *Nominal Interest Rates in the 19th Century*   133

5-4   The Nominal Interest Rate and the Demand for Money   134

The Cost of Holding Money   134

Future Money and Current Prices   134

5-5   The Social Costs of Inflation   136

The Layman's View and the Classical Response   136

▶ CASE STUDY *What Economists and the Public Say about Inflation*   137

The Costs of Expected Inflation   138

The Costs of Unexpected Inflation   139

One Benefit of Inflation   140

5-6   Hyperinflation   141

The Costs of Hyperinflation   141

▶ CASE STUDY *Wars, Economic Disruption and Hyperinflation*   142

The Causes of Hyperinflation   143

▶ CASE STUDY *Hyperinflation in Interwar Germany*   144

▶ CASE STUDY *Hyperinflation in Zimbabwe*   146

5-7   Conclusion: The Classical Dichotomy   147

Appendix: The Cagan Model: How Current and Future Money Affect the Price Level   150

Chapter 6 The Open Economy   153

▶ CASE STUDY *The Increasing Globalization of the World Economy*   155

6-1   The International Flows of Capital and Goods   156

The Role of Net Exports   156

International Capital Flows and the Trade Balance   157

International Flows of Goods and Capital: An Example   159

GDP, GNP, the Trade Balance and the Current Account   160

▶ FYI *The Irrelevance of Bilateral Trade Balances*   161

▶ CASE STUDY *The Current Account Balance and the Trade Balance in Some European Countries*   163

6-2   Saving and Investment in a Small Open Economy   164

Capital Mobility and the World Interest Rate   164

The Model   165

How Policies Influence the Trade Balance   166

Evaluating Economic Policy   169

▶ CASE STUDY *The US Trade Deficit*   169

▶ CASE STUDY *Why Doesn't Capital Flow to Poor Countries?*   172

6-3   Exchange Rates   173

Nominal and Real Exchange Rates   173

The Real Exchange Rate and the Trade Balance   175

The Determinants of the Real Exchange Rate   176

How Policies Influence the Real Exchange Rate   177

The Effects of Trade Policies   180

The Determinants of the Nominal Exchange Rate   181

▶ CASE STUDY *Inflation and Nominal Exchange Rates*   *182*

The Special Case of Purchasing Power Parity   183

▶ CASE STUDY *Big Mac PPP*   *185*

6-4   Conclusion: Exchange Rates, the Trade Balance and Capital Flows   187

Appendix: The Large Open Economy   191

Net Capital Outflow   191

The Model   193

Policies in the Large Open Economy   195

Conclusion   199

Chapter 7 Unemployment   201

7-1   Job Loss, Job Finding and the Natural Rate of Unemployment   202

7-2   Job Search and Frictional Unemployment   204

Government Policy and Frictional Unemployment   205

▶ CASE STUDY *Unemployment Benefit and the Rate of Job Finding*   *206*

7-3   Real-Wage Rigidity and Structural Unemployment   207

Minimum-Wage Laws   208

▶ CASE STUDY *The Secrets to Happiness: Some European Evidence*   *210*

Unions and Collective Bargaining   211

Efficiency Wages   212

▶ FYI *The Natural Rate of Unemployment and the NAIRU*   *213*

▶ CASE STUDY *Henry Ford's $5 Workday*   *214*

7-4   Labour-Market Experience: The United Kingdom   215

The Duration of Unemployment   215

Variation in the UK Unemployment Rate across Demographic Groups   216

Trends in UK Unemployment   217

Transitions Into and Out of the Labour Force   220

7-5   Labour-Market Experience: Continental Europe   221

The Rise in European Unemployment   221

Variation in European Unemployment Rates across Demographic Groups   224

▶ CASE STUDY *The European Social Model: Must It Necessarily Raise Unemployment?*   *226*

▶ CASE STUDY *Reforming French Labour Markets: I Predict a Riot*   *226*

7-6   Conclusion   227

part 3 Growth Theory: The Economy in the Very Long Run 231

Chapter 8 Economic Growth I: Capital Accumulation and Population Growth 233

8-1 The Accumulation of Capital 235
The Supply and Demand for Goods 235
Growth in the Capital Stock and the Steady State 237
Approaching the Steady State: A Numerical Example 240
▶ CASE STUDY *The Miracle of Japanese and German Growth* 242
How Saving Affects Growth 243
▶ CASE STUDY *Saving and Investment around the World* 244

8-2 The Golden Rule Level of Capital 246
Comparing Steady States 246
Finding the Golden Rule Steady State: A Numerical Example 249
The Transition to the Golden Rule Steady State 251

8-3 Population Growth 253
The Steady State with Population Growth 254
The Effects of Population Growth 255
▶ CASE STUDY *Population Growth around the World* 257
Alternative Perspectives on Population Growth 258

8-4 Conclusion 260

Chapter 9 Economic Growth II: Technology, Empirics and Policy 265

9-1 Technological Progress in the Solow Model 266
The Efficiency of Labour 266
The Steady State with Technological Progress 267
The Effects of Technological Progress 268

9-2 From Growth Theory to Growth Empirics 269
Balanced Growth 269
Convergence 270
Factor Accumulation versus Production Efficiency 271
▶ CASE STUDY *Is Free Trade Good for Economic Growth?* 272

9-3 Policies to Promote Growth 273
Evaluating the Rate of Saving 274
Changing the Rate of Saving 275
Allocating the Economy's Investment 276
Establishing the Right Institutions 278
▶ CASE STUDY *The Colonial Origins of Modern Institutions* 279
Encouraging Technological Progress 280

▶ CASE STUDY *The Worldwide Slowdown in Economic Growth: 1972–2011* 281

▶ CASE STUDY *A Tale of Two Growth Experiences* 283

9-4 Beyond the Solow Model: Endogenous Growth Theory 285

The Basic Model 286

A Two-Sector Model 287

The Microeconomics of Research and Development 288

▶ CASE STUDY *Economic Growth as a Process of Creative Destruction* 289

9-5 Conclusion 290

Appendix: Accounting for the Sources of Economic Growth 294

Increases in the Factors of Production 294

Technological Progress 296

The Sources of Growth 298

▶ CASE STUDY *Growth in the East Asian Tigers* 298

part 4 Business Cycle Theory: The Economy in the Short Run 301

Chapter 10 Introduction to Economic Fluctuations 303

10-1 The Facts about the Business Cycle 305

GDP and Its Components 305

Unemployment and Okun's Law 307

Leading Economic Indicators 310

▶ CASE STUDY *The Conference Board Index of Leading Economic Indicators* 310

10-2 Time Horizons in Macroeconomics 312

How the Short Run and Long Run Differ 312

▶ CASE STUDY *Why Are Prices Sticky?* 313

The Model of Aggregate Supply and Aggregate Demand 313

10-3 Aggregate Demand 314

The Quantity Equation as Aggregate Demand 315

Why the Aggregate Demand Curve Slopes Downward 315

Shifts in the Aggregate Demand Curve 316

10-4 Aggregate Supply 317

The Long Run: The Vertical Aggregate Supply Curve 317

The Short Run: The Horizontal Aggregate Supply Curve 318

From the Short Run to the Long Run 320

▶ CASE STUDY *Gold, the Pound Sterling and the UK Contraction of the 1920s* 321

10-5 Stabilization Policy 323

Shocks to Aggregate Demand 323

Shocks to Aggregate Supply 324

▶ CASE STUDY *How OPEC Helped Cause Stagflation in the 1970s and Euphoria in the 1980s* 326

10-6 Conclusion 328

Chapter 11 Aggregate Demand I: Building the *IS–LM* Model   331

11-1 The Goods Market and the *IS* Curve   333

The Keynesian Cross   333

▶ CASE STUDY *The Dwindling Popularity of Fiscal Policy as a Means to Fine-Tune the Economy   340*

▶ CASE STUDY *Increasing Government Purchases to Stimulate the Economy: The Obama Spending Plan   342*

The Interest Rate, Investment and the *IS* Curve   343

How Fiscal Policy Shifts the *IS* Curve   345

A Loanable-Funds Interpretation of the *IS* Curve   345

11-2 The Money Market and the *LM* Curve   348

The Theory of Liquidity Preference   348

▶ CASE STUDY *Does a Monetary Tightening Raise or Lower Interest Rates?   350*

Income, Money Demand and the *LM* Curve   352

How Monetary Policy Shifts the *LM* Curve   353

A Quantity-Equation Interpretation of the *LM* Curve   354

11-3 Conclusion: The Short-Run Equilibrium   355

Chapter 12 Aggregate Demand II: Applying the *IS-LM* Model   359

12-1 Explaining Fluctuations with the *IS-LM* Model   360

How Fiscal Policy Shifts the *IS* Curve and Changes the Short-Run Equilibrium   360

How Monetary Policy Shifts the *LM* Curve and Changes the Short-Run Equilibrium   361

The Interaction between Monetary and Fiscal Policy   363

Shocks in the *IS-LM* Model   365

▶ CASE STUDY *The International Decline in GDP Growth in 2001   366*

What Is the Central Bank's Policy Instrument: The Money Supply or the Interest Rate?   367

12-2 *IS-LM* as a Theory of Aggregate Demand   368

From the *IS-LM* Model to the Aggregate Demand Curve   368

The *IS-LM* Model in the Short Run and Long Run   371

12-3 The Great Depression   373

The Spending Hypothesis: Shocks to the *IS* Curve   374

The Money Hypothesis: A Shock to the *LM* Curve   376

The Money Hypothesis Again: The Effects of Falling Prices   377

Could the Depression Happen Again?   379

▶ CASE STUDY *The Japanese Slump of the 1990s   380*

▶ CASE STUDY *The Financial Crisis and Economic Downturn of 2008 and 2009   381*

▶ FYI *The Liquidity Trap   382*

12-4 Conclusion   384

Appendix: The Simple Algebra of the *IS-LM* Model and the Aggregate Demand Curve   388

The *IS* Curve 388

The *LM* Curve 389

The Aggregate Demand Curve 390

▶ CASE STUDY *The Effectiveness of Monetary and Fiscal Policy* 391

Chapter 13 The Open Economy Revisited: The Mundell–Fleming Model and the Exchange-Rate Regime 393

13-1 The Mundell–Fleming Model 395

The Key Assumption: Small Open Economy with Perfect Capital Mobility 395

The Goods Market and the *IS** Curve 395

The Money Market and the *LM** Curve 396

Putting the Pieces Together 399

13-2 The Small Open Economy under Floating Exchange Rates 399

Fiscal Policy 400

Monetary Policy 401

Trade Policy 402

13-3 The Small Open Economy under Fixed Exchange Rates 404

How a Fixed-Exchange-Rate System Works 404

▶ CASE STUDY *The International Gold Standard* 406

Fiscal Policy 407

Monetary Policy 408

▶ CASE STUDY *Devaluation and European Recovery from the Great Depression* 409

Trade Policy 409

Policy in the Mundell–Fleming Model: A Summary 410

13-4 Interest-Rate Differentials 411

Country Risk and Exchange-Rate Expectations 411

Differentials in the Mundell–Fleming Model 412

▶ CASE STUDY *International Financial Crisis: Mexico 1994–1995* 414

▶ CASE STUDY *International Financial Crisis: East Asia 1997–1998* 415

13-5 Should Exchange Rates Be Floating or Fixed? 416

Pros and Cons of Different Exchange-Rate Systems 416

▶ CASE STUDY *The Debate over the Euro* 417

Speculative Attacks, Currency Boards, 'Dollarization' and 'Euroization' 419

▶ CASE STUDY *International Financial Crisis: The Speculative Attack on the European Exchange Rate Mechanism, 1992* 420

The Impossible Trinity 422

▶ CASE STUDY *European Monetary Union: Squaring the Triangle?* 423

▶ CASE STUDY *The Chinese Currency Controversy* 424

13-6 From the Short Run to the Long Run: The Mundell–Fleming Model with a Changing Price Level 425

13-7 Conclusion 428

Appendix: A Short-Run Model of the Large Open Economy 431

Fiscal Policy 433

Monetary Policy   434

A Rule of Thumb   434

Chapter 14 Aggregate Supply and the Short-Run Trade-Off between Inflation and Unemployment   437

14-1 Three Models of Aggregate Supply   438

The Sticky-Price Model   439

The Sticky-Wage Model   440

▶ CASE STUDY *The Cyclical Behaviour of the Real Wage*   443

The Imperfect-Information Model   444

▶ CASE STUDY *International Differences in the Aggregate Supply Curve*   446

Summary and Implications   447

14-2 Inflation, Unemployment and the Phillips Curve   449

Deriving the Phillips Curve from the Aggregate Supply Curve   449

▶ FYI *The History of the Modern Phillips Curve*   451

Adaptive Expectations and Inflation Inertia   451

Two Causes of Rising and Falling Inflation   452

▶ CASE STUDY *Inflation and Unemployment in the United Kingdom*   453

The Short-Run Trade-Off between Inflation and Unemployment   455

Disinflation and the Sacrifice Ratio   456

▶ FYI *How Precise Are Estimates of the Natural Rate of Unemployment?*   457

Rational Expectations and the Possibility of Painless Disinflation   458

▶ CASE STUDY *The Sacrifice Ratio in Practice: The Thatcher Disinflation*   460

Hysteresis and the Challenge to the Natural-Rate Hypothesis   461

14-3 Conclusion   462

Appendix: A Big, Comprehensive Model   466

part 5 Macroeconomic Policy Debates   469

Chapter 15 Stabilization Policy   471

15-1 Should Policy Be Active or Passive?   472

Lags in the Implementation and Effects of Policies   472

The Difficult Job of Economic Forecasting   474

▶ CASE STUDY *Mistakes in Forecasting*   475

Ignorance, Expectations and the Lucas Critique   477

The Historical Record   478

▶ CASE STUDY *The Remarkable Stability of the Modern Economy*   478

15-2 Should Policy Be Conducted by Rule or by Discretion?   480

Distrust of Policy Makers and the Political Process   480

The Time Inconsistency of Discretionary Policy   481

Rules for Monetary Policy   483

The Taylor Rule of Monetary Policy   484

15-3 Inflation Targeting: Rule or Constrained Discretion? 485

The Taylor Rule and Inflation Targeting 486

15-4 Central Bank Independence 487

15-5 Inflation Targeting and Central Bank Independence 489

The European Central Bank 489

The Bank of England 490

The Riksbank 491

The Norges Bank 492

The US Federal Reserve System 492

15-6 Conclusion: Making Policy in an Uncertain World 493

Appendix: Time Inconsistency and the Trade-Off between Inflation and Unemployment 496

Chapter 16 Government Debt 499

16-1 The Size of the Government Debt 501

16-2 Problems in Measurement 503

Measurement Problem 1: Inflation 503

Measurement Problem 2: Capital Assets 504

Measurement Problem 3: Uncounted Liabilities 505

Measurement Problem 4: The Business Cycle 505

▶ FYI *Measuring National Indebtedness: General Government Gross Debt or Public Sector Net Debt? 506*

Summing Up 507

16-3 The Traditional View of Government Debt 508

▶ CASE STUDY *The Laffer Curve and Supply-Side Economics 509*

▶ FYI *Taxes and Incentives 510*

16-4 The Ricardian View of Government Debt 512

The Basic Logic of Ricardian Equivalence 513

Consumers and Future Taxes 514

▶ CASE STUDY *Why Do Parents Leave Bequests? 516*

Making a Choice 516

▶ FYI *Ricardo on Ricardian Equivalence 517*

16-5 Other Perspectives on Government Debt 517

Balanced Budgets versus Optimal Fiscal Policy 518

Fiscal Effects on Monetary Policy 519

International Dimensions 520

▶ CASE STUDY *Indexed Bonds 520*

16-6 Fiscal Sustainability, Budget Deficits and the Debt-to-GDP Ratio 523

▶ CASE STUDY *The Stability and Growth Pact: A Sneak Preview 526*

▶ CASE STUDY *The 'Golden Rule' of UK Public Finance 527*

▶ FYI *Ponzi Finance 528*

16-7 Conclusion 529

Chapter 17 Common Currency Areas and European Economic and Monetary Union 533

17-1 Common Currency Areas 534

17-2 The Benefits of a Single Currency 535
Reduction in Transactions Costs in Trade 535
Reduction in Price Discrimination 536
Reduction in Foreign-Exchange-Rate Variability 537

17-3 The Costs of a Single Currency 537
Loss of Monetary Policy Sovereignty 537
Asymmetric Demand Shocks 537
Asymmetric Supply Shocks 541
Loss of Fiscal Policy Sovereignty 541

17-4 The Theory of Optimum Currency Areas 543
Characteristics that Reduce the Costs of a Single Currency 544
Characteristics that Increase the Benefits of a Single Currency 547

17-5 Is Europe an Optimum Currency Area? 548
Summing Up: Is Europe an Optimum Currency Area? 553

17-6 Fiscal Policy and Common Currency Areas 554
Fiscal Federalism 554
National Fiscal Policies in a Currency Union: The Free-Rider Problem 555
The Stability and Growth Pact 557
▶ CASE STUDY *The Euro Area Crisis* 559

17-7 Conclusion 560

part 6 More on the Microeconomics behind Macroeconomics 565

Chapter 18 Consumption 567

18-1 John Maynard Keynes and the Consumption Function 568
Keynes's Conjectures 568
The Early Empirical Successes 570
Secular Stagnation, Simon Kuznets and the Consumption Puzzle 570

18-2 Irving Fisher and Intertemporal Choice 572
The Intertemporal Budget Constraint 572
▶ FYI *Present Value, or Why European Lottery Prizes Are Worth More than US Lottery Prizes* 575
Consumer Preferences 576
Optimization 577
How Changes in Income Affect Consumption 578

How Changes in the Real Interest Rate Affect Consumption   579

Constraints on Borrowing   581

▶ CASE STUDY *The High Japanese Saving Rate*   *583*

18-3 Franco Modigliani and the Life-Cycle Hypothesis   584

The Hypothesis   585

Implications   585

▶ CASE STUDY *The Consumption and Saving of the Elderly*   *587*

18-4 Milton Friedman and the Permanent-Income Hypothesis   589

The Hypothesis   589

Implications   590

▶ CASE STUDY *The Contrasting Effects of Permanent and
Temporary Tax Changes*   *591*

18-5 Robert Hall and the Random-Walk Hypothesis   592

The Hypothesis   592

Implications   592

▶ CASE STUDY *Do Predictable Changes in Income Lead to Predictable
Changes in Consumption?*   *593*

18-6 David Laibson and the Pull of Instant Gratification   594

▶ CASE STUDY *How to Encourage People to Save More: A Proposal from the Field of
Behavioural Economics*   *595*

18-7 Conclusion   596

Chapter 19 Investment   601

19-1 Business Fixed Investment   602

The Rental Price of Capital   603

The Cost of Capital   604

The Determinants of Investment   606

Taxes and Investment   608

The Stock Market and Tobin's q 609

▶ CASE STUDY *The Stock Market as an Economic Indicator*   *610*

Alternative Views of the Stock Market: The Efficient Markets Hypothesis versus
Keynes's Beauty Contest   612

Financing Constraints   614

▶ CASE STUDY *Banking Crises and Credit Crunches*   *615*

19-2 Residential Investment   615

The Stock Equilibrium and the Flow Supply   616

Changes in Housing Demand   617

19-3 Inventory Investment   618

Reasons for Holding Inventories   618

The Accelerator Model of Inventories   619

Inventories and the Real Interest Rate   620

19-4 Conclusion   620

Chapter 20 The Financial System: Opportunities and Dangers   623

20-1 What Does the Financial System Do?   624

Financing Investment   624

Sharing Risk   625

Dealing with Asymmetric Information   626

Fostering Economic Growth   628

▶ CASE STUDY *Microfinance: Professor Yunus's Profound Idea*   629

20-2 Financial Crises   630

The Anatomy of a Crisis   630

▶ FYI *The TED Spread*   632

▶ CASE STUDY *Who Should Be Blamed for the Financial Crisis of 2008 and 2009?*   635

Policy Responses to a Crisis   636

Policies to Prevent Crises   639

▶ FYI *CoCo Bonds*   640

▶ CASE STUDY *The European Sovereign Debt Crisis*   642

20-3 Conclusion   643

Epilogue What We Know, What We Don't   647

The Four Most Important Lessons of Macroeconomics   647

Lesson 1: In the Long Run, a Country's Capacity to Produce Goods and Services Determines the Standard of Living of its Residents   648

Lesson 2: In the Short Run, Aggregate Demand Influences the Amount of Goods and Services that a Country Produces   648

Lesson 3: In the Long Run, the Rate of Money Growth Determines the Rate of Inflation, But It Does Not Affect the Rate of Unemployment   649

Lesson 4: In the Short Run, Policy Makers Who Control Monetary and Fiscal Policy Face a Trade-off Between Inflation and Unemployment   650

The Four Most Important Unresolved Questions of Macroeconomics   650

Question 1: How Should Policy Makers Try to Promote Growth in the Economy's Natural Level of Output?   650

Question 2: Should Policy Makers Try to Stabilize the Economy?   651

Question 3: How Costly Is Inflation, and How Costly Is Reducing Inflation?   653

Question 4: How Big a Problem Are Government Budget Deficits?   654

Conclusion   655

Glossary   657

Index   669

preface

An economist must be 'mathematician, historian, statesman, philosopher, in some degree . . . as aloof and incorruptible as an artist, yet sometimes as near the earth as a politician'. So remarked John Maynard Keynes, the great British economist who, as much as anyone, could be called the father of macroeconomics. No single statement summarizes better what it means to be an economist.

As Keynes's assessment suggests, students who aim to learn economics need to draw on many disparate talents. The job of helping students find and develop these talents falls to lecturers and textbook authors. When writing this textbook for intermediate-level courses in macroeconomics, our goal was to make macroeconomics understandable, relevant and (believe it or not) fun. Those of us who have chosen to be professional macroeconomists have done so because we are fascinated by the field. More importantly, we believe that the study of macroeconomics can illuminate much about the world, and that the lessons learned, if properly applied, can make the world a better place. We hope this book conveys not only our profession's accumulated wisdom, but also its enthusiasm and sense of purpose.

This Book's Approach

Although macroeconomists share a common body of knowledge, they do not all have the same perspective on how that knowledge is best taught. So let's begin by setting out five of our objectives, which together define this book's approach to the field.

First, we try to offer a balance between short-run and long-run issues in macroeconomics. All economists agree that public policies and other events influence the economy over different time horizons. We live in our own short run, but we also live in the long run that our parents bequeathed to us. As a result, courses in macroeconomics need to cover both short-run topics, such as the business cycle and stabilization policy, and long-run topics, such as economic growth, the natural rate of unemployment, persistent inflation and the effects of government debt. Neither time horizon trumps the other.

Second, we integrate the insights of Keynesian and classical theories. Although Keynes's *General Theory* provides the foundation for much of our current understanding of economic fluctuations, it is important to remember that classical economics provides the right answers to many fundamental questions. In this book we incorporate many of the contributions of the classical economists before Keynes and the new classical economists of the past two decades. Substantial coverage is given, for example, to the loanable-funds theory of the interest rate, the quantity theory of money and the problem of time inconsistency. At the same time, we recognize that many of the ideas of Keynes and the new Keynesians are necessary for understanding economic fluctuations. Substantial coverage is given also to the *IS-LM* model of aggregate demand, the short-run trade-off between inflation and unemployment, and modern theories of wage and price rigidity.

Third, we present macroeconomics using a variety of simple models. Instead of pretending that there is one model that is complete enough to explain all facets of the economy, we encourage students to learn how to use and compare a set of prominent models. This approach has the pedagogical value that each model can be kept relatively simple and presented within one or two chapters. More important, this approach asks students to think like economists, who always keep various models in mind when analysing economic events or public policies.

Fourth, we emphasize that macroeconomics is an empirical discipline, motivated and guided by a wide array of experience. This book contains numerous case studies that use macroeconomic theory to shed light on real-world data or events. To highlight the broad applicability of the basic theory, we have drawn the case studies both from current issues facing the world's economies and from dramatic historical episodes. The case studies teach the reader how to apply economic principles to issues involving the European and global economies, the island of Yap, the land of Oz and items in today's newspapers.

Fifth, we have tried to write a book that has a distinctively European focus. Although we discuss important aspects of the global economy, and important economies such as those of the US and Japan, we have attempted to relate macroeconomic analysis to an environment that will be familiar and interesting to a European student. We also examine some important issues relevant to the European economy, such as the single European currency, and use European examples whenever possible in our discussion of the macroeconomy and economic institutions. The case studies also draw largely – although not exclusively – on European material.

What's New in the Second European Edition?

This new European edition is an updated version of the 1st European edition and brings in the latest relevant material from the US 8th edition of *Macroeconomics* whilst also updating the book from a European perspective.

A significant change since the 1st European edition concerns the effects of the global financial crisis of 2008–2009 and how this has affected policy makers and regulators. This has led to a reorganization of some of the material in this new edition. For example, monetary policy makers at the central banks have engaged in a variety of unconventional measures to prop up a weak banking system and promote recovery from the deep recession. Understanding these policies requires a strong background in the details of the monetary system. As a result, this edition covers the topic earlier in the book than it did previously. A complete treatment of the monetary system and the tools of monetary policy (formerly in Chapter 19) can now be found in Chapter 4. The second part of the original Chapter 4 now forms Chapter 5, with consequential changes in chapter numbering thereafter.

The biggest change in the book is the addition of a new Chapter 20, 'The Financial System: Opportunities and Dangers'. Over the past several years, in the aftermath of the financial crisis and economic downturn of 2008 and 2009, economists have developed a renewed appreciation of the crucial linkages between the financial system and the broader economy. Chapter 20 gives students a deeper look at this topic. It begins by discussing the functions of the financial system. It then discusses the causes and effects of financial crises, as well as the government policies that aim to deal with crises and to prevent future ones.

In addition, the following changes have been made:

- Numerous tables and figures have been updated with new data where that is available, and, where the EU has widened, those new countries have been included.

- There are many new and substantially adapted cases in the light of the recent worldwide economic turmoil. Reviewers of this second European edition have been keen that we do not focus on the EU to the exclusion of the US, and, where US cases have resonance in Europe, these are included. New 'Case Studies' and new 'For Your Information' sections to this edition are:

  Chapter 3: FYI: The Growing Gap between Rich and Poor in the US; The Financial System: Markets, Intermediaries, and the Crisis of 2008–2009

  Chapter 4: Case Study: Quantitative Easing and the Exploding Monetary Base in the US

  Chapter 5: Case Study: Hyperinflation in Zimbabwe

  Chapter 10: Case Study: The Conference Board Index of Leading Economic Indicators

  Chapter 11: Case Study: Increasing Government Purchases to Stimulate the Economy: The Obama Spending Plan

  Chapter 12: Case Study: The Financial Crisis and Economic Downturn of 2008 and 2009

  Chapter 13: Case Study: The Debate over the Euro

  Chapter 15: Case Study: Mistakes in Forecasting

  Chapter 17: Case Study: The Euro Area crisis

  Chapter 20: Case Studies: Microfinance: Professor Yunus's Profound Idea; Who Should Be Blamed for the Financial Crisis of 2008 and 2009?; The European Sovereign Debt Crisis

  Chapter 20: FYI: The TED Spread; CoCo bonds

  With the exception of the Chapter 17 Case Study, the new cases and FYI boxes will be familiar to users of the US 8th edition, although all cases are adapted for the European market where appropriate.

- Two appendices on large open economies originally from the US 8th edition, but treating the Euro Area as such an economy, are included in this new edition.

As always, all the changes that we made, and the many others that we considered, were evaluated keeping in mind the benefits of brevity. From our own experience as students, we know that long books are less likely to be read. Our goal in this book is to offer the clearest, most up-to-date, most accessible course in macroeconomics in the fewest words possible.

The Arrangement of Topics

Our strategy for teaching macroeconomics is first to examine the long run when prices are flexible and then to examine the short run when prices are sticky. This approach has several advantages. First, because the classical dichotomy permits the separation of real and monetary issues, the long-run material is easier for students to understand. Second, when students begin studying short-run fluctuations, they understand fully the long-run equilibrium around which the economy is fluctuating. Third, beginning with market-clearing models makes clearer the link between macroeconomics and microeconomics. Fourth, students learn first the material that is less controversial among macroeconomists. For all these reasons, the strategy of beginning with long-run classical models simplifies the teaching of macroeconomics.

Let's now move from strategy to tactics. What follows is a whirlwind tour of the book.

Part 1: Introduction

The introductory material in Part 1 is brief so that students can get to the core topics quickly. Chapter 1 discusses the broad questions that macroeconomists address and the economist's approach of building models to explain the world. Chapter 2 introduces the key data of macroeconomics, emphasizing gross domestic product, the consumer price index and the unemployment rate.

Part 2: Classical Theory: The Economy in the Long Run

Part 2 examines the long run over which prices are flexible. Chapter 3 presents the basic classical model of national income. In this model, the factors of production and the production technology determine the level of income, and the marginal products of the factors determine its distribution to households. In addition, the model shows how fiscal policy influences the allocation of the economy's resources among consumption, investment and government purchases, and it highlights how the real interest rate equilibrates the supply and demand for goods and services.

Money and the price level are introduced next. Chapter 4 examines the monetary system and the tools of monetary policy. Chapter 5 begins the discussion of the effects of monetary policy. Because prices are assumed to be fully flexible, the chapters present the prominent ideas of classical monetary theory: the quantity theory of money, the inflation tax, the Fisher effect, the social costs of inflation and the causes and costs of hyperinflation.

The study of open-economy macroeconomics begins in Chapter 6. Maintaining the assumption of full employment, this chapter presents models to explain the trade balance and the exchange rate. Various policy issues are addressed: the relationship between the budget deficit and the trade deficit, the macroeconomic impact of protectionist trade policies and the effect of monetary policy on the value of a currency in the market for foreign exchange.

Chapter 7 relaxes the assumption of full employment by discussing the dynamics of the labour market and the natural rate of unemployment. It examines various causes of unemployment, including job search, minimum-wage laws, union power and efficiency wages. It also presents some important facts about patterns of unemployment.

Part 3: Growth Theory: The Economy in the Very Long Run

Part 3 makes the classical analysis of the economy dynamic by developing the tools of modern growth theory. Chapter 8 introduces the Solow growth model as a description of how the economy evolves over time. This chapter emphasizes the roles of capital accumulation and population growth. Chapter 9 then adds technological progress to the Solow model. It uses the model to discuss growth experiences around the world as well as public policies that influence the level and growth of the standard of living. Finally, Chapter 9 introduces students to the modern theories of endogenous growth.

Part 4: Business Cycle Theory: The Economy in the Short Run

Part 4 examines the short run when prices are sticky. It begins in Chapter 10 by examining some of the key facts that describe short-run fluctuations in economic activity. The chapter then introduces the model of aggregate supply and aggregate demand, as well as the role of stabilization policy. Subsequent chapters refine the ideas introduced in this chapter.

Chapters 11 and 12 look more closely at aggregate demand. Chapter 11 presents the Keynesian cross and the theory of liquidity preference, and uses these models as building blocks for developing the *IS-LM* model. Chapter 12 uses the *IS-LM* model to explain economic fluctuations and the aggregate demand curve. It concludes with an extended case study of the Great Depression.

The study of short-run fluctuations continues in Chapter 13, which focuses on aggregate demand in an open economy. This chapter presents the Mundell-Fleming model and shows how monetary and fiscal policies affect the economy under floating and fixed-exchange-rate systems. It also discusses the debate over whether exchange rates should be floating or fixed.

Chapter 14 looks more closely at aggregate supply. It examines various approaches to explaining the short-run aggregate supply curve and discusses the short-run trade-off between inflation and unemployment.

Part 5: Macroeconomic Policy Debates

Once the student has command of standard long-run and short-run models of the economy, the book uses these models as the foundation for discussing some of the key debates over economic policy. Chapter 15 considers the debate over how policy makers should respond to short-run economic fluctuations. It emphasizes two broad questions. Should monetary and fiscal policy be active or passive? Should policy be conducted by rule or by discretion? The chapter presents arguments on both sides of these questions and discusses current policy issues such as central bank independence and inflation targeting.

Chapter 16 focuses on the various debates over government debt. It gives some sense about the magnitude of government indebtedness, discusses why measuring budget deficits is not always straightforward, recaps the traditional view of the effects of government debt, presents Ricardian equivalence as an alternative view and discusses various other perspectives on government debt. We also discuss fiscal policy rules such as the European Stability and Growth Pact and the UK 'Golden Rule' of public finance. As in the previous chapter, students are not handed conclusions, but are given the tools with which to evaluate the alternative viewpoints on their own.

Chapter 17 uses the macroeconomic tools developed in previous chapters to analyse issues relating to common currency areas – situations where a group of countries adopt the same currency and have a single monetary policy. We spend some time analysing the costs and benefits for a group of countries to adopt a single, common currency and some of the issues regarding fiscal policy that arise in this connection. Rather than discuss these issues in an abstract way, throughout the discussion we focus on the European Economic and Monetary Union (EMU) in order to illustrate the analysis. We analyse whether or not Europe is an 'optimum currency area' and, in a case study, analyse the recent Euro Area crisis.

Part 6: More on the Microeconomics behind Macroeconomics

After developing theories to explain the economy in the long run and in the short run, and then applying those theories to macroeconomic policy debates, the book turns to several topics that refine our understanding of the economy. The last chapters analyse more fully the microeconomics behind macroeconomics. These chapters can be presented at the end of a course, or they can be covered earlier, depending on the preferences of the lecturer.

Chapter 18 presents the various theories of consumer behaviour, including the Keynesian consumption function, Fisher's model of inter-temporal choice, Modigliani's life-cycle hypothesis, Friedman's permanent-income hypothesis, Hall's random-walk hypothesis and Laibson's model of instant gratification. Chapter 19 examines the theory behind the investment function.

Chapter 20 discusses the financial system and its linkages to the overall economy. It begins by examining what the financial system does: financing investment, sharing risk, dealing with asymmetric information, and fostering economic growth. It then discusses the causes of financial crises, their macro-economic impact, and the policies that might mitigate their effects and reduce their likelihood.

Epilogue

The book ends with a brief epilogue that reviews the broad lessons about which most macroeconomists agree and discusses some of the most important open questions. Regardless of which chapters a lecturer chooses to cover, this capstone chapter can be used to remind students how the many models and themes of macroeconomics relate to one another. Here and throughout the book, we emphasize that despite the disagreements among macroeconomists, there is much that we know about how the economy works.

Alternative Routes through the Text

Although we have organized the material in the way that we prefer to teach intermediate-level macroeconomics, we understand that other lecturers have different preferences. We tried to keep this in mind as we wrote the book, so that it would offer a degree of flexibility. Here are a few ways that lecturers might consider rearranging the material:

- Some lecturers are eager to cover short-run economic fluctuations. For such a course, we recommend covering Chapters 1 to 5, so that students are grounded in the basics of classical theory, and then jumping to Chapters 10, 11, 12 and 14, to cover the model of aggregate demand and aggregate supply.

- Some lecturers are eager to cover long-run economic growth. These lecturers can cover Chapters 8 and 9 immediately after Chapter 3.

- A lecturer who wants to defer (or even skip) open-economy macro-economics can put off Chapters 6, 13 and 17 without loss of continuity.

- A lecturer who wants to emphasize the microeconomic foundations of macroeconomics can teach Chapters 18 and 19 early in the course, such as immediately after Chapter 7 (or even earlier).

We hope we have embedded a sufficient degree of flexibility into the book for it to complement well a variety of approaches to the field.

Learning Tools

We have tried to make the book user-friendly in a number of ways.

Case Studies

Economics comes to life when it is applied to understanding actual events. Therefore, the numerous case studies are an important learning tool, integrated closely with the theoretical material presented in each chapter. The frequency with which these case studies occur ensures that a student does not have to grapple with an overdose of theory before seeing the theory applied.

FYI Boxes

These boxes present ancillary material 'for your information'. We use these boxes to clarify difficult concepts, to provide additional information about the tools of economics and to show how economics relates to our daily lives.

Graphs

Understanding graphical analysis is a key part of learning macroeconomics, and we have worked hard to make the figures easy to follow. We often use comment boxes within figures that describe briefly and draw attention to the important points that the figures illustrate. They should help students both learn and review the material.

Mathematical Notes

We use occasional mathematical footnotes to keep more difficult material out of the body of the text. These notes make an argument more rigorous or present a proof of a mathematical result. They can easily be skipped by those students who have not been introduced to the necessary mathematical tools.

Chapter Summaries

Every chapter ends with a brief, non-technical summary of its major lessons. Students can use the summaries to place the material in perspective and to review for examinations.

Key Concepts

Learning the language of a field is a major part of any course. Within the chapter, each key concept is in **bold type** when it is introduced. At the end of the chapter, the key concepts are listed for review.

Questions for Review

After studying a chapter, students can immediately test their understanding of its basic lessons by answering the Questions for Review.

Problems and Applications

Every chapter includes Problems and Applications designed for coursework assignments. Some of these are numerical applications of the theory in the chapter. Others encourage the student to go beyond the material in the chapter by addressing new issues that are closely related to the chapter topics.

Chapter Appendices

Several chapters include appendices that offer additional material, sometimes at a higher level of mathematical sophistication. These are designed so that lecturers can cover certain topics in greater depth if they wish. The appendices can be skipped altogether without loss of continuity.

Glossary

To help students become familiar with the language of macroeconomics, a glossary of more than 250 terms is provided at the back of the book.

Translations

The English-language version of this book has been used in dozens of countries. To make the book more accessible for students around the world, editions are (or soon will be) available in 15 other languages: Armenian, Chinese, French, German, Greek, Hungarian, Indonesian, Italian, Japanese, Korean, Portuguese, Romanian, Russian, Spanish and Ukrainian. In addition, a Canadian adaptation co-authored with William Scarth (McMaster University) is available. Lecturers who would like information about these versions of the book should contact Worth Publishers.

Acknowledgements

We would like to thank:

Dr David McCausland
University of Aberdeen, UK

for his excellent work in updating this new edition, and

Dr Alexandros Zangelidis
University of Aberdeen, UK

for his careful assistance.

A number of reviewers have given up their scarce time to help us improve the economics and pedagogy of this text. We are grateful to the following people who provided us with detailed feedback for the first European edition: Dr Toke Aidt, Dr Yunus Aksoy, Dr Rakesh Bissoonddeal, Dr Derick Boyd, Dr David Domeij, Dr Giulio Fella, Professor John Fender, Dr Martin Floden, Dr Christopher J Gerry, Dr Emanuel Kohlsheen, Professor Oliver Landmann, Dr Stephen McKnight, Dr Karen Mumford, Dr Geethanjali, Mr Oliver Taylor, and Dr Chris Tsoukis. We would also like to acknowledge the many lecturers around Europe who helped inform the second European edition of this book and in particular:

Dr Fredrik N. G. Andersson
Lund University, Sweden

Dr Vincent Hogan
University College Dublin, Ireland

Professor Asbjørn Rødseth
University of Oslo, Norway

Dr Marc Schramm
Utrecht University, Netherlands

Dr Niels-Henrik Topp
University of Copenhagen, Denmark

Dr James Watson
University of East Anglia, UK

The people at Worth Publishers have continued to be congenial and dedicated. In particular, Sarah Dorger, the Economics Editor who co-ordinated the revision process for this edition; Steven Rigolosi, Associate Publisher; Tracey Kuehn, Director of Print and Digital Development; Lukia Kliossis, Media Editor; and Mary Walsh, Associate Development Editor.

Thank you also to those at Palgrave Macmillan who have been helpful in the development of this text, especially Jaime Marshall, Helen Bugler, Nikini Jayatunga, Elizabeth Stone and Isobel Munday, and all the sales representatives who contributed useful feedback.

Our wives, Deborah and Anita, provided, as always, the right mix of moral support, criticism and encouragement.

Finally, we should like to thank our children, Catherine, Nicholas and Peter Mankiw, and Ben, Oliver and Harriet Taylor. They helped immensely by providing a pleasant distraction and by reminding us that textbooks are written for the next generation.

N. Gregory Mankiw
Cambridge, Massachusetts, USA

Mark P. Taylor
Kenilworth, Warwickshire, England

December 2013

companion website resources

www.worthpublishers.com/mankiwtaylor2e

The companion website provides a range of activities to aid the lecturer and motivate the student throughout the course.

For students the site offers opportunities to practise and review key concepts through:

- *Self-test questions.* Students can test their knowledge of the material in the book by taking multiple-choice tests on any chapter or combination of chapters.

- *Web links.* For each chapter web links are suggested to guide and encourage students to further their understanding of macroeconomics.

- *Flashcards.* For each chapter flashcards test key vocabulary.

For lecturers the site offers many resources and teaching materials to help enhance their course, including:

- *Lecture PowerPoint Slides.* These feature graphs with effective animation, careful explanations of the core material, additional case studies and data, helpful notes to the lecturer and innovative pedagogical features. Designed to be customized or used 'as is', they include easy instructions for lecturers who have little experience with PowerPoint.

- *Lecturers' Resource Manual.* This contains Additional Case Studies, Case Study Extensions, Advanced Topics and Additional Readings for every chapter.

- *Solutions Manual.* This includes solutions to all of the Questions for Review and Problems and Applications contained within the textbook.

- *Test Bank.* Over 2500 multiple-choice questions, numerical problems and short-answer graphical questions to accompany each chapter of the text, for lecturers to set in assessments or examinations.

- *Image Gallery.* Lecturers have access to all of the textbook illustrations and tables.

PART I

Introduction

CHAPTER 1

The Science of Macroeconomics

The whole of science is nothing more than the refinement of everyday thinking.
— *Albert Einstein*

When Albert Einstein made the above observation about the nature of science, he was probably referring to physics, chemistry and other natural sciences. But the statement is equally true when applied to social sciences such as economics. As a participant in the economy, and as a citizen in a democracy, you cannot help but think about economic issues as you go about your life or when you enter the voting booth. But, if you are like most people, your everyday thinking about economics has probably been casual rather than rigorous (or at least it was before you took your first economics course). The goal of studying economics is to refine that thinking. This book aims to help you in that endeavour, focusing on the part of the field called macroeconomics, which studies the forces that influence the economy as a whole.

1-1 What Macroeconomists Study

Why have some countries experienced rapid growth in incomes over the past century while others stay mired in poverty? Why do some countries have high rates of inflation while others maintain stable prices? Why do some countries have higher rates of unemployment than others? Why do all countries experience recessions and depressions – recurrent periods of falling incomes and rising unemployment – and how can government policy reduce the frequency and severity of these episodes? **Macroeconomics** attempts to answer these and many related questions.

To appreciate the importance of macroeconomics, you need only read the newspaper or listen to the news. Every day you can see headlines such as '*Euro Area (Eurozone) unemployment touches fresh high*', '*Britain's rating cut sparks new sterling fears*' or '*Euro Area recovery stutters as France weakens*'. Although these macroeconomic events may seem abstract, they touch all our lives. University graduates looking for jobs hope that the economy will boom and that firms will be taking on new staff. Investment by firms may be cut back if the cost of borrowing rises, and exports may suffer if the changes in the exchange rate makes their products less competitive. Businesses need to forecast how the demand for their products will be affected if consumers' income falls, or they are unable to get loans to fund their purchases.

Because the state of the economy affects everyone, macroeconomic issues play a central role in national political debates. Voters are aware of how the economy is doing, and they know that government policy can affect the economy in powerful ways. As a result, government popularity often rises when the economy is doing well and falls when it is performing poorly.

Macroeconomic issues are also at the centre of world politics, and international news is filled with macroeconomic questions. Should the United Kingdom leave the European Union? Why is the unemployment rate so much higher in Germany, France, Spain and many other Continental European countries than it is in the UK or the US? Why is the US running very large trade deficits and how does this affect other countries? How can poor nations raise their standard of living? When world leaders meet, these topics are often high on their agenda.

Although the job of making economic policy belongs to world leaders, the task of explaining how the economy as a whole functions falls to macroeconomists. Towards this end, macroeconomists collect data on incomes, prices, unemployment and many other variables from different time periods and different countries. They then attempt to formulate general theories that help to explain these data. Like astronomers studying the evolution of stars or biologists studying the evolution of species, macroeconomists cannot conduct controlled experiments in a laboratory. Instead, they must make use of the data that history provides them with. Macroeconomists observe that economies differ from one another and that they change over time. These observations provide both the motivation for developing macroeconomic theories and the data for testing them.

To be sure, macroeconomics is a young and imperfect science. The macroeconomist's ability to predict the future course of economic events is no better than the meteorologist's ability to predict next month's weather. But, as you will see, macroeconomists do know a great deal about how economies work. This knowledge is useful for explaining economic events and for formulating economic policy.

Every era has its own economic problems. Consider, for example, the macroeconomic history of the United Kingdom and Germany over the last 60 or 70 years. In the immediate post-war period, with the memory of the high unemployment rates that had prevailed in the 1930s still fresh in people's minds, the UK government committed itself to maintaining low unemployment and largely used expansionary fiscal policy (higher government expenditure and/or lower taxation) in an attempt to achieve this. While this policy did have an effect on unemployment by increasing the total amount of goods and services demanded, it also led to perennial balance of payments crises, as people responded to increased government spending or tax cuts by demanding more imports as well as home-produced goods, so that the UK imported far more than it exported. Thus, throughout the 1950s and 1960s, successive British governments wrestled with the problem of keeping unemployment low while avoiding excessive balance of payments deficits. In the 1970s, as UK inflation moved into double figures following the oil price shocks of 1973–1974 and 1978–1979, the government abandoned the promise of full employment and turned its attention to trying to control inflation. From the late 1970s onwards, under Prime Minister Margaret Thatcher, it tried to do this largely by attempting to control the money supply. While Mrs Thatcher did succeed in bringing down inflation, from around 20 per cent in 1980 to about 5 per cent in 1983, this was at the cost of significantly increasing unemployment, from around 6 per cent of the labour force when Mrs Thatcher took office in 1979, to approximately double that figure in 1983. Moreover, controlling the money supply turned out to be difficult and the government looked for other means of controlling inflation. In the late 1980s and early 1990s, it tried to use the exchange rate as a policy instrument by linking it to the value of European currencies – a policy that came to an abrupt end in 1992 when the foreign exchange markets launched a massive speculative attack on sterling, forcing the link to be broken. From the mid-1990s until the late 2000s, the UK enjoyed a sustained period of low inflation coupled with steady income growth, and used a macroeconomic policy of inflation targeting, whereby the Bank of England raised interest rates whenever its forecasts of inflation exceeded a certain target level. This period of sustained growth came to an abrupt end with the financial crisis of 2008 and the bankruptcy or near bankruptcy of many financial institutions. An era characterized by rising house prices, cheap credit and lax regulation gave way to a period of falling house prices, constrained credit and increasing calls for financial regulation. The spectre of the Great Depression of the 1930s reared its head again. The period of protracted downturn that persists to this day has challenged policy makers to find an appropriate balance between fiscal and monetary stimulus needed to prevent a recurrence of the mass unemployment during the Great Depression against the need to control the greatly expanded levels of government debt.

Let us now compare the UK experience with that of Germany. Following World War II, Germany split into two countries, known simply as West Germany and East Germany, until in 1990 the two countries were reunited. West Germany was a democratic nation that grew out of the post-war sectors controlled by the US, the UK and France, as opposed to East Germany which was a socialist state and satellite state of the Soviet Union. Compared with the UK, West Germany's post-war experience with controlling inflation, keeping unemployment low and maintaining relatively high economic growth was, by and large, much happier. Indeed, West Germany's post-war macroeconomic policy success was a major argument for linking the value of sterling to the Deutschmark in the late 1980s. In 1990, however, when West Germany and East Germany were reunited into a single country, a choice had to be made as to the rate at which the currency of the former East Germany, the Ostmark, would be exchanged for the Deutschmark. East German prices were three or four times the level of West German prices, but, for political reasons, the Ostmark's exchange rate was fixed at 1 Deutschmark. As a result, East German producers could not withstand the competition from cheaper West German producers and the East German region became persistently depressed. To maintain East German incomes through the

1990s required large budgetary transfers of roughly 4 per cent of German GDP annually to the former East from the former West. This was a major reason why Germany for many years after reunification had both high unemployment and large government budget deficits.

Notwithstanding Germany's travails over unification, however, the UK experience of steady income growth and stable inflation from the mid-1990s, based largely on a policy of inflation targeting, was not unusual among many developed countries, including the US and much of Europe. Indeed, by the mid-2000s, many came to believe that the familiar cycle of boom and bust – rapid expansion of the economy combined with spiralling inflation, followed by a sudden fall in both output and inflation – had finally been laid to rest. Meanwhile, the introduction of a common currency, the euro, between many major European countries, introduced in 1999, was approaching its first decade of operation without any major crises. Between 2007 and 2008, however, the world experienced a dramatic financial crisis that triggered a sharp recession in many countries from which they are still struggling to recover. In Europe, the financial crisis and the ensuing recession opened up serious problems with the functioning of the euro, and the implications for macroeconomic policy are still being worked out as this book is being written.

As these two cases make clear, macroeconomic circumstances change over time, sometimes radically. The basic principles of macroeconomics do not change from decade to decade, but the macroeconomist must apply these principles with flexibility and creativity to meet changing circumstances.

CASE STUDY

Inflation and Unemployment: Some European Comparisons

Economists use many types of data to measure the performance of an economy. Two important macroeconomic variables are the inflation rate and the unemployment rate. The **inflation rate** measures how fast prices are rising. The **unemployment rate** measures the fraction of the labour force that is out of work. Macroeconomists study how these variables are determined, why they vary over time and across countries, and how they interact with one another.

Table 1-1 shows the unemployment rate for a number of European economies, as well as for the US, over the period 2003–2012. Perhaps the most striking feature of Table 1-1 is the relatively high rates of unemployment in many Continental European countries compared with the UK and the US. Taken together, in the 17 countries that have adopted the euro as their common currency and make up the Euro Area,[1] the unemployment rate diminished a little

---

[1] The 17 Euro Area countries referred to here are Belgium, Germany, Spain, France, Ireland, Italy, Luxembourg, the Netherlands, Austria, Portugal, Finland, Greece, Slovenia, Cyprus, Malta, Slovakia and Estonia.

TABLE 1-1

European and US Unemployment Rates 2003–2012

	2003	2004	2005	2006	2007	2008	2009	2010	2011	2012
European Union (27 countries)	9.1	9.3	9.0	8.3	7.2	7.1	9.0	9.7	9.7	10.5
Euro Area (17 countries)	9.0	9.3	9.2	8.5	7.6	7.6	9.6	10.1	10.2	11.4
Belgium	8.2	8.4	8.5	8.3	7.5	7.0	7.9	8.3	7.2	7.3
Bulgaria	13.7	12.1	10.1	9.0	6.9	5.6	6.8	10.3	11.3	12.2
Czech Republic	:	:	:	:	:	:	6.7	7.3	6.7	7.0
Denmark	5.4	5.5	4.8	3.9	3.8	3.4	6.0	7.5	7.6	7.5
Germany	9.8	10.5	11.3	10.3	8.7	7.5	7.8	7.1	5.9	5.5
Estonia	10.1	9.7	7.9	5.9	4.6	5.5	13.8	16.9	12.5	10.2
Ireland	4.6	4.5	4.4	4.5	4.7	6.4	12.0	13.9	14.7	14.8
Greece	9.7	10.5	9.9	8.9	8.3	7.7	9.5	12.6	17.7	24.3
Spain	11.4	10.9	9.2	8.5	8.3	11.3	18.0	20.1	21.7	25.0
France	8.9	9.3	9.3	9.2	8.4	7.8	9.5	9.7	9.6	10.2
Italy	8.4	8.0	7.7	6.8	6.1	6.7	7.8	8.4	8.4	10.7
Cyprus	4.2	4.7	5.5	4.7	4.1	3.8	5.5	6.5	7.9	12.1
Latvia	11.3	11.2	9.6	7.3	6.5	8.0	18.2	19.8	16.2	14.9
Lithuania	12.4	11.3	8.0	5.2	3.8	5.3	13.6	18.0	15.3	13.3
Luxembourg	3.8	5.0	4.6	4.6	4.2	4.9	5.1	4.6	4.8	5.0
Hungary	5.8	6.1	7.2	7.5	7.4	7.8	10.0	11.2	10.9	10.9
Malta	7.7	7.2	7.3	6.9	6.5	6.0	6.9	6.9	6.5	6.5
Netherlands	4.2	5.1	5.3	4.4	3.6	3.1	3.7	4.5	4.4	5.3
Austria	4.3	4.9	5.2	4.8	4.4	3.8	4.8	4.4	4.2	4.3
Poland	19.8	19.1	17.9	13.9	9.6	7.1	8.1	9.7	9.7	10.1
Portugal	7.1	7.5	8.6	8.6	8.9	8.5	10.6	12.0	12.9	15.9
Romania	6.8	8.0	7.2	7.3	6.4	5.8	6.9	7.3	7.4	7.0
Slovenia	6.7	6.3	6.5	6.0	4.9	4.4	5.9	7.3	8.2	9.0
Slovakia	17.7	18.4	16.4	13.5	11.2	9.6	12.1	14.5	13.6	14.0
Finland	9.0	8.8	8.4	7.7	6.9	6.4	8.2	8.4	7.8	7.7
Sweden	6.6	7.4	7.7	7.1	6.1	6.2	8.3	8.6	7.8	8.0
United Kingdom	5.0	4.7	4.8	5.4	5.3	5.6	7.6	7.8	8.0	7.9
Norway	4.2	4.3	4.5	3.4	2.5	2.5	3.2	3.6	3.3	3.2
Croatia	14.2	13.7	12.7	11.2	9.0	8.4	9.1	11.8	13.5	15.8
United States	6.0	5.5	5.1	4.6	4.6	5.8	9.3	9.6	8.9	8.1

Source: Eurostat.
Unemployment in the 2000s has been higher in many Continental European countries than in the UK or the US, although it has also been relatively low in a few European countries such as Norway and the Netherlands.

over the 2004–2008 period, but then increased to over 11 per cent in 2012. More particularly, Portugal, Greece and Spain all had unemployment rates exceeding 15 per cent in 2012 – nearly twice the rate of unemployment in the UK and the US.

In addition, although non-Europeans sometimes speak as if the economies that make up Europe are a homogeneous group, this is clearly not true. For example, while the French unemployment rate has typically remained at 8 to 9 per cent over the 2003–2012 period, in the Netherlands unemployment has never exceeded 5.3 per cent over the same period. While unemployment rates in some countries, such as Ireland, rose sharply in the second part of the decade, others, such as Germany, have had remarkable successes in bringing unemployment rates down. On the other hand, Norway, outside the European Union, has enjoyed one of the lowest rates of unemployment, never exceeding 4.5 per cent, and, in 2012, the lowest at just 3.2 per cent.

The picture is a little more homogeneous if one compares consumer price index (Harmonized Index of Consumer Prices, or HICP) inflation rates, as in Table 1-2. In the Euro Area as a whole, inflation was 2.5 per cent in 2012 (not dissimilar to the UK's 2.8 per cent and the US's 2.1 per cent), and was in excess of 4 per cent in only three of the individual European countries listed. Even with inflation, however, one can discern some variation in performance across Europe.

TABLE 1-2

European and US Inflation Rates 2003-2012

	2003	2004	2005	2006	2007	2008	2009	2010	2011	2012
European Union (27 countries)	2.1	2.3	2.3	2.3	2.4	3.7	1.0	2.1	3.1	2.6
Euro Area (17 countries)	2.1	2.2	2.2	2.2	2.1	3.3	0.3	1.6	2.7	2.5
Belgium	1.5	1.9	2.5	2.3	1.8	4.5	0.0	2.3	3.4	2.6
Bulgaria	2.3	6.1	6.0	7.4	7.6	12.0	2.5	3.0	3.4	2.4
Czech Republic	−0.1	2.6	1.6	2.1	3.0	6.3	0.6	1.2	2.1	3.5
Denmark	2.0	0.9	1.7	1.9	1.7	3.6	1.1	2.2	2.7	2.4
Germany	1.0	1.8	1.9	1.8	2.3	2.8	0.2	1.2	2.5	2.1
Estonia	1.4	3.0	4.1	4.4	6.7	10.6	0.2	2.7	5.1	4.2
Ireland	4.0	2.3	2.2	2.7	2.9	3.1	−1.7	−1.6	1.2	1.9
Greece	3.4	3.0	3.5	3.3	3.0	4.2	1.3	4.7	3.1	1.0
Spain	3.1	3.1	3.4	3.6	2.8	4.1	−0.2	2.0	3.1	2.4
France	2.2	2.3	1.9	1.9	1.6	3.2	0.1	1.7	2.3	2.2
Italy	2.8	2.3	2.2	2.2	2.0	3.5	0.8	1.6	2.9	3.3
Cyprus	4.0	1.9	2.0	2.2	2.2	4.4	0.2	2.6	3.5	3.1
Latvia	2.9	6.2	6.9	6.6	10.1	15.3	3.3	−1.2	4.2	2.3
Lithuania	−1.1	1.2	2.7	3.8	5.8	11.1	4.2	1.2	4.1	3.2

TABLE **1-2** *Continued*

	2003	2004	2005	2006	2007	2008	2009	2010	2011	2012
Luxembourg	2.5	3.2	3.8	3.0	2.7	4.1	0.0	2.8	3.7	2.9
Hungary	4.7	6.8	3.5	4.0	7.9	6.0	4.0	4.7	3.9	5.7
Malta	1.9	2.7	2.5	2.6	0.7	4.7	1.8	2.0	2.5	3.2
Netherlands	2.2	1.4	1.5	1.7	1.6	2.2	1.0	0.9	2.5	2.8
Austria	1.3	2.0	2.1	1.7	2.2	3.2	0.4	1.7	3.6	2.6
Poland	0.7	3.6	2.2	1.3	2.6	4.2	4.0	2.7	3.9	3.7
Portugal	3.3	2.5	2.1	3.0	2.4	2.7	−0.9	1.4	3.6	2.8
Romania	15.3	11.9	9.1	6.6	4.9	7.9	5.6	6.1	5.8	3.4
Slovenia	5.7	3.7	2.5	2.5	3.8	5.5	0.9	2.1	2.1	2.8
Slovakia	8.4	7.5	2.8	4.3	1.9	3.9	0.9	0.7	4.1	3.7
Finland	1.3	0.1	0.8	1.3	1.6	3.9	1.6	1.7	3.3	3.2
Sweden	2.3	1.0	0.8	1.5	1.7	3.3	1.9	1.9	1.4	0.9
United Kingdom	1.4	1.3	2.1	2.3	2.3	3.6	2.2	3.3	4.5	2.8
Iceland	1.4	2.3	1.4	4.6	3.6	12.8	16.3	7.5	4.2	6.0
Norway	2.0	0.6	1.5	2.5	0.7	3.4	2.3	2.3	1.2	0.4
Switzerland	:	:	:	1.0	0.8	2.3	−0.7	0.6	0.1	−0.7
Croatia	2.4	2.1	3.0	3.3	2.7	5.8	2.2	1.1	2.2	3.4
United States	2.3	2.7	3.7	3.2	2.6	4.4	−0.8	2.4	3.8	2.1

Source: Eurostat.
European inflation performance has been at least as good as that of the US over the past decade or so.

While Romania has made consistent progress bringing inflation down through-out the 2003–2012 period, other countries, such as Iceland and the Baltic states, experienced double-digit inflation during the middle part of the period.

This examination of European unemployment and inflation throws up a number of macroeconomic issues. While European inflation rates are relatively homogeneous, a major issue of concern is why Continental European unemployment rates tend, on average, to be so high compared with those of the UK and the US. This is an issue to which we shall return later in the book. ■

CASE STUDY

The Historical Performance of the UK Economy

Another important macroeconomic variable is real gross domestic product (GDP). **Real GDP** measures the total income of everyone in the economy (adjusted for the level of prices). As a summary of total economic activity, real GDP is a good barometer of the state of the economy, and macroeconomists spend a great deal of time trying to understand its long-term growth rate and its short-term fluctuations. For this reason, it is often instructive to look at macro-economic data over very long periods of time.

FIGURE **1-1**

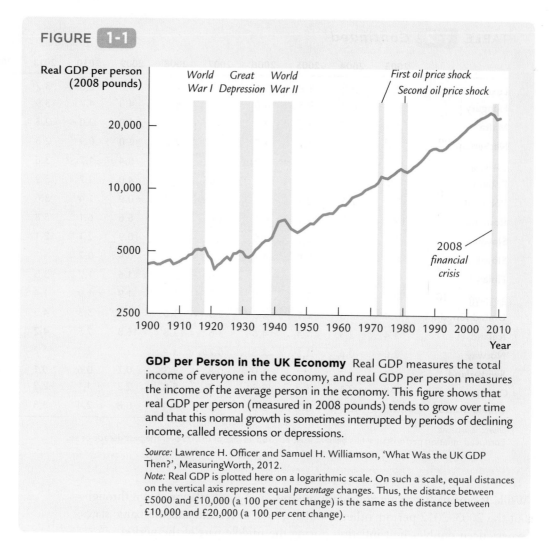

GDP per Person in the UK Economy Real GDP measures the total income of everyone in the economy, and real GDP per person measures the income of the average person in the economy. This figure shows that real GDP per person (measured in 2008 pounds) tends to grow over time and that this normal growth is sometimes interrupted by periods of declining income, called recessions or depressions.

Source: Lawrence H. Officer and Samuel H. Williamson, 'What Was the UK GDP Then?', MeasuringWorth, 2012.
Note: Real GDP is plotted here on a logarithmic scale. On such a scale, equal distances on the vertical axis represent equal *percentage* changes. Thus, the distance between £5000 and £10,000 (a 100 per cent change) is the same as the distance between £10,000 and £20,000 (a 100 per cent change).

Figure 1-1 shows real GDP per person in the UK since 1900. Two aspects of this figure are noteworthy. First, real GDP grows over time. Real GDP per person in the UK today is about five times higher than it was in 1900. This growth in average income allows UK citizens to enjoy a much higher standard of living than their great-grandparents did. Second, although real GDP rises in most years, this growth is not steady. There are repeated periods during which real GDP falls. Such periods are called **recessions** if they are mild and **depressions** if they are more severe. Not surprisingly, periods of declining income are associated with substantial economic hardship.

Figure 1-2 shows the UK inflation rate over the same period. You can see that inflation varies substantially over time. In the first half of the 20th century, periods of falling prices, called **deflation**, were almost as common as periods of rising prices. In the past half-century, inflation has been the norm, becoming most severe during the 1970s: in 1975, inflation was about 25 per cent, and although it declined slightly for a few years, it closed the decade at a rate perilously close

FIGURE 1-2

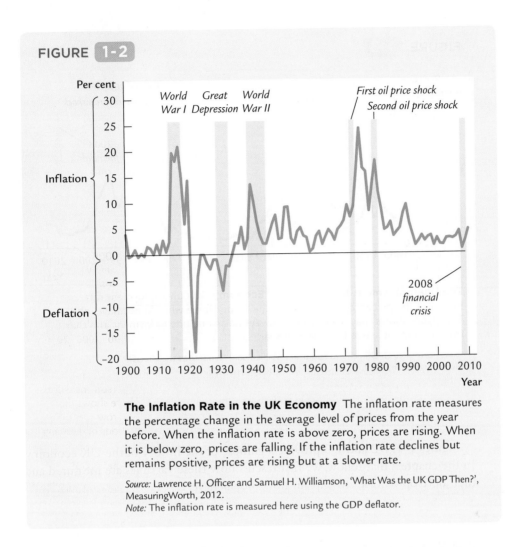

The Inflation Rate in the UK Economy The inflation rate measures the percentage change in the average level of prices from the year before. When the inflation rate is above zero, prices are rising. When it is below zero, prices are falling. If the inflation rate declines but remains positive, prices are rising but at a slower rate.

Source: Lawrence H. Officer and Samuel H. Williamson, 'What Was the UK GDP Then?', MeasuringWorth, 2012.
Note: The inflation rate is measured here using the GDP deflator.

to 20 per cent. Since the early 1990s, the UK inflation rate has been about 2 or 3 per cent per year, indicating that prices have been fairly stable.

Figure 1-3 shows the UK unemployment rate.[2] Notice that there is always some unemployment in the economy. In addition, although there is no long-term trend, the amount of unemployment varies from year to year. Recessions and depressions are associated with unusually high unemployment. The highest rates of unemployment were reached during the depression years of the 1930s, although the unemployment rate again attained double figures during much of the 1980s and early 1990s. The worst economic downturn since the Great Depression occurred in the aftermath of the financial crisis of 2008 and 2009, when unemployment rose substantially.

---

[2] The figures for the UK unemployment rate in Table 1-1 are slightly different from those reported in Figure 1-3 because of slightly different definitions. In particular, the figures in Table 1-1 are harmonized to allow valid comparisons across countries, while the figures in Figure 1-3 have been computed to allow valid comparisons through time.

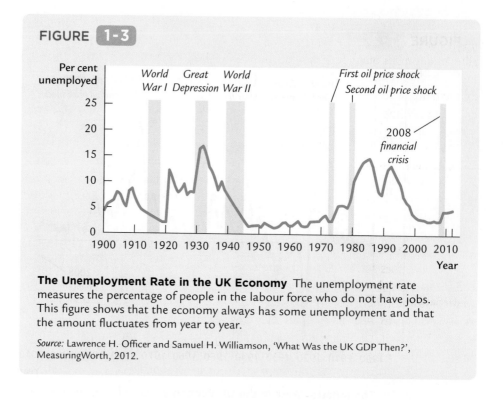

The Unemployment Rate in the UK Economy The unemployment rate measures the percentage of people in the labour force who do not have jobs. This figure shows that the economy always has some unemployment and that the amount fluctuates from year to year.

Source: Lawrence H. Officer and Samuel H. Williamson, 'What Was the UK GDP Then?', MeasuringWorth, 2012.

Figures 1-1, 1-2 and 1-3 provide a glimpse of the history of the UK economy. In the chapters that follow, we first discuss how these variables are measured and then develop theories to explain how they behave. ■

1-2 How Economists Think

Although economists often study politically charged issues, they try to address these issues with a scientist's objectivity. Like any science, economics has its own set of tools – terminology, data and a way of thinking – that can seem foreign and arcane to the layman. The best way to become familiar with these tools is to practise using them, and this book affords you ample opportunity to do so. To make these tools less forbidding, however, let's discuss a few of them here.

Theory as Model Building

Young children learn much about the world around them by playing with toy versions of real objects. For instance, they often put together models of cars, trains or planes. These models are far from realistic, but the model builder learns a lot from them nonetheless. The model illustrates the essence of the real object it is designed to resemble. (In addition, for many children, building models is fun.)

Economists also use **models** to understand the world, but an economist's model is more likely to be made of symbols and equations than plastic and glue. Economists build their 'toy economies' to help explain economic variables, such as GDP, inflation and unemployment. Economic models illustrate, often in mathematical terms, the relationships among the variables. They are useful because they help us to dispense with irrelevant details and to focus on important connections. (In addition, for many economists, building models is fun.)

Models have two kinds of variables: endogenous variables and exogenous variables. **Endogenous variables** are those variables that a model tries to explain. **Exogenous variables** are those variables that a model takes as given. The purpose of a model is to show how the exogenous variables affect the endogenous variables. In other words, as Figure 1-4 illustrates, exogenous variables come from outside the model and serve as the model's input, whereas endogenous variables are determined within the model and are the model's output.

To make these ideas more concrete, let's review the most celebrated of all economic models – the model of supply and demand. Imagine that an economist were interested in figuring out what factors influence the price of pizza and the quantity of pizza sold. He or she would develop a model that described the behaviour of pizza buyers, the behaviour of pizza sellers and their interaction in the market for pizza. For example, the economist supposes that the quantity of pizza demanded by consumers Q^d depends on the price of pizza P and on aggregate income Y. This relationship is expressed in the equation

$$Q^d = D(P, Y),$$

where $D(\ )$ represents the demand function. Similarly, the economist supposes that the quantity of pizza supplied by pizzerias Q^s depends on the price of pizza P and on the price of materials P_m, such as cheese, tomatoes, flour and anchovies. This relationship is expressed as

$$Q^s = S(P, P_m),$$

where $S(\ )$ represents the supply function. Finally, the economist assumes that the price of pizza adjusts to bring the quantity supplied and quantity demanded into balance:

$$Q^s = Q^d.$$

FIGURE 1-4

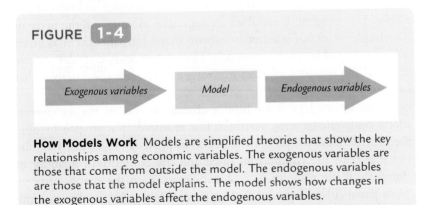

How Models Work Models are simplified theories that show the key relationships among economic variables. The exogenous variables are those that come from outside the model. The endogenous variables are those that the model explains. The model shows how changes in the exogenous variables affect the endogenous variables.

FIGURE 1-5

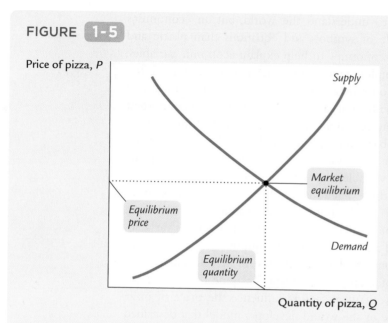

The Model of Supply and Demand The most famous economic model is that of supply and demand for a good or service – in this case, pizza. The demand curve is a downward-sloping curve relating the price of pizza to the quantity of pizza that consumers demand. The supply curve is an upward-sloping curve relating the price of pizza to the quantity of pizza that pizzerias supply. The price of pizza adjusts until the quantity supplied equals the quantity demanded. The point where the two curves cross is the market equilibrium, which shows the equilibrium price of pizza and the equilibrium quantity of pizza.

These three equations compose a model of the market for pizza.

The economist illustrates the model with a supply-and-demand diagram, as in Figure 1-5. The demand curve shows the relationship between the quantity of pizza demanded and the price of pizza, while holding aggregate income constant. The demand curve slopes downward because a higher price of pizza encourages consumers to switch to other foods and buy less pizza. The supply curve shows the relationship between the quantity of pizza supplied and the price of pizza, while holding the price of materials constant. The supply curve slopes upward because a higher price of pizza makes selling pizza more profitable, which encourages pizzerias to produce more of it. The equilibrium for the market is the price and quantity at which the supply and demand curves intersect. At the equilibrium price, consumers choose to buy the amount of pizza that pizzerias choose to produce.

This model of the pizza market has two exogenous variables and two endogenous variables. The exogenous variables are aggregate income and the price of materials. The model does not attempt to explain them, but takes them as given (perhaps to be explained by another model). The endogenous variables are the price of pizza and the quantity of pizza exchanged. These are the variables that the model attempts to explain.

The model can be used to show how a change in one of the exogenous variables affects both endogenous variables. For example, if aggregate income increases, then the demand for pizza increases, as in panel (a) of Figure 1-6. The model shows that both the equilibrium price and the equilibrium quantity of pizza rise. Similarly, if the price of materials increases, then the supply of pizza decreases, as in panel (b) of Figure 1-6. The model shows that in this case the equilibrium price of pizza rises and the equilibrium quantity of pizza falls. Thus,

FIGURE 1-6

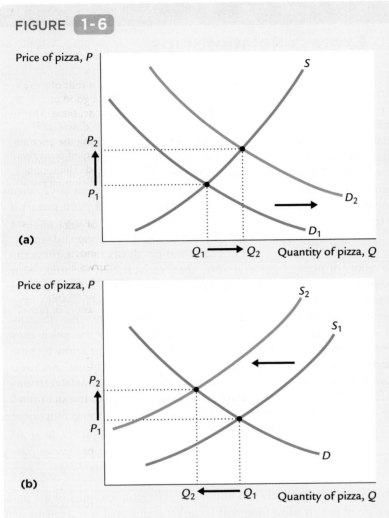

(a)

(b)

Changes in Equilibrium In panel (a), a rise in aggregate income causes the demand for pizza to increase: at any given price, consumers now want to buy more pizza. This is represented by a rightward shift in the demand curve from D_1 to D_2. The market moves to the new intersection of supply and demand. The equilibrium price rises from P_1 to P_2, and the equilibrium quantity of pizza rises from Q_1 to Q_2. In panel (b), a rise in the price of materials decreases the supply of pizza: at any given price, pizzerias find that the sale of pizza is less profitable and therefore choose to produce less pizza. This is represented by a leftward shift in the supply curve from S_1 to S_2. The market moves to the new intersection of supply and demand. The equilibrium price rises from P_1 to P_2, and the equilibrium quantity falls from Q_1 to Q_2.

the model shows how changes in aggregate income or in the price of materials affect price and quantity in the market for pizza.

Like all models, this model of the pizza market makes simplifying assumptions. The model does not take into account, for example, that every pizzeria is in a different location so that, for each customer, one pizzeria may be more convenient than the others. Or there may be other reasons why a customer prefers a particular pizzeria – the decor or the music that is played there perhaps. For reasons like this, pizzerias may retain some customer loyalty and thus may have some ability to set their own prices. Although the model assumes that there is a single price for pizza, in fact there could be a different price at every pizzeria.

How should we react to the model's lack of realism? Should we discard the simple model of pizza supply and pizza demand? Should we attempt to build a more complex model that allows for diverse pizza prices? The answers to these questions depend on our purpose. If our goal is to explain how the price of cheese affects the average price of pizza and the amount of pizza sold, then the

FYI

Using Functions to Express Relationships among Variables

All economic models express relationships among economic variables. Often these relationships are expressed as functions. A *function* is a mathematical concept that shows how one variable depends on a set of other variables. For example, in the model of the pizza market, we said that the quantity of pizza demanded depends on the price of pizza and on aggregate income. To express this, we use functional notation to write

$$Q^d = D(P, Y).$$

This equation says that the quantity of pizza demanded Q^d is a function of the price of pizza P and aggregate income Y. In functional notation, the variable preceding the parentheses denotes the function. In this case, $D(\ )$ is the function expressing how the variables in parentheses determine the quantity of pizza demanded.

If we knew more about the pizza market, we could give a numerical formula for the quantity of pizza demanded. We might be able to write

$$Q^d = 60 - 10P + 2Y.$$

In this case, the demand function is

$$D(P, Y) = 60 - 10P + 2Y.$$

For any price of pizza and aggregate income, this function gives the corresponding quantity of pizza demanded. For example, if aggregate income is €10 and the price of pizza is €2, then the quantity of pizza demanded is 60 pizzas; if the price of pizza rises to €3, the quantity of pizza demanded falls to 50 pizzas.

Functional notation allows us to express the general idea that variables are related, even when we do not have enough information to write the precise numerical relationship. For example, we might know that the quantity of pizza demanded falls when the price rises from €2 to €3, but we might not know by how much it falls. In this case, functional notation is useful: as long as we know that a relationship among the variables exists, we can remind ourselves of that relationship using functional notation.

diversity of pizza prices is probably not important. The simple model of the pizza market does a good job of addressing that issue. Yet if our goal is to explain why towns with three pizzerias have lower pizza prices than towns with one pizzeria, the simple model is less useful.

The art in economics is in judging when a simplifying assumption (such as assuming a single price of pizza) clarifies our thinking and when it misleads us. Simplification is a necessary part of building a useful model: any model constructed to be completely realistic would be too complicated for anyone to understand. Yet models lead to incorrect conclusions if they assume away features of the economy that are crucial to the issue at hand. Economic modelling therefore requires care and common sense.

A Multitude of Models

Macroeconomists study many facets of the economy. For example, they examine the role of saving in economic growth, the impact of minimum wage laws on unemployment, the effect of inflation on interest rates, and the influence of trade policy on the trade balance and exchange rate.

Although economists use models to address all these issues, no single model can answer all questions. Just as carpenters use different tools for different tasks, economists use different models to explain different economic phenomena. Students of macroeconomics, therefore, must keep in mind that there is no single 'correct' model that is useful for all purposes. Instead, there are many models, each of which is useful for shedding light on a different facet of the economy. The field of macroeconomics is like a Swiss army knife – a set of complementary but distinct tools that can be applied in different ways in different circumstances.

This book presents many different models that address different questions and make different assumptions. Remember that a model is only as good as its assumptions and that an assumption that is useful for some purposes may be misleading for others. When using a model to address a question, the economist must keep in mind the underlying assumptions and judge if they are reasonable for studying the matter at hand.

Prices: Flexible versus Sticky

Throughout this book, one group of assumptions will prove especially important – those concerning the speed at which wages and prices adjust to changing economic conditions. Economists normally presume that the price of a good or a service moves quickly to bring quantity supplied and quantity demanded into balance. In other words, they assume that markets are normally in equilibrium, so the price of any good or service is found where the supply and demand curves intersect. This assumption is called **market clearing** and is central to the model of the pizza market discussed earlier. For answering most questions, economists use market-clearing models.

Yet the assumption of *continuous* market clearing is not entirely realistic. For markets to clear continuously, prices must adjust instantly to changes in supply and demand. In fact, many wages and prices adjust slowly. Labour contracts often set wages for up to three years. Many firms leave their product prices the same for long periods of time – for example, magazine publishers typically change their prices only every three or four years. Although market-clearing models assume that all wages and prices are **flexible**, in the real world some wages and prices are **sticky**.

The apparent stickiness of prices does not make market-clearing models useless. After all, prices are not stuck forever; eventually, they do adjust to changes in supply and demand. Market-clearing models might not describe the economy at every instant, but they do describe the equilibrium towards which the economy gravitates. Therefore, most macroeconomists believe that price flexibility is a good assumption for studying long-run issues, such as the growth in real GDP that we observe from decade to decade.

For studying short-run issues, such as year-to-year fluctuations in real GDP and unemployment, the assumption of price flexibility is less plausible. Over short periods, many prices in the economy are fixed at predetermined levels. Therefore, most macroeconomists believe that price stickiness is a better assumption for studying the short-run behaviour of the economy.

F Y I

Nobel Macroeconomists

The Nobel Prize in economics is announced every October. Many winners have been macroeconomists whose work we study in this book. Here are a few of them, together with some of their own words about how they chose their field of study:

Edmund Phelps, awarded the 2006 Nobel Prize 'for his analysis of intertemporal trade-offs in macroeconomic policy': 'What launched me into economics . . . was the usual thing: top-drawer instruction. What drove me on and on in the study of economics was also rather common, it seems. As others have commented about their experience, I kept hoping that if I took just one more course the hidden harmony of economics would be revealed to me and I would be released from its dismal prison. In my own case, however, this gap in understanding was specific. I had a vague sense that the microeconomics taught in one set of courses was not communicating with the macroeconomics in the other courses!'

Edward Prescott,[3] *awarded the 2004 Nobel Prize 'for his contributions to dynamic macroeconomics: the time consistency of economic policy and the driving forces behind business cycles'*: 'Through discussion with [my father], I learned a lot about the way businesses operated. This was one reason why I liked my microeconomics course so much in my first year [at university]. The price theory that I learned in that course rationalised what I had learned from him about the way businesses operate.'

George Akerlof,[4] *awarded the 2001 Nobel Prize 'for his analyses of markets with asymmetric information'*: 'I was convinced that I wanted to be either an economist or an historian. Really, for me it was a distinction without a difference. If I was going to be an historian, then I would be an economic historian. And if I was to be an economist I would consider history as the basis for my economics.'

Robert Mundell, awarded the 1999 Nobel Prize 'for his analysis of monetary and fiscal policy under different exchange rate regimes and his analysis of optimum currency areas': 'I have been very lucky in my career. I was

lucky first of all to find a profession that suited me. As an undergraduate . . . I fell in love with economic theory. It was the right choice for me.'

Robert Lucas, awarded the 1995 Nobel Prize 'for having developed and applied the hypothesis of rational expectations, and thereby having transformed macroeconomic analysis and deepened our understanding of economic policy': 'In school, science was an unending and not very well organised list of things other people had discovered long ago. In college, I learned something about the process of scientific discovery, but what I learned did not attract me as a career possibility . . . What I liked thinking about were politics and social issues.'

Robert Solow, awarded the 1987 Nobel Prize 'for his contributions to the theory of economic growth': 'I came back [to college after being in the army] and, almost without thinking about it, signed up to finish my undergraduate degree as an economics major. The time was such that I had to make a decision in a hurry. No doubt I acted as if I were maximizing an infinite discounted sum of one-period utilities, but you couldn't prove it by me. To me it felt as if I were saying to myself: "What the hell."'

Franco Modigliani, awarded the 1985 Nobel Prize 'for his pioneering analyses of saving and of financial markets': 'For a while it was thought that I should study medicine because my father was a physician . . . I went to the registration window to sign up for medicine, but then I closed my eyes and thought of blood! I got pale just thinking about blood and decided under those conditions I had better keep away from medicine . . . Casting about for something to do, I happened to get into some economics activities. I knew some German and was asked to translate from German into Italian some articles for one of the trade associations. Thus I began to be exposed to the economic problems that were in the German literature.'

James Tobin, awarded the 1981 Nobel Prize 'for his analysis of financial markets and their relations to

---

[3] Awarded the prize jointly with Finn Kydland.
[4] Awarded the prize jointly with Michael Spence and Joseph Stiglitz.

expenditure decisions, employment, production and prices': 'I was attracted to the field for two reasons. One was that economic theory is a fascinating intellectual challenge, on the order of mathematics or chess. I liked analytics and logical argument . . . The other reason was the obvious relevance of economics to understanding and perhaps overcoming the Great Depression.'

Milton Friedman, awarded the 1976 Nobel Prize 'for his achievements in the fields of consumption analysis, monetary history and theory and for his demonstration of the complexity of stabilization policy': 'I graduated from college in 1932 . . . The dominant problem of the time was economics. How to get out of the depression? How to reduce unemployment?

What explained the paradox of great need on the one hand and unused resources on the other? Under the circumstances, becoming an economist seemed more relevant to the burning issues of the day than becoming an applied mathematician or an actuary.'

Simon Kuznets, awarded the 1971 Nobel Prize 'for his empirically founded interpretation of economic growth which has led to new and deepened insight into the economic and social structure and process of development': 'I first became interested in economics . . . as a discipline that provided the key to social structure and social man literature.'

If you want to learn more about the Nobel Prize and its winners, go to www.nobelprize.org.[5]

---

[5] The first quotation is from Professor Phelps's autobiographical essay, 'A Life in Economics', in Arnold Heertje, ed., *The Makers of Modern Economics*, vol. 2, Aldershot, UK, and Brookfield, VT: Edward Elgar, 1995. The quotations by Professors Akerlof, Kuznets, Mundell and Prescott are from the Nobel website. The others (Friedman, Lucas, Modigliani, Solow and Tobin) are from William Breit and Barry T. Hirsch, eds, *Lives of the Laureates*, 4th edn, Cambridge, MA: The MIT Press, 2004.

Microeconomic Thinking and Macroeconomic Models

Microeconomics is the study of how households and firms make decisions and how these decision makers interact in the marketplace. A central principle of microeconomics is that households and firms optimize – they do the best they can for themselves given their objectives and the constraints they face. In microeconomic models, households choose their purchases to maximize their level of satisfaction, which economists call *utility*, and firms make production decisions to maximize their profits.

Because economy-wide events arise from the interaction of many households and many firms, macroeconomics and microeconomics are inextricably linked. When we study the economy as a whole, we must consider the decisions of individual economic actors. For example, to understand what determines total consumer spending, we must think about a family deciding how much to spend today and how much to save for the future. To understand what determines total investment spending, we must think about a firm deciding whether or not to build a new factory. Because aggregate variables are the sum of the variables describing many individual decisions, macroeconomic theory rests on a microeconomic foundation.

Although microeconomic decisions underlie all economic models, in many models the optimizing behaviour of households and firms is implicit rather than explicit. The model of the pizza market we discussed earlier is an example. Households' decisions about how much pizza to buy underlie the demand for pizza, and pizzerias' decisions about how much pizza to produce underlie the supply of pizza. Presumably, households make their decisions to maximize utility, and pizzerias make their decisions to maximize profit. Yet the model did not focus on how these microeconomic decisions are made; it left these decisions in the background. Similarly, although microeconomic decisions lie behind all macroeconomic phenomena, macroeconomic models do not necessarily focus on the optimizing behaviour of households and firms, but sometimes leave that behaviour in the background.

1-3 How This Book Proceeds

This book has six parts. This chapter and the next make up Part I, the Introduction. Chapter 2 discusses how economists measure economic variables, such as aggregate income, the inflation rate and the unemployment rate.

Part II, Classical Theory: The Economy in the Long Run, presents the classical model of how the economy works. The key assumption of the classical model is that prices are flexible. That is, with rare exceptions, the classical model assumes that markets clear. Because the assumption of price flexibility describes the economy only in the long run, classical theory is best suited for analysing a time horizon of at least several years.

Part III, Growth Theory: The Economy in the Very Long Run, builds on the classical model. It maintains the assumption of market clearing, but adds a new emphasis on growth in the capital stock, the labour force and technological knowledge. Growth theory is designed to explain how the economy evolves over a period of several decades.

Part IV, Business Cycle Theory: The Economy in the Short Run, examines the behaviour of the economy when prices are sticky. The non-market-clearing model developed here is designed to analyse short-run issues, such as the reasons for economic fluctuations and the influence of government policy on those fluctuations. It is best suited to analysing the changes in the economy we observe from month to month or from year to year.

The last two parts of the book cover various topics to supplement, reinforce and refine our long-run and short-run analyses. Part V, Topics in Macroeconomic Theory, presents advanced material of a somewhat theoretical nature, including models of consumer behaviour and theories of firms' investment decisions.

Part VI, Topics in Macroeconomic Policy, considers what role the government should have in the economy. It discusses the policy debates over stabilization policy, government debt and financial crises. In addition, it discusses the various economic issues relating to the adoption of a common currency (such as the euro).

Summary

1. Macroeconomics is the study of the economy as a whole – including growth in incomes, changes in prices and the rate of unemployment. Macroeconomists attempt both to explain economic events and to devise policies to improve economic performance.

2. To understand the economy, economists use models — theories that simplify reality in order to reveal how exogenous variables influence endogenous variables. The art in the science of economics is in judging whether or not a model captures the important economic relationships for the matter at hand. Because no single model can answer all questions, macroeconomists use different models to look at different issues.

3. A key feature of a macroeconomic model is whether it assumes that prices are flexible or sticky. According to most macroeconomists, models with flexible prices describe the economy in the long run, whereas models with sticky prices offer a better description of the economy in the short run.

4. Microeconomics is the study of how firms and individuals make decisions and how these decision makers interact. Because macroeconomic events arise from many microeconomic interactions, all macroeconomic models must be consistent with microeconomic foundations, even if those foundations are only implicit.

KEY CONCEPTS

Macroeconomics	Depression	Market clearing
Inflation rate	Deflation	Flexible and sticky prices
Unemployment rate	Models	Microeconomics
Real GDP	Endogenous variables	
Recession	Exogenous variables	

QUESTIONS FOR REVIEW

1. Explain the difference between macroeconomics and microeconomics. How are these two fields related?

2. Why do economists build models?

3. What is a market-clearing model? When is it appropriate to assume that markets clear?

PROBLEMS AND APPLICATIONS

1. What macroeconomic issues have been in the news lately?

2. What do you think are the defining characteristics of a science? Does the study of the economy have these characteristics? Do you think macroeconomics should be called a science? Why, or why not?

3. Use the model of supply and demand to explain how a fall in the price of lemonade would affect the price of cola and the quantity of lemonade sold. In your explanation, identify the exogenous and endogenous variables.

4. How often does the price you pay for a haircut change? What does your answer imply about the usefulness of market-clearing models for analysing the market for haircuts?

The Data of Macroeconomics

It is a capital mistake to theorise before one has data. Insensibly one begins to twist facts to suit theories, instead of theories to fit fact.

— *Sherlock Holmes (Sir Arthur Conan Doyle,* A Scandal in Bohemia*)*

Scientists, economists and detectives have much in common: they all want to figure out what is going on in the world around them. To do this, they rely on theory and observation. They build theories in an attempt to make sense of what they see happening. They then turn to more systematic observation to evaluate the validity of those theories. Only when theory and evidence come into line do they feel they understand the situation. This chapter discusses the types of observation that economists use to develop and test their theories.

Casual observation is one source of information about what is happening in the economy. When you go shopping, you see how fast prices are rising. When you look for a job, you learn whether or not firms are recruiting. Because we are all participants in the economy, we get some sense of economic conditions as we go about our lives.

A century ago, economists monitoring the economy had little more to go on than these casual observations. Such fragmentary information made economic policy making all the more difficult. One person's anecdote would suggest the economy was moving in one direction, while a different person's anecdote would suggest it was moving in another. Economists needed some way to combine many individual experiences into a coherent whole. There was an obvious solution: as the old quip goes, the plural of 'anecdote' is 'data'.

Today, economic data offer a systematic and objective source of information, and almost every day the newspapers have a story about some newly released statistic. Most of these statistics are produced by the government. Various government agencies survey households and firms to learn about their economic activity — how much they are earning, what they are buying, what prices they are charging, whether they have a job or are looking for work, and so on. From these surveys, various statistics are computed that summarize the state of the economy. Economists use these statistics to study the economy; policy makers use them to monitor developments and formulate policies.

This chapter focuses on the three statistics that economists and policy makers use most often. **Gross domestic product** (**GDP**) tells us the nation's total income and the total expenditure on its output of goods and services. The consumer price index (CPI) measures the level of prices. The **unemployment rate** tells us the fraction of workers who are unemployed. In the following pages, we see how these statistics are computed and what they tell us about the economy.

2-1 Measuring the Value of Economic Activity: Gross Domestic Product

Gross domestic product is often considered the best measure of how well the economy is performing. All advanced industrialized economies have a government agency that is responsible for computing this statistic, usually every three months, from a large number of primary data sources.[1] The purpose of GDP is to summarize in a single number the euro value of economic activity in a given period of time.

There are two ways to view this statistic. One way to view GDP is as *the total income of everyone in the economy*. Another way to view GDP is as *the total expenditure on the economy's output of goods and services*. From either viewpoint, it is clear why GDP is a gauge of economic performance. GDP measures something people care about – their incomes. Similarly, an economy with a large output of goods and services can better satisfy the demands of households, firms and the government.

How can GDP measure both the economy's income and its expenditure on output? The reason is that these two quantities are really the same: for the economy as a whole, income must equal expenditure. That fact, in turn, follows from an even more fundamental one: because every transaction has a buyer and a seller, every euro of expenditure by a buyer must become a euro of income to a seller. When James paints Joanna's house for €1000, that €1000 is income to James and expenditure by Joanna. The transaction contributes €1000 to GDP, regardless of whether we are adding up all income or adding up all expenditure.

To understand the meaning of GDP more fully, we turn to **national income accounting**, the accounting system used to measure GDP and many related statistics.

Income, Expenditure and the Circular Flow

Imagine an economy that produces a single good, for example, bread, from a single input, labour. Figure 2-1 illustrates all the economic transactions that occur between households and firms in this economy.

The inner loop in Figure 2-1 represents the flows of bread and labour. The households sell their labour to the firms. The firms use the labour of their workers to produce bread, which the firms in turn sell to the households. Hence, labour flows from households to firms, and bread flows from firms to households.

---

[1] The European statistical agency Eurostat collects data from all European Union and many non-EU countries. In the UK the central statistical agency is the Office for National Statistics (ONS).

FIGURE 2-1

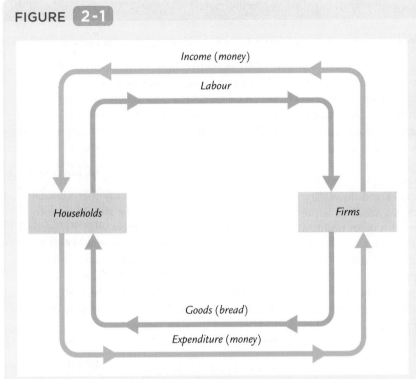

Income (money)

Labour

Households

Firms

Goods (bread)

Expenditure (money)

The Circular Flow This figure illustrates the flows between firms and households in an economy that produces one good, bread, from one input, labour. The inner loop represents the flows of labour and bread: households sell their labour to firms, and the firms sell the bread they produce to households. The outer loop represents the corresponding flows of money: households pay the firms for the bread, and the firms pay wages and profit to the households. In this economy, GDP is both the total expenditure on bread and the total income from the production of bread.

The outer loop in Figure 2-1 represents the corresponding flow of money. The households buy bread from the firms. The firms use some of the revenue from these sales to pay the wages of their workers, and the remainder is the profit belonging to the owners of the firms (who themselves are part of the household sector). Hence, expenditure on bread flows from households to firms, and income in the form of wages and profit flows from firms to households.

GDP measures the flow of money in this economy. We can compute it in two ways. GDP is the total income from the production of bread, which equals the sum of wages and profit – the top half of the circular flow of money. GDP is also the total expenditure on purchases of bread – the bottom half of the circular flow of money. To compute GDP, we can look at either the flow of money from firms to households or the flow of money from households to firms.

These two ways of computing GDP must be equal because the expenditure of buyers on products is, by the rules of accounting, income to the sellers of those products. Every transaction that affects expenditure must affect income, and every transaction that affects income must affect expenditure. For example, suppose that a firm produces and sells one more loaf of bread to a household. Clearly this transaction raises total expenditure on bread, but it also has an equal effect on total income. If the firm produces the extra loaf without taking on any more labour (such as by making the production process more efficient), then profit increases. If the firm produces the extra loaf by taking on more labour, then wages increase. In both cases, expenditure and income increase equally.

F Y I

Stocks and Flows

Many economic variables measure a quantity of something – a quantity of money, a quantity of goods and so on. Economists distinguish between two types of quantity variables: stocks and flows. A **stock** is a quantity measured at a given point in time, whereas a **flow** is a quantity measured per unit of time.

A bathtub, shown in Figure 2-2, is the classic example used to illustrate stocks and flows. The amount of water in the bath is a stock: it is the quantity of water in the bath at a given point in time. The amount of water coming out of the tap is a flow: it is the quantity of water being added to the bath per unit of time. Note that we measure stocks and flows in different units. We say that the bathtub contains 200 *litres* of water, but that water is coming out of the tap at 20 *litres per minute*.

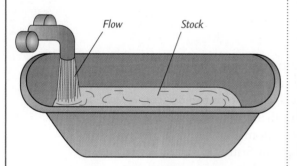

Figure 2-2 Stocks and Flows The amount of water in a bathtub is a stock: it is a quantity measured at a given moment in time. The amount of water coming out of the tap is a flow: it is a quantity measured per unit of time.

GDP is probably the most important flow variable in economics: it tells us how much money is flowing around the economy's circular flow per unit of time. When you hear someone say that GDP in the European Union (EU) countries (all 27 of them added together) is about €11 trillion (i.e. €11,000,000,000,000), you should understand that this means that it is €11 trillion *per year*. (Equivalently, we could say that EU GDP is €350,000 per second, but we should have to be careful to qualify the statement with 'per second' because the usual practice is to speak of GDP per year and that is what will be understood unless we explicitly state otherwise.)

Stocks and flows are often related. In the bathtub example, these relationships are clear. The stock of water in the bath represents the accumulation of the flow out of the tap, and the flow of water represents the change in the stock. When building theories to explain economic variables, it is often useful to determine whether the variables are stocks or flows and whether any relationships link them.

Here are some examples of related stocks and flows that we study in future chapters:

- A person's wealth is a stock; his income and expenditure are flows.

- The number of unemployed people is a stock; the number of people losing their jobs is a flow.

- The amount of capital in the economy is a stock; the amount of investment is a flow.

- The government debt is a stock; the government budget deficit is a flow.

Rules for Computing GDP

In an economy that produces only bread, we can compute GDP by adding up the total expenditure on bread. Real economies, however, include the production and sale of a vast number of goods and services. To compute GDP for such a complex economy, it will be helpful to have a more precise definition: *Gross domestic product (GDP) is the market value of all final goods and services produced within an economy in a given period of time.* To see how this definition is applied, let's discuss some of the rules that economists follow in constructing this statistic.

Adding Apples and Oranges An advanced economy produces many different goods and services – pizzas, haircuts, cars, computers and so on. GDP combines the value of these goods and services into a single measure. The diversity of products in the economy complicates the calculation of GDP because different products have different values.

Suppose, for example, that the economy produces four apples and three oranges. How do we compute GDP? We could simply add apples and oranges and conclude that GDP equals seven pieces of fruit. But this makes sense only if we thought apples and oranges had equal value, which is generally not true. (This would be even clearer if the economy had produced four watermelons and three grapes.)

To compute the total value of different goods and services, the national income accounts use market prices because these prices reflect how much people are willing to pay for a good or service. Thus, if apples cost €0.50 each and oranges cost €1.00 each, GDP would be

$$
\begin{aligned}
GDP &= (\text{Price of Apples} \times \text{Quantity of Apples}) \\
&\quad + (\text{Price of Oranges} \times \text{Quantity of Oranges}) \\
&= (\text{€}0.50 \times 4) + (\text{€}1.00 \times 3) \\
&= \text{€}5.00.
\end{aligned}
$$

GDP equals €5.00 – the value of all the apples, €2.00, plus the value of all the oranges, €3.00.

Used Goods When Renault makes a car and sells it for €50,000, that €50,000 is added to France's GDP. But what about when a Parisian, Jean-Olivier, sells his two-year-old Renault for €25,000 in order to buy a new car? That €25,000 is not part of French GDP. GDP measures the value of currently produced goods and services. The sale of the used Renault reflects the transfer of an asset, not an addition to the economy's income. Thus, the sale of used goods is not included as part of GDP.

The Treatment of Inventories Imagine that a bakery takes on workers to produce more bread, pays their wages and then fails to sell the additional bread. How does this transaction affect GDP?

The answer depends on what happens to the unsold bread. Let's first suppose that the bread goes stale and cannot be sold. In this case, the firm has paid more in wages, but has not received any additional revenue, so the firm's profit is reduced by the amount that wages have increased. Total expenditure in the economy has not changed because no one buys the bread. Total income has not changed either – although more is distributed as wages and less as profit. Because the transaction affects neither expenditure nor income, it does not alter GDP.

Now suppose, instead, that the bread (which, because of a secret additive, has a long shelf life) is put into inventory to be sold later.[2] In this case, the transaction is treated differently. The owners of the firm are assumed to have 'purchased' the

---

[2] Another common term for inventory is 'stock' – hence the term 'stocktaking', which means 'counting inventories'. Economists prefer to use the term 'inventory', however, presumably to avoid confusion with the term 'stock' as we defined it earlier, meaning *any* variable that is measured at a point in time (although inventory is, of course, a stock in the sense that it is measured at a point in time).

bread for the firm's inventory, and the firm's profit is not reduced by the additional wages it has paid. Because the higher wages raise total income, and greater spending on inventory raises total expenditure, the economy's GDP rises.

What happens later when the firm sells the bread out of inventory? This case is much like the sale of a used good. There is spending by bread consumers, but there is inventory disinvestment by the firm. This negative spending by the firm offsets the positive spending by consumers, so the sale out of inventory does not affect GDP.

The general rule is that when a firm increases its inventory of goods, this investment in inventory is counted as an expenditure by the firm's owners. Thus, production for inventory increases GDP just as much as production for final sale. A sale out of inventory, however, is a combination of positive spending (the purchase) and negative spending (inventory disinvestment), so it does not influence GDP. This treatment of inventories ensures that GDP reflects the economy's current production of goods and services.

Intermediate Goods and Value Added Many goods are produced in stages: raw materials are processed into intermediate goods by one firm and then sold to another firm for final processing. How should we treat such products when computing GDP? For example, suppose a cattle farmer sells 100 grams of meat to McDonald's for €0.50, and then McDonald's sells you a hamburger for €1.50. Should GDP include both the meat and the hamburger (a total of €2.00), or just the hamburger (€1.50)?

The answer is that GDP includes only the value of final goods. Thus, the hamburger is included in GDP, but the meat is not: GDP increases by €1.50, not by €2.00. The reason is that the value of intermediate goods is already included as part of the market price of the final goods in which they are used. To add the intermediate goods to the final goods would be double counting – that is, the meat would be counted twice. Hence, GDP is the total value of final goods and services produced.

One way to compute the value of all final goods and services is to sum the value added at each stage of production. The **value added** of a firm equals the value of the firm's output less the value of the intermediate goods that the firm purchases. In the case of the hamburger, the value added of the farmer is €0.50 (assuming that the farmer bought no intermediate goods), and the value added of McDonald's is €1.50 − €0.50, or €1.00. Total value added is €0.50 + €1.00, which equals €1.50. For the economy as a whole, the sum of all value added must equal the value of all final goods and services. Hence, GDP is also the total value added of all firms in the economy.

To return to our example of Jean-Olivier and the sale of his used Renault, what if Jean-Olivier sells his car for €25,000 to a used car dealer, who then sells it to someone else for €35,000? Is that part of GDP? The answer is that only the value that has been added to the car by the dealer is part of GDP, in this case €35,000 − €25,000 = €10,000. That €10,000 of value added represents the value of the service the used car dealer has provided in buying the car and finding a purchaser for it (plus perhaps cleaning and servicing it).

Housing Services and Other Imputations Although most goods and services are valued at their market prices when computing GDP, some are not sold in the marketplace and therefore do not have market prices. If GDP is to include the value of these goods and services, we must use an estimate of their value. Such an estimate is called an **imputed value**.

Imputations are especially important for determining the value of housing. A person who rents a house is buying housing services and providing income for the landlord; the rent is part of GDP, both as expenditure by the renter and as income for the landlord. Many people, however, live in their own homes. Although they do not pay rent to a landlord, they are enjoying housing services similar to those that renters purchase. To take account of the housing services enjoyed by home-owners, GDP includes the 'rent' that these homeowners 'pay' to themselves. Of course, homeowners do not in fact pay themselves this rent. National statistical agencies typically estimate what the market rent for a house would be if it were rented and include that imputed rent as part of GDP. This imputed rent is included both in the homeowner's expenditure and in the homeowner's income.

Imputations also arise in valuing government services. For example, police officers, firefighters and Members of Parliament provide services to the public. Giving a value to these services is difficult because they are not sold in a market-place and therefore do not have a market price. The national income accounts include these services in GDP by valuing them at their cost. That is, the wages of these public servants are used as a measure of the value of their output.

In many cases, an imputation is called for in principle but, to keep things simple, is not made in practice. Because GDP includes the imputed rent on owner-occupied houses, one might expect it also to include the imputed rent on cars, lawnmowers, fridges, jewellery and other durable goods owned by households. Yet the value of these rental services is left out of GDP. In addition, some of the output of the economy is produced and consumed at home and never enters the marketplace. For example, meals cooked at home are similar to meals cooked at a restaurant, yet the value added in meals at home is left out of GDP.

Finally, no imputation is made for the value of goods and services sold in the *black economy*. The black economy (also sometimes called the *underground economy* or the *shadow economy*) is the part of the economy that people hide from the government, either because they wish to evade taxation or because the activity is illegal. Examples include builders or plumbers who are paid in cash and under-report their earnings to the tax authorities, or domestic workers such as gardeners or cleaners paid 'off the books'. The illegal drug trade is another example. Although the black economy is not accounted for in official GDP figures, economists do attempt to measure it and – even allowing for inevitable inaccuracies in its measurement – it can be both sizeable as a proportion of GDP, and highly variable from country to country (see the next case study).[3] Because the imputations necessary for computing GDP are only approximate, and because the value of many goods and services is left out altogether, GDP is an imperfect measure of economic activity. These imperfections are most problematic when comparing standards of living across countries. Yet as long as the magnitude of these imperfections remains fairly constant over time, GDP is useful for comparing economic activity from year to year.

---

[3] In September 2006 Greece became the first country to include estimates of the black economy in its official GDP figures and raised its estimate of GDP by 25 per cent.

The Size of the Black Economy: Some International Estimates

The size of the black economy is very difficult to measure because, by definition, it is 'off the books'. Macroeconomists, however, have not been deterred by the difficulty of this task and have devised various ways of estimating the size of the black economy. For example, in one study, researchers noted that there is usually a stable relationship between the income of a household and the amount of money it spends on food. They then observed that, for every £100 of reported income, self-employed workers tended to spend 1.5 times as much as other workers on food, suggesting that the self-employed were under-reporting their income to the authorities by about a third.[4]

In Table 2-1 we list some recent estimates of the black economy for selected countries. In Greece and Italy, as much as 27–30 per cent of economic activity is

TABLE 2-1	
Estimated Size of the Black Economy for Selected Countries (per cent of GDP)	
Austria	8.6
Belgium	22.2
Denmark	18.2
France	14.8
Germany	14.8
Greece	30.1
Ireland	16.0
Italy	27.2
Netherlands	13.8
Norway	19.4
Portugal	22.8
Spain	23.0
Sweden	19.5
United Kingdom	13.0
United States	8.8
Japan	11.3

Source: Friedrich Schneider and Dominik H. Enste, 'Shadow Economies: Size, Causes, and Consequences', *Journal of Economic Literature*, 2000, vol. 38, pp. 77–114.
The black economy varies from country to country, but can represent a sizeable proportion of GDP.

---

[4] C.A. Pissarides and G. Weber, 'An Expenditure-Based Estimate of Britain's Black Economy', *Journal of Public Economics*, 1989, vol. 39, pp. 17–32.

estimated to be 'off the books', while in France and Germany the figure is closer to 15 per cent. The estimated size of the black economy is smallest for the UK, Japan and the US, with estimates of about 13, 11 and 9 per cent, respectively. While these estimates may be subject to considerable measurement error, they do give some idea of the magnitude of the black economy and how it varies from country to country. ■

Real GDP versus Nominal GDP

Economists use the rules just described to compute GDP, which values the economy's total output of goods and services. But is GDP a good measure of economic well-being? Consider once again the economy that produces only apples and oranges. In this economy, GDP is the sum of the value of all the apples produced and the value of all the oranges produced. That is,

$$\text{GDP} = (\text{Price of Apples} \times \text{Quantity of Apples})$$
$$+ (\text{Price of Oranges} \times \text{Quantity of Oranges}).$$

Notice that GDP can increase either because prices rise or because quantities rise.

It is easy to see that GDP computed this way is not a good gauge of economic well-being. That is, this measure does not accurately reflect how well the economy can satisfy the demands of households, firms and the government. If all prices doubled without any change in quantities, GDP would double. Yet it would be misleading to say that the economy's ability to satisfy demands has doubled, because the quantity of every good produced remains the same. Economists call the value of goods and services measured at current prices **nominal GDP**.

A better measure of economic well-being would tally the economy's output of goods and services and would not be influenced by changes in prices. For this purpose, economists use **real GDP**, which is the value of goods and services measured using a constant set of prices. That is, real GDP shows what would have happened to expenditure on output if quantities had changed but prices had not.

To see how real GDP is computed, imagine we wanted to compare output in 2013 with output in subsequent years for our apple-and-orange economy. We could begin by choosing a set of prices, called *base-year prices*, such as the prices that prevailed in 2013. Goods and services are then added up using these base-year prices to value the different goods in both years. Real GDP for 2013 would be

$$\text{Real GDP} = (\text{2013 Price of Apples} \times \text{2013 Quantity of Apples})$$
$$+ (\text{2013 Price of Oranges} \times \text{2013 Quantity of Oranges}).$$

Similarly, real GDP in 2014 would be

$$\text{Real GDP} = (\text{2013 Price of Apples} \times \text{2014 Quantity of Apples})$$
$$+ (\text{2013 Price of Oranges} \times \text{2014 Quantity of Oranges}).$$

And real GDP in 2015 would be

$$\text{Real GDP} = (\text{2013 Price of Apples} \times \text{2015 Quantity of Apples})$$
$$+ (\text{2013 Price of Oranges} \times \text{2015 Quantity of Oranges}).$$

Notice that 2013 prices are used to compute real GDP for all three years. Because the prices are held constant, real GDP varies from year to year only if the quantities produced vary. Because a society's ability to provide economic satisfaction for its members ultimately depends on the quantities of goods and services produced, real GDP provides a better measure of economic well-being than nominal GDP.

The GDP Deflator

From nominal GDP and real GDP we can compute a third statistic: the GDP deflator. The **GDP deflator**, also called the *implicit price deflator for GDP*, is the ratio of nominal GDP to real GDP:

$$\text{GDP Deflator} = \frac{\text{Nominal GDP}}{\text{Real GDP}}.$$

The GDP deflator reflects what is happening to the overall level of prices in the economy.

To understand this better, consider again an economy with only one good, bread. If P is the price of bread and Q is the quantity sold, then nominal GDP is the total number of euros spent on bread in that year, $P \times Q$. Real GDP is the number of loaves of bread produced in that year times the price of bread in some base year, $P_{base} \times Q$. The GDP deflator is the price of bread in that year relative to the price of bread in the base year, P/P_{base}.

The definition of the GDP deflator allows us to separate nominal GDP into two parts: one part measures quantities (real GDP) and the other measures prices (the GDP deflator). That is,

$$\text{Nominal GDP} = \text{Real GDP} \times \text{GDP Deflator}.$$

Nominal GDP measures the current money value of the output of the economy. Real GDP measures output valued at constant prices. The GDP deflator measures the price of output relative to its price in the base year. We can also write this equation as

$$\text{Real GDP} = \frac{\text{Nominal GDP}}{\text{GDP Deflator}}.$$

In this form, you can see how the deflator earns its name: it is used to deflate (that is, take inflation out of) nominal GDP to yield real GDP.

Chained-Volume Measures of Real GDP

We have been discussing real GDP as if the prices used to compute this measure never change from their base-year values. If this were truly the case, over time the prices would become more and more dated. For instance, the price of computers (comparing like with like) has fallen substantially in recent years, while the price of a year at university has risen. When valuing the production of computers and education, it would be misleading to use the prices that prevailed 10 or 20 years ago.

F Y I

Two Arithmetic Tricks for Working with Percentage Changes

For manipulating many relationships in economics, there is an arithmetic trick that is useful to know: *the percentage change of a product of two variables is approximately the sum of the percentage changes in each of the variables.*

To see how this trick works, consider an example. Let P denote the GDP deflator and Y denote real GDP. Nominal GDP is $P \times Y$. The trick states that

$$\text{Percentage Change in } (P \times Y)$$
$$= (\text{Percentage Change in } P)$$
$$+ (\text{Percentage Change in } Y).$$

For instance, suppose that in one year, real GDP is 100 and the GDP deflator is 2; the next year, real GDP is 103 and the GDP deflator is 2.1. We can calculate that real GDP rose by 3 per cent and that the GDP deflator rose by 5 per cent. Nominal GDP rose from 200 the first year to 216.3 the second year, an increase of 8.15 per cent. Notice that the growth in nominal GDP (8.15 per cent) is approximately the sum of the growth in the GDP deflator (5 per cent) and the growth in real GDP (3 per cent).[5]

A second arithmetic trick follows as a corollary to the first: *the percentage change of a ratio is approximately the percentage change in the numerator minus the percentage change in the denominator.* Again, consider an example. Let Y denote GDP and L denote the population, so that Y/L is GDP per person. The second trick states:

$$\text{Percentage Change in } (Y/L)$$
$$= (\text{Percentage Change in } Y)$$
$$- (\text{Percentage Change in } L).$$

For instance, suppose that in the first year, Y is 100,000 and L is 100, so Y/L is 1000; in the second year, Y is 110,000 and L is 103, so Y/L is 1068. Notice that the growth in GDP per person (6.8 per cent) is approximately the growth in income (10 per cent) minus the growth in population (3 per cent).

---

[5]*Mathematical note:* The proof that this trick works begins with the chain rule from calculus:

$$d(PY) = Y\,dP + P\,dY.$$

Now divide both sides of this equation by PY to obtain:

$$d(PY)/(PY) = dP/P + dY/Y.$$

Notice that all three terms in this equation are percentage changes.

To solve this problem, the UK Office for National Statistics (ONS) used to update periodically the prices used to compute real GDP. About every five years, a new base year was chosen. The prices were then held fixed and used to measure year-to-year changes in the production of goods and services until the base year was updated once again.

In 2003, the ONS announced a new policy for dealing with changes in the base year. In particular, it now emphasizes *chained-volume* measures of real GDP. With these new measures, the base year changes continuously over time. In essence, average prices in 2012 and 2013 are used to measure real growth from 2012 to 2013; average prices in 2013 and 2014 are used to measure real growth from 2013 to 2014; and so on. These various year-to-year growth rates are then put together to form a 'chain' that can be used to compare the output of goods and services between any two dates.

This new chained-volume measure of real GDP is better than the more traditional measure (the constant-price measure) because it ensures that the prices used to compute real GDP are never far out of date. For most purposes, however, the differences are not important. It turns out that the two measures of real GDP are highly correlated with each other. As a practical matter, both measures of real GDP reflect the same thing: economy-wide changes in the production of goods and services.

Chained-volume measures of real GDP are recommended by Eurostat, the statistical agency of the European Union, and they are now calculated by many European countries (France and Luxembourg, for example, have published them since 1999, and the Netherlands since 1982). They were first published by the US in 1996.

The Components of Expenditure and the National Income Accounts

Economists and policy makers care not only about the economy's total output of goods and services, but also about the allocation of this output among alternative uses. In most European countries, the convention is adopted in the national income accounts of dividing GDP into three broad categories of spending:

- final consumption expenditure
- gross capital formation
- net exports.[6]

As we shall see, macroeconomists often prefer a slightly different categorization of GDP, but, for the moment, let's take a closer look at these standard national accounts categories.

Final consumption expenditure is spending on goods and services purely for their own sake (i.e. with the aim of consuming them!). This is further broken down according to who is doing the consumption – namely households, non-profit institutions serving households and general government:

- Household consumption is divided into four subcategories in the national accounts: non-durable goods, durable goods, semi-durable goods and services:
  - Non-durable goods are goods that last only a short time, such as food and beverages.
  - Durable goods are goods that can be used repeatedly over a period considerably longer than one year, and they usually have a 'high' price relative to other goods. Examples of durable goods are 'big-ticket items' such as cars and televisions, and 'white goods' (i.e. large domestic electrical appliances, such as fridges, washing machines and tumble dryers).
  - Semi-durable goods also have an expected lifetime that exceeds a year, but it is less than that for durable goods, and their price tends to be lower than that of a durable good. Clothing, shoes and sports equipment are examples

---

[6] Members of the European Union calculate their national accounts using a common set of conventions and definitions developed by Eurostat in 1995 and known as the European System of Accounts, or ESA95.

of semi-durables. If you want to make yourself a cup of coffee and listen to a CD (perhaps you lost your iPod), you will need a non-durable good (coffee), a durable good (a CD player) and a semi-durable good (a CD).

- Services include the work done for consumers by individuals and firms, such as haircuts, waiter services and massages. If you buy a cup of coffee sitting outside a café on the Champs-Elysées in Paris, part of the money you pay will be for the services of the waiter who brings you the coffee.

■ Non-profit institutions serving households (NPISH) are very similar to households in that they do not aim to make profits; in effect, they consume on behalf of households. Examples of NPISH are academic establishments (such as universities), trades unions, churches and religious societies, social clubs (that are run by their own members rather than as profit-making businesses) and charities.

■ General government consumption includes spending by both local and central government on goods and services such as items of military equipment and the services that government workers provide. It does not include transfer payments to individuals, such as social security and unemployment benefits. Because transfer payments reallocate existing income and are not made in exchange for goods and services, they are not part of GDP.

In addition, final consumption expenditure includes an allowance for net tourism in the national accounts. When Danish tourists visit Rome to see the Colosseum, they buy Italian goods and services (e.g. ice cream and hotel services). When Italians visit Barcelona to admire the wonderful cathedral, they buy Spanish goods and services. Net tourist consumption is the amount of consumption done in the domestic economy by foreign tourists less the amount of consumption done by domestic residents when they go on holiday and become tourists in foreign countries.

Gross capital formation is actually a fancy way of saying total investment (i.e. the total amount of spending that is aimed at providing something in the future). When a firm invests in building a new factory, it does so in order to produce goods in the future that can be sold at a profit. When the government invests in building a new motorway, it does so in order to provide improved transport services to the economy in the future. Gross capital formation is broken down into two main subcategories: gross fixed capital formation and inventory investment.

■ Gross fixed capital formation is further broken down into business fixed investment, general government fixed investment and fixed investment in dwellings (or residential fixed investment):

- Business fixed investment is the purchase of new factories and equipment by firms.

- General government fixed investment is the purchase of schools, motorways and similar items by local and central government.

- Residential fixed investment is the purchase of new housing by households and landlords.

■ Inventory investment is the increase in firms' inventories of goods (if inventories are falling, inventory investment is negative).

Net exports are the value of goods and services exported to other countries minus the value of goods and services that foreigners provide us with. Net exports are positive when the value of our exports is greater than the value of our imports, and negative when the value of our imports is greater than the value of our exports. Net exports represent the net expenditure from abroad on our goods and services, which provides income for domestic producers.

Now, as we pointed out before, macroeconomists usually like to adjust these standard national accounts categories slightly when they are thinking about the macroeconomy. What are these adjustments and why do macroeconomists make them?

First, because government spending can be used by the government as a tool with which to influence the economy, macroeconomists usually find it useful to fish government spending on consumption and investment out of the final consumption expenditure and gross capital formation expenditure categories (which may then be referred to simply as investment and consumption) and define a new category of total government purchases. Second, for most macroeconomic analysis, the distinction between households and non-profit institutions serving households is not important because they tend to behave similarly, and so lumping the final consumption expenditure of households and NPISH together is a useful simplification. Third, although the national accounts include net tourism as a component of final consumption, from a macroeconomist's point of view, net tourism is better classified as part of net exports, since selling an ice cream to an American tourist in Rome has the same effect on the economy as exporting ice cream to the United States (and selling hotel services to foreign tourists is not very different from selling, say, insurance services to foreign households).

What we are then left with is a category of **investment** that includes only investment by firms (business fixed investment plus changes in inventories) and households (in the form of residential buildings); a category of **consumption** that includes consumption by households plus consumption by members of households through clubs, societies and charities (NPISH); a category of net exports that includes an allowance for net tourism; and a category of **government purchases** that includes general government consumption expenditure and general government investment expenditure. Hence, we can define the macroeconomist's four categories of expenditure as:

- Consumption (C) = household final consumption expenditure *plus* final consumption expenditure of NPISH

- Investment (I) = business investment *plus* residential investment *plus* inventory investment

- Government purchases (G) = general government consumption *plus* general government investment

- Net exports (NX) = exports *minus* imports *plus* net tourism.

Because all expenditure in the economy must fall into one of these four categories, they must add up to total GDP. Thus, letting Y stand for GDP,

$$Y = C + I + G + NX.$$

FYI

What Is Investment?

Newcomers to macroeconomics are sometimes confused by how macroeconomists use familiar words in new and specific ways. One example is the term 'investment'. The confusion arises because what looks like investment for an individual may not be investment for the economy as a whole. The general rule is that the economy's investment does not include purchases that merely reallocate existing assets among different individuals. Investment, as macroeconomists use the term, creates new capital.

Let's consider some examples. Suppose we observe these two events:

■ Smith buys for himself a 150-year-old Victorian house.

■ Jones builds for herself a brand new contemporary house.

What is the total investment here? Two houses, one house or zero?

A macroeconomist seeing these two transactions counts only the Jones house as investment. Smith's transaction has not created new housing for the economy; it has merely reallocated existing housing. Smith's purchase is investment for Smith, but it is disinvestment for the person selling the house. By contrast, Jones has added new housing to the economy; her new house is counted as investment.

Similarly, consider these two events:

■ Richard Branson buys £5 million in British Petroleum shares from the Duke of Westminster on the London Stock Exchange.

■ Cadbury Schweppes sells £50 million in shares to the public and uses the proceeds to build a new chocolate factory.

Here, investment is £50 million. In the first transaction, Richard Branson is investing in BP shares, and the Duke of Westminster is disinvesting; there is no investment for the economy. In contrast, Cadbury Schweppes is using some of the economy's output of goods and services to add to its stock of capital; hence, its new factory is counted as investment.

In words, GDP is the sum of consumption, investment, government purchases and net exports. Strictly speaking, this equation should be written as an *identity*, or ≡ (an equation that must hold because of the way the variables are defined) and is therefore called the **national income accounts identity**. However, we shall follow normal practice and use the usual equals sign, =, instead of an identity sign.

CASE STUDY

GDP and Its Components

In 2010 the GDP of the United Kingdom totalled about £1458 billion. This number is so large that it is almost impossible to comprehend. We can make it easier to understand by dividing it by the 2010 UK population of about 62 million. In this way, we obtain GDP per person – the amount of expenditure for every man, woman and child – which equalled £23,516 in 2010. How did this GDP get used? Table 2-2 shows that consumption made up about two-thirds of GDP (64.3 per cent, to be precise), or £15,112 per person. Investment was £2887 per person (12.3 per cent of GDP). Government purchases were

£6161 per person (26.4 per cent of total expenditure). Each Brit on average bought £7693 of goods imported from abroad and produced £7048 of goods that were exported to other countries – a gap of £645 per person. Hence, net exports were negative (−2.7 per cent of GDP). Furthermore, because the average Brit earned less from selling to foreigners than she spent on foreign goods, she must have financed the difference by taking out loans from foreigners (or, equivalently, by selling them some of her assets). Thus, the average UK resident borrowed £645 from abroad in 2010.

In Figure 2-3, we show the breakdown of GDP into private consumption (C), investment (I), government expenditure (G) and net exports (NX) in 2010 for 12 other European countries. Because the components of GDP are all positive for the first eight countries, Denmark, the Netherlands, Switzerland, Germany, Finland, Norway, Ireland and Sweden, we can represent the data in a pie chart, which shows well how GDP is shared out among the various components of expenditure. In broad terms, the picture is similar to that for the UK, with private consumption expenditure taking the largest slice of the national pie, at around 50–60 per cent of GDP. For the last four countries, France, Italy, Spain and Greece, however, we have to use a bar chart to represent the shares of expenditure because net exports are negative. Nevertheless, the bar charts again show that consumption takes the biggest share of GDP. Note, however, that in the countries with negative net exports, consumption tends to account for a higher share of GDP: the last

TABLE 2-2

UK GDP and the Components of Expenditure 2010

	Total (billions of pounds)	Per Person (pounds)	%
Gross Domestic Product	1458	23,516	100
Consumption (1)	937	15,112	64.3
Investment	179	2887	12.3
Business fixed investment	119	1920	
Residential fixed investment	53	854	
Inventory investment	7	113	
Government Expenditure	382	6161	26.4
General government consumption	337	5435	
General government investment	45	726	
Net Exports	−40	−645	−2.7
Exports	437	7048	
Imports	477	7693	

Source: UK Office for National Statistics.
Note: (1) Consumption by households and by non-profit institutions providing services to households.

FIGURE 2-3

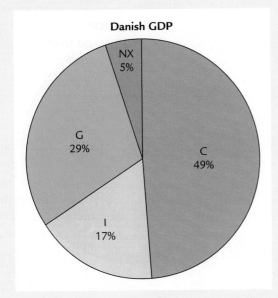

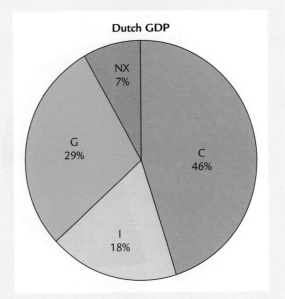

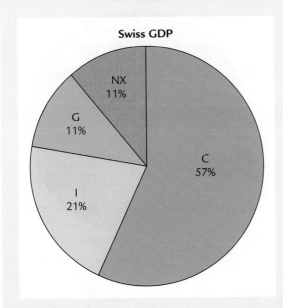

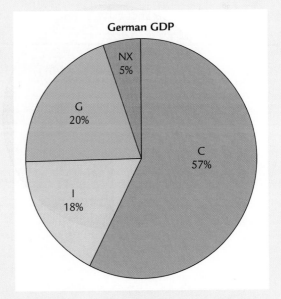

The Breakdown of GDP into its Main Components for Some European Countries in 2010

Source: Eurostat.
Notes:
(C) Private consumption
(I) Investment
(G) Government expenditure
(NX) Net exports

FIGURE **2-3** *Continued*

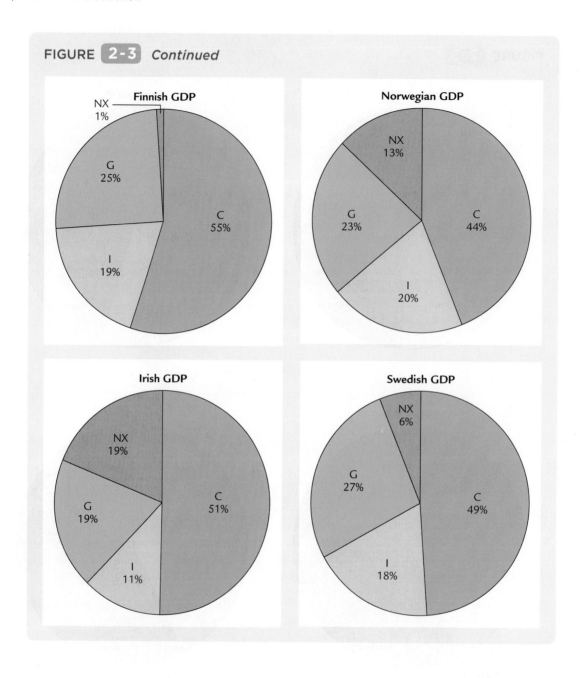

four countries shown in Figure 2-3 all had higher consumption levels as a percentage of GDP than the first eight countries. In general, countries that have lower consumption have bigger net exports, since lower consumption means – all other things being equal – that there is less demand for imports and that more of GDP can be exported. Conversely, countries with relatively high consumption will tend to have low net exports, other things equal. Thus, as we saw earlier, the UK's relatively high level of consumption of just over 64 per cent of GDP was accompanied by negative net exports of about

FIGURE **2-3** *Continued*

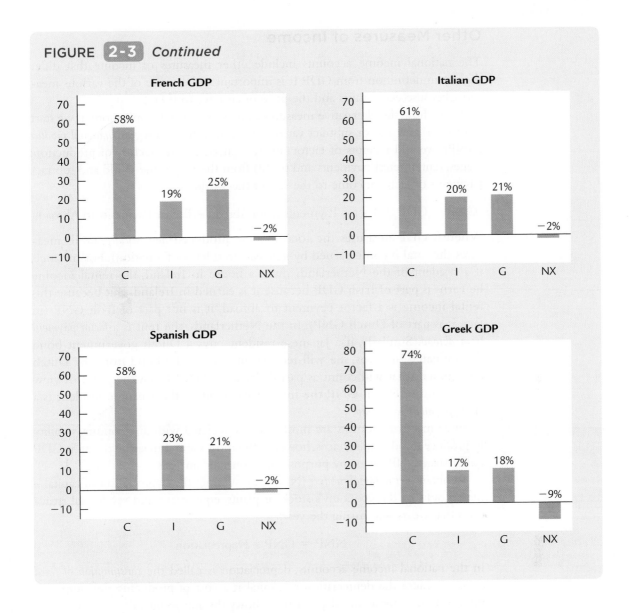

3 per cent of GDP in 2010. Similarly, in Greece, for example, consumption was nearly three-quarters of its GDP in 2010 and its net exports were −9 per cent of national income. Germany and Switzerland had consumption levels of 57 per cent of GDP, which was only slightly less than that of France or Spain, and nevertheless managed healthy levels of net exports of 5 per cent and 11 per cent of their GDP respectively, but this is because government expenditure as a percentage of GDP was relatively low in these countries in 2010.

These data come from the UK Office of National Statistics and from Eurostat. You can find more recent data on UK GDP at its website (www.statistics.gov uk) and on GDP for other members of the EU at the Eurostat website http://epp.eurostat.ec.europa.eu. ■

Other Measures of Income

The national income accounts include other measures of income that differ slightly in definition from GDP. It is important to be aware of the various measures, because economists and the press often refer to them.

To see how the alternative measures of income relate to one another, we start with GDP and add or subtract various quantities. To obtain *gross national product* (GNP), we add receipts of factor income (income from factors of production: wages, rent, interest payments and profit) from the rest of the world and subtract payments of factor income to the rest of the world:

GNP = GDP + Factor Payments from Abroad − Factor Payments to Abroad.

Whereas GDP measures the total income produced *domestically*, GNP measures the total income earned by *nationals* (residents of a nation). For instance, if a resident of the Netherlands owns a house in Ireland, the rental income he earns is part of Irish GDP because it is earned in Ireland. But because this rental income is a factor payment to abroad, it is not part of Irish GNP (in fact, it is part of Dutch GNP). In the Netherlands, the rent is a *factor payment from abroad*. Similarly, if a Japanese resident buys a Dutch government bond denominated in euros, she will receive interest on the bond from the Dutch government that will count as part of Japanese GNP. From the point of view of computing Dutch GNP, the interest payment to the Japanese resident is a *factor payment to abroad*.

Since macroeconomists are most often concerned with an economy's ability to produce goods and services, however, the most natural measure to use is GDP rather than GNP for many purposes in economic analysis.

To obtain *net national product* (NNP), we subtract the depreciation of capital – the amount of the economy's stock of plants, equipment and residential structures that wears out during the year:

NNP = GNP − Depreciation.

In the national income accounts, depreciation is called the *consumption of fixed capital*. Because the depreciation of capital is a cost of producing the output of the economy, subtracting depreciation shows the net result of economic activity. However, because of the difficulties in obtaining reliable estimates of the consumption of fixed capital (depreciation), GDP remains the most widely used measure of economic activity.

CASE STUDY

Real GDP per Person across the European Union

Eurostat, the statistical agency of the European Union, collects statistics from member countries of the EU (plus a few other countries) primarily so that comparisons can be made across the EU. This is why it is important for all

EU members to use the same conventions when they are constructing their national statistics. In Table 2-3 we have listed data obtained from Eurostat on real GDP per person in 2011 for all members of the EU, plus a few others. How do we interpret these figures? Eurostat has done two things to the real GDP figures. First, it has made a purchasing power parity adjustment. In other words, it has adjusted them to put them into a common currency and also take account of price differences in different countries. Second, it has expressed them as an index, such that a value of 100 is equal to the average level of real GDP across all 27 member countries in 2011. Therefore, the UK figure of 109 means that the average UK resident was about 9 per cent better off than the EU-wide average. It is also interesting to note that most of the countries that joined the EU prior to 2004 (the 'EU-15') are relatively rich: of the EU-15, only Greece, Portugal and Spain had levels of income per capita lower than the EU-wide average, while *all* the countries that joined in 2004 or subsequently did so.

The real GDP per person index figure of 271 for Luxembourg in 2011 is particularly impressive: it seems that the average resident of Luxembourg was

TABLE 2-3

Real GDP per Person in the European Union and Selected Countries 2011

Countries That Joined the European Union Before 2004		Countries That Have Joined the European Union Since 2004	
Austria	129	Bulgaria	46
Belgium	119	Cyprus	94
Finland	114	Czech Republic	80
Denmark	125	Estonia	67
France	108	Hungary	66
Germany	121	Latvia	58
Greece	79	Lithuania	66
Ireland	129	Malta	85
Italy	100	Poland	64
Luxembourg	271	Romania	49
Portugal	77	Slovakia	73
Netherlands	131	Slovenia	84
Spain	98		
Sweden	127	Other Countries	
United Kingdom	109	United States	148

Source: Eurostat.
Notes: Real GDP per person in 2011 is measured at purchasing power parity (i.e. after adjusting for price-level differences and, where necessary, differences in currency). Figures are expressed as an index with 100 equal to the average across the 27 member countries of the EU in 2011.

two-and-a-quarter times better off than the EU-wide average! Luxembourg, however, is an unusual case, where GDP in fact gives a misleading view of how rich a country actually is. This is because Luxembourg is a very small country and a very high proportion of its labour force (about 40 per cent) lives just across its borders, in Germany, France and Belgium. These workers are classed as non-resident in Luxembourg and are therefore not taken into account when calculating GDP per person, even though they contribute to the formation of value added and earn wages and salaries. Thus, when GDP per person is calculated, because these non-resident workers are omitted from the denominator, the resulting figure looks very large. Adjusting for this effect is not straightforward, however. In 2011, the resident population of Luxembourg was about 500,000 and its labour force comprised about 215,000 resident workers and about 135,000 workers who were non-residents living across the border. Thus, the 2011 GDP per person figure has been derived by dividing total GDP by the total population figure of about 500,000, whereas, allowing for the 135,000 or so cross-border workers, perhaps it should be divided by 635,000 (= 500,000 + 135,000). However, this ignores the fact that those 135,000 cross-border workers will have non-working dependants (e.g. school-age children) who are not in the labour force. In Luxembourg, the number of *resident* people not in the labour force was about 285,000 (= 500,000 − 215,000), or about 130 per cent of the resident labour force of 215,000. If we assume a similar proportion of non-working dependants among the cross-border workers, we need to add about 175,500 (130 per cent of 135,000) to the total number of people directly involved in the production of the national output of Luxembourg, either because they work in Luxembourg or because they are a non-working dependant of someone else who works there. Thus, the total number of people dependent on Luxembourg national output is the sum of the resident population (about 500,000) plus the number of non-resident workers (about 135,000) plus the number of people dependent on the non-resident workers (by our estimate about 175,500), bringing it to 810,500 (= 500,000 + 135,000 + 175,500). Adjusting the index of 271 to allow for this (i.e. multiplying by 500,000/810,500) reduces it to about 170. On this estimate, Luxembourg was still a very rich country, with GDP per person dependent on that GDP about 70 per cent greater than the EU average – significantly richer than both Switzerland and the United States. ∎

Seasonal Adjustment

Because real GDP and the other measures of income reflect how well the economy is performing, economists are interested in studying the quarter-to-quarter fluctuations in these variables. Yet when we start to do so, one fact leaps out: all these measures of income exhibit a regular seasonal pattern. The output of the economy rises during the year, reaching a peak in the fourth quarter (October, November and December), and then falling in the first quarter (January, February and March) of the next year.

It is not surprising that real GDP follows a seasonal cycle. Some of these changes are attributable to changes in our ability to produce: for example, building houses is more difficult during the cold weather of winter than during other seasons. In addition, people have seasonal tastes: they have preferred times for such activities as annual holidays and Christmas shopping.

When economists study fluctuations in real GDP and other economic variables, they often want to eliminate the portion of fluctuations due to predictable seasonal changes. Statisticians have developed methods of adjusting data for these predictable changes, so that many of the economic statistics reported in the newspapers are *seasonally adjusted*. This means that the data have been adjusted to remove the regular seasonal fluctuations. (The precise statistical procedures used are too elaborate to bother with here, but in essence they involve subtracting those changes in income that are predictable just from the change in season.) Therefore, when you observe a rise or fall in real GDP or any other data series, you must look beyond the seasonal cycle for the explanation.

2-2 Measuring the Cost of Living: The Consumer Price Index

A pound or a euro today does not buy as much as it did even a few years ago. The cost of almost everything has gone up. This increase in the overall level of prices is called *inflation*, and it is one of the primary concerns of economists and policy makers. In later chapters we examine in detail the causes and effects of inflation. Here we discuss how economists measure changes in the cost of living.

The Price of a Basket of Goods

The most commonly used measure of the level of prices is the consumer price index (CPI). The government statistical agency has the job of computing the CPI. It begins by collecting the prices of thousands of goods and services. Just as GDP turns the quantities of many goods and services into a single number measuring the value of production, the CPI turns the prices of many goods and services into a single index measuring the overall level of prices.

How should economists aggregate the many prices in the economy into a single index that reliably measures the price level? They could simply compute an average of all prices. Yet this approach would treat all goods and services equally. Because people buy more chicken than caviar, the price of chicken should have a greater weight in the CPI than the price of caviar. The statistical agency weights different items by computing the price of a basket of goods and services purchased by a typical consumer. The CPI is the price of this basket of goods and services relative to the price of the same basket in some base year.

For example, suppose that the typical consumer buys 5 apples and 2 oranges every month. Then the basket of goods consists of 5 apples and 2 oranges, and the CPI is

$$CPI = \frac{(5 \times \text{Current Prices of Apples})}{(5 \times 2012 \text{ Prices of Apples})} + \frac{(2 \times \text{Current Price of Oranges})}{(2 \times 2012 \text{ Price of Oranges})}.$$

In this CPI, 2012 is the base year. The index tells us how much it costs now to buy 5 apples and 2 oranges relative to how much it cost to buy the same basket of fruit in 2012.

The CPI is the most closely watched index of prices, but it is not the only such index. Another is the producer price index, which measures the price of a typical basket of goods bought by firms rather than consumers. In addition to these overall price indices, the statistical agency computes price indices for specific types of goods, such as food, housing and energy.

The CPI versus the GDP Deflator

Earlier in this chapter we saw another measure of prices – the implicit price deflator for GDP, which is the ratio of nominal GDP to real GDP. The GDP deflator and the CPI give somewhat different information about what is happening to the overall level of prices in the economy. There are three key differences between the two measures.

The first difference is that the GDP deflator measures the prices of all goods and services produced, whereas the CPI measures the prices of only the goods and services bought by consumers. Thus, an increase in the price of goods bought only by firms or the government will show up in the GDP deflator but not in the CPI.

The second difference is that the GDP deflator includes only those goods produced domestically. Imported goods are not part of GDP and do not show up in the GDP deflator. Hence, an increase in the price of a Toyota made in Japan and sold in this country affects the CPI, because the Toyota is bought by consumers, but it does not affect the GDP deflator.

The third and most subtle difference results from the way the two measures aggregate the many prices in the economy. The CPI assigns fixed weights to the prices of different goods, whereas the GDP deflator assigns changing weights. In other words, the CPI is computed using a fixed basket of goods, whereas the GDP deflator allows the basket of goods to change over time as the composition of GDP changes. The following example shows how these approaches differ. Suppose that major frosts destroy the economy's apple crop. The quantity of apples produced falls to zero, and the price of the few apples that remain on greengrocers' shelves is driven sky-high. Because apples are no longer part of GDP, the increase in the price of apples does not show up in the GDP deflator. But because the CPI is computed with a fixed basket of goods that includes apples, the increase in the price of apples causes a substantial rise in the CPI.

Economists call a price index with a fixed basket of goods a *Laspeyres index* and a price index with a changing basket a *Paasche index*. Economic theorists have studied the properties of these different types of price indices to determine which is a better measure of the cost of living. The answer, it turns out, is that neither is clearly superior. When prices of different goods are changing by different amounts, a Laspeyres (fixed basket) index tends to overstate the increase in the cost of living because it does not take into account that consumers have the opportunity to substitute less expensive goods for more expensive ones. By contrast, a Paasche (changing basket) index tends to understate the increase in the cost of living. Although it accounts for the substitution of alternative goods, it does not reflect the reduction in consumers' welfare that may result from such substitutions.

The example of the destroyed apple crop shows the problems with Laspeyres and Paasche price indices. Because the CPI is a Laspeyres index, it overstates the impact of the increase in apple prices on consumers: by using a fixed basket of goods, it ignores consumers' ability to substitute other fruit for apples (e.g. oranges). By contrast, because the GDP deflator is a Paasche index, it understates the impact on consumers: the GDP deflator shows no rise in prices, yet surely the higher price of apples makes consumers worse off.[7]

Luckily, the difference between the GDP deflator and the CPI is usually not large in practice.

Does the CPI Overstate Inflation?

The CPI is a closely watched measure of inflation. For example, both the Bank of England and the European Central Bank attempt to achieve a target rate of inflation as measured by the CPI, and may change interest rates in order to try to achieve this target.

Because so much depends on the CPI, it is important to ensure that this measure of the price level is accurate. Many economists believe that, for a number of reasons, the CPI tends to overstate inflation.

One problem is the substitution bias we have already discussed. Because the CPI measures the price of a fixed basket of goods, it does not reflect the ability of consumers to substitute cheaper goods for more expensive goods in their basket. Thus, when relative prices change, the true cost of living rises less rapidly than the CPI.

A second problem is the introduction of new goods. When a new good is introduced into the marketplace, consumers are better off because they have more products from which to choose. In effect, the introduction of new goods increases the real value of the euro. Yet this increase in the purchasing power of the euro is not reflected in a lower CPI.

A third problem is unmeasured changes in quality. When a firm changes the quality of a good it sells, not all of the good's price change reflects a change in the cost of living. Government statistical agencies often try to account for changes in the quality of goods over time. For example, if a car manufacturer increases the horsepower of a particular car model from one year to the next, then the CPI will reflect the change: the quality-adjusted price of the car will not rise as fast as the unadjusted price. Yet many changes in quality, such as comfort or safety, are hard to measure. If unmeasured quality improvement (rather

---

[7] Because a Laspeyres index overstates inflation and a Paasche index understates inflation, one might strike a compromise by taking an average of the two measured rates of inflation. This is the approach taken by another type of index, called a *Fisher index*.

than unmeasured quality deterioration) is typical, then the measured CPI rises faster than it should.

Clearly, getting a perfect measure of inflation is impossible. For these reasons, macroeconomists often factor in the fact that the CPI overstates inflation. For example, this is one reason why attempting to achieve zero measured inflation is not recommended by most macroeconomists.

The Consumer Price Index and the Retail Price Index: A Study of European Harmony

Before the end of 2003, it was more usual in the UK to measure prices using an index known as the Retail Price Index (RPI). In December 2003, however, the UK Chancellor of the Exchequer announced that all policy announcements concerning inflation and prices would relate to the CPI rather than the RPI, so that movements in the CPI became the main measure of inflation, although the RPI continues to be used in the UK for a variety of purposes, such as the indexation of pensions and other state benefits, and for valuing index-linked government bonds. What is the difference between the CPI and the RPI, and why the switch?

The RPI is a price index constructed in the way described above, and differs from the CPI mainly in the goods and services included in the basket and in the coverage of households. In particular, the CPI excludes a number of items that are included in RPI, mainly related to housing, such as council tax and house mortgage interest payments. These items are excluded because if council taxes rise, or mortgage payments rise due to an increase in interest rates, then the inflation rate as measured by the RPI will rise, even though underlying inflationary pressures in the economy may not have changed. Also, the CPI covers all private households, whereas the RPI excludes the top 4 per cent by income and pensioner households who derive at least three-quarters of their income from state benefits. The argument for excluding such households in the RPI is that they may spend their money on items that are not typical of the general population; the argument for including them in the CPI is in order to be consistent across different countries when measuring inflation, since it is not common to make adjustments like this in many countries. The CPI also includes the residents of institutional households such as student hostels, and also foreign visitors to the UK. This means that it covers some items that are not in the RPI, such as stockbrokers' fees, university accommodation fees and foreign students' university tuition fees. The two indices also differ in some of the very fine details of the way in which prices are measured (such as allowance for quality adjustment). In general, the two measures move very closely, although in recent years the CPI has tended to rise more slowly than the RPI – by an average of around 0.5 per cent a year over the period 1997–2012, as is evident in Figure 2-4. This is mainly due to the CPI's exclusion of most

FIGURE 2-4

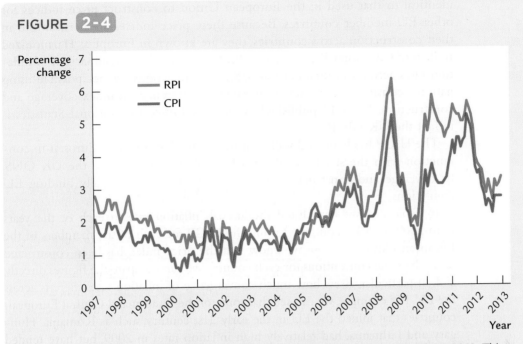

The UK Retail Price Index and the Consumer Price Index, 1997–2012 This figure shows the percentage change in the RPI and the CPI for the UK every year from 1997 to 2012. Although these two measures of prices diverge at times, they usually tell the same story about how quickly prices are rising.

Source: UK Office for National Statistics.

housing costs that are included in RPI, which have been rising relatively rapidly in the UK during these years.[8]

What was the point of introducing the CPI? One reason is that some economists believe that it is closer to the concept of the overall price level employed in macroeconomic analysis – although others would argue that it may be misleading in the way in which it understates housing costs by excluding mortgage interest payments and council taxes. The main reason for its adoption, however, is that the construction methodology of the CPI is

---

[8] Another, more technical reason why the CPI tends to be less than the RPI is that the conventions for constructing the CPI which have been adopted across Europe (the Harmonized Index of Consumer Prices) include using geometric rather than arithmetic averages. In an arithmetic average, we add together values and divide by the number of them we have. So, for example, if one price increased by 25 per cent from the base period and another price decreased by 20 per cent, their index values would be 125 and 80 respectively, and the arithmetic average of these two values would be $(125 + 80)/2 = 102.5$, indicating an 'average' price increase of 2.5 per cent. In a geometric average, if we have, say, n values, we take the product of the n values (i.e. multiply them all together) and then take the n-th root (i.e. find the number that, multiplied by itself n times, would yield a number equal to the product of the n values). Thus, in the previous example where we had individual index values of 125 and 80, the geometric average would be $\sqrt{(125 \times 80)} = 100$, indicating that the 'average' increase has been zero. In general, a geometric average is always less than an arithmetic average, so this builds in a bias for the CPI to be less than the RPI.

identical to that used in the European Union to construct price indices for other EU member countries. Because these price indices are harmonized in their construction across countries, they are known in Europe as Harmonized Indices of Consumer Prices, or HICPs. This allows direct comparison of inflation rates across EU member states. Such comparisons are not possible using national consumer price indices because of differences in index coverage and construction. The CPI published by the UK Office for National Statistics is in fact the UK HICP.

The HICP has been and will continue to be developed by Eurostat in conjunction with the statistical offices of member states, such as the UK ONS. Its coverage and construction are set out in a series of legally binding EU regulations.

In Table 2-4 we have listed the annual inflation rate in each of the years from 2009 to 2012, computed using the HICP for each of the members of the European Union. Because we know that the price index has been constructed using the same conventions for each country, we can compare the figures directly and, in particular, assess how much convergence of inflation rates there is across the EU. For example, we can see that some of the Eastern and Central European countries that joined the EU in the early 21st century, such as Romania, Hungary and Lithuania, had relatively high inflation rates in 2009, but have tended towards the EU average by the end of the period. We can also assess the impact of the international financial crisis of 2008 on inflation rates across the EU: in the two years immediately after the crisis inflation rates were held back to very low levels by historical standards, and some countries, such as Ireland, had negative inflation rates.

Measures of inflation based on price indices such as the CPI and the RPI are sometimes used to protect the real value of pensions. For example, if a person retires with a pension of, say, £20,000 a year, and inflation rises by, say, 2 per cent, the pension provider may agree to increase the pension by 2 per cent in the following year, in this case to £20,400. This is called indexation. Now, the choice of which measure of inflation to use when indexing a pension may be important since, as we have seen, the UK RPI has, over the past 15 years or so, tended to record inflation about 0.5 per cent or so higher per year than the CPI. So using the CPI rather than the RPI will tend to reduce the amount of increase in pension that the pension provider grants in order to compensate for inflation. Over time, the effect of this choice on the value of the amount of the pension paid can be significant. Suppose, for example, that the RPI measures an average inflation rate of 2.5 per cent over the period you are in retirement and receiving a pension, while the CPI records only an average of 2.0 per cent. If your pension is indexed by the RPI, it will have risen by 28 per cent after ten years, but if the pension is linked to the CPI, it will have risen by only 22 per cent – a difference of 6 per cent. And after 20 years, the difference is even bigger: your pension will have risen by about 50 per cent in cash terms if it is indexed by the CPI but by about 65 per cent if it is linked to the RPI, a difference of 15 per cent. In April 2011, the UK government announced that it was going to do exactly this for public sector pensions – link their indexed

TABLE 2-4

Annual Inflation Rate in Selected European Countries, 2009–2012

	2009	2010	2011	2012
Belgium	0	2.3	3.4	2.6
Bulgaria	2.5	3.0	3.4	2.4
Czech Republic	0.6	1.2	2.1	3.5
Denmark	1.1	2.2	2.7	2.4
Germany	0.2	1.2	2.5	2.1
Estonia	0.2	2.7	5.1	4.2
Ireland	−1.7	−1.6	1.2	1.9
Greece	1.3	4.7	3.1	1.0
Spain	−0.2	2.0	3.1	2.4
France	0.1	1.7	2.3	2.2
Italy	0.8	1.6	2.9	3.3
Cyprus	0.2	2.6	3.5	3.1
Latvia	3.3	−1.2	4.2	2.3
Lithuania	4.2	1.2	4.1	3.2
Luxembourg	0	2.8	3.7	2.9
Hungary	4.0	4.7	3.9	5.7
Malta	1.8	2.0	2.5	3.2
Netherlands	1.0	0.9	2.5	2.8
Austria	0.4	1.7	3.6	2.6
Poland	4.0	2.7	3.9	3.7
Portugal	−0.9	1.4	3.6	2.8
Romania	5.6	6.1	5.8	3.4
Slovenia	0.9	2.1	2.1	2.8
Slovakia	0.9	0.7	4.1	3.7
Finland	1.6	1.7	3.3	3.2
Sweden	1.9	1.9	1.4	0.9
United Kingdom	2.2	3.3	4.5	2.8
Iceland	16.3	7.5	4.2	6.0
Norway	2.3	2.3	1.2	0.4
Switzerland	−0.7	0.6	0.1	−0.7

Source: Eurostat.
Note: Figures show the annual increase in the Harmonized Index of Consumer Prices in 2009, 2010, 2011 and 2012.

value to the CPI rather than, as previously, the RPI, with consequent savings to public spending on pensions.[9] ■

[9] The UK Office for Budget Responsibility has in fact forecast that the long-run difference between RPI and CPI measure of inflation may in the future be as high as 1.5 per cent per year in the UK. See Ruth Miller, *The Long-Run Difference between RPI and CPI Inflation*, Office of Budget Responsibility Working paper No. 2, November 2011, available at: http://cdn.budgetresponsibility.independent.gov.uk/Working-paper-No2-The-long-run-difference-between-RPI-and-CPI-inflation.pdf.

2-3 Measuring Joblessness: The Unemployment Rate

Drawing M. Stevens; © 1980 The New Yorker Magazine, Inc.

'Well, so long, Eddie. The recession's over.'

One aspect of economic performance is how well an economy uses its resources. Because an economy's workers are its chief resource, keeping workers employed is a paramount concern of economic policy makers. The unemployment rate is the statistic that measures the percentage of those people wanting to work who do not have jobs.

There are two ways of measuring the unemployment rate in the economy. Perhaps the simplest is the *claimant count* method. This involves counting the number of people who, on any given day, are claiming unemployment benefit payments from the government. Since a government agency is paying out the benefits, it will be easy to gather data on the number of claimants. The government also has a good idea of the total labour force in employment, since it is receiving income tax payments from them. Adding to this the number of unemployment benefit claimants is a measure of the total labour force, and expressing the claimant count as a proportion of the labour force is a measure of the unemployment rate.

Since the government already has all the data necessary to compute the unemployment rate based on the claimant count, it is relatively cheap and easy to do. Unfortunately, there are a number of important drawbacks with this method.

One obvious problem is that it is subject to changes in the rules the government applies for eligibility to unemployment benefit. Suppose the government gets tougher and changes the rules so that fewer people are now entitled to unemployment benefit. The claimant count will go down and so will the measured unemployment rate, even though there has been no change in the number of people with or without work. The opposite would happen if the government became more lenient, and relaxed the rules so that more people became eligible. As it happens, governments do often change the rules on unemployment benefit eligibility. In the UK, for example, there have been about 30 changes to the eligibility rules since the early 1980s, all but one of which have reduced the claimant count and so reduced the measured unemployment rate based on this measure. For example, anyone on a government training programme (largely school leavers who have not found a job), anyone looking for part-time work, and anyone who left the workforce for a while and now wishes to return to employment (for example, women who have brought up a family) would be excluded from measured unemployment in the UK using the claimant count method, even though they may be of working age and are able and available for work at current wage rates.

A more reliable method, which is recommended by the International Labour Organization (ILO), and which is now used in well over 100 countries, including all members of the European Union as well as the United States and Japan, measures unemployment through the use of questionnaire surveys.[10] In the UK, this is called the *Labour Force Survey*; it is carried out every three months and covers about 60,000 households. Based on the responses to survey questions, each adult (16 years and older) in each household is placed into one of three categories:

- *Employed*
- *Unemployed*
- *Not in the labour force (or 'economically inactive').*

A person is considered employed if he or she spent some of the previous week working at a paid job. A person is unemployed if he or she fits the ILO definition of an unemployed person: someone who is without a job and who is willing to start work within the next two weeks, and either has been looking for work within the past four weeks or was waiting to start a job. A person who does not fit either of the first two categories, such as a full-time student, housewife/house husband or retiree, is economically inactive (not in the labour force).

Notice that a person who wants a job but has given up looking – a *discouraged worker* – is counted as being economically inactive.

The **labour force** is defined as the sum of the employed and unemployed, and the unemployment rate is defined as the percentage of the labour force that is unemployed. That is,

$$\text{Labour Force} = \text{Number of Employed} + \text{Number of Unemployed},$$

and

$$\text{Unemployment Rate} = \frac{\text{Number of Unemployed}}{\text{Labour Force}} \times 100.$$

A related statistic is the **labour-force participation rate**, the percentage of the adult population that is in the labour force:

$$\text{Labour-Force Participation Rate} = \frac{\text{Labour Force}}{\text{Adult Population}} \times 100.$$

Figure 2-5 shows the UK adult population aged 16 years and older of 50.6 million in autumn 2012, broken down into the three categories, as follows:

- Labour Force = 32.1 + 2.5 = 34.6 million
- Unemployment Rate = (2.5/34.6) × 100 = 7.2 per cent
- Labour-Force Participation Rate = (34.6/50.6) × 100 = 68.4 per cent.

---

[10] The International Labour Organization is a specialized agency of the United Nations and has its headquarters in Geneva. The ILO formulates international labour standards in the form of conventions and recommendations. You can find out more about it on its website, www.ilo.org.

FIGURE 2-5

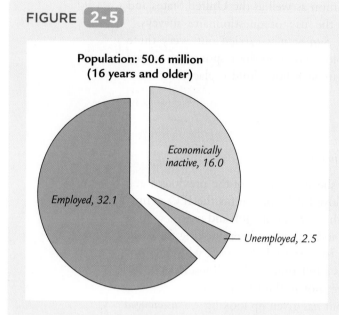

Population: 50.6 million (16 years and older)

Economically inactive, 16.0

Employed, 32.1

Unemployed, 2.5

The Three Groups of the UK Population in 2012 When the Office for National Statistics surveys the population, it places all adults into one of three categories: employed, unemployed or economically inactive. This figure shows the number of people in each category in 2012.

Source: UK Office for National Statistics, Labour Force Survey, February 2013.

Hence, in autumn 2012, nearly two-thirds of the UK adult population (63.4 per cent) were in the labour force, and 7.8 per cent of those in the labour force did not have a job.

CASE STUDY

Trends in Labour-Force Participation in the UK

The data on the labour market collected by national statistical agencies reflect not only economic developments, such as the booms and busts of the business cycle, but also a variety of social changes. Longer-term social changes in the roles of men and women in society, for example, are evident in the data on labour-force participation.

Figure 2-6 shows the labour-force participation rates of men and women in the United Kingdom from 1971 to 2012. The overall participation rate, including both men and women aged 16 and over, has remained remarkably constant over this 40-year period, at around 63 per cent. However, when we break down the participation rates by gender, a different story emerges. At the beginning of the period, the female participation rate was about 45 per cent, and it steadily increased to about 57 per cent in 2012. The trend for male participation in the labour force, on the other hand, goes the opposite way: from a value of just over 83 per cent in 1971, the UK male participation rate declines steadily to around 70 per cent in 2012. As measured by labour-force participation, men and women are playing a much more equal role in the UK economy in the early 21st century than they were 40 years before.

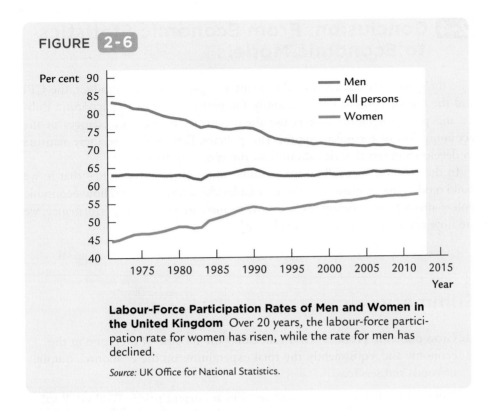

FIGURE 2-6

Labour-Force Participation Rates of Men and Women in the United Kingdom Over 20 years, the labour-force participation rate for women has risen, while the rate for men has declined.

Source: UK Office for National Statistics.

There are many reasons for this change. In part, it is due to new technologies, such as the washing machine, tumble dryer, fridge, freezer and dishwasher, which have reduced the amount of time required to complete routine household tasks. In part, it is due to improved birth control, which has reduced the number of children born to the typical family. And in part, this change in the role of women is due to changing political and social attitudes. Together these developments have had a profound impact, as demonstrated by these data.

Although the increase in women's labour-force participation is easily explained, the fall in men's participation may seem puzzling. There are several developments at work. First, more young men now stay in education longer than their fathers and grandfathers did. Second, older men now retire earlier and live longer. Third, with more women employed, more fathers now stay at home to bring up their children. Full-time students, retirees and stay-at-home fathers are all counted as out of the labour force or economically inactive.

Looking ahead, many economists believe that labour-force participation for both men and women may gradually decline over the next several decades. The reason is demographic. People today are living longer and having fewer children than did their counterparts in previous generations. As a result, the elderly are representing an increasing share of the population. Because the elderly are more often retired and less often members of the labour force, the rising elderly share of the population will tend to reduce the economy's labour-force participation rate. ■

2-4 Conclusion: From Economic Statistics to Economic Models

The three statistics discussed in this chapter – gross domestic product, the CPI and the unemployment rate – quantify the performance of the economy. Public and private decision makers use these statistics to monitor changes in the economy and to formulate appropriate policies. Economists use these statistics to develop and test theories about how the economy works.

In the chapters that follow we examine some of these theories – that is, we build models that explain how these variables are determined and how economic policy affects them. Having learned how to measure economic performance, we are now ready to learn how to explain it.

Summary

1. Gross domestic product (GDP) measures the income of everyone in the economy and, equivalently, the total expenditure on the economy's output of goods and services.

2. Nominal GDP values goods and services at current prices. Real GDP values goods and services at constant prices. Real GDP rises only when the amount of goods and services has increased, whereas nominal GDP can rise either because output has increased or because prices have increased.

3. GDP is the sum of four categories of expenditure: consumption, investment, government purchases and net exports.

4. The consumer price index (CPI) measures the price of a fixed basket of goods and services purchased by a typical consumer. Like the GDP deflator, which is the ratio of nominal GDP to real GDP, the CPI measures the overall level of prices.

5. The unemployment rate shows what fraction of those who would like to work do not have a job.

K E Y   C O N C E P T S

Gross domestic product (GDP)

Consumer price index (CPI)

Unemployment rate

National income accounting

Stocks and flows

Value added

Imputed value

Nominal versus real GDP

GDP deflator

Net exports

Investment

Consumption

Government purchases

National income accounts identity

Labour force

Labour-force participation rate

QUESTIONS FOR REVIEW

1. List the two things that GDP measures. How can GDP measure two things at once?

2. What does the CPI measure?

3. List the three categories used by the Labour Force Survey to classify the adult population in the economy.

4. Explain the two ways the UK Office for National Statistics measures unemployment.

PROBLEMS AND APPLICATIONS

1. Look at the newspapers for the past few days. What new economic statistics have been released? How do you interpret these statistics?

2. Obtain a recent copy of *The Economist* and find the section towards the back on data and statistics. Use it to compare the latest unemployment figures for the UK, the US, Denmark, Germany, France, the Netherlands and Spain.

3. In this chapter, we discussed in a case study how real GDP per capita may be a misleading guide to how rich the residents of Luxembourg are, because a high proportion of the labour force actually resides in other countries. Can you suggest a better measure?

4. A farmer grows a kilo of wheat and sells it to a miller for €1.00. The miller turns the wheat into flour and then sells the flour to a baker for €3.00. The baker uses the flour to make bread and sells the bread to an engineer for €6.00. The engineer eats the bread. What is the value added by each person? What is GDP?

5. Suppose a woman marries her butler. After they are married, her husband continues to wait on her as before, and she continues to support him as before (but as a husband rather than as an employee). How does the marriage affect GDP? How should it affect GDP?

6. Place each of the following transactions in one of the four components of expenditure for the German economy: consumption, investment, government purchases and net exports (BMW is a German car manufacturer):

a. BMW sells a car to a German household.

b. BMW sells a car to a US resident.

c. BMW sells a car to the German government.

d. BMW makes a car to be sold next year.

7. Find data on GDP and its components for your country, and compute the percentage of GDP for the following components for 1985, 1995 and 2005.

a. Consumption expenditure by households and non-profit institutions serving households

b. Business fixed investment

c. Government purchases (investment plus consumption)

d. Exports

e. Imports.

Do you see any stable relationships in the data?

Do you see any trends? (*Hint:* A good place to look for data is on the website of the Office for National Statistics, www.statistics.gov.uk (for UK data) or on the website of Eurostat, http://epp.eurostat.cec.eu.int (for other EU countries).

8. Consider an economy that produces and consumes bread and cars. In the following table are data for two different years.

	Year 2000	Year 2010
Price of a car	€50,000	€60,000
Price of a loaf of bread	€1	€20
Number of cars produced	100	120
Number of loaves of bread produced	500,000	400,000

a. Using the year 2000 as the base year, compute the following statistics for each year: nominal GDP, real GDP, the implicit price deflator for GDP and a fixed-weight price index such as the CPI.

b. By how much have prices risen between year 2000 and year 2010? Compare the answers given by the Laspeyres and Paasche price indices. Explain the difference.

c. Suppose the government is thinking of indexing state retirement pensions, so that it will increase the pension paid to offset changes in the cost of living. The government minister responsible asks you for your advice as to whether to use the GDP deflator or the CPI. Which do you advise her to use? Why?

9. Harriet consumes only apples. In year 1, red apples cost €1 each, green apples cost €2 each, and Harriet buys 10 red apples. In year 2, red apples cost €2, green apples cost €1, and Harriet buys 10 green apples.

a. Compute a CPI for apples for each year. Assume that year 1 is the base year in which the consumer basket is fixed. How does your index change from year 1 to year 2?

b. Compute Harriet's nominal spending on apples in each year. How does it change from year 1 to year 2?

c. Using year 1 as the base year, compute Harriet's real spending on apples in each year. How does it change from year 1 to year 2?

d. Defining the implicit price deflator as nominal spending divided by real spending, compute the deflator for each year. How does the deflator change from year 1 to year 2?

e. Suppose that Harriet is equally happy eating red or green apples. How much has the true cost of living increased for Harriet? Compare this answer with your answers to parts (a) and (d). What does this example tell you about Laspeyres and Paasche price indexes?

10. Consider how each of the following events is likely to affect the real GDP of the country concerned. Do you think the change in real GDP reflects a similar change in economic well-being?

a. A freak hurricane in northern France forces Disneyland Paris to shut down for a month.

b. The discovery of a new, easy-to-grow strain of wheat increases British farm harvests.

c. Increased hostility between unions and management sparks a rash of strikes in Italy.

d. Firms throughout the German economy experience falling demand, causing them to lay off workers.

e. The European Parliament passes new environmental laws that prohibit EU firms from using production methods that emit large quantities of pollution.

f. Irish university students drop out of university to take jobs painting houses.

g. Greek fathers reduce their working weeks in order to spend more time with their children.

11. The environmental campaign group Friends of the Earth say this on their website (www.foe.co.uk):

GDP, rather than leading us down the right path, points us in a completely random direction. It is no measure of progress. It increases with polluting activities and then again with their clean-up. It takes no account of income distribution, or the depletion or degradation of natural resources, and treats crime, divorce and other elements of social breakdown as economic gains. GDP is merely a gross tally of products and services bought and sold, with no distinctions between transactions that add to well-being, and those that diminish it. It is as if a business tried to assess its financial condition by simply adding up all 'business activity', lumping together income and expenses, assets and liabilities.

Is Friends of the Earth right? If so, why do we care about GDP?

PART 2

Classical Theory: The Economy in the Long Run

CHAPTER 3

National Income: Where It Comes From and Where It Goes

A large income is the best recipe for happiness I ever heard of.

— *Jane Austen,* Mansfield Park

Most of us would probably agree that a large income is not the *only* ingredient in the recipe for happiness, but it certainly helps. Whether the issue is alleviating the misery of poverty, as in the very poor developing countries, or improving general living standards – as in the relatively rich countries of Europe and North America – it helps to have a higher level of national income. This is why the most important macroeconomic variable is gross domestic product (GDP). As we have seen, GDP measures both a nation's total output of goods and services and its total income. To appreciate the significance of GDP, one need only take a quick look at international data: compared with their poorer counterparts, nations with a high level of GDP per person have everything from better childhood nutrition to more televisions per household. A large GDP does not ensure that all a nation's citizens are happy, but it may be the best recipe for happiness that macroeconomists have to offer.

This chapter addresses four groups of questions about the sources and uses of a nation's GDP:

- How much do the firms in the economy produce? What determines a nation's total income?

- Who gets the income from production? How much goes to compensate workers, and how much goes to compensate owners of capital?

- Who buys the output of the economy? How much do households purchase for consumption, how much do households and firms purchase for investment, and how much does the government buy for public purposes?

- What equilibrates the demand for and supply of goods and services? What ensures that desired spending on consumption, investment and government purchases equals the level of production?

To answer these questions, we must examine how the various parts of the economy interact.

A good place to start is the circular flow diagram. In Chapter 2 we traced the circular flow of money in a hypothetical economy that produced one product, bread, from labour services. Figure 3-1 more accurately reflects how real economies function. It shows the linkages among the economic actors – households, firms and the government – and how money flows between them through the various markets in the economy.

Let's look at the flow of money from the viewpoints of these economic actors. Households receive income and use it to pay taxes to the government, to consume goods and services, and to save through the financial markets. Firms receive revenue from the sale of goods and services and use it to pay for the factors of production. Households and firms borrow in financial markets to buy investment goods, such as houses and factories. The government receives revenue from taxes and uses it to pay for government purchases. Any excess of tax revenue over government spending is called public saving, which can be either positive (a *budget surplus*) or negative (a *budget deficit*).

In this chapter we develop a basic classical model to explain the economic interactions depicted in Figure 3-1. We begin with firms and look at what determines their level of production (and, thus, the level of national income). Then we examine how the markets for the factors of production distribute this income to

FIGURE 3-1

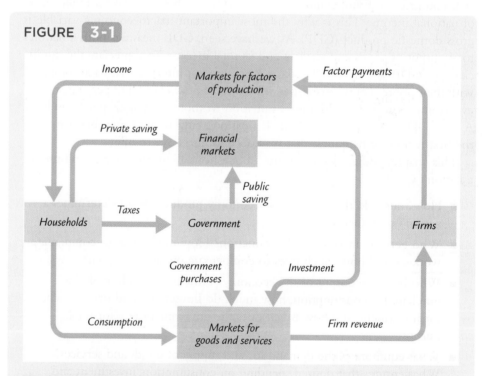

The Circular Flow of Money through the Economy This figure is a more realistic version of the circular flow diagram found in Chapter 2. Each yellow box represents an economic actor – households, firms and the government. Each blue box represents a type of market – the markets for goods and services, the markets for the factors of production, and financial markets. The green arrows show the flow of money between the economic actors through the three types of markets.

households. Next, we consider how much of this income households consume and how much they save. In addition to discussing the demand for goods and services arising from the consumption of households, we discuss the demand arising from investment and government purchases. Finally, we come full circle and examine how the demand for goods and services (the sum of consumption, investment and government purchases) and the supply of goods and services (the level of production) are brought into balance.

3-1 What Determines the Total Production of Goods and Services?

An economy's output of goods and services – its GDP – depends on (1) its quantity of inputs, called the factors of production, and (2) its ability to turn inputs into output, as represented by the production function. We discuss each of these in turn.

The Factors of Production

Factors of production are the inputs used to produce goods and services. The two most important factors of production are capital and labour. Capital is the set of tools that workers use: the construction worker's crane, the accountant's calculator and the personal computers that were used when writing this book. Labour is the time people spend working. We use the symbol K to denote the amount of capital, and the symbol L to denote the amount of labour.

In this chapter we take the economy's factors of production as given. In other words, we assume that the economy has a fixed amount of capital and a fixed amount of labour. We write

$$K = \overline{K},$$

$$L = \overline{L}.$$

The overbar means that each variable is fixed at some level. In Chapter 8 we examine what happens when the factors of production change over time, as they do in the real world. For now, to keep our analysis simple, we assume fixed amounts of capital and labour.

We also assume here that the factors of production are fully utilized – that is, that no resources are wasted. Again, in the real world, part of the labour force is unemployed and some capital lies idle. In Chapter 7 we examine the reasons for unemployment, but for now we assume that capital and labour are fully employed.

The Production Function

The available production technology determines how much output is produced from given amounts of capital and labour. Economists express the available technology using a **production function**. Letting Y denote the amount of output, we write the production function as

$$Y = F(K, L).$$

This equation states that output is a function of the amount of capital and the amount of labour.

The production function reflects the available technology for turning capital and labour into output. If someone invents a better way to produce a good, the result is more output from the same amounts of capital and labour. Thus, technological change alters the production function.

Many production functions have a property called **constant returns to scale**. A production function has constant returns to scale if an increase of an equal percentage in all factors of production causes an increase in output of the same percentage. If the production function has constant returns to scale, we have 10 per cent more output when we increase both capital and labour by 10 per cent. Mathematically, a production function has constant returns to scale if

$$zY = F(zK, zL)$$

for any positive number z. This equation says that, if we multiply both the amount of capital and the amount of labour by some number z, output is also multiplied by z. In the next section we see that the assumption of constant returns to scale has an important implication for how the income from production is distributed.

As an example of a production function, consider production at a bakery. The kitchen and its equipment are the bakery's capital, the workers taken on to make the bread are its labour, and the loaves of bread are its output. The bakery's production function shows that the number of loaves produced depends on the amount of equipment and the number of workers. If the production function has constant returns to scale, then doubling the amount of equipment and the number of workers doubles the amount of bread produced.

The Supply of Goods and Services

We can now see that the factors of production and the production function together determine the quantity of goods and services supplied, which in turn equals the economy's output. To express this mathematically, we write

$$Y = F(\overline{K}, \overline{L})$$
$$= \overline{Y}.$$

In this chapter, because we assume that the supplies of capital and labour and the technology are fixed, output is also fixed (at a level denoted here as $\overline{Y}$). When we discuss economic growth in Chapters 8 and 9, we will examine how increases in capital and labour and improvements in the production technology lead to growth in the economy's output.

3-2 How Is National Income Distributed to the Factors of Production?

As we discussed in Chapter 2, the total output of an economy equals its total income. Because the factors of production and the production function together determine the total output of goods and services, they also determine national income. The circular flow diagram in Figure 3-1 shows that this national income flows from firms to households through the markets for the factors of production.

In this section we continue developing our model of the economy by discussing how these factor markets work. Economists have long studied factor markets to understand the distribution of income. For example, Karl Marx, the noted 19th-century economist, spent much time trying to explain the incomes of capital and labour. The political philosophy of communism was in part based on Marx's now-discredited theory.

Here we examine the modern theory of how national income is divided among the factors of production. It is based on the classical (18th-century) idea that prices adjust to balance supply and demand, applied here to the markets for the factors of production, together with the more recent (19th-century) idea that the demand for each factor of production depends on the marginal productivity of that factor. This theory, called the *neoclassical theory of distribution*, is accepted by most economists today as the best place to start in understanding how the economy's income is distributed from firms to households.

Factor Prices

The distribution of national income is determined by factor prices. **Factor prices** are the amounts paid to the factors of production. In an economy where the two factors of production are capital and labour, the two factor prices are the wages workers earn and the rent the owners of capital collect.

As Figure 3-2 illustrates, the price each factor of production receives for its services is in turn determined by the supply and demand for that factor. Because we have assumed that the economy's factors of production are fixed, the factor supply curve in Figure 3-2 is vertical. Regardless of the factor price, the quantity of the factor supplied to the market is the same. The intersection of the downward-sloping factor demand curve and the vertical supply curve determines the equilibrium factor price.

To understand factor prices and the distribution of income, we must examine the demand for the factors of production. Because factor demand arises from the thousands of firms that use capital and labour, we now look at the decisions faced by a typical firm about how much of these factors to employ.

The Decisions Facing the Competitive Firm

The simplest assumption to make about a typical firm is that it is **competitive**. A competitive firm is small relative to the markets in which it trades, so it has

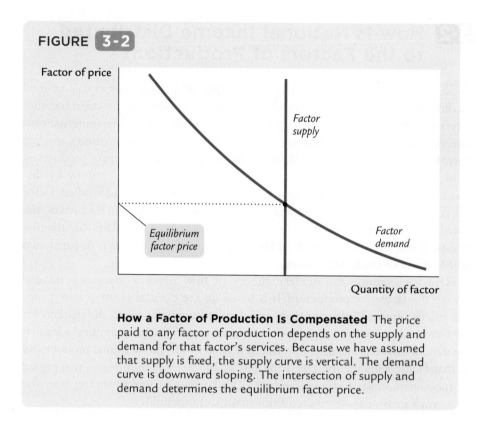

FIGURE 3-2

How a Factor of Production Is Compensated The price paid to any factor of production depends on the supply and demand for that factor's services. Because we have assumed that supply is fixed, the supply curve is vertical. The demand curve is downward sloping. The intersection of supply and demand determines the equilibrium factor price.

little influence on market prices. For example, our firm produces a good and sells it at the market price. Because many firms produce this good, our firm can sell as much as it wants without causing the price of the good to fall, or it can stop selling altogether without causing the price of the good to rise. Similarly, our firm cannot influence the wages of the workers it employs because many other local firms also employ workers. The firm has no reason to pay more than the market wage, and if it tried to pay less, its workers would take jobs elsewhere. Therefore, the competitive firm takes the prices of its output and its inputs as given by market conditions.

To make its product, the firm needs two factors of production, capital and labour. As we did for the aggregate economy, we represent the firm's production technology with the production function

$$Y = F(K, L),$$

where Y is the number of units produced (the firm's output), K the number of machines used (the amount of capital), and L the number of hours worked by the firm's employees (the amount of labour). The firm produces more output if it uses more machines or if its employees work more hours.

The firm sells its output at a price P, takes on workers at a wage W, and rents capital at a rate R. Notice that, when we speak of firms renting capital, we are assuming that households own the economy's stock of capital. In this analysis, households rent out their capital, just as they sell their labour. The firm obtains both factors of production from the households that own them.[1]

The goal of the firm is to maximize profit. **Profit** is revenue minus costs – it is what the owners of the firm keep after paying for the costs of production. Revenue equals $P \times Y$, the selling price of the good P multiplied by the amount of the good the firm produces, Y. Costs include both labour costs and capital costs. Labour costs equal $W \times L$, the wage W times the amount of labour L. Capital costs equal $R \times K$, the rental price of capital R times the amount of capital K. We can write

$$\text{Profit} = \text{Revenue} - \text{Labour Costs} - \text{Capital Costs}$$
$$= PY - WL - RK.$$

To see how profit depends on the factors of production, we use the production function $Y = F(K, L)$ to substitute for Y to obtain

$$\text{Profit} = PF(K, L) - WL - RK.$$

This equation shows that profit depends on the product price P, the factor prices W and R, and the factor quantities L and K. The competitive firm takes the product price and the factor prices as given and chooses the amounts of labour and capital that maximize profit.

The Firm's Demand for Factors

We now know that our firm will hire labour and rent capital in the quantities that maximize profit. But what are those profit-maximizing quantities? To answer this question, we first consider the quantity of labour and then the quantity of capital.

The Marginal Product of Labour The more labour the firm employs, the more output it produces. The **marginal product of labour (MPL)** is the extra amount of output the firm gets from one extra unit of labour, holding the amount of capital fixed. We can express this using the production function:

$$MPL = F(K, L + 1) - F(K, L).$$

The first term on the right-hand side is the amount of output produced with K units of capital and $L + 1$ units of labour; the second term is the amount of output produced with K units of capital and L units of labour. This equation states that the marginal product of labour is the difference between the amount of output produced with $L + 1$ units of labour and the amount produced with only L units of labour.

---

[1] This is a simplification. In the real world, the ownership of capital is indirect because firms own capital and households own the firms. That is, real firms have two functions: owning capital and producing output. To help us understand how the factors of production are compensated, however, we assume that firms only produce output and that households own capital directly.

Most production functions have the property of **diminishing marginal product:** holding the amount of capital fixed, the marginal product of labour decreases as the amount of labour increases. Consider again the production of bread at a bakery. As a bakery hires more labour, it produces more bread. The *MPL* is the amount of extra bread produced when an extra unit of labour is taken on. As more labour is added to a fixed amount of capital, however, the *MPL* falls. Fewer additional loaves are produced by each additional worker compared to the worker hired just before him, because workers are less productive when the kitchen is more crowded. In other words, holding the size of the kitchen fixed, each additional worker adds fewer loaves of bread to the bakery's output.

Figure 3-3 graphs the production function. It illustrates what happens to the amount of output when we hold the amount of capital constant and vary the amount of labour. This figure shows that the marginal product of labour is the slope of the production function. As the amount of labour increases, the production function becomes flatter, indicating diminishing marginal product.

From the Marginal Product of Labour to Labour Demand When the competitive, profit-maximizing firm is deciding whether to hire an additional unit of labour, it considers how that decision would affect profits. It therefore compares the extra revenue from the increased production that results from the added labour to the extra cost of higher spending on wages. The increase in revenue from an additional unit of labour depends on two variables: the marginal product of labour and the price of the output. Because an extra unit of labour

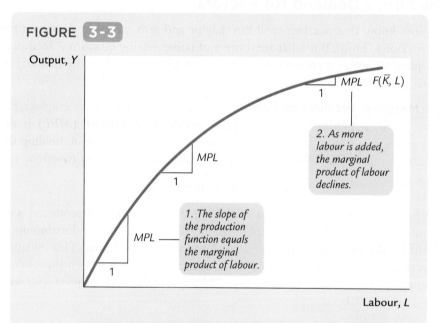

FIGURE 3-3

The Production Function This curve shows how output depends on labour input, holding the amount of capital constant. The marginal product of labour *MPL* is the change in output when the labour input is increased by 1 unit. As the amount of labour increases, the production function becomes flatter, indicating diminishing marginal product.

produces *MPL* units of output and each unit of output sells for *P* euros, the extra revenue is $P \times MPL$. The extra cost of hiring one more unit of labour is the wage *W*. Thus, the change in profit from hiring an additional unit of labour is

$$\Delta\text{Profit} = \Delta\text{Revenue} - \Delta\text{Cost}$$
$$= (P \times MPL) - W.$$

The symbol Δ (called *delta*) denotes the change in a variable.

We can now answer the question we asked at the beginning of this section: How much labour does the firm take on? The firm's manager knows that if the extra revenue $P \times MPL$ exceeds the wage *W*, an extra unit of labour increases profit. Therefore, the manager continues to take on labour until the next unit is no longer be profitable – that is, until the *MPL* falls to the point where the extra revenue equals the wage. The competitive firm's demand for labour is determined by

$$P \times MPL = W.$$

We can also write this as

$$MPL = W/P.$$

W/P is the **real wage** – the payment to labour measured in units of output rather than in euros. To maximize profit, the firm takes on labour up to the point at which the marginal product of labour equals the real wage.

For example, consider a bakery again. Suppose the price of bread *P* is €2 per loaf, and a worker earns a wage *W* of €20 per hour. The real wage W/P is 10 loaves per hour. In this example, the firm keeps taking on workers as long as the additional worker produces at least 10 loaves per hour. When the *MPL* falls to 10 loaves per hour or less, taking on additional workers is no longer profitable.

Figure 3-4 shows how the marginal product of labour depends on the amount of labour employed (holding the firm's capital stock constant). That is, this figure graphs the *MPL* schedule. Because the *MPL* diminishes as the amount of labour increases, this curve slopes downward. For any given real wage, the firm takes on labour up to the point at which the *MPL* equals the real wage. Hence, the *MPL* schedule is also the firm's labour demand curve.

The Marginal Product of Capital and Capital Demand The firm decides how much capital to rent in the same way it decides how much labour to take on. The **marginal product of capital (MPK)** is the amount of extra output the firm gets from an extra unit of capital, holding the amount of labour constant:

$$MPK = F(K + 1, L) - F(K, L).$$

Thus, the marginal product of capital is the difference between the amount of output produced with $K + 1$ units of capital and that produced with only *K* units of capital.

Like labour, capital is subject to diminishing marginal product. Once again, consider the production of bread at a bakery. The first few ovens installed in the kitchen will be very productive. However, if the bakery installs more and more ovens, while holding its labour force constant, it will eventually contain more

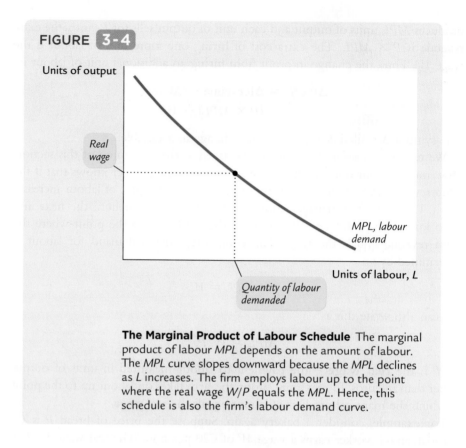

FIGURE 3-4

The Marginal Product of Labour Schedule The marginal product of labour *MPL* depends on the amount of labour. The *MPL* curve slopes downward because the *MPL* declines as *L* increases. The firm employs labour up to the point where the real wage *W/P* equals the *MPL*. Hence, this schedule is also the firm's labour demand curve.

ovens than its employees can operate effectively. Hence, the marginal product of the last few ovens is lower than that of the first few.

The increase in profit from renting an additional machine is the extra revenue from selling the output of that machine minus the machine's rental price:

$$\Delta\text{Profit} = \Delta\text{Revenue} - \Delta\text{Cost} = (P \times MPK) - R.$$

To maximize profit, the firm continues to rent more capital until the *MPK* falls to equal the real rental price:

$$MPK = R/P.$$

The **real rental price of capital** is the rental price measured in units of goods rather than in euros.

To sum up, the competitive, profit-maximizing firm follows a simple rule about how much labour to employ and how much capital to rent. *The firm demands each factor of production until that factor's marginal product falls to equal its real factor price.*

The Division of National Income

Having analysed how a firm decides how much of each factor to employ, we can now explain how the markets for the factors of production distribute the economy's total income. If all firms in the economy are competitive and profit maximizing, then each factor of production is paid its marginal contribution to the production process. The real wage paid to each worker equals the *MPL*, and the real rental price paid to each owner of capital equals the *MPK*. The total real wages paid to labour are therefore *MPL* × *L*, and the total real return paid to capital owners is *MPK* × *K*.

The income that remains after the firms have paid the factors of production is the **economic profit** of the owners of the firms. Real economic profit is expressed as

$$\text{Economic Profit} = Y - (MPL \times L) - (MPK \times K).$$

Because we want to examine the distribution of national income, we rearrange the terms as follows:

$$Y = (MPL \times L) + (MPK \times K) + \text{Economic Profit}.$$

Total income is divided among the return to labour, the return to capital and economic profit.

How large is economic profit? The answer is surprising: if the production function has the property of constant returns to scale, as is often thought to be the case, then economic profit must be zero. That is, nothing is left after the factors of production are paid. This conclusion follows from a famous mathematical result called *Euler's theorem*,[2] which states that if the production function has constant returns to scale, then

$$F(K, L) = (MPK \times K) + (MPL \times L).$$

If each factor of production is paid its marginal product, then the sum of these factor payments equals total output. In other words, constant returns to scale, profit maximization and competition together imply that economic profit is zero.

If economic profit is zero, how can we explain the existence of 'profit' in the economy? The answer is that the term 'profit' as normally used is different from economic profit. We have been assuming that there are three types of agents: workers, owners of capital and owners of firms. Total income is divided among wages, return to capital and economic profit. In the real world, however, most firms own rather than rent the capital they use. Because firm owners and capital owners are the same people, economic profit and the return to capital are often lumped together. If we call this alternative definition **accounting profit**, we can say that

$$\text{Accounting Profit} = \text{Economic Profit} + (MPK \times K).$$

Under our assumptions – constant returns to scale, profit maximization and competition – economic profit is zero. If these assumptions approximately describe the world, then the 'profit' in the national income accounts must be mostly the return to capital.

We can now answer the question posed at the beginning of this chapter about how the income of the economy is distributed from firms to households. Each factor of production is paid its marginal product, and these factor payments exhaust total output. *Total output is divided between the payments to capital and the payments to labour, depending on their marginal productivities.*

---

[2] *Mathematical note:* To prove Euler's theorem, begin with the definition of constant returns to scale: $zY = F(zK, zL)$. Now differentiate with respect to z and then evaluate at $z = 1$.

CASE STUDY

The Black Death and Factor Prices

According to the neoclassical theory of distribution, factor prices equal the marginal products of the factors of production. Because the marginal products depend on the quantities of the factors, a change in the quantity of any one factor alters the marginal products of all the factors. Therefore, a change in the supply of a factor alters equilibrium factor prices and the distribution of income.

Fourteenth-century Europe provides a grisly natural context in which to study how factor quantities affect factor prices. The outbreak of the bubonic plague – the Black Death – in 1348 reduced the population of Europe by about one-third within a few years. Because the marginal product of labour increases as the amount of labour falls, this massive reduction in the labour force should have raised the marginal product of labour and equilibrium real wages. (That is, the economy should have moved to the left along the curves in Figures 3-3 and 3-4.) The evidence confirms the theory: real wages approximately doubled during the plague years. The peasants who were fortunate enough to survive the plague enjoyed economic prosperity.

The reduction in the labour force caused by the plague should also have affected the return to land, the other major factor of production in medieval Europe. With fewer workers available to farm the land, an additional unit of land would have produced less additional output, and so land rents should have fallen. Once again, the theory is confirmed: real rents fell by 50 per cent or more during this period. While the peasant classes prospered, the landed classes suffered reduced incomes.[3] ∎

The Cobb–Douglas Production Function

What production function describes how actual economies turn capital and labour into GDP? One production function that is very widely used in economics was developed by a professor of economics (Paul Douglas) and a mathematician (Charles Cobb) in the 1920s. Looking at data for the US economy, Douglas noticed a surprising fact: the division of national income between capital and labour had been roughly constant over a long period. In other words, as the economy grew more prosperous over time, the total income of workers and the total income of capital owners grew at almost exactly the same rate. This observation caused Douglas to wonder what conditions might lead to constant factor shares.

Douglas asked Cobb what production function, if any, would produce constant factor shares if factors always earned their marginal products. The production function would need to have the property that

$$\text{Capital Income} = MPK \times K = \alpha Y, \quad \text{and}$$

$$\text{Labour Income} = MPL \times L = (1 - \alpha)Y,$$

[3] Carlo M. Cipolla, *Before the Industrial Revolution: European Society and Economy, 1000–1700*, 2nd edn, New York: Norton, 1980, pp. 200–202.

where α is a constant between zero and one that measures capital's share of income. That is, α determines what share of income goes to capital and what share goes to labour. Cobb showed that the function with this property is

$$F(K, L) = A\,K^{\alpha}L^{1-\alpha}.$$

where A is a parameter greater than zero that measures the productivity of the available technology. This function became known as the **Cobb–Douglas production function**.

Let's take a closer look at some of the properties of this production function. First, the Cobb–Douglas production function has constant returns to scale. That is, if capital and labour are increased by the same proportion, then output increases by that proportion as well.[4]

Next, consider the marginal products for the Cobb–Douglas production function. The marginal product of labour is[5]

$$MPL = (1 - \alpha)\,A\,K^{\alpha}L^{-\alpha}.$$

and the marginal product of capital is

$$MPK = \alpha A\,K^{\alpha-1}L^{1-\alpha}.$$

From these equations, recalling that α is between zero and one, we can see what causes the marginal products of the two factors to change. An increase in the amount of capital raises the MPL and reduces the MPK. Similarly, an increase in the amount of labour reduces the MPL and raises the MPK. A technological advance that increases the parameter A raises the marginal product of both factors proportionately.

The marginal products for the Cobb–Douglas production function can also be written as[6]

$$MPL = (1 - \alpha)Y/L,$$

$$MPK = \alpha Y/K.$$

---

[4] *Mathematical note:* To prove that the Cobb–Douglas production function has constant returns to scale, examine what happens when we multiply capital and labour by a constant z:

$$F(zK, zL) = A(zK)^{\alpha}(zL)^{1-\alpha}.$$

Expanding terms on the right,

$$F(zK, zL) = Az^{\alpha}K^{\alpha}z^{1-\alpha}L^{1-\alpha}.$$

Rearranging to bring like terms together, we get

$$F(zK, zL) = Az^{\alpha}z^{1-\alpha}K^{\alpha}L^{1-\alpha}.$$

Since $z^{\alpha}z^{1-\alpha} = z$, our function becomes

$$F(zK, zL) = zA\,K^{\alpha}L^{1-\alpha}.$$

But $A\,K^{\alpha}L^{1-\alpha} = F(K, L)$. Thus,

$$F(zK, zL) = zF(K, L) = zY.$$

Hence, the amount of output Y increases by the same factor z, which implies that this production function has constant returns to scale.

[5] *Mathematical note:* Obtaining the formulas for the marginal products from the production function requires a bit of calculus. To find the MPL, differentiate the production function with respect to L. This is done by multiplying by the exponent $(1 - \alpha)$, and then subtracting 1 from the old exponent to obtain the new exponent, $-\alpha$. Similarly, to obtain the MPK, differentiate the production function with respect to K.

[6] *Mathematical note:* To check these expressions for the marginal products, substitute the production function for Y to show that these expressions are equivalent to the earlier formulas for the marginal products.

The *MPL* is proportional to output per worker, and the *MPK* is proportional to output per unit of capital. Y/L is called *average labour productivity*, and Y/K is called *average capital productivity*. If the production function is Cobb–Douglas, then the marginal productivity of a factor is proportional to its average productivity.

We can now verify that if factors earn their marginal products, then the parameter α indeed tells us how much income goes to labour and how much goes to capital. The total amount paid to labour, which we have seen is $MPL \times L$, is simply $(1 - \alpha)Y$. Therefore, $(1 - \alpha)$ is labour's share of output. Similarly, the total amount paid to capital, $MPK \times K$, is αY, and α is capital's share of output. The ratio of labour income to capital income is a constant, $(1 - \alpha)/\alpha$, just as Douglas observed. The factor shares depend only on the parameter α, not on the amounts of capital or labour, or on the state of technology as measured by the parameter A.

In fact, for the industrialized countries of Europe and North America, it turns out that the labour share of income tends to be stable over time at around the level of around 70 per cent of total income, consistent with a Cobb–Douglas production function in which the parameter α is around 0.3. In Figure 3-5, for example, we have graphed labour's share of total income in the United Kingdom

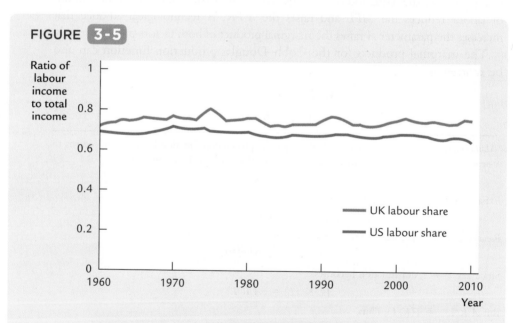

FIGURE 3-5

The Ratio of Labour Income to Total Income in the US and the UK
Labour income in the US and the UK has remained about 0.7–0.75 of total income over a long period of time. This approximate constancy of factor shares is consistent with the Cobb–Douglas production function.

Source: UK Office for National Statistics (*Economic Trends, Annual Supplement*) and US Bureau of Economic Affairs.
Notes: Labour income is income from employment and self-employment.
Total income is labour income plus gross operating surpluses of corporations.

FYI

The Growing Gap between Rich and Poor in the US

The approximate constancy of the labour and capital shares in US data has a simple meaning: the distribution of income between workers and owners of capital has not radically changed over the course of its history. There is, however, another way to look at the data on the income distribution that shows more substantial changes. If we look within labour income, we find that the gap between the earnings of high-wage workers and the earnings of low-wage workers has grown substantially since the 1970s. As a result, income inequality in the US today is much greater than it was four decades ago. Since this rise in income inequality is also a facet of many other developed economies, it is important to investigate possible reasons that might explain it.

So, what has caused this growing income disparity between rich and poor? Economists do not have a definitive answer, but one diagnosis comes from economists Claudia Goldin and Lawrence Katz in their book *The Race Between Education and Technology*.[7] Their bottom line is that 'the sharp rise in inequality was largely due to an educational slowdown'.

According to Goldin and Katz, for the past century technological progress in the US has been a steady force not only increasing average living standards, but also increasing the demand for skilled workers relative to unskilled workers. Skilled workers are needed to apply and manage new technologies, while less skilled workers are more likely to become obsolete.

For much of the 20th century, however, skill-biased technological change was outpaced by advances in educational attainment. In other words, while technological progress increased the demand for skilled workers, the US educational system increased the supply of them even faster. As a result, skilled workers did not benefit disproportionately from economic growth.

But recently things have changed. Over the last few decades, technological advance has kept up its pace, while educational advancement in the US has slowed down. The cohort of workers born in 1950 averaged 4.67 more years of schooling than the cohort born in 1900, representing an increase of 0.93 years of schooling in each decade. By contrast, the cohort born in 1975 had only 0.74 more years of schooling than that born in 1950, an increase of only 0.30 years per decade. That is, the pace of educational advance has fallen by 68 per cent.

Because growth in the supply of skilled workers has slowed, their wages have grown relative to those of the unskilled. This is evident in Goldin and Katz's estimates of the financial return to education. In 1980, each year of college raised a person's wage by 7.6 per cent. In 2005, each year of college yielded an additional 12.9 per cent. Over this time period, the rate of return from each year of graduate school has risen even more – from 7.3 to 14.2 per cent.

The implication of this analysis for public policy is that reversing the rise in income inequality will likely require putting more of society's resources into education (which economists call *human capital*). The implication for personal decision making is that college and university are investments well worth making.

[7] Claudia Goldin and Lawrence F. Katz, *The Race Between Education and Technology*, Cambridge, MA: Belknap Press, 2011.

over the 20-year period 1991–2010. Labour's income share is indeed fairly stable at around 0.7, implying an α of around 0.3.

The Cobb–Douglas production function is not the last word in explaining the economy's production of goods and services or the distribution of national income between capital and labour. It is, however, a good place to start.

CASE STUDY

UK Labour Productivity as the Key Determinant of Real Wages

The neoclassical theory of distribution tells us that the real wage W/P equals the marginal product of labour. The Cobb-Douglas production function tells us that the marginal product of labour is proportional to average labour productivity Y/L. If this theory is right, then workers should enjoy rapidly rising living standards when labour productivity is growing robustly. Is this true?

Table 3-1 presents some data on growth in productivity and real wages for the UK economy. From 1963 to 2010, productivity as measured by output per hour of work grew about 1.9 per cent per year. Real wages grew at almost the same rate: 1.8 per cent per year. With a growth rate of 2.0 per cent per year, productivity and real wages double about every 36 years.

TABLE 3-1

Growth in Labour Production and Real Wages in the UK

Time Period	Growth Rate of Productivity	Growth Rate of Real Wages
1963–2003	2.1	2.0
1963–1973	2.8	3.1
1973–1995	1.75	1.5
1995–2003	1.6	1.7
2003–2010	0.7	0.6

Source: UK Office for National Statistics.
Notes: Growth in productivity is measured here as the annualized rate of change in output per worker.
Growth in real wages is measured as the annualized rate of change in average wages deflated by the Retail Price Index.

Productivity growth varies over time. Table 3-1 also shows the rates of growth for four shorter periods of time. From 1963 to 1973, average productivity growth was high, at 2.8 per cent per year, but so was real wage growth, at 3.1 per cent per year. Notice that from 1973 to 1995 growth in productivity, at 1.75 per cent per year, was slow compared with the period before 1973, but was accompanied by a slowdown in real wage growth to 1.5 per cent per year. Over the period 1995–2003 productivity growth averaged about 1.6 per cent per year and was accompanied by closely matching growth in real wages of 1.7 per cent per year. Over the more recent period 2003–2010, productivity growth slowed to just 0.7 per cent per year, but the growth rate of real wages slowed down by almost the same amount, to just 0.6 per cent per year.

Theory and history both confirm the close link between labour productivity and real wages. This lesson is the key to understanding why workers today are better off than workers in previous generations. ■

3-3 What Determines the Demand for Goods and Services?

We have seen what determines the level of production and how the income from production is distributed to workers and owners of capital. We now continue our tour of the circular flow diagram, Figure 3-1, and examine how the output from production is used.

In Chapter 2 we identified the four components of GDP:

- Consumption (C)
- Investment (I)
- Government purchases (G)
- Net exports (NX).

The circular flow diagram contains only the first three components. For now, to simplify the analysis, we assume our economy is a *closed economy* – a country that does not trade with other countries. Thus, net exports are always zero. (We examine the macroeconomics of *open economies* in Chapter 6.)

A closed economy has three uses for the goods and services it produces. These three components of GDP are expressed in the national income accounts identity:

$$Y = C + I + G.$$

Households consume some of the economy's output; firms and households use some of the output for investment; and the government buys some of the output for public purposes. We want to see how GDP is allocated among these three uses.

Consumption

When we eat food, wear clothing or go to the cinema we are consuming some of the output of the economy. As we show in a case study below, all forms of consumption together make up about 60–65 per cent of GDP in the UK and around 60 per cent on average in the major European economies. Because consumption is so large, macroeconomists have devoted much energy to studying how households decide how much to consume. Chapter 17 examines this work in detail. Here we consider the simplest story of consumer behaviour.

Households receive income from their labour and their ownership of capital, pay taxes to the government and then decide how much of their after-tax income to consume and how much to save. As we discussed in Section 3-2, the income that households receive equals the output of the economy Y. The government then taxes households an amount T. (Although the government imposes many kinds of taxes, such as personal and corporate income taxes and sales taxes, for our purposes we can lump all these taxes together.) We define income after the payment of all taxes, $Y - T$, as **disposable income**. Households divide their disposable income between consumption and saving.

We assume that the level of consumption depends directly on the level of disposable income – the higher disposable income is, the greater the level of consumption. Thus,

$$C = C(Y - T).$$

This equation states that consumption is a function of disposable income. The relationship between consumption and disposable income is called the **consumption function**.

The **marginal propensity to consume (MPC)** is the amount by which consumption changes when disposable income increases by one euro. The MPC is between zero and one: an extra euro of income increases consumption, but by less than one euro. Thus, if households obtain an extra euro of income, they save a portion of it. For example, if the MPC is 0.7, then households spend €0.70 of each additional euro of disposable income on consumer goods and services, and save €0.30.

Figure 3-6 illustrates the consumption function. The slope of the consumption function tells us how much consumption increases when disposable income increases by one euro. That is, the slope of the consumption function is the MPC.

FIGURE **3-6**

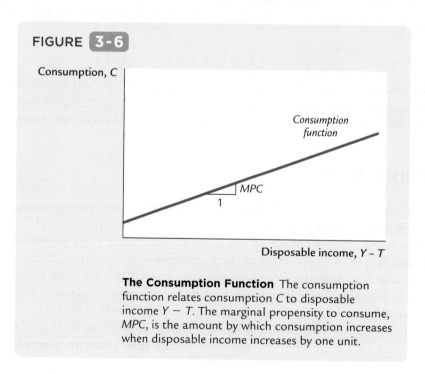

The Consumption Function The consumption function relates consumption C to disposable income $Y - T$. The marginal propensity to consume, MPC, is the amount by which consumption increases when disposable income increases by one unit.

Investment

Both firms and households purchase investment goods. Firms buy investment goods to add to their stock of capital and to replace existing capital as it wears out. Households buy new houses, which are also part of investment. Total investment in the UK averages about 17 per cent of GDP and is around 17–20 per cent of GDP in most European countries (see the case study on page 81).

The quantity of investment goods demanded depends on the **interest rate**, which measures the cost of the funds used to finance investment. For an investment project to be profitable, its return (the revenue from increased future production of goods and services) must exceed its cost (the payments for borrowed funds). If the interest rate rises, fewer investment projects are profitable, and the quantity of investment goods demanded falls.

For example, suppose a firm is considering whether it should build a €1 million factory that would yield a return of €100,000 per year, or 10 per cent. The firm compares this return with the cost of borrowing the €1 million. If the interest rate is below 10 per cent, the firm borrows the money in financial markets and makes the investment. If the interest rate is above 10 per cent, the firm forgoes the investment opportunity and does not build the factory.

The firm makes the same investment decision even if it does not have to borrow the €1 million, but rather uses its own funds. The firm can always deposit this money in a bank or a money market fund and earn interest on it. Building the factory is more profitable than the deposit if and only if the interest rate is less than the 10 per cent return on the factory.

A person wanting to buy a new house faces a similar decision. The higher the interest rate, the greater the cost of carrying a mortgage. A €100,000 mortgage costs €8000 per year if the interest rate is 8 per cent and €10,000 per year if the interest rate is 10 per cent. As the interest rate rises, the cost of owning a home rises, and the demand for new homes falls.

When studying the role of interest rates in the economy, economists distinguish between the nominal interest rate and the real interest rate. This distinction is relevant when the overall level of prices is changing. The **nominal interest rate** is the interest rate as usually reported: it is the rate of interest that investors pay to borrow money. The **real interest rate** is the nominal interest rate corrected for the effects of inflation. If the nominal interest rate is 8 per cent and the inflation rate is 3 per cent, then the real interest rate is 5 per cent. In Chapter 5 we discuss the relation between nominal and real interest rates in detail. Here it is sufficient to note that the real interest rate measures the true cost of borrowing and, thus, determines the quantity of investment.

We can summarize this discussion with an equation relating investment I to the real interest rate r:

$$I = I(r).$$

Figure 3-7 shows this investment function. It slopes downward because, as the interest rate rises, the quantity of investment demanded falls.

F Y I

The Many Different Interest Rates

If you look in the business section of a newspaper, you will find many different interest rates reported. By contrast, throughout this book, we will talk about 'the' interest rate, as if there were only one interest rate in the economy. The only distinction we will make is between the nominal interest rate (which is not corrected for inflation) and the real interest rate (which is corrected for inflation). Almost all the interest rates reported in the newspaper are nominal.

Why does the newspaper report so many interest rates? The various interest rates differ in two main ways:

1. *Term.* Some loans in the economy are for short periods of time, even as short as overnight. Other loans are for 30 years or even longer. The interest rate on a loan depends on its term. Long-term interest rates are usually, but not always, higher than short-term interest rates.

2. *Credit risk.* In deciding whether to make a loan, a lender must take into account the probability that the borrower will repay. The law allows borrowers to default on their loans by declaring bankruptcy. The higher the perceived probability of default, the higher the interest rate. Because the safest credit risk is the government, government bonds tend to pay a low interest rate. At the other extreme, financially shaky corporations can raise funds only by issuing *junk bonds,* which pay a high interest rate to compensate for the high risk of default.

When you see two different interest rates in the newspaper, you can almost always explain the difference by considering the term and the credit risk.

Although there are many different interest rates in the economy, macroeconomists can usually ignore these distinctions. The various interest rates tend to move up and down together. The assumption that there is only one interest rate is, for our purposes, a useful simplification.

FIGURE 3-7

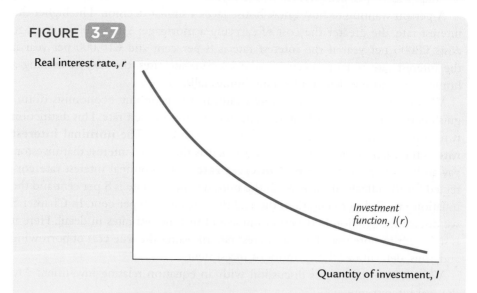

The Investment Function The investment function relates the quantity of investment I to the real interest rate r. Investment depends on the real interest rate because the interest rate is the cost of borrowing. The investment function slopes downward: when the interest rate rises, fewer investment projects are profitable.

Government Purchases

Government purchases are the third component of the demand for goods and services. The central government buys guns, missiles and the services of government employees. Local governments buy library books, build schools and employ teachers. Governments at all levels build roads and other public works. All these transactions make up government purchases of goods and services, which account for about 20 per cent of GDP in the UK (and indeed averages around 15–20 per cent in most European countries – see the case study below).

These purchases are only one type of government spending. The other type is transfer payments to households, such as unemployment benefit and state pension payments to the elderly. Unlike government purchases, transfer payments are not made in exchange for some of the economy's output of goods and services. Therefore, they are not included in the variable G.

Transfer payments affect the demand for goods and services indirectly. Transfer payments are the opposite of taxes: they increase households' disposable income, just as taxes reduce disposable income. Thus, an increase in transfer payments financed by an increase in taxes leaves disposable income unchanged. We can now revise our definition of T to equal taxes minus transfer payments. Disposable income, $Y - T$, includes both the negative impact of taxes and the positive impact of transfer payments.

If government purchases equal taxes minus transfers, then $G = T$, and the government has a *balanced budget*. If G exceeds T, the government runs a *budget deficit*, which it funds by issuing government debt – that is, by borrowing in the financial markets. If G is less than T, the government runs a *budget surplus*, which it can use to repay some of its outstanding debt.

Here we do not try to explain the political process that leads to a particular fiscal policy – that is, to the level of government purchases and taxes. Instead, we take government purchases and taxes as exogenous variables. To denote that these variables are fixed outside our model of national income, we write

$$G = \overline{G},$$
$$T = \overline{T}.$$

We do, however, want to examine the impact of fiscal policy on the variables determined within the model, the endogenous variables. The endogenous variables here are consumption, investment and the interest rate.

To see how the exogenous variables affect the endogenous variables, we must complete the model. This is the subject of the next section.

CASE STUDY

Consumption, Investment and Government Purchases in European Countries

In Chapter 2 we identified the four components of GDP as consumption (C), investment (I), government purchases (G) and net exports (NX):

$$Y = C + I + G + NX.$$

In Table 3-2 we have shown the percentage of 2012 GDP going to private consumption, investment expenditure and government purchases in a number of European countries, as well as for the US for purposes of comparison.

TABLE 3-2

Consumption, Investment and Government Purchases as a Percentage of GDP: Some European Comparisons

	Private Consumption	Investment Expenditure	Government Purchases
Belgium	52.7	20.7	24.7
Bulgaria	64.3	21.4	15.5
Czech Republic	50	23.6	20.7
Denmark	49.5	17.5	28.7
Germany	57.6	17.6	19.5
Estonia	51.7	25.0	19.6
Ireland	47.6	9.8	17.6
Greece	73.7	13.1	17.8
Spain	59.4	19.3	20.0
France	57.7	20.2	24.7
Italy	61.1	18.2	20.1
Cyprus	66.8	12.8	20.1
Latvia	62.1	23.5	15.3
Lithuania	64.4	16.7	17.7
Luxembourg	31.2	19.2	17.0
Hungary	54.2	17.2	20.6
Malta	60.4	14.6	21.5
Netherlands	45.5	16.8	28.4
Austria	54.5	21.5	18.7
Poland	60.9	19.7	17.9
Portugal	66.3	15.8	18.3
Romania	62.2	26.6	15.8
Slovenia	58.3	17.4	20.6
Slovakia	57.3	21.5	17.6
Finland	56.3	19.4	24.8
Sweden	48.3	18.8	26.9
United Kingdom	65.6	14.1	22.2
Iceland	53.6	14.4	25.5
Norway	40.3	20.5	21.5
Switzerland	57.9	20	11.2
Croatia	59.1	18.1	19.6
Former Yugoslav Republic of Macedonia	75.3	20.7	17.9
United States	70.9	15.8	16.5

Source: Eurostat. Figures are for 2012.

For the countries listed in Table 3-2, consumption averaged a little under 60 per cent of GDP, while investment expenditure and government expenditure on goods and services each averaged around 20 per cent. Consumption was relatively higher as a percentage of GDP in the UK and the US, at about 65 and 70 per cent respectively, and was significantly lower (less than 50 per cent of GDP) in the Scandinavian countries of Denmark, Norway and Sweden as well as in the Netherlands. However, the relatively lower share of private consumption expenditure in the Netherlands and in two of the Scandinavian countries, Denmark and Sweden, was made up for in part by relatively high government spending on goods and services, which approached 30 per cent of GDP in both cases. ■

3-4 What Brings the Supply and Demand for Goods and Services into Equilibrium?

We have now come full circle in the circular flow diagram, Figure 3-1. We began by examining the supply of goods and services, and we have just discussed the demand for them. How can we be certain that all these flows balance? In other words, what ensures that the sum of consumption, investment and government purchases equals the amount of output produced? We will see that, in this classical model, the interest rate is the price that has the crucial role of equilibrating supply and demand.

There are two ways to think about the role of the interest rate in the economy. We can consider how the interest rate affects the supply and demand for goods or services, or we can consider how the interest rate affects the supply and demand for loanable funds. As we will see, these two approaches are two sides of the same coin.

Equilibrium in the Market for Goods and Services: The Supply and Demand for the Economy's Output

The following equations summarize the discussion of the demand for goods and services in Section 3-3:

$$Y = C + I + G,$$
$$C = C(Y - T),$$
$$I = I(r),$$
$$G = \overline{G},$$
$$T = \overline{T}.$$

The demand for the economy's output comes from consumption, investment and government purchases. Consumption depends on disposable income; investment depends on the real interest rate; and government purchases and taxes are the exogenous variables set by fiscal policy makers.

To this analysis, let's add what we learned about the supply of goods and services in Section 3-1. There we saw that the factors of production and the production function determine the quantity of output supplied to the economy:

$$Y = F(\overline{K}, \overline{L})$$
$$= \overline{Y}.$$

Now let's combine these equations describing the supply and demand for output. If we substitute the consumption function and the investment function into the national income accounts identity, we obtain

$$Y = C(Y - T) + I(r) + G.$$

Because the variables G and T are fixed by policy, and the level of output Y is fixed by the factors of production and the production function, we can write

$$Y = C(\overline{Y} - \overline{T}) + I(r) + \overline{G}.$$

This equation states that the supply of output equals its demand, which is the sum of consumption, investment and government purchases.

Notice that the interest rate r is the only variable not already determined in the last equation. This is because the interest rate still has a key role to play: it must adjust to ensure that the demand for goods equals the supply. The greater the interest rate, the lower the level of investment, and thus the lower the demand for goods and services, $C + I + G$. If the interest rate is too high, investment is too low, and the demand for output falls short of the supply. If the interest rate is too low, investment is too high, and the demand exceeds the supply. *At the equilibrium interest rate, the demand for goods and services equals the supply.*

This conclusion may seem somewhat mysterious: how does the interest rate get to the level that balances the supply and demand for goods and services? The best way to answer this question is to consider how financial markets fit into the story.

Equilibrium in the Financial Markets: The Supply and Demand for Loanable Funds

Because the interest rate is the cost of borrowing and the return to lending in financial markets, we can better understand the role of the interest rate in the economy by thinking about the financial markets. To do this, rewrite the national income accounts identity as

$$Y - C - G = I.$$

The term $Y - C - G$ is the output that remains after the demands of consumers and the government have been satisfied; it is called **national saving** or simply **saving** (S). In this form, the national income accounts identity shows that saving equals investment.

To understand this identity more fully, we can split national saving into two parts – one part representing the saving of the private sector and the other representing the saving of the government:

$$S = (Y - T - C) + (T - G) = I.$$

The term $(Y - T - C)$ is disposable income minus consumption, which is **private saving**. The term $(T - G)$ is government revenue minus government spending, which is **public saving**. (If government spending exceeds government revenue, the government runs a budget deficit, and public saving is negative.) National saving is the sum of private and public saving. The circular flow diagram in Figure 3-1 reveals an interpretation of this equation: this equation states that the flows into the financial markets (private and public saving) must balance the flows out of the financial markets (investment).

To see how the interest rate brings financial markets into equilibrium, substitute the consumption function and the investment function into the national income accounts identity:

$$Y - C(Y - T) - G = I(r).$$

Next, note that G and T are fixed by policy and Y is fixed by the factors of production and the production function:

$$\overline{Y} - C(\overline{Y} - \overline{T}) - \overline{G} = I(r),$$
$$\overline{S} = I(r).$$

The left-hand side of this equation shows that national saving depends on income Y and the fiscal policy variables G and T. For fixed values of Y, G and T, national saving S is also fixed. The right-hand side of the equation shows that investment depends on the interest rate.

Figure 3-8 graphs saving and investment as a function of the interest rate. The saving function is a vertical line because in this model saving does not depend on the interest rate (we relax this assumption later). The investment function slopes downward: the higher the interest rate, the fewer investment projects are profitable.

From a quick glance at Figure 3-8, one might think it was a supply-and-demand diagram for a particular good. In fact, saving and investment can be interpreted in terms of supply and demand. In this case, the 'good' is **loanable funds**, and its 'price' is the interest rate. Saving is the supply of loanable funds – households lend their saving to investors or deposit their saving in a bank that then loans the funds out. Investment is the demand for loanable funds – investors borrow from the public directly by selling bonds, or indirectly by borrowing from banks. Because investment depends on the interest rate, the quantity of loanable funds demanded also depends on the interest rate.

The interest rate adjusts until the amount that firms want to invest equals the amount that households want to save. If the interest rate is too low, investors want more of the economy's output than households want to save. Equivalently, the quantity of loanable funds demanded exceeds the quantity supplied. When this happens, the interest rate rises. Conversely, if the interest rate is too high,

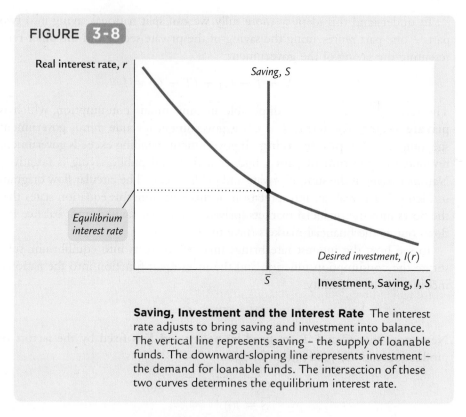

FIGURE 3-8

Saving, Investment and the Interest Rate The interest rate adjusts to bring saving and investment into balance. The vertical line represents saving – the supply of loanable funds. The downward-sloping line represents investment – the demand for loanable funds. The intersection of these two curves determines the equilibrium interest rate.

households want to save more than firms want to invest; because the quantity of loanable funds supplied is greater than the quantity demanded, the interest rate falls. The equilibrium interest rate is found where the two curves cross. *At the equilibrium interest rate, households' desire to save balances firms' desire to invest, and the quantity of loanable funds supplied equals the quantity demanded.*[8]

Changes in Saving: The Effects of Fiscal Policy

We can use our model to show how fiscal policy affects the economy. When the government changes its spending or the level of taxes, it affects the demand for the economy's output of goods and services and alters national saving, investment and the equilibrium interest rate.

An Increase in Government Purchases Consider first the effects of an increase in government purchases by an amount ΔG. The immediate impact is to increase the demand for goods and services by ΔG. But since total output is fixed by the factors of production, the increase in government purchases must be met by a decrease in some other category of demand. Because disposable income $Y - T$ is unchanged, consumption C is unchanged. The increase in government purchases must be met by an equal decrease in investment.

[8] In practice, this will occur in the financial sector of the economy, where households place their savings, investors borrow money and the supply and demand for loanable funds is balanced by financial institutions (such as banks) bidding among one another for funds.

The Financial System: Markets, Intermediaries, and the Crisis of 2008–2009

The model presented in this chapter represents the economy's financial system with a single market – the market for loanable funds. Those who have some income they don't want to consume immediately bring their saving to this market. Those who have investment projects they want to undertake finance them by borrowing in this market. The interest rate adjusts to bring saving and investment into balance.

The actual financial system is rather more complicated than this description. As in this model, the goal of the system is to channel resources from savers into various forms of investment. But the system includes a large variety of mechanisms to facilitate this transfer of resources.

One piece of the financial system is the set of *financial markets* through which households can directly provide resources for investment. Two important financial markets are the market for *bonds* and the market for *stocks*. A person who buys a bond from, say, Apple Corporation, becomes a creditor of the company, while a person who buys newly issued stock from Apple becomes a part owner of the company. (A purchase of stock on a stock exchange, however, represents a transfer of ownership shares from one person to another and does not provide new funds for investment projects.) Raising investment funds by issuing bonds is called *debt finance*, and raising funds by issuing stock is called *equity finance*.

Another piece of the financial system is the set of *financial intermediaries* through which households can indirectly provide resources for investment. As the term suggests, a financial

intermediary stands between the two sides of the market and helps direct financial resources toward their best use. Banks are the best-known type of financial intermediary. They take deposits from savers and use these deposits to make loans to those who have investments to make. Other examples of financial intermediaries include mutual funds, pension funds and insurance companies. In contrast to financial markets, when a financial intermediary is involved, the saver is often unaware of the investments that his or her saving is financing.

In 2007 and 2008, the world financial system experienced a historic crisis. Many banks and other financial intermediaries had previously made loans to homeowners, called *mortgages*, and had purchased many mortgage-backed securities (financial instruments whose value derives from a pool of mortgages). A large decline in housing prices throughout the United States, however, caused many homeowners to default on their mortgages, which in turn led to large losses at these financial institutions. Many banks and other financial intermediaries found themselves nearly bankrupt, and the financial system started having trouble performing its key functions. The crisis quickly spread globally; a number of European banks also found themselves in trouble and world stock markets fell.

We will examine more fully the financial crisis of 2007–2008 later in the book. For our purposes in this chapter, and as a building block for further analysis, representing the entire financial system by a single market for loanable funds is a useful simplification.

To induce investment to fall, the interest rate must rise. Hence, the increase in government purchases causes the interest rate to increase and investment to decrease. Government purchases are said to **crowd out** investment.

To grasp the effects of an increase in government purchases, consider the impact on the market for loanable funds. Because the increase in government purchases is not accompanied by an increase in taxes, the government finances the additional spending by borrowing – that is, by reducing public saving. With private saving

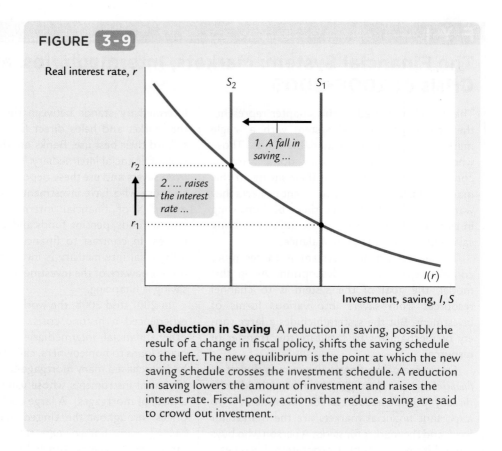

FIGURE 3-9

A Reduction in Saving A reduction in saving, possibly the result of a change in fiscal policy, shifts the saving schedule to the left. The new equilibrium is the point at which the new saving schedule crosses the investment schedule. A reduction in saving lowers the amount of investment and raises the interest rate. Fiscal-policy actions that reduce saving are said to crowd out investment.

unchanged, this government borrowing reduces national saving. As Figure 3-9 shows, a reduction in national saving is represented by a leftward shift in the supply of loanable funds available for investment. At the initial interest rate, the demand for loanable funds exceeds the supply. The equilibrium interest rate rises to the point where the investment schedule crosses the new saving schedule. Thus, an increase in government purchases causes the interest rate to rise from r_1 to r_2.

CASE STUDY

Wars and Interest Rates in the United Kingdom, 1730–1920

Wars are traumatic – both for those who fight them and for a nation's economy. Because the economic changes accompanying them are often significant, wars provide a natural experiment with which economists can test their theories. We can learn about the economy by seeing how in wartime the endogenous variables respond to the major changes in the exogenous variables.

One exogenous variable that changes substantially in wartime is the level of government purchases. Figure 3-10 shows military spending as a percentage of GDP for the United Kingdom from 1730 to 1919. This graph shows, as one would expect, that government purchases rose suddenly and dramatically during the seven wars of this period.

FIGURE 3-10

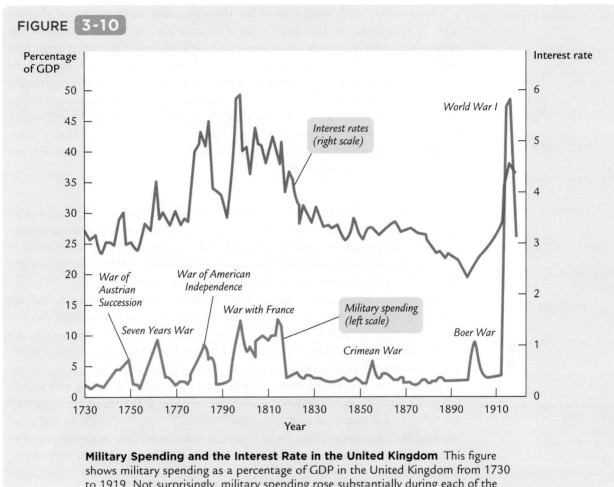

Military Spending and the Interest Rate in the United Kingdom This figure shows military spending as a percentage of GDP in the United Kingdom from 1730 to 1919. Not surprisingly, military spending rose substantially during each of the seven wars of this period. This figure also shows that the interest rate tended to rise when military spending rose.

Source: Series constructed from various sources described in Robert J. Barro, 'Government Spending, Interest Rates, Prices, and Budget Deficits in the United Kingdom, 1701–1918', *Journal of Monetary Economics,* September 1987, vol. 20, pp. 221–248.

Our model predicts that this wartime increase in government purchases — and the increase in government borrowing to finance the wars — should have raised the demand for goods and services, reduced the supply of loanable funds and raised the interest rate. To test this prediction, Figure 3-10 also shows the interest rate on long-term government bonds, called *consols* in the United Kingdom. A positive association between military purchases and interest rates is apparent in this figure. These data support the model's prediction: interest rates do tend to rise when government purchases increase.[9]

---

[9] Daniel K. Benjamin and Levis A. Kochin, 'War, Prices, and Interest Rates: A Martial Solution to Gibson's Paradox', in M. D. Bordo and A. J. Schwartz, eds, *A Retrospective on the Classical Gold Standard, 1821–1931,* Chicago: University of Chicago Press, 1983, pp. 587–612; Robert J. Barro, 'Government Spending, Interest Rates, Prices, and Budget Deficits in the United Kingdom, 1701–1918', *Journal of Monetary Economics,* September 1987, vol. 20, pp. 221–248.

One problem with using wars to test theories is that many economic changes may be occurring at the same time. For example, in World War II, while government purchases increased dramatically, rationing also restricted consumption of many goods. In addition, the risk of defeat in the war and default by the government on its debt presumably increases the interest rate the government must pay. Economic models predict what happens when one exogenous variable changes and all the other exogenous variables remain constant. In the real world, however, many exogenous variables may change at once. Unlike controlled laboratory experiments, the natural experiments on which economists must rely are not always easy to interpret. ■

A Decrease in Taxes Now consider a reduction in taxes of ΔT. The immediate impact of the tax cut is to raise disposable income and thus to raise consumption. Disposable income rises by ΔT, and consumption rises by an amount equal to ΔT times the marginal propensity to consume MPC. The higher the MPC, the greater the impact of the tax cut on consumption.

Because the economy's output is fixed by the factors of production, and the level of government purchases is fixed by the government, the increase in consumption must be met by a decrease in investment. For investment to fall, the interest rate must rise. Hence, a reduction in taxes, like an increase in government purchases, crowds out investment and raises the interest rate.

We can also analyse the effect of a tax cut by looking at saving and investment. Because the tax cut raises disposable income by ΔT, consumption goes up by $MPC \times \Delta T$. National saving S, which equals $Y - C - G$, falls by the same amount as consumption rises. As in Figure 3-9, the reduction in saving shifts the supply of loanable funds to the left, which increases the equilibrium interest rate and crowds out investment.

Changes in Investment Demand

So far, we have discussed how fiscal policy can change national saving. We can also use our model to examine the other side of the market – the demand for investment. In this section we look at the causes and effects of changes in investment demand.

One reason investment demand might increase is technological innovation. Suppose, for example, that someone invents a new technology, such as the railway or the computer. Before a firm or household can take advantage of the innovation, it must buy investment goods. The invention of the railway had no value until railway engines were produced and tracks were laid. The idea of the computer was not productive until computers were manufactured. Thus, technological innovation leads to an increase in investment demand.

Investment demand may also change because the government encourages or discourages investment through the tax laws. For example, suppose that the government increases personal income taxes and uses the extra revenue to provide tax cuts for those who invest in new capital. Such a change in the tax laws makes more investment projects profitable and, like a technological innovation, increases the demand for investment goods.

FIGURE 3-11

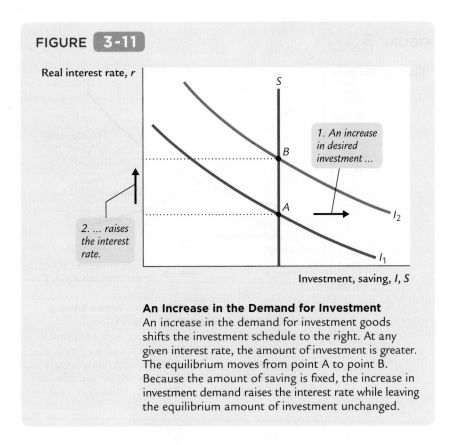

Real interest rate, r

S

B

1. An increase in desired investment ...

A

2. ... raises the interest rate.

I_2

I_1

Investment, saving, I, S

An Increase in the Demand for Investment
An increase in the demand for investment goods shifts the investment schedule to the right. At any given interest rate, the amount of investment is greater. The equilibrium moves from point A to point B. Because the amount of saving is fixed, the increase in investment demand raises the interest rate while leaving the equilibrium amount of investment unchanged.

Figure 3-11 shows the effects of an increase in investment demand. At any given interest rate, the demand for investment goods (and also for loanable funds) is higher. This increase in demand is represented by a shift in the investment schedule to the right. The economy moves from the old equilibrium, point A, to the new equilibrium, point B.

The surprising implication of Figure 3-11 is that the equilibrium amount of investment is unchanged. Under our assumptions, the fixed level of saving determines the amount of investment; in other words, there is a fixed supply of loanable funds. An increase in investment demand merely raises the equilibrium interest rate.

We would reach a different conclusion, however, if we modified our simple consumption function and allowed consumption (and its flip side, saving) to depend on the interest rate. Because the interest rate is the return to saving (as well as the cost of borrowing), a higher interest rate might reduce consumption and increase saving. If so, the saving schedule would be upward sloping rather than vertical.

With an upward-sloping saving schedule, an increase in investment demand would raise both the equilibrium interest rate and the equilibrium quantity of investment. Figure 3-12 shows such a change. The increase in the interest rate causes households to consume less and save more. The decrease in consumption frees resources for investment.

FIGURE 3-12

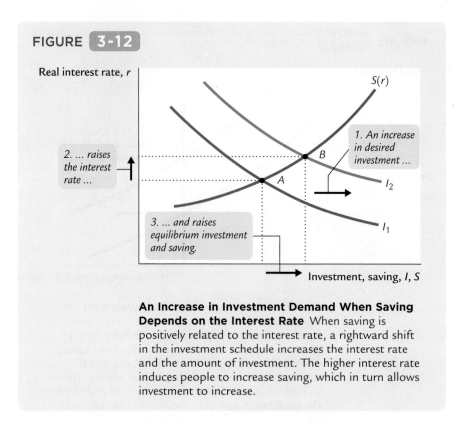

An Increase in Investment Demand When Saving Depends on the Interest Rate When saving is positively related to the interest rate, a rightward shift in the investment schedule increases the interest rate and the amount of investment. The higher interest rate induces people to increase saving, which in turn allows investment to increase.

3-5 Conclusion

In this chapter we have developed a model that explains the production, distribution and allocation of the economy's output of goods and services. The model relies on the classical assumption that prices adjust to equilibrate supply and demand. In this model, factor prices equilibrate factor markets, and the interest rate equilibrates the supply and demand for goods and services (or, equivalently, the supply and demand for loanable funds). Because the model incorporates all the interactions illustrated in the circular flow diagram in Figure 3-1, it is sometimes called a *general equilibrium model*.

Throughout the chapter, we have discussed various applications of the model. The model can explain how income is divided among the factors of production and how factor prices depend on factor supplies. We have also used the model to discuss how fiscal policy alters the allocation of output among its alternative uses − consumption, investment and government purchases − and how it affects the equilibrium interest rate.

At this point it is useful to review some of the simplifying assumptions we have made in this chapter. In the following chapters we relax some of these assumptions to address a greater range of questions.

■ We have ignored the role of money, the asset with which goods and services are bought and sold. In Chapters 4 and 5 we discuss how money affects the economy and the influence of monetary policy.

■ We have assumed that there is no trade with other countries. In Chapter 6 we consider how international interactions affect our conclusions.

■ We have assumed that the labour force is fully employed. In Chapter 7 we examine the reasons for unemployment and see how public policy influences the level of unemployment.

■ We have assumed that the capital stock, the labour force and the production technology are fixed. In Chapters 8 and 9 we see how changes over time in each of these lead to growth in the economy's output of goods and services.

■ We have ignored the role of short-run sticky prices. In Chapters 10 to 13 we develop a model of short-run fluctuations that includes sticky prices. We then discuss how the model of short-run fluctuations relates to the model of national income developed in this chapter.

Before going on to these chapters, go back to the beginning of this one and make sure you can answer the four groups of questions about national income that begin the chapter.

Summary

1. The factors of production and the production technology determine the economy's output of goods and services. An increase in one of the factors of production or a technological advance raises output.

2. Competitive, profit-maximizing firms take on labour until the marginal product of labour equals the real wage. Similarly, these firms rent capital until the marginal product of capital equals the real rental price. Therefore, each factor of production is paid its marginal product. If the production function has constant returns to scale, all output is used to compensate the inputs.

3. The economy's output is used for consumption, investment and government purchases. Consumption depends positively on disposable income. Investment depends negatively on the real interest rate. Government purchases and taxes are the exogenous variables of fiscal policy.

4. The real interest rate adjusts to equilibrate the supply and demand for the economy's output – or, equivalently, to equilibrate the supply of loanable funds (saving) and the demand for loanable funds (investment). A decrease in national saving, perhaps because of an increase in government purchases or a decrease in taxes, reduces the equilibrium amount of investment and raises the interest rate. An increase in investment demand, perhaps because of a technological innovation or a tax incentive for investment, also raises the interest rate. An increase in investment demand increases the quantity of investment only if higher interest rates stimulate additional saving.

KEY CONCEPTS

Factors of production

Production function

Constant returns to scale

Factor prices

Competition

Profit

Marginal product of labour (MPL)

Diminishing marginal product

Real wage

Marginal product of capital (MPK)

Real rental price of capital

Economic profit versus accounting profit

Cobb–Douglas production function

Disposable income

Consumption function

Marginal propensity to consume (MPC)

Interest rate

Nominal interest rate

Real interest rate

National saving (saving)

Private saving

Public saving

Loanable funds

Crowding out

QUESTIONS FOR REVIEW

1. What determines the amount of output an economy produces?

2. Explain how a competitive, profit-maximizing firm decides how much of each factor of production to demand.

3. What is the role of constant returns to scale in the distribution of income?

4. Write down a Cobb–Douglas production function for which capital earns one-quarter of total income.

5. What determines consumption and investment?

6. Explain the difference between government purchases and transfer payments. Give two examples of each.

7. What makes the demand for the economy's output of goods and services equal the supply?

8. Explain what happens to consumption, investment and the interest rate when the government increases taxes.

PROBLEMS AND APPLICATIONS

1. Use the neoclassical theory of distribution to predict the impact on the real wage and the real rental price of capital of each of the following events:

   a. A wave of immigration increases the labour force.

   b. An earthquake destroys some of the capital stock.

   c. A technological advance improves the production function.

2. If a 10 per cent increase in both capital and labour causes output to increase by less than 10 per cent, the production function is said to exhibit *decreasing returns to scale*. If it causes output to increase by more than 10 per cent, the production function is said to exhibit *increasing returns to scale*. Why might a production function exhibit decreasing or increasing returns to scale?

3. Suppose that an economy's production function is Cobb–Douglas with parameter $\alpha = 0.3$.

   a. What fractions of income do capital and labour receive in most of the advanced economies of Europe and North America?

   b. Suppose that immigration raises the labour force by 10 per cent. What happens to total output (in per cent)? The rental price of capital? The real wage?

c. Suppose that a gift of capital from abroad raises the capital stock by 10 per cent. What happens to total output (in per cent)? The rental price of capital? The real wage?

d. Suppose that a technological advance raises the value of the parameter A by 10 per cent. What happens to total output (in per cent)? The rental price of capital? The real wage?

4. Figure 3-5 shows that in UK and US data, labour's share of total income is approximately a constant over time. Table 3-1 shows that the trend in the real wage closely tracks the trend in labour productivity. How are these facts related? Could the first fact be true without the second also being true?

5. According to the neoclassical theory of distribution, the real wage earned by any worker equals that worker's marginal productivity. Let's use this insight to examine the incomes of two groups of workers: farmers and barbers.

a. Over the past century, the productivity of farmers has risen substantially because of technological progress. According to the neoclassical theory, what should have happened to their real wage?

b. In what units is the real wage discussed in part (a) measured?

c. Over the same period, the productivity of barbers has remained constant. What should have happened to their real wage?

d. In what units is the real wage in part (c) measured?

e. Suppose workers can move freely between being farmers and being barbers. What does this mobility imply for the wages of farmers and barbers?

f. What do your previous answers imply for the price of haircuts relative to the price of food?

g. Who benefits from technological progress in farming – farmers or barbers?

6. (This problem requires the use of calculus.) Consider a Cobb–Douglas production function with three inputs. K is capital (the number of machines), L is labour (the number of workers) and H is human capital (the number of college degrees among the workers). The production function is

$$Y = K^{1/3}L^{1/3}H^{1/3}.$$

a. Derive an expression for the marginal product of labour. How does an increase in the amount of human capital affect the marginal product of labour?

b. Derive an expression for the marginal product of human capital. How does an increase in the amount of human capital affect the marginal product of human capital?

c. What is the income share paid to labour? What is the income share paid to human capital? In the national income accounts of this economy, what share of total income do you think workers would appear to receive? (*Hint:* Consider where the return to human capital shows up.)

d. An unskilled worker earns the marginal product of labour, whereas a skilled worker earns the marginal product of labour plus the marginal product of human capital. Using your answers to (a) and (b), find the ratio of the skilled wage to the unskilled wage. How does an increase in the amount of human capital affect this ratio? Explain.

e. Some people argue that the government should pay university fees for all students as a way of creating a more egalitarian society. Others argue that this policy helps only those who are able to go to college. Do your answers to the preceding questions shed light on this debate?

7. The government raises taxes by €100 billion. If the marginal propensity to consume is 0.6, what happens to the following? Do they rise or fall? By what amounts?

a. Public saving.

b. Private saving.

c. National saving.

d. Investment.

8. Suppose that an increase in consumer confidence raises consumers' expectations about their future income and thus increases the amount they want to consume today. This might be interpreted as an upward shift in the consumption function. How does this shift affect investment and the interest rate?

9. Consider an economy described by the following equations:

$$Y = C + I + G$$

$$Y = 5000$$

$$G = 1000$$

$$T = 1000$$

$$C = 250 + 0.75(Y - T)$$

$$I = 1000 - 50r.$$

a. In this economy, compute private saving, public saving and national saving.

b. Find the equilibrium interest rate.

c. Now suppose that G rises to 1250. Compute private saving, public saving and national saving.

d. Find the new equilibrium interest rate.

10. Suppose that the government increases taxes and government purchases by equal amounts. What happens to the interest rate and investment in response to this balanced budget change? Does your answer depend on the marginal propensity to consume?

11. When the government subsidizes investment, such as with an investment tax credit, the subsidy often applies to only some types of investment. This question asks you to consider the effect of such a change. Suppose there are two types of investment in the economy: business investment and residential investment. And suppose that the government institutes an investment tax credit only for business investment.

a. How does this policy affect the demand curve for business investment? The demand curve for residential investment?

b. Draw the economy's supply and demand for loanable funds. How does this policy affect the supply and demand for loanable funds? What happens to the equilibrium interest rate?

c. Compare the old and the new equilibrium. How does this policy affect the total quantity of investment? The quantity of business investment? The quantity of residential investment?

12. If consumption depended on the interest rate, how would that affect the conclusions reached in this chapter about the effects of fiscal policy?

13. Macroeconomic data do not show a strong correlation between investment and interest rates. Let's examine why this might be so. Use our model in which the interest rate adjusts to equilibrate the supply of loanable funds (which is upward sloping) and the demand for loanable funds (which is downward sloping).

a. Suppose the demand for loanable funds were stable, but the supply fluctuated from year to year. What might cause these fluctuations in supply? In this case, what correlation between investment and interest rates would you find?

b. Suppose the supply of loanable funds were stable, but the demand fluctuated from year to year. What might cause these fluctuations in demand? In this case, what correlation between investment and interest rates would you find now?

c. Suppose that both supply and demand in this market fluctuated over time. If you were to construct a scatter plot of investment and the interest rate, what would you find?

d. Which of the above three cases seems most empirically realistic to you?

CHAPTER 4

The Monetary System: What It Is and How It Works

There have been three great inventions since the beginning of time: fire, the wheel, and central banking.

– Will Rogers

The two arms of macroeconomic policy are monetary and fiscal policy. Fiscal policy encompasses the government's decisions about spending and taxation, as we saw in the previous chapter. Monetary policy refers to decisions about the nation's system of coin, currency and banking. Fiscal policy is usually made by elected representatives, such as the US Congress, British Parliament, or Japanese Diet. Monetary policy is made by central banks, which are typically set up by elected representatives but allowed to operate independently. Examples include the US Federal Reserve, the Bank of England, and the European Central Bank. Will Rogers was exaggerating when he said that central banking was one of the three greatest inventions of all time, but he is right that these policy-making institutions have a great influence over the lives and livelihoods of citizens of all nations around the world.

Much of this book is aimed at understanding the effects and desired role of monetary and fiscal policy. This chapter begins our analysis of monetary policy. We address three related questions. First, what is money? Second, what is the role of a nation's banking system in determining the amount of money in the economy? Third, how does a nation's central bank influence the system of banking and the money supply?

This chapter's introduction to the monetary system provides the foundation for understanding monetary policy. In the next chapter, consistent with the focus of this part of book, we examine the long-run effects of monetary policy. The short-run effects of monetary policy are more complex. We start discussing that topic in Chapter 10, but it will take several chapters to develop a complete explanation. This chapter gets us ready. Both the long-run and short-run analysis of monetary policy must be grounded on a firm understanding of what money is, how banks affect it and how central banks control it.

4-1 What Is Money?

When we say that a person has a lot of money, we usually mean that he or she is wealthy. By contrast, economists use the term *money* in a more specialized way. To an economist, money does not refer to all wealth, but only to one type: **money** is the stock of assets that can be readily used to make transactions. Roughly speaking, the euros (or pounds) in the hands of the public make up the nation's stock of money.

The Functions of Money

Money has three purposes. It is a store of value, a unit of account and a medium of exchange.

As a **store of value**, money is a way to transfer purchasing power from the present to the future. If I work today and earn €100, I can hold the money and spend it tomorrow, next week or next month. Of course, money is an imperfect store of value: if prices are rising, the amount you can buy with any given quantity of money is falling. Even so, people hold money because they can trade the money for goods and services at some time in the future.

As a **unit of account**, money provides the terms in which prices are quoted and debts are recorded. Microeconomics teaches us that resources are allocated according to relative prices – the prices of goods relative to other goods – yet shops post their prices in money terms. A car dealer tells you that a car costs €20,000, not 400 shirts (even though it may amount to the same thing). Similarly, most debts require the debtor to deliver a specified number of money in the future, not a specified amount of some commodity. Money is the yardstick with which we measure economic transactions.

As a **medium of exchange**, money is what we use to buy goods and services. When we walk into a shop, we are confident that the shopkeeper will accept our money in exchange for the items they are selling. The ease with which money is converted into other things – goods and services – is sometimes called money's *liquidity*.

To understand better the functions of money, try to imagine an economy without it: a barter economy. In such a world, trade requires the *double coincidence of wants* – the unlikely situation of two people each having a good that the other wants at the right time and place to make an exchange. A barter economy permits only simple transactions.

Money makes more indirect transactions possible. A bricklayer uses his wages to buy books; the bookshop owner uses the revenue from the sale of books to buy a used car; the used car dealer uses the profits from his business to have an extension built on his house; and the firm that builds the extension uses the money paid to them to do the work to pay the wages of the bricklayer. In a complex, modern economy, trade is usually indirect and requires the use of money.

The Types of Money

Money takes many forms. In advanced economies we make transactions with an item whose sole function is to act as money: currency. These pieces of brightly coloured paper – with maps of Europe, strange symbols and perhaps even the portrait of a monarch or president – would have little value if they were not widely accepted as money. Money that has no intrinsic value is called **fiat money** because it is established as money by government decree, or fiat.

Although fiat money is the norm in most economies today, most societies in the past have used for money a commodity with some intrinsic value. Money of this sort is called **commodity money**. The most widespread example of commodity money is gold. When people use gold as money (or use paper money that is redeemable for gold), the economy is said to be on a gold standard. Gold is a form of commodity money because it can be used for various purposes – jewellery, watch cases, dental fillings, and so on – as well as for transactions. The gold standard was common throughout the world during the late 19th century.

"I married him for his money. As it turned out, it was 'funny money'. He's doing five to ten for counterfeiting."

Paro Lini/Cartoonstock.com

Cigarette Money

An unusual form of commodity money developed in some prisoner-of-war (POW) camps in Europe during World War II. The Red Cross supplied the prisoners with various goods – food, clothing, cigarettes, and so on. Yet these rations were allocated without close attention to personal preferences, so the allocations were often inefficient. One prisoner may have preferred chocolate, while another may have preferred cheese, and a third may have wanted a new shirt. The differing tastes and endowments of the prisoners led them to trade with one another.

Barter proved to be an inconvenient way to allocate these resources, however, because it required a double coincidence of wants. In other words, a barter system was not the easiest way to ensure that each prisoner received the goods he valued most. Even the limited economy of the POW camp needed some form of money to facilitate transactions.

Eventually, cigarettes became the established 'currency' in which prices were quoted and with which trades were made. A shirt, for example, cost about 80 cigarettes. Services were also quoted in cigarettes: some prisoners offered to do other prisoners' laundry for two cigarettes per garment. Even non-smokers were happy to accept cigarettes in exchange, knowing they could trade the cigarettes in the future for some good they did enjoy. Within the POW camp the cigarette became the store of value, the unit of account and the medium of exchange.[1] ■

How Fiat Money Evolves

It is not surprising that some form of commodity money arises to facilitate exchange: people are willing to accept a commodity currency such as gold because it has intrinsic value. The development of fiat money, however, is more perplexing. What would make people begin to value something that is intrinsically useless?

To understand how the evolution from commodity money to fiat money takes place, imagine an economy in which people carry around bags of gold. When a purchase is made, the buyer measures out the appropriate amount of gold. If the seller is convinced that the weight and purity of the gold are right, the buyer and seller make the exchange.

The government might first get involved in the monetary system to help people reduce transaction costs. Using raw gold as money is costly because it takes time to verify the purity of the gold and to measure the correct quantity. To reduce these costs, the government can mint gold coins of known purity and weight. The coins are easier to use than gold bullion because their values are widely recognized.

The next step is for the government to accept gold from the public in exchange for gold certificates – pieces of paper that can be redeemed for a certain quantity of gold. If people believe the government's promise to redeem the paper notes for gold, the notes are just as valuable as the gold itself (hence the phrase, 'as good as gold'). In addition, because the notes are lighter than gold (and gold coins), they are easier to use in transactions. Eventually, no one carries gold around at all, and these gold-backed government notes become the monetary standard.

Finally, the gold backing becomes irrelevant. If no one ever bothers to redeem the notes for gold, no one cares if the option is abandoned. As long as everyone continues to accept the paper notes in exchange, they will have value and serve as money. Thus, the system of commodity money evolves into a system of fiat money. Notice that, in the end, the use of money in exchange is a social convention: everyone values fiat money because they expect everyone else to value it.

CASE STUDY

Money and Social Conventions on the Island of Yap

The economy of Yap, a small island in the Pacific, once had a type of money that was something between commodity and fiat money. The traditional medium of exchange in Yap was *fei,* stone wheels up to 4 metres in diameter. These stones

---

[1] R. A. Radford, 'The Economic Organisation of a POW Camp', *Economica*, November 1945, pp. 189–201. The use of cigarettes as money is not limited to this example. In the Soviet Union in the late 1980s, American cigarettes were preferred to the ruble in the large black economy.

had holes in the centre so that they could be carried on poles and used for exchange. Large stone wheels are not a convenient form of money. The stones were heavy, so it took substantial effort for a new owner to take his *fei* home after completing a transaction. Although the monetary system facilitated exchange, it did so at great cost.

Eventually, it became common practice for the new owner of the *fei* not to bother to take physical possession of the stone. Instead, the new owner accepted a claim to the *fei* without moving it. In future bargains, he traded this claim for goods that he wanted. Having physical possession of the stone became less important than having legal claim to it.

This practice was put to a test when a valuable stone was lost at sea during a storm. Because the owner lost his money by accident rather than through negligence, everyone agreed that his claim to the *fei* remained valid. Even generations later, when no one alive had ever seen this stone, the claim to this *fei* was still valued in exchange.[2] ■

How the Quantity of Money Is Controlled

The quantity of money available in an economy is called the **money supply**. For commodity money, the money supply is simply the quantity of that commodity. In an economy that uses fiat money, such as most economies today, the government controls the supply of money: legal restrictions give the government a monopoly on the printing of money. Just as the level of taxation and the level of government purchases are policy instruments of the government, so is the supply of money. The control over the money supply is called **monetary policy**.

In most advanced economies, monetary policy is delegated to an institution called the **central bank**. The central bank of the Euro Area (also known as the Eurozone; the 17 countries that have adopted the euro as their currency) is the **European Central Bank** (often referred to as the ECB). In the United Kingdom, the central bank is the **Bank of England**, while in the United States it is the **Federal Reserve** (often called the Fed). Central bank decisions over monetary policy are usually made by a committee. In the ECB this committee is called the Governing Council, while the corresponding committees in the Bank of England and the Fed are the Monetary Policy Committee (MPC) and the Federal Open Market Committee (FOMC), respectively. These committees meet regularly to discuss and set monetary policy.

The primary way in which a central bank controls the supply of money is through **open-market operations** – the purchase and sale of government bonds. When the central bank wants to increase the money supply, it creates money and uses it to buy government bonds from the public. Because this money has left the central bank and entered into the hands of the public, the purchase of bonds increases the quantity of money in circulation. Conversely, when the central bank

---

[2] Norman Angell, *The Story of Money*, New York: Frederick A. Stokes Company, 1929, pp. 88–89.

> **F Y I**
>
> # How Do Credit Cards Fit into the Monetary System?
>
> What about credit cards? We need to think about these even more carefully, because credit cards are not really a method of payment, but a method of *deferring* payment. When you buy clothes with a credit card, the bank that issued the card pays the clothes shop what it is due – you have effectively borrowed from the bank. At a later date, you will have to repay the bank (perhaps with interest). When the time comes to pay your credit card bill, you will probably do so by direct transfer from your current account (or possibly by writing a cheque against your current account or by using your debit card over the Internet). The balance in this current account is part of the economy's stock of money.
>
> Notice that credit cards are very different from debit cards, which automatically withdraw funds from a bank account to pay for items bought. Why does a shopkeeper accept payment by credit card? Because he or she gets their money immediately by having their bank account credited for the price of the clothes even though you do not have to pay the credit card company back immediately. Again, it is the underlying movement in the shopkeeper's bank balance that matters.
>
> Although credit cards are not a form of money, they are still important for analysing the monetary system. Because people with credit cards can pay many of their bills all at once at the end of the month, rather than sporadically as they make purchases, they may hold less money on average than people without credit cards. Thus, the increased popularity of credit cards may reduce the amount of money that people choose to hold. In other words, credit cards are not part of the supply of money, but they may affect the demand for money.

wants to decrease the money supply, it sells some government bonds from its own portfolio. This open-market sale of bonds takes some money out of the hands of the public and, thus, decreases the quantity of money in circulation.

Later in the chapter we discuss in detail how the ECB, the Bank of England and the Fed control the supply of money. For our current discussion, these details are not crucial. It is sufficient to assume that the central bank directly controls the supply of money.

How the Quantity of Money Is Measured

One goal of this chapter is to determine how the money supply affects the economy; we turn to that topic in the next section. As a background for that analysis, let's first discuss how economists measure the quantity of money.

Because money is the stock of assets used for transactions, the quantity of money is the quantity of those assets. In simple economies, this quantity is easy to measure. In the POW camp, the quantity of money was the quantity of cigarettes in the camp. But how can we measure the quantity of money in more complex economies? The answer is not obvious, because no single asset is used for all transactions. People can use various assets, such as cash in their wallets or deposits in their current accounts, to make transactions, although some assets are more convenient than others.

The most obvious asset to include in the quantity of money is **currency** – the sum of outstanding paper money and coins – and the majority of day-to-day transactions still use currency as the medium of exchange.

However, most places where people want to buy things or pay for services (shops, department stores, restaurants, cafés, garages, travel agencies, and so on) nowadays also accept payment by debit card, which allows money to be transferred electronically between your current account and the current account of the shop owner (or café owner, or whatever). Another, more old-fashioned way of transferring money between current accounts is to write a personal cheque, and personal cheques are indeed still widely accepted as a means of payment (though rapidly being replaced by debit cards in the early 21st century).

So is a debit card money? Not really – it is the bank account on which the debit card draws which contains the money. A debit card is simply a means of transferring money between accounts. The same is true of a cheque. Although a cheque may seem to be similar in some ways to paper money – it is also written on paper and is made out for a certain sum of money – it is only accepted by a shopkeeper or a restaurateur because it is a means of transferring money from your bank account to his or hers. Thus, although a cheque and a credit card can both be used to pay for goods and services, neither of them is money – they are each a method of transferring money between bank accounts.

Wealth held in your current account is almost as convenient for buying things as wealth held in your wallet. To measure the money stock, therefore, you might want to include **demand deposits** – balances in bank accounts that depositors can access on demand simply by using their debit card or writing a cheque. Once you start to consider balances in current accounts as part of the money stock, you are led to consider the large variety of other accounts that people hold at banks and other financial institutions. Bank depositors usually cannot write cheques or use their debit cards against the balances in their savings accounts, but they can easily transfer funds from savings into current accounts. In addition, depositors in money market funds (investment funds that take depositors' money and invest in a portfolio of interest-bearing assets, such as government and company bonds) can often write cheques and use debit cards against their balances (although usually with some restriction on the frequency, size and notice required for the withdrawal). Thus, these other accounts should plausibly be counted as part of the money stock.

In a complex economy, it is not easy, in general, to draw a line between assets that can be called 'money' and assets that cannot. Figure 4-1 shows the main measures of the money supply for the Euro Area and for the UK, and the proportions of their constituents as they stood at the end of 2012. For the Euro Area, economists often refer to one of three main measures, of which the narrowest measure is M1, and is comprised of currency (the number of euro notes and coins in circulation) plus overnight deposits. Next there is M2, an intermediate measure comprised of M1 plus longer-term deposits; and finally there is M3, a broad measure comprised of M2 plus other money market instruments, such as repurchase agreements and shares in money market funds. In the UK, there is now only one main money supply measure that is regularly quoted and that is called M4, a broad measure similar to – but not identical to – the Euro Area M3. An important point to note from Figure 4-1 is that currency comprises quite a small proportion of the overall money stock, however it is measured.

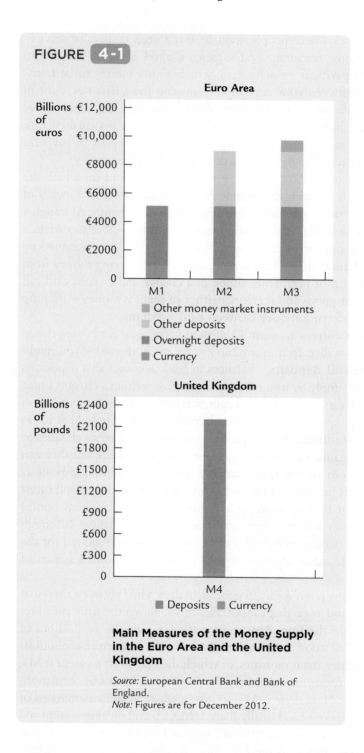

FIGURE 4-1

Main Measures of the Money Supply in the Euro Area and the United Kingdom

Source: European Central Bank and Bank of England.
Note: Figures are for December 2012.

For our purposes in this book, however, we need not dwell on the differences between the various measures of money. The important point is that the money stock for an advanced economy includes not only currency but also deposits in banks and other financial institutions that can be readily accessed and used to buy goods and services.

4-2 The Role of Banks in the Monetary System

Earlier in this chapter, we introduced the concept of 'money supply' in a highly simplified manner. We defined the quantity of money as the number of euros held by the public, and we assumed that the central bank controls the supply of money by increasing or decreasing the number of euros in circulation through open-market operations. Although this explanation is a good first approximation, it is incomplete because it omits the role of the banking system in determining the money supply. We now present a more complete explanation.

In this section, we see that the money supply is determined not only by central bank policy but also by the behaviour of households (which hold money) and banks (in which money is held). We begin by recalling that the money supply includes both currency in the hands of the public and deposits at banks, such as current accounts, that households can use on demand for transactions. That is, letting M denote the money supply, C currency and D demand deposits, we can write

$$\text{Money Supply} = \text{Currency} + \text{Demand Deposits},$$

$$M = C + D.$$

To understand the money supply, we must understand the interaction between currency and demand deposits, and how central bank policy influences these two components of the money supply.

100 Per Cent Reserve Banking

We begin by imagining a world without banks. In such a world, all money takes the form of currency, and the quantity of money is simply the amount of currency that the public holds. For this discussion, suppose that there is €1000 of currency in the economy.

Now introduce banks. At first, suppose that banks accept deposits, but do not make loans. The only purpose of the banks is to provide a safe place for depositors to keep their money.

The deposits that banks have received but have not lent out are called **reserves**. Some reserves are held in the vaults of local banks throughout the country, but most are held at a central bank. In our hypothetical economy, all deposits are held as reserves: banks simply accept deposits, place the money in reserve, and leave the money there until the depositor makes a withdrawal or writes a cheque against the balance. This system is called **100 per cent-reserve banking**.

Suppose that households deposit the economy's entire €1000 in First European Bank. First European Bank's **balance sheet** – its accounting statement of assets and liabilities – looks like this:

First European Bank's Balance Sheet

Assets		Liabilities	
Reserves	1000	Deposits	1000

The bank's assets are the €1000 it holds as reserves; the bank's liabilities are the €1000 it owes to depositors. Unlike banks in our economy, this bank is not making loans, so it will not earn profit from its assets. The bank presumably charges depositors a small fee to cover its costs.

What is the money supply in this economy? Before the creation of First European Bank, the money supply was the €1000 of currency. After the creation of First European Bank, the money supply is the €1000 of demand deposits. A euro deposited in a bank reduces the currency by one euro and raises deposits by one euro, so the money supply remains the same. *If banks hold 100 per cent of deposits in reserve, the banking system does not affect the supply of money.*

Fractional Reserve Banking

Now imagine that banks start to use some of their deposits to make loans – for example, to families who are buying houses or to firms that are investing in new plants and equipment. The advantage to banks is that they can charge interest on the loans. The banks must keep some reserves on hand so that reserves are available whenever depositors want to make withdrawals. But as long as the amount of new deposits approximately equals the amount of withdrawals, a bank does not need to keep all its deposits in reserve. Thus, bankers have an incentive to make loans. When they do so, we have **fractional reserve banking**, a system under which banks keep only a fraction of their deposits in reserve.

Here is First European Bank's balance sheet after it makes a loan:

<table>
<tr><th colspan="4">First European Bank's Balance Sheet</th></tr>
<tr><th colspan="2">Assets</th><th colspan="2">Liabilities</th></tr>
<tr><td>Reserves</td><td>200</td><td>Deposits</td><td>1000</td></tr>
<tr><td>Loans</td><td>800</td><td></td><td></td></tr>
</table>

This balance sheet assumes that the *reserve–deposit ratio* – the fraction of deposits kept in reserve – is 20 per cent. First European Bank keeps €200 of the €1000 in deposits in reserve and lends out the remaining €800.

Notice that First European Bank increases the supply of money by €800 when it makes this loan. Before the loan is made, the money supply is €1000, equalling the deposits in First European Bank. After the loan is made, the money supply is €1800: the depositor still has a demand deposit of €1000, but now the borrower holds €800 in currency. *Thus, in a system of fractional reserve banking, banks create money.*

The creation of money does not stop with First European Bank. If the borrower deposits the €800 in another bank (or if the borrower uses the €800 to pay someone who then deposits it), the process of money creation continues. Here is the balance sheet of Second European Bank:

<table>
<tr><th colspan="4">Second European Bank's Balance Sheet</th></tr>
<tr><th colspan="2">Assets</th><th colspan="2">Liabilities</th></tr>
<tr><td>Reserves</td><td>160</td><td>Deposits</td><td>€800</td></tr>
<tr><td>Loans</td><td>640</td><td></td><td></td></tr>
</table>

Second European Bank receives the €800 in deposits, keeps 20 per cent, or €160, in reserve, and then loans €640. Thus, Second European Bank creates €640 of money. If this €640 is eventually deposited in Third European Bank, this bank keeps 20 per cent, or €128, in reserve and loans €512, resulting in this balance sheet:

Third European Bank's Balance Sheet

Assets		Liabilities	
Reserves	€128	Deposits	€640
Loans	€512		

The process goes on and on. With each deposit and loan, more money is created.

Although this process of money creation can continue for ever, it does not create an infinite amount of money. Letting rr denote the reserve–deposit ratio, the amount of money that the original €1000 creates is

$$\text{Original Deposit} = €1000$$

$$\text{First European Bank Lending} = (1 - rr) \times €1000$$

$$\text{Second European Bank Lending} = (1 - rr)^2 \times €1000$$

$$\text{Third European Bank Lending} = (1 - rr)^3 \times €1000$$

$$\cdot$$
$$\cdot$$
$$\cdot$$

$$\text{Total Money Supply} = [1 + (1 - rr) + (1 - rr)^2$$
$$+ (1 - rr)^3 + \ldots] \times €1000$$
$$= (1/rr) \times €1000$$

Each €1 of reserves generates €$(1/rr)$ of money. In our example, $rr = 0.2$, so the original €1000 generates €5000 of money.[3]

The banking system's ability to create money is the primary difference between banks and other financial institutions. As we first discussed in Chapter 3, financial markets have the important function of transferring the economy's resources from those households that wish to save some of their income for the future to those households and firms that wish to borrow to buy investment goods to be used in future production. The process of transferring funds from savers to borrowers is called **financial intermediation**. Many institutions in the economy act as financial intermediaries: the most prominent examples are the stock market, the bond market and the banking system. Yet, of these financial institutions,

---

[3] *Mathematical note:* The last step in the derivation of the total money supply uses the algebraic result for the sum of an infinite geometric series. According to this result, if x is a number between -1 and 1, then

$$1 + x + x^2 + x^3 + \ldots = 1/(1 - x).$$

In this application, $x = (1 - rr)$.

only banks have the legal authority to create assets (such as current accounts) that are part of the money supply. Therefore, banks are the only financial institutions that directly influence the money supply.

Note that, although the system of fractional reserve banking creates money, it does not create wealth. When a bank loans some of its reserves, it gives borrowers the ability to make transactions and therefore increases the supply of money. The borrowers are also undertaking a debt obligation to the bank, however, so the loan does not make them wealthier. In other words, the creation of money by the banking system increases the economy's liquidity, not its wealth.

Bank Capital, Leverage and Capital Requirements

The model of the banking system presented so far is simplified. That is not necessarily a problem: after all, all models are simplified. But it is worth drawing attention to one particular simplifying assumption.

In the bank balance sheets we have just examined, a bank takes in deposits and uses those deposits to make loans or to hold reserves. Based on this discussion, you might think that it does not take any resources to open a bank. That is untrue, however. Starting a bank requires some capital. That is, the bank owners must start with some financial resources to get the business going. Those resources are called **bank capital** or, equivalently, the equity of the bank's owners.

Here is what a more realistic balance sheet for a bank would look like:

Real European Bank's Balance Sheet

Assets		Liabilities and Owners' Equity	
Reserves	€200	Deposits	€750
Loans	€500	Debt	€200
Securities	€300	Capital (owners' equity)	€50

The bank obtains resources from its owners, who provide capital, and also by taking in deposits and issuing debt. It uses these resources in three ways. Some funds are held as reserves; some are used to make bank loans; and some are used to buy financial securities, such as government or corporate bonds. The bank allocates its resources among these asset classes, taking into account the risk and return that each offers and any regulations that restrict its choices. The reserves, loans, and securities on the left-hand side of the balance sheet must equal, in total, the deposits, debt, and capital on the right-hand side of the balance sheet.

This business strategy relies on a phenomenon called **leverage**, which is the use of borrowed money to supplement existing funds for purposes of investment. The *leverage ratio* is the ratio of the bank's total assets (the left-hand side of the balance sheet) to bank capital (the one item on the right-hand side of the balance sheet that represents the owners' equity). In this example, the leverage ratio is €1000/€50, or 20. This means that for every euro of capital that the bank owners have contributed, the bank has €20 of assets and, thus, €19 of deposits and debts.

One implication of leverage is that, in bad times, a bank can lose much of its capital very quickly. To see how, let's continue with this numerical example. If the bank's assets fall in value by a mere 5 per cent, then the €1000 of assets are now worth only €950. Because the depositors and debt holders have the legal right to be paid first, the value of the owners' equity falls to zero. That is, when the leverage ratio is 20, a 5 per cent fall in the value of the bank assets leads to a 100 per cent fall in bank capital. The fear that bank capital may be running out, and thus that depositors may not be fully repaid, is typically what generates bank runs when there is no deposit insurance.

One of the restrictions that bank regulators put on banks is that the banks must hold sufficient capital. The goal of such a **capital requirement** is to ensure that banks will be able to pay off their depositors. The amount of capital required depends on the kind of assets a bank holds. If the bank holds safe assets such as government bonds, regulators require less capital than if the bank holds risky assets such as loans to borrowers whose credit is of dubious quality.

4-3 How Central Banks Influence the Money Supply

Now that we have seen what money is and how the banking system affects the amount of money in the economy, we are ready to examine how the central bank influences the banking system and the money supply. This influence is the essence of monetary policy.

A Model of the Money Supply

Now that we have seen how banks create money, let's examine in more detail what determines the money supply. Here we present a model of the money supply under fractional reserve banking. The model has three exogenous variables:

- The **monetary base** B is the total number of euros held by the public as currency C and by the banks as reserves R. It is directly controlled by the central bank.
- The **reserve–deposit ratio** rr is the proportion of deposits that banks hold in reserve. It is determined by the business policies of banks and the laws regulating banks.
- The **currency–deposit ratio** cr is the amount of currency C people hold as a proportion of their holdings of demand deposits D. It reflects the preferences of households about the form of money they wish to hold.

Our model shows how the money supply depends on the monetary base, the reserve–deposit ratio and the currency–deposit ratio. It allows us to examine how central bank policy and the choices of banks and households influence the money supply.

We begin with the definitions of the money supply and the monetary base:

$$M = C + D,$$
$$B = C + R.$$

The first equation states that the money supply is the sum of currency and demand deposits. The second equation states that the monetary base is the sum of currency and bank reserves. To solve for the money supply as a function of the three exogenous variables (B, rr and cr), we begin by dividing the first equation by the second to obtain

$$\frac{M}{B} = \frac{C + D}{C + R}.$$

Then divide both the top and bottom of the expression on the right by D:

$$\frac{M}{B} = \frac{C/D + 1}{C/D + R/D}.$$

Note that C/D is the currency–deposit ratio cr, and that R/D is the reserve–deposit ratio rr. Making these substitutions, and bringing the B from the left to the right-hand side of the equation, we obtain

$$M = \frac{cr + 1}{cr + rr} \times B.$$

This equation shows how the money supply depends on the three exogenous variables.

We can now see that the money supply is proportional to the monetary base. The factor of proportionality, $(cr + 1)/(cr + rr)$, is denoted m and is called the **money multiplier**. We can write

$$M = m \times B.$$

Each euro of the monetary base produces m euros of money. Because the monetary base has a multiplied effect on the money supply, the monetary base is sometimes called **high-powered money**.

We can now see how changes in the three exogenous variables – B, rr and cr – cause the money supply to change.

1. The money supply is proportional to the monetary base. Thus, an increase in the monetary base increases the money supply by the same percentage.

2. The lower the reserve–deposit ratio, the more loans banks make, and the more money banks create from every euro of reserves. Thus, a decrease in the reserve–deposit ratio raises the money multiplier and the money supply.

3. The lower the currency–deposit ratio, the fewer euros of the monetary base the public holds as currency, the more base euros banks hold as reserves, and the more money banks can create. Thus, a decrease in the currency–deposit ratio raises the money multiplier and the money supply.

With this model in mind, we can discuss the ways in which the central bank influences the money supply.

The Three Instruments of Monetary Policy

Earlier in this chapter, we made the simplifying assumption that the central bank controls the money supply directly. In fact, the central bank controls the money supply indirectly, by altering either the monetary base or the reserve–deposit ratio. To do this, the central bank has at its disposal three instruments of monetary policy: open-market operations, the refinancing rate and reserve requirements.

How Central Banks Change the Monetary Base The central bank can change the amount of money that is circulating in the economy by buying and selling bonds – a process known as **open-market operations**. If the central bank wants to increase the money supply, it can create currency and use it to buy bonds from the public in the bond market. After the purchase, the extra currency is in the hands of the public. Thus, an open-market purchase of bonds by the central bank increases the money supply. If, on the other hand, the central bank wants to decrease the money supply, it can sell bonds from its portfolio to the public. After the sale, the currency it receives for the bonds are out of the hands of the public. Thus, an open-market sale of bonds by the central bank decreases the money supply. To be precise, the open-market operations discussed in these simple examples are called *outright* open-market operations, because they each involve an outright sale or purchase of non-monetary assets to or from the banking sector, without a corresponding agreement to reverse the transaction at a later date.

The central bank of an economy will set an interest rate at which it is willing to lend to commercial banks on a short-term basis. The term for this interest rate differs across central banks, although, for simplicity, in this chapter we shall in general follow the practice of the European Central Bank and refer to it as the **refinancing rate**.

The way in which the central bank lends to the banking sector is through a special form of open-market operations. Above, we discussed the use of outright open-market operations. Although outright open-market operations have traditionally been used by central banks to regulate the money supply, central banks nowadays more often use a slightly more sophisticated form of open-market operations that involves buying bonds or other assets from banks and at the same time agreeing to sell them back later. When it does this, the central bank has effectively made a loan and taken the bonds or other assets as collateral or security on the loan. The central bank will have a list of eligible assets that it will accept as collateral – 'safe' assets, such as government bonds or assets issued by large corporations, on which the risk of default by the issuer is negligible. The interest rate that the central bank charges on the loan is the refinancing rate. Because the central bank has bought the assets but the seller has agreed to buy them back later at an agreed price, this kind of open-market operation is often called a repurchase agreement, or 'repo' for short. To see how the central bank uses repos as a means of controlling the money supply and how this is affected by the refinancing rate, we need to look a little more closely at the way commercial banks lend money to one another and borrow from the central bank.

As discussed above, banks need to carry enough reserves to cover their lending, and will generally aim for a certain ratio of reserves to deposits, known as the reserve ratio. The minimum reserve ratio may be set by the central bank, but even if this is not the case, banks will still have a reserve ratio which they consider prudent. Since deposits and withdrawals at banks can fluctuate randomly, some banks may find that they have an excess of reserves one day (i.e., their reserve ratio is above the level the bank considers prudent, or above the minimum reserve ratio, or both), while other banks may find that they are short of reserves and their reserve ratio is too low. Therefore, the commercial banks in an economy will generally lend money to one another on a short-term basis – from overnight to a couple of weeks – so that banks with excess reserves can lend them to banks who have inadequate reserves to cover their lending. This market for short-term reserves is – perhaps not surprisingly – called the money market. If there is a general shortage of liquidity in the money market (because the banks together have done a lot of lending), then the short-term interest rate at which they lend to one another will begin to rise, while it will begin to fall if there is excess liquidity among banks. The central bank closely monitors the money market and may intervene in it to affect the supply of liquidity to banks, which in turn affects their lending and hence affects the money supply.

Suppose, for example, that there is a shortage of liquidity in the market because the banks have been increasing their lending and they need to increase their reserves. A commercial bank may then attempt to obtain liquidity from the central bank by selling assets to the central bank and, at the same time, agreeing to purchase them back a short time later. In this type of open-market operation, the central bank effectively lends money to the bank and takes the assets as collateral on the loan. Because the commercial bank is legally bound to repurchase the assets at a set price, this is called a **repurchase agreement**, and the difference between the price at which the bank sells the assets to the central bank and the price at which it agrees to buy them back, expressed as an annualized percentage of the selling price, is called the repurchase or **repo rate** by the Bank of England and the refinancing rate by the European Central Bank (ECB). The ECB's refinancing rate is thus the rate at which it will lend to the banking sector of the Euro Area, while the repo rate is the rate at which the Bank of England lends short-term to the UK banking sector.

In the example given, the central bank added liquidity to the banking system by lending reserves to banks. This would have the effect of increasing the money supply. Because the loans made through open-market operations are typically very short-term, however, with a maturity of two weeks at most, the banks are constantly having to repay the loans and borrow again, or 'refinance' the loans. If the central bank wants to mop up liquidity, it can simply decide not to renew some of the loans. In practice, however, the central bank will set a reference rate of interest – the Bank of England's repo rate or the ECB's refinancing rate – and will conduct open-market operations (adding or mopping up liquidity) close to this reference rate.

In the US, the interest rate at which the Federal Reserve lends to the banking sector (corresponding to the ECB's refinancing rate or the Bank of England's repo rate) is called the **discount rate**.

Now we can see why the setting of the central bank's refinancing rate is the key instrument of monetary policy. If the central bank raises the refinancing rate, commercial banks will try to rein in their lending rather than borrow reserves from the central bank, and so the money supply will fall. If the central bank lowers the refinancing rate, banks will feel freer to lend, knowing that they will be able to borrow more cheaply from the central bank in order to meet their reserve requirements, and so the money supply will tend to rise.

How Central Banks Change Reserve Requirements The central bank may also influence the money supply with **reserve requirements**, which are regulations on the minimum amount of reserves that banks must hold against deposits. Reserve requirements influence how much money the banking system can create with each euro or with each pound of reserves. An increase in reserve requirements means that banks must hold more reserves and, therefore, can lend out less of each euro that is deposited; as a result, it raises the reserve ratio, lowers the money multiplier and decreases the money supply. Conversely, a decrease in reserve requirements lowers the reserve ratio, raises the money multiplier and increases the money supply.

Central banks have traditionally tended to use changes in reserve requirements only rarely because frequent changes would disrupt the business of banking. When the central bank increases reserve requirements, for instance, some banks find themselves short of reserves, even though they have seen no change in deposits. As a result, they have to curtail lending until they build their level of reserves to the new required level. In fact, the Bank of England no longer sets minimum reserve requirements at all. The European Central Bank does set minimum reserve requirements, but it applies them to the average reserve ratio over a specified period rather than at a single point in time. It does this to stop the amount of lending fluctuating wildly, in order to maintain stability in the money market. Hence, the ECB uses reserve requirements in order to maintain stability in the money market rather than as an instrument of policy by which to increase or decrease the money supply.

CASE STUDY

Quantitative Easing and the Exploding Monetary Base in the US

Figure 4-2 shows the monetary base in the US from 1960 to 2011. You can see that something extraordinary happened in the last few years of this period. From 1960 to 2007, the monetary base grew gradually over time. But then from 2007 to 2011 it spiked up substantially, approximately tripling over just a few years.

This huge increase in the monetary base is attributable to actions the Federal Reserve took during the financial crisis and economic downturn of this period. With the financial markets in turmoil, the Fed pursued its job as a lender of last resort with historic vigour. It began by buying large quantities of mortgage-backed securities. Its goal was to restore order to the mortgage market so that would-be homeowners could borrow. Later, the Fed pursued a policy of buying long-term government bonds to keep their prices up and long-term interest rates down. This policy, called *quantitative easing*, is a kind of open-market operation.

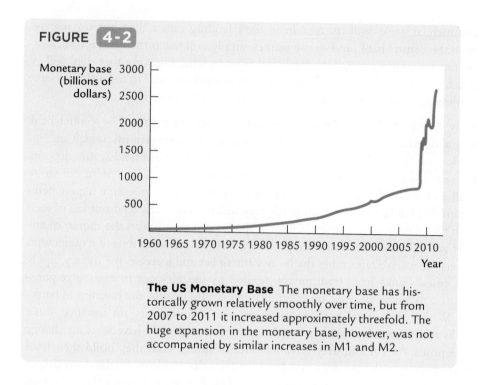

FIGURE 4-2

The US Monetary Base The monetary base has historically grown relatively smoothly over time, but from 2007 to 2011 it increased approximately threefold. The huge expansion in the monetary base, however, was not accompanied by similar increases in M1 and M2.

But rather than buying short-term Treasury bills, as the Fed normally does in an open-market operation, it bought longer-term and somewhat riskier securities. These open-market purchases led to the substantial increase in the monetary base.

The huge expansion in the monetary base, however, did not lead to a similar increase in broader measures of the money supply. While the monetary base increased about 200 per cent from 2007 to 2011, M1 increased by only 40 per cent, and M2 increased by only 25 per cent. These figures show that the tremendous expansion in the monetary base was accompanied by a large decline in the money multiplier. Why did this decline occur?

The model of the money supply presented earlier in this chapter shows that a key determinant of the money multiplier is the reserve ratio *rr*. From 2007 to 2011, the reserve ratio increased substantially because banks chose to hold substantial quantities of excess reserves. That is, rather than making loans, the banks kept much of their available funds in reserve. This decision prevented the normal process of money creation that occurs in a system of fractional reserve banking.

Why did banks choose to hold so much in excess reserves? Part of the reason is that banks had made many bad loans leading up to the financial crisis; when this fact became apparent, bankers tried to tighten their credit standards and make loans only to those they were confident could repay. In addition, interest rates had fallen to such low levels that making loans was not as profitable as it normally is. Banks did not lose much by leaving their financial resources idle as excess reserves.

Although the explosion in the monetary base did not lead to a similar explosion in the money supply, some observers feared that it still might. As the economy recovered from the economic downturn and interest rates rose to normal levels, they argued, banks could reduce their holdings of excess reserves by making loans. The money supply would start growing, perhaps too quickly.

Policy makers at the Federal Reserve, however, thought they could handle this problem if and when it arose. One possibility was to drain the banking system of reserves by engaging in the opposite open-market operation that had created them in the first place—that is, by selling the Treasury bonds and other securities in the Fed's portfolio. Another policy option for the Fed was to increase the interest rate it pays on reserves. A higher interest on reserves would make holding reserves more profitable for banks, thereby discouraging bank lending and keeping the money multiplier low.

Which of these 'exit strategies' the Fed would use in the aftermath of the monetary base explosion is still to be determined. ∎

Problems in Controlling the Money Supply

Through the setting of its refinancing rate and the associated open-market operations, the central bank can effect an important degree of control over the money supply. Yet the central bank's control of the money supply is not precise. The central bank has to wrestle with two problems, each of which arises because much of the money supply is created by the system of fractional reserve banking.

The first problem is that the central bank does not control the amount of money that households choose to hold as deposits in banks. The more money households deposit, the more reserves banks have, and the more money the banking system can create. And the less money households deposit, the less reserves banks have, and the less money the banking system can create. To see why this is a problem, suppose that one day people begin to lose confidence in the banking system and, therefore, decide to withdraw deposits and hold more currency. When this happens, the banking system loses reserves and creates less money. The money supply falls, even without any central bank action.

The second problem of monetary control is that the central bank does not control the amount that bankers choose to lend. When money is deposited in a bank, it creates more money only when the bank lends it out. Because banks can choose to hold **excess reserves** instead, the central bank cannot be sure how much money the banking system will create. For instance, suppose that one day bankers become more cautious about economic conditions and decide to make fewer loans and hold greater reserves. In this case, the banking system creates less money than it otherwise would. Because of the bankers' decision, the money supply falls.

Hence, in a system of fractional reserve banking, the amount of money in the economy depends in part on the behaviour of depositors and bankers. Because the central bank cannot control or perfectly predict this behaviour, it cannot perfectly control the money supply.

US Bank Failures, the Money Supply and the Great Depression

Between August 1929 and March 1933, the US money supply fell by 28 per cent. As we shall discuss in Chapter 11, some economists believe that this large decline in the money supply was the primary cause of the Great Depression. But we have not yet discussed why the US money supply fell so dramatically.

In Table 4-1, US figures on the three variables that determine the money supply – the monetary base, the reserve–deposit ratio and the currency–deposit ratio – are shown for 1929 and 1933. You can see that the fall in the money supply cannot be attributed to a fall in the monetary base: in fact, the monetary base rose by 19 per cent over this period. Instead, the money supply fell because the money multiplier fell by 38 per cent. The money multiplier fell because the currency–deposit and reserve–deposit ratios both rose substantially.

Most economists attribute the fall in the money multiplier to the large number of bank failures in the US in the early 1930s. From 1930 to 1933, more than 9000 US banks suspended operations, often defaulting on their depositors. The bank failures caused the money supply to fall by altering the behaviour of both depositors and bankers.

Bank failures raised the currency–deposit ratio by reducing public confidence in the banking system. People feared that bank failures would continue, and they began to view currency as a more desirable form of money than demand deposits. When they withdrew their deposits, they drained the banks of reserves. The process of money creation reversed itself, as banks responded to lower reserves by reducing their outstanding balance of loans.

TABLE 4-1

The Money Supply and Its Determinants: 1929 and 1933

	August 1929	March 1933
Money Supply	26.5	19.0
Currency	3.9	5.5
Demand deposits	22.6	13.5
Monetary Base	7.1	8.4
Currency	3.9	5.5
Reserves	3.2	2.9
Money Multiplier	3.7	2.3
Reserve-deposit ratio	0.14	0.21
Currency-deposit ratio	0.17	0.41

Source: Adapted from Milton Friedman and Anna Schwartz, *A Monetary History of the United States, 1867–1960*, Princeton, NJ: Princeton University Press, 1963, Appendix A.

In addition, the bank failures raised the reserve–deposit ratio by making bankers more cautious. Having just observed many bank runs, bankers became apprehensive about operating with a small amount of reserves. They therefore increased their holdings of reserves to well above the legal minimum. Just as households responded to the banking crisis by holding more currency relative to deposits, bankers responded by holding more reserves relative to loans. Together these changes caused a large fall in the money multiplier.

Although it is easy to explain why the money supply fell, it is more difficult to decide whether to blame the US central bank, the Federal Reserve. One might argue that the monetary base did not fall, so the central bank should not be blamed. Critics of central bank policy during this period make two counterarguments. First, they claim that the central bank should have taken a more vigorous role in preventing bank failures by acting as a *lender of last resort* when banks needed cash during bank runs. This would have helped maintain confidence in the banking system and prevented the large fall in the money multiplier. Second, they point out that the central bank could have responded to the fall in the money multiplier by increasing the monetary base even more than it did. Either of these actions may well have prevented such a large fall in the money supply, which in turn might have reduced the severity of the Great Depression.

Since the 1930s, many policies have been put into place that make such a large and sudden fall in the money multiplier less likely today. Most importantly, most developed countries today have a system of deposit insurance that protects depositors when a bank fails. Under a European Union Directive of 1994, for example, member countries of the European Union must have in place a system of deposit insurance that provides cover to depositors of up to £85,000 in the UK and €100,000 in most European countries. This policy maintains public confidence in the banking system, thus preventing large swings in the currency–deposit ratio and helping to stabilize the banking system and the money supply. ∎

4-4 Conclusion

You should now understand what money is and how central banks affect its supply. Yet this accomplishment, valuable as it is, is only the first step toward understanding monetary policy. The next and more interesting step is to see how changes in the money supply influence the economy. We begin our study of that question in the next chapter. As we examine the effects of monetary policy, we move toward an appreciation of what central bankers can do to improve the functioning of the economy and, just as important, an appreciation of what they cannot do. But be forewarned: it will not be until the end of the book before all the pieces of the puzzle fall into place.

Summary

1. Money is the stock of assets used for transactions. It serves as a store of value, a unit of account and a medium of exchange. Different sorts of assets are used as money: commodity money systems use an asset with intrinsic value, whereas fiat money systems use an asset whose sole function is to serve as money. In modern economies, a central bank is responsible for controlling the supply of money.

2. The system of fractional reserve banking creates money, because each euro of reserves generates many euros of demand deposits.

3. To start a bank, the owners must contribute some of their own financial resources, which become the bank's capital. Because banks are highly leveraged, however, a small decline in the value of their assets can potentially have a major impact on the value of bank capital. Bank regulators require that banks hold sufficient capital to ensure that depositors can be repaid.

4. The supply of money depends on the monetary base, the reserve–deposit ratio and the currency–deposit ratio. An increase in the monetary base leads to a proportionate increase in the money supply. A decrease in the reserve–deposit ratio or in the currency–deposit ratio increases the money multiplier and thus the money supply.

5. The central bank changes the money supply using three policy instruments. It can increase the monetary base by making an open-market purchase of bonds or by lowering the refinancing rate. It can reduce the reserve–deposit ratio by relaxing reserve requirements.

KEY CONCEPTS

Money

Store of value

Unit of account

Medium of exchange

Fiat money

Commodity money

Gold standard

Money supply

Monetary policy

Central bank

Federal Reserve

Open-market operations

Currency

Demand deposits

Reserves

100 per cent reserve banking

Balance sheet

Fractional reserve banking

Financial intermediation

Bank capital

Leverage

Capital requirement

Monetary base

Reserve–deposit ratio

Currency–deposit ratio

Money multiplier

High-powered money

Discount rate

Reserve requirements

Excess reserves

Interest on reserves

QUESTIONS FOR REVIEW

1. Describe the functions of money.

2. What is fiat money? What is commodity money?

3. What are open-market operations, and how do they influence the money supply?

4. Explain how banks create money.

5. What are the various ways in which the central banks can influence the money supply?

6. Why might a banking crisis lead to a fall in the money supply?

PROBLEMS AND APPLICATIONS

1. What are the three functions of money? Which of the functions do the following items satisfy? Which do they not satisfy?

   a. A credit card

   b. A painting by Rembrandt

   c. A bus pass

2. An economy has a monetary base of €1000. Calculate the money supply in each of the following four scenarios.

   a. All money is held as currency.

   b. All money is held as demand deposits. Banks hold 100 per cent of deposits as reserves.

   c. All money is held as demand deposits. Banks hold 20 per cent of deposits as reserves.

   d. People hold equal amount of currency and demand deposits. Banks hold 20 per cent of deposits as reserves.

   The central bank decides to increase the money supply by 10 per cent. In each of the above four scenarios, how much should it increase the monetary base?

3. As a case study in the chapter discusses, the US money supply fell from 1929 to 1933 because both the currency–deposit ratio and the reserve–deposit ratio increased. Use the model of the money supply and the data in Table 4-1 to answer the following hypothetical questions about this episode.

   a. What would have happened to the money supply if the currency–deposit ratio had risen but the reserve–deposit ratio had remained the same?

   b. What would have happened to the money supply if the reserve–deposit ratio had risen but the currency–deposit ratio had remained the same?

   c. Which of the two changes was more responsible for the fall in the money supply?

4. Give an example of a bank balance sheet with a leverage ratio of 10. If the value of the bank's assets rises by 5 per cent, what happens to the value of the owners' equity in this bank? How large a decline in the value of bank assets would it take to reduce this bank's capital to zero?

CHAPTER 5

Inflation: Its Causes, Effects and Social Costs

Lenin is said to have declared that the best way to destroy the Capitalist System was to debauch the currency. . . . Lenin was certainly right. There is no subtler, no surer means of overturning the existing basis of society than to debauch the currency. The process engages all the hidden forces of economic law on the side of destruction, and does it in a manner which not one man in a million is able to diagnose.

– John Maynard Keynes

One of the most popular chocolate bars sold in the UK is the Mars Bar. In 1979, a Mars Bar sold for £0.15, the price of a pint of beer in a pub was £0.34 and the average UK family house exchanged hands for £20,000. In 2012, a Mars Bar cost about £0.35, a pint of beer about £3.00 and the average UK house price was £170,000. This overall increase in prices is called **inflation**, and it is the subject of this chapter.

The rate of inflation – the percentage change in the overall level of prices – varies greatly over time and across countries. In the UK, according to the GDP deflator, prices rose by an average of 3.5 per cent per year in the 1960s, reaching 13 per cent per year in the 1970s, 7.5 per cent per year in the 1980s, 3.5 per cent per year in the 1990s, and averaged around 2.0 per cent per year during the period 2000–2012. Even when the inflation problem became severe during the 1970s, however, it was nothing compared with the episodes of extraordinarily high inflation, called **hyperinflation**, that other countries have experienced from time to time. A classic example is Germany in 1923, when prices increased an average of 500 per cent *per month*. More recent examples of hyperinflation have occurred in some of the formerly centrally planned economies of Central and Eastern Europe, following the break-up of the Soviet Union in the late 1980s and early 1990s. In Ukraine in 1993, for example, inflation exceeded 10,000 per cent per year. But even that rate of inflation is dwarfed by the extreme hyperinflation in the African country of Zimbabwe, where, in 2008, inflation is estimated to have reached a level in excess of 200 million per cent per year.

In this chapter we examine the classical theory of the causes, effects, and social costs of inflation. The theory is 'classical' in the sense that it assumes that prices are flexible. As we first discussed in Chapter 1, most economists believe this assumption describes the behaviour of the economy in the long run. By contrast, many prices are thought to be sticky in the short run, and from Chapter 10 we will incorporate this fact into our analysis. For now, we ignore short-run price stickiness. As we will see, the classical theory of inflation not only provides a good description of the long run, it also provides a useful foundation for the short-run analysis we develop later.

The 'hidden forces of economic law' that lead to inflation are not as mysterious as Keynes claims in the quotation that opens this chapter. Inflation is simply an increase in the average level of prices, and a price is the rate at which money is exchanged for a good or a service. To understand inflation, therefore, we must understand money – what it is, what affects its supply and demand, and what influence it has on the economy. In the previous chapter, we introduced the economist's concept of 'money' and discussed how, in most modern economies, a central bank set up by the government controls the quantity of money in the hands of the public. This chapter begins in Section 5-1 by showing that the quantity of money determines the price level and that the rate of growth in the quantity of money determines the rate of inflation.

Inflation in turn has numerous effects of its own on the economy. Section 5-2 discusses the revenue that governments can raise by printing money, sometimes called the *inflation tax*. Section 5-3 examines how inflation affects the nominal interest rate. Section 5-4 discusses how the nominal interest rate in turn affects the quantity of money people wish to hold and, thereby, the price level.

After completing our analysis of the causes and effects of inflation, in Section 5-5 we address what is perhaps the most important question about inflation: Is it a major social problem? Does inflation amount to 'overturning the existing basis of society', as the chapter's opening quotation suggests?

Finally, in Section 5-6, we discuss the dramatic case of hyperinflation. Hyperinflations are interesting to examine because they show clearly the causes, effects, and costs of inflation. Just as geologists learn much by studying earthquakes, economists learn much by studying how hyperinflations begin and end.

5-1 The Quantity Theory of Money

In Chapter 4 we defined what money is and learned that the quantity of money available in the economy is called the money supply. We also saw how the money supply is determined by the banking system and the policy decisions of the central bank. With that foundation, we can now start to examine the broad macroeconomic effects of monetary policy. To do this, we need a theory of how the quantity of money is related to other economic variables, such as prices and incomes. The theory we will now develop, called the *quantity theory of money*, has its roots in the work of the early monetary theorists, including the British philosopher and economist David Hume (1711–76). It remains the leading explanation for how money affects the economy in the long run.

Transactions and the Quantity Equation

People hold money to buy goods and services. The more money they need for such transactions, the more money they hold. Thus, the quantity of money in the economy is related to the number of euros or pounds exchanged in transactions.

The link between transactions and money is expressed in the following equation, called the **quantity equation**:

$$\text{Money} \times \text{Velocity} = \text{Price} \times \text{Transactions},$$

$$M \times V = P \times T.$$

Let's examine each of the four variables in this equation.

The right-hand side of the quantity equation tells us about transactions. T represents the total number of transactions during some period of time, say, a year. In other words, T is the number of times in a year that goods or services are exchanged for money. P is the price of a typical transaction – the number of pounds or euros exchanged. The product of the price of a transaction and the number of transactions, PT, equals the number of pounds or euros exchanged in a year.

The left-hand side of the quantity equation tells us about the money used to make the transactions. M is the quantity of money. V is called the **transactions velocity of money** and measures the rate at which money circulates in the economy. In other words, velocity tells us the number of times a unit of money (a euro or a pound) changes hands in a given period of time.

For example, suppose that 60 loaves of bread are sold in a given year at €1.00 per loaf. Then T equals 60 loaves per year, and P equals €1.00 per loaf. The total number of euros exchanged is

$$PT = €1.00/\text{loaf} \times 60 \text{ loaves/year} = €60/\text{year}.$$

The right-hand side of the quantity equation equals €60 per year, which is the euro value of all transactions.

Suppose further that the quantity of money in the economy is €20. By rearranging the quantity equation, we can compute velocity as

$$V = PT/M$$

$$= (€60/\text{year})/(€20)$$

$$= 3 \text{ times per year.}$$

That is, for €60 of transactions per year to take place with €20 of money, each euro must change hands three times per year.

The quantity equation is an *identity*: the definitions of the four variables make it true. The equation is useful because it shows that if one of the variables changes, one or more of the others must also change to maintain the equality. For example, if the quantity of money increases and the velocity of money remains unchanged, then either the price or the number of transactions must rise.

From Transactions to Income

When studying the role of money in the economy, economists usually use a slightly different version of the quantity equation than the one just introduced. The problem with the first equation is that the number of transactions is difficult to measure. To solve this problem, the number of transactions T is replaced by the total output of the economy Y.

Transactions and output are related, because the more the economy produces, the more goods are bought and sold. They are not the same, however. When one person sells a used car to another person, for example, they make a transaction using money, even though the used car is not part of current output. Nonetheless, the monetary value of transactions is roughly proportional to the monetary value of output.

If Y denotes the amount of output and P denotes the price of one unit of output, then the monetary value of output is PY. We encountered measures for these variables when we discussed the national income accounts in Chapter 2: Y is real GDP, P the GDP deflator, and PY nominal GDP. The quantity equation becomes

$$\text{Money} \times \text{Velocity} = \text{Price} \times \text{Output},$$

$$M \times V = P \times Y.$$

Because Y is also total income, V in this version of the quantity equation is called the **income velocity of money**. The income velocity of money tells us the number of times a unit of money enters someone's income in a given period of time. This version of the quantity equation is the most common, and it is the one we use from now on.

The Money Demand Function and the Quantity Equation

When we analyse how money affects the economy, it is often useful to express the quantity of money in terms of the quantity of goods and services it can buy. This amount, M/P, is called **real money balances**.

Real money balances measure the purchasing power of the stock of money. For example, consider an economy that produces only bread. If the quantity of money is €20, and the price of a loaf is €1.00, then real money balances are 20 loaves of bread. That is, at current prices, the stock of money in the economy is able to buy 20 loaves.

A **money demand function** is an equation showing the determinants of the quantity of real money balances that people wish to hold. A simple money demand function is

$$(M/P)^{\mathrm{d}} = kY,$$

where k is a constant that tells us how much money people want to hold for every unit of income. This equation states that the quantity of real money balances demanded is proportional to real income.

The money demand function is like the demand function for a particular good. Here, the 'good' is the convenience of holding real money balances. Just as owning a car makes it easier for a person to travel, holding money makes it easier to make transactions. Therefore, just as higher income leads to a greater demand for cars, higher income also leads to a greater demand for real money balances.

This money demand function offers another way to view the quantity equation. To see this, add to the money demand function the condition that the demand for real money balances $(M/P)^d$ must equal the supply M/P. Therefore,

$$M/P = kY.$$

A simple rearrangement of terms changes this equation into

$$M(1/k) = PY,$$

which can be written as

$$MV = PY,$$

where $V = 1/k$. These few steps of simple mathematics show the link between the demand for money and the velocity of money. When people want to hold a lot of money for each unit of income (k is large), money changes hands infrequently (V is small). Conversely, when people want to hold only a little money (k is small), money changes hands frequently (V is large). In other words, the money demand parameter k and the velocity of money V are opposite sides of the same coin.

The Assumption of Constant Velocity

The quantity equation can be viewed as a definition: it defines velocity V as the ratio of nominal GDP, PY, to the quantity of money M. Yet, if we make the additional assumption that the velocity of money is constant, then the quantity equation becomes a useful theory about the effects of money, called the **quantity theory of money**.

As with many of the assumptions in economics, the assumption of constant velocity is only an approximation to reality. Velocity does change if the money demand function changes. For example, when the cashpoint machine (also known as an ATM, which stands for automated teller machine, or a 'hole in the wall') was introduced, people could reduce their average money holdings, which meant a fall in the money demand parameter k and an increase in velocity V. Nonetheless, experience shows that the assumption of constant velocity is a useful one in many situations. Let's assume, therefore, that velocity is constant, and see what this assumption implies about the effects of the money supply on the economy.

With this assumption included, the quantity equation can be seen as a theory of what determines nominal GDP. The quantity equation says

$$M\bar{V} = PY,$$

where the bar over V means that velocity is fixed. Therefore, a change in the quantity of money (M) must cause a proportionate change in nominal GDP (PY). That is, if velocity is fixed, the quantity of money determines the monetary value of the economy's output in terms of euros or pounds.

Money, Prices and Inflation

We now have a theory to explain what determines the economy's overall level of prices. The theory has three building blocks:

1. The factors of production and the production function determine the level of output Y. We borrow this conclusion from Chapter 3.

2. The money supply M determines the nominal value of output, PY. This conclusion follows from the quantity equation and the assumption that the velocity of money is fixed.

3. The price level P is then the ratio of the nominal value of output, PY, to the level of output Y.

In other words, the productive capability of the economy determines real GDP, the quantity of money determines nominal GDP, and the GDP deflator is the ratio of nominal GDP to real GDP.

This theory explains what happens when the central bank changes the supply of money. Because velocity is fixed, any change in the supply of money leads to a proportionate change in nominal GDP. Because the factors of production and the production function have already determined real GDP, the change in nominal GDP must represent a change in the price level. Hence, the quantity theory implies that the price level is proportional to the money supply.

Because the inflation rate is the percentage change in the price level, this theory of the price level is also a theory of the inflation rate. The quantity equation, written in percentage-change form, is

$$\text{\% Change in } M + \text{\% Change in } V = \text{\% Change in } P + \text{\% Change in } Y.$$

Consider each of these four terms. First, the percentage change in the quantity of money M is under the control of the central bank. Second, the percentage change in velocity V reflects shifts in money demand; we have assumed that velocity is constant, so the percentage change in velocity is zero. Third, the percentage change in the price level P is the rate of inflation; this is the variable in the equation that we would like to explain. Fourth, the percentage change in output Y depends on growth in the factors of production and on technological progress, which for our present purposes we are taking as given. This analysis tells us that (except for a constant that depends on exogenous growth in output) the growth in the money supply determines the rate of inflation.

Thus, the quantity theory of money states that the central bank, which controls the money supply, has ultimate control over the rate of inflation. If the central bank keeps the money supply stable, the price level will be stable. If the central bank increases the money supply rapidly, the price level will rise rapidly.

CASE STUDY

Inflation and Money Growth

'Inflation is always and everywhere a monetary phenomenon.' So wrote Milton Friedman, the American economist who won the Nobel Prize in economics in 1976. The quantity theory of money leads us to agree that the growth in the quantity of money is the primary determinant of the inflation rate. Yet Friedman's claim is empirical, not theoretical. To evaluate his claim, and to judge the usefulness of our theory, we need to look at data on money and prices.

Figure 5-1 examines the average rate of inflation and the average rate of money growth in 180 countries, during the period 2003–2011. The data verify the link between money growth and inflation. Countries with high money growth (such as Turkey) tend to have high inflation, and countries with low money growth (such as Singapore) tend to have low inflation.

If we looked at monthly data on money growth and inflation, rather than data over a long period of time, we would not see as close a connection between these two variables. This theory of inflation works best in the long run, not in the short run. We examine the short-run impact of changes in the quantity of money when we turn to economic fluctuations in Part IV of this book. ■

FIGURE 5-1

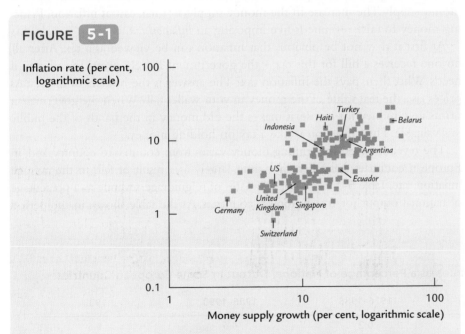

The Relationship Between Money Growth and Inflation In this scatterplot, each point represents a country. The horizontal axis shows the average growth in the money supply (as measured by currency plus demand deposits) during the period 2003–2011, and the vertical axis shows the average rate of inflation (as measured by the CPI). Once again, the positive correlation is evidence for the quantity theory's prediction that high money growth leads to high inflation.

Source: World Bank.
Notes: Countries with negative growth rates have been dropped from the data. Averages cover the period 2003–2011.

5-2 Seigniorage: The Revenue from Printing Money

So far, we have seen how growth in the money supply causes inflation. With inflation as a consequence, what would ever induce a central bank to increase the money supply so much? Here we examine one answer to this question.

Let's start with an indisputable fact: all governments spend money. Some of this spending is to buy goods and services (such as roads and a police force), and some is to provide transfer payments (for the poor and elderly, for example). A government can finance its spending in three ways. First, it can raise revenue through taxes, such as personal and corporate income taxes. Second, it can borrow from the public by selling government bonds. Third, it can print money.

The revenue raised by printing money is called **seigniorage**. The term comes from *seigneur*, the French word for 'feudal lord'. In the Middle Ages, European lords had the exclusive right on their manor to coin money. Today this right belongs to the central government, and it is one source of revenue.

When the government prints money to finance expenditure, it increases the money supply. The increase in the money supply, in turn, causes inflation. Printing money to raise revenue is like imposing an *inflation tax*.

At first it may not be obvious that inflation can be viewed as a tax. After all, no one receives a bill for this tax – the government merely prints the money it needs. Who, then, pays the inflation tax? The answer is the holders of money. As prices rise, the real value of the money in your wallet falls. When the government prints new money for its use, it makes the old money in the hands of the public less valuable. Thus, inflation is like a tax on holding money.

The revenue raised by printing money varies from country to country and, in European countries, has fallen over time, largely as a result of falls in the average inflation rate. Table 5-1 lists some estimates of seigniorage revenue as a percentage of national output for five European countries. As the table shows, in the period

---

TABLE 5-1

Seigniorage Revenues as a Percentage of National Output in Some European Countries

	1976–1985	1986–1990	1993
Germany	0.2	0.6	0.5
Greece	3.4	1.5	0.7
Italy	2.6	0.7	0.5
Portugal	3.4	1.9	0.6
Spain	2.9	0.8	0.6

Source: Rudiger Dornbusch, 'The European Monetary System, the Dollar and the Yen', in F. Giavazzi, S. Micossi and M. Miller, eds, *The European Monetary System,* 1988, Cambridge: Cambridge University Press; Daniel Gros, 'Seigniorage and EMS Discipline', in P. De Grauwe and L. Papademos, eds, *The European Monetary System in the 1990s,* 1990, London: Longman; Daniel Gros and Niels Thygesen, *European Monetary Integration: From the European Monetary System Towards Monetary Union,* 1992, London: Longman.
Note: Seigniorage revenue is expressed as a percentage of GNP.

1976–1985, the governments of the southern European countries of Greece, Portugal, Italy and Spain each generated about 3 per cent of GDP through seigniorage, while over the period 1986–1990, when these countries achieved lower average inflation rates, seigniorage revenues more than halved. By 1993, seigniorage revenue in all four countries was close to the German level of 0.5 per cent of national output.

In countries experiencing hyperinflation, however, seigniorage is often the government's chief source of revenue – indeed, the need to print money to finance expenditure is a primary cause of hyperinflation.

As the economist John Maynard Keynes observed in his 1923 book, *A Tract on Monetary Reform*:

> Inflation is the form of taxation which the public find hardest to evade and even the weakest government can enforce, when it can enforce nothing else . . . The burden of the tax is well spread, cannot be evaded, costs nothing to collect and falls, in a rough sort of way, in proportion to the wealth of the victim. No wonder its superficial advantages have attracted Ministers of Finance. . .

Note, however, Keynes's use of the term 'superficial advantages' in this quotation: relying on the inflation tax as the major source of government revenue is an easy and superficially attractive policy for the reasons Keynes mentions, but it is also dangerous and foolhardy because it is certain to result in a high inflation rate, and eventually hyperinflation. This is because the inflation caused by printing money also affects the real value of the seigniorage revenue, so that the government has to print more and more money to maintain its spending, and so inflation spirals higher and higher.

CASE STUDY

The Inflation Tax and Money Growth on the Island of Yap

We discussed in a case study in Chapter 4 how the islanders of Yap in the Pacific Ocean used large stone wheels as money. The Yapese valued these large stones because their size made them difficult to steal and because their supply was more or less fixed since they had to be brought to Yap by sea in a perilous journey from the Island of Palau, 210 kilometres away, using only rough outrigger canoes and navigating by the stars. Although it became common practice just to exchange the title to a stone rather than to lug the stone about, this did not matter so long as the titles exactly matched the stones (even if at least one of them was at the bottom of the sea).

However, in 1874, an Irish-American man called David O'Keefe worked out that with modern ships and navigation methods, it was relatively cheap and easy for him to ship large amounts of the stones from Palau to Yap. Over time, he imported thousands of new stones, becoming a man of considerable wealth and influence on the island. But, through dramatically increasing the Yapese money supply, he also dramatically raised inflation and debased the value of the stones. In effect, O'Keefe became rich by appropriating seigniorage (the difference between what it cost him to ship the stones and their value on the Island of Yap) and imposing an inflation tax on the Yapese.

Today the stones are almost worthless, except as a tourist curiosity, and the accepted currency on the Island of Yap is the US dollar.[1] ∎

5-3 Inflation and Interest Rates

As we first discussed in Chapter 3, interest rates are among the most important macroeconomic variables. In essence, they are the prices that link the present and the future. Here we discuss the relationship between inflation and interest rates.

Two Interest Rates: Real and Nominal

Suppose you deposit your savings in a bank account that pays 8 per cent interest annually. Next year, you withdraw your savings and the accumulated interest. Are you 8 per cent richer than you were when you made the deposit a year earlier?

The answer depends on what 'richer' means. Certainly, you have 8 per cent more money than you had before. But if prices have risen, each unit of money buys less, and your purchasing power has not risen by 8 per cent. If the inflation rate was 5 per cent over the year, then the amount of goods you can buy has increased by only 3 per cent. And if the inflation rate was 10 per cent, then your purchasing power has fallen by 2 per cent.

Economists call the interest rate that the bank pays the **nominal interest rate**, and the increase in your purchasing power the **real interest rate**. If i denotes the nominal interest rate, r the real interest rate and π the rate of inflation, then the relationship among these three variables can be written as

$$r = i - \pi.$$

The real interest rate is the difference between the nominal interest rate and the rate of inflation.[2]

The Fisher Effect

Rearranging terms in our equation for the real interest rate, we can show that the nominal interest rate is the sum of the real interest rate and the inflation rate:

$$i = r + \pi.$$

The equation written in this way is called the **Fisher equation**, after economist Irving Fisher (1867–1947). It shows that the nominal interest rate can change for two reasons: because the real interest rate changes or because the inflation rate changes.

---

[1] Curiously, O'Keefe's life was the subject of a bestselling 1950 novel by Laurence Klingman and Gerald Green, entitled *His Majesty O'Keefe*, as well as a 1954 Hollywood film of the same name, starring Burt Lancaster.

[2] *Mathematical note*: This equation relating the real interest rate, nominal interest rate and inflation rate is only an approximation. The exact formula is $(1 + r) = (1 + i)/(1 + \pi)$. The approximation in the text is reasonably accurate as long as r, i and π are relatively small (say, less than 20 per cent per year).

Once we separate the nominal interest rate into these two parts, we can use this equation to develop a theory that explains the nominal interest rate. Chapter 3 showed that the real interest rate adjusts to equilibrate saving and investment. The quantity theory of money shows that the rate of money growth determines the rate of inflation. The Fisher equation then tells us to add the real interest rate and the inflation rate together to determine the nominal interest rate.

The quantity theory and the Fisher equation together tell us how money growth affects the nominal interest rate. *According to the quantity theory, an increase in the rate of money growth of 1 per cent causes a 1 per cent increase in the rate of inflation. According to the Fisher equation, a 1 per cent increase in the rate of inflation, in turn, causes a 1 per cent increase in the nominal interest rate.* The one-for-one relation between the inflation rate and the nominal interest rate is called the **Fisher effect**.

CASE STUDY

Inflation and Nominal Interest Rates

How useful is the Fisher effect in explaining interest rates? To answer this question we look at two types of data on inflation and nominal interest rates.

Figure 5-2 shows the variation over time in the nominal interest rate and the inflation rate in the United Kingdom during the period 1975–2012. You

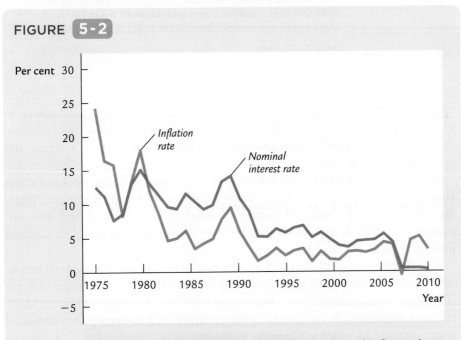

FIGURE 5-2

Inflation and Nominal Interest Rates Over Time This figure plots the nominal interest rate (on three-month UK Treasury bills) and the inflation rate (as measured by the RPI) in the United Kingdom since 1975. It shows the Fisher effect: higher inflation leads to a higher nominal interest rate.

Source: Bank of England and UK Office for National Statistics.

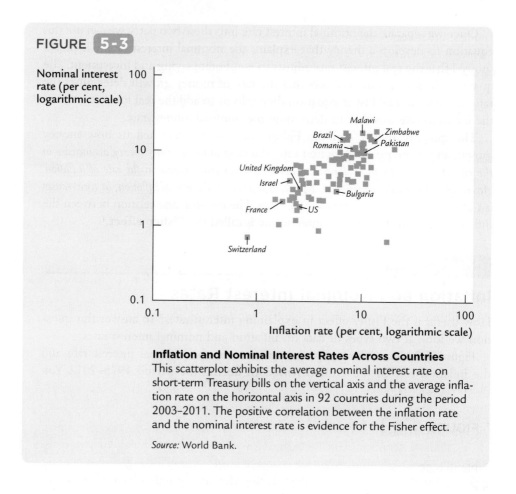

FIGURE 5-3

Inflation and Nominal Interest Rates Across Countries
This scatterplot exhibits the average nominal interest rate on short-term Treasury bills on the vertical axis and the average inflation rate on the horizontal axis in 92 countries during the period 2003–2011. The positive correlation between the inflation rate and the nominal interest rate is evidence for the Fisher effect.

Source: World Bank.

can see that the Fisher effect has done a good job of explaining fluctuations in the nominal interest rate over the past 40 years. When inflation is high, nominal interest rates are typically high, and when inflation is low, nominal interest rates are typically low as well.

Similar support for the Fisher effect comes from examining the variation across countries. As Figure 5-3 shows, a nation's inflation rate and its nominal interest rate are related. Countries with high inflation tend to have high nominal interest rates as well, and countries with low inflation tend to have low nominal interest rates. ■

The link between inflation and interest rates is well known to financial investment firms. Because bond prices move inversely with interest rates, one can get rich by predicting correctly the direction in which interest rates will move. Many financial investment firms hire economists to monitor monetary policy and news about inflation to anticipate changes in interest rates.

Two Real Interest Rates: *Ex Ante* and *Ex Post*

When a borrower and lender agree on a nominal interest rate, they do not know what the inflation rate over the term of the loan will be. Therefore, we must distinguish between two concepts of the real interest rate: the real interest rate the borrower and lender expect when the loan is made, called the ***ex ante* real interest rate**, and the real interest rate actually realized, called the ***ex post* real interest rate**.

Although borrowers and lenders cannot predict future inflation with certainty, they do have some expectation about what the inflation rate will be. Let π denote actual future inflation and π^e the expectation of future inflation. The *ex ante* real interest rate is $i - \pi^e$, and the *ex post* real interest rate is $i - \pi$. The two real interest rates differ when actual inflation π differs from expected inflation π^e.

How does this distinction between actual and expected inflation modify the Fisher effect? Clearly, the nominal interest rate cannot adjust to actual inflation, because actual inflation is not known when the nominal interest rate is set. The nominal interest rate can adjust only to expected inflation. The Fisher effect is more precisely written as

$$i = r + \pi^e.$$

The *ex ante* real interest rate r is determined by equilibrium in the market for goods and services, as described by the model in Chapter 3 (see Section 3-4). The nominal interest rate i moves one-for-one with changes in expected inflation π^e.

Nominal Interest Rates in the 19th Century

Although recent data show a positive relationship between nominal interest rates and inflation rates, this finding is not universal. In data from economies like those of the United Kingdom and the United States during the late 19th and early 20th centuries, high nominal interest rates did not accompany high inflation. The apparent absence of any Fisher effect during this time puzzled Irving Fisher. He suggested that inflation 'caught merchants napping'.

How should we interpret the absence of an apparent Fisher effect in 19th-century data? Does this period of history provide evidence against the adjustment of nominal interest rates to inflation? Recent research suggests that this period has little to tell us about the validity of the Fisher effect. The reason is that the Fisher effect relates the nominal interest rate to *expected* inflation, and, according to this research, inflation at this time was largely unexpected.

Although expectations are not observable, we can draw inferences about them by examining the persistence of inflation. In recent experience, inflation has been very persistent: when it is high one year, it tends to be high the next year as well. Therefore, when people have observed high inflation, it has been rational for them to expect high inflation in the future. By contrast, during the 19th century, when the gold standard was in effect, inflation had little persistence. High inflation in one year was just as likely to be followed the next year by low inflation as by high inflation. Therefore, high inflation did not imply high expected inflation and did not lead to high nominal interest rates. So, in a sense, Fisher was right to say that inflation 'caught merchants napping'.[3] ■

---

[3] Robert B. Barsky, 'The Fisher Effect and the Forecastability and Persistence of Inflation', *Journal of Monetary Economics*, January 1987, vol. 19, pp. 3–24.

5-4 The Nominal Interest Rate and the Demand for Money

The quantity theory is based on a simple money demand function: it assumes that the demand for real money balances is proportional to income. Although the quantity theory is a good place to start when analysing the effects of money on the economy, it is not the whole story. Here, we add another determinant of the quantity of money demanded – the nominal interest rate.

The Cost of Holding Money

The money you hold in your wallet does not earn interest. If, instead of holding that money, you used it to buy government bonds or deposited it in a savings account, you would earn the nominal interest rate. The nominal interest rate is the opportunity cost of holding money: it is what you give up by holding money rather than bonds.

Another way to see that the cost of holding money equals the nominal interest rate is by comparing the real returns on alternative assets. Assets other than money, such as government bonds, earn the real return r. Money earns an expected real return of $-\pi^e$, because its real value declines at the rate of inflation. When you hold money, you give up the difference between these two returns. Thus, the cost of holding money is $r - (-\pi^e)$, which the Fisher equation tells us is the nominal interest rate i.

Just as the quantity of bread demanded depends on the price of bread, the quantity of money demanded depends on the price of holding money. Hence, the demand for real money balances depends both on the level of income and on the nominal interest rate. We write the general money demand function as

$$(M/P)^d = L(i, Y).$$

The letter L is used to denote money demand because money is the economy's most liquid asset (the asset most easily used to make transactions). This equation states that the demand for the liquidity of real money balances is a function of income and the nominal interest rate. The higher the level of income Y, the greater the demand for real money balances. The higher the nominal interest rate i, the lower the demand for real money balances.

Future Money and Current Prices

Money, prices and interest rates are now related in several ways. Figure 5-4 illustrates the linkages we have discussed. As the quantity theory of money explains, money supply and money demand together determine the equilibrium price level. Changes in the price level are, by definition, the rate of inflation. Inflation, in turn, affects the nominal interest rate through the Fisher effect. But now, because the nominal interest rate is the cost of holding money, the nominal interest rate feeds back to affect the demand for money.

FIGURE 5-4

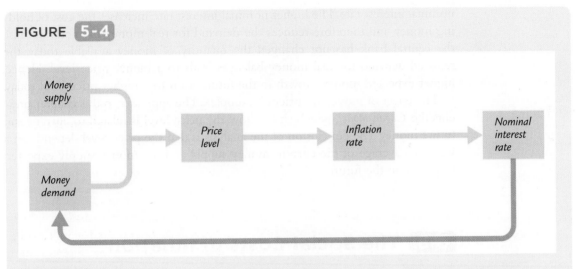

The Linkages Among Money, Prices and Interest Rates This figure illustrates the relationships among money, prices and interest rates. Money supply and money demand determine the price level. Changes in the price level determine the inflation rate. The inflation rate influences the nominal interest rate. Because the nominal interest rate is the cost of holding money, it may affect money demand. This last link (shown as a blue line) is omitted from the basic quantity theory of money.

Consider how the introduction of this last link affects our theory of the price level. First, equate the supply of real money balances M/P to the demand $L(i, Y)$:

$$M/P = L(i, Y).$$

Next, use the Fisher equation to write the nominal interest rate as the sum of the real interest rate and expected inflation:

$$M/P = L(r + \pi^e, Y).$$

This equation states that the level of real money balances depends on the expected rate of inflation.

The last equation tells a more sophisticated story about the determination of the price level than does the quantity theory. The quantity theory of money says that today's money supply determines today's price level. This conclusion remains partly true: if the nominal interest rate and the level of output are held constant, the price level moves proportionately with the money supply. Yet the nominal interest rate is not constant; it depends on expected inflation, which in turn depends on growth in the money supply. The presence of the nominal interest rate in the money demand function yields an additional channel through which money supply affects the price level.

This general money-demand equation implies that the price level depends not only on today's money supply, but also on the money supply expected in the future. To see why, suppose the central bank announces that it will increase the money supply in the future, but it does not change the money supply today. This announcement causes people to expect higher money growth and higher inflation. Through the Fisher effect, this increase in expected inflation raises the nominal interest rate. The higher nominal interest rate increases the cost of holding money and therefore reduces the demand for real money balances. Because the central bank has not changed the quantity of money available today, the reduced demand for real money balances leads to a higher price level. Hence, higher expected money growth in the future leads to a higher price level today.

The effect of money on prices is complex. The appendix to this chapter presents the *Cagan model,* which shows how the price level is related to current and future money. The conclusion of the analysis is that the price level depends on a weighted average of the current money supply and the money supply expected to prevail in the future.

5-5 The Social Costs of Inflation

Our discussion of the causes and effects of inflation does not tell us much about the social problems that result from inflation. We turn to those problems now.

The Layman's View and the Classical Response

If you ask the average person why inflation is a social problem, he will probably answer that inflation makes him poorer. 'Each year my boss gives me a pay rise, but prices go up and that takes some of my pay rise away from me.' The implicit assumption in this statement is that if there were no inflation, he would get the same raise and be able to buy more goods.

This complaint about inflation is a common fallacy. As we know from Chapter 3, the purchasing power of labour – the real wage – depends on the marginal productivity of labour, not on how much money the government chooses to print. If the central bank reduces inflation by slowing the rate of money growth, workers will not see their real wage increasing more rapidly. Instead, when inflation slows, firms will increase the prices of their products less each year and, as a result, will give their workers smaller pay rises.

According to the classical theory of money, a change in the overall price level is like a change in the units of measurement. It is as if we switched from measuring distances in metres to measuring them in centimetres: numbers get larger, but nothing really changes. Imagine that tomorrow morning you wake up and find that, for some reason, all money figures in the economy have been multiplied by a hundred. The price of everything you buy has increased a hundredfold, but so has your wage and the value of your savings. What difference would such a price increase make to your life? All numbers would have an extra two zeros at the end, but nothing else would change. Your economic well-being depends on relative prices, not the overall price level.

Why, then, is a persistent increase in the price level a social problem? It turns out that the costs of inflation are subtle. Indeed, economists disagree about the size of the social costs. To the surprise of many laymen, some economists argue that the costs of inflation are small – at least for the moderate rates of inflation that most countries have experienced in recent years.[4]

What Economists and the Public Say about Inflation

As we have been discussing, laymen and economists hold very different views about the costs of inflation. Economist Robert Shiller has documented this difference of opinion in a US survey of the two groups. The survey results are striking, for they show how the study of economics changes a person's attitudes.

In one question, Shiller asked people whether their 'biggest gripe about inflation' was that 'inflation hurts my real buying power, it makes me poorer'. Of the general public, 77 per cent agreed with this statement, compared to only 12 per cent of economists. Shiller also asked people whether they agreed with the following statement: 'When I see projections about how many times more a college education will cost, or how many times more the cost of living will be in coming decades, I feel a sense of uneasiness; these inflation projections really make me worry that my own income will not rise as much as such costs will.' Among the general public, 66 per cent said they fully agreed with this statement, while only 5 per cent of economists agreed with it.

Survey respondents were asked to judge the seriousness of inflation as a policy problem: 'Do you agree that preventing high inflation is an important national priority, as important as preventing drug abuse or preventing deterioration in the quality of our schools?' Fifty-two per cent of laymen, but only 18 per cent of economists, fully agreed with this view. Apparently, inflation worries the public much more than it does the economics profession.

The public's distaste for inflation may be psychological. Shiller asked those surveyed if they agreed with the following statement: 'I think that if my pay went up I would feel more satisfaction in my job, more sense of fulfilment, even if prices went up just as much.' Of the public, 49 per cent fully or partly agreed with this statement, compared with 8 per cent of economists.

Do these survey results mean that laymen are wrong and economists are right about the costs of inflation? Not necessarily. But economists do have the advantage of having given the issue more thought. So let's now consider what some of the costs of inflation might be.[5] ■

---

[4] See, for example, Chapter 2 of Alan Blinder, *Hard Heads, Soft Hearts: Tough-Minded Economics for a Just Society*, Reading, MA: Addison Wesley, 1987.

[5] Robert J. Shiller, 'Why Do People Dislike Inflation?', in Christina D. Romer and David H. Romer, eds, *Reducing Inflation: Motivation and Strategy*, Chicago: University of Chicago Press, 1997.

The Costs of Expected Inflation

Consider first the case of expected inflation. Suppose that every month the price level rose by 1 per cent. What would be the social costs of such a steady and predictable 12 per cent annual inflation?

One cost is the distortion of the inflation tax on the amount of money people hold. As we have already discussed, a higher inflation rate leads to a higher nominal interest rate, which in turn leads to lower real money balances. If people are to hold lower money balances on average, they must make more frequent trips to the bank to withdraw money – for example, they might withdraw €50 twice a week rather than €100 once a week to cater for a given pattern of expenses. The inconvenience of reducing money holding is metaphorically called the **shoe-leather cost** of inflation, because walking to the bank more often causes one's shoes to wear out more quickly.

A second cost of inflation arises because high inflation induces firms to change their posted prices more often. Changing prices is sometimes costly: for example, it may require printing and distributing a new catalogue. These costs are called **menu costs**, because the higher the rate of inflation, the more often restaurants have to print new menus.

A third cost of inflation arises because firms facing menu costs change prices infrequently; therefore, the higher the rate of inflation, the greater the variability in relative prices. For example, suppose a firm issues a new catalogue every January. If there is no inflation, then the firm's prices relative to the overall price level are constant over the year. Yet if inflation is 1 per cent per month, then from the beginning to the end of the year the firm's relative prices fall by 12 per cent. Sales from this catalogue will tend to be low early in the year (when its prices are relatively high) and high later in the year (when its prices are relatively low). Hence, when inflation induces variability in relative prices, it leads to microeconomic inefficiencies in the allocation of resources.

A fourth cost of inflation results from the tax laws. Many provisions of the tax system do not take into account the effects of inflation. Inflation can alter individuals' tax liability, often in ways that policy makers did not intend.

One example of the failure of the tax system to deal with inflation is the tax treatment of capital gains. Suppose you buy some company shares today and sell them a year from now at the same real price. It would seem reasonable for the government not to levy a tax, because you have earned no real income from this investment. Indeed, if there is no inflation, a zero tax liability would be the outcome. But suppose the rate of inflation is 12 per cent and you initially paid €100 per share; for the real price to be the same a year later, you must sell the shares for €112 each. In this case, the tax system, which ignores the effects of inflation, says that you have earned €12 per share in income, and the government taxes you on this capital gain. The problem, of course, is that the tax system measures income as the nominal rather than the real capital gain. In this example, and in many others, inflation distorts how taxes are levied.

A fifth cost of inflation is the inconvenience of living in a world with a changing price level. Money is the yardstick with which we measure economic transactions.

When there is inflation, that yardstick is changing in length. To continue the analogy, suppose that the government passed a law specifying that a metre would equal 100 cm in 2014, 98 cm in 2015, 96 cm in 2016, and so on. Although the law would not lead to any ambiguity, it would be highly inconvenient. When someone measured a distance in metres, it would be necessary to specify whether the measurement was in 2014 metres or 2015 metres; to compare distances measured in different years, one would need to make an 'inflation' correction. Similarly, the monetary unit – the euro or the pound – is a less useful measure when its value is always changing. The changing value of money requires that we correct for inflation when comparing figures expressed in pounds or euros from different times.

For example, a changing price level complicates personal financial planning. One important decision that all households face is how much of their income to consume today and how much to save for retirement. A euro saved today and invested at a fixed nominal interest rate will yield a fixed euro amount in the future. Yet the real value of that euro amount – which will determine the retiree's living standard – depends on the future price level. Deciding how much to save would be much simpler if people could count on the price level in 30 years' time being similar to its level today.

The Costs of Unexpected Inflation

Unexpected inflation has an effect that is more pernicious than any of the costs of steady, anticipated inflation: it arbitrarily redistributes wealth among individuals. You can see how this works by examining long-term loans. Most loan agreements specify a nominal interest rate, which is based on the rate of inflation expected at the time of the agreement. If inflation turns out differently from what was expected, the *ex post* real return that the debtor pays to the creditor differs from what both parties anticipated. On the one hand, if inflation turns out to be higher than expected, the debtor wins and the creditor loses because the debtor repays the loan with less valuable euros. On the other hand, if inflation turns out to be lower than expected, the creditor wins and the debtor loses because the repayment is worth more than the two parties anticipated.

Consider, for example, a person taking out a mortgage in order to buy a house or a flat. That person will have the choice of a variable-rate mortgage or a fixed-rate mortgage. With a variable-rate mortgage, the lender can change the interest rate to link it to the level of interest rates in the economy, and so, through the Fisher effect, to the level of inflation. With a fixed-rate mortgage, the interest rate is fixed at an agreed rate for an agreed period – for example, ten years. If inflation is low, say, 2 per cent per year, and has been for some time, and the fixed-rate mortgage rate is, say, 5 per cent, then the creditor can reasonably expect to receive a real return of about 3 per cent per year, and the debtor is expected to pay this real return. If, in fact, the inflation rate immediately rises to 4 per cent, the *ex post* real return on the fixed-rate mortgage will drop to only 1 per cent. This unanticipated inflation would benefit the debtor at the expense of the creditor. Not surprisingly, because of the riskiness of fixed-rate mortgages, lenders tend to charge a higher rate of interest for a fixed-rate mortgage than for a variable-rate mortgage.

Unanticipated inflation also hurts individuals on fixed pensions. Workers and firms sometimes agree on a fixed nominal pension when the worker retires (or even earlier). Because the pension is deferred earnings, the worker is essentially providing the firm a loan: the worker provides labour services to the firm while young, but does not get fully paid until old age. Like any creditor, the worker is hurt when inflation is higher than anticipated. Like any debtor, the firm is hurt when inflation is lower than anticipated.

These situations provide a clear argument against variable inflation. The more variable the rate of inflation, the greater the uncertainty that both debtors and creditors face. Because most people are *risk averse* – they dislike uncertainty – the unpredictability caused by highly variable inflation hurts almost everyone.

Given these effects of uncertain inflation, it is puzzling that nominal contracts are so prevalent. One might expect debtors and creditors to protect themselves from this uncertainty by writing contracts in real terms – that is, by indexing to some measure of the price level. In economies with high and variable inflation, indexation is often widespread; sometimes this indexation takes the form of writing contracts using a more stable foreign currency. In economies with moderate inflation, indexation is less common. Yet even in moderate-inflation countries, some long-term obligations are indexed. For example, in the UK, public sector and state retirement pensions are adjusted annually in response to changes in the consumer price index, and the UK government issues inflation-indexed bonds (i.e. bonds that pay a certain real rate of interest).

Finally, in thinking about the costs of inflation, it is important to note a widely documented but little understood fact: high inflation is variable inflation. That is, countries with high average inflation also tend to have inflation rates that change greatly from year to year. The implication is that if a country decides to pursue a high-inflation monetary policy, it will likely have to accept highly variable inflation as well. As we have just discussed, highly variable inflation increases uncertainty for both creditors and debtors by subjecting them to arbitrary and potentially large redistributions of wealth.

One Benefit of Inflation

So far, we have discussed the many costs of inflation. These costs lead many economists to conclude that monetary policy makers should aim for zero inflation. Yet there is another side to the story. Some economists believe that a little inflation – say, 2 or 3 per cent per year – can be a good thing.

The argument for moderate inflation starts with the observation that cuts in nominal wages are rare: firms are reluctant to cut their workers' nominal wages, and workers are reluctant to accept such cuts. A 2 per cent wage cut in a zero-inflation world is, in real terms, the same as a 3 per cent rise with 5 per cent inflation, but workers do not always see it that way. The 2 per cent wage cut may seem to be an insult, whereas the 3 per cent rise is, after all, still a rise. Empirical studies confirm that nominal wages rarely fall.

This finding suggests that some inflation may make labour markets work better. The supply and demand for different kinds of labour are always changing.

Sometimes an increase in supply or decrease in demand leads to a fall in the equilibrium real wage for a group of workers. If nominal wages cannot be cut, then the only way to cut real wages is to allow inflation to do the job. Without inflation, the real wage will be stuck above the equilibrium level, resulting in higher unemployment.

For this reason, some economists argue that inflation 'greases the wheels' of labour markets. Only a little inflation is needed: an inflation rate of 2 per cent lets real wages fall by 2 per cent per year, or 20 per cent per decade, without cuts in nominal wages. Such automatic reductions in real wages are impossible with zero inflation.[6]

5-6 Hyperinflation

Hyperinflation is often defined as inflation that exceeds 50 per cent per month, which is just over 1 per cent per day. Compounded over many months, this rate of inflation leads to very large increases in the price level. An inflation rate of 50 per cent per month implies a more than one hundredfold increase in the price level over a year, and a more than two million-fold increase over three years. Here we consider the costs and causes of such extreme inflation.

The Costs of Hyperinflation

Although economists debate whether the costs of moderate inflation are large or small, no one doubts that hyperinflation exacts a high toll on society. The costs are qualitatively the same as those we discussed earlier. When inflation reaches extreme levels, however, these costs are more apparent because they are so severe.

The shoe-leather costs associated with reduced money holding, for instance, are serious under hyperinflation. Business executives devote much time and energy to cash management when cash loses its value quickly. By diverting this time and energy from more socially valuable activities, such as production and investment decisions, hyperinflation makes the economy run less efficiently.

Menu costs also become larger under hyperinflation. Firms have to change prices so often that normal business practices, such as printing and distributing catalogues with fixed prices, become impossible. In one restaurant during the German hyperinflation of the 1920s, a waiter would stand up on a table every 30 minutes to call out the new prices.

Similarly, relative prices do not do a good job of reflecting true scarcity during hyperinflations. When prices change frequently by large amounts, it is hard for customers to shop around for the best price. Highly volatile and rapidly rising prices can alter behaviour in many ways. According to one report, when patrons entered a pub during the German hyperinflation, they would often buy two jugs of beer.

---

[6] For a recent paper examining this benefit of inflation, see George A. Akerlof, William T. Dickens and George L. Perry, 'The Macroeconomics of Low Inflation', *Brookings Papers on Economic Activity*, 1996, vol. 1, pp. 1–76.

Although the second jug of beer would lose value by getting warm over time, it would lose value less rapidly than the money left sitting in the patron's wallet.

Tax systems are also distorted by hyperinflation – but in ways that are different from the distortions of moderate inflation. In most tax systems there is a delay between the time a tax is levied and the time the tax is paid to the government. This short delay does not matter much under low inflation. By contrast, during hyperinflation, even a short delay greatly reduces real tax revenue. By the time the government gets the money it is due, the money has fallen in value. As a result, once hyperinflations start, the real tax revenue of the government often falls substantially.

Finally, no one should underestimate the sheer inconvenience of living with hyperinflation. When carrying money to the shops is as burdensome as carrying the groceries back home, the monetary system is not doing its best to facilitate exchange. The government tries to overcome this problem by adding more and more zeros to the paper currency, but often it cannot keep up with the exploding price level.

Eventually, these costs of hyperinflation become intolerable. Over time, money loses its role as a store of value, unit of account and medium of exchange. Barter becomes more common. And more stable unofficial monies – cigarettes, the US dollar or the euro – start to replace the official money.

CASE STUDY

Wars, Economic Disruption and Hyperinflation

Whenever governments need to spend heavily and are forced to the printing presses to finance their spending, high inflation is just around the corner. Often, governments find themselves in this situation in times of war, since they cannot cut expenditure (because they are spending mainly on the military and to do so would lead to defeat) and they cannot raise enough through taxes (because resources are directed towards fighting rather than normal economic activity) – so they face a big budget deficit (the difference between government expenditure and government tax revenue). In normal times, a deficit is financed by government borrowing (selling government bonds), but in wartime it is typically difficult and expensive to borrow, especially if the war is going badly for the government in question. The only alternative is to print money.

A similar effect arises when there is severe social and economic disruption in an economy, such as in the aftermath of a war, when a defeated country finds its productive potential severely damaged because many of its factories have been destroyed or converted to armaments production, and much of its workforce has been killed in the war. The government is then tempted to spend heavily in order to reinvigorate the economy, but finds it difficult to raise money through borrowing or raising taxes, and is therefore forced to finance its expenditure by printing money.

Hyperinflation was seen in the United States during the War of Independence in the 18th century, when the revolutionary government financed the war against Britain by printing fiat money. It was also seen in several European countries – Austria, Hungary, Germany, Poland and Russia – in the 1920s, in the aftermath of World War I.

More recently, the break-up of the Soviet Union in the late 1980s meant that many countries that were formerly either part of the Soviet Union (such as Ukraine) or part of the communist bloc (like Poland) were ill-equipped to cope with the sudden move from communist central planning to a capitalist economy. The demand for goods previously sold to other countries in the communist bloc virtually dried up overnight. Some governments tried to make up for these shortfalls by providing subsidies to state enterprises in order to keep them from going bankrupt, and also so that they could invest in new plant and equipment to replace the obsolete equipment they had been working with under central planning. With a shortfall in tax revenue because of the fall in economic activity in the economy, and because governments found it difficult to raise money by borrowing, this meant the printing of fiat money was needed to cover the inevitable government deficits that ensued. This led to very high levels of inflation in many of the formerly centrally planned economies, in some cases reaching hyperinflation levels. In Poland, for example, prices increased by more than 600 per cent per year in 1989, and in Ukraine in 1993 inflation exceeded 10,000 per cent per year. ■

The Causes of Hyperinflation

Why do hyperinflations start, and how do they end? This question can be answered at different levels.

The most obvious answer is that hyperinflations are due to excessive growth in the supply of money. When the central bank prints money, the price level rises. When it prints money rapidly enough, the result is hyperinflation. To stop the hyperinflation, the central bank must reduce the rate of money growth.

This answer is incomplete, however, for it leaves open the question of why central banks in hyperinflating economies choose to print so much money. To address this deeper question, we must turn our attention from monetary to fiscal policy. Most hyperinflations begin when the government has inadequate tax revenue to pay for its spending. Although the government might prefer to finance this budget deficit by issuing debt, it may find itself unable to borrow, perhaps because lenders view the government as a bad credit risk. To cover the deficit, the government turns to the only mechanism at its disposal – the printing press. The result is rapid money growth and hyperinflation.

Once the hyperinflation is under way, the fiscal problems become even more severe. Because of the delay in collecting tax payments,

'It's inflation, Miss Borgia
-Too much money chasing too few poisons.'

Alan de la Nougerede/Cartoonstock.com

real tax revenue falls as inflation rises. Thus, the government's need to rely on seigniorage is self-reinforcing. Rapid money creation leads to hyperinflation, which leads to a larger budget deficit, which leads to even more rapid money creation.

The end of hyperinflation almost always coincides with fiscal reforms. Once the magnitude of the problem becomes apparent, the government musters the political will to reduce government spending and increase taxes. These fiscal reforms reduce the need for seigniorage, which allows a reduction in money growth. Hence, even if inflation is always and everywhere a monetary phenomenon, the end of hyperinflation is often a fiscal phenomenon as well.[7]

Hyperinflation in Interwar Germany

After World War I, Germany experienced one of history's most spectacular examples of hyperinflation. At the war's end, the Allies demanded that Germany pay substantial reparations. These payments led to fiscal deficits in Germany, which the German government eventually financed by printing large quantities of money.

Panel (a) of Figure 5-5 shows the quantity of money and the general price level in Germany from January 1922 to December 1924. During this period both money and prices rose at a remarkable rate. For example, the price of a daily newspaper rose from 0.30 marks in January 1921 to 1 mark in May 1922, to 8 marks in October 1922, to 100 marks in February 1923, and to 1000 marks in September 1923. Then, in the autumn of 1923, prices took off: the newspaper sold for 2000 marks on October 1, 20,000 marks on October 15, 1 million marks on October 29, 15 million marks on November 9, and 70 million marks on November 17. In December 1923 the money supply and prices abruptly stabilized.[8]

Just as fiscal problems caused the German hyperinflation, a fiscal reform ended it. At the end of 1923, the number of government employees was cut by one-third, and the reparations payments were temporarily suspended and eventually reduced. At the same time, a new central bank, the Rentenbank, replaced the old central bank, the Reichsbank. The Rentenbank was committed to not financing the government by means of printing money.

According to our theoretical analysis of money demand, an end to a hyperinflation should lead to an increase in real money balances as the cost of holding money falls. Panel (b) of Figure 5-5 shows that real money balances in Germany did fall as inflation increased, and then increased again

---

[7] For more on these issues, see Thomas J. Sargent, 'The End of Four Big Inflations', in Robert Hall, ed., *Inflation*, Chicago: University of Chicago Press, 1983, pp. 41–98; Rudiger Dornbusch and Stanley Fischer, 'Stopping Hyperinflations: Past and Present', *Weltwirtschaftliches Archiv*, April 1986, vol. 122, pp. 1–47.

[8] The data on newspaper prices are from Michael Mussa, 'Sticky Individual Prices and the Dynamics of the General Price Level', *Carnegie-Rochester Conference on Public Policy*, autumn 1981, vol. 15, pp. 261–296.

FIGURE 5-5

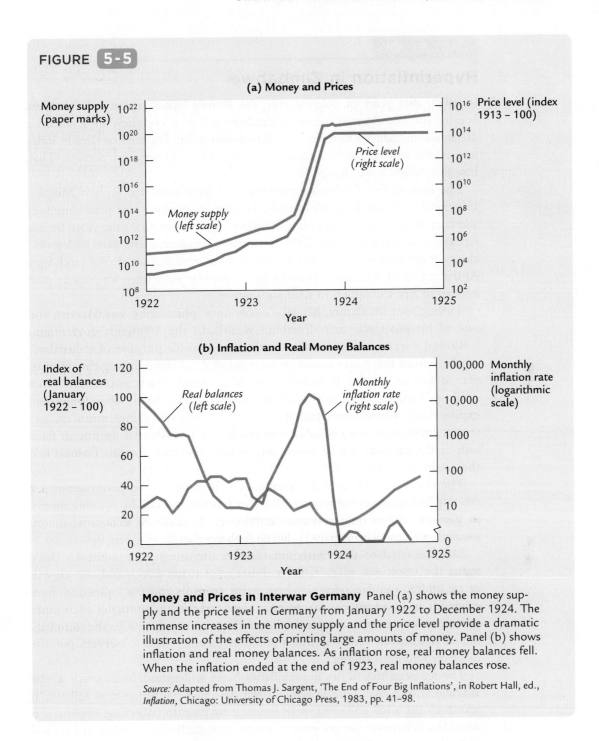

Money and Prices in Interwar Germany Panel (a) shows the money supply and the price level in Germany from January 1922 to December 1924. The immense increases in the money supply and the price level provide a dramatic illustration of the effects of printing large amounts of money. Panel (b) shows inflation and real money balances. As inflation rose, real money balances fell. When the inflation ended at the end of 1923, real money balances rose.

Source: Adapted from Thomas J. Sargent, 'The End of Four Big Inflations', in Robert Hall, ed., *Inflation*, Chicago: University of Chicago Press, 1983, pp. 41–98.

as inflation fell. Yet the increase in real money balances was not immediate. Perhaps the adjustment of real money balances to the cost of holding money is a gradual process. Or perhaps it took time for people in Germany to believe that the inflation had ended, so that expected inflation fell more gradually than actual inflation. ■

CASE STUDY

Hyperinflation in Zimbabwe

In 1980, after years of colonial rule, the former British colony of Rhodesia became the new African nation of Zimbabwe. A new currency, the Zimbabwe dollar, was introduced to replace the Rhodesian dollar. For the first decade, inflation in the new nation was modest – about 10 to 20 per cent per year. That, however, would soon change.

The hero of the Zimbabwe independence movement was Robert Mugabe. In general elections in 1980, Mugabe became the nation's first prime minister and later, after a government reorganization, its president. Over the years, he was repeatedly re-elected. In his 2008 re-election, however, there were widespread claims of electoral fraud and threats against voters who supported rival candidates. At the age of 84, Mugabe was no longer as popular as he once was; but he gave no sign of any willingness to relinquish power.

Throughout his tenure, Mugabe's economic philosophy was Marxist, and one of his goals was to redistribute wealth. In the 1990s his government instituted a series of land reforms with the ostensible purpose of redistributing land from the white minority who ruled Zimbabwe during the colonial era in favour of the historically disenfranchised black population. One result of these reforms was widespread corruption. Many abandoned and expropriated white farms ended up in the hands of cabinet ministers and senior government officials. Another result was a substantial decline in farm output. Productivity fell because many of the experienced white farmers fled the country.

The decline in the economy's output led to a fall in the government's tax revenue. The government responded to this revenue shortfall by printing money to pay the salaries of government employees. As textbook economic theory predicts, the monetary expansion led to higher inflation.

Mugabe tried to deal with inflation by imposing price controls. Once again, the result was predictable: a shortage of many goods and the growth of an underground economy where price controls and tax collection were evaded. The government's tax revenue declined further, inducing even more monetary expansion and yet higher inflation. In July 2008, the officially reported inflation rate was 231 million per cent. Other observers put the inflation rate even higher.

The repercussions of this hyperinflation were widespread. In an article in the *Washington Post*, one Zimbabwean citizen describes the situation as follows: 'If you don't get a bill collected in 48 hours, it isn't worth collecting, because it is worthless. Whenever we get money, we must immediately spend it, just go and buy what we can. Our pension was destroyed ages ago. None of us have any savings left.'

The Zimbabwe hyperinflation finally ended in March 2009, when the government abandoned its own money. The US dollar became the nation's official currency. Inflation quickly stabilized. Zimbabwe still had its problems, but at least hyperinflation was not among them. ∎

5-7 Conclusion: The Classical Dichotomy

Over the course of this and the previous chapter, we have studied the meaning of money and the impact of the money supply on inflation and various other variables. This analysis builds on our model of national income in Chapter 3. Let's now step back and examine a key assumption that has been implicit in our discussion.

In Chapter 3 we explained many macroeconomic variables. Some of these variables were *quantities,* such as real GDP and the capital stock; others were *relative prices*, such as the real wage and the real interest rate. But all these variables had one thing in common: they measured a physical (rather than a monetary) quantity. Real GDP is the quantity of goods and services produced in a given year, and the capital stock is the quantity of machines and structures available at a given time. The real wage is the quantity of output a worker earns for each hour of work, and the real interest rate is the quantity of output a person earns in the future by lending one unit of output today. All variables measured in physical units, such as quantities and relative prices, are called **real variables**.

In this chapter we examined **nominal variables** – variables expressed in terms of money. The economy has many nominal variables, such as the price level, the inflation rate and the money wage a person earns.

At first it may seem surprising that we were able to explain real variables without introducing nominal variables or the existence of money. In Chapter 3 we studied the level and allocation of the economy's output without mentioning the price level or the rate of inflation. Our theory of the labour market explained the real wage without explaining the nominal wage.

Economists call this theoretical separation of real and nominal variables the **classical dichotomy**. It is the hallmark of classical macroeconomic theory. The classical dichotomy is an important insight because it simplifies economic theory. In particular, it allows us to examine real variables, as we have done, while ignoring nominal variables. The classical dichotomy arises because, in classical economic theory, changes in the money supply do not influence real variables. This irrelevance of money for real variables is called **monetary neutrality**. For many purposes – in particular, for studying long-run issues – monetary neutrality is approximately correct.

Yet monetary neutrality does not fully describe the world in which we live. Beginning in Chapter 10, we discuss departures from the classical model and monetary neutrality. These departures are crucial for understanding many macroeconomic phenomena, such as short-run economic fluctuations.

Summary

1. The quantity theory of money assumes that the velocity of money is stable and concludes that nominal GDP is proportional to the stock of money. Because the factors of production and the production function determine

real GDP, the quantity theory implies that the price level is proportional to the quantity of money. Therefore, the rate of growth in the quantity of money determines the inflation rate.

2. Seigniorage is the revenue that the government raises by printing money. It is a tax on money holding. Although seigniorage is quantitatively small in most economies, it is often a major source of government revenue in economies experiencing hyperinflation.

3. The nominal interest rate is the sum of the real interest rate and the inflation rate. The Fisher effect says that the nominal interest rate moves one-for-one with expected inflation.

4. The nominal interest rate is the opportunity cost of holding money. Thus, one might expect the demand for money to depend on the nominal interest rate. If it does, then the price level depends on both the current quantity of money and the quantities of money expected in the future.

5. The costs of expected inflation include shoe-leather costs, menu costs, the cost of relative price variability, tax distortions and the inconvenience of making inflation corrections. In addition, unexpected inflation causes arbitrary redistributions of wealth between debtors and creditors. One possible benefit of inflation is that it improves the functioning of labour markets by allowing real wages to reach equilibrium levels without cuts in nominal wages.

6. During hyperinflations, most of the costs of inflation become severe. Hyperinflations typically begin when governments finance large budget deficits by printing money. They end when fiscal reforms eliminate the need for seigniorage.

7. According to classical economic theory, money is neutral: the money supply does not affect real variables. Therefore, classical theory allows us to study how real variables are determined, without any reference to the money supply. The equilibrium in the money market then determines the price level and, as a result, all other nominal variables. This theoretical separation of real and nominal variables is called the classical dichotomy.

KEY CONCEPTS

Inflation	Money demand function	Shoe-leather costs
Hyperinflation	Quantity theory of money	Menu costs
Quantity equation	Seigniorage	Real and nominal variables
Transactions velocity of money	Nominal and real interest rates	Classical dichotomy
Income velocity of money	Fisher equation and Fisher effect	Monetary neutrality
Real money balances	*Ex ante* and *ex post* real interest rates	

QUESTIONS FOR REVIEW

1. Write the quantity equation and explain it.

2. What does the assumption of constant velocity imply?

3. Who pays inflation tax?

4. If inflation rises from 6 to 8 per cent, what happens to real and nominal interest rates according to the Fisher effect?

5. List all the costs of inflation you can think of, and rank them according to how important you think they are.

6. Explain the roles of monetary and fiscal policy in causing and ending hyperinflations.

7. Define the terms *real variable* and *nominal variable*, and give an example of each.

PROBLEMS AND APPLICATIONS

1. During World War II, both Germany and England had plans for a paper weapon: they each printed the other's currency, with the intention of dropping large quantities by aeroplane. Why might this have been an effective weapon?

2. Someone once said that 'inflation is repudiation of debt'. What might have been meant by this? Do you agree? Why, or why not? Does it matter whether the inflation is expected or unexpected?

3. Some economic historians have noted that during the period of the gold standard, gold discoveries were most likely to occur after a long deflation. Why might this be true?

4. Suppose that consumption depends on the level of real money balances (on the grounds that real money balances are part of wealth). Show that if real money balances depend on the nominal interest rate, then an increase in the rate of money growth affects consumption, investment and the real interest rate. Does the nominal interest rate adjust more than one-for-one or less than one-for-one to expected inflation? This deviation from the classical dichotomy and the Fisher effect is called the *Mundell–Tobin effect*. How might you decide whether the Mundell–Tobin effect is important in practice?

5. Use the internet to identify a country that has had high inflation over the past year and another country that has had low inflation. (*Hint:* One useful website is www.economist.com/markets/indicators/.) For these two countries, find the rate of money growth and the current level of the nominal interest rate. Relate your findings to the theories presented in this chapter.

The Cagan Model: How Current and Future Money Affect the Price Level

In this chapter we showed that if the quantity of real money balances demanded depends on the cost of holding money, the price level depends on both the current money supply and the future money supply. This appendix develops the *Cagan model* to show more explicitly how this works.[9]

To keep the mathematics as simple as possible, we posit a money demand function that is linear in the natural logarithms of all the variables. The money demand function is

$$m_t - p_t = -\gamma(p_{t+1} - p_t), \tag{A1}$$

where m_t is the log of the quantity of money at time t; p_t is the log of the price level at time t; and γ is a parameter that governs the sensitivity of money demand to the rate of inflation. By the property of logarithms, $m_t - p_t$ is the log of real money balances, and $p_{t+1} - p_t$ is the inflation rate between period t and period $t + 1$. This equation states that if inflation goes up by 1 percentage point, real money balances fall by γ per cent.

We have made a number of assumptions in writing the money demand function in this way. First, by excluding the level of output as a determinant of money demand, we are implicitly assuming that it is constant. Second, by including the rate of inflation rather than the nominal interest rate, we are assuming that the real interest rate is constant. Third, by including actual inflation rather than expected inflation, we are assuming perfect foresight. All of these assumptions are to keep the analysis as simple as possible.

We want to solve Equation A1 to express the price level as a function of current and future money. To do this, note that Equation A1 can be rewritten as

$$p_t = \left(\frac{1}{1 + \gamma}\right)m_t + \left(\frac{\gamma}{1 + \gamma}\right)p_{t+1}. \tag{A2}$$

This equation states that the current price level p_t is a weighted average of the current money supply m_t and the next period's price level p_{t+1}. The next period's price level will be determined the same way as this period's price level:

$$p_{t+1} = \left(\frac{1}{1 + \gamma}\right)m_{t+1} + \left(\frac{\gamma}{1 + \gamma}\right)p_{t+2}. \tag{A3}$$

---

[9] This model is derived from Phillip Cagan, 'The Monetary Dynamics of Hyperinflation', in Milton Friedman, ed., *Studies in the Quantity Theory of Money*, Chicago: University of Chicago Press, 1956.

Now substitute Equation A3 for p_{t+1} in Equation A2 to obtain

$$p_t = \frac{1}{1+\gamma} m_t + \frac{\gamma}{(1+\gamma)^2} m_{t+1} + \frac{\gamma^2}{(1+\gamma)^2} p_{t+2} \qquad (A4)$$

Equation A4 states that the current price level is a weighted average of the current money supply, the next period's money supply and the following period's price level. Once again, the price level in $t+2$ is determined as in Equation A2:

$$p_{t+2} = \left(\frac{1}{1+\gamma}\right) m_{t+2} + \left(\frac{\gamma}{1+\gamma}\right) p_{t+3} \qquad (A5)$$

Now substitute Equation A5 into Equation A4 to obtain

$$p_t = \frac{1}{1+\gamma} m_t + \frac{\gamma}{(1+\gamma)^2} m_{t+1} + \frac{\gamma^2}{(1+\gamma)^3} m_{t+2} + \frac{\gamma^3}{(1+\gamma)^3} p_{t+3}. \qquad (A6)$$

By now you see the pattern. We can continue to use Equation A2 to substitute for the future price level. If we do this an infinite number of times, we find

$$p_t = \left(\frac{1}{1+\gamma}\right)\left[m_t + \left(\frac{\gamma}{1+\gamma}\right) m_{t+1} + \left(\frac{\gamma}{1+\gamma}\right)^2 m_{t+2} + \left(\frac{\gamma}{1+\gamma}\right)^3 m_{t+3} + \dots \right] \quad (A7)$$

where '...' indicates an infinite number of analogous terms. According to Equation A7, the current price level is a weighted average of the current money supply and all future money supplies.

Note the importance of γ, the parameter governing the sensitivity of real money balances to inflation. The weights on the future money supplies decline geometrically at rate $\gamma/(1+\gamma)$. If γ is small, then $\gamma/(1+\gamma)$ is small, and the weights decline quickly. In this case, the current money supply is the primary determinant of the price level. (Indeed, if γ equals zero, then we obtain the quantity theory of money: the price level is proportional to the current money supply, and the future money supplies do not matter at all.) If γ is large, then $\gamma/(1+\gamma)$ is close to 1, and the weights decline slowly. In this case, the future money supplies play a key role in determining today's price level.

Finally, let's relax the assumption of perfect foresight. If the future is not known with certainty, then we should write the money demand function as

$$m_t - p_t = -\gamma(Ep_{t+1} - p_t), \qquad (A8)$$

where Ep_{t+1} is the expected price level. Equation A8 states that real money balances depend on expected inflation. By following steps similar to those above, we can show that

$$p_t = \left(\frac{1}{1+\gamma}\right)\left[m_t + \left(\frac{\gamma}{1+\gamma}\right) Em_{t+1} + \left(\frac{\gamma}{1+\gamma}\right)^2 Em_{t+2} + \left(\frac{\gamma}{1+\gamma}\right)^3 Em_{t+3} + \dots \right].$$
$$(A9)$$

Equation A9 states that the price level depends on the current money supply and expected future money supplies.

Some economists use this model to argue that *credibility* is important for ending hyperinflation. Because the price level depends on both current and expected future money, inflation depends on both current and expected future money growth. Therefore, to end high inflation, both money growth and expected money growth must fall. Expectations, in turn, depend on credibility – the perception that the central bank is committed to a new, more stable policy.

How can a central bank achieve credibility in the midst of hyperinflation? Credibility is often achieved by removing the underlying cause of the hyperinflation – the need for seigniorage. Thus, a credible fiscal reform is often necessary for a credible change in monetary policy. This fiscal reform might take the form of reducing government spending and making the central bank more independent from the government. Reduced spending decreases the need for seigniorage, while increased independence allows the central bank to resist government demands for seigniorage.

MORE PROBLEMS AND APPLICATIONS

1. In the Cagan model, if the money supply is expected to grow at some constant rate μ (so that $Em_{t+s} = m_t + s\mu$), then Equation A9 can be shown to imply that $p_t = m_t + \gamma\mu$.

   a. Interpret this result.

   b. What happens to the price level p_t when the money supply m_t changes, Holding the money growth rate μ constant?

   c. What happens to the price level p_t when the money growth rate μ changes, holding the current money supply m_t constant?

   d. If a central bank is about to reduce the rate of money growth μ, but wants to hold the price level p_t constant, what should it do with m_t? Can you see any practical problems that might arise in following such a policy?

   e. How do your previous answers change in the special case where money demand does not depend on the expected rate of inflation (so that $\gamma = 0$)?

CHAPTER 6

The Open Economy

Whether the advantages which one country has over another be natural or acquired is in this respect of no consequence. As long as the one country has those advantages, and the other wants them, it will always be more advantageous for the latter rather to buy of the former than to make.

— *Adam Smith,* The Wealth of Nations

An important feature of European economies is their degree of openness, that is, the value of transactions that the country engages in with the rest of the world as a percentage of GDP. In previous chapters we simplified our analysis by assuming a closed economy. In fact, most economies are open: they export goods and services abroad, they import goods and services from abroad, and they borrow and lend in world financial markets. Figure 6-1 gives some sense of the importance of these international interactions by showing imports and exports as a percentage of GDP for a number of European countries and the US in 2011. To create a measure of openness, we have taken an average of exports and imports (i.e. added them together and divided by 2) and then expressed the resulting figure as a percentage of GDP. As the figure shows, trade accounts for about 28 per cent of French GDP, around one-third of UK and Norwegian GDP, and roughly 50 per cent of German, Danish and Swedish GDP. In the Netherlands, Belgium and Ireland – the most open economies – exports and imports are actually around 80 per cent per cent of GDP or above.[1]

At the other extreme, exports and imports account for less than 16 per cent of US GDP – less than half of the corresponding figure for the UK. While these statistics are striking, you probably notice the openness of the economy in which you live on a day-to-day basis, since, even if you never leave your home town, you are an active participant in a global economy. When you go to the supermarket, for instance, you might choose between apples grown locally and grapes grown in South Africa. When you make a deposit into your bank account, the bank might lend those funds to your next-door neighbour or to a Japanese company building a factory outside Tokyo. Because the economy is integrated

---

[1] Note that this does not contradict the national accounting identity, since exports *plus* imports (divided by 2) can be a large number, while exports *minus* imports (which is a component of aggregate demand) may be much smaller in magnitude.

FIGURE 6-1

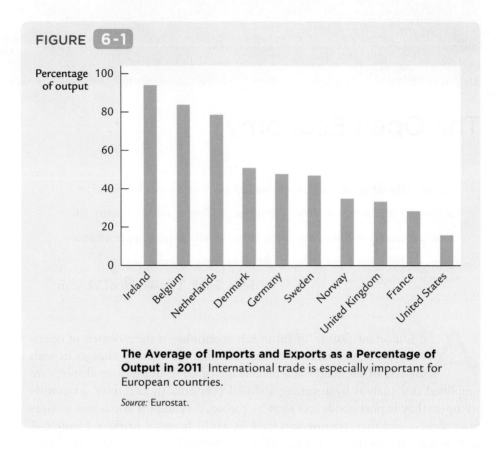

The Average of Imports and Exports as a Percentage of Output in 2011 International trade is especially important for European countries.

Source: Eurostat.

with many others around the world, consumers have more goods and services from which to choose, and savers have more opportunities to invest their wealth.

This chapter begins our study of open-economy macroeconomics. We begin in Section 6-1 with questions of measurement. To understand how an open economy works, we must understand the key macroeconomic variables that measure the interactions among countries. Accounting identities reveal a key insight: the flow of goods and services across national borders is always matched by an equivalent flow of funds to finance capital accumulation.

In Section 6-2 we examine the determinants of these international flows. We develop a model of the small open economy that corresponds to our model of the closed economy in Chapter 3. The model shows the factors that determine whether a country is a borrower or a lender in world markets, and how policies at home and abroad affect the flows of capital and goods.

In Section 6-3 we extend the model to discuss the prices at which a country makes exchanges in world markets. We examine what determines the price of domestic goods relative to foreign goods. We also examine what determines the rate at which the domestic currency trades for foreign currencies. Our model shows how protectionist trade policies – policies designed to protect domestic industries from foreign competition – influence the amount of international trade and the exchange rate.

We shall assume in this chapter that the open economy has its own currency, and that the rate at which that currency exchanges for other national currencies is freely determined in the foreign exchange market. In Chapter 17 we shall discuss the case where a group of countries shares the same currency and participate in a monetary union.

CASE STUDY

The Increasing Globalization of the World Economy

Figure 6-2 shows an index of the total real value of goods and services exported from all countries in the world over the period 1950–2011, as well as an index of world real GDP over the same period (both indices are set to 100 in 1950).[2] World real GDP grew impressively over this period, by a factor of about 9, or at an annual average growth rate of about 3.6 per cent a year. But the growth in world exports over the same period was notably larger: they rose by a factor of 34, representing an average annual growth rate of about 6 per cent a year.

This increase in international trade was partly due to improvements in transportation, such as the introduction of the long-distance and wide-body jet aircraft. In 1950 the average merchant ship carried less than 10,000 tonnes of cargo; in the early 21st century, many ships carry more than 100,000 tonnes. The increase in international trade has also been influenced by advances in

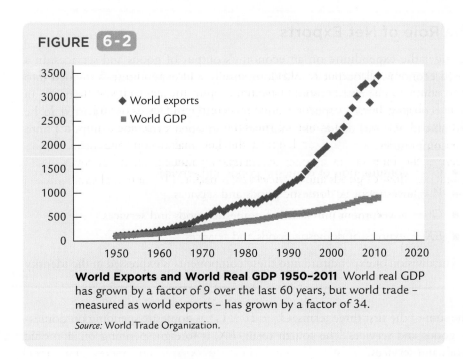

FIGURE 6-2

World Exports and World Real GDP 1950–2011 World real GDP has grown by a factor of 9 over the last 60 years, but world trade – measured as world exports – has grown by a factor of 34.

Source: World Trade Organization.

---

[2] We have shown only exports because, at the world level, the total value of exports must be the same as the total value of imports.

telecommunications, which have allowed businesses to reach overseas customers more easily. Furthermore, technological progress has fostered international trade by changing the kinds of goods that economies produce. Goods produced with modern technology are often much lighter and easier to transport than goods produced 50 years ago. Consumer electronics, for instance, have low weight for every euro of value, which makes them easy to produce in one country and sell in another. National and international trade policies have also been a factor in increasing international trade. The pattern of increasing trade illustrated in Figure 6-2 is a phenomenon that most economists and policy makers would endorse and encourage. ■

6-1 The International Flows of Capital and Goods

The key macroeconomic difference between open and closed economies is that, in an open economy, a country's spending in any given year need not equal its output of goods and services. A country can spend more than it produces by borrowing from abroad, or it can spend less than it produces and lend the difference to foreigners. To understand this more fully, let's take another look at national income accounting, which we first discussed in Chapter 2.

The Role of Net Exports

Consider the expenditure on an economy's output of goods and services. In a closed economy, all output is sold domestically, and expenditure is divided into three components: consumption, investment and government purchases. In an open economy, some output is sold domestically and some is exported to be sold abroad. We can divide expenditure on an open economy's output Y into four components:

- C^d — consumption of domestic goods and services
- I^d — investment in domestic goods and services
- G^d — government purchases of domestic goods and services
- EX — exports of domestic goods and services.

The division of expenditure into these components is expressed in the identity

$$Y = C^d + I^d + G^d + EX.$$

The sum of the first three terms, $C^d + I^d + G^d$, is domestic spending on domestic goods and services. The fourth term, EX, is foreign spending on domestic goods and services.

A bit of manipulation can make this identity more useful. Note that domestic spending on *all* goods and services equals domestic spending on *domestic* goods and services and domestic spending on *foreign* goods and services. Hence, total consumption C equals consumption of domestic goods and services C^d plus consumption of foreign goods and services C^f; total investment I equals investment in domestic goods and services I^d plus investment in foreign goods and services I^f; and total government purchases G equals government purchases of domestic goods and services G^d plus government purchases of foreign goods and services G^f. Thus,

$$C = C^d + C^f,$$

$$I = I^d + I^f,$$

$$G = G^d + G^f.$$

We substitute these three equations into the identity above:

$$Y = (C - C^f) + (I - I^f) + (G - G^f) + EX.$$

We can rearrange to obtain

$$Y = C + I + G + EX - (C^f + I^f + G^f).$$

The sum of domestic spending on foreign goods and services $(C^f + I^f + G^f)$ is expenditure on imports (IM). We can thus write the national income accounts identity as

$$Y = C + I + G + EX + IM.$$

Because spending on imports is included in domestic spending $(C + I + G)$, and because goods and services imported from abroad are not part of a country's output, this equation subtracts spending on imports. Defining **net exports** to be exports minus imports $(NX = EX - IM)$, the identity becomes

$$Y = C + I + G + NX.$$

This equation states that expenditure on domestic output is the sum of consumption, investment, government purchases and net exports. This is the most common form of the national income accounts identity; it should be familiar from Chapter 2.

The national income accounts identity shows how domestic output, domestic spending and net exports are related. In particular,

$$NX = Y - (C + I + G)$$

Net Exports = Output − Domestic Spending.

This equation shows that in an open economy, domestic spending need not equal the output of goods and services. *If output exceeds domestic spending, we export the difference: net exports are positive. If output falls short of domestic spending, we import the difference: net exports are negative.*

International Capital Flows and the Trade Balance

In an open economy, as in the closed economy we discussed in Chapter 3, financial markets and goods markets are closely related. To see the relationship, we must rewrite the national income accounts identity in terms of saving and investment. Begin with the identity

$$Y = C + I + G + NX.$$

Subtract C and G from both sides to obtain

$$Y - C - G = I + NX.$$

Recall from Chapter 3 that $Y - C - G$ is national saving S, the sum of private saving, $Y - T - C$, and public saving, $T - G$, where T stands for taxes. Therefore,

$$S = I + NX.$$

Subtracting I from both sides of the equation, we can write the national income accounts identity as

$$S - I = NX.$$

This form of the national income accounts identity shows that an economy's net exports must always equal the difference between its saving and its investment.

Let's look more closely at each part of this identity. The easy part is the right-hand side, NX, the net export of goods and services. Another name for net exports is the **trade balance**, because it tells us how our trade in goods and services departs from the benchmark of equal imports and exports.

The left-hand side of the identity is the difference between domestic saving and domestic investment, $S - I$, which we will call **net capital outflow**. (It is sometimes called *net foreign investment*.) Net capital outflow equals the amount that domestic residents are lending abroad minus the amount that foreigners are lending to us. If net capital outflow is positive, the economy's saving exceeds its investment, and it is lending the excess to foreigners. If the net capital outflow is negative, the economy is experiencing a capital inflow: investment exceeds saving, and the economy is financing this extra investment by borrowing from abroad. Thus, net capital outflow reflects the international flow of funds to finance capital accumulation.

The national income accounts identity shows that net capital outflow always equals the trade balance. That is,

$$\text{Net Capital Outflow} = \text{Trade Balance}$$

$$S - I = NX.$$

If $S - I$ and NX are positive, we have a **trade surplus**. In this case, we are net lenders in world financial markets, and we are exporting more goods than we are importing. If $S - I$ and NX are negative, we have a **trade deficit**. In this case, we are net borrowers in world financial markets, and we are importing more goods than we are exporting. If $S - I$ and NX are exactly zero, we are said to have **balanced trade** because the value of imports equals the value of exports.

The national income accounts identity shows that the international flow of funds to finance capital accumulation and the international flow of goods and services are two sides

TABLE **6-1**

International Flows of Goods and Capital: Summary

This table shows the three outcomes that an open economy can experience.

Trade Surplus	Balanced Trade	Trade Deficit
Exports > Imports	Exports = Imports	Exports < Imports
Net Exports > 0	Net Exports = 0	Net Exports < 0
$Y > C + I + G$	$Y = C + I + G$	$Y < C + I + G$
Saving > Investment	Saving = Investment	Saving < Investment
Net Capital Outflow > 0	Net Capital Outflow = 0	Net Capital Outflow < 0

of the same coin. If domestic saving exceeds domestic investment, the surplus saving is used to make loans to foreigners. Foreigners require these loans because we are providing them with more goods and services than they are providing us. That is, we are running a trade surplus. If investment exceeds saving, the extra investment must be financed by borrowing from abroad. These foreign loans enable us to import more goods and services than we export. That is, we are running a trade deficit. Table 6-1 summarizes these points.

Note that the international flow of capital can take many forms. It is easiest to assume — as we have done so far — that when we run a trade deficit, foreigners make loans to us. This happens, for example, when a foreign company buys the debt (i.e. bonds) issued by a domestic corporation or by the domestic government. But the flow of capital can also take the form of foreigners buying domestic assets, such as when a foreign citizen buys shares in a domestic company. Whether foreigners buy domestically issued debt or domestically owned assets, they obtain a claim to the future returns to domestic capital. In both cases, foreigners end up owning some of the domestic capital stock.

International Flows of Goods and Capital: An Example

The equality of net exports and net capital outflow is an identity: it must hold by the way the variables are defined and the numbers are added up. But it is easy to miss the intuition behind this important relationship. The best way to understand it is to consider an example.

Imagine that a Dutch manufacturer, Dirck, sells a consumer good (e.g. a clock) to a Japanese consumer for 5000 yen. Because Dirck is a resident of the Netherlands, the sale represents a Dutch export. Other things equal, Dutch net exports rise. What else happens to make the identity hold? It depends on what Dirck does with the 5000 yen.

Suppose Dirck decides to stuff the 5000 yen in his mattress. In this case, Dirck has allocated some of his saving to an investment in the Japanese economy (in the form of the Japanese currency) rather than to an investment in the Dutch economy. Thus, Dutch saving exceeds Dutch investment. The rise in Dutch net exports is matched by a rise in the Dutch net capital outflow.

If Dirck wants to invest in Japan, however, he is unlikely to make currency his asset of choice. He might use the 5000 yen to buy some shares in, say, the Sony Corporation, or he might buy a bond issued by the Japanese government. In either case, some of Dutch saving is flowing abroad. Once again, the Dutch net capital outflow exactly balances Dutch net exports.

The opposite situation occurs in Japan. When the Japanese consumer buys the Dutch machinery, Japan's purchases of goods and services ($C + I + G$) rise, but there is no change in what Japan has produced (Y). The transaction reduces Japan's saving ($S = Y - C - G$) for a given level of investment (I). While the Netherlands experiences a net capital outflow, Japan experiences a net capital inflow.

Now let's change the example. Suppose that instead of investing his 5000 yen in a Japanese asset, Dirck uses it to buy something made in Japan, such as a Sony PlayStation 4. In this case, imports into the Netherlands rise. Together, the clock export and the PlayStation 4 import represent balanced trade between Japan and the Netherlands. Because exports and imports rise equally, net exports and net capital outflow are both unchanged.

A final possibility is that Dirck exchanges his 5000 yen for euros at a local bank. But this does not change the situation: the bank now has to do something with the 5000 yen. It can buy Japanese assets (a Dutch net capital outflow); it can buy a Japanese good (a Dutch import); or it can sell the yen to another resident of the Netherlands who wants to make such a transaction. If you follow the money, you can see that, in the end, Dutch net exports must equal Dutch net capital outflow.

GDP, GNP, the Trade Balance and the Current Account

We started our discussion of the open economy from the national accounts identity, with GDP as our measure of national income. In particular, we broke down the components of GDP into consumption, investment, government expenditure and net exports:

$$Y = C + I + G + NX,$$

where Y denotes GDP:

$$GDP = C + I + G + NX.$$

Now, recall that in Chapter 2 we discussed an alternative measure of national income, namely *gross national product*, or GNP. Whereas GDP measures the total income produced *domestically*, GNP measures the total income earned by *nationals* (residents of a country). Thus, if residents of Country A own assets in Country B on which they receive an income, then the income from those assets is counted into the GNP of Country A. Even though that income is not produced domestically in Country A (and so is *not* part of Country A GDP), it is income to the nationals of Country A (and so *is* part of Country A GNP). Thus, to obtain

F Y I

The Irrelevance of Bilateral Trade Balances

The trade balance we have been discussing measures the difference between a nation's exports and its imports with the rest of the world. Sometimes you might hear in the media a report on a nation's trade balance with a specific other nation. This is called a *bilateral* trade balance. For example, the UK's bilateral trade balance with China equals exports that the United Kingdom sells to China minus imports that the United Kingdom buys from China.

The overall trade balance is, as we have seen, inextricably linked to a nation's saving and investment. That is not true of a bilateral trade balance. Indeed, a nation can have large trade deficits and surpluses with specific trading partners, while having balanced trade overall.

For example, suppose the world has three countries: the United States, China and the Netherlands. The Netherlands sells €100 billion in machine tools to the United States; the United States sells €100 billion in wheat to China; and China sells €100 billion in toys to the Netherlands. In this case, the Netherlands has a bilateral trade deficit with China; China has a bilateral trade deficit with the United States; and the United States has a bilateral trade deficit with the Netherlands. But each of the three

nations has balanced trade overall, exporting and importing €100 billion in goods.

Bilateral trade deficits receive more attention in the political arena than they deserve. This is in part because international relations are conducted country to country, so politicians and diplomats are naturally drawn to statistics measuring country-to-country economic transactions. Most economists, however, believe that bilateral trade balances are not very meaningful. From a macroeconomic standpoint, it is a nation's trade balance with all foreign nations put together that matters.

The same lesson applies to individuals as it does to nations. Your own personal trade balance is the difference between your income and your spending, and you may be concerned if these two variables are out of line. But you should not be concerned with the difference between your income and spending with a particular person or firm. Economist Robert Solow once explained the irrelevance of bilateral trade balances as follows: 'I have a chronic deficit with my barber, who doesn't buy a darned thing from me.' But that does not stop Professor Solow from living within his means, or getting a haircut when he needs it.

gross national product (GNP), we add to GDP receipts of factor income (wages, rent, interest payments and profit) from the rest of the world and subtract payments of factor income to the rest of the world:

GNP = GDP + Factor Payments from Abroad − Factor Payments to Abroad.

Or, if we define *net factor income from abroad,* as equal to *factor payments from abroad* minus *factor payments to abroad,* and denote this as *NFIA,* then we can write:

$$GNP = GDP + NFIA.$$

Now, since GDP = $C + I + G + NX$, we can see that

$$GNP = C + I + G + NX + NFIA.$$

There is, however, one more aspect of foreign transactions that we need to mention here: *unilateral transfers.* Unilateral transfers are payments made (or goods and services rendered) for which nothing in return is recorded in the national accounts. Typical examples of unilateral transfers for European countries would include foreign aid payments to developing countries and payments into (or grants from) the European Union budget. If we take the sum of net exports and net factor income from abroad, and add to it *net* unilateral transfers (unilateral transfers paid *into* the country minus unilateral transfers paid *out* by the country), the result is called the *current account balance:*

$$\text{Current Account Balance} = \text{Net Exports} + \text{Net Factor Income from Abroad} + \text{Net Unilateral Transfers.}$$

The current account balance is an important concept because, if the nationals of a country are receiving a large amount of income on assets that they own abroad, this may outweigh the fact that they import far more than they export – in other words, it is possible to have a zero or even positive current account balance, but a negative trade balance. In effect, this means that domestic residents of the country are spending more than is being produced domestically, but are able to pay for the shortfall out of their income from abroad. This might be the case, for example, in a country with an ageing population. The residents of the country may in the past have acquired a great deal of overseas assets in the forms of foreign government bonds and shares in foreign companies, so that the country is able to use this factor income from abroad to pay for the consumption of its ageing population, which has many retired people who are consuming more than they are producing.

Alternatively, countries may have a positive trade balance and a low or even negative current account balance. Take the example of a country that has received a great deal of foreign direct investment over the years (i.e. foreign companies setting up their factories and offices in the country concerned). Governments often encourage direct investment because it provides employment and training for the labour force and generally raises economic activity in the economy; however, the profits that those companies earn will be paid back to the owners of the company, who are located overseas. This will tend to raise *net factor payments to abroad* (i.e. reduce *net factor income from abroad*) and so worsen the current account. Thus, a country with a highly productive manufacturing sector, but which has enjoyed high levels of foreign direct investment, may be characterized by a positive trade balance and much worse performance – perhaps even a deficit – on the current account balance.

Although the current account is an important concept in macroeconomics, in this book we will in fact concentrate on net exports, or the trade balance, as our measure of a country's current transactions with the rest of world. Effectively, we shall assume that net factor income from abroad is zero (and similarly for net unilateral transfers). The basic insights gained from the open economy models we shall develop using the trade balance would be largely unchanged if we were to use the concept of the current account instead, and a good principle of economic modelling is that models should always be kept as simple as possible for the purpose in hand. If you later take a more advanced course in macroeconomics or in international macroeconomics, you will learn a lot more about how economists model the current account. For now, we will stick with the trade balance.

The Current Account Balance and the Trade Balance in Some European Countries

In Table 6-2 we have listed the current account balance in 2011 for several European countries, as well as its constituent parts of net exports, net factor income from abroad and net unilateral transfers. Two immediately striking features of the table are the very large current account surpluses earned by Germany and the Netherlands in 2011, and the very large current account deficits of France and the UK. The UK, in fact, ran a sizeable trade deficit of 34.1 billion euros, which was, however, offset by the large amount of net factor income from abroad: 34.9 billion euros. Nevertheless, after allowing for unilateral transfers, the UK ran a current account deficit of 24.6 billion euros in 2011 – about 1.4 per cent of UK GDP.

In contrast to the UK, Ireland recorded a large trade *surplus* of 34.8 billion euros in 2011. Therefore, despite the very large *negative* net factor income from abroad – the Irish actually paid out 31.8 billion euros more to foreigners in factor payments than they received in 2011 – Ireland achieved a current account *surplus* of 1.8 billion euros (roughly 1.1 per cent of the Irish GDP). This largely reflects the high degree of direct investment that the Irish economy has enjoyed over the years, resulting from Ireland's vibrant economy and the very attractive tax breaks that the government has offered to overseas firms wishing to set up production in Ireland and use it as their European base. Over 1000 overseas companies have established operations in Ireland over the past 25 years, including major corporations such as the pharmaceuticals company Pfizer, and the information technology companies Apple and Intel. According to the latest figures, direct investment by overseas companies brings with it employment for the local labour force (over 146,000 people), an increase in exports (over €115 billion) and a general boost

TABLE 6-2

The Current Account Balance in 2011 for Some European Countries (billions of euros)

	Net Exports	+	Net Factor Income from Abroad	+	Unilateral Transfers	=	Current Account Balance
Belgium	−5.5		6.8		−6.5		−5.2
Denmark	12.9		4.9		−4.2		13.6
Germany	132.3		48.4		−33.5		147.2
France	−49.3		46.9		−36.6		−39.0
Ireland	34.8		−31.8		−1.2		1.8
Netherlands	58.9		13.9		−10.9		61.9
Sweden	22.7		10.0		−5.1		27.6
United Kingdom	−34.1		34.9		−25.4		−24.6

Source: Eurostat.

to the economy (it generates €19 billion of expenditure), but it also means that the profits from those companies will be sent overseas to their owners.[3] ■

6-2 Saving and Investment in a Small Open Economy

So far in our discussion of the international flows of goods and capital, we have rearranged accounting identities. That is, we have defined some of the variables that measure transactions in an open economy, and we have shown the links among these variables that follow from their definitions. Our next step is to develop a model that explains the behaviour of these variables. We can then use the model to answer questions such as how the trade balance responds to changes in policy.

Capital Mobility and the World Interest Rate

Below, we present a model of the international flows of capital and goods. Because the trade balance equals the net capital outflow, which in turn equals saving minus investment, our model focuses on saving and investment. To develop this model, we use some elements that should be familiar from Chapter 3, but in contrast to the Chapter 3 model, we do not assume that the real interest rate equilibrates saving and investment. Instead, we allow the economy to run a trade deficit and borrow from other countries, or to run a trade surplus and lend to other countries.

If the real interest rate does not adjust to equilibrate saving and investment in this model, what *does* determine the real interest rate? We answer this question here by considering the simple case of a **small open economy** with perfect capital mobility. By 'small' we mean that this economy is a small part of the world market and thus, by itself, can have only a negligible effect on the world interest rate. By 'perfect capital mobility' we mean that residents of the country have full access to world financial markets. In particular, the government does not impede international borrowing or lending.

Because of this assumption of perfect capital mobility, the interest rate in our small open economy, r, must equal the **world interest rate** r^*, the real interest rate prevailing in world financial markets:

$$r = r^*.$$

Residents of the small open economy need never borrow at any interest rate above r^*, because they can always get a loan at r^* from abroad. Similarly, residents of this economy need never lend at any interest rate below r^*, because they can always earn r^* by lending abroad. Thus, the world interest rate determines the interest rate in our small open economy.

---

[3] IDA Annual Report 2011 – Impact of FDI (Foreign Direct Investment), available at: www.idaireland.com/news-media/publications/annual-reports/accesible-versions/2011/impact-of-fdi.html.

Let us discuss for a moment what determines the world real interest rate. In a closed economy, the equilibrium of domestic saving and domestic investment determines the interest rate. Barring interplanetary trade, the world economy is a closed economy. Therefore, the equilibrium of world saving and world investment determines the world interest rate. Our small open economy has a negligible effect on the world real interest rate because, being a small part of the world, it has a negligible effect on world saving and world investment. Hence, our small open economy takes the world interest rate as exogenously given.

The Model

To build the model of the small open economy, we take three assumptions from Chapter 3:

■ The economy's output Y is fixed by the factors of production and the production function. We write this as

$$Y = \bar{Y} = F(\bar{K}, \bar{L}).$$

■ Consumption C is positively related to disposable income $Y - T$. We write the consumption function as

$$C = C(Y - T).$$

■ Investment I is negatively related to the real interest rate r. We write the investment function as

$$I = I(r).$$

These are the three key parts of our model. If you do not understand these relationships, review Chapter 3 before continuing.

We can now return to the accounting identity and write it as

$$NX = (Y - C - G) - I,$$
$$NX = S - I.$$

Substituting the Chapter 3 assumptions recapped above, and the assumption that the interest rate equals the world interest rate, we obtain

$$NX = \bar{Y} - C(\bar{Y} - T) - G - I(r^*)$$
$$= \bar{S} - I(r^*).$$

This equation shows that the trade balance NX depends on those variables that determine saving S and investment I. Because saving depends on fiscal policy (lower government purchases G or higher taxes T raise national saving) and investment depends on the world real interest rate r^* (a higher interest rate makes some investment projects unprofitable), the trade balance depends on these variables as well.

FIGURE 6-3

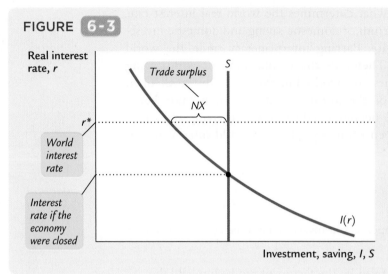

Saving and Investment in a Small Open Economy In a closed economy, the real interest rate adjusts to equilibrate saving and investment. In a small open economy, the interest rate is determined in world financial markets. The difference between saving and investment determines the trade balance. Here there is a trade surplus, because at the world interest rate, saving exceeds investment.

In Chapter 3 we graphed saving and investment as in Figure 6-3. In the closed economy studied in that chapter, the real interest rate adjusts to equilibrate saving and investment – that is, the real interest rate is found where the saving and investment curves cross. In the small open economy, however, the real interest rate equals the world real interest rate. *The trade balance is determined by the difference between saving and investment at the world interest rate.*

At this point, you might wonder about the mechanism that causes the trade balance to equal the net capital outflow. The determinants of the capital flows are easy to understand. When saving falls short of investment, investors borrow from abroad; when saving exceeds investment, the excess is lent to other countries. But what causes those who import and export to behave in a way that ensures that the international flow of goods exactly balances this international flow of capital? For now we leave this question unanswered, but we return to it in Section 6-3, when we discuss the determination of exchange rates.

How Policies Influence the Trade Balance

Suppose that the economy begins in a position of balanced trade. That is, at the world interest rate, investment I equals saving S, and net exports NX equal zero. Let's use our model to predict the effects of government policies at home and abroad.

Fiscal Policy at Home Consider first what happens to the small open economy if the government expands domestic spending by increasing government purchases. The increase in G reduces national saving, because $S = Y - C - G$. With an unchanged world real interest rate, investment remains the same. Therefore, saving falls below investment, and some investment must now be financed by borrowing from abroad. Because $NX = S - I$, the fall in S implies a fall in NX. The economy now runs a trade deficit.

FIGURE 6-4

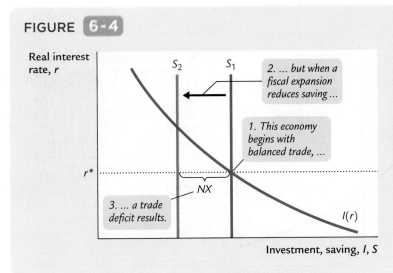

A Fiscal Expansion at Home in a Small Open Economy An increase in government purchases or a reduction in taxes reduces national saving and thus shifts the saving schedule to the left, from S_1 to S_2. The result is a trade deficit.

The same logic applies to a decrease in taxes. A tax cut lowers T, raises disposable income $Y - T$, stimulates consumption and reduces national saving. (Even though some of the tax cut finds its way into private saving, public saving falls by the full amount of the tax cut; in total, saving falls.) Because $NX = S - I$, the reduction in national saving in turn lowers NX.

Figure 6-4 illustrates these effects. A fiscal policy change that increases private consumption C or public consumption G reduces national saving ($Y - C - G$) and, therefore, shifts the vertical line that represents saving from S_1 to S_2. Because NX is the distance between the saving schedule and the investment schedule at the world interest rate, this shift reduces NX. *Hence, starting from balanced trade, a change in fiscal policy that reduces national saving leads to a trade deficit.*

Fiscal Policy Abroad Consider now what happens to a small open economy when foreign governments increase their government purchases. If these foreign countries are a small part of the world economy, then their fiscal change has a negligible impact on other countries. But if these foreign countries are a large part of the world economy, their increase in government purchases reduces world saving. The decrease in world saving causes the world interest rate to rise, just as we saw in our closed economy model (remember, Earth is a closed economy).

The increase in the world interest rate raises the cost of borrowing and, thus, reduces investment in our small open economy. Because there has been no change in domestic saving, saving S now exceeds investment I, and some of our saving begins to flow abroad. Since $NX = S - I$, the reduction in I must also increase NX. Hence, reduced saving abroad leads to a trade surplus at home.

Figure 6-5 illustrates how a small open economy starting from balanced trade responds to a foreign fiscal expansion. Because the policy change is occurring abroad, the domestic saving and investment schedules remain the same. The only change is an increase in the world interest rate from r_1^* to r_2^*. The trade balance is the difference between the saving and investment schedules; because saving

FIGURE 6-5

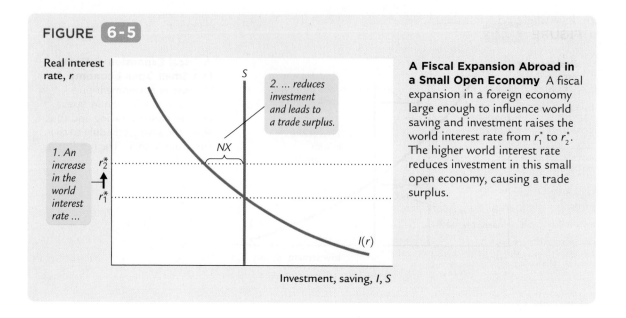

FIGURE **6-5**

Real interest rate, r

2. ... reduces investment and leads to a trade surplus.

1. An increase in the world interest rate ...

NX

r_2^*

r_1^*

S

$I(r)$

Investment, saving, I, S

A Fiscal Expansion Abroad in a Small Open Economy A fiscal expansion in a foreign economy large enough to influence world saving and investment raises the world interest rate from r_1^* to r_2^*. The higher world interest rate reduces investment in this small open economy, causing a trade surplus.

exceeds investment at r_2^*, there is a trade surplus. *Hence, starting from balanced trade, an increase in the world interest rate due to a fiscal expansion abroad leads to a trade surplus.*

Shifts in Investment Demand Consider what happens to our small open economy if its investment schedule shifts outward − that is, if the demand for investment goods at every interest rate increases. This shift would occur if, for example, the government changed the tax laws to encourage investment by providing an investment tax credit. Figure 6-6 illustrates the impact of a shift in

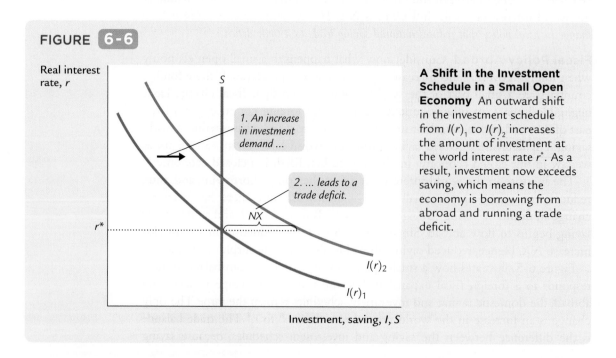

FIGURE **6-6**

Real interest rate, r

1. An increase in investment demand ...

2. ... leads to a trade deficit.

NX

r^*

S

$I(r)_2$

$I(r)_1$

Investment, saving, I, S

A Shift in the Investment Schedule in a Small Open Economy An outward shift in the investment schedule from $I(r)_1$ to $I(r)_2$ increases the amount of investment at the world interest rate r^*. As a result, investment now exceeds saving, which means the economy is borrowing from abroad and running a trade deficit.

the investment schedule. At a given world interest rate, investment is now higher. Because saving is unchanged, some investment must now be financed by borrowing from abroad. Capital flows into the economy to finance the increased investment, so that the net capital outflow is negative. Put differently, because $NX = S - I$, the increase in I implies a decrease in NX. *Hence, starting from balanced trade, an outward shift in the investment schedule causes a trade deficit.*

Evaluating Economic Policy

Our model of the open economy shows that the flow of goods and services measured by the trade balance is inextricably connected to the international flow of funds for capital accumulation. The net capital outflow is the difference between domestic saving and domestic investment. Thus, the impact of economic policies on the trade balance can always be found by examining their impact on domestic saving and domestic investment. Policies that increase investment or decrease saving tend to cause a trade deficit, and policies that decrease investment or increase saving tend to cause a trade surplus.

Our analysis of the open economy has been positive, not normative. That is, our analysis of how economic policies influence the international flows of capital and goods has not told us whether these policies are desirable. Evaluating economic policies and their impact on the open economy is a frequent topic of debate among economists and policy makers.

When a country runs a trade deficit, policy makers must confront the question of whether it represents a national problem. Most economists view a trade deficit not as a problem in itself, but perhaps as a symptom of a problem. A trade deficit could be a reflection of low saving. In a closed economy, low saving leads to low investment and a smaller future capital stock. In an open economy, low saving leads to a trade deficit and a growing foreign debt, which eventually must be repaid. In both cases, high current consumption leads to lower future consumption, implying that future generations bear the burden of low national saving.

Yet trade deficits are not always a reflection of economic malady. When poor rural economies develop into modern industrial economies, they sometimes finance their high levels of investment with foreign borrowing. In these cases, trade deficits are a sign of economic development. For example, South Korea ran large trade deficits throughout the 1970s, and it became one of the success stories of economic growth. The lesson is that one cannot judge economic performance from the trade balance alone. Instead, one must look at the underlying causes of the international flows.

CASE STUDY

The US Trade Deficit

Although, as we discussed earlier, the US economy is much more closed than the typical European economy in terms of the percentage of GDP accounted for by international trade, the sheer size of the US economy means that US trade deficits or surpluses can be a very important feature of the world economy. In fact, during the 1980s, 1990s and early 2000s, the United States ran very large trade deficits. Panel (a) of Figure 6-7 documents this experience by showing US net exports as a percentage of GDP. The exact size of the trade deficit fluctuated over time, but it was large throughout these two and a half decades. In 2004,

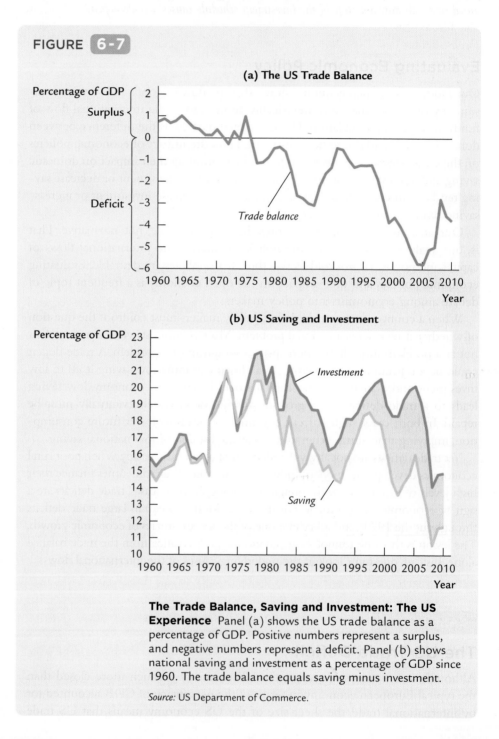

FIGURE 6-7

The Trade Balance, Saving and Investment: The US Experience Panel (a) shows the US trade balance as a percentage of GDP. Positive numbers represent a surplus, and negative numbers represent a deficit. Panel (b) shows national saving and investment as a percentage of GDP since 1960. The trade balance equals saving minus investment.

Source: US Department of Commerce.

the US trade deficit was about 4 per cent of US GDP. But US GDP is equal to about 92 per cent of the total GDP of all 27 members of the European Union put together, or about 6½ times the GDP of the United Kingdom, so that 4 per cent of US GDP is a very large number indeed – about $593 billion. As accounting identities require, this huge trade deficit had to be financed by borrowing from abroad (or, equivalently, by selling US assets abroad). During this period, the United States went from being the world's largest creditor to the world's largest debtor.

What caused the US trade deficit? There is no single explanation. But to understand some of the forces at work, it helps to look at national saving and domestic investment, as shown in panel (b) of the figure. Keep in mind that the trade deficit is the difference between saving and investment.

The start of the trade deficit coincided with a fall in US national saving. This development can be explained by the expansionary fiscal policy in the 1980s. In the early 1980s, the US government substantially cut personal income taxes. Because these tax cuts were not met with equal cuts in government spending, the government budget went into deficit. These budget deficits were among the largest ever experienced in the US in a period of peace and prosperity. According to our model, such a policy should reduce national saving, thereby causing a trade deficit. And, in fact, that is exactly what happened. Because the US government budget and trade balance went into deficit at roughly the same time, these shortfalls were called the *twin deficits*.

Things started to change in the 1990s, when the US government got its fiscal house in order by introducing tax increases and reining in government spending. In addition to these policy changes, rapid US productivity growth in the late 1990s raised incomes and, thus, further increased tax revenue. These developments moved the US government budget from deficit to surplus, which in turn caused US national saving to rise.

In contrast to what our model predicts, the increase in US national saving did not coincide with a shrinking trade deficit, because domestic investment rose at the same time. The likely explanation is that the boom in information technology caused an expansionary shift in the US investment function. Even though fiscal policy was pushing the trade deficit towards surplus, the investment boom was an even stronger force pushing the trade balance towards deficit.

In the early 2000s, fiscal policy once again put downward pressure on national saving. With President George W. Bush in the White House, tax cuts were signed into law in 2001 and 2003, while the 'war on terror' led to substantial increases in government spending. The federal government was again running budget deficits. National saving fell to historic lows, and the trade deficit reached historic highs.

A few years later, the trade deficit started to shrink somewhat, as the economy experienced a substantial decline in housing prices (a phenomenon examined in Case Studies in Chapters 12 and 18). Lower housing prices led to a substantial decline in residential investment. The trade deficit fell from 5.8 per cent of GDP at its peak in 2006 to 3.6 per cent in 2010.

The history of the US trade deficit shows that this trade deficit, by itself, does not tell us much about what is happening in the economy. We have to look deeper at saving, investment, and the policies and events that cause them to change over time.[4] Another issue concerns how the US is able to finance such a large deficit by borrowing huge amounts from the rest of the world. We have not yet studied the exchange rate in detail, but common sense dictates that if the US were to find itself unable to borrow on world markets to finance the huge trade deficit, there would be a massive excess supply of US dollars in the foreign exchange market and the external value of the dollar would collapse. So who is lending money to the US in order to finance the trade deficit? We discuss this in the next case study. ■

CASE STUDY

Why Doesn't Capital Flow to Poor Countries?

The US trade deficit discussed in the previous case study represents a flow of capital into the United States from the rest of the world. Which countries were the source of these capital flows? Because the world is a closed economy, the capital must be coming from those countries that were running trade surpluses. In 2010, this group included many nations that were far poorer than the United States, such as Russia, Malaysia, Venezuela and China. In these nations, saving exceeded investment in domestic capital. These countries were sending funds abroad to countries such as the United States, where investment in domestic capital exceeded saving.

From one perspective, the direction of international capital flows is a paradox. Recall our discussion of production functions in Chapter 3. There, we established that an empirically realistic production function is the Cobb–Douglas form:

$$F(K, L) = AK^{\alpha}L^{1-\alpha},$$

where K is capital, L is labour, A is a variable representing the state of technology, and α is a parameter that determines capital's share of total income. For this production function, the marginal product of capital is

$$MPK = \alpha A(K/L)^{\alpha-1}.$$

The marginal product of capital tells us how much extra output an extra unit of capital would produce. Because α is capital's share, it must be less than 1, so $\alpha - 1 < 0$. This means that an increase in K/L decreases MPK. In other words, holding other variables constant, the more capital a nation has, the less valuable an extra unit of capital is. This phenomenon of diminishing marginal product says that capital should be more valuable where capital is scarce.

This prediction, however, seems at odds with the international flow of capital represented by trade imbalances. Capital does not seem to flow to those nations where it should be most valuable. Instead of capital-rich countries such as the United States lending to capital-poor countries, we often observe the opposite. Why is that?

---

[4] For more on this topic, see Catherine L. Mann, *Is the US Trade Deficit Sustainable?*, Washington, DC: Institute for International Economics, 1999.

One reason is that there are important differences among nations other than their accumulation of capital. Poor nations have not only lower levels of capital accumulation (represented by K/L), but also inferior production capabilities (represented by the variable A). For example, compared with rich nations, poor nations may have less access to advanced technologies, lower levels of education (or *human capital*) or less efficient economic policies. Such differences could mean less output for given inputs of capital and labour; in the Cobb–Douglas production function, this is translated into a lower value of the parameter A. If so, then capital need not be more valuable in poor nations, even though capital is scarce.

A second reason why capital might not flow to poor nations is that property rights are often not enforced. Corruption is typically much higher; revolutions, coups and expropriation of wealth are more common; and governments often default on their debts. So even if capital is more valuable in poor nations, foreigners may avoid investing their wealth there simply because they are afraid of losing it. Moreover, local investors face similar incentives. Imagine that you lived in a poor nation and you happened to be lucky enough to have some wealth to invest; you might well decide that putting it in a safe country such as the United States was your best option, even if capital is less valuable there than in your home country.

Whichever of these two reasons is correct, the challenge for poor nations is to find ways to reverse the situation. If these nations offered the same production efficiency and legal protections as the US economy, the direction of international capital flows would likely reverse. The US trade deficit would become a trade surplus, and capital would flow to these emerging nations. Such a change would help the poor of the world escape poverty.[5] ■

6-3 Exchange Rates

Having examined the international flows of capital and of goods and services, we now extend the analysis by considering the prices that apply to these transactions. The *exchange rate* between two countries is the price at which residents of those countries trade with each other. In this section we first examine precisely what the exchange rate measures, and we then discuss how exchange rates are determined.

Nominal and Real Exchange Rates

Economists distinguish between two exchange rates: the nominal exchange rate and the real exchange rate. Let's discuss each in turn and see how they are related.

The Nominal Exchange Rate The **nominal exchange rate** is the relative price of the currency of two countries. For example, if the exchange rate between the euro and the Japanese yen is 140 yen per euro, then you can

---

[5] For more on this topic, see Robert E. Lucas, 'Why Doesn't Capital Flow from Rich to Poor Countries?', *American Economic Review*, 1990, vol. 80, pp. 92–96.

exchange one euro for 140 yen in world markets for foreign currency. A Japanese who wants to obtain euros would pay 140 yen for each euros he bought. A Frenchman who wants to obtain yen would get 140 yen for each euro he paid. When people refer to 'the exchange rate' between two countries, they usually mean the nominal exchange rate.

You can find nominal exchange rates reported in many newspapers.[6] Often they are reported in different ways. For example, the sterling–euro rate may be quoted as 1.189 euros per British pound, or as 0.8410 pounds per euro. Because 0.8410 equals 1/1.189, these two ways of expressing the exchange rate are equivalent. In this book, we shall usually express the exchange rate as the foreign price of domestic currency. For example, if we think of, say, the Netherlands as the domestic economy, then the exchange rate is expressed as units of foreign currency (e.g. pounds, yen or dollars) per euro. This is equivalent to thinking of the exchange rate as the price of a euro in the currency concerned (e.g. a rate of 0.8410 pounds per euro means that a euro is worth £0.8410 or 84.10 pence).

Suppose that the exchange rate were to move from 0.6847 pounds per euro to 0.6900 pounds per euro. Such a rise in the exchange rate is called an *appreciation* of the euro, because the euro is now worth more in terms of the UK pound; a fall in the exchange rate is called a *depreciation*. When the domestic currency appreciates, it buys more of the foreign currency; when it depreciates, it buys less. An appreciation is sometimes called a *strengthening* of the currency, and a depreciation is sometimes called a *weakening* of the currency. The advantage of defining the nominal exchange rate as the foreign price of domestic currency is that an increase in the exchange rate (e.g. from 140 to 145) then implies an appreciation of the domestic currency (e.g. more yen per euro), while a fall in the exchange rate (e.g. from 140 to 135) implies a depreciation of the domestic currency.

A word of caution: the definition of the exchange rate is often a source of confusion for students. You should make sure you understand what is meant by 'the foreign price of domestic currency'. If you are living (or studying) in the Euro Area (Eurozone), then it is the price of one euro in the currency of any other country. If you are outside the Euro Area, then you should think of the exchange rate as the foreign currency price of one unit of *your* country's currency (e.g. dollars per UK pound if you are in the UK). So long as you are consistent in your choice of the economy that you label 'domestic' and think of the exchange rate as the foreign price of one unit of the currency of that economy, you cannot go wrong.

The Real Exchange Rate The **real exchange rate** is the relative price of the goods of two countries. That is, the real exchange rate tells us the rate at which we can trade the goods of one country for the goods of another. The real exchange rate is sometimes called the *terms of trade*.

To see the relation between the real and nominal exchange rates, consider a single good produced in many countries: cars. Suppose a French car costs €10,000 and a similar Japanese car costs 2,800,000 yen. To compare the prices of the two cars, we must convert them into a common currency. If a euro is worth 140 yen,

---

[6] *The Economist* has an online currency converter on its website (www.economist.com) that allows you to get the latest exchange rates between any two currencies in the world.

then the French car costs 1,400,000 yen. Comparing the price of the French car (1,400,000 yen) and the price of the Japanese car (2,800,000 yen), we conclude that the French car costs one-half of what the Japanese car costs. In other words, at current prices, we can exchange two French cars for one Japanese car.

We can summarize our calculation as follows:

$$\text{Real Exchange Rate} = \frac{(140 \text{ yen/euro}) \times (10,000 \text{ euros/French Car})}{(2,800,000 \text{ yen/Japanese Car})}$$

$$= 0.5 \frac{\text{Japanese Car}}{\text{French Car}}.$$

At these prices and this exchange rate, we obtain one-half of a Japanese car per French car. More generally, we can write this calculation as

$$\text{Real Exchange Rate} = \frac{\text{Nominal Exchange Rate} \times \text{Price of Domestic Good}}{\text{Price of Foreign Good}}.$$

The rate at which we exchange foreign and domestic goods depends on the prices of the goods in the local currencies and on the rate at which the currencies are exchanged.

This calculation of the real exchange rate for a single good suggests how we should define the real exchange rate for a broader basket of goods. Suppose we want to compute the real exchange rate between France and Japan (thinking of France as the domestic economy). Let e be the nominal exchange rate (the number of yen per euro), P be the price level in France (measured in euros), and P^* be the price level in Japan (measured in yen). Then the real exchange rate ε is

$$\text{Real Exchange Rate} = \text{Nominal Exchange Rate} \times \text{Ratio of Price Levels},$$

$$\varepsilon = e \times (P/P^*).$$

The real exchange rate between two countries is computed from the nominal exchange rate and the price levels in the two countries. *If the real exchange rate is high, foreign goods are relatively cheap and domestic goods are relatively expensive. If the real exchange rate is low, foreign goods are relatively expensive and domestic goods are relatively cheap.*

The Real Exchange Rate and the Trade Balance

What macroeconomic influence does the real exchange rate exert? To answer this question, remember that the real exchange rate is nothing more than a relative price. Just as the relative price of hamburgers and pizza determines which you choose for lunch, the relative price of domestic and foreign goods affects the demand for these goods.

Suppose, first, that the real exchange rate is low. In this case, because domestic goods are

FIGURE 6-8

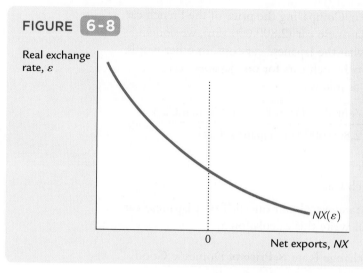

Real exchange rate, ε

$NX(\varepsilon)$

0

Net exports, NX

Net Exports and the Real Exchange Rate The figure shows the relationship between the real exchange rate and net exports: the lower the real exchange rate, the less expensive are domestic goods relative to foreign goods, and thus the greater are the net exports. Note that a portion of the horizontal axis measures negative values of NX: because imports can exceed exports, net exports can be less than zero.

relatively cheap, domestic residents will want to purchase fewer imported goods. For the same reason, foreigners will want to buy many of our goods. As a result of both of these actions, the quantity of our net exports demanded will be high.

The opposite occurs if the real exchange rate is high. Because domestic goods are expensive relative to foreign goods, domestic residents will want to buy many imported goods, and foreigners will want to buy few of our goods. Therefore, the quantity of our net exports demanded will be low.

We write this relationship between the real exchange rate and net exports as

$$NX = NX(\varepsilon).$$

This equation states that net exports are a function of the real exchange rate. Figure 6-8 illustrates the negative relationship between the trade balance and the real exchange rate.

The Determinants of the Real Exchange Rate

We now have all the pieces needed to construct a model that explains what factors determine the real exchange rate. In particular, we combine the relationship between net exports and the real exchange rate we just discussed with the model of the trade balance we developed earlier in the chapter. We can summarize the analysis as follows:

■ The real exchange rate is related to net exports. When the real exchange rate is lower, domestic goods are less expensive relative to foreign goods, and net exports are greater.

■ The trade balance (net exports) must equal the net capital outflow, which in turn equals saving minus investment. Saving is fixed by the consumption function and fiscal policy; investment is fixed by the investment function and the world interest rate.

FIGURE 6-9

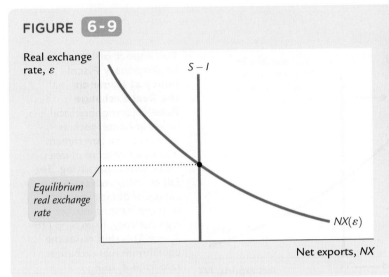

How the Real Exchange Rate is Determined The real exchange rate is determined by the intersection of the vertical line representing saving minus investment and the downward-sloping net-exports schedule. At this intersection, the quantity of domestic currency supplied for the flow of capital abroad equals the quantity of domestic money demanded for the net export of goods and services.

Figure 6-9 illustrates these two conditions. The line showing the relationship between net exports and the real exchange rate slopes downward because a low real exchange rate makes domestic goods relatively inexpensive. The line representing the excess of saving over investment, $S - I$, is vertical because neither saving nor investment depends on the real exchange rate. The crossing of these two lines determines the equilibrium exchange rate.

Figure 6-9 looks like an ordinary supply-and-demand diagram. In fact, you can think of this diagram as representing the supply and demand for foreign currency exchange. The vertical line, $S - I$, represents the net capital outflow and thus the supply of domestic currency to be exchanged into foreign currency and invested abroad. The downward-sloping line, NX, represents the net demand for domestic currency coming from foreigners who want domestic currency to buy our goods. *At the equilibrium real exchange rate, the supply of domestic currency available from the net capital outflow balances the demand for domestic currency by foreigners buying our net exports.*

How Policies Influence the Real Exchange Rate

We can use this model to show how the changes in economic policy we discussed earlier affect the real exchange rate.

Fiscal Policy at Home What happens to the real exchange rate if the government reduces national saving by increasing government purchases or cutting taxes? As we discussed earlier, this reduction in saving lowers $S - I$ and thus NX. That is, the reduction in saving causes a trade deficit.

Figure 6-10 shows how the equilibrium real exchange rate adjusts to ensure that NX falls. The change in policy shifts the vertical $S - I$ line to the left, lowering the supply of domestic currency to be invested abroad. The lower supply causes the equilibrium real exchange rate to rise from ε_1 to ε_2 – that is, the

FIGURE 6-10

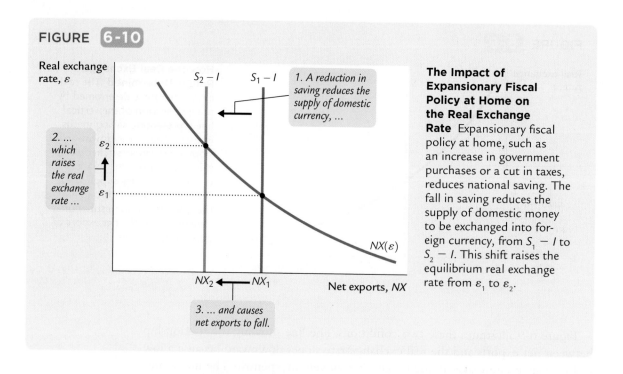

The Impact of Expansionary Fiscal Policy at Home on the Real Exchange Rate Expansionary fiscal policy at home, such as an increase in government purchases or a cut in taxes, reduces national saving. The fall in saving reduces the supply of domestic money to be exchanged into foreign currency, from $S_1 - I$ to $S_2 - I$. This shift raises the equilibrium real exchange rate from ε_1 to ε_2.

domestic currency becomes more valuable. Because of the rise in the value of the domestic currency, domestic goods become more expensive relative to foreign goods, which causes exports to fall and imports to rise. The change in exports and the change in imports both act to reduce net exports.

Fiscal Policy Abroad What happens to the real exchange rate if foreign governments increase government purchases or cut taxes? This change in fiscal policy reduces world saving and raises the world interest rate. The increase in the world interest rate reduces domestic investment I, which raises $S - I$ and thus NX. That is, the increase in the world interest rate causes a trade surplus.

Figure 6-11 shows that this change in policy shifts the vertical $S - I$ line to the right, raising the supply of domestic currency to be invested abroad. The equilibrium real exchange rate falls. That is, the domestic currency becomes less valuable, and domestic goods become less expensive relative to foreign goods.

Shifts in Investment Demand What happens to the real exchange rate if investment demand at home increases, perhaps because the government introduces a policy of allowing tax relief against company expenditure on investment? At the given world interest rate, the increase in investment demand leads to higher investment. A higher value of I means lower values of $S - I$ and NX. That is, the increase in investment demand causes a trade deficit.

Figure 6-12 shows that the increase in investment demand shifts the vertical $S - I$ line to the left, reducing the supply of euros to be invested abroad. The equilibrium real exchange rate rises. Hence, when the investment tax relief

FIGURE 6-11

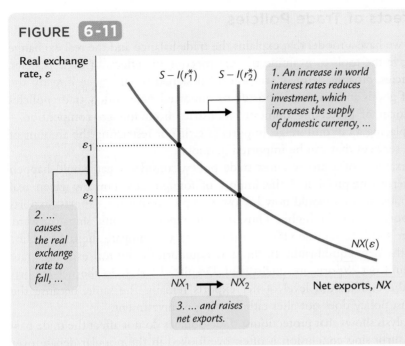

Real exchange rate, ε

$S - I(r_1^*)$ $S - I(r_2^*)$

1. An increase in world interest rates reduces investment, which increases the supply of domestic currency, ...

ε_1

ε_2

2. ... causes the real exchange rate to fall, ...

$NX(\varepsilon)$

NX_1 → NX_2 Net exports, NX

3. ... and raises net exports.

The Impact of Expansionary Fiscal Policy Abroad on the Real Exchange Rate Expansionary fiscal policy abroad reduces world saving and raises the world interest rate from r_1^* to r_2^*. The increase in the world interest rate reduces investment at home, which in turn raises the supply of domestic currency to be exchanged into foreign currencies. As a result, the equilibrium real exchange rate falls from ε_1 to ε_2.

FIGURE 6-12

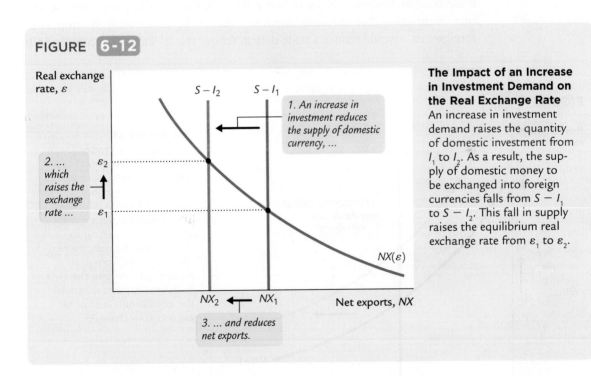

Real exchange rate, ε

$S - I_2$ $S - I_1$

1. An increase in investment reduces the supply of domestic currency, ...

2. ... which raises the exchange rate ...

ε_2

ε_1

$NX(\varepsilon)$

NX_2 ← NX_1 Net exports, NX

3. ... and reduces net exports.

The Impact of an Increase in Investment Demand on the Real Exchange Rate An increase in investment demand raises the quantity of domestic investment from I_1 to I_2. As a result, the supply of domestic money to be exchanged into foreign currencies falls from $S - I_1$ to $S - I_2$. This fall in supply raises the equilibrium real exchange rate from ε_1 to ε_2.

makes investing in the domestic economy more attractive, it also increases the value of the domestic currency necessary to make these investments. When the domestic currency appreciates, domestic goods become more expensive relative to foreign goods, and net exports fall.

The Effects of Trade Policies

Now that we have a model that explains the trade balance and the real exchange rate, we have the tools to examine the macroeconomic effects of trade policies. Trade policies, broadly defined, are policies designed to influence directly the amount of goods and services exported or imported. Most often, trade policies take the form of protecting domestic industries from foreign competition — either by placing a tax on foreign imports (a tariff) or restricting the amount of goods and services that can be imported (a quota).

As an example of a protectionist trade policy, consider what would happen if the government prohibited the import of foreign cars. For any given real exchange rate, imports would now be lower, implying that net exports (exports minus imports) would be higher. Thus, the net-exports schedule shifts outward, as in Figure 6-13. To see the effects of the policy, we compare the old equilibrium and the new equilibrium. In the new equilibrium, the real exchange rate is higher, and net exports are unchanged. Despite the shift in the net-exports schedule, the equilibrium level of net exports remains the same, because the protectionist policy does not alter either saving or investment.

This analysis shows that protectionist trade policies do not affect the trade balance. This surprising conclusion is often overlooked in the popular debate over trade policies. Because a trade deficit reflects an excess of imports over exports, one might guess that reducing imports — such as by prohibiting the import of foreign cars — would reduce a trade deficit. Yet our model shows that protectionist

FIGURE 6-13

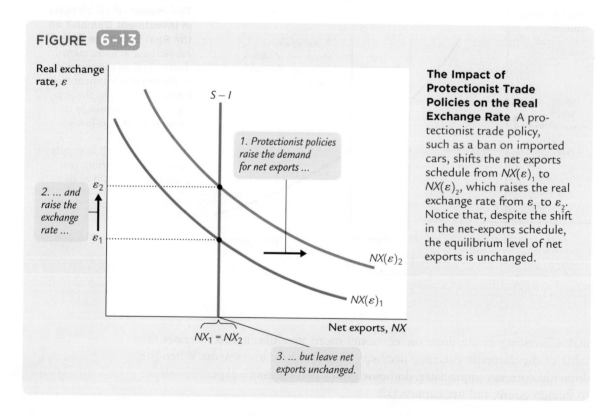

The Impact of Protectionist Trade Policies on the Real Exchange Rate A protectionist trade policy, such as a ban on imported cars, shifts the net exports schedule from $NX(\varepsilon)_1$ to $NX(\varepsilon)_2$, which raises the real exchange rate from ε_1 to ε_2. Notice that, despite the shift in the net-exports schedule, the equilibrium level of net exports is unchanged.

policies lead only to an appreciation of the real exchange rate. The increase in the price of domestic goods relative to foreign goods tends to lower net exports by stimulating imports and depressing exports. Thus, the appreciation offsets the increase in net exports that is directly attributable to the trade restriction.

Although protectionist trade policies do not alter the trade balance, they do affect the amount of trade. As we have seen, because the real exchange rate appreciates, the goods and services we produce become more expensive relative to foreign goods and services. We therefore export less in the new equilibrium. Because net exports are unchanged, we must import less as well. (The appreciation of the exchange rate does stimulate imports to some extent, but this only partly offsets the decrease in imports due to the trade restriction.) Thus, protectionist policies reduce both the quantity of imports and the quantity of exports.

This fall in the total amount of trade is the reason economists almost always oppose protectionist policies. International trade benefits all countries by allowing each country to specialize in what it produces best, and by providing each country with a greater variety of goods and services. Protectionist policies diminish these gains from trade. Although these policies benefit certain groups within society – for example, a ban on imported cars helps domestic car producers – society on average is worse off when policies reduce the amount of international trade.

The Determinants of the Nominal Exchange Rate

Having seen what determines the real exchange rate, we now turn our attention to the nominal exchange rate – the rate at which the currencies of two countries trade. Recall the relationship between the real and the nominal exchange rate:

Real Exchange Rate = Nominal Exchange Rate × Ratio of Price Levels

$$\varepsilon = e \times (P/P^*).$$

We can write the nominal exchange rate as

$$e = \varepsilon \times (P^*/P).$$

This equation shows that the nominal exchange rate depends on the real exchange rate and the price levels in the two countries. Given the value of the real exchange rate, if the domestic price level P rises, then the nominal exchange rate e will fall: because a euro is worth less, a euro will buy fewer yen. However, if the Japanese price level P^* rises, then the nominal exchange rate will increase: because the yen is worth less, a euro will buy more yen.

It is instructive to consider changes in exchange rates over time. The exchange rate equation can be written

% Change in e = % Change in ε + % Change in P^* − % Change in P.

The percentage change in ε is the change in the real exchange rate. The percentage change in P is the domestic inflation rate π, and the percentage change in P^* is the foreign country's inflation rate π^*. Thus, the percentage change in the nominal exchange rate is

$$\text{\% Change in } e = \text{\% Change in } \varepsilon + (\pi^* - \pi)$$

$$\frac{\text{Percentage Change in}}{\text{Nominal Exchange Rate}} = \frac{\text{Percentage Change in}}{\text{Real Exchange Rate}} + \frac{\text{Difference in}}{\text{Inflation Rates.}}$$

This equation states that the percentage change in the nominal exchange rate between the currencies of two countries equals the percentage change in the real exchange rate plus the difference in their inflation rates. *If a foreign country has a high rate of inflation relative to the domestic country, the domestic currency will buy an increasing amount of the foreign currency over time. If a foreign country has a low rate of inflation relative to the domestic country, the domestic currency will buy a decreasing amount of the foreign currency over time.*

This analysis shows how monetary policy affects the nominal exchange rate. We know from Chapter 5 that high growth in the money supply leads to high inflation. Here, we have just seen that one consequence of high inflation is a depreciating currency: high π implies falling e. In other words, just as growth in the amount of money raises the price of goods measured in terms of money, it also tends to raise the price of foreign currencies measured in terms of the domestic currency.

CASE STUDY

Inflation and Nominal Exchange Rates

If we look at data on exchange rates and price levels of different countries, we quickly see the importance of inflation for explaining changes in the nominal exchange rate. The most dramatic examples come from periods of very high inflation. For example, the price level in Mexico rose by 2300 per cent between 1983 and 1988. Because of this inflation, the number of pesos a person could buy with a US dollar rose from 144 in 1983 to 2281 in 1988.

The same relationship holds true for countries with more moderate inflation. Figure 6-14 is a scatterplot showing the relationship between inflation and the exchange rate for 15 countries. On the horizontal axis is the difference between each country's average inflation rate and the average inflation rate of the United States, over the period 1980–2011. On the vertical axis is the average percentage change in the exchange rate between each country's currency and the US dollar. The positive relationship between these two variables is clear in this figure. Countries with relatively high inflation tend to have depreciating currencies, and countries with relatively low inflation tend to have appreciating currencies.

As an example, consider the exchange rate between Swiss francs and US dollars. Both Switzerland and the United States have experienced inflation over the past 20 years, so both the Swiss franc and the dollar buy fewer goods than they once did. But, as Figure 6-14 shows, inflation in Switzerland has been lower than inflation in the United States. This means that the value of the Swiss franc

FIGURE 6-14

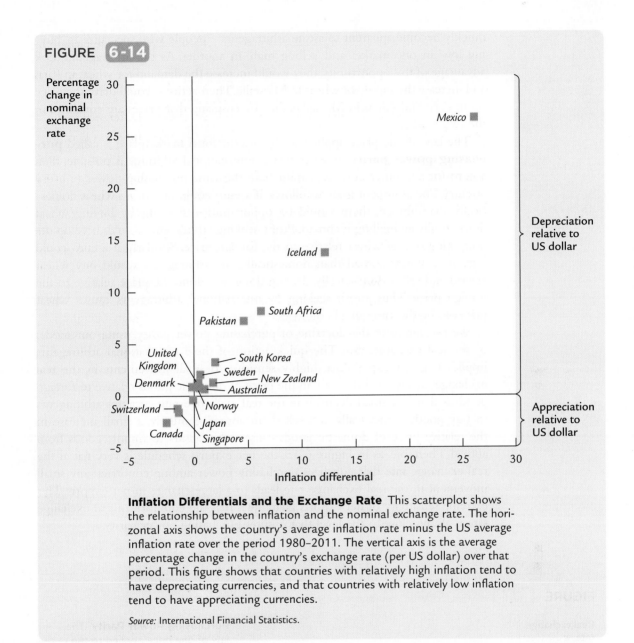

Inflation Differentials and the Exchange Rate This scatterplot shows the relationship between inflation and the nominal exchange rate. The horizontal axis shows the country's average inflation rate minus the US average inflation rate over the period 1980–2011. The vertical axis is the average percentage change in the country's exchange rate (per US dollar) over that period. This figure shows that countries with relatively high inflation tend to have depreciating currencies, and that countries with relatively low inflation tend to have appreciating currencies.

Source: International Financial Statistics.

has fallen less than the value of the dollar. Therefore, the number of Swiss francs exchanging for a US dollar has been falling over time. ■

The Special Case of Purchasing Power Parity

A famous hypothesis in economics, called the *law of one price,* states that the same good cannot sell for different prices in different locations at the same time. If a tonne of wheat sold for less in Paris than in Marseille, it would be profitable to buy wheat in Paris and then sell it in Marseille. This profit opportunity would quickly become apparent to astute arbitrageurs – people who specialize in 'buying low' in one market and 'selling high' in another. As the arbitrageurs took advantage of this opportunity, they would increase the demand for wheat in Paris and increase the supply of wheat in Marseille. Their actions would drive the price up in Paris and down in Marseille, thereby ensuring that prices are equalized in the two markets.

The law of one price applied to the international marketplace is called **purchasing power parity**. It states that if international arbitrage is possible, then a euro (or any other currency) must have the same purchasing power in every country. The argument goes as follows. If a euro could buy more wheat domestically than abroad, there would be opportunities to profit by buying wheat domestically and selling it abroad. Profit-seeking arbitrageurs would drive up the domestic price of wheat relative to the foreign price. Similarly, if a euro could buy more wheat abroad than domestically, the arbitrageurs would buy wheat abroad and sell it domestically, driving down the domestic price relative to the foreign price. Thus, profit seeking by international arbitrageurs causes wheat prices to be the same in all countries.

We can interpret the doctrine of purchasing power parity using our model of the real exchange rate. The quick action of these international arbitrageurs implies that net exports are highly sensitive to small movements in the real exchange rate. A small decrease in the price of domestic goods relative to foreign goods – that is, a small decrease in the real exchange rate – causes arbitrageurs to buy goods domestically and sell them abroad. Similarly, a small increase in the relative price of domestic goods causes arbitrageurs to import goods from abroad. Therefore, as in Figure 6-15, the net-exports schedule is very flat at the real exchange rate that equalizes purchasing power among countries: any small movement in the real exchange rate leads to a large change in net exports. This extreme sensitivity of net exports guarantees that the equilibrium real exchange rate is always close to the level that ensures purchasing power parity.

FIGURE 6-15

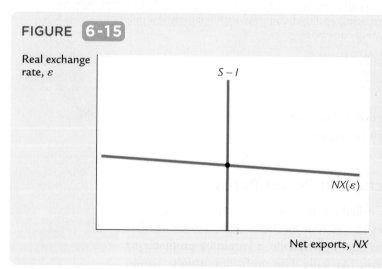

Real exchange rate, ε

$S - I$

$NX(\varepsilon)$

Net exports, NX

Purchasing Power Parity The law of one price applied to the international marketplace suggests that net exports are highly sensitive to small movements in the real exchange rate. This high sensitivity is reflected here with a very flat net-exports schedule.

Purchasing power parity has two important implications. First, because the net-exports schedule is flat, changes in saving or investment do not influence the real or nominal exchange rate. Second, because the real exchange rate is fixed, all changes in the nominal exchange rate result from changes in price levels.

Is this doctrine of purchasing power parity realistic? Most economists believe that, despite its appealing logic, purchasing power parity does not provide a completely accurate description of the world. First, many goods are not easily traded. A haircut can be more expensive in Tokyo than in London, yet there is no room for international arbitrage because it is impossible to transport haircuts. Second, even tradable goods are not always perfect substitutes. Some consumers prefer Toyotas, and others prefer Mercedes. Thus, the relative price of Toyotas and Mercedes can vary to some extent without leaving any profit opportunities. For these reasons, real exchange rates do in fact vary over time.

Although the doctrine of purchasing power parity does not describe the world perfectly, it does provide a reason why movement in the real exchange rate will be limited. There is much validity to its underlying logic: the further the real exchange rate drifts from the level predicted by purchasing power parity, the greater the incentive for individuals to engage in international arbitrage in goods. Although we cannot rely on purchasing power parity to eliminate all changes in the real exchange rate, this doctrine does provide a reason to expect that fluctuations in the real exchange rate will typically be small or temporary.[7]

CASE STUDY

Big Mac PPP

The general idea behind purchasing power parity (PPP) is that a unit of currency should be able to buy the same basket of goods in one country as the equivalent amount of foreign currency, at the going exchange rate, can buy in a foreign country, so that there is parity in the purchasing power of the unit of currency across the two economies. One very simple way of gauging whether there may be discrepancies from PPP is to compare the prices of similar or identical goods from the basket in the two countries. For example, *The Economist* newspaper publishes the prices of McDonald's Big Mac hamburgers around the world and compares them in a common currency, the US dollar, at the market exchange rate, as a means of gauging whether that exchange rate overvalues or undervalues a currency relative to the dollar (the supposition being that the currency would be valued just right if the dollar price of the burger were the same as in the US). Table 6-3 presents the prices in January 2013, when a Big Mac sold on average for $4.37 in the United States. For example, at the going exchange rate, a Big

---

[7] To learn more about purchasing power parity, see Alan M. Taylor and Mark P. Taylor, 'The Purchasing Power Parity Debate', *Journal of Economic Perspectives*, 2004, vol. 18, pp. 135–158.

TABLE 6-3

International Prices of a Big Mac Hamburger

Country	Dollar Price of a Big Mac	% Overvaluation (+) or Undervaluation (−)
Denmark	$5.18	+18.69
Sweden	$7.62	+74.54
Euro Area	$4.88	+11.69
United Kingdom	$4.25	−2.73
New Zealand	$4.32	−0.98
Turkey	$4.78	+9.39
Mexico	$2.90	−33.49
South Korea	$3.41	−21.95
Australia	$4.90	+12.21
South Africa	$2.03	−53.61
Japan	$3.51	−19.54
Poland	$2.94	−32.61
China	$2.57	−41.10

Source: © The Economist Newspaper Limited, London, July 26, 2012.
Note: Prices and exchange rates as at 7 January 2013.
Dollar prices are computed as the local currency price converted to dollars at the market dollar exchange rate.

Mac cost the peso equivalent of $2.90 in Mexico City. But if 'Big Mac PPP' held, the price in Mexico City should have been the peso equivalent of the US price of $4.37. Hence, according to the Big Mac PPP standard, the Mexican peso was undervalued by about 33.49 per cent. According to the Big Mac index, therefore, given that China was the home of the cheapest burger, this implied that the Chinese yuan was 41.1 per cent undervalued. On the other hand, the average price of a Big Mac in the Euro Area countries was $4.88, suggesting that the euro was 11.69 per cent overvalued against the dollar. In contrast, the Japanese yen was 19.54 per cent undervalued by the Big Mac PPP standard.

While the Big Mac index is an immediately engaging and fun way to think about exchange rates, it is easy to come up with good reasons why the prices of burgers might differ internationally – most of which are related to the fact that many of the inputs into a Big Mac cannot be traded internationally, or not easily at least: each contains a high service component – the wages of the person serving the food and drink – and a high property rental component – the cost of providing you with somewhere to sit and munch your two beef patties on a sesame seed bun with secret-recipe sauce. Neither the service-sector labour nor the property (nor the sauce) is easily arbitraged internationally, and advocates of PPP have tended to base their view largely on arguments relating to international goods arbitrage. Thus, while these indices may give a light-hearted and suggestive idea of the relative value of currencies, they should be treated with caution. ■

6-4 Conclusion: Exchange Rates, the Trade Balance and Capital Flows

In this chapter we have seen how a small open economy works. We have examined the determinants of the international flow of funds for capital accumulation and the international flow of goods and services. We have also examined the determinants of a country's real and nominal exchange rates. Our analysis shows how various policies – monetary policies, fiscal policies and trade policies – affect the trade balance, capital flows and the exchange rate.

The key assumption of our small open economy model is that the economy under examination is too small to influence world interest rates and that it possesses its own national currency that trades for other currencies at the market exchange rate. This model is a reasonable approximation to European economies that have retained their national currencies, such as Sweden, Denmark, Switzerland and the United Kingdom. It is less directly applicable to the 17 European countries that have adopted the euro as their currency, because these countries effectively have fixed exchange rates with one another. Moreover, we cannot simply treat the whole Euro Area as one 'large open economy', as we may be tempted to do with the US, for example, because, for one thing, the Euro Area countries do not have a common fiscal policy and so cannot be treated as the same economy when analysing macroeconomic policy. We therefore need to develop a theory relating specifically to the case where a group of countries have formed a so-called monetary union and adopted a common currency. We shall postpone this for later in the book (to Chapter 17), because we need to develop quite a lot of macroeconomic tools in order to do such a theory justice. Nevertheless, the model developed in this chapter gets us quite a long way towards understanding the economics of the open economy, and it gives us a foundation upon which to build.

Summary

1. Net exports are the difference between exports and imports. They are equal to the difference between what we produce and what we demand for consumption, investment and government purchases.

2. The net capital outflow is the excess of domestic saving over domestic investment. The trade balance is the amount received for our net exports of goods and services. The national income accounts identity shows that the net capital outflow always equals the trade balance.

3. The impact of any policy on the trade balance can be determined by examining its impact on saving and investment. Policies that raise saving or lower investment lead to a trade surplus, and policies that lower saving or raise investment lead to a trade deficit.

4. The nominal exchange rate is the rate at which people trade the currency of one country for the currency of another country. The real exchange rate is the rate at which people trade the goods produced by the two countries. The real exchange rate equals the nominal exchange rate multiplied by the ratio of the price levels in the two countries.

5. Because the real exchange rate is the price of domestic goods relative to foreign goods, an appreciation of the real exchange rate tends to reduce net exports. The equilibrium real exchange rate is the rate at which the quantity of net exports demanded equals the net capital outflow.

6. The nominal exchange rate is determined by the real exchange rate and the price levels in the two countries. Other things being equal, a high rate of inflation leads to a depreciating currency.

KEY CONCEPTS

Net exports

Trade balance

Net capital outflow

Trade surplus and trade deficit

Balanced trade

Small open economy

World interest rate

Nominal exchange rate

Real exchange rate

Purchasing power parity

QUESTIONS FOR REVIEW

1. What are the net capital outflow and the trade balance? Explain how they are related.

2. Define the nominal exchange rate and the real exchange rate.

3. If a small open economy cuts defence spending, what happens to saving, investment, the trade balance, the interest rate and the exchange rate?

4. If a small open economy bans the import of Japanese DVD players, what happens to saving, investment, the trade balance, the interest rate and the exchange rate?

5. If Europe has low inflation and Mexico has high inflation, what will happen to the exchange rate between the euro and the Mexican peso?

PROBLEMS AND APPLICATIONS

1. Use the model of the small open economy to predict what would happen to the trade balance, the real exchange rate and the nominal exchange rate in response to each of the following events.

   a. A fall in consumer confidence about the future induces consumers to spend less and save more.

   b. The introduction of a stylish line of Toyotas makes some consumers prefer foreign cars over domestic cars.

   c. The introduction of cashpoint machines (ATMs) reduces the demand for money.

2. Consider an economy described by the following equations:

$$Y = C + I + G + NX$$
$$Y = 5000$$
$$G = 1000$$
$$T = 1000$$

$C = 250 + 0.75(Y - T),$

$I = 1000 - 50r,$

$NX = 500 - 500\varepsilon$

$r = r^* = 5.$

a. In this economy, solve for national saving, investment, the trade balance and the equilibrium exchange rate.

b. Suppose now that G rises to 1250. Solve for national saving, investment, the trade balance and the equilibrium exchange rate. Explain what you find.

c. Now suppose that the world interest rate rises from 5 to 10 per cent. (G is again 1000.) Solve for national saving, investment, the trade balance and the equilibrium exchange rate. Explain what you find.

3. The country of Labassecour is a small open economy. Suddenly, a change in world fashions makes the exports of Labassecour unpopular.

a. What happens in Labassecour to saving, investment, net exports, the interest rate and the exchange rate?

b. The citizens of Labassecour like to travel abroad. How will this change in the exchange rate affect them?

c. The fiscal policy makers of Labassecour want to adjust taxes to maintain the exchange rate at its previous level. What should they do? If they do this, what are the overall effects on saving, investment, net exports and the interest rate?

4. In 2005, US Federal Reserve Governor Ben Bernanke said in a speech:

Over the past decade a combination of diverse forces has created a significant increase in the global supply of saving – a global saving glut – which helps to explain both the increase in the US current account deficit [a broad measure of the trade deficit] and the relatively low level of long-term real interest rates in the world today.

Is this statement consistent with the models you have learned? Explain.

5. What will happen to the trade balance and the real exchange rate of a small open economy when government purchases increase, such as during a war? Does your answer depend on whether this is a local war or a world war?

6. A case study in this chapter concludes that if poor nations offered better production efficiency and legal protections, the trade balance in rich nations such as the United States would move towards surplus. Let's consider why this might be the case.

a. If the world's poor nations offer better production efficiency and legal protection, what would happen to the investment demand function in those countries?

b. How would the change you describe in part (a) affect the demand for loanable funds in world financial markets?

c. How would the change you describe in part (b) affect the world interest rate?

d. How would the change in the world interest rate you describe in part (c) affect the trade balance in rich nations?

7. Suppose the government is considering placing a tariff on the import of Japanese luxury cars. Discuss the economics and politics of such a policy. In particular, how would the policy affect the country's trade deficit? How would it affect the exchange rate? Who would be hurt by such a policy? Who would benefit?

8. Suppose that some foreign countries begin to subsidize investment by instituting investment tax relief.

a. What happens to world investment demand as a function of the world interest rate?

b. What happens to the world interest rate?

c. What happens to investment in our small open economy?

d. What happens to our trade balance?

e. What happens to our real exchange rate?

9. Suppose a friend tells you that travelling in Mexico is much cheaper now than it was five years ago. 'Five years ago,' says your friend, 'a UK pound bought 11 pesos; this year, a pound buys 22 pesos.' Is your friend right or wrong? Given that total inflation over this period was about 25 per cent in the United Kingdom and 100 per cent in Mexico, has it become more or less expensive for UK residents to travel in Mexico? Write your answer using a concrete example – such as the price of a British pork pie versus the price of a Mexican taco – that will convince your friend.

10. You read in a newspaper that the nominal interest rate is 12 per cent per year in Sweden and 8 per cent per year in the United Kingdom. Suppose that the real interest rates are equalized in the two countries and that purchasing power parity holds.

a. Using the Fisher equation (discussed in Chapter 4), what can you infer about expected inflation in Sweden and in the United Kingdom?

b. What can you infer about the expected change in the exchange rate between the Swedish krona and the UK pound?

c. A friend proposes a get-rich-quick scheme: borrow from a UK bank at 8 per cent, deposit the money in a Swedish bank at 12 per cent, and make a 4 per cent profit. What's wrong with this scheme?

The Large Open Economy

When analysing policy for a large country such as the United States, or a large group of countries with a common currency such as the Euro Area (Euro-zone), we need to combine the closed economy logic of Chapter 3 and the small-open-economy logic of this chapter. This appendix presents a model of an economy between these two extremes, called the *large open economy*.

Net Capital Outflow

The key difference between the small and large open economies is the behaviour of the net capital outflow. In the model of the small open economy, capital flows freely into or out of the economy at a fixed world interest rate r^*. The model of the large open economy makes a different assumption about international capital flows. To understand this assumption, keep in mind that the net capital outflow is the amount that domestic investors lend abroad minus the amount that foreign investors lend here.

Imagine that you are a European investor deciding where to invest your funds. You could invest domestically (for example, by making loans to Euro Area companies), or you could invest abroad (by making loans to foreign companies). Many factors may affect your decision, but surely one of them is the interest rate you can earn. The higher the interest rate you can earn domestically, the less attractive you would find foreign investment.

Investors abroad face a similar decision. They have a choice between investing in their home country and lending to someone in the Euro Area. The higher the interest rate in the Euro Area, the more willing foreigners are to lend to Euro Area companies and to buy Euro Area assets.

Thus, because of the behaviour of both domestic and foreign investors, the net flow of capital to other countries, which we'll denote as CF, is negatively related to the domestic real interest rate r. As the interest rate rises, less of our saving flows abroad, and more funds for capital accumulation flow in from other countries. We write this as

$$CF = CF(r).$$

This equation states that the net capital outflow is a function of the domestic interest rate. Figure 6-16 illustrates this relationship. Notice that CF can be either positive or negative, depending on whether the economy is a lender or borrower in world financial markets.

To see how this CF function relates to our previous models, consider Figure 6-17. This figure shows two special cases: a vertical CF function and a horizontal CF function.

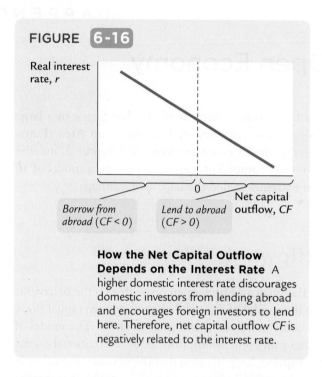

FIGURE 6-16

How the Net Capital Outflow Depends on the Interest Rate A higher domestic interest rate discourages domestic investors from lending abroad and encourages foreign investors to lend here. Therefore, net capital outflow CF is negatively related to the interest rate.

The closed economy is the special case shown in panel (a) of Figure 6-17. In the closed economy, there is no international borrowing or lending, and the interest rate adjusts to equilibrate domestic saving and investment. This means that $CF = 0$ at all interest rates. This situation would arise if investors here and abroad were unwilling to hold foreign assets, regardless of the return. It might also arise if the government prohibited its citizens from transacting in foreign financial markets, as some governments do.

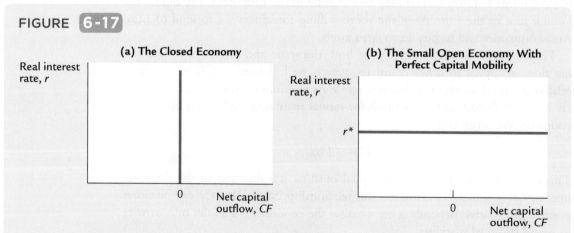

FIGURE 6-17

Two Special Cases In the closed economy, shown in panel (a), the net capital outflow is zero for all interest rates. In the small open economy with perfect capital mobility, shown in panel (b), the net capital outflow is perfectly elastic at the world interest rate r^*.

The small open economy with perfect capital mobility is the special case shown in panel (b) of Figure 6-17. In this case, capital flows freely into and out of the country at the fixed world interest rate r^*. This situation would arise if investors here and abroad bought whatever asset yielded the highest return and if this economy were too small to affect the world interest rate. The economy's interest rate would be fixed at the interest rate prevailing in world financial markets.

Why isn't the interest rate of a large open economy such as the Euro Area fixed by the world interest rate? There are two reasons. The first is that the Euro Area is large enough to influence world financial markets. The more the Euro Area lends abroad, the greater is the supply of loans in the world economy, and the lower interest rates become around the world. The more the Euro Area borrows from abroad (that is, the more negative CF becomes), the higher are world interest rates. We use the label 'large open economy' because this model applies to an economy large enough to affect world interest rates.

There is, however, a second reason the interest rate in an economy may not be fixed by the world interest rate: capital may not be perfectly mobile. That is, investors here and abroad may prefer to hold their wealth in domestic rather than foreign assets. Such a preference for domestic assets could arise because of imperfect information about foreign assets or because of government impediments to international borrowing and lending. In either case, funds for capital accumulation will not flow freely to equalize interest rates in all countries. Instead, the net capital outflow will depend on domestic interest rates relative to foreign interest rates. Euro Area investors will lend abroad only if Euro Area interest rates are comparatively low, and foreign investors will lend in the Euro Area only if Euro Area interest rates are comparatively high. The large-open-economy model, therefore, may apply even to a small economy if capital does not flow freely into and out of the economy.

Hence, either because the large open economy affects world interest rates, or because capital is imperfectly mobile, or perhaps for both reasons, the CF function slopes downward. Except for this new downward-sloping CF function, the model of the large open economy resembles the model of the small open economy. We put all the pieces together in the next section.

The Model

To understand how the large open economy works, we need to consider two key markets: the market for loanable funds (where the interest rate is determined) and the market for foreign exchange (where the exchange rate is determined). The interest rate and the exchange rate are two prices that guide the allocation of resources.

The Market for Loanable Funds An open economy's saving S is used in two ways: to finance domestic investment I and to finance the net capital outflow CF. We can write

$$S = I + CF.$$

Consider how these three variables are determined. National saving is fixed by the level of output, fiscal policy, and the consumption function. Invest-

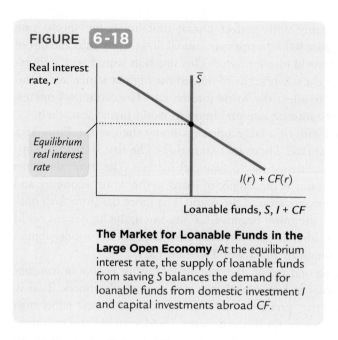

FIGURE 6-18

Real interest rate, r

$\overline{S}$

Equilibrium real interest rate

$I(r) + CF(r)$

Loanable funds, $S, I + CF$

The Market for Loanable Funds in the Large Open Economy At the equilibrium interest rate, the supply of loanable funds from saving S balances the demand for loanable funds from domestic investment I and capital investments abroad CF.

ment and net capital outflow both depend on the domestic real interest rate. We can write

$$S = I(r) + CF(r).$$

Figure 6-18 shows the market for loanable funds. The supply of loanable funds is national saving. The demand for loanable funds is the sum of the demand for domestic investment and the demand for foreign investment (net capital outflow). The interest rate adjusts to equilibrate supply and demand.

The Market for Foreign Exchange Next, consider the relationship between the net capital outflow and the trade balance. The national income accounts identity tells us

$$NX = S - I.$$

Because NX is a function of the real exchange rate, and because $CF = S - I$, we can write

$$NX(\varepsilon) = CF.$$

Figure 6-19 shows the equilibrium in the market for foreign exchange. Once again, the real exchange rate is the price that equilibrates the trade balance and the net capital outflow.

The last variable we should consider is the nominal exchange rate. As before, the nominal exchange rate is the real exchange rate times the ratio of the price levels:

$$e = \varepsilon \times (P^*/P).$$

The real exchange rate is determined as in Figure 6-19, and the price levels are determined by monetary policies here and abroad, as we discussed in Chapter 5. Forces that move the real exchange rate or the price levels also move the nominal exchange rate.

FIGURE 6-19

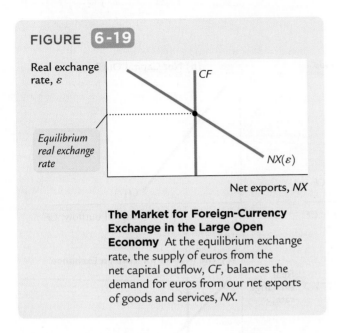

Real exchange rate, ε

CF

Equilibrium real exchange rate

$NX(\varepsilon)$

Net exports, NX

The Market for Foreign-Currency Exchange in the Large Open Economy At the equilibrium exchange rate, the supply of euros from the net capital outflow, CF, balances the demand for euros from our net exports of goods and services, NX.

Policies in the Large Open Economy

We can now consider how economic policies influence the large open economy. Figure 6-20 shows the three diagrams we need for the analysis. Panel (a) shows the equilibrium in the market for loanable funds; panel (b) shows the relationship between the equilibrium interest rate and the net capital outflow; and panel (c) shows the equilibrium in the market for foreign exchange.

Fiscal Policy at Home Consider the effects of expansionary fiscal policy — an increase in government purchases or a decrease in taxes. Figure 6-21 shows what happens. The policy reduces national saving S, thereby reducing the supply of loanable funds and raising the equilibrium interest rate r. The higher interest rate reduces both domestic investment I and the net capital outflow CF. The fall in the net capital outflow reduces the supply of euros to be exchanged into foreign currency. The exchange rate appreciates, and net exports fall.

Note that the impact of fiscal policy in this model combines its impact in the closed economy and its impact in the small open economy. As in the closed economy, a fiscal expansion in a large open economy raises the interest rate and crowds out investment. As in the small open economy, a fiscal expansion causes a trade deficit and an appreciation in the exchange rate.

One way to see how the three types of economy are related is to consider the identity

$$S = I + NX.$$

In all three cases, expansionary fiscal policy reduces national saving S. In the closed economy, the fall in S coincides with an equal fall in I, and NX stays constant at zero. In the small open economy, the fall in S coincides with an equal fall in NX, and I remains constant at the level fixed by the world interest rate.

FIGURE 6-20

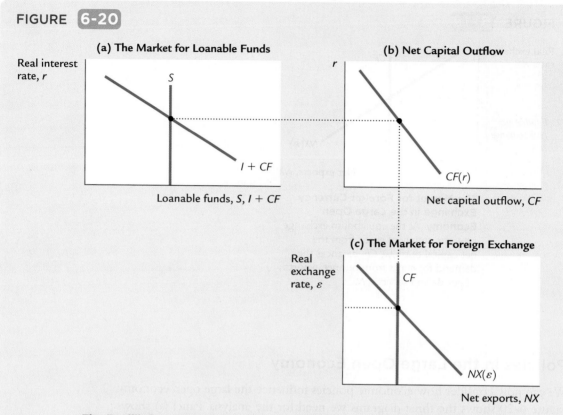

The Equilibrium in the Large Open Economy Panel (a) shows that the market for loanable funds determines the equilibrium interest rate. Panel (b) shows that the interest rate determines the net capital outflow, which in turn determines the supply of euros to be exchanged into foreign currency. Panel (c) shows that the real exchange rate adjusts to balance this supply of euros with the demand coming from net exports.

The large open economy is the intermediate case: both I and NX fall, each by less than the fall in S.

Shifts in Investment Demand Suppose that the investment demand schedule shifts outward, perhaps due to the intoduction of an investment tax credit. Figure 6-22 shows the effect. The demand for loanable funds rises, raising the equilibrium interest rate. The higher interest rate reduces the net capital outflow: domestic residents make fewer loans abroad, and foreigners make more loans to the Euro Area. The fall in the net capital outflow reduces the supply of euros in the market for foreign exchange. The exchange rate appreciates, and net exports fall.

Trade Policies Figure 6-23 shows the effect of a trade restriction, such as an import quota. The reduced demand for imports shifts the net exports schedule outward in panel (c). Because nothing has changed in the market for loanable funds, the interest rate remains the same, which in turn implies

FIGURE 6-21

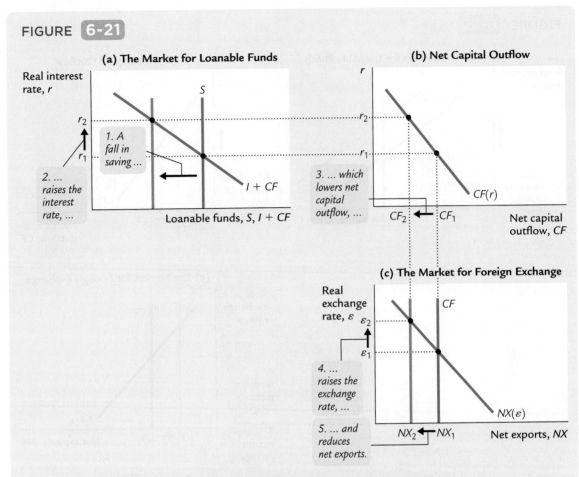

A Reduction in National Saving in the Large Open Economy Panel (a) shows that a reduction in national saving lowers the supply of loanable funds. The equilibrium interest rate rises. Panel (b) shows that the higher interest rate lowers the net capital outflow. Panel (c) shows that the reduced capital outflow means a reduced supply of euros in the market for foreign-currency exchange. The reduced supply of euros causes the real exchange rate to appreciate and net exports to fall.

that the net capital outflow remains the same. The shift in the net-exports schedule causes the exchange rate to appreciate. The rise in the exchange rate makes Euro Area goods expensive relative to foreign goods, which depresses exports and stimulates imports. In the end, the trade restriction does not affect the trade balance.

Shifts in Net Capital Outflow There are various reasons that the CF schedule might shift. One reason is fiscal policy abroad. For example, suppose that UK pursues a fiscal policy that raises UK saving. This policy reduces the UK interest rate. The lower UK interest rate discourages Euro Area investors from lending in the UK and encourages British investors to lend in the Euro Area. For any given Euro Area interest rate, the Euro Area net capital outflow falls.

FIGURE 6-22

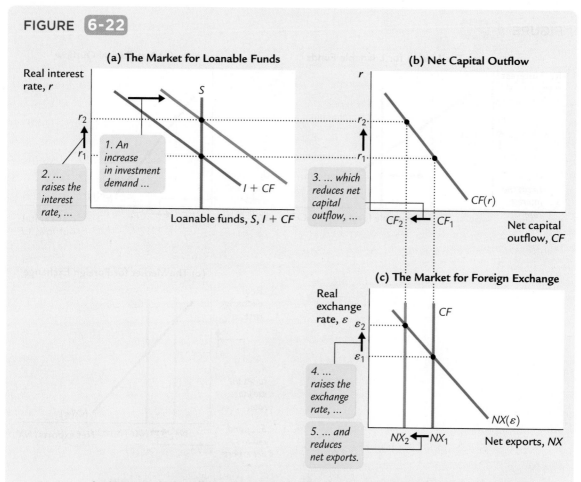

An Increase in Investment Demand in the Large Open Economy Panel (a) shows that an increase in investment demand raises the interest rate. Panel (b) shows that the higher interest rate lowers the net capital outflow. Panel (c) shows that a lower capital outflow causes the real exchange rate to appreciate and net exports to fall.

Another reason the *CF* schedule might shift is political instability abroad. Suppose that a war or revolution breaks out in another country. Investors around the world will try to withdraw their assets from that country and seek a 'safe haven' in a stable area such as the Euro Area. The result is a reduction in the Euro Area net capital outflow.

Figure 6-24 shows the impact of a leftward shift in the *CF* schedule. The reduced demand for loanable funds lowers the equilibrium interest rate. The lower interest rate tends to raise net capital outflow, but because this only partly mitigates the shift in the *CF* schedule, *CF* still falls. The reduced level of net capital outflow reduces the supply of euros in the market for foreign exchange. The exchange rate appreciates, and net exports fall.

FIGURE 6-23

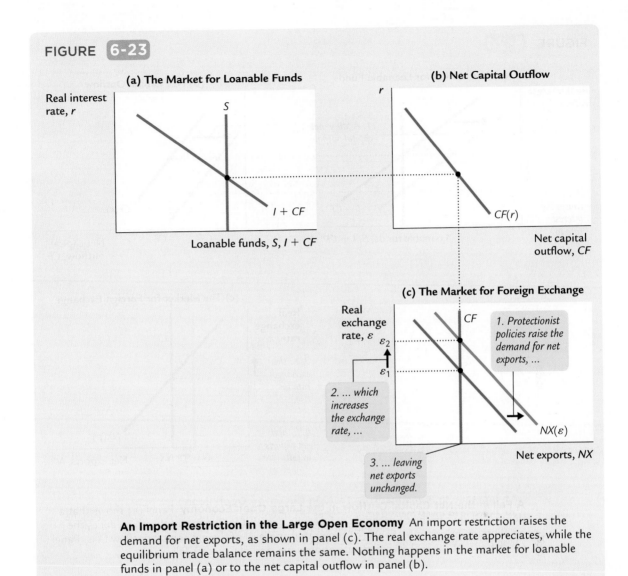

(a) The Market for Loanable Funds

Real interest rate, r

S

$I + CF$

Loanable funds, $S, I + CF$

(b) Net Capital Outflow

r

$CF(r)$

Net capital outflow, CF

(c) The Market for Foreign Exchange

Real exchange rate, ε

ε_2

ε_1

CF

$NX(\varepsilon)$

Net exports, NX

1. Protectionist policies raise the demand for net exports, ...

2. ... which increases the exchange rate, ...

3. ... leaving net exports unchanged.

An Import Restriction in the Large Open Economy An import restriction raises the demand for net exports, as shown in panel (c). The real exchange rate appreciates, while the equilibrium trade balance remains the same. Nothing happens in the market for loanable funds in panel (a) or to the net capital outflow in panel (b).

Conclusion

How different are large and small open economies? Certainly, policies affect the interest rate in a large open economy, unlike in a small open economy. But, in other ways, the two models yield similar conclusions. In both large and small open economies, policies that raise saving or lower investment lead to trade surpluses. Similarly, policies that lower saving or raise investment lead to trade deficits. In both economies, protectionist trade policies cause the exchange rate to appreciate and do not influence the trade balance. Because the results are so similar, for most questions one can use the simpler model of the small open economy, even if the economy being examined is not really small.

FIGURE 6-24

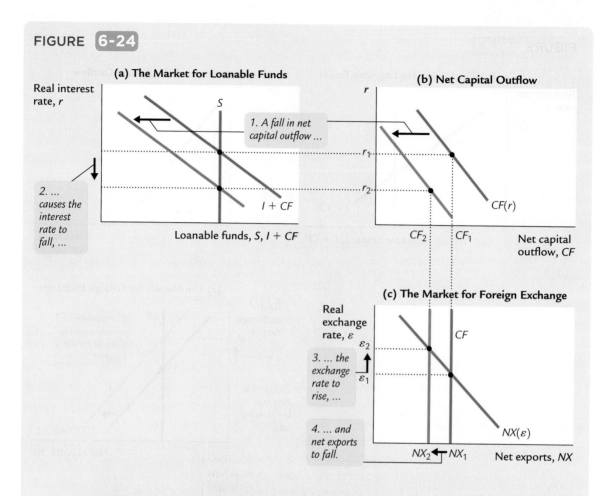

(a) The Market for Loanable Funds

Real interest rate, r

S

1. A fall in net capital outflow ...

$I + CF$

r_1

r_2

2. ... causes the interest rate to fall, ...

Loanable funds, S, $I + CF$

(b) Net Capital Outflow

r

r_1

r_2

$CF(r)$

CF_2 CF_1

Net capital outflow, CF

(c) The Market for Foreign Exchange

Real exchange rate, ε

ε_2

CF

3. ... the exchange rate to rise, ...

ε_1

4. ... and net exports to fall.

$NX(\varepsilon)$

NX_2 NX_1

Net exports, NX

A Fall in the Net Capital Outflow in the Large Open Economy Panel (a) shows that a downward shift in the CF schedule reduces the demand for loans and thereby reduces the equilibrium interest rate. Panel (b) shows that the level of the net capital outflow falls. Panel (c) shows that the real exchange rate appreciates and net exports fall.

CHAPTER 7

Unemployment

A man willing to work, and unable to find work, is perhaps the saddest sight that fortune's inequality exhibits under the sun.

— *Thomas Carlyle,* Chartism

Unemployment is the macroeconomic problem that affects people most directly and severely. For most people, the loss of a job means a reduced living standard and psychological distress. It is no surprise that unemployment is a frequent topic of political debate and that politicians often claim that their proposed policies would help create jobs.

Economists study unemployment to identify its causes and to help improve the public policies that affect the unemployed. Some of these policies, such as job training programmes, help people to find employment. Others, such as unemployment benefit, alleviate some of the hardships that the unemployed face. Further policies affect the prevalence of unemployment inadvertently. Laws mandating a high minimum wage, for instance, are widely thought to raise unemployment among the least skilled and experienced members of the labour force.

Our discussions of the labour market so far have ignored unemployment. In particular, the model of national income in Chapter 3 was built with the assumption that the economy was always at full employment. In reality, of course, not everyone in the labour force has a job all the time: all free-market economies experience some unemployment.

Figure 7-1 shows the rate of unemployment — the percentage of the labour force unemployed — in France, Germany, Italy and the United Kingdom from 1960 to 2011. This graph makes clear that, although the rate of unemployment fluctuates from year to year, it is always greater than zero.

In this chapter we begin our study of unemployment by discussing why there is always some unemployment and what determines its level. We do not study what determines the year-to-year fluctuations in the rate of unemployment until Part Four of this book, which examines short-run economic fluctuations. Here we examine the determinants of the **natural rate of unemployment** — the average rate of unemployment around which the economy fluctuates. The natural rate is the rate of unemployment towards which the economy gravitates in the long run, given all the labour-market imperfections that impede workers from instantly finding jobs. In the economies of the UK and other European countries, there is some evidence that this equilibrium rate may itself have shifted

FIGURE **7-1**

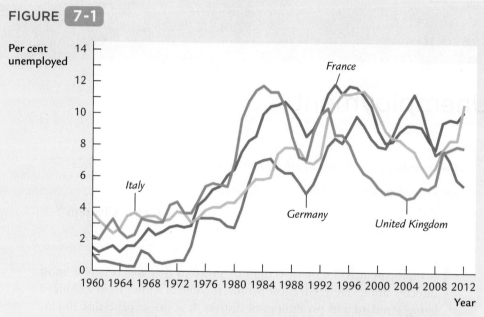

Unemployment in Four European Countries 1960–2012 This figure shows the unemployment rate in the four largest nations in Europe. The figure shows that the unemployment rate in France, Germany and Italy has risen substantially over time, and has, in recent years, fallen less in those three countries than it has in the United Kingdom. Since the onset of the Euro Area crisis in 2008 the trends have changed, with the unemployment rate in the UK rising to the levels of Continental Europe. Interestingly, in the last two years of these figures Germany has diverged away from the other three European countries with unemployment figures there declining to just below 6 per cent.

Source: Eurostat.

over time, due to structural changes in the economy. In Figure 7-1, for example, we can see that there are substantial swings in the unemployment rate that persist for several years at a time. This is an issue to which we shall return.

7-1 Job Loss, Job Finding and the Natural Rate of Unemployment

Every day some workers lose or leave their jobs, and some unemployed workers are hired. This perpetual ebb and flow determines the fraction of the labour force that is unemployed. In this section, we develop a model of labour-force dynamics that shows what determines the natural rate of unemployment.[1]

---

[1] Robert E. Hall, 'A Theory of the Natural Rate of Unemployment and the Duration of Unemployment', *Journal of Monetary Economics*, 1979, vol. 5, pp. 153–169.

We start with some notation. Let L denote the labour force, E the number of employed workers, and U the number of unemployed workers. Because every worker is either employed or unemployed, the labour force is the sum of the employed and the unemployed:

$$L = E + U.$$

In this notation, the rate of unemployment is U/L.

To see what factors determine the unemployment rate, we assume that the labour force L is fixed, and focus on the transition of individuals in the labour force between employment E and unemployment U. This is illustrated in Figure 7-2. Let s denote the *rate of job separation*, the fraction of employed individuals who lose their job each month. Let f denote the *rate of job finding*, the fraction of unemployed individuals who find a job each month. Together, the rate of job separation s and the rate of job finding f determine the rate of unemployment.

If the unemployment rate is neither rising nor falling — that is, if the labour market is in a steady state — then the number of people finding jobs must equal the number of people losing jobs. The number of people finding jobs is fU and the number of people losing jobs is sE, so we can write the steady-state condition as

$$fU = sE.$$

We can use this equation to find the steady-state unemployment rate. From our definition of the labour force, we know that $E = L - U$; that is, the number of employed equals the labour force minus the number of unemployed. If we substitute $(L - U)$ for E in the steady-state condition, we find

$$fU = s(L - U).$$

FIGURE 7-2

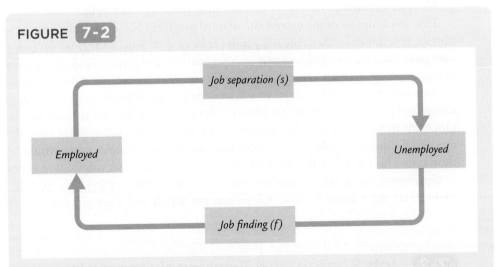

The Transitions between Employment and Unemployment In every period, a fraction s of the employed lose their jobs, and a fraction f of the unemployed find jobs. The rates of job separation and job finding determine the rate of unemployment.

To get closer to solving for the unemployment rate, divide both sides of this equation by L to obtain

$$f\frac{U}{L} = s\left(1 - \frac{U}{L}\right).$$

Now we can solve for U/L to find

$$\frac{U}{L} = \frac{s}{s + f}.$$

This can also be written as

$$\frac{U}{L} = \frac{1}{1 + f/s}.$$

This equation shows that the steady-state rate of unemployment U/L depends on the rates of job separation s and job finding f. The higher the rate of job separation, the higher the unemployment rate. The higher the rate of job finding, the lower the unemployment rate.

Here is a numerical example. Suppose that 1 per cent of the employed lose their jobs each month ($s = 0.01$). This means that, on average, jobs last 100 months, or about 8 years. Suppose further that 20 per cent of the unemployed find a job each month ($f = 0.20$), so that spells of unemployment last 5 months on average. Then the steady-state rate of unemployment is

$$\frac{U}{L} = \frac{0.01}{0.01 + 0.20}$$

$$= 0.0476.$$

The rate of unemployment in this example is about 5 per cent.

This simple model of the natural rate of unemployment has an important implication for government policy. *Any policy aimed at lowering the natural rate of unemployment must either reduce the rate of job separation or increase the rate of job finding. Similarly, any policy that affects the rate of job separation or job finding also changes the natural rate of unemployment.*

Although this model is useful in relating the unemployment rate to job separation and job finding, it fails to answer a central question: why is there unemployment in the first place? If a person could always find a job quickly, then the rate of job finding would be very high and the rate of unemployment would be near zero. This model of the unemployment rate assumes that job finding is not instantaneous, but it fails to explain why. In the next two sections, we examine two underlying reasons for unemployment: job search and wage rigidity.

7-2 Job Search and Frictional Unemployment

One reason for unemployment is that it takes time to match workers and jobs. The equilibrium model of the aggregate labour market discussed in Chapter 3 assumes that all workers and all jobs are identical, and therefore that all workers are equally well suited for all jobs. If this were true and the labour market were in equilibrium, a job loss would not cause unemployment: a laid-off worker would immediately find a new job at the market wage.

In fact, workers have different preferences and abilities, and jobs have different attributes. Furthermore, the flow of information about job candidates and job vacancies is imperfect, and the geographic mobility of workers is not instantaneous. For all these reasons, searching for an appropriate job takes time and effort, and this tends to reduce the rate of job finding. Indeed, because different jobs require different skills and pay different wages, unemployed workers may not accept the first job offer they receive. The unemployment caused by the time it takes workers to search for a job is called **frictional unemployment**.

Some frictional unemployment is inevitable in a changing economy. For many reasons, the types of goods that firms and households demand vary over time. As the demand for goods shifts, so does the demand for the labour that produces those goods. The invention of the personal computer, for example, reduced the demand for typewriters and, as a result, for labour by typewriter manufacturers. At the same time, it increased the demand for labour in the electronics industry. Economists call a change in the composition of demand among industries or regions a **sectoral shift**. Because sectoral shifts are always occurring, and because it takes time for workers to change sectors, there is always frictional unemployment.

Sectoral shifts are not the only cause of job separation and frictional unemployment. In addition, workers find themselves unexpectedly out of work when their firms fail, when their job performance is deemed unacceptable, or when their particular skills are no longer needed. Workers may also quit their jobs to change careers or to move to different parts of the country. Regardless of the cause of the job separation, it will take time and effort for the worker to find a new job. As long as the supply and demand for labour among firms is changing, frictional unemployment is unavoidable.

Government Policy and Frictional Unemployment

Many public policies seek to decrease the natural rate of unemployment by reducing frictional unemployment. Government employment agencies disseminate information about job opportunities in order to match jobs and workers more efficiently. Publicly funded retraining programmes are designed to ease the transition of workers from declining to growing industries. If these programmes succeed at increasing the rate of job finding, they decrease the natural rate of unemployment.

Other government programmes inadvertently increase the amount of frictional unemployment. One of these is **unemployment insurance**. Under this programme, unemployed workers can collect a fraction of their wages for a certain period after losing their jobs. The money paid to the unemployed worker is called unemployment benefit.

By softening the economic hardship of unemployment, unemployment insurance increases the amount of frictional unemployment and raises the natural rate. The unemployed who receive unemployment-insurance benefits are less pressed to search for new employment and are more likely to turn down unattractive job offers. Both of these changes in behaviour reduce the rate of job finding. In addition, because workers know that their incomes are partially protected by unemployment insurance, they are less likely to seek jobs with stable employment prospects and are less likely to bargain for guarantees of job security. These behavioural changes raise the rate of job separation.

That unemployment insurance raises the natural rate of unemployment does not necessarily imply that the policy is ill-advised. The programme has the benefit of reducing workers' uncertainty about their incomes. Moreover, inducing workers to reject unattractive job offers may lead to a better matching between workers and jobs. Evaluating the costs and benefits of different systems of unemployment insurance is a difficult task that continues to be a topic of much research.

Economists who study unemployment insurance often propose reforms that would reduce the amount of unemployment. One common proposal is to require a firm that lays off a worker to bear the full cost of that worker's unemployment benefits. Such a system is called *100 per cent experience rated*, because the rate that each firm pays into the unemployment-insurance system fully reflects the unemployment experience of its own workers. Most current programmes are *partially experience rated*. Under this system, when a firm lays off a worker, it is charged for only part of the worker's unemployment benefits; the remainder comes from the programme's general revenue. Because a firm pays only a fraction of the cost of the unemployment it causes, it has an incentive to lay off workers when its demand for labour is temporarily low. By reducing that incentive, the proposed reform may reduce the prevalence of temporary layoffs.

CASE STUDY

Unemployment Benefit and the Rate of Job Finding

Many studies have examined the effect of unemployment insurance and the payment of unemployment benefits on job search. The most persuasive studies use data on the experiences of unemployed individuals, rather than economy-wide rates of unemployment. Individual data often yield sharp results that are open to few alternative explanations. Nevertheless, European studies have tended to come up with conflicting results. The issue is hard to settle empirically for the simple reason that there is typically no random variation in unemployment benefits that can be used to investigate the issue of causality. If people with high benefits behave differently from people with low benefits, there is usually no way to find out whether the difference reflects causality or whether it simply reflects the fact that the two groups consist of different individuals.

In a large-scale Norwegian analysis of virtually all registered unemployment spells in Norway during the 1990s, however, the authors were able to exploit particular features of the Norwegian unemployment insurance system that in fact do entail elements of random assignment in unemployment benefits. The researchers found that when unemployed workers become ineligible for benefits, they are more likely to find jobs. In particular, the probability of a person finding a job rises by 40 to 60 per cent in the few months before his or her benefits are due to run out.

One possible explanation is that an absence of benefits increases the search effort of unemployed workers. Another possibility is that workers without benefits are more likely to accept job offers that would otherwise be declined because of low wages or poor working conditions.[2] ■

7-3 Real-Wage Rigidity and Structural Unemployment

A second reason for unemployment is **wage rigidity** – the failure of wages to adjust to a level at which labour supply equals labour demand. In the equilibrium model of the labour market, as outlined in Chapter 3, the real wage adjusts to equilibrate labour supply and labour demand. Yet wages are not always flexible. Sometimes the real wage is stuck above the market-clearing level.

Figure 7-3 shows why wage rigidity leads to unemployment. When the real wage is above the level that equilibrates supply and demand, the quantity of labour supplied exceeds the quantity demanded. Firms must in some way ration the scarce jobs among workers. Real-wage rigidity reduces the rate of job finding and raises the level of unemployment.

The unemployment resulting from wage rigidity and job rationing is sometimes called **structural unemployment**. Workers are unemployed not because

FIGURE 7-3

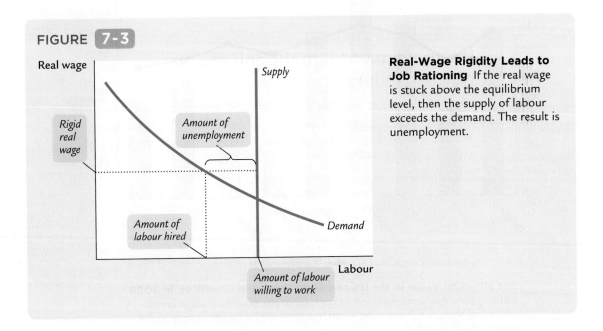

Real-Wage Rigidity Leads to Job Rationing If the real wage is stuck above the equilibrium level, then the supply of labour exceeds the demand. The result is unemployment.

---

[2] Knut Røed and Tao Zhang, 'Does Unemployment Compensation Affect Unemployment Duration?', *Economic Journal*, 2003, vol. 113, pp. 190–206.

they are actively searching for the jobs that best suit their individual skills, but because there is a fundamental mismatch between the number of people who want to work and the number of jobs that are available. At the going wage, the quantity of labour supplied exceeds the quantity of labour demanded, so many workers are simply waiting for jobs to open up.

To understand wage rigidity and structural unemployment, we must examine why the labour market does not clear. When the real wage exceeds the equilibrium level and the supply of workers exceeds the demand, we might expect firms to lower the wages they pay. Structural unemployment arises because firms fail to reduce wages despite an excess supply of labour. We now turn to three causes of this wage rigidity: minimum-wage laws, the monopoly power of unions and efficiency wages.

Minimum-Wage Laws

The government causes wage rigidity when it prevents wages from falling to equilibrium levels. Minimum-wage laws set a legal minimum on the wages that firms pay their employees. The US and a number of European countries have a statutory national minimum wage. In Figure 7-4 we show the national minimum

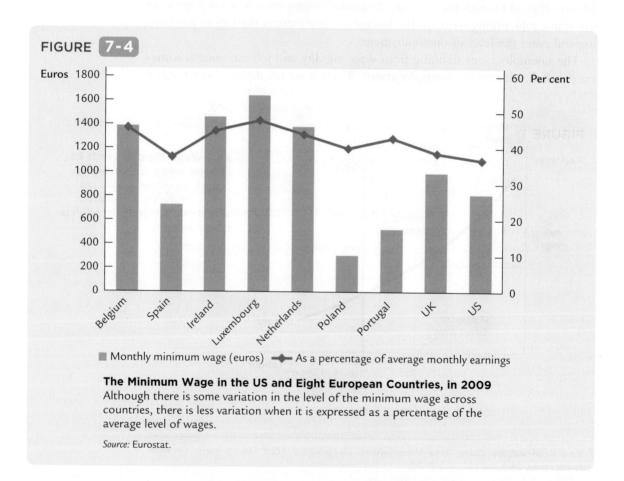

FIGURE 7-4

The Minimum Wage in the US and Eight European Countries, in 2009
Although there is some variation in the level of the minimum wage across countries, there is less variation when it is expressed as a percentage of the average level of wages.

Source: Eurostat.

wage in 2009 in eight European countries, as well as the US, expressed both as monthly earnings in euros and as a percentage of average monthly earnings in each economy. While the level of the minimum wage varies quite a lot across countries, it tends to be between about one-third and one-half of the economy-wide average wage. For example, in Poland, minimum monthly earnings were only just over €300, while in the US the minimum wage was more than two and a half times greater, at about €815 per month, and in the UK it was about three times greater, at about €995 per month. However, the Polish minimum wage was 40 per cent of the Polish average wage, slightly more than the figure of 38.6 per cent for the UK, and the 36.7 per cent figure for the US. In fact, although the US is the richest country, it had the lowest minimum wage as a proportion of the average wage. Luxembourg and Ireland had the most generous national minimum wages, in both money terms (about €1642 and €1462 per month, respectively) and relative terms (around 45 per cent of the economy-wide average wage).

For most workers, the minimum wage is not binding, because they earn well above the minimum. Yet for some workers, especially the unskilled and inexperienced, the minimum wage raises their wage above its equilibrium level and, therefore, reduces the quantity of their labour that firms demand.

Economists believe that the minimum wage has its greatest impact on the level of unemployment of youths (i.e. people aged roughly between the ages of 15 and 24). The equilibrium wages of youths tend to be low for two reasons. First, because youths are among the least skilled and least experienced members of the labour force, they tend to have low marginal productivity. Second, youths often take some of their 'compensation' in the form of on-the-job training rather than as direct pay. An apprenticeship is a classic example of training offered in place of wages. For both these reasons, the wage at which the supply of youth workers equals the demand is low. The minimum wage is therefore more often binding for youths than for others in the labour force.

Many economists have studied the impact of the minimum wage on youth employment. These researchers compare the variation in the minimum wage over time with the variation in the number of youths with jobs. These studies find that a 10 per cent increase in the minimum wage reduces teenage employment by 1 to 3 per cent.[3]

The minimum wage is a perennial source of political debate. Advocates of a higher minimum wage view it as a means of raising the income of the working poor. Certainly, the minimum wage provides only a meagre standard of living. While minimum-wage advocates often admit that the policy causes unemployment for some workers, they argue that this cost is worth bearing to raise others out of poverty.

---

[3] Much of this research has been conducted using US data, although a study employing data for 20 countries, of which 15 were European, found similar results: David Neumark and William Wascher, 'Minimum Wages, Labor Market Institutions, and Youth Employment: A Cross-National Analysis', *Finance and Economics Discussion Series* 2003–23, Board of Governors of the Federal Reserve System (2003). It should be noted, however, that the magnitude of employment effects is controversial. For research suggesting negligible employment effects, see David Card and Alan Krueger, *Myth and Measurement: The New Economics of the Minimum Wage*, Princeton, NJ: Princeton University Press, 1995.

Opponents of a higher minimum wage claim that it is not the best way to help the working poor. They contend not only that the increased labour costs would raise unemployment, but also that the minimum wage is poorly targeted. Many minimum-wage earners are youths from middle-class homes working for discretionary spending money, rather than heads of households working to support their families.

CASE STUDY

The Secrets to Happiness: Some European Evidence

Why are some people more satisfied with their lives than others? This is a deep and difficult question, most often left to philosophers, psychologists and self-help gurus. But part of the answer is macroeconomic. Recent research has shown that people are happier when they are living in a country with low inflation and low unemployment.

From 1975 to 1991, a survey called the Euro-Barometer Survey Series asked 264,710 people living in 12 European countries about their happiness and overall satisfaction with life. One question asked: 'On the whole, are you very satisfied, fairly satisfied, not very satisfied or not at all satisfied with the life you lead?' To see what determines happiness, the answers to this question were correlated with individual and macroeconomic variables. Other things equal, people are more satisfied with their lives if they are rich, educated, married, in school, self-employed, retired, female, and young or old (as opposed to middle-aged). They are less satisfied if they are unemployed, divorced or living with adolescent children. (Some of these correlations may reflect the effects, rather than causes, of happiness: for example, a happy person may find it easier than an unhappy one to keep a job and a spouse.)

Beyond these individual characteristics, the economy's overall rates of unemployment and inflation also play a significant role in explaining reported happiness. An increase in the unemployment rate of 4 percentage points is large enough to move 11 per cent of the population down from one life-satisfaction category to another. The overall unemployment rate reduces satisfaction, even after controlling for an individual's employment status. That is, the employed in a high-unemployment nation are less happy than their counterparts in a low-unemployment nation, perhaps because they are more worried about job loss or perhaps out of sympathy with their fellow citizens.

High inflation is also associated with lower life satisfaction, although the effect is not as large. A 1.7 percentage point increase in inflation reduces happiness by as much as about a 1 percentage point increase in unemployment. The commonly cited 'misery index', which is the sum of the inflation and unemployment rates, apparently gives too much weight to inflation relative to unemployment.[4] ■

---

[4] Rafael Di Tella, Robert J. MacCulloch and Andrew J. Oswald, 'Preferences over Inflation and Unemployment: Evidence from Surveys of Happiness', *American Economic Review*, 2001, vol. 91, pp. 335–341.

Unions and Collective Bargaining

A second cause of wage rigidity is the monopoly power of unions. Table 7-1 shows the importance of unions in a range of major countries, ranked by the percentage of workers covered by collective wage bargaining through unions. Note that some workers may be covered by a trades union collective agreement without actually being a member of a union. The United States heads the list, with only 13.6 per cent of workers covered by collective bargaining. At the other extreme, in Austria, Belgium, Finland, France, and Sweden, 90 per cent or more of workers are unionized. The United Kingdom, with a little less than 33 per cent of its workers covered by collective bargaining, is closer to the North American than the Continental European models.

The wages of unionized workers are determined not by the equilibrium of supply and demand, but by bargaining between union leaders and firm management. Often, the final agreement raises the wage above the equilibrium level and allows the firm to decide how many workers to employ. The result is a reduction in the number of workers hired, a lower rate of job finding and an increase in structural unemployment.

TABLE 7-1

Percentage of Workers Covered by Collective Bargaining

Country	Year	Percentage
United States	2009	13.6
Japan	2008	16.0
United Kingdom	2009	32.7
Canada	2009	31.6
Switzerland	2008	48.0
New Zealand	2007	17.0
Spain	2008	84.5
Netherlands	2008	82.3
Norway	2008	74.0
Portugal	2009	45.0
Australia	2007	40.0
Sweden	2008	91.0
Belgium	2008	96.0
Germany	2009	62.0
France	2008	90.0
Finland	2007	90.0
Austria	2009	99.0

Source: Organisation for Economic Co-operation and Development (OECD) Database on Trade Unions, as reported in J. Visser, S. Martin and P. Tergeist, 'Trade Union Member and Union Density in OECD Countries', OECD Labour Force Statistics, 2010, available at: www.oecd.org/els/emp/UnionDensity_Sourcesandmethods.pdf.

Unions can also influence the wages paid by firms whose workforces are not unionized, because the threat of unionization can keep wages above the equilibrium level. Most firms dislike unions. Unions not only raise wages, but also increase the bargaining power of labour on many other issues, such as hours of employment and working conditions. A firm may choose to pay its workers high wages to keep them happy and discourage them from forming a union.

The unemployment caused by unions and the threat of unionization are examples of conflict between different groups of workers – **insiders** and **outsiders**. Those workers already employed by a firm, the insiders, typically try to keep their firm's wages high. The unemployed, the outsiders, bear part of the cost of higher wages, because they might be hired at a lower wage. These two groups inevitably have conflicting interests. The effect of any bargaining process on wages and employment depends crucially on the relative influence of each group.

The conflict between insiders and outsiders is resolved differently in different countries. In some countries, wage bargaining takes place at the level of the firm or plant. In other countries, wage bargaining takes place at the national level – with the government often playing a key role. In the United Kingdom, national-level bargaining was once the main type of collective bargaining, but it has declined dramatically in importance since the mid-1980s, so that most workers are now covered by localized bargaining. In Sweden, however, national-level wage bargaining remains the norm. Despite a highly unionized labour force (over 80 per cent), however, Sweden has not experienced extraordinarily high unemployment throughout its history. One possible explanation is that the centralization of wage bargaining and the role of the government in the bargaining process give more influence to the outsiders, which keeps wages closer to the equilibrium level.

Efficiency Wages

Efficiency-wage theories propose a third cause of wage rigidity in addition to minimum-wage laws and unionization. These theories hold that high wages make workers more productive. The influence of wages on worker efficiency may explain the failure of firms to cut wages, despite an excess supply of labour. Even though a wage reduction would lower a firm's wage bill, it would also – if these theories are correct – lower worker productivity and the firm's profits.

Economists have proposed various theories to explain how wages affect worker productivity. One efficiency-wage theory, which is applied mostly to poorer countries, holds that wages influence nutrition. Better-paid workers can afford a more nutritious diet, and healthier workers are more productive. A firm may decide to pay a wage above the equilibrium level to maintain a healthy workforce. Obviously this consideration is not important for employers in wealthier countries, such as most of Europe and North America, because the equilibrium wage is well above the level necessary to maintain good health.

FYI

The Natural Rate of Unemployment and the NAIRU

Sometimes economists use the term **non-accelerating inflation rate of unemployment**, or its acronym, the **NAIRU**, to denote the equilibrium unemployment level. In many ways, the NAIRU and the natural rate of unemployment are similar concepts, in that they both denote an equilibrium level of unemployment towards which the economy reverts and at which there are no inflationary pressures arising from the labour market – hence the term *non-accelerating* inflation rate of unemployment (although *non-increasing* or *stable* inflation rate of unemployment would probably have been a better term for the equilibrium rate). However, some economists would still distinguish between the two by arguing that the natural rate of unemployment assumes a competitive labour market in which the labour market clears and there is no involuntary unemployment (in the sense that anyone who is willing to work for the going wage rate will be employed), apart from some frictional unemployment as people search for jobs; whereas the NAIRU is largely due to various labour-market imperfections, such as real-wage rigidity, and is composed of both frictional and structural unemployment, so that there may be some people who are willing to

work for the going wage but simply cannot find employment. To these economists, the natural rate is the lower bound that the NAIRU would attain in the absence of labour-market imperfections.

To a large extent, the broader concept of the NAIRU has now largely superseded the strict interpretation of the natural rate of unemployment, and the term 'natural rate of unemployment' has come to denote simply the equilibrium rate of unemployment, which may be affected by labour-market imperfections, such as the influence of trades unions. In this book, we will adhere to this broader usage of the term 'natural rate' as simply denoting the equilibrium rate.

There are pluses and minuses to this broader usage of the term 'natural rate of unemployment'. On the one hand, it obviates the need for an ugly (and ill-named) acronym. On the other hand, the adjective 'natural' does suggest that there is something natural and normal about unemployment, whereas, in fact, losing one's job and becoming unemployed is one of the most unnatural and devastating things that can happen to someone in their life, as the epigraph at the beginning of this chapter notes.

A second efficiency–wage theory, which is more relevant for developed countries, holds that high wages reduce labour turnover. Workers quit jobs for many reasons – to accept better positions at other firms, to change careers or to move to other parts of the country. The more a firm pays its workers, the greater is their incentive to stay with the firm. By paying a high wage, a firm reduces the frequency at which its workers quit, thereby decreasing the time and money spent hiring and training new workers.

A third efficiency–wage theory holds that the average quality of a firm's workforce depends on the wage it pays its employees. If a firm reduces its wage, the best employees may take jobs elsewhere, leaving the firm with inferior employees who have fewer alternative opportunities. Economists recognize this unfavourable sorting as an example of *adverse selection* – the tendency of people with more information (in this case, the workers, who know their own outside opportunities) to self-select in a way that disadvantages people with less information (the firm). By paying a wage above the equilibrium level, the firm may reduce adverse selection, improve the average quality of its workforce and thereby increase productivity.

A fourth efficiency-wage theory holds that a high wage improves worker effort. This theory posits that firms cannot perfectly monitor their employees' work effort, and that employees must themselves decide how hard to work. Workers can choose to work hard, or they can choose to shirk and risk getting caught and fired. Economists recognize this possibility as an example of *moral hazard* – the tendency of people to behave inappropriately when their behaviour is imperfectly monitored. The firm can reduce the problem of moral hazard by paying a high wage. The higher the wage, the greater the cost to the worker of getting fired. By paying a higher wage, a firm induces more of its employees not to shirk and thus increases their productivity.

Although these four efficiency-wage theories differ in detail, they share a common theme: because a firm operates more efficiently if it pays its workers a high wage, the firm may find it profitable to keep wages above the level that balances supply and demand. The result of this higher-than-equilibrium wage is a lower rate of job finding and greater unemployment.[5]

CASE STUDY

Henry Ford's $5 Workday

In 1914 the US car manufacturer, the Ford Motor Company, started paying its workers $5 per day. At that time, $5 was worth about £1, and UK prices have risen by a factor of about 50 since then, so $5 a day translates into about £1250 a year in 1914 pounds and about £12,500 (or about €18,000) a year today. This might not seem like much nowadays, but back then this was about twice the going American wage of $2 to $3 per day, so Ford's wage was well above the equilibrium level. Not surprisingly, long lines of job seekers waited outside the Ford plant gates, hoping for a chance to earn this high wage.

What was Ford's motive? Henry Ford later wrote, 'We wanted to pay these wages so that the business would be on a lasting foundation. We were building for the future. A low wage business is always insecure ... The payment of five dollars a day for an eight hour day was one of the finest cost cutting moves we ever made.'

From the standpoint of traditional economic theory, Ford's explanation seems peculiar. He was suggesting that *high* wages imply *low* costs. But perhaps Ford had discovered efficiency-wage theory. Perhaps he was using the high wage to increase worker productivity.

Evidence suggests that paying such a high wage did benefit the company. According to an engineering report written at the time, 'The Ford high wage does away with all the inertia and living force resistance ... The workingmen are absolutely docile, and it is safe to say that since the last day of 1913, every single day has seen major reductions in Ford shops' labour costs.' Absenteeism fell by 75 per cent,

[5] For more extended discussions of efficiency wages, see Janet Yellen, 'Efficiency Wage Models of Unemployment', *American Economic Review Papers and Proceedings*, May 1984, pp. 200–205; and Lawrence Katz, 'Efficiency Wages: A Partial Evaluation', *NBER Macroeconomics Annual*, 1986, pp. 235–276.

suggesting a large increase in worker effort. Alan Nevins, a historian who studied the early Ford Motor Company, wrote: 'Ford and his associates freely declared on many occasions that the high wage policy had turned out to be good business. By this they meant that it had improved the discipline of the workers, given them a more loyal interest in the institution, and raised their personal efficiency.' ∎

7-4 Labour-Market Experience: The United Kingdom

So far we have developed the theory behind the natural rate of unemployment. We began by showing that the economy's steady-state unemployment rate depends on the rates of job separation and job finding. Then we discussed two reasons why job finding is not instantaneous: the process of job search (which leads to frictional unemployment) and wage rigidity (which leads to structural unemployment). Wage rigidity, in turn, arises from minimum-wage laws, unionization and efficiency wages.

With these theories as background, we now examine some additional facts about unemployment, focusing first on the case of UK labour markets, before turning to an analysis of European labour markets. These facts will help us to evaluate our theories and assess public policies aimed at reducing unemployment.

The Duration of Unemployment

When a person becomes unemployed, is the spell of unemployment likely to be short or long? The answer to this question is important because it indicates the reasons for the unemployment and what policy response is appropriate. On the one hand, if most unemployment is short-term, one might argue that it is frictional and perhaps unavoidable. Unemployed workers may need some time to search for the job that is best suited to their skills and tastes. On the other hand, long-term unemployment cannot easily be attributed to the time it takes to match jobs and workers: we would not expect this matching process to take many months. Long-term unemployment is more likely to be structural unemployment, representing a mismatch between the number of jobs available and the number of people who want to work. Thus, data on the duration of unemployment can affect our view about the reasons for unemployment.

The answer to our question turns out to be subtle. The data show that most spells of unemployment are short, but that most months of unemployment are attributable to the long-term unemployed. To see how both these facts can be true, consider the following example. Suppose that ten people are unemployed for part of a given year. Of these ten people, eight are unemployed for 1 month, and two are unemployed for 12 months, totalling 32 months of unemployment.

In this example, most spells of unemployment are short: eight of the ten unemployment spells, or 80 per cent, end in 1 month. Yet most months of unemployment are attributable to the long-term unemployed: 24 of the 32 months of unemployment, or 75 per cent, are experienced by the two workers who are unemployed for 12 months. Depending on whether we look at spells of unemployment or months of unemployment, most unemployment can appear to be short-term or long-term.

This evidence on the duration of unemployment has an important implication for public policy. If the goal is to lower substantially the natural rate of unemployment, policies must aim at the long-term unemployed, because these individuals account for a large amount of unemployment. Yet policies must be carefully targeted, because the long-term unemployed constitute a small minority of those who become unemployed. Most people who become unemployed find work within a short time.

Variation in the UK Unemployment Rate across Demographic Groups

The rate of unemployment varies substantially across different groups within the population. Table 7-2 presents the overall UK unemployment rate, as well as the unemployment rates broken down by gender and for those aged 15–24 years at the end of 2011.

Table 7-2 shows that in 2011 the overall unemployment rate was 8 per cent, while the unemployment rate among those aged 15–24 was 21.1 per cent, showing that younger workers have much higher unemployment rates than older ones. To explain this difference, recall our model of the natural rate of unemployment. The model isolates two possible causes for a high rate of unemployment: a low rate of job finding and a high rate of job separation. When economists study data on the transition of individuals between employment and unemployment, they find that those groups with high unemployment tend to have high rates of job separation. They find less variation across groups in the rate of job finding. For example, an employed white male is four times more likely to become unemployed if he is a teenager than if he is middle-aged; once unemployed, his rate of job finding is not closely related to his age.

TABLE 7-2

UK Unemployment Rates 2011

	Percentage
Overall	8.0
Men	8.7
Women	7.3
Aged 15-24	21.1

Source: Eurostat.

These findings help to explain the higher unemployment rates for younger workers. Younger workers have only recently entered the labour market, and they are often uncertain about their career plans. It may be best for them to try different types of jobs before making a long-term commitment to a specific occupation. If so, we should expect a higher rate of job separation and a higher rate of frictional unemployment for this group.

The fact that the measured unemployment rate is lower for women in the UK (7.3 per cent) than for men (8.7 per cent) should be treated with caution. Homemakers are not counted as part of the labour force (despite the fact that they may work harder and longer than many people counted as being employed), and it is still the case that a higher proportion of women fulfil this role than men. Hence, if a woman has difficulty finding a job, she is more likely to cease looking for employment and drop out of the labour force altogether. Or, if her partner is unemployed and she has spent some time as a housewife and bringing up children, she may be discouraged by her partner's lack of success in finding a job. Indeed, this phenomenon is sometimes called the *discouraged worker effect*. It is also reflected in the fact that participation rates among women (the percentage of working-age women who are economically active in the sense of being employed or actively seeking a job) are much lower than for men. At the end of 2011, for example, about 83 per cent of working-age men in the UK were economically active, compared to about 71 per cent of women.

Trends in UK Unemployment

Since about 1980, the natural rate of unemployment in the United Kingdom has not been stable. Unfortunately, economists do not agree on how the natural rate should be measured. In Table 7-3, however, we have listed some estimates of the equilibrium that are probably worth considering, as they were calculated by Professor Stephen Nickell, a leading labour economist and a member of the Bank of England's interest rate-setting committee, the Monetary Policy

---

TABLE 7-3

Estimates of the Equilibrium UK Unemployment Rate

	1969–1973	1974–1981	1981–1986	1986–1990	1991–1997	1994–1998	1997–2000	2000–2005
Average Unemployment (%)	3.9	5.8	11.3	8.9	8.8	7.9	6.1	5.0
Equilibrium Unemployment (%)	3.8	7.5	9.5	9.6	8.9	6.9	5.7	5.0

Source: 1969–2000 Stephen J. Nickell, 'Has UK Labour Market Performance Changed?', speech given to the Society of Business Economists, 2005, available at the Bank of England website, www.bankofengland.co.uk. 2000–2005 UK Office of National Statistics and authors' calculations.

Committee, for six years until June 2006. As you will see, in Professor Nickell's estimation, the equilibrium rate was around 4 per cent in the late 1960s to early 1970s, rose to nearer 6 per cent in the period 1974–1981 and reached a peak of over 11 per cent in the early 1980s. Since then, it has declined progressively, and had reached around 5 per cent by 2005. (Actually, the estimate of 5 per cent for the 2000–2005 period is our estimate rather than Stephen Nickell's, but since inflation has been stable over this period it seems reasonable to estimate the equilibrium rate by the average rate.) Why has the natural rate shown such instability during this period? Although economists do not have a conclusive explanation for these changes, they have proposed several hypotheses.

Demographics One explanation stresses the changing composition of the UK labour force. After World War II, birth rates rose dramatically, and the increase in births in the 1950s led to a rise in the number of young workers in the 1970s. Younger workers have higher unemployment rates, however, so when the baby-boom generation entered the labour force, they increased the average level of unemployment. Then, as the baby-boom workers aged, the average age of the labour force increased, lowering the average unemployment rate in the 1990s.

This demographic change, however, cannot explain fully the trends in unemployment because similar trends are apparent for fixed demographic groups. For example, for UK men between the ages of 25 and 49, the unemployment rate was above 10 per cent in 1993, and did not fall below 5 per cent until 2000. Thus, while demographic changes may be part of the story of rising unemployment over this period, there must be other explanations of the long-term trend as well.

Sectoral Shifts A second explanation is based on changes in the prevalence of sectoral shifts. The greater the amount of reallocation among regions and industries, the greater the rate of job separation and the higher the level of frictional unemployment. One source of sectoral shifts during the 1970s and early 1980s was the great volatility in oil prices caused by OPEC, the international oil cartel. These large changes in oil prices may have required reallocating labour between more-energy-intensive and less-energy-intensive sectors. If so, oil-price volatility may have increased unemployment during this period. The increase in oil-price volatility in the early 2000s, however, did not cause a similar rise in the natural rate of unemployment, but this may be because the UK economy, like all advanced economies, is now significantly less oil-intensive (as measured by oil consumption per unit of GDP) than it was in the 1980s.

Productivity A third explanation for the trends in unemployment emphasizes the link between unemployment and productivity. As Chapter 9 discusses more fully, the 1970s witnessed a slowdown in productivity growth in the UK, while the 1990s saw a pickup in productivity growth. These productivity changes roughly coincide with changes in unemployment. Perhaps slowing productivity during the 1970s raised the natural rate of unemployment, and accelerating productivity during the 1990s growth lowered it.

Why such an effect would occur, however, is not obvious. In standard theories of the labour market, higher productivity means greater labour demand and thus higher real wages, but unemployment is unchanged. This prediction is consistent with the long-term data, which show consistent upward trends in productivity and real wages, but no trend in unemployment. Yet suppose that workers are slow to catch on to news about productivity. When productivity changes, workers may only gradually alter the real wages they ask from their employers, making real wages sluggish in response to labour demand. An acceleration in productivity growth, such as that experienced during the 1990s, will increase labour demand and, with a sluggish real wage, reduce the amount of unemployment.

The Decline in Unionization We saw in Table 7-1 that the UK is closer to the US than many Continental European countries in terms of union coverage, with about 33 per cent of workers with wage agreements covered by union bargaining. This figure – the level of 'union coverage' – has been falling over time, from a peak of around 70 per cent in 1980. As we remarked earlier, however, workers may find a trades union negotiating wage agreements on their behalf even if they are not members of a union. This is because the employer may recognize the union as representing the majority of its workers, although not all of them. Figures for actual union membership – what labour economists call 'union density' – are therefore lower than figures for coverage. Currently, less than 30 per cent of UK workers are members of a trades union, and, as we show in Table 7-4, this figure has also been falling steadily over time, from a peak of around 50 per cent in 1980.

The dramatic fall in unionization in the UK since 1980 is unique in its scale among the major industrialized countries. How did it come about? There are three important factors.

First, the UK government in the 1980s, led by Prime Minister Margaret Thatcher, introduced a number of laws that moved the balance of power in disputes over pay and working conditions away from the unions and towards employers, and also made it harder for unions to organize. In effect, therefore, the new legislation made it less easy and less attractive for workers to join a union.

Second, the most heavily unionized sectors of the economy were in the former nationalized industries. During the Thatcher years, many former public-sector firms, such as gas, electricity and railways, were privatized and broken up into smaller firms. This made it more difficult for the unions to enforce national agreements, and it also meant that they were faced with private-sector employers,

---

TABLE **7-4**

UK Trades Union Density

	1970	1975	1980	1985	1990	1995	2000	2005	2010
Percentage of Workers Who Are Union Members	44	48	50	45	38	32.4	29.8	28.6	26.6

Source: 1970–1990 Stephen J. Nickell, 'Has UK Labour Market Performance Changed?', speech given to the Society of Business Economists, 2001, available at the Bank of England website, www.bankofengland.co.uk. 1995–2010 UK Office for National Statistics (ONS).

who, it might be argued, took a tougher stance on unions and were more likely to avail themselves of the new anti-trades union legislation.

Third, many of the most highly unionized sectors, such as coal and shipbuilding, have been in relative decline during these years, and employment in those sectors has fallen.

The decline in unionization among the UK workforce, arising largely from these three factors, has undoubtedly reduced the natural rate of unemployment in the UK since 1980.

Changes in the Unemployment Benefit System The UK has also seen quite radical changes in its unemployment benefits system since 1980. In particular, the average level of weekly unemployment benefit relative to average weekly earnings fell from around 18 per cent to 10 per cent in 2011. Again, this was due largely to reforms in the benefit system brought about during the Thatcher administration. Other reforms included reducing the coverage of the benefit system (for example, the general entitlement of those aged 16–17 years was removed in 1988), reducing the duration over which benefits could be received and increasing the strictness with which the benefit rules are applied. Furthermore, the unemployment benefit and income support (IS) for unemployed people were replaced in 1996 by the Jobseeker's Allowance (JSA). This change brought stricter enforcement of eligibility conditions, and also intended to increase the search activity of jobseekers and, hence, raise inflows into employment.

It seems clear that these reforms to the benefit system are expected to reduce the natural rate of unemployment in the UK.[6] Indeed, recent evidence suggests that the introduction of JSA in the UK has reduced the claimant count by about 8 percentage points. However, this reduction was primarily driven by a flow to non-claimant non-employment, which was largely evident among those with low initial levels of job search activity. Therefore, there is no empirical evidence that JSA actually increased job search activity or moves into employment.[7]

Transitions Into and Out of the Labour Force

So far we have ignored an important aspect of labour-market dynamics: the movement of individuals into and out of the labour force. Our model of the natural rate of unemployment assumes that the labour force is fixed. In this case, the sole reason for unemployment is job separation, and the sole reason for leaving unemployment is job finding.

In fact, movements into and out of the labour force are important. About one-third of the unemployed have only recently entered the labour force. Some of these entrants are young workers still looking for their first jobs; others have worked before but had left the labour force temporarily. In addition, not all

---

[6] For further discussion of these issues, see Stephen J. Nickell, 'Has UK Labour Market Performance Changed?', speech given to the Society of Business Economists, 2001, available at the Bank of England website, www.bankofengland.co.uk.

[7] Alan Manning, 'You Can't Always Get What You Want: The Impact of the UK Jobseeker's Allowance', *Labour Economics*, 2009, vol. 16, pp. 239–250.

unemployment ends with job finding: almost half of all spells of unemployment end in the unemployed person's withdrawal from the labour market.

Individuals entering and leaving the labour force make unemployment statistics more difficult to interpret. On the one hand, some individuals calling themselves unemployed may not be looking for jobs seriously and, perhaps, should best be viewed as out of the labour force. Their 'unemployment' may not represent a social problem. On the other hand, some individuals may want jobs, but, after unsuccessful searches, have given up looking. These **discouraged workers** are counted as being out of the labour force and do not show up in unemployment statistics. Even though their joblessness is unmeasured, it may be a social problem nevertheless.

7-5 Labour-Market Experience: Continental Europe

Although our discussion so far has focused largely on the United Kingdom, many fascinating and sometimes puzzling phenomena become apparent when we examine the labour-market experience of the Continental European economies.

The Rise in European Unemployment

Look again at Figure 7-1, which shows the rate of unemployment from 1960 to 2011 in three of the largest Continental European countries – France, Germany and Italy – as well as for the United Kingdom. As you can see, the rate of unemployment in the three Continental European countries has risen substantially. For France and Germany, the change is particularly pronounced: unemployment averaged about 2 per cent in the 1960s and about 10 per cent in the early 21st century. The most striking difference with the UK's unemployment experience was the sustained fall in the UK unemployment level from the early 1990s and during the early 2000s. However, from the onset of the Euro Area (Eurozone) crises in 2008, this has been reversed with unemployment in the UK rising to levels similar to those in Continental Europe.

In Figure 7-5, we show the average levels of unemployment for three periods, 1983–1991, 1992–2005 and 2006–2011, for a wider range of European countries, as well as the US and Japan. While there is a range of unemployment rates across Europe, with notably lower rates for countries such as the Denmark, Luxembourg and the Netherlands in the more recent period, the average rates are very high. Indeed, the unemployment rate across the EU15 and EU27 countries in the 2006–2011 period was around 8.5 per cent.[8]

What is the cause of the high levels of European unemployment? For the period up to the financial crisis in 2008, no one knows for sure, but there is a

---

[8] The EU15 countries are: Austria, Belgium, Denmark, Finland, France, Germany, Greece, Ireland, Italy, Luxembourg, Portugal, Spain, Sweden, the Netherlands and the United Kingdom. The EU27 includes the following additional countries: Bulgaria, Cyprus, Czech Republic, Estonia, Hungary, Latvia, Lithuania, Malta, Slovakia, Slovenia, Poland, and Romania.

FIGURE 7-5

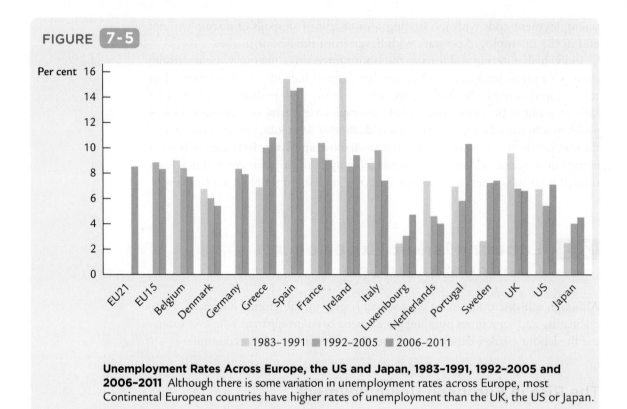

Unemployment Rates Across Europe, the US and Japan, 1983–1991, 1992–2005 and 2006–2011 Although there is some variation in unemployment rates across Europe, most Continental European countries have higher rates of unemployment than the UK, the US or Japan.

Source: Eurostat.

leading theory. Many economists believe that the problem can be traced to the interaction between long-standing policies and a recent shock. The long-standing policies were generous benefits for unemployed workers and various labour-market policies that protected employment and restricted the flexibility of the labour market. The recent shock was a technologically driven fall in the demand for unskilled workers relative to skilled workers.

There is no question that most European countries have generous systems of unemployment benefit for those without jobs. Although there are difficulties in comparing like with like, the ratio of unemployment benefit to average wages (the replacement ratio) in France and Germany, for example, is about twice the UK level, and in many Continental European countries it is even higher. The duration over which unemployment benefit is paid is also generally higher in Continental Europe than it is in the UK or the US.

In some sense, those living on the dole, especially the long-term unemployed who have been out of work for a year or more, are really out of the labour force: given the employment opportunities available, taking a job is less attractive than remaining without work. Yet these people are often counted as unemployed in government statistics.

The other aspect of Continental European labour markets is their lack of flexibility due to various labour-market laws. In many European countries, largely in order to pay for generous unemployment benefit systems, there are very high rates of social insurance charges and other employment taxes that must be paid by the employer on top of the worker's wages. These non-wage costs make recruiting expensive. Once they have recruited a worker, moreover, a firm will find making him or her redundant extremely difficult and costly because of the legal protection that workers enjoy and the compensation they can demand from the firm, even if they have only been employed for a few months. These factors make firms reluctant to take workers on, and, instead, they substitute capital (machines) for workers. In addition, as we saw earlier (in Table 7-1), the degree of union coverage is very much higher throughout Continental Europe than it is in either the UK or North America. But union leaders are not paid to represent unemployed workers. As we noted earlier, they are paid to represent the *insiders* – union members in paid employment – rather than *outsiders*. Thus, if unions force up wage costs, there are high non-wage costs to taking workers on and, because of labour-market laws (and also, perhaps, because of the threat of a union-led strike), it is very costly to fire employees if there is a downturn in demand, so it is little wonder that firms may be reluctant to hire workers and that high levels of unemployment persist.

There is also no question that the demand for unskilled workers has fallen relative to the demand for skilled workers. This change in demand is probably due to changes in technology: computers, for example, increase the demand for workers who can use them and reduce the demand for those who cannot. In the UK and the US, this change in demand has been reflected in wages rather than unemployment: since the mid-1980s, the wages of unskilled workers have fallen substantially relative to the wages of skilled workers. In Continental Europe, however, the welfare state provides unskilled workers with an alternative to working for low wages. As the wages of unskilled workers fall, more workers view the dole as their best available option. The result is higher unemployment.

This diagnosis of high Continental European unemployment does not suggest an easy remedy. Reducing the magnitude of government benefits for the unemployed would encourage workers to get off the dole and accept low-wage jobs. But it would also exacerbate economic inequality – the very problem that welfare-state policies were designed to address.[9]

The financial crisis that erupted in 2008 had severe repercussions for the European labour markets. The current economic climate across Europe is depicted by austerity policies, a low level of household consumption, bank liquidity problems, limited private investment, a lack of confidence and reduced/negative expectations in the financial market, as well as high public deficits and debts. Not surprisingly, in countries where labour flexibility is very high, such as the UK, unemployment has increased dramatically. The adoption of a proactive policy stance towards a flexible and lightly regulated labour market in the UK

---

[9] For more discussion of these issues, see Paul Krugman, 'Past and Prospective Causes of High Unemployment', in *Reducing Unemployment: Current Issues and Policy Options,* August 1994, Federal Reserve Bank of Kansas City.

has meant more lenient hiring and firing rules and therefore greater flexibility for employers to adjust their labour demand. Hence, in periods of economic downturn, employers can lay off workers and adjust the size of their production to the limited demand they face with greater ease compared with employers in Continental Europe. Along with a very strong flexible labour market, countries affected the most by the crisis can also be described by high levels of inequality, greater exposure to foreign banks, a stronger reliance on the housing sector, less incisive labour market policies and expenditure, lower trade union density, higher levels of private debt, and lower levels of savings. Such countries are Spain, Ireland, Portugal, Greece, Italy and the UK, followed by others EU members.

Interestingly, since 2010 Germany appears to have diverged from the other countries, with its unemployment rate showing a declining trend and the latest unemployment rate figures slightly less than 6 per cent. The German labour market managed to recover very quickly from the 2008–2009 economic crisis and unemployment continued its long-run structural decline in 2010 and 2011. The German labour market 'miracle' is at least partly attributed to a series of reforms introduced ten years ago that include: (i) structural labour market reforms, which strengthened work incentives and improved the matching of unemployed workers to jobs; (ii) pension reforms; (iii) increased firm-level working-time flexibility and the use of working-time accounts; and (iv) short-time work schemes. However, the flipside of Germany's high employment rate is low-paid and unstable jobs. Specifically, the share of wages, salaries and benefits in total national income ('labour share') has fallen, contributing to rising inequality. In addition, there is an increasing share of employees under precarious contracts.

Variation in European Unemployment Rates across Demographic Groups

Figure 7-6 presents the overall unemployment rate, as well as the unemployment rates broken down by gender and for those aged 15–24 years, in a number of European countries at the end of 2011. A striking feature of Figure 7-6 is that, as we saw in our analysis of unemployment and demographic groups in the UK, the rate of youth unemployment is higher in every case – and, in many cases, substantially higher – than the overall unemployment rate. In France and Italy, for example, where the overall unemployment rate was approximately 9.6 and 8.4 per cent respectively, youth unemployment was around 22.8 and 29.1 per cent respectively. Even Luxembourg, with its relatively low unemployment rate of about 4.8 per cent, had more than triple that percentage of youth unemployment. Clearly, the tendency of younger workers to have much higher unemployment rates than older ones is a feature of Continental European as well as UK labour markets. We discussed earlier how this is consistent with our model of the natural rate of unemployment, given that younger workers are relatively inexperienced and are usually less certain about their career plans, implying a relatively higher rate of frictional youth unemployment.

FIGURE **7-6**

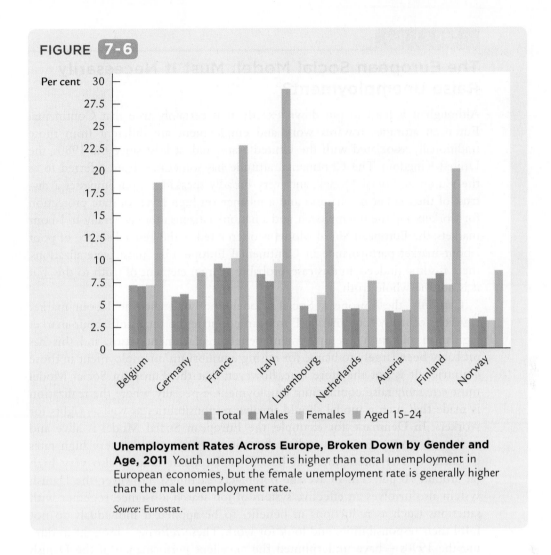

Unemployment Rates Across Europe, Broken Down by Gender and Age, 2011 Youth unemployment is higher than total unemployment in European economies, but the female unemployment rate is generally higher than the male unemployment rate.

Source: Eurostat.

On the other hand, female unemployment rates are also higher than the male unemployment rate in over half of the European countries depicted in Figure 7-6. This is in contrast to the situation in the UK, where (as we discussed earlier) the female unemployment rate was lower than the male unemployment rate (see Table 7-2). What is generating this difference between the UK and Continental Europe? Again, there is no clear-cut answer, but we can think of at least two reasons why we observe this phenomenon. First, recall how we suggested earlier that the lower UK female unemployment rate may be due in part to the discouraged worker effect. However, because of the relatively more generous unemployment benefit system in Continental European countries, the discouraged worker effect will be less important, since leaving the workforce means giving up substantial unemployment benefits. Second, because of the significant non-wage costs borne by Continental European employers, they may be especially reluctant to take on female workers who are likely to have children and become entitled to maternity leave, for example.

The European Social Model: Must It Necessarily Raise Unemployment?

Although it is hard to pin down exactly, it is certainly true that Continental European attitudes towards work and employment are different from those traditionally associated with the United States and, at least since the 1980s, the United Kingdom. The Continental attitude has sometimes been referred to as the 'European Social Model', and, very broadly speaking, it encompasses a distrust of the market mechanism and a reliance on high levels of state protection for workers and the unemployed, and a nation's citizens more generally. In labour markets, the European Social Model is often cited as the general source of poor labour-market performance in Continental Europe. Like most generalizations, there is some (indeed, in this case, probably a large) element of truth to this, but it is not the whole truth.

Certainly, the European Social Model does underlie the labour-market rigidities of many Continental European countries, in terms of labour-market legislation and high unemployment benefit replacement ratios, and this has probably been largely to blame for raising equilibrium unemployment in those countries. It is not therefore true, however, that the European Social Model must *necessarily* raise equilibrium employment, especially where the realization is made that such a model should involve responsibilities as well as rights for workers. In Denmark, for example, the European Social Model is alive and well, with a very generous welfare benefit system funded by very high rates of taxation. The unemployment benefit replacement ratio is also very high (at around 70 per cent of average before-tax earnings). However, the Danish system also involves an effective system of job search assistance, together with sanctions (such as reductions in benefit) to be applied if individuals do not fulfil their responsibilities and look for work. These reforms – brought in during the 1990s – have underpinned the excellent performance of the Danish labour market, where unemployment in 2011 was around 8 per cent, close to the UK level. ∎

Reforming French Labour Markets: I Predict a Riot

If the rigidity of Continental European labour markets has resulted in an increase in unemployment, should politicians not reform those markets, as successive UK governments have been doing in their labour markets since the 1980s? This is more easily said than done, as the experience of attempted labour market reform in France in 2006 makes clear.

In early 2006, French unemployment was running at around 9.5 per cent. Among young people the rate was even higher, at around 23 per cent. As we have noted, one major reason why Continental European (including French) unemployment is so high is because of rigidities in the labour market that raise the costs of both hiring and firing. This has made firms over the years more and more reluctant to take people on, preferring instead to hire more machines. This is particularly true of young workers, who typically have less experience and so will need training or who may turn out to be unsuitable for the job, and so on, all of which makes them risky to hire.

In an effort to reduce unemployment among young people, therefore, in 2006 French Prime Minister Dominique de Villepin introduced a radical change in labour-market law in the form of a new work contract, known as the 'First Employment Contract' – the Contrat Première Embauche (CPE) – for workers under 26 years of age. The CPE allowed a two-year trial period for a new under-26 worker, during which time employers could end a contract without explanation. It was designed to reduce the reluctance of firms to take on younger workers and was also backed up by an increase in state support for employers taking them on.

However, Monsieur Villepin's new initiative resulted in mass protests, with both students and trades unions denouncing the measure as a means of 'institutionalizing insecurity' and victimizing the young. Moreover, opinion polls suggested that a majority of the French people agreed. On two occasions, strikes and protest marches drew as many as three million people onto the streets. Students occupied campuses and closed their universities for up to a month, and staged spontaneous invasions of many roads, airports and main-line railway stations. Finally, on Monday 10 April, President Jacques Chirac gave in to the popular protest, overruled his prime minister and repealed the CPE. ■

7-6 Conclusion

Unemployment represents wasted resources. Unemployed workers have the potential to contribute to national income, but are not doing so. Those searching for jobs to suit their skills are happy when the search is over, and those waiting for jobs in firms that pay above-equilibrium wages are happy when positions open up.

Unfortunately, neither frictional unemployment nor structural unemployment can be reduced easily. The government cannot make job search instantaneous, and it cannot easily bring wages closer to equilibrium levels. Zero unemployment is not a plausible goal for free-market economies.

Yet public policy is not powerless in the fight to reduce unemployment. Job-training programmes, the unemployment-insurance system, the minimum wage and the laws governing collective bargaining are often topics of political debate. The policies we choose are likely to have important effects on the economy's natural rate of unemployment.

Summary

1. The natural rate of unemployment is the steady-state rate of unemployment. It depends on the rate of job separation and the rate of job finding.

2. Because it takes time for workers to search for the job that best suits their individual skills and tastes, some frictional unemployment is inevitable. Various government policies, such as unemployment insurance, alter the amount of frictional unemployment.

3. Structural unemployment results when the real wage remains above the level that equilibrates labour supply and labour demand. Minimum-wage legislation is one cause of wage rigidity. Unions and the threat of unionization are another. Finally, efficiency-wage theories suggest that, for various reasons, firms may find it profitable to keep wages high, despite an excess supply of labour.

4. The unemployment rates among demographic groups differ substantially. In particular, the unemployment rates for younger workers are much higher than for older workers in most countries. This results from a difference in the rate of job separation, rather than from a difference in the rate of job finding.

5. The natural rate of unemployment in the United Kingdom has exhibited long-term trends. In particular, it rose from the 1960s to the 1970s and early 1980s, and then started drifting downward again in the 1990s and early 2000s. Various explanations have been proposed, but the two most important factors are probably the decline in the unionization of the labour force and the reform of the unemployment benefit system.

6. Individuals who have recently entered the labour force, including both new entrants and re-entrants, make up about one-third of the unemployed. Transitions into and out of the labour force make unemployment statistics more difficult to interpret.

7. Prior to the financial crisis in 2008, Continental European levels of unemployment tended to be much higher than in the UK or the US. Major reasons for this were the more generous unemployment benefit systems of many European countries that still exist, combined with various laws that protect employment and reduce labour-market flexibility. However, from the onset of the Euro Area crisis in 2008, unemployment in the UK, a country traditionally characterized by a very strong flexible labour market, has risen to levels similar to those in Continental Europe.

KEY CONCEPTS

Natural rate of unemployment

Frictional unemployment

Sectoral shift

Unemployment insurance

Wage rigidity

Structural unemployment

Insiders versus outsiders

Non-accelerating rate of unemployment (NAIRU)

Efficiency wages

Discouraged workers

QUESTIONS FOR REVIEW

1. What determines the natural rate of unemployment?

2. Describe the difference between frictional unemployment and structural unemployment.

3. Give three explanations why the real wage may remain above the level that equilibrates labour supply and labour demand.

4. How do economists explain the fall in the natural rate of unemployment in the UK in the 1990s and early 2000s?

5. Why have Continental European countries tended to have higher rates of unemployment than the UK or the US?

PROBLEMS AND APPLICATIONS

1. Answer the following questions about your own experience in the labour force:

   a. When you or one of your friends is looking for a part-time job, how many weeks does it typically take? After you find a job, how many weeks does it typically last?

   b. From your estimates, calculate (in a rate per week) your rate of job finding f and your rate of job separation s. (*Hint:* If f is the rate of job finding, then the average spell of unemployment is $1/f$.)

   c. What is the natural rate of unemployment for the population you represent?

2. In this chapter we saw that the steady-state rate of unemployment is $U/L = s/(s + f)$. Suppose that the unemployment rate does not begin at this level. Show that unemployment will evolve over time and reach this steady state. (*Hint:* Express the change in the number of unemployed as a function of s, f and U. Then show that if unemployment is above the natural rate, unemployment falls, and if unemployment is below the natural rate, unemployment rises.)

3. The residents of a certain hall of residence have collected the following data: people who live in the hall can be classified as either involved in a relationship or uninvolved. Among involved people, 10 per cent experience a break-up of their relationship every month. Among uninvolved people, 5 per cent will enter into a relationship every month. What is the steady-state fraction of residents who are uninvolved?

4. Suppose that the government passes legislation making it more difficult for firms to fire work-

ers. (An example is a law requiring severance pay for fired workers.) If this legislation reduces the rate of job separation without affecting the rate of job finding, how would the natural rate of unemployment change? Do you think it is plausible that the legislation would not affect the rate of job finding? Why, or why not?

5. Consider an economy with the following Cobb–Douglas production function:

$$Y = K^{1/3}L^{2/3}.$$

The economy has 1000 units of capital and a labour force of 1000 workers.

   a. Derive the equation describing labour demand in this economy as a function of the real wage and the capital stock. (*Hint:* Review Chapter 3.)

   b. If the real wage can adjust to equilibrate labour supply and labour demand, what is the real wage? In this equilibrium, what are employment, output and the total amount earned by workers?

   c. Now suppose that the government, concerned about the welfare of the working class, passes a law requiring firms to pay workers a real wage of 1 unit of output. How does this wage compare to the equilibrium wage?

   d. The government cannot dictate how many workers firms hire at the mandated wage. Given this fact, what are the effects of this law? Specifically, what happens to employment, output and the total amount earned by workers?

e. Will the government succeed in its goal of helping the working class? Explain.

f. Do you think this analysis provides a good way of thinking about a minimum-wage law? Why, or why not?

6. Suppose that a country experiences a reduction in productivity – that is, an adverse shock to the production function.

a. What happens to the labour demand curve?

b. How would this change in productivity affect the labour market – that is, employment, unemployment and real wages – if the labour market were always in equilibrium?

c. How would this change in productivity affect the labour market if unions prevented real wages from falling?

7. In any city at any time, some of the stock of usable office space is vacant. This vacant office space is unemployed capital. How would you explain this phenomenon? Is it a social problem?

PART 3

Growth Theory: The Economy in the Very Long Run

CHAPTER 8

Economic Growth I: Capital Accumulation and Population Growth

The question of growth is nothing new but a new disguise for an age-old issue, one which has always intrigued and preoccupied economics: the present versus the future.

— James Tobin, 'Economic Growth as an Objective of Government Policy'

If you have ever spoken with your grandparents about what their lives were like when they were young, most likely you learned an important lesson about economic growth: material standards of living have improved substantially over time for most families in most countries. This advance comes from rising incomes, which have allowed people to consume greater quantities of goods and services.

To measure economic growth, economists use data on gross domestic product (GDP), which measures the total income of everyone in the economy. The real GDP of the United Kingdom today is more than three times its level 50 years ago, while real GDP per person has grown by only a slightly lower multiple (a factor of around two and three-quarters) over the same period. In any given year, we also observe large differences in the standard of living among countries. Table 8-1 shows income per person in 2011 for 26 countries (these figures are calculated by the World Bank, and, as is customary in international income comparisons of this kind, they are given in US dollars). Norway tops the list, with an income of $98,102 per person. Burundi has an income per person of only $271 – barely 0.28 per cent of the figure for Norway.

Our goal in this part of the book is to understand what causes these differences in income over time and across countries. In Chapter 3 we identified the factors of production – capital and labour – and the production technology as the sources of the economy's output and, thus, of its total income. Differences in income, then, must come from differences in capital, labour and technology.

Our primary task in this chapter and the next is to develop a theory of economic growth called the **Solow growth model**. Our analysis in Chapter 3 enabled us to describe how the economy produces and uses its output at one

TABLE 8-1

International Differences in the Standard of Living

Country	Income Per Person (2011)
Norway	$98,102
Switzerland	$83,383
Denmark	$59,852
Sweden	$57,091
Netherlands	$50,076
Ireland	$48,423
United States	$48,112
Japan	$45,903
Germany	$44,060
France	$42,377
United Kingdom	$39,038
Italy	$36,103
Spain	$31,943
Croatia	$14,180
Poland	$13,463
Russia	$13,089
Brazil	$12,594
Mexico	$10,047
China	$ 5445
Indonesia	$ 3495
Nigeria	$ 1502
India	$ 1489
Vietnam	$ 1407
Pakistan	$ 1189
Bangladesh	$ 743
Burundi	$ 271

Source: The World Bank.

point in time. The analysis was static – a snapshot of the economy. To explain why national income grows, and why some economies grow faster than others, we must broaden our analysis so that it describes changes in the economy over time. By developing such a model, we make our analysis dynamic – more like a film than a photograph. The Solow growth model shows how saving, population growth and technological progress affect the level of an economy's output and its growth over time. In this chapter we analyse the roles of saving and population growth. In the next chapter we introduce technological progress.[1]

---

[1] The Solow growth model is named after economist Robert Solow and was developed in the 1950s and 1960s. In 1987, Solow won the Nobel Prize in economics for his work in economic growth. The model was introduced in Robert M. Solow, 'A Contribution to the Theory of Economic Growth', *Quarterly Journal of Economics*, 1956, pp. 65–94. Sometimes the Solow growth model is loosely referred to as the 'neoclassical growth model'.

8-1 The Accumulation of Capital

The Solow growth model is designed to show how growth in the capital stock, growth in the labour force and advances in technology interact in an economy, and how they affect a nation's total output of goods and services. We will build this model in a series of steps. Our first step is to examine how the supply and demand for goods determine the accumulation of capital. In this first step, we assume that the labour force and technology are fixed. We then relax these assumptions by introducing changes in the labour force (later in this chapter) and then changes in technology (in the following chapter).

The Supply and Demand for Goods

The supply and demand for goods played a central role in our static model of the closed economy in Chapter 3. The same is true for the Solow model. By considering the supply and demand for goods, we can see what determines how much output is produced at any given time and how this output is allocated among alternative uses.

The Supply of Goods and the Production Function The supply of goods in the Solow model is based on the production function, which states that output (Y) depends on the capital stock (K) and the labour force (L):

$$Y = F(K, L).$$

The Solow growth model assumes that the production function has constant returns to scale. This assumption is often considered realistic and, as we will see shortly, it helps to simplify the analysis. Recall that a production function has constant returns to scale if

$$zY = F(zK, zL)$$

for any positive number z. That is, if both capital and labour are multiplied by z, the amount of output is also multiplied by z.

Production functions with constant returns to scale allow us to analyse all quantities in the economy relative to the size of the labour force. To see that this is true, set $z = 1/L$ in the preceding equation to obtain

$$Y/L = F(K/L, 1).$$

This equation shows that the amount of output per worker Y/L is a function of the amount of capital per worker K/L. (The number '1' is constant and thus can be ignored.) The assumption of constant returns to scale implies that the size of the economy — as measured by the number of workers — does not affect the relationship between output per worker and capital per worker.

Because the size of the economy does not matter, it will prove convenient to denote all quantities in per-worker terms. We designate quantities per worker

FIGURE 8-1

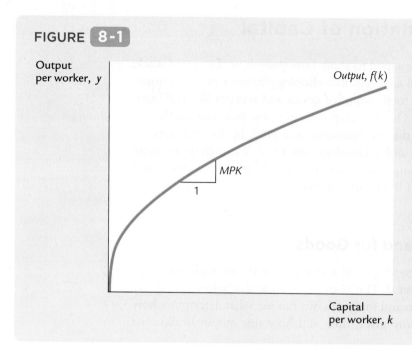

Output per worker, y

Output, $f(k)$

MPK

1

Capital per worker, k

The Production Function The production function shows how the amount of capital per worker k determines the amount of output per worker $y = f(k)$. The slope of the production function is the marginal product of capital: if k increases by 1 unit, y increases by MPK units. The production function becomes flatter as k increases, indicating diminishing marginal product of capital.

with lower-case letters, so $y = Y/L$ is output per worker, and $k = K/L$ is capital per worker. We can then write the production function as

$$y = f(k),$$

where we define $f(k) = F(k, 1)$. Figure 8-1 illustrates this production function.

The slope of this production function shows how much extra output a worker produces when given an extra unit of capital. This amount is the marginal product of capital MPK. Mathematically, we write

$$MPK = f(k + 1) - f(k).$$

Note that in Figure 8-1, as the amount of capital increases, the production function becomes flatter, indicating that the production function exhibits diminishing marginal product of capital. When k is low, the average worker has only a little capital to work with, so an extra unit of capital is very useful and produces a lot of additional output. When k is high, the average worker has a lot of capital, so an extra unit increases production only slightly.

The Demand for Goods and the Consumption Function The demand for goods in the Solow model comes from consumption and investment. In other words, output per worker y is divided between consumption per worker c and investment per worker i:

$$y = c + i.$$

This equation is the per-worker version of the national income accounts identity for an economy. Notice that it omits government purchases (which we can ignore for present purposes) and net exports (because we are assuming a closed economy).

The Solow model assumes that each year people save a fraction s of their income and consume a fraction $(1 - s)$. We can express this idea with the following consumption function:

$$c = (1 - s)y,$$

where s, the saving rate, is a number between zero and one. Keep in mind that various government policies can potentially influence a nation's saving rate, so one of our goals is to find what saving rate is desirable. For now, however, we just take the saving rate s as given.

To see what this consumption function implies for investment, substitute $(1 - s)y$ for c in the national income accounts identity:

$$y = (1 - s)y + i.$$

Rearrange the terms to obtain

$$i = sy.$$

This equation shows that investment equals saving, as we first saw in Chapter 3. Thus, the rate of saving s is also the fraction of output devoted to investment.

We have now introduced the two main ingredients of the Solow model — the production function and the consumption function — which describe the economy at any moment in time. For any given capital stock k, the production function $y = f(k)$ determines how much output the economy produces, and the saving rate s determines the allocation of that output between consumption and investment.

Growth in the Capital Stock and the Steady State

At any moment, the capital stock is a key determinant of the economy's output, but the capital stock can change over time, and those changes can lead to economic growth. In particular, two forces influence the capital stock: investment and depreciation. *Investment* refers to the expenditure on new plant and equipment, and it causes the capital stock to rise. *Depreciation* refers to the wearing out of old capital, and it causes the capital stock to fall. Let's consider each of these in turn.

As we have already noted, investment per worker i equals sy. By substituting the production function for y, we can express investment per worker as a function of the capital stock per worker:

$$i = sf(k).$$

This equation relates the existing stock of capital k to the accumulation of new capital i. Figure 8-2 shows this relationship. This figure illustrates how, for any value of k, the amount of output is determined by the production function $f(k)$, and the allocation of that output between consumption and saving is determined by the saving rate s.

FIGURE 8-2

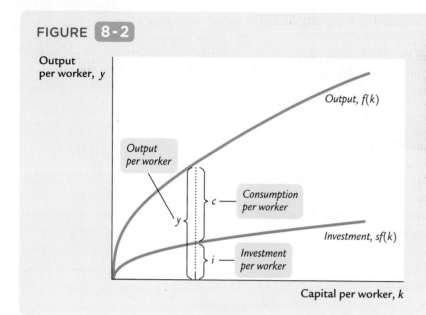

Output per worker, y

Output, $f(k)$

Output per worker

y

c — Consumption per worker

Investment, $sf(k)$

i — Investment per worker

Capital per worker, k

Output, Consumption and Investment The saving rate s determines the allocation of output between consumption and investment. For any level of capital k, output is $f(k)$, investment is $sf(k)$ and consumption is $f(k) - sf(k)$.

To incorporate depreciation into the model, we assume that a certain fraction δ of the capital stock wears out each year. Here δ (the lower-case Greek letter delta) is called the *depreciation rate*. For example, if capital lasts an average of 25 years, then the depreciation rate is 4 per cent per year ($\delta = 0.04$). The amount of capital that depreciates each year is δk. Figure 8-3 shows how the amount of depreciation depends on the capital stock.

FIGURE 8-3

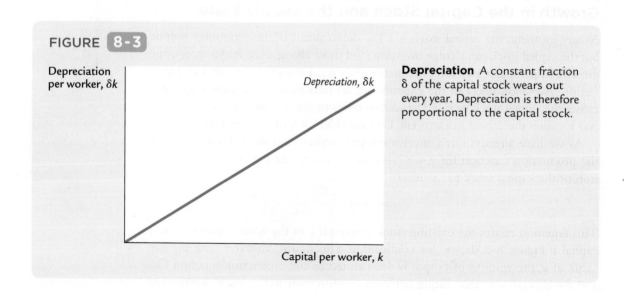

Depreciation per worker, δk

Depreciation, δk

Capital per worker, k

Depreciation A constant fraction δ of the capital stock wears out every year. Depreciation is therefore proportional to the capital stock.

We can express the impact of investment and depreciation on the capital stock with this equation:

$$\text{Change in Capital Stock} = \text{Investment} - \text{Depreciation}$$
$$\Delta k = I - \delta k,$$

where Δk is the change in the capital stock between one year and the next. Because investment i equals $sf(k)$, we can write this as

$$\Delta k = sf(k) - \delta k.$$

Figure 8-4 graphs the terms of this equation — investment and depreciation — for different levels of the capital stock k. The higher the capital stock, the greater the amounts of output and investment. Yet the higher the capital stock, the greater also the amount of depreciation.

As Figure 8-4 shows, there is a single capital stock k^* at which the amount of investment equals the amount of depreciation. If the economy finds itself at this level of the capital stock, the capital stock will not change, because the two forces acting on it — investment and depreciation — just balance. That is, at k^*, $\Delta k = 0$, so the capital stock k and output $f(k)$ are steady over time (rather than growing or shrinking). Thus we call k^* the steady-state level of capital.

The **steady state** is significant for two reasons. As we have just seen, an economy at the steady state will stay there. In addition, and just as important, an economy *not* at the steady state will go there. That is, regardless of the level of capital with which the economy begins, it ends up with the steady-state level of capital. In this sense, *the steady state represents the long-run equilibrium of the economy.*

FIGURE 8-4

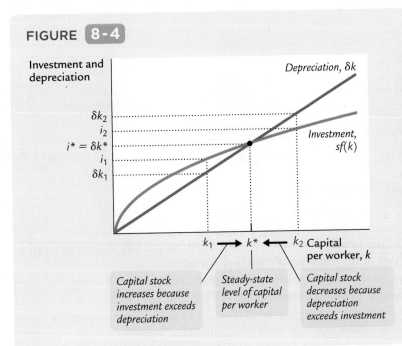

Investment, Depreciation and the Steady State
The steady-state level of capital k^* is the level at which investment equals depreciation, indicating that the amount of capital will not change over time. Below k^*, investment exceeds depreciation, so the capital stock grows. Above k^*, investment is less than depreciation, so the capital stock shrinks.

To see why an economy always ends up at the steady state, suppose that the economy starts with less than the steady-state level of capital, such as level k_1 in Figure 7-4. In this case, the level of investment exceeds the amount of depreciation. Over time, the capital stock will rise and will continue to rise – along with output $f(k)$ – until it approaches the steady state k^*.

Similarly, suppose that the economy starts with more than the steady-state level of capital, such as level k_2. In this case, investment is less than depreciation: capital is wearing out faster than it is being replaced. The capital stock will fall, again approaching the steady-state level. Once the capital stock reaches the steady state, investment equals depreciation, and there is no pressure for the capital stock to either increase or decrease.

Approaching the Steady State: A Numerical Example

Let's use a numerical example to see how the Solow model works and how the economy approaches the steady state. For this example, we assume that the production function is

$$Y = K^{1/2}L^{1/2}.$$

You will recognize this as the Cobb–Douglas production function (from Chapter 3), with the capital-share parameter α equal to $1/2$. To derive the per-worker production function $f(k)$, divide both sides of the production function by the labour force L:

$$\frac{Y}{L} = \frac{K^{1/2}L^{1/2}}{L}.$$

Rearrange to obtain

$$\frac{Y}{L} = \left(\frac{K}{L}\right)^{1/2}.$$

Because $y = Y/L$ and $k = K/L$, this equation becomes

$$y = k^{1/2},$$

which can also be written as

$$y = \sqrt{k}.$$

This form of the production function states that output per worker is equal to the square root of the amount of capital per worker.

To complete the example, let's assume that 30 per cent of output is saved ($s = 0.3$), that 10 per cent of the capital stock depreciates every year ($\delta = 0.1$), and that the economy starts off with 4 units of capital per worker ($k = 4$). Given these numbers, we can now examine what happens to this economy over time.

We begin by looking at the production and allocation of output in the first year, when the economy has 4 units of capital. Here are the steps we follow.

- According to the production function $y = \sqrt{k}$, the 4 units of capital per worker k produce 2 units of output per worker y.
- Because 30 per cent of output is saved and invested, and 70 per cent is consumed, $i = 0.6$ and $c = 1.4$.
- Because 10 per cent of the capital stock depreciates, $\delta k = 0.4$.
- With investment of 0.6 and depreciation of 0.4, the change in the capital stock is $\Delta k = 0.2$.

Thus, the economy begins its second year with 4.2 units of capital per worker.

We can do the same calculations for each subsequent year. Table 8-2 shows how the economy progresses. Every year, because investment exceeds depreciation, new capital is added and output grows. Over many years, the economy approaches a steady state with 9 units of capital per worker. In this steady state, investment of 0.9 exactly offsets depreciation of 0.9, so that the capital stock and output are no longer growing.

TABLE 8-2

Approaching the Steady State: A Numerical Example
Assumptions: $y = \sqrt{k}$; $s = 0.3$; $\delta = 0.1$; initial $k = 4.0$

Year	k	y	c	i	δk	Δk
1	4.000	2.000	1.400	0.600	0.400	0.200
2	4.200	2.049	1.435	0.615	0.420	0.195
3	4.395	2.096	1.467	0.629	0.440	0.189
4	4.584	2.141	1.499	0.642	0.458	0.184
5	4.768	2.184	1.529	0.655	0.477	0.178
⋮						
10	5.602	2.367	1.657	0.710	0.560	0.150
⋮						
25	7.321	2.706	1.894	0.812	0.732	0.080
⋮						
100	8.962	2.994	2.096	0.898	0.896	0.002
⋮						
∞	9.000	3.000	2.100	0.900	0.900	0.000

Following the progress of the economy for many years is one way to find the steady-state capital stock, but there is another way that requires fewer calculations. Recall that

$$\Delta k = sf(k) - \delta k.$$

This equation shows how k evolves over time. Because the steady state is (by definition) the value of k at which $\Delta k = 0$, we know that

$$0 = sf(k^*) - \delta k^*,$$

or, equivalently,

$$\frac{k^*}{f(k^*)} = \frac{s}{\delta}.$$

This equation provides a way of finding the steady-state level of capital per worker, k^*. Substituting the numbers and production function from our example, we obtain

$$\frac{k^*}{\sqrt{k^*}} = \frac{0.3}{0.1}.$$

Now square both sides of this equation to find

$$k^* = 9.$$

The steady-state capital stock is 9 units per worker. This result confirms the calculation of the steady state in Table 8-2.

The Miracle of Japanese and German Growth

Japan and Germany are two success stories of economic growth. Although today they are economic superpowers, in 1945 the economies of both countries were in a shambles. World War II had destroyed much of their capital stocks. In the decades after the war, however, these two countries experienced some of the most rapid growth rates on record. Between 1948 and 1972, output per person grew at 8.2 per cent per year in Japan and 5.7 per cent per year in Germany, compared to only 2.2 per cent per year in the United States.

Are the post-war experiences of Japan and Germany so surprising from the standpoint of the Solow growth model? Consider an economy in steady state. Now suppose that a war destroys some of the capital stock. (That is, suppose the capital stock drops from k^* to k_1 in Figure 8-4.) Not surprisingly, the level of output falls immediately. But if the saving rate – the fraction of output devoted to saving and investment – is unchanged, the economy will then experience a period of high growth. Output grows because, at the lower capital stock, more capital is added by investment than is removed by depreciation. This high growth continues until the economy approaches its former steady state. Hence, although destroying part of the capital stock immediately reduces output, it is followed by higher-than-normal growth. The 'miracle' of rapid growth in Japan and Germany, as it is often described in the business press, is what the Solow model predicts for countries in which war has greatly reduced the capital stock. ∎

How Saving Affects Growth

The explanation of Japanese and German growth after World War II is not quite as simple as suggested in the preceding case study. Another relevant fact is that both Japan and Germany save and invest a high fraction of their output. To understand more fully the international differences in economic performance, we must consider the effects of different saving rates.

Consider what happens to an economy when its saving rate increases. Figure 8-5 shows such a change. The economy is assumed to begin in a steady state, with saving rate s_1 and capital stock k_1^*. When the saving rate increases from s_1 to s_2, the $sf(k)$ curve shifts upward. At the initial saving rate s_1 and the initial capital stock k_2^*, the amount of investment just offsets the amount of depreciation. Immediately after the saving rate rises, investment is higher, but the capital stock and depreciation are unchanged. Therefore, investment exceeds depreciation. The capital stock will gradually rise until the economy reaches the new steady state k_2^*, which has a higher capital stock and a higher level of output than the old steady state.

FIGURE 8-5

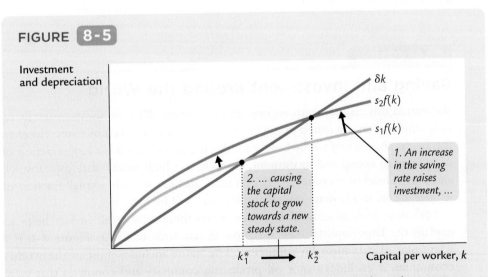

An Increase in the Saving Rate An increase in the saving rate s implies that the amount of investment for any given capital stock is higher. It therefore shifts the saving function upward. At the initial steady state k_1^*, investment now exceeds depreciation. The capital stock rises until the economy reaches a new steady state k_2^*, with more capital and output.

The Solow model shows that the saving rate is a key determinant of the steady-state capital stock. *If the saving rate is high, the economy will have a large capital stock and a high level of output in the steady state. If the saving rate is low, the economy will have a small capital stock and a low level of output in the steady state.* This conclusion sheds light on many discussions of fiscal policy. As we saw in Chapter 3, a government budget deficit can reduce national saving and crowd out investment. Now we can see that the long-run consequences of a reduced saving rate are a lower capital stock and lower national income. This is why many economists are critical of persistent budget deficits.

What does the Solow model say about the relationship between saving and economic growth? Higher saving leads to faster growth in the Solow model, but only temporarily. An increase in the rate of saving raises growth only until the economy reaches the new steady state. If the economy maintains a high saving rate, it will maintain a large capital stock and a high level of output, but it will not maintain a high rate of growth for ever. Policies that alter the steady-state growth rate of income per person are said to have a *growth effect;* we will see examples of such policies in the next chapter. By contrast, a higher saving rate is said to have a *level effect,* because only the level of income per person – and not its growth rate – is influenced by the saving rate in the steady state.

Now that we understand how saving and growth interact, we can explain more fully the impressive economic performance of Germany and Japan after World War II. Not only were their initial capital stocks low because of the war, but their steady-state capital stocks were high because of their high saving rates. Both these facts help to explain the rapid growth of these two countries in the 1950s and 1960s.

Saving and Investment around the World

We started this chapter with an important question: Why are some countries so rich while others are mired in poverty? Our analysis has taken us a step closer to the answer. According to the Solow model, if a nation devotes a large fraction of its income to saving and investment, it will have a high steady-state capital stock and a high level of income. If a nation saves and invests only a small fraction of its income, its steady-state capital and income will be low.

Let's now look at some data to see if this theoretical result in fact helps to explain the large international variation in standards of living. Figure 8-6 is a scatterplot of data from 96 countries. (The figure includes most of the world's economies. It excludes major oil-producing countries and countries that were communist during much of this period, because their experiences are explained by their special circumstances.) The data show a positive relationship between the fraction of output devoted to investment and the level of income per person. That is, countries with high rates of investment, such as the United Kingdom, the United States and Japan, usually have high incomes, whereas countries with low rates of investment, such as Ethiopia and Burundi, have low incomes. Thus, the

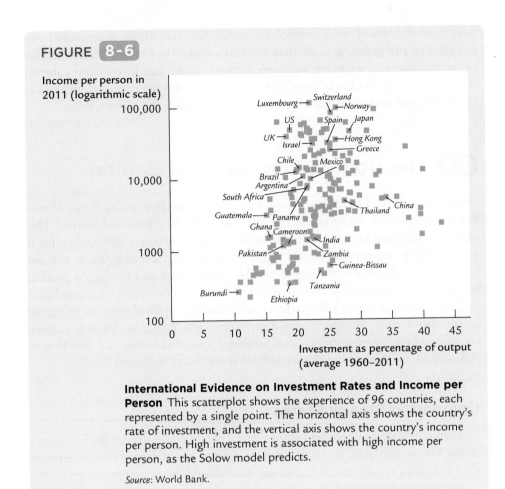

FIGURE 8-6

International Evidence on Investment Rates and Income per Person This scatterplot shows the experience of 96 countries, each represented by a single point. The horizontal axis shows the country's rate of investment, and the vertical axis shows the country's income per person. High investment is associated with high income per person, as the Solow model predicts.

Source: World Bank.

data are consistent with the Solow model's prediction that the investment rate is a key determinant of whether a country is rich or poor.

The strong correlation shown in this figure is an important fact, but it raises as many questions as it resolves. One might naturally ask why rates of saving and investment vary so much from country to country. There are many potential answers, such as tax policy, retirement patterns, the development of financial markets and cultural differences. In addition, political stability may play a role: not surprisingly, rates of saving and investment tend to be low in countries with frequent wars, revolutions and coups. Saving and investment also tend to be low in countries with poor political institutions, as measured by estimates of official corruption. A final interpretation of the evidence in Figure 8-6 is reverse causation: perhaps high levels of income somehow foster high rates of saving and investment. Unfortunately, there is no consensus among economists about which of the many possible explanations is most important.

The association between investment rates and income per person is strong, and it is an important clue as to why some countries are rich and others poor, but it is not the whole story. The correlation between these two variables is far from perfect. Mexico and Zambia, for instance, have had similar investment rates, but income per person is more than ten times higher in Mexico. There must be other determinants of living standards beyond saving and investment. Later in this chapter, and also in the next one, we return to the international differences in income per person to see what other variables enter the picture. ∎

8-2 The Golden Rule Level of Capital

So far, we have used the Solow model to examine how an economy's rate of saving and investment determines its steady-state levels of capital and income. This analysis might lead you to think that higher saving is always a good thing, for it always leads to greater income. Yet suppose a nation had a saving rate of 100 per cent. That would lead to the largest possible capital stock and the largest possible income. But if all this income is saved and none is ever consumed, what good is it?

This section uses the Solow model to discuss the optimal amount of capital accumulation from the standpoint of economic well-being. In the next chapter, we discuss how government policies influence a nation's saving rate. But first, in this section, we present the theory behind these policy decisions.

Comparing Steady States

To keep our analysis simple, let's assume that a policy maker can set the economy's saving rate at any level. By setting the saving rate, the policy maker determines the economy's steady state. What steady state should the policy maker choose?

When choosing a steady state, the policy maker's goal is to maximize the well-being of the individuals who make up the society. Individuals themselves do not care about the amount of capital in the economy, or even the amount of output. They care about the amount of goods and services they can consume. Thus, a benevolent policy maker would want to choose the steady state with the highest level of consumption. The steady-state value of k that maximizes consumption is called the **Golden Rule level of capital** and is denoted k^*_{gold}.[2]

How can we tell whether an economy is at the Golden Rule level? To answer this question, we must first determine steady-state consumption per worker. Then we can see which steady state provides the most consumption.

To find steady-state consumption per worker, we begin with the national income accounts identity

$$y = c + i$$

and rearrange it as

$$c = y - i.$$

---

[2] Edmund Phelps, 'The Golden Rule of Accumulation: A Fable for Growthmen', *American Economic Review*, 1961, vol. 51, pp. 638–643.

Consumption is simply output minus investment. Because we want to find steady-state consumption, we substitute steady-state values for output and investment. Steady-state output per worker is $f(k^*)$, where k^* is the steady-state capital stock per worker. Furthermore, because the capital stock is not changing in the steady state, investment is equal to depreciation δk^*. Substituting $f(k^*)$ for y, and δk^* for i, we can write steady-state consumption per worker as

$$c^* = f(k^*) - \delta k^*.$$

According to this equation, steady-state consumption is what is left of steady-state output after paying for steady-state depreciation. This equation shows that an increase in steady-state capital has two opposing effects on steady-state consumption. On the one hand, more capital means more output. On the other hand, more capital also means that more output must be used to replace capital that is wearing out.

Figure 8-7 graphs steady-state output and steady-state depreciation as a function of the steady-state capital stock. Steady-state consumption is the gap between output and depreciation. This figure shows that there is one level of the capital stock – the Golden Rule level k^*_{gold} – that maximizes consumption.

When comparing steady states, we must keep in mind that higher levels of capital affect both output and depreciation. If the capital stock is below the Golden Rule level, an increase in the capital stock raises output more than

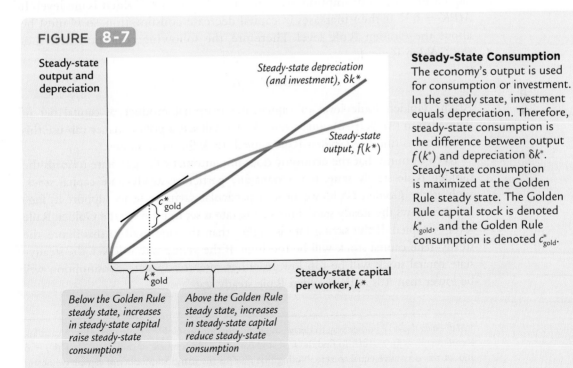

FIGURE 8-7

Steady-state output and depreciation

Steady-state depreciation (and investment), δk^*

Steady-state output, $f(k^*)$

c^*_{gold}

k^*_{gold}

Steady-state capital per worker, k^*

Below the Golden Rule steady state, increases in steady-state capital raise steady-state consumption

Above the Golden Rule steady state, increases in steady-state capital reduce steady-state consumption

Steady-State Consumption
The economy's output is used for consumption or investment. In the steady state, investment equals depreciation. Therefore, steady-state consumption is the difference between output $f(k^*)$ and depreciation δk^*. Steady-state consumption is maximized at the Golden Rule steady state. The Golden Rule capital stock is denoted k^*_{gold}, and the Golden Rule consumption is denoted c^*_{gold}.

depreciation, so that consumption rises. In this case, the production function is steeper than the δk^* line, so the gap between these two curves — which equals consumption — grows as k^* rises. By contrast, if the capital stock is above the Golden Rule level, an increase in the capital stock reduces consumption, since the increase in output is smaller than the increase in depreciation. In this case, the production function is flatter than the δk^* line, so the gap between the curves — consumption — shrinks as k^* rises. At the Golden Rule level of capital, the production function and the δk^* line have the same slope, and consumption is at its greatest level.

We can now derive a simple condition that characterizes the Golden Rule level of capital. Recall that the slope of the production function is the marginal product of capital MPK. The slope of the δk^* line is δ. Because these two slopes are equal at k^*_{gold}, the Golden Rule is described by the equation

$$MPK = \delta.$$

At the Golden Rule level of capital, the marginal product of capital equals the depreciation rate.

To make the point somewhat differently, suppose that the economy starts at some steady-state capital stock k^* and that the policy maker is considering increasing the capital stock to $k^* + 1$. The amount of extra output from this increase in capital would be $f(k^* + 1) - f(k^*)$, the marginal product of capital MPK. The amount of extra depreciation from having 1 more unit of capital is the depreciation rate δ. Thus, the net effect of this extra unit of capital on consumption is $MPK - \delta$. If $MPK - \delta > 0$, then increases in capital increase consumption, so k^* must be below the Golden Rule level. If $MPK - \delta < 0$, then increases in capital decrease consumption, so k^* must be above the Golden Rule level. Therefore, the following condition describes the Golden Rule:

$$MPK - \delta = 0.$$

At the Golden Rule level of capital, the marginal product of capital net of depreciation ($MPK - \delta$) equals zero. As we will see, a policy maker can use this condition to find the Golden Rule capital stock for an economy.[3]

Keep in mind that the economy does not automatically gravitate towards the Golden Rule steady state. If we want any particular steady-state capital stock, such as the Golden Rule, we need a particular saving rate to support it. Figure 8-8 shows the steady state if the saving rate is set to produce the Golden Rule level of capital. If the saving rate is higher than the one used in this figure, the steady-state capital stock will be too high. If the saving rate is lower, the steady-state capital stock will be too low. In either case, steady-state consumption will be lower than it is at the Golden Rule steady state.

---

[3] *Mathematical note:* Another way to derive the condition for the Golden Rule uses a bit of calculus. Recall that $c^* = f(k^*) - \delta k^*$. To find the k^* that maximizes c^*, differentiate to find $dc^*/dk^* = f'(k^*) - \delta$ and set this derivative equal to zero. Noting that $f'(k^*)$ is the marginal product of capital, we obtain the Golden Rule condition in the text.

FIGURE 8-8

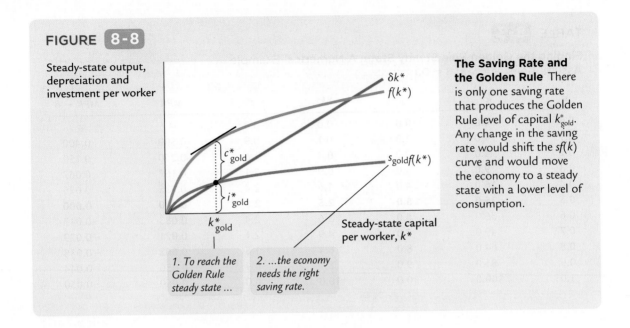

Steady-state output, depreciation and investment per worker

δk^*

$f(k^*)$

c^*_{gold}

$s_{gold}f(k^*)$

i^*_{gold}

k^*_{gold}

Steady-state capital per worker, k^*

1. To reach the Golden Rule steady state ...

2. ...the economy needs the right saving rate.

The Saving Rate and the Golden Rule There is only one saving rate that produces the Golden Rule level of capital k^*_{gold}. Any change in the saving rate would shift the $sf(k)$ curve and would move the economy to a steady state with a lower level of consumption.

Finding the Golden Rule Steady State: A Numerical Example

Consider the decision of a policy maker choosing a steady state in the following economy. The production function is the same as in our earlier example:

$$y = \sqrt{k}.$$

Output per worker is the square root of capital per worker. Depreciation δ is again 10 per cent of capital. This time, the policy maker chooses the saving rate s and thus the economy's steady state.

To see the outcomes available to the policy maker, recall that the following equation holds in the steady state:

$$\frac{k^*}{f(k^*)} = \frac{s}{\delta}.$$

In this economy, this equation becomes

$$\frac{k^*}{\sqrt{k^*}} = \frac{s}{0.1}.$$

Squaring both sides of this equation yields a solution for the steady-state capital stock. We find

$$k^* = 100s^2.$$

Using this result, we can compute the steady-state capital stock for any saving rate.

Table 8-3 presents calculations showing the steady states that result from various saving rates in this economy. We see that higher saving leads to a higher

TABLE 8-3

Finding the Golden Rule Steady State: A Numerical Example
Assumptions: $y = \sqrt{k}$; $\delta = 0.1$

s	k^*	y^*	δk^*	c^*	MPK	$MPK - \delta$
0.0	0.0	0.0	0.0	0.0	∞	∞
0.1	1.0	1.0	0.1	0.9	0.500	0.400
0.2	4.0	2.0	0.4	1.6	0.250	0.150
0.3	9.0	3.0	0.9	2.1	0.167	0.067
0.4	16.0	4.0	1.6	2.4	0.125	0.025
0.5	**25.0**	**5.0**	**2.5**	**2.5**	**0.100**	**0.000**
0.6	36.0	6.0	3.6	2.4	0.083	−0.017
0.7	49.0	7.0	4.9	2.1	0.071	−0.029
0.8	64.0	8.0	6.4	1.6	0.062	−0.038
0.9	81.0	9.0	8.1	0.9	0.056	−0.044
1.0	100.0	10.0	10.0	0.0	0.050	−0.050

capital stock, which in turn leads to higher output and higher depreciation. Steady-state consumption, the difference between output and depreciation, first rises with higher saving rates and then declines. Consumption is highest when the saving rate is 0.5. Hence, a saving rate of 0.5 produces the Golden Rule steady state.

Recall that another way to identify the Golden Rule steady state is to find the capital stock at which the net marginal product of capital ($MPK - \delta$) equals zero. For this production function, the marginal product is[4]

$$MPK = \frac{1}{2\sqrt{k}}.$$

Using this formula, the last two columns of Table 8-3 present the values of MPK and $MPK - \delta$ in the different steady states. Note that the net marginal product of capital is exactly zero when the saving rate is at its Golden Rule value of 0.5. Because of diminishing marginal product, the net marginal product of capital is greater than zero whenever the economy saves less than this amount, and it is less than zero whenever the economy saves more.

This numerical example confirms that the two ways of finding the Golden Rule steady state – looking at steady-state consumption or looking at the marginal product of capital – give the same answer. If we want to know whether an actual economy is currently at, above or below its Golden Rule capital stock, the second method is usually more convenient, because it is relatively straightforward

---

[4] *Mathematical note:* To derive this formula, note that the marginal product of capital is the derivative of the production function with respect to k.

to estimate the marginal product of capital. By contrast, evaluating an economy with the first method requires estimates of steady-state consumption at many different saving rates; such information is harder to obtain. Thus, when we apply this kind of analysis to the US economy in the next chapter, we will evaluate US saving by examining the marginal product of capital. Before engaging in that policy analysis, however, we need to proceed further in our development and understanding of the Solow model.

The Transition to the Golden Rule Steady State

Let's now make our policy maker's problem more realistic. So far, we have been assuming that the policy maker can simply choose the economy's steady state and jump there immediately. In this case, the policy maker would choose the steady state with highest consumption – the Golden Rule steady state. But now suppose that the economy has reached a steady state other than the Golden Rule. What happens to consumption, investment and capital when the economy makes the transition between steady states? Might the impact of the transition deter the policy maker from trying to achieve the Golden Rule?

We must consider two cases: the economy might begin with more capital than in the Golden Rule steady state, or with less. It turns out that the two cases offer very different problems for policy makers. (As we will see in the next chapter, the second case – too little capital – describes most actual economies.)

Starting with Too Much Capital We first consider the case in which the economy begins at a steady state with more capital than it would have in the Golden Rule steady state. In this case, the policy maker should pursue policies aimed at reducing the rate of saving in order to reduce the capital stock. Suppose that these policies succeed and that at some point – call it time t_0 – the saving rate falls to the level that will eventually lead to the Golden Rule steady state.

Figure 8-9 shows what happens to output, consumption and investment when the saving rate falls. The reduction in the saving rate causes an immediate increase in consumption and a decrease in investment. Because investment and depreciation were equal in the initial steady state, investment will now be less than depreciation, which means the economy is no longer in a steady state. Gradually, the capital stock falls, leading to reductions in output, consumption and investment. These variables continue to fall until the economy reaches the new steady state. Because we are assuming that the new steady state is the Golden Rule steady state, consumption must be higher than it was before the change in the saving rate, even though output and investment are lower.

Note that, compared to the old steady state, consumption is higher not only in the new steady state, but also along the entire path to it. When the capital stock exceeds the Golden Rule level, reducing saving is clearly a good policy, for it increases consumption at every point in time.

Starting with Too Little Capital When the economy begins with less capital than in the Golden Rule steady state, the policy maker must raise the saving

FIGURE **8-9**

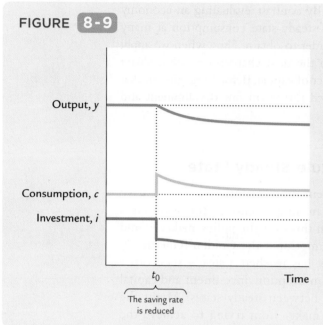

Reducing Saving When Starting with More Capital Than in the Golden Rule Steady State This figure shows what happens over time to output, consumption and investment when the economy begins with more capital than the Golden Rule level and the saving rate is reduced. The reduction in the saving rate (at time t_0) causes an immediate increase in consumption and an equal decrease in investment. Over time, as the capital stock falls, output, consumption and investment fall together. Because the economy began with too much capital, the new steady state has a higher level of consumption than the initial steady state.

Output, y

Consumption, c

Investment, i

t_0 Time

The saving rate is reduced

rate to reach the Golden Rule. Figure 8-10 shows what happens. The increase in the saving rate at time t_0 causes an immediate fall in consumption and a rise in investment. Over time, higher investment causes the capital stock to rise. As capital accumulates, output, consumption and investment gradually increase, eventually approaching the new steady-state levels. Because the initial steady state

FIGURE **8-10**

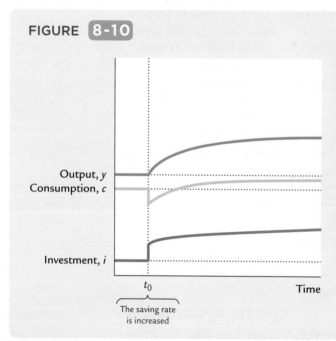

Increasing Saving When Starting with Less Capital Than in the Golden Rule Steady State This figure shows what happens over time to output, consumption and investment when the economy begins with less capital than the Golden Rule and the saving rate is increased. The increase in the saving rate (at time t_0) causes an immediate drop in consumption and an equal jump in investment. Over time, as the capital stock grows, output, consumption and investment increase together. Because the economy began with less capital than the Golden Rule, the new steady state has a higher level of consumption than the initial steady state.

Output, y
Consumption, c

Investment, i

t_0 Time

The saving rate is increased

was below the Golden Rule, the increase in saving eventually leads to a higher level of consumption than that which prevailed initially.

Does the increase in saving that leads to the Golden Rule steady state raise economic welfare? Eventually it does, because the new steady-state level of consumption is higher than the initial level. But achieving that new steady state requires an initial period of reduced consumption. Note the contrast to the case in which the economy begins above the Golden Rule. *When the economy begins above the Golden Rule, reaching the Golden Rule produces higher consumption at all points in time. When the economy begins below the Golden Rule, reaching the Golden Rule requires initially reducing consumption to increase consumption in the future.*

When deciding whether to try to reach the Golden Rule steady state, policy makers have to take into account that current consumers and future consumers are not always the same people. Reaching the Golden Rule achieves the highest steady-state level of consumption and so benefits future generations. But when the economy is initially below the Golden Rule, reaching the Golden Rule requires raising investment and thus lowering the consumption of current generations. Thus, when choosing whether to increase capital accumulation, the policy maker faces a trade-off between the welfare of different generations. A policy maker who cares more about current generations than about future generations may decide not to pursue policies to reach the Golden Rule steady state. By contrast, a policy maker who cares about all generations equally will choose to reach the Golden Rule. Even though current generations will consume less, an infinite number of future generations will benefit by moving to the Golden Rule.

Thus, optimal capital accumulation depends crucially on how we weigh the interests of current and future generations. The biblical Golden Rule tells us, 'Do unto others as you would have them do unto you.' If we heed this advice, we give all generations equal weight. In this case, it is optimal to reach the Golden Rule level of capital – which is why it is called the 'Golden Rule'.

8-3 Population Growth

The basic Solow model shows that capital accumulation, by itself, cannot explain sustained economic growth: high rates of saving lead to high growth temporarily, but the economy eventually approaches a steady state in which capital and output are constant. To explain the sustained economic growth that we observe in most parts of the world, we must expand the Solow model to incorporate the other two sources of economic growth – population growth and technological progress. In this section we add population growth to the model.

Instead of assuming that the population is fixed, as we did in Sections 7-1 and 7-2, we now suppose that the population and the labour force grow at the same constant rate of n per period. For example, the UK population grows about 0.7 per cent per year, so $n = 0.007$. This means that if 30 million people are working one year, then 30.21 million (1.007×30) are working the next year, and 30.42 million (1.007×30.21) the year after that, and so on.

The Steady State with Population Growth

How does population growth affect the steady state? To answer this question, we must discuss how population growth, along with investment and depreciation, influences the accumulation of capital per worker. As we noted before, investment raises the capital stock, and depreciation reduces it. But now there is a third force acting to change the amount of capital per worker: the growth in the number of workers causes capital per worker to fall.

We continue to let lower-case letters stand for quantities per worker. Thus, $k = K/L$ is capital per worker, and $y = Y/L$ is output per worker. Keep in mind, however, that the number of workers is growing over time.

The change in the capital stock per worker is

$$\Delta k = i - (\delta + n)k.$$

This equation shows how investment, depreciation and population growth influence the per-worker capital stock. Investment increases k, whereas depreciation and population growth decrease k. We saw this equation earlier in this chapter for the special case of a constant population ($n = 0$).

We can think of the term $(\delta + n)k$ as defining *break-even investment* – the amount of investment necessary to keep the capital stock per worker constant. Break-even investment includes the depreciation of existing capital, which equals δk. It also includes the amount of investment necessary to provide new workers with capital. The amount of investment necessary for this purpose is nk, because there are n new workers for each existing worker, and because k is the amount of capital for each worker. The equation shows that population growth reduces the accumulation of capital per worker much the way that depreciation does. Depreciation reduces k by wearing out the capital stock, whereas population growth reduces k by spreading the capital stock more thinly among a larger population of workers.[5]

Our analysis with population growth now proceeds much as it did previously. First, we substitute $sf(k)$ for i. The equation can then be written as

$$\Delta k = sf(k) - (\delta + n)k.$$

To see what determines the steady-state level of capital per worker, we use Figure 8-11, which extends the analysis of Figure 8-4 to include the effects of population growth. An economy is in a steady state if capital per worker k is unchanging. As before, we designate the steady-state value of k as k^*. If k is less than k^*, investment is greater than break-even investment, so k rises. If k is greater than k^*, investment is less than break-even investment, so k falls.

---

[5] *Mathematical note:* Formally deriving the equation for the change in k requires a bit of calculus. Note that the change in k per unit of time is $dk/dt = d(K/L)/dt$. After applying the chain rule, we can write this as $dk/dt = (1/L)(dK/dt) - (K/L^2)(dL/dt)$. Now use the following facts to substitute in this equation: $dK/dt = I - \delta K$ and $(dL/dt)/L = n$. After a bit of manipulation, this produces the equation in the text.

FIGURE 8-11

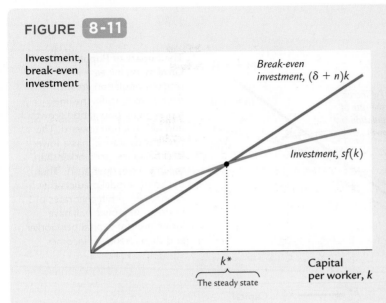

Population Growth in the Solow Model Depreciation and population growth are two reasons the capital stock per worker shrinks. If n is the rate of population growth and δ is the rate of depreciation, then $(\delta + n)k$ is *break-even investment* – the amount of investment necessary to keep constant the capital stock per worker k. For the economy to be in a steady state, investment $sf(k)$ must offset the effects of depreciation and population growth $(\delta + n)k$. This is represented by the crossing of the two curves.

In the steady state, the positive effect of investment on the capital stock per worker exactly balances the negative effects of depreciation and population growth. That is, at k^*, $\Delta k = 0$ and $i^* = \delta k^* + nk^*$. Once the economy is in the steady state, investment has two purposes. Some of it (δk^*) replaces the depreciated capital, and the rest (nk^*) provides the new workers with the steady-state amount of capital.

The Effects of Population Growth

Population growth alters the basic Solow model in three ways. First, it brings us closer to explaining sustained economic growth. In the steady state with population growth, capital per worker and output per worker are constant. Because the number of workers is growing at rate n, however, *total* capital and *total* output must also be growing at rate n. Hence, although population growth cannot explain sustained growth in the standard of living (because output per worker is constant in the steady state), it can help to explain sustained growth in total output.

Second, population growth gives us another explanation for why some countries are rich and others are poor. Consider the effects of an increase in population growth. Figure 8-12 shows that an increase in the rate of population growth from n_1 to n_2 reduces the steady-state level of capital per worker from k_1^* to k_2^*. Because k^* is lower, and because $y^* = f(k^*)$, the level of output per worker y^* is also lower. Thus, the Solow model predicts that countries with higher population growth will have lower levels of GDP per person. Notice that a change in the population growth rate, like a change in the saving rate,

FIGURE 8-12

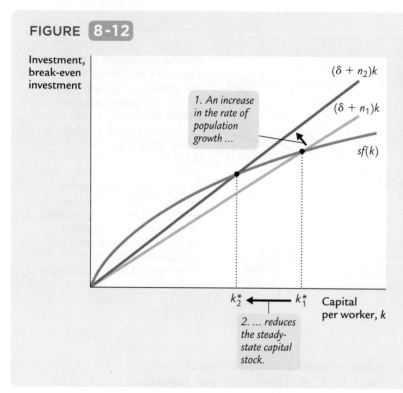

Investment,
break-even
investment

1. *An increase
in the rate of
population
growth ...*

$(\delta + n_2)k$

$(\delta + n_1)k$

$sf(k)$

k_2^* ← k_1^* Capital
per worker, k

2. *... reduces
the steady-
state capital
stock.*

The Impact of Population Growth An increase in the rate of population growth from n_1 to n_2 shifts the line representing population growth and depreciation upward. The new steady state k_2^* has a lower level of capital per worker than the initial steady state k_1^*. Thus, the Solow model predicts that economies with higher rates of population growth will have lower levels of capital per worker and therefore lower incomes.

has a level effect on income per person, but does not affect the steady-state growth rate of income per person.

Finally, population growth affects our criterion for determining the Golden Rule (consumption-maximizing) level of capital. To see how this criterion changes, note that consumption per worker is

$$c = y - i.$$

Because steady-state output is $f(k^*)$ and steady-state investment is $(\delta + n)k^*$, we can express steady-state consumption as

$$c^* = f(k^*) - (\delta n)k^*.$$

Using an argument largely the same as before, we conclude that the level of k^* that maximizes consumption is the one at which

$$MPK = \delta + n,$$

or, equivalently,

$$MPK - \delta = n.$$

In the Golden Rule steady state, the marginal product of capital net of depreciation equals the rate of population growth.

Population Growth around the World

Let's return now to the question of why standards of living vary so much around the world. The analysis we have just completed suggests that population growth may be one of the answers. According to the Solow model, a nation with a high rate of population growth will have a low steady-state capital stock per worker, and thus also a low level of income per worker. In other words, high population growth tends to impoverish a country because it is hard to maintain a high level of capital per worker when the number of workers is growing quickly. To see whether the evidence supports this conclusion, we look again at cross-country data.

Figure 8-13 is a scatterplot of data for the same 96 countries examined in the previous case study (and in Figure 8-6). The figure shows that countries with high rates of population growth tend to have low levels of income per

FIGURE 8-13

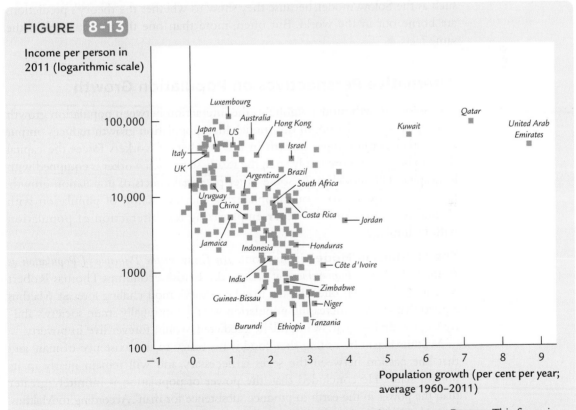

International Evidence on Population Growth and Income per Person This figure is a scatterplot of data from 96 countries. It shows that countries with high rates of population growth tend to have low levels of income per person, as the Solow model predicts.

Source: World Bank.

person. The international evidence is consistent with our model's prediction that the rate of population growth is one determinant of a country's standard of living.

This conclusion is not lost on policy makers. Those trying to pull the world's poorest nations out of poverty, such as the advisers sent to developing nations by the World Bank, often advocate reducing fertility by increasing education about birth-control methods and expanding women's job opportunities. Towards the same end, China has followed the totalitarian policy of allowing only one child per couple. These policies to reduce population growth should, if the Solow model is right, raise income per person in the long run.

In interpreting the cross-country data, however, it is important to keep in mind that correlation does not imply causation. The data show that low population growth is typically associated with high levels of income per person, and the Solow model offers one possible explanation for this fact, but other explanations are also possible. It is conceivable that high income encourages low population growth, perhaps because birth-control techniques are more readily available in richer countries. The international data can help us evaluate a theory of growth, such as the Solow model, because they show us whether the theory's predictions are borne out in the world. But often, more than one theory can explain the same facts. ■

Alternative Perspectives on Population Growth

The Solow growth model highlights the interaction between population growth and capital accumulation. In this model, high population growth reduces output per worker because rapid growth in the number of workers forces the capital stock to be spread more thinly, so in the steady state, each worker is equipped with less capital. The model omits some other potential effects of population growth. Here we consider two – one emphasizing the interaction of population with natural resources, and the other emphasizing the interaction of population with technology.

The Malthusian Model In his book *An Essay on the Principle of Population as It Affects the Future Improvement of Society*, the British economist Thomas Robert Malthus (1766–1834) offered what may be history's most chilling forecast. Malthus argued that an ever-increasing population would continually strain society's ability to provide for itself. Mankind, he predicted, would forever live in poverty.

Malthus began by noting that 'food is necessary to the existence of man' and that 'the passion between the sexes is necessary and will remain nearly in its present state'. He concluded that 'the power of population is infinitely greater than the power in the earth to produce subsistence for man'. According to Malthus, the only check on population growth was 'misery and vice'. Attempts by charities or governments to alleviate poverty were counterproductive, he argued, because they merely allowed the poor to have more children, placing even greater strains on society's productive capabilities.

Although the Malthusian model may have described the world when Malthus lived, its prediction that mankind would remain in poverty forever has proven very wrong. The world population has increased about sixfold over the past two centuries, but average living standards are much higher. Because of economic growth, chronic hunger and malnutrition are less common now than they were in Malthus's day. Famines occur from time to time, but they are more often the result of an unequal income distribution or political instability than of an inadequate production of food.

Malthus failed to see that growth in humanity's ingenuity would more than offset the effects of a larger population. Pesticides, fertilizers, mechanized farm equipment, new crop varieties and other technological advances that Malthus never imagined have allowed each farmer to feed ever greater numbers of people. Even with more mouths to feed, fewer farmers are necessary because each farmer is so productive. In addition, although the 'passion between the sexes' is just as strong now as it was in Malthus's day, the link between passion and population growth that Malthus assumed has been broken by modern birth control. Many advanced nations, such as those in Western Europe, are now experiencing fertility below replacement rates. Over the next century, shrinking populations may be more likely than rapidly expanding ones. There is now little reason to think that an ever-expanding population will overwhelm food production and doom mankind to poverty.[6]

The Kremerian Model While Malthus saw population growth as a threat to rising living standards, economist Michael Kremer has suggested that world population growth is a key driver of advancing economic prosperity. If there are more people, Kremer argues, then there are more scientists, inventors and engineers to contribute to innovation and technological progress.

As evidence for this hypothesis, Kremer begins by noting that over the broad span of human history, world growth rates have increased together with world population. For example, world growth was more rapid when the world population was 1 billion (which occurred around the year 1800) than it was when the population was only 100 million (around 500 BC). This fact is consistent with the hypothesis that having more people induces more technological progress.

Kremer's second, more compelling piece of evidence comes from comparing regions of the world. The melting of the polar ice caps at the end of the Ice Age, around 10,000 BC, flooded the land bridges and separated the world into several distinct regions that could not communicate with one another for thousands of years. If technological progress is more rapid when there are more people to discover things, then the more populous regions should have experienced more rapid growth.

And, indeed, they did. The most successful region of the world in 1500 (when Columbus re-established technological contact) included the 'Old World' civilizations of the large Eurasia–Africa region. Next in technological development

---

[6] For modern analyses of the Malthusian model, see Oded Galor and David N. Weil, 'Population, Technology, and Growth: From Malthusian Stagnation to the Demographic Transition and Beyond', *American Economic Review*, 2000, vol. 90, pp. 806–828; and Gary D. Hansen and Edward C. Prescott, 'Malthus to Solow', *American Economic Review*, 2002, vol. 92, pp. 1205–1217.

were the Aztec and Mayan civilizations in the Americas, followed by the hunter-gatherers of Australia, and then the people of Tasmania, who lacked even fire-making and most stone and bone tools.

The least populous isolated region was Flinders Island, a tiny island between Tasmania and Australia. With few people to contribute new innovations, Flinders Island had the least technological advance, and, in fact, seemed to regress. Around 3000 BC, human society on Flinders Island died out completely. Kremer concludes from this evidence that a large population is a prerequisite for technological advance.[7]

8-4 Conclusion

This chapter has started the process of building the Solow growth model. The model as developed so far shows how saving and population growth determine the economy's steady-state capital stock and its steady-state level of income per person. As we have seen, it sheds light on many features of actual growth experiences – why Germany and Japan grew so rapidly after being devastated by World War II, why countries that save and invest a high fraction of their output are richer than countries that save and invest a smaller fraction, and why countries with high rates of population growth are poorer than countries with low rates of population growth.

What the model cannot do, however, is explain the persistent growth in living standards we observe in most countries. In the model we have now, when the economy reaches its steady state, output per worker stops growing. To explain persistent growth, we need to introduce technological progress into the model. That is our first job in the next chapter.

Summary

1. The Solow growth model shows that, in the long run, an economy's rate of saving determines the size of its capital stock and thus its level of production. The higher the rate of saving, the higher the stock of capital and the higher the level of output.

2. In the Solow model, an increase in the rate of saving has a level effect on income per person: it causes a period of rapid growth, but eventually that growth slows as the new steady state is reached. Thus, although a high saving rate yields a high steady-state level of output, saving by itself cannot generate persistent economic growth.

---

[7] Michael Kremer, 'Population Growth and Technological Change: One Million B.C. to 1990', *Quarterly Journal of Economics*, 1993, vol. 108, pp. 681–716.

3. The level of capital that maximizes steady-state consumption is called the Golden Rule level. If an economy has more capital than in the Golden Rule steady state, then reducing saving will increase consumption at all points in time. By contrast, if the economy has less capital than in the Golden Rule steady state, then reaching the Golden Rule requires increased investment and thus lower consumption for current generations.

4. The Solow model shows that an economy's rate of population growth is another long-run determinant of the standard of living. According to the Solow model, the higher the rate of population growth, the lower the steady-state levels of capital per worker and output per worker. Other theories highlight other effects of population growth. Malthus suggested that population growth will strain the natural resources necessary to produce food; Kremer suggested that a large population may promote technological progress.

KEY CONCEPTS

Solow growth model   Steady state   Golden Rule level of capital

QUESTIONS FOR REVIEW

1. In the Solow model, how does the saving rate affect the steady-state level of income? How does it affect the steady-state rate of growth?

2. Why might an economic policy maker choose the Golden Rule level of capital?

3. Might a policy maker choose a steady state with more capital than in the Golden Rule steady state? With less capital than in the Golden Rule steady state? Explain your answers.

4. In the Solow model, how does the rate of population growth affect the steady-state level of income? How does it affect the steady-state rate of growth?

PROBLEMS AND APPLICATIONS

1. Country A and country B both have the production function

$$Y = F(K, L) = K^{1/2}L^{1/2}.$$

a. Does this production function have constant returns to scale? Explain.

b. What is the per-worker production function $y = f(k)$?

c. Assume that neither country experiences population growth or technological progress, and

that 5 per cent of capital depreciates each year. Assume further that country A saves 10 per cent of output each year and country B saves 20 per cent of output each year. Using your answer from part (b) and the steady-state condition that investment equals depreciation, find the steady-state level of capital per worker for each country. Then find the steady-state levels of income per worker and consumption per worker.

d. Suppose that both countries start off with a capital stock per worker of 2. What are the levels of income per worker and consumption per worker? Remembering that the change in the capital stock is investment less depreciation, use a calculator or a computer spreadsheet to show how the capital stock per worker will evolve over time in both countries. For each year, calculate income per worker and consumption per worker. How many years will it be before the consumption in country B is higher than the consumption in country A?

2. In the discussion of German and Japanese post-war growth, the text describes what happens when part of the capital stock is destroyed in a war. By contrast, suppose that a war does not affect the capital stock directly, but that casualties reduce the labour force.

   a. What is the immediate impact on total output and on output per person?

   b. Assuming that the saving rate is unchanged and that the economy was in a steady state before the war, what happens subsequently to output per worker in the post-war economy? Is the growth rate of output per worker after the war smaller or greater than normal?

3. Consider an economy described by the production function

$$Y = F(K, L) = K^{0.3}L^{0.7}.$$

   a. What is the per-worker production function?

   b. Assuming no population growth or technological progress, find the steady-state capital stock per worker, output per worker and consumption per worker as a function of the saving rate and the depreciation rate.

   c. Assume that the depreciation rate is 10 per cent per year. Make a table showing steady-state capital per worker, output per worker and consumption per worker for saving rates of 0 per cent, 10 per cent, 20 per cent, 30 per cent, and so on. (You will need a calculator with an exponent key for this.) What saving rate maximizes output per worker? What saving rate maximizes consumption per worker?

   d. (*Harder*) Use calculus to find the marginal product of capital. Add to your table the marginal product of capital net of depreciation for each of the saving rates. What does your table show?

4. 'Devoting a larger share of national output to investment would help restore rapid productivity growth and rising living standards.' Do you agree with this claim? Explain.

5. One view of the consumption function is that workers have high propensities to consume and capitalists have low propensities to consume. To explore the implications of this view, suppose that an economy consumes all wage income and saves all capital income. Show that if the factors of production earn their marginal product, this economy reaches the Golden Rule level of capital. (*Hint:* Begin with the identity that saving equals investment. Then use the steady-state condition that investment is just enough to keep up with depreciation and population growth, and the fact that saving equals capital income in this economy.)

6. Data from the European Union's statistical office shows that in the 20-year period between 1975 and 1995, the EU population grew by around 0.3 per cent per year. From 1995 to 2025, however, this growth is expected to fall to an annual growth rate of only about 0.2 per cent per year. Use the Solow model to forecast the effect of this slowdown in population growth on the growth of total output and the growth of output per person. Consider the effects both in the steady state and in the transition between steady states.

7. In the Solow model, population growth leads to steady-state growth in total output, but not in output per worker. Do you think this would still be true if the production function exhibited increasing or decreasing returns to scale? Explain. (For the definitions of increasing and decreasing returns to scale, see Chapter 3, Problems and Applications, Problem 2.)

8. Consider how unemployment would affect the Solow growth model. Suppose that output is produced according to the production function

$$Y = K^{\alpha} [(1 - u)L]^{1-\alpha}$$

where K is capital, L is the labour force and u is the natural rate of unemployment. The national saving rate is s, the labour force grows at rate n, and capital depreciates at rate δ.

   a. Express output per worker ($y = Y/L$) as a function of capital per worker ($k = K/L$) and the natural rate of unemployment. Describe the steady state of this economy.

b. Suppose that some change in government policy reduces the natural rate of unemployment. Describe how this change affects output, both immediately and over time. Is the steady-state effect on output larger or smaller than the immediate effect? Explain.

9. Choose two countries that interest you – one rich and one poor. What is the income per person in each country? Find some data on country characteristics that might help explain the difference in income: investment rates, population growth rates, educational attainment, and so on. (*Hint:* The website of the World Bank, www.worldbank.org, is one place to find such data.) How might you figure out which of these factors is most responsible for the observed income difference?

CHAPTER 9

Economic Growth II: Technology, Empirics and Policy

Is there some action a government could take that would lead the Indian
economy to grow like Indonesia's or Egypt's? If so, what exactly? If not, what
is it about the 'nature of India' that makes it so? The consequences for human
welfare involved in questions like these are simply staggering: Once one starts
to think about them, it is hard to think about anything else.

— Robert E. Lucas, Jr. 'On the Mechanics of Economic Development',
Journal of Monetary Economics, *1988, vol. 22, p. 5.*

This chapter continues our analysis of the forces governing long-run economic growth. With the basic version of the Solow growth model as our
starting point, we take on four new tasks.

Our first task is to make the Solow model more general and more realistic.
In Chapter 3 we saw that capital, labour and technology are the key determinants of a nation's production of goods and services. In Chapter 8 we developed
the Solow model to show how changes in capital (saving and investment) and
changes in the labour force (population growth) affect the economy's output. We
are now ready to add the third source of growth – changes in technology – into
the mix. The Solow model does not explain technological progress, but takes it as
exogenously given and shows how it interacts with other variables in the process
of economic growth.

Our second task is to move from theory to empirics. That is, we consider how
well the Solow model fits the facts. Over the past two decades, a large literature
has examined the predictions of the Solow model and other models of economic
growth. It turns out that the glass is both half full and half empty. The Solow
model can shed much light on international growth experiences, but it is far
from the last word on the subject.

Our third task is to examine how a nation's public policies can influence the
level and growth of its citizens' standard of living. In particular, we address five
questions: Should our society save more or save less? How can policy influence
the rate of saving? Are there some types of investment that policy should especially encourage? What institutions ensure that the economy's resources are put
to their best use? How can policy increase the rate of technological progress?

The Solow growth model provides the theoretical framework within which we consider these policy issues.

Our fourth and final task is to consider what the Solow model leaves out. As we have discussed previously, models help us to understand the world by simplifying it. After completing an analysis of a model, therefore, it is important to consider whether we have oversimplified matters. In the last section, we examine a new set of theories, called *endogenous growth theories,* which hope to explain the technological progress that the Solow model takes as exogenous.

9-1 Technological Progress in the Solow Model

So far, our presentation of the Solow model has assumed an unchanging relationship between the inputs of capital and labour and the output of goods and services. Yet the model can be modified to include exogenous technological progress, which over time expands society's ability to produce.

The Efficiency of Labour

To incorporate technological progress, we must return to the production function that relates total capital K and total labour L to total output Y. Thus far, the production function has been

$$Y = F(K, L).$$

We now write the production function as

$$Y = F(K, L \times E),$$

where E is a new (and somewhat abstract) variable called the **efficiency of labour**. The efficiency of labour is meant to reflect society's knowledge about production methods: as the available technology improves, the efficiency of labour rises. For instance, the efficiency of labour rose when assembly-line production transformed manufacturing in the early 20th century, and it rose again when computerization was introduced in the late 20th century. The efficiency of labour also rises when there are improvements in the health, education or skills of the labour force.

The term $L \times E$ measures the *effective number of workers.* It takes into account the number of workers L and the efficiency of each worker E. This new production function states that total output Y depends on the inputs of capital K and effective workers $L \times E$.

The essence of this approach to modelling technological progress is that increases in the efficiency of labour E are analogous to increases in the labour force L. Suppose, for example, that an advance in production methods makes the efficiency of labour E double between 1980 and 2010. This means that a single worker in 2010 is, *in effect,* as productive as two workers were in 1980. That is, even if the actual number of workers (*L*) stays the same from 1980 to 2010, the effective number of workers (*L* × *E*) doubles, and the economy will benefit from an increased production of goods and services.

The simplest assumption about technological progress is that it causes the efficiency of labour *E* to grow at some constant rate *g*. For example, if *g* = 0.02, then each unit of labour becomes 2 per cent more efficient each year: output increases as if the labour force had increased by an additional 2 per cent. This form of technological progress is called *labour augmenting,* and *g* is called the rate of **labour-augmenting technological progress**. Because the labour force *L* is growing at rate *n,* and the efficiency of each unit of labour *E* is growing at rate *g,* the effective number of workers *L* × *E* is growing at rate *n* + *g*.

The Steady State with Technological Progress

Because technological progress is modelled here as labour-augmenting, it has effects similar to those of population growth. Although technological progress does not cause the actual number of workers to increase, each worker in effect comes with more units of labour over time. Thus, technological progress causes the effective number of workers to increase. The analytic tools we used in Chapter 7 to study the Solow model with population growth are easily adapted to study the Solow model with labour-augmenting technological progress.

We begin by reconsidering our notation. Previously, we analysed the economy in terms of quantities per worker; now we analyse the economy in terms of quantities per effective worker. We now let $k = K/(L \times E)$ stand for capital per effective worker, and $y = Y/(L \times E)$ stand for output per effective worker. With these definitions, we can again write $y = f(k)$.

Our analysis of the economy proceeds just as it did when we examined population growth. The equation showing the evolution of *k* over time now changes to

$$\Delta k = sf(k) - (\delta + n + g)k.$$

As before, the change in the capital stock Δk equals investment $sf(k)$ minus break-even investment $(\delta + n + g)k$. Now, however, because $k = K/(L \times E)$, break-even investment includes three terms: to keep *k* constant, δk is needed to replace depreciating capital, nk is needed to provide capital for new workers, and gk is needed to provide capital for the new 'effective workers' created by technological progress.[1]

As shown in Figure 9-1, the inclusion of technological progress does not substantially alter our analysis of the steady state. There is one level of *k*, denoted k^*, at which capital per effective worker and output per effective worker are constant. As before, this steady state represents the long-run equilibrium of the economy.

---

[1] *Mathematical note:* This model with technological progress is a strict generalization of the model analysed in Chapter 8. In particular, if the efficiency of labour is constant at $E = 1$, then $g = 0$, and the definitions of *k* and *y* reduce to our previous definitions. In this case, the more general model considered here simplifies precisely to the Chapter 8 version of the Solow model.

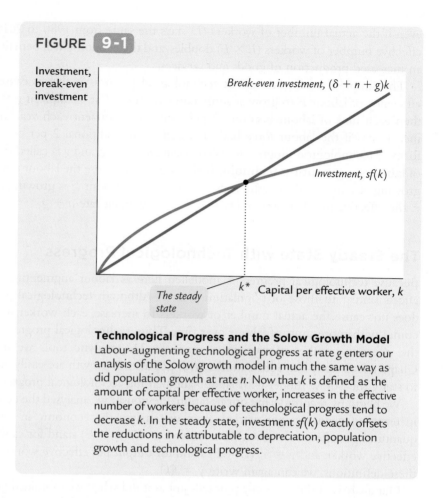

FIGURE 9-1

Investment, break-even investment

Break-even investment, $(\delta + n + g)k$

Investment, $sf(k)$

The steady state

k^* Capital per effective worker, k

Technological Progress and the Solow Growth Model
Labour-augmenting technological progress at rate g enters our analysis of the Solow growth model in much the same way as did population growth at rate n. Now that k is defined as the amount of capital per effective worker, increases in the effective number of workers because of technological progress tend to decrease k. In the steady state, investment $sf(k)$ exactly offsets the reductions in k attributable to depreciation, population growth and technological progress.

The Effects of Technological Progress

Table 9-1 shows how four key variables behave in the steady state with technological progress. As we have just seen, capital per effective worker k is constant in the steady state. Because $y = f(k)$, output per effective worker is also constant. It is these quantities per effective worker that are steady in the steady state.

From this information, we can also infer what is happening to other variables, those not expressed per effective worker. For instance, consider output per actual worker $Y/L = y \times E$. Because y is constant in the steady state and E is growing at rate g, output per worker must also be growing at rate g in the steady state. Similarly, the economy's total output is $Y = y \times (E \times L)$. Because y is constant in the steady state, E is growing at rate g and L is growing at rate n, total output grows at rate $n + g$ in the steady state.

With the addition of technological progress, our model can finally explain the sustained increases in standards of living that we observe. That is, we have shown that technological progress can lead to sustained growth in output per worker. By contrast, a high rate of saving leads to a high rate of growth only until the steady state is reached. Once the economy is in steady state, the rate of growth of output per worker depends only on the rate of technological progress. *According to the Solow model, only technological progress can explain sustained growth and persistently rising living standards.*

TABLE 9-1

Steady-State Growth Rates in the Solow Model with Technological Progress

Variable	Symbol	Steady-State Growth Rate
Capital per effective worker	$k = K/(E \times L)$	0
Output per effective worker	$y = Y/(E \times L) = f(k)$	0
Output per worker	$Y/L = y \times E$	g
Total output	$Y = y \times (E \times L)$	$n + g$

The introduction of technological progress also modifies the criterion for the Golden Rule. The Golden Rule level of capital is now defined as the steady state that maximizes consumption per effective worker. Following the same arguments that we have used before, we can show that steady-state consumption per effective worker is

$$c^* = f(k^*) - (\delta + n + g)k^*.$$

Steady-state consumption is maximized if

$$MPK = \delta + n + g,$$

or

$$MPK - \delta = n + g.$$

That is, at the Golden Rule level of capital, the net marginal product of capital, $MPK - \delta$, equals the rate of growth of total output, $n + g$. Because actual economies experience both population growth and technological progress, we must use this criterion to evaluate whether they have more or less capital than they would at the Golden Rule steady state.

9-2 From Growth Theory to Growth Empirics

So far in this chapter we have introduced exogenous technological progress into the Solow model to explain sustained growth in standards of living. Let's now discuss what happens when the theory is forced to confront the facts.

Balanced Growth

According to the Solow model, technological progress causes the values of many variables to rise together in the steady state. This property, called *balanced growth*, does a good job of describing the long-run data for the advanced industrialized economies of Europe and North America.

Consider, first, output per worker Y/L and the capital stock per worker K/L. According to the Solow model, in the steady state, both these variables grow at g, the rate of technological progress. UK data since the mid-20th century, for example, show that output per worker and the capital stock per worker have in fact grown at approximately the same rate – about 2 per cent per year. To put it another way, the capital-output ratio has remained approximately constant over time.

Technological progress also affects factor prices. Problem 3(d) at the end of the chapter asks you to show that, in the steady state, the real wage grows at the rate of technological progress. The real rental price of capital, however, is constant over time. Again, these predictions hold true for the United Kingdom. Since the 1950s, the real wage has increased about 2 per cent per year; it has increased by about the same amount as real GDP per worker. Yet the real rental price of capital (measured as real capital income divided by the capital stock) has remained about the same.

The Solow model's prediction about factor prices – and the success of this prediction – is especially noteworthy when contrasted with Karl Marx's theory of the development of capitalist economies. Marx predicted that the return to capital would decline over time and that this would lead to economic and political crisis. Economic history has not supported Marx's prediction, which partly explains why we now study Solow's theory of growth rather than Marx's.

Convergence

If you travel round the world, you will see tremendous variation in living standards. The world's poor countries have average levels of income per person that are less than one-tenth the average levels in the world's rich countries. These differences in income are reflected in almost every measure of the quality of life – from the number of televisions and telephones per household to the infant mortality rate and life expectancy.

Much research has been devoted to the question of whether economies converge over time. In particular, do economies that start off poor subsequently grow faster than economies that start off rich? If they do, then the world's poor economies will tend to catch up with the world's rich economies. This property of catch-up is called *convergence*. If there is no convergence, then countries that start off behind are likely to remain poor.

The Solow model makes clear predictions about when convergence should occur. According to the model, whether two economies will converge depends on why they differ in the first place. On the one hand, suppose two economies happen by historical accident to start off with different capital stocks, but have the same steady state, as determined by their saving rates, population growth rates and the efficiency of labour. In this case, we should expect the two economies to converge; the poorer economy with the smaller capital stock will naturally grow more quickly to reach the steady state. (In a case study in Chapter 8, we applied this logic to explain rapid growth in Germany and Japan after World War II.) On the other hand, if two economies have different steady states, perhaps because the economies have different rates of saving, then we should not expect convergence. Instead, each economy will approach its own steady state.

Experience is consistent with this analysis. In samples of economies with similar cultures and policies, studies find that economies converge to one another at a rate of about 2 per cent per year. That is, the gap between rich and poor economies closes by about 2 per cent each year. An example is the regions of European countries, such as the UK regions of the West Midlands, the South-West, Scotland, Northern Ireland, and so on, or the Italian regions of Piedmont, Tuscany, Lombardy, and so on. For historical reasons, most notably the two world wars of the 20th century, income levels varied greatly between the various European regions in the mid-20th century, both within and across countries. Yet these differences have largely disappeared over time — convergence has been at the rate of about 2 per cent per year. A similar result holds across American states and Japanese prefectures.

When we examine data for larger groups of countries, a more complex picture emerges. When researchers examine only data on income per person, they find little evidence of convergence: countries that start off poor do not grow faster on average than countries that start off rich. This finding suggests that different countries have different steady states. If statistical techniques are used to control for some of the determinants of the steady state, such as saving rates, population growth rates and accumulation of human capital (education), then once again the data show convergence at a rate of about 2 per cent per year. In other words, the economies of the world exhibit *conditional convergence:* they appear to be converging to their own steady states, which in turn are determined by such variables as saving, population growth and human capital.[2]

Factor Accumulation versus Production Efficiency

As a matter of accounting, international differences in income per person can be attributed to either (1) differences in the factors of production, such as the quantities of physical and human capital, or (2) differences in the efficiency with which economies use their factors of production. That is, a worker in a poor country may be poor because he lacks tools and skills, or because the tools and skills he has are not being put to their best use. To describe this issue in terms of the Solow model, the question is whether the large gap between rich and poor is explained by differences in capital accumulation (including human capital) or differences in the production function.

Much research has attempted to estimate the relative importance of these two sources of income disparities. The exact answer varies from study to study, but both factor accumulation and production efficiency appear important. Moreover, a common finding is that they are positively correlated: nations with high levels of physical and human capital also tend to use those factors efficiently.[3]

[2] Robert Barro and Xavier Sala-i-Martin, 'Convergence across States and Regions', *Brookings Papers on Economic Activity*, 1991, no. 1, pp. 107–182; N. Gregory Mankiw, David Romer and David N. Weil, 'A Contribution to the Empirics of Economic Growth', *Quarterly Journal of Economics*, 1992, pp. 407–437.

[3] Robert E. Hall and Charles I. Jones, 'Why Do Some Countries Produce So Much More Output Per Worker Than Others?' *Quarterly Journal of Economics*, 1999, vol. 114, pp. 83–116; Peter J. Klenow and Andres Rodriguez-Clare, 'The Neoclassical Revival in Growth Economics: Has It Gone Too Far?', *NBER Macroeconomics Annual*, 1997, pp. 73–103.

There are several ways to interpret this positive correlation. One hypothesis is that an efficient economy may encourage capital accumulation. For example, a person in a well-functioning economy may have greater resources and incentive to stay in education and accumulate human capital. Another hypothesis is that capital accumulation may induce greater efficiency. If there are positive externalities to physical and human capital, then countries that save and invest more will appear to have better production functions (unless the research study accounts for these externalities, which is hard to do). Thus, greater production efficiency may cause greater factor accumulation, or the other way round.

A final hypothesis is that both factor accumulation and production efficiency are driven by a common third variable. Perhaps the common third variable is the quality of the nation's institutions, including the government's policy making process. As one economist put it, when governments screw up, they screw up big time. The outcomes from poorly designed policies, such as high inflation, excessive budget deficits, widespread market interference and rampant corruption often go hand in hand with poor levels of factor accumulation and low levels of production efficiency. We should not be surprised that economies exhibiting these maladies both accumulate less capital and fail to use the capital they have as efficiently as they might.

CASE STUDY

Is Free Trade Good for Economic Growth?

At least since the time of the great 18th-century British economist Adam Smith, economists have advocated free trade as a policy that promotes national prosperity. Here is how Smith put the argument in his 1776 classic, *The Wealth of Nations:*

> It is a maxim of every prudent master of a family, never to attempt to make at home what it will cost him more to make than to buy. The tailor does not attempt to make his own shoes, but buys them of the shoemaker. The shoemaker does not attempt to make his own clothes but employs a tailor. . .
>
> What is prudence in the conduct of every private family can scarce be folly in that of a great kingdom. If a foreign country can supply us with a commodity cheaper than we ourselves can make it, better buy it of them with some part of the produce of our own industry employed in a way in which we have some advantage.

Today, economists make the case with greater rigour, relying on David Ricardo's theory of comparative advantage, as well as more modern theories of international trade. According to these theories, a nation open to trade can achieve greater production efficiency and a higher standard of living by specializing in those goods for which it has a comparative advantage.

A sceptic might point out that this is just theory. What about the evidence? Do nations that permit free trade in fact enjoy greater prosperity? A large literature addresses precisely this question.

One approach is to look at international data to see if countries that are open to trade typically enjoy greater prosperity. The fact is that they do. Economists Andrew Warner and Jeffrey Sachs studied the period 1970 to 1989. They report that among developed nations, the open economies grew at 2.3 per cent per year, while the closed economies grew at 0.7 per cent per year. Among developing nations, the open economies grew at 4.5 per cent per year, while the closed economies again grew at 0.7 per cent per year. These findings are consistent with Smith's view that trade enhances prosperity, but they are not conclusive. Correlation does not prove causation. Perhaps being closed to trade is correlated with various other restrictive government policies, and it is those other policies that retard growth.

A second approach is to look at what happens when closed economies remove their trade restrictions. Once again, Smith's hypothesis fairs well. Throughout history, when nations open themselves up to the world economy, the typical result is a subsequent increase in economic growth. This occurred in Japan in the 1850s, South Korea in the 1960s and Vietnam in the 1990s. But once again, correlation does not prove causation. Trade liberalization is often accompanied by other reforms, and it is hard to disentangle the effects of trade from the effects of the other reforms.

A third approach to measuring the impact of trade on growth, proposed by economists Jeffrey Frankel and David Romer, is to look at the impact of geography. Some countries trade less simply because they are geographically disadvantaged. For example, New Zealand is disadvantaged compared with Belgium because it is further from other populous countries. Similarly, landlocked countries are disadvantaged compared with countries that have their own seaports. Because these geographical characteristics are correlated with trade, but arguably uncorrelated with other determinants of economic prosperity, they can be used to identify the causal impact of trade on income. (The statistical technique, which you may have studied in an econometrics course, is called *instrumental variables*.) After analysing the data, Frankel and Romer concluded that 'a rise of one percentage point in the ratio of trade to GDP increases income per person by at least one-half percentage point. Trade appears to raise income by spurring the accumulation of human and physical capital and by increasing output for given levels of capital.'

The overwhelming weight of evidence from this body of research is that Adam Smith was right. Openness to international trade is beneficial for economic growth.[4] ∎

9-3 Policies to Promote Growth

So far we have used the Solow model to uncover the theoretical relationships among the different sources of economic growth, and we have discussed some of the empirical work that describes actual growth experiences. We can now use the theory and evidence to help guide our thinking about economic policy.

---

[4] Jeffrey D. Sachs and Andrew Warner, 'Economic Reform and the Process of Global Integration', *Brookings Papers on Economic Activity*, 1995, pp. 1–95; Jeffrey A. Frankel and David Romer, 'Does Trade Cause Growth?', *American Economic Review*, June 1999, vol. 89, pp. 379–399.

Evaluating the Rate of Saving

According to the Solow growth model, how much a nation saves and invests is a key determinant of its citizens' standard of living. So let's begin our policy discussion with a natural question: Is the rate of saving in the UK economy too low, too high or about right?

As we have seen, the saving rate determines the steady-state levels of capital and output. One particular saving rate produces the Golden Rule steady state, which maximizes consumption per worker, and thus economic well-being. The Golden Rule provides the benchmark against which we can compare the UK economy.

To decide whether the UK economy is at, above or below the Golden Rule steady state, we need to compare the marginal product of capital net of depreciation $(MPK - \delta)$ with the growth rate of total output $(n + g)$. As we established in Section 9-1, at the Golden Rule steady state, $MPK - \delta = n + g$. If the economy is operating with less capital than in the Golden Rule steady state, then diminishing marginal product tells us that $MPK - \delta > n + g$. In this case, increasing the rate of saving will increase capital accumulation and economic growth, and, eventually, lead to a steady state with higher consumption (although consumption will be lower for part of the transition to the new steady state). On the other hand, if the economy has more capital than in the Golden Rule steady state, then $MPK - \delta < n + g$. In this case, capital accumulation is excessive: reducing the rate of saving would lead to higher consumption both immediately and in long run.

To make this comparison for a real economy, such as the UK economy, we need an estimate of the growth rate of output $(n + g)$ and an estimate of the net marginal product of capital $(MPK - \delta)$. Real GDP in the United Kingdom grows at an average rate of 2.5 per cent per year, so $n + g = 0.025$. We can estimate the net marginal product of capital from the following three facts:

1. The capital stock is about 2.5 times one year's GDP.
2. Depreciation of capital is about 10 per cent of GDP.
3. Capital income is about 30 per cent of GDP.

Using the notation of our model (and the result from Chapter 3 that capital owners earn income of MPK for each unit of capital), we can write these facts as

1. $k = 2.5y$,
2. $\delta k = 0.1y$,
3. $MPK \times k = 0.3y$.

We solve for the rate of depreciation δ by dividing equation 2 by equation 1:

$$\delta k/k = (0.1y)/(2.5y),$$

$$\delta = 0.04.$$

And we solve for the marginal product of capital MPK by dividing equation 3 by equation 1:

$$(MPK \times k)/k = (0.3y)/(2.5y),$$

$$MPK = 0.12.$$

Thus, about 4 per cent of the capital stock depreciates each year, and the marginal product of capital is about 12 per cent per year. The net marginal product of capital, $MPK = \delta$, is about 8 per cent per year.

We can now see that the return to capital ($MPK - \delta = 8$ per cent per year) is well in excess of the economy's average growth rate ($n + g = 2.5$ per cent per year). This fact, together with our previous analysis, indicates that the capital stock in the UK economy is well below the Golden Rule level. In other words, if the United Kingdom saved and invested a higher fraction of its income, it would grow more rapidly and eventually reach a steady state with higher consumption.

This conclusion is not unique to the UK economy. When calculations similar to those above are carried out for the other advanced economies of Europe or North America, the results are similar. The possibility of excessive saving and capital accumulation beyond the Golden Rule level is intriguing as a matter of theory, but it appears not to be a problem that actual economies face. In practice, economists are more often concerned with insufficient saving. It is this kind of calculation that provides the intellectual foundation for this concern.[5]

Changing the Rate of Saving

The preceding calculations show that to move the UK economy towards the Golden Rule steady state, policy makers should increase national saving. But how can they do that? We saw in Chapter 3 that, as a matter of sheer accounting, higher national saving means higher public saving, higher private saving or some combination of the two. Much of the debate over policies to increase growth centres on which of these options is likely to be most effective.

The most direct way in which the government affects national saving is through public saving – the difference between what the government receives in tax revenue and what it spends. When the government's spending exceeds its revenue, the government runs a *budget deficit*, which represents negative public saving. As we saw in Chapter 3, a budget deficit raises interest rates and crowds out investment; the resulting reduction in the capital stock is part of the burden of the national debt on future generations.

---

[5] For more on this topic and some international evidence, see Andrew B. Abel, N. Gregory Mankiw, Lawrence H. Summers and Richard J. Zeckhauser, 'Assessing Dynamic Efficiency: Theory and Evidence', *Review of Economic Studies*, 1989, vol. 56, pp. 1–19.

Conversely, if the government spends less than it raises in revenue, it runs a *budget surplus*, which it can use to retire some of the national debt and stimulate investment.

The government also affects national saving by influencing private saving – the amount saved by households and firms. In particular, how much people decide to save depends on the incentives they face, and these incentives are altered by a variety of public policies. Many economists argue that high tax rates on capital – including tax on firms' profits (corporation tax), income tax and inheritance tax – discourage private saving by reducing the rate of return that savers earn. On the other hand, most countries allow tax exemption on any income that is paid into a retirement pension fund. Governments also frequently offer preferential treatment to income that is earned (in the form of interest, dividends and capital gains) in special savings accounts (in the UK, an example is the individual savings account, or ISA scheme). These are policies specifically designed to encourage private saving. Some economists have proposed increasing the incentive to save by replacing the current system of income taxation with a system of consumption taxation.

Many disagreements over public policy are rooted in different views about how much private saving responds to incentives. For example, suppose that the government were to expand the amount that people can put into tax-exempt retirement pension schemes. Would people respond to the increased incentive to save by saving more? Or would people merely transfer saving done in other forms into these accounts – reducing tax revenue and thus public saving without any stimulus to private saving? The desirability of the policy depends on the answers to these questions. Unfortunately, despite much research on this issue, no consensus has emerged.

Allocating the Economy's Investment

The Solow growth model makes the simplifying assumption that there is only one type of capital. In the real world, of course, there are many types. Private businesses invest in traditional types of capital, such as bulldozers and steel plants, and newer types of capital, such as computers and robots. The government invests in various forms of public capital, called *infrastructure*, such as roads, bridges and sewer systems.

In addition, there is *human capital* – the knowledge and skills that workers acquire through education, from primary and secondary school education to on-the-job training for adults in the labour force. Although the capital variable in the Solow model is usually interpreted as including only physical capital, in many ways human capital is analogous to physical capital. Like physical capital, human capital raises our ability to produce goods and services. Raising the level of human capital requires investment in the form of teachers, libraries and student time. Recent research on economic growth has emphasized that human capital is at least as important as physical capital in explaining international differences in standards of living. One way of modelling this fact is to give the variable we call 'capital' a broader definition that includes both human and physical capital.[6]

Policy makers trying to stimulate economic growth must confront the issue of what kinds of capital the economy needs most. In other words, what kinds of capital yield the highest marginal products? To a large extent, policy makers can rely on the marketplace to allocate the pool of saving to alternative types of investment. Those industries with the highest marginal products of capital will naturally be most willing to borrow at market interest rates to finance new investment. Many economists advocate that the government should merely create a 'level playing field' for different types of capital – for example, by ensuring that the tax system treats all forms of capital equally. The government can then rely on the market to allocate capital efficiently.

Other economists have suggested that the government should actively encourage particular forms of capital. Suppose, for instance, that technological advance occurs as a by-product of certain economic activities. This would happen if new and improved production processes are devised during the process of building capital (a phenomenon called *learning by doing*), and if these ideas become part of society's pool of knowledge. Such a by-product is called a *technological externality* (or a *knowledge spillover*). In the presence of such externalities, the social returns to capital exceed the private returns, and the benefits of increased capital accumulation to society are greater than the Solow model suggests.[7] Moreover, some types of capital accumulation may yield greater externalities than others. If, for example, installing robots yields greater technological externalities than building a new steel mill, then perhaps the government should use the tax laws to encourage investment in robots. The success of such an *industrial policy,* as it is sometimes called, requires that the government is able to measure accurately the externalities of different economic activities, so it can give the correct incentive to each activity.

Most economists are sceptical about industrial policies for two reasons. First, measuring the externalities from different sectors is so difficult as to be virtually impossible. If policy is based on poor measurements, its effects might be close to random and, thus, worse than no policy at all. Second, the political process is far from perfect. Once the government gets into the business of rewarding specific industries with subsidies and tax breaks, the rewards are as likely to be based on political clout and effective lobbying as on the magnitude of externalities.

---

[6] Earlier in this chapter, when we were interpreting K as only physical capital, human capital was folded into the efficiency-of-labour parameter E. The alternative approach suggested here is to include human capital as part of K instead, so E represents technology, but not human capital. If K is given this broader interpretation, then much of what we call labour income is really the return to human capital. As a result, the true capital share is much larger than the traditional Cobb–Douglas value of about 1/3. For more on this topic, see N. Gregory Mankiw, David Romer and David N. Weil, 'A Contribution to the Empirics of Economic Growth', *Quarterly Journal of Economics,* 1992, pp. 407–437.

[7] Paul Romer, 'Crazy Explanations for the Productivity Slowdown', *NBER Macroeconomics Annual,* 1987, vol. 2, pp. 163–201.

One type of capital that necessarily involves the government is public capital. Local and national governments are always deciding whether to borrow to finance new roads, bridges and public transport systems. Would a higher level of infrastructure investment make the economy substantially more productive? One problem with answering this question is that measuring the marginal product of public capital is very difficult. Private capital generates an easily measured rate of profit for the firm owning the capital, whereas the benefits of public capital are more diffuse. Moreover, while private capital investment is made by investors spending their own money, the allocation of resources for public capital involves the political process and taxpayer funding. So, public spending decisions may represent political rather than purely economic considerations.

Establishing the Right Institutions

As we discussed earlier in this chapter, economists who study international differences in the standard of living attribute some of these differences to the inputs of physical and human capital, and some to the productivity with which these inputs are used. One reason that nations may have different levels of production efficiency is that they have different institutions that guide the allocation of scarce resources. Creating the right institutions is important for ensuring that resources are allocated to their best use.

A nation's legal tradition is an example of such an institution. Some countries – largely the United Kingdom and its former colonies, such as the United States, Australia, India and Singapore, and various other English-speaking or Commonwealth countries – have English-style common law systems. Other nations, including most Continental European countries and many countries that have been linked with them historically, such as most of the Latin American countries, as well as Japan and South Korea, have legal systems based on civil law, which traces its origins back to ancient Roman law. One way of characterizing the difference between the two traditions is to note that common law is based on an unwritten code, and develops largely by custom and precedents set by the courts in individual legal cases. In civil law countries, government legislation is seen as the primary source of law, and courts thus base their judgments on the provisions of codes and statutes. By contrast, in the common law system, cases are the primary source of law, while statutes are only seen as incursions into the common law and thus interpreted narrowly.

Studies have found that legal protections for shareholders and creditors are stronger in the English-style common law legal systems than in civil law systems. As a result, the English-style countries have better developed capital markets. Nations with more developed capital markets, in turn, experience more rapid growth because it is easier for small and start-up companies to finance investment projects, leading to a more efficient allocation of the nation's capital.[8]

---

[8] Rafael La Porta, Florencio Lopez-de-Silanes, Andrei Shleifer and Robert Vishny, 'Law and Finance', *Journal of Political Economy*, 1998, vol. 106, pp. 1113–1155; Ross Levine and Robert G. King, 'Finance and Growth: Schumpeter Might Be Right', *Quarterly Journal of Economics*, 1993, vol. 108, pp. 717–737.

Another important institutional difference across countries is the quality of government itself. Ideally, governments should provide a 'helping hand' to the market system, protecting property rights, enforcing contracts, promoting competition, prosecuting fraud, and so on. Yet governments sometimes diverge from this ideal and act more like a 'grabbing hand', using the authority of the state to enrich a few powerful individuals at the expense of the broader community. Empirical studies have shown that the extent of corruption in a nation is indeed a significant determinant of economic growth.[9]

Adam Smith, the great 18th-century British economist, was well aware of the role of institutions in economic growth. He once wrote, 'Little else is requisite to carry a state to the highest degree of opulence from the lowest barbarism but peace, easy taxes, and a tolerable administration of justice: all the rest being brought about by the natural course of things.' Unfortunately, many nations do not enjoy these three simple advantages.

CASE STUDY

The Colonial Origins of Modern Institutions

International data show a remarkable correlation between latitude and economic prosperity: nations closer to the equator typically have lower levels of income per person than nations farther from the equator. This fact is true in the northern and southern hemispheres.

What explains the correlation? Some economists have suggested that the tropical climates near the equator have a direct negative impact on productivity. In the heat of the tropics, agriculture is more difficult and disease is more prevalent. This makes the production of goods and services more challenging.

Although the direct impact of geography is one reason tropical nations tend to be poor, it is not the whole story. Research by economists Daron Acemoglu, Simon Johnson and James Robinson in the early 21st century has suggested an indirect mechanism – the impact of geography on institutions. Here is their explanation, presented in several steps:

1. In the 17th, 18th and 19th centuries, tropical climates presented European settlers with an increased risk of disease, especially from malaria and yellow fever. As a result, when Europeans were colonizing much of the rest of the world, they avoided settling in tropical areas, such as much of Africa and Central America. The European settlers preferred areas with more moderate climates and better health conditions, such as the United States, Canada and New Zealand.

2. In those areas where Europeans settled in large numbers, the settlers established European-like institutions that protected individual property rights and limited the power of government. By contrast, in tropical climates, the colonial powers often set up 'extractive' institutions, including authoritarian governments, so

---

[9] Paulo Mauro, 'Corruption and Growth', *Quarterly Journal of Economics*, 1995, vol. 110, pp. 681–712.

they could take advantage of the area's natural resources. These institutions enriched the colonizers, but they did little to foster economic growth.

3. Although the era of colonial rule is now long over, the early institutions that the European colonizers established are strongly correlated with the modern institutions in the former colonies. In tropical nations, where the colonial powers set up extractive institutions, there is typically less protection of property rights even today. When the colonizers left, the extractive institutions remained and were simply taken over by new ruling elites.

4. The quality of institutions is a key determinant of economic performance. Where property rights are well protected, people have more incentive to make the investments that lead to economic growth. Where property rights are less respected, as is typically the case in tropical nations, investment and growth lag behind.

This research suggests that much of the international variation in living standards that we observe today is a result of the long reach of history.[10] ∎

Encouraging Technological Progress

The Solow model shows that sustained growth in income per worker must come from technological progress. The Solow model, however, takes technological progress as exogenous; it does not explain it. Unfortunately, the determinants of technological progress are not well understood.

Despite this limited understanding, many public policies are designed to stimulate technological progress. Most of these policies encourage the private sector to devote resources to technological innovation. For example, the patent system gives a temporary monopoly to inventors of new products; the tax code offers tax breaks for firms engaging in research and development; and government agencies directly subsidize basic research in universities. In addition, as discussed above, proponents of industrial policy argue that the government should take a more active role in promoting specific industries that are key for rapid technological advance.

In the late 20th and early 21st century, the encouragement of technological progress has taken on an international dimension. Many of the companies that engage in research to advance technology are located in countries in Europe, North America and other developed nations. Developing nations such as China have an incentive to 'free-ride' on this research by not strictly enforcing intellectual property rights. That is, Chinese companies often use the ideas developed abroad without compensating the patent holders. Some developed countries have strenuously objected to this practice, and China has promised to step up enforcement. If intellectual property rights were better enforced around the world, firms would have more incentive to engage in research, and this would promote worldwide technological progress.

---

[10] Daron Acemoglu, Simon Johnson and James A. Robinson, 'The Colonial Origins of Comparative Development: An Empirical Investigation', *American Economic Review*, 2001, vol. 91, pp. 1369–1401.

CASE STUDY

The Worldwide Slowdown in Economic Growth: 1972–2011

Beginning in the early 1970s, and lasting until the mid-1990s, world policy makers faced a perplexing problem: a global slowdown in economic growth. Table 9-2 presents data on the growth in real GDP per person for the seven major world economies (the 'G7'). Growth in the United Kingdom fell from 2.2 per cent before 1972 to 1.5 per cent from 1972 to 1995, and although the UK enjoyed a period of higher growth from 1995 to 2004, it has now slipped back to 0.28 per cent for the period 2004–2011. Growth in France likewise declined from 4.3 per cent in the early part of the period to 0.34 per cent recently. Other countries experienced similar or more severe declines. Accumulated over many years, even a small change in the rate of growth has a large effect on economic well-being. Real income in the UK in the first decade of the 21st century is almost 22 per cent lower than it would have been had growth remained at its previous level.

Why did this slowdown occur? Studies have shown that it was attributable to a fall in the rate at which the production function was improving over time. The appendix to this chapter explains how economists measure changes in the production function with a variable called *total factor productivity,* which is closely related to the efficiency of labour in the Solow model. There are, however, many hypotheses to explain this fall in productivity growth. Here are four of them.

Measurement Problems One possibility is that the productivity slowdown did not really occur, and that it shows up in the data because the data are flawed.

TABLE 9-2

Growth around the World

Country	Growth in Output Per Person (per cent per year)			
	1948–1972	1972–1995	1995–2004	2004–2011
Canada	2.9	1.8	2.4	0.55
France	4.3	1.6	1.7	0.34
West Germany	5.7	2.0		
Germany			1.2	1.6
Italy	4.9	2.3	1.5	−0.6
Japan	8.2	2.6	1.2	0.33
United Kingdom	2.4	1.8	2.5	0.27
United States	2.2	1.5	2.2	0.28

Source: Angus Maddison, *Phases of Capitalist Development*, 1982, Oxford: Oxford University Press; *OECD National Accounts*; and *World Bank: World Development Indicators*.

As you may recall from Chapter 2, one problem in measuring inflation is correcting for changes in the quality of goods and services. The same issue arises when measuring output and productivity. For instance, if technological advance leads to *more* computers being built, then the increase in output and productivity is easy to measure. But if technological advance leads to *faster* computers being built, then output and productivity have increased, but that increase is more subtle and harder to measure. Government statisticians try to correct for changes in quality, but, despite their best efforts, the resulting data are far from perfect.

Unmeasured quality improvements mean that our standard of living is rising more rapidly than the official data indicate. This issue should make us suspicious of the data, but by itself it cannot explain the productivity slowdown. To explain a *slowdown* in growth, one must argue that the measurement problems got *worse*. There is some indication that this might be so. As history passes, fewer people work in industries with tangible and easily measured output, such as agriculture, and more work in industries with intangible and less easily measured output, such as medical services. Yet few economists believe that measurement problems were the full story.

Oil Prices When the productivity slowdown began around 1973, the obvious hypothesis to explain it was the large increase in oil prices caused by the actions of the OPEC oil cartel. The primary piece of evidence was the timing: productivity growth slowed at the same time that oil prices skyrocketed. Over time, however, this explanation has appeared less likely. One reason is that the accumulated shortfall in productivity seems too large to be explained by an increase in oil prices – petroleum-based products are not that large a fraction of the typical firm's costs. In addition, if this explanation were right, productivity should have sped up when political turmoil in OPEC caused oil prices to plummet in 1986. Unfortunately, that did not happen.

Worker Quality Some economists suggest that the productivity slowdown might have been caused by changes in the labour force. In the early 1970s, the large baby-boom generation started leaving school and taking jobs. At the same time, changing social norms encouraged many women to leave full-time housework and enter the labour force. Both these developments lowered the average level of experience among workers, which in turn lowered average productivity.

Other economists point to changes in worker quality, as gauged by human capital. Although the educational attainment of the labour force continued to rise throughout this period, it was not increasing as rapidly as it had in the past. Moreover, declining performance on some standardized tests suggests that the quality of education was declining. If so, this could explain slowing productivity growth.

The Depletion of Ideas Still other economists suggest that the world started to run out of new ideas about how to produce in the early 1970s, pushing the economy into an age of slower technological progress. These economists often argue that the anomaly is not the period since 1970, but the preceding two decades. In the late 1940s, the economy had a large backlog of ideas that had not been fully implemented because of the Great Depression of the 1930s and

World War II in the first half of 1940s. After the economy used up this backlog, the argument goes, a slowdown in productivity growth was likely. Indeed, although the growth rates in the 1970s, 1980s and early 1990s were disappointing compared with those of the 1950s and 1960s, they were not lower than average growth rates from 1870 to 1950.

As any good doctor will tell you, sometimes a patient's illness goes away on its own, even if the doctor has failed to come up with a convincing diagnosis and remedy. This seems to be the outcome of the productivity slowdown. In the middle of the 1990s, economic growth took off, at least in the English-speaking countries of the United States, Canada and the United Kingdom, in large part because of advances in computer and information technology, including the Internet. Yet this period of rapid growth was then offset by the financial crisis and deep recession in 2008–2009 (a topic we will discuss in Chapters 12 and 20). Overall, the period from 1995 to 2010 shows a continuation of the relatively slow growth experienced from 1972 to 1995.[11] ∎

CASE STUDY

A Tale of Two Growth Experiences

'It was the best of times, it was the worst of times.' So begins Charles Dickens' novel *A Tale of Two Cities*. The description might easily be applied to the growth experience across the G7 in the decade from 1995. Beginning in the middle of the 1990s, in the UK, the US and Canada, economic growth took off, as shown in the third column of Table 9-2. In the United Kingdom, for example, output per person accelerated from 1.8 to 2.5 per cent per year. On the other hand, over the same period, the growth rate collapsed even further in Japan, and stagnated or fell further in the Continental European countries. Why were the growth experiences across the G7 so diverse?

As we discussed in Chapter 1, the unification of Germany in 1990 brought with it a number of economic problems, which Germany was still trying to resolve at the turn of the 21st century; the decline in the German growth rate over this period is therefore not surprising. In much of the rest of Europe, the major project of the late 1990s was the adoption of a single European currency – the euro. We shall discuss the European Monetary Union (EMU) in more detail in Chapter 17. For now, it is sufficient to note that certain criteria were laid down for membership (called the 'Maastricht criteria'), requiring, among other things, that government budget deficits and the level of government debt relative to GDP should be at 'prudent levels': no more than 3 per cent and 60 per cent of GDP, respectively. In an attempt to satisfy the Maastricht criteria, the governments of France and Italy pursued strongly deflationary fiscal policies during the late 1990s, resulting in a fall in their growth rates.

---

[11] For various views on the growth slowdown, see 'Symposium: The Slowdown in Productivity Growth', *Journal of Economic Perspectives*, Fall 1988, vol. 2, pp. 3–98.

The causes of the Japanese growth collapse in the last decade or so are a little more debatable. Some economists have argued that Japan's ageing population, combined with statutory reductions in the working week, reduced the productivity of Japanese workers. Others argue that it was a fall in aggregate demand, combined with interest rates so low that they could not be lowered any further, making expansionary monetary policy impossible – a 'liquidity trap' situation that Keynes had referred to as a theoretical possibility back in the 1930s.

What about the growth acceleration seen in the UK and North America during this time? As with the slowdown in economic growth in the 1970s, the UK–North American acceleration in the 1990s is hard to explain definitively. But part of the credit goes to advances in computer and information technology, including the Internet.

Observers of the computer industry often cite Moore's law, which states that computer processing power doubles about every 18 months. This is not an inevitable law of nature, but an empirical regularity describing the rapid technological progress this industry has enjoyed. In the 1980s and early 1990s, economists were surprised that the rapid progress in computing did not have a larger effect on the overall economy. Economist Robert Solow once quipped that 'we can see the computer age everywhere but in the productivity statistics'.

One reason why the productivity benefits of computers may have been delayed is that it took time for firms to figure out how best to use the technology. Whenever firms change their production systems and train workers to use a technology, they disrupt the existing means of production. Measured productivity can fall for a while before the economy reaps the benefits. Indeed, some economists even suggest that the spread of computers can help to explain the productivity slowdown that began in the 1970s.

Economic history provides some support for the idea that new technologies influence growth with a long lag. The electric light bulb was invented in 1879. But it took several decades before electricity had a big economic impact. For businesses to reap large productivity gains, they had to do more than just replace steam engines with electric motors; they had to rethink the entire organization of factories. Similarly, replacing the typewriters on desks with computers and word-processing programs, as was common in the 1980s, may have had small productivity effects. Only later, when the Internet and other advanced applications were invented, did the computers yield large economic gains.

Eventually, advances in technology should show up in economic growth, as was the case in the second half of the 1990s. This extra growth occurs through three channels. First, because the computer industry is part of the economy, productivity growth in that industry directly affects overall productivity growth. Second, because computers are a type of capital good, falling computer prices allow firms to accumulate more computing capital for every dollar of investment spending; the resulting increase in capital accumulation raises growth in all sectors that use computers as a factor of production. Third, the innovations in the computer industry may induce other industries to re-evaluate their own production methods, and this re-evaluation in turn leads to productivity growth in those industries.

The big, open question is how long the computer industry will remain an engine of growth. Will Moore's law describe the future as well as it has described the past? Will the technological advances (e.g. advanced processors, tablets, three-dimensional printing, cloud computing, etc.) experienced in the first part of the 21st century be as profound as the Internet was during the late 20th century? Stay tuned.[12] ■

9-4 Beyond the Solow Model: Endogenous Growth Theory

A chemist, a physicist and an economist are all trapped on a desert island, trying to figure out how to open a can of food.

'Let's heat the can over the fire until it explodes,' says the chemist.

'No, no,' says the physicist. 'Let's drop the can onto the rocks from the top of a high tree.'

'I have an idea,' says the economist. 'First, we assume a can opener. . .'

This old joke takes aim at how economists use assumptions to simplify – and sometimes oversimplify – the problems they face. It is particularly apt when evaluating the theory of economic growth. One goal of growth theory is to explain the persistent rise in living standards that we observe in most parts of the world. The Solow growth model shows that such persistent growth must come from technological progress. But where does technological progress come from? In the Solow model, it is just assumed!

The preceding two case studies on the productivity slowdown of the 1970s and speed-up of the 1990s suggest that changes in the pace of technological progress are tremendously important. To understand fully the process of economic growth, we need to go beyond the Solow model and develop models that explain technological advance. Models that do this often go by the label **endogenous growth theory**, because they reject the Solow model's assumption of exogenous technological change. Although the field of endogenous growth theory is large and sometimes complex, here we get a quick taste of this modern research.[13]

---

[12] For more on this topic, see the symposium on 'Computers and Productivity', *Journal of Economic Perspectives*, Fall 2000. On the parallel between electricity and computers, see Paul A. David, 'The Dynamo and the Computer: A Historical Perspective on the Modern Productivity Paradox', *American Economic Review*, 1990, vol. 80, no. 2, pp. 355–361.

[13] This section provides a brief introduction to the large and fascinating literature on endogenous growth theory. Early and important contributions to this literature include Paul M. Romer, 'Increasing Returns and Long-Run Growth', *Journal of Political Economy*, October 1986, vol. 94, pp. 1002–1037; and Robert E. Lucas, Jr., 'On the Mechanics of Economic Development', *Journal of Monetary Economics*, 1988, vol. 22, pp. 3–42. The reader can learn more about this topic in the undergraduate textbook by David N. Weil, *Economic Growth*, 2nd edn, Upper Saddle River, NJ: Prentice Hall, 2008.

The Basic Model

To illustrate the idea behind endogenous growth theory, let's start with a particularly simple production function:

$$Y = AK,$$

where Y is output, K is the capital stock and A is a constant measuring the amount of output produced for each unit of capital. Notice that this production function does not exhibit the property of diminishing returns to capital. One extra unit of capital produces A extra units of output, regardless of how much capital there is. This absence of diminishing returns to capital is the key difference between this endogenous growth model and the Solow model.

Now let's see what this production function says about economic growth. As before, we assume a fraction s of income is saved and invested. We therefore describe capital accumulation with an equation similar to those we used previously:

$$\Delta K = sY - \delta K.$$

This equation states that the change in the capital stock (ΔK) equals investment (sY) minus depreciation (δK). Combining this equation with the $Y = AK$ production function, we obtain, after a bit of manipulation,

$$\Delta Y/Y = \Delta K/K = sA - \delta.$$

This equation shows what determines the growth rate of output $\Delta Y/Y$. Notice that, as long as $sA > \delta$, the economy's income grows forever, even without the assumption of exogenous technological progress.

Thus, a simple change in the production function can alter dramatically the predictions about economic growth. In the Solow model, saving leads to growth temporarily, but diminishing returns to capital eventually force the economy to approach a steady state in which growth depends only on exogenous technological progress. By contrast, in this endogenous growth model, saving and investment can lead to persistent growth.

But is it reasonable to abandon the assumption of diminishing returns to capital? The answer depends on how we interpret the variable K in the production function $Y = AK$. If we take the traditional view that K includes only the economy's stock of plants and equipment, then it is natural to assume diminishing returns. Giving ten computers to each worker does not make the worker ten times as productive as he or she is with one computer.

Advocates of endogenous growth theory, however, argue that the assumption of constant (rather than diminishing) returns to capital is more palatable if K is interpreted more broadly. Perhaps the best case for the endogenous growth model is to view knowledge as a type of capital. Clearly, knowledge is an important input into the economy's production – both its production of goods and services and its production of new knowledge. Compared to other forms of capital, however, it is less natural to assume that knowledge exhibits the property of diminishing returns. (Indeed, the increasing pace of scientific and technological innovation over the past few centuries has led some economists to argue that there are increasing returns to knowledge.) If we accept the view that knowledge is a type of capital, then this endogenous growth model with its assumption of constant returns to capital becomes a more plausible description of long-run economic growth.

A Two-Sector Model

Although the $Y = AK$ model is the simplest example of endogenous growth, the theory has gone well beyond this. One line of research has tried to develop models with more than one sector of production in order to offer a better description of the forces that govern technological progress. To see what we might learn from such models, let's sketch out an example.

The economy has two sectors, which we can call manufacturing firms and research universities. Firms produce goods and services, which are used for consumption and investment in physical capital. Universities produce a factor of production called 'knowledge', which is then freely used in both sectors. The economy is described by the production function for firms, the production function for universities and the capital-accumulation equation:

$$Y = F[K, (1 - u)LE] \text{ (production function in manufacturing firms)},$$

$$\Delta E = g(u)E \qquad \text{(production function in research universities)},$$

$$\Delta K = sY - \delta K \qquad \text{(capital accumulation)},$$

where u is the fraction of the labour force (L) in universities (and $1 - u$ is the fraction in manufacturing), E is the stock of knowledge (which in turn determines the efficiency of labour), and g is a function that shows how the growth in knowledge depends on the fraction of the labour force in universities. The rest of the notation is standard. As usual, the production function for the manufacturing firms is assumed to have constant returns to scale: if we double both the amount of physical capital (K) and the effective number of workers in manufacturing $[(1 - u)LE]$, we double the output of goods and services (Y).

This model is a cousin of the $Y = AK$ model. Most importantly, this economy exhibits constant (rather than diminishing) returns to capital, as long as capital is broadly defined to include knowledge. In particular, if we double both physical capital K and knowledge E, then we double the output of both sectors in the economy. As a result, like the $Y = AK$ model, this model can generate persistent growth without the assumption of exogenous shifts in the production function. Here, persistent growth arises endogenously because the creation of knowledge in universities never slows down.

At the same time, however, this model is also a cousin of the Solow growth model. If u, the fraction of the labour force in universities, is held constant, then the efficiency of labour E grows at the constant rate $g(u)$. This result of constant growth in the efficiency of labour at rate g is precisely the assumption made in the Solow model with technological progress. Moreover, the rest of the model – the manufacturing production function and the capital-accumulation equation – also resembles the rest of the Solow model. As a result, for any given value of u, this endogenous-growth model works just like the Solow model.

There are two key decision variables in this model. As in the Solow model, the fraction of output used for saving and investment, s, determines the steady-state stock of physical capital. In addition, the fraction of labour in universities, u, determines the growth in the stock of knowledge. Both s and u affect the level of income, although only u affects the steady-state growth rate of income. Thus, this model of endogenous growth takes a small step in the direction of showing which societal decisions determine the rate of technological change.

The Microeconomics of Research and Development

The two-sector endogenous growth model just presented takes us closer to understanding technological progress, but it still tells only a rudimentary story about the creation of knowledge. If one thinks about the process of research and development for even a moment, three facts become apparent. First, although knowledge is largely a public good (that is, a good freely available to everyone), much research is done in firms that are driven by the profit motive. Second, research is profitable because innovations give firms temporary monopolies, either because of the patent system or because there is an advantage to being the first firm on the market with a new product. Third, when one firm innovates, other firms build on that innovation to produce the next generation of innovations. These (essentially microeconomic) facts are not easily connected with the (essentially macroeconomic) growth models we have discussed so far.

Some endogenous growth models try to incorporate these facts about research and development. Doing this requires modelling the decisions that firms face as they engage in research, and modelling the interactions among firms that have some degree of monopoly power over their innovations. Going into more detail about these models is beyond the scope of this book. But it should be clear already that one virtue of these endogenous growth models is that they offer a more complete description of the process of technological innovation.

One question these models are designed to address is whether, from the standpoint of society as a whole, private profit-maximizing firms tend to engage in too little or too much research. In other words, is the social return to research (which is what society cares about) greater or smaller than the private return (which is what motivates individual firms)? It turns out that, as a theoretical matter, there are effects in both directions. On the one hand, when a firm creates a new technology, it makes other firms better off by giving them a base of knowledge on which to build in future research. As Isaac Newton famously remarked, 'If I have seen farther than others, it is because I was standing on the shoulders of giants.' On the other hand, when one firm invests in research, it can also make other firms worse off by merely being first to discover a technology that another firm would have invented. This duplication of research effort has been called the 'stepping on toes' effect. Whether firms left to their own devices do too little or too much research depends on whether the positive 'standing on shoulders' externality or the negative 'stepping on toes' externality is more prevalent.

Although theory alone is ambiguous about whether research effort is more or less than optimal, the empirical work in this area is usually less so. Many studies have suggested the 'standing on shoulders' externality is important and, as a result, the social return to research is large – often in excess of 40 per cent per year. This is an impressive rate of return, especially when compared to the return to physical capital, which we earlier estimated to be about 8 per cent per year. In the judgement of some economists, this finding justifies substantial government subsidies to research.[14]

CASE STUDY

Economic Growth as a Process of Creative Destruction

In his 1942 book *Capitalism, Socialism, and Democracy*, economist Joseph Schumpeter suggested that economic progress comes through a process of 'creative destruction'. According to Schumpeter, the driving force behind progress is the entrepreneur with an idea for a new product, a new way to produce an old product, or some other innovation. When the entrepreneur's firm enters the market, it has some degree of monopoly power over its innovation; indeed, it is the prospect of monopoly profits that motivates the entrepreneur. The entry of the new firm is good for consumers, who now have an expanded range of choices, but it is often bad for incumbent producers, who may find it hard to compete with the entrant. If the new product is sufficiently better than old ones, the incumbents may even be driven out of business. Over time, the process keeps renewing itself. The entrepreneur's firm becomes an incumbent, enjoying high profitability until its product is displaced by another entrepreneur, with the next generation of innovation.

History confirms Schumpeter's thesis that there are winners and losers from technological progress. For example, in England in the early 19th century, an important innovation was the invention and spread of machines that could produce textiles using unskilled workers at low cost. This technological advance was good for consumers, who could clothe themselves more cheaply. Yet skilled knitters in England saw their jobs threatened by new technology, and they responded by organizing violent revolts. The rioting workers, called Luddites, smashed the weaving machines used in the wool and cotton mills and set the homes of the mill owners on fire (a less than creative form of destruction). Today, the term 'Luddite' refers to anyone who opposes technological progress.

A more recent example of creative destruction entails the production of wristwatches. The Swiss watch industry, based in Geneva, evolved in the 19th and 20th centuries into the major producer of watches in the world. In the 1980s, however, the industry very nearly became defunct because of the intense competition it experienced from Japanese producers such as Casio, who were

---

[14] For an overview of the empirical literature on the effects of research, see Zvi Griliches, 'The Search for R&D Spillovers', *Scandinavian Journal of Economics*, 1991, vol. 94, pp. 29–47.

marketing watches based on a new technology. The new electronic watches worked by counting the vibrations of a tiny piece of quartz when an electric current was passed through it. This meant that a high-precision (and expensive) mechanical movement was no longer necessary for a watch to be reliable; in fact, the new quartz watches were much more accurate than mechanical watches and sold for a fraction of the price. It seemed that, apart from a few luxury watch producers such as Rolex, Switzerland would no longer be a home for watch production. Not only was there a new technology to contend with, but wage rates in the Far East were very much lower than in Northern Europe, making the prospect of competing with the Japanese producers seem futile.

Swiss engineer Nicolas Hayek, however, saw the challenge from the Far East as an opportunity to revitalize the Swiss industry. He founded his own company in Geneva, producing watches that embodied the new quartz technology, but which also used innovative design and production methods. Hayek and his team designed a watch that contained very few moving parts, and produced it with a series of robots which created a plastic watch case in one swift motion and embedded many of the watch parts into it at the same time, so that watches could be 'printed' every three seconds, thereby dramatically reducing the cost of production. Hayek's new company was called SWATCH, and his watches – bright, cheerful, cheap and reliable affairs that contrasted dramatically with the expensive and conservative traditional image of Swiss watches – were branded as SWATCHES. To date, something like 200 million SWATCHES have been sold worldwide, re-establishing Switzerland as the world's largest watch manufacturer.

Faced with the prospect of being the victims of creative destruction, incumbent producers who lack the innovative flair of Nicolas Hayek often look to the political process to stop the entry of new, more efficient competitors. The original Luddites wanted the British government to save their jobs by restricting the spread of the new textile technology; instead, Parliament sent troops to suppress the Luddite riots.

Schumpeter's vision of how capitalist economies work has merit as a matter of economic history. Moreover, it has inspired some recent work in the theory of economic growth. One line of endogenous growth theory, pioneered by economists Philippe Aghion and Peter Howitt, builds on Schumpeter's insights by modelling technological advance as a process of entrepreneurial innovation and creative destruction.[15] ∎

9-5 Conclusion

Long-run economic growth is the single most important determinant of the economic well-being of a nation's citizens. Everything else that macroeconomists study – unemployment, inflation, trade deficits, and so on – pales in comparison.

Fortunately, economists know quite a lot about the forces that govern economic growth. The Solow growth model and the more recent endogenous

---

[15] Philippe Aghion and Peter Howitt, 'A Model of Growth through Creative Destruction', *Econometrica*, 1992, vol. 60, pp. 323–351.

growth models show how saving, population growth and technological progress interact in determining the level and growth of a nation's standard of living. Although these theories offer no magic recipe to ensure an economy achieves rapid growth, they do offer much insight, and they provide the intellectual framework for much of the debate over public policy aimed at promoting long-run economic growth.

Summary

1. In the steady state of the Solow growth model, the growth rate of income per person is determined solely by the exogenous rate of technological progress.

2. Many empirical studies have examined to what extent the Solow model can help explain long-run economic growth. The model can explain much of what we see in the data, such as balanced growth and conditional convergence. Recent studies have also found that international variation in standards of living is attributable to a combination of capital accumulation and the efficiency with which capital is used.

3. In the Solow model with population growth and technological progress, the Golden Rule (consumption-maximizing) steady state is characterized by equality between the net marginal product of capital ($MPK - \delta$) and the steady-state growth rate of total income ($n + g$). In most advanced economies, the net marginal product of capital is well in excess of the growth rate, indicating that the economy has much less capital than it would have in the Golden Rule steady state.

4. Policy makers often claim that their nations should devote a larger percentage of their output to saving and investment. Increased public saving and tax incentives for private saving are two ways to encourage capital accumulation. Policy makers can also promote economic growth by setting up the right legal and financial institutions so resources are allocated efficiently, and by ensuring proper incentives to encourage research and technological progress.

5. In the early 1970s, the rate of growth of income per person fell substantially in most industrialized countries. The cause of this slowdown is not well understood. In the mid-1990s, the growth rates of the UK, the US and Canada increased, most likely because of advances in information technology. (Continental European growth rates did not rebound largely because of problems surrounding German unification and deflationary fiscal policy in preparation for the single European currency.)

6. Modern theories of endogenous growth attempt to explain the rate of technological progress, which the Solow model takes as exogenous. These models try to explain the decisions that determine the creation of knowledge through research and development.

KEY CONCEPTS

Efficiency of labour   Labour-augmenting technological progress   Endogenous growth theory

QUESTIONS FOR REVIEW

1. In the Solow model, what determines the steady-state rate of growth of income per worker?

2. In the steady state of the Solow model, at what rate does output per person grow? At what rate does capital per person grow? How does this compare with the experience of your country?

3. What data would you need to determine whether an economy has more or less capital than in the Golden Rule steady state?

4. How can policy makers influence a nation's saving rate?

5. What has happened to the rate of productivity growth in your country over the past 40 years? How might you explain this phenomenon?

6. How does endogenous growth theory explain persistent growth without the assumption of exogenous technological progress? How does this differ from the Solow model?

PROBLEMS AND APPLICATIONS

1. An economy described by the Solow growth model has the following production function:

$$y = \sqrt{k}.$$

a. Solve for the steady-state value of y as a function of s, n, g and δ.

b. A developed country has a saving rate of 28 per cent and a population growth rate of 1 per cent per year. A less-developed country has a saving rate of 10 per cent and a population growth rate of 4 per cent per year. In both countries, $i = 0.02$ and $\delta = 0.04$. Find the steady-state value of y for each country.

c. What policies might the less-developed country pursue to raise its level of income?

2. In the United Kingdom, the capital share of GDP is about 30 per cent; the average growth in output is about 2.5 per cent per year; the depreciation rate is about 4 per cent per year; and the capital–output ratio is about 2.5. Suppose that the production function is Cobb–Douglas, so that the capital share in output is

constant, and that the UK has been in a steady state. (For a discussion of the Cobb–Douglas production function, see Chapter 3.)

a. What must the saving rate be in the initial steady state? (*Hint*: Use the steady-state relationship, $sy = (\delta + n + g)k$.)

b. What is the marginal product of capital in the initial steady state?

c. Suppose that public policy raises the saving rate so that the economy reaches the Golden Rule level of capital. What will the marginal product of capital be at the Golden Rule steady state? Compare the marginal product at the Golden Rule steady state to the marginal product in the initial steady state. Explain.

d. What will the capital–output ratio be at the Golden Rule steady state? (*Hint*: For the Cobb–Douglas production function, the capital–output ratio is related to the marginal product of capital.)

e. What must the saving rate be to reach the Golden Rule steady state?

3. Prove each of the following statements about the steady state of the Solow model with population growth and technological progress.

a. The capital–output ratio is constant.

b. Capital and labour each earn a constant share of an economy's income. (*Hint*: Recall the definition $MPK = f(k + 1) - f(k)$.)

c. Total capital income and total labour income both grow at the rate of population growth plus the rate of technological progress, $n + g$.

d. The real rental price of capital is constant, and the real wage grows at the rate of technological progress g. (*Hint*: The real rental price of capital equals total capital income divided by the capital stock, and the real wage equals total labour income divided by the labour force.)

4. Two countries, Richland and Poorland, are described by the Solow growth model. They have the same Cobb–Douglas production function, $F(K, L) = A K^\alpha L^{1-\alpha}$, but with different quantities of capital and labour. Richland saves 32 per cent of its income, while Poorland saves 10 per cent. Richland has population growth of 1 per cent per year, while Poorland has population growth of 3 per cent. (The numbers in this problem are chosen to be approximately realistic descriptions of rich and poor nations.) Both nations have technological progress at a rate of 2 per cent per year and depreciation at a rate of 5 per cent per year.

a. What is the per worker production function $f(k)$?

b. Solve for the ratio of Richland's steady-state income per worker to Poorland's. (*Hint*: The parameter α will play a role in your answer.)

c. If the Cobb–Douglas parameter α takes the conventional value of about 1/3, how much higher should income per worker be in Richland compared to Poorland?

d. Income per worker in Richland is actually 16 times income per worker in Poorland. Can you explain this fact by changing the value of the parameter α? What must it be? Can you think of any way of justifying such a value for this parameter? How else might you explain the large difference in income between Richland and Poorland?

5. The amount of education the typical person receives varies substantially among countries. Suppose you were to compare a country with a highly educated labour force and a country with a less educated labour force. Assume that education affects only the level of the efficiency of labour. Also assume that the countries are otherwise the same: they have the same saving rate, the same depreciation rate, the same population growth rate and the same rate of technological progress. Both countries are described by the Solow model and are in their steady states. What would you predict for the following variables?

a. The rate of growth of total income.

b. The level of income per worker.

c. The real rental price of capital.

d. The real wage.

6. This question asks you to analyse in more detail the two-sector endogenous growth model presented in the text.

a. Rewrite the production function for manufactured goods in terms of output per effective worker and capital per effective worker.

b. In this economy, what is break-even investment (the amount of investment needed to keep capital per effective worker constant)?

c. Write down the equation of motion for k, which shows Δk as saving minus break-even investment. Use this equation to draw a graph showing the determination of steady-state k. (*Hint*: This graph will look much like those we used to analyse the Solow model.)

d. In this economy, what is the steady-state growth rate of output per worker Y/L? How do the saving rate s and the fraction of the labour force in universities u affect this steady-state growth rate?

e. Using your graph, show the impact of an increase in u. (*Hint*: This change affects both curves.) Describe both the immediate and the steady-state effects.

f. Based on your analysis, is an increase in u an unambiguously good thing for the economy? Explain.

Accounting for the Sources of Economic Growth

In Chapter 3 we linked the output of the economy to the factors of production – capital and labour – and to the production technology. Here we develop a technique called *growth accounting* that divides the growth in output into three different sources: increases in capital, increases in labour and advances in technology. This breakdown provides us with a measure of the rate of technological change.

Increases in the Factors of Production

We first examine how increases in the factors of production contribute to increases in output. To do this, we start by assuming there is no technological change, so the production function relating output Y to capital K and labour L is constant over time:

$$Y = F(K, L).$$

In this case, the amount of output changes only because the amount of capital or labour changes.

Increases in Capital First, consider changes in capital. If the amount of capital increases by ΔK units, by how much does the amount of output increase? To answer this question, we need to recall the definition of the marginal product of capital MPK:

$$MPK = F(K + 1, L) - F(K, L).$$

The marginal product of capital tells us how much output increases when capital increases by 1 unit. Therefore, when capital increases by ΔK units, output increases by approximately $MPK \times \Delta K$.[16]

For example, suppose that the marginal product of capital is 1/5; that is, an additional unit of capital increases the amount of output produced by one-fifth of a unit. If we increase the amount of capital by 10 units, we can compute the amount of additional output as follows:

$$\Delta Y = MPK \times \Delta K$$

$$= 1/5 \, \frac{\text{units of output}}{\text{unit of capital}} \times 10 \text{ units of capital}$$

$$= 2 \text{ units of output.}$$

---

[16] Note the word 'approximately' here. This answer is only an approximation because the marginal product of capital varies: it falls as the amount of capital increases. An exact answer would take into account that each unit of capital has a different marginal product. If the change in K is not too large, however, the approximation of a constant marginal product is very accurate.

By increasing capital by 10 units, we obtain 2 more units of output. Thus, we use the marginal product of capital to convert changes in capital into changes in output.

Increases in Labour Next, consider changes in labour. If the amount of labour increases by ΔL units, by how much does output increase? We answer this question the same way we answered the question about capital. The marginal product of labour MPL tells us how much output changes when labour increases by 1 unit – that is,

$$MPL = F(K, L + 1) - F(K, L).$$

Therefore, when the amount of labour increases by ΔL units, output increases by approximately $MPL \times \Delta L$.

For example, suppose that the marginal product of labour is 2; that is, an additional unit of labour increases the amount of output produced by 2 units. If we increase the amount of labour by 10 units, we can compute the amount of additional output as follows:

$$\Delta Y = MPL \times \Delta L$$

$$= 2 \, \frac{\text{units of output}}{\text{unit of labour}} \times 10 \text{ units of labor}$$

$$= 20 \text{ units of output}.$$

By increasing labour by 10 units, we obtain 20 more units of output. Thus, we use the marginal product of labour to convert changes in labour into changes in output.

Increases in Capital and Labour Finally, let's consider the more realistic case in which both factors of production change. Suppose that the amount of capital increases by ΔK, and the amount of labour increases by ΔL. The increase in output then comes from two sources: more capital and more labour. We can divide this increase into the two sources using the marginal products of the two inputs:

$$\Delta Y = (MPK \times \Delta K) + (MPL + \Delta L).$$

The first term in parentheses is the increase in output resulting from the increase in capital, and the second term in parentheses is the increase in output resulting from the increase in labour. This equation shows us how to attribute growth to each factor of production.

We now want to convert this last equation into a form that is easier to interpret and apply to the available data. First, with some algebraic rearrangement, the equation becomes[17]

$$\frac{\Delta Y}{Y} = \left(\frac{MPL \times K}{Y}\right)\frac{\Delta K}{K} + \left(\frac{MPL \times L}{Y}\right)\frac{\Delta L}{L}.$$

---

[17] *Mathematical note:* to see that this is equivalent to the previous equation, note that we can multiply both sides of this equation by Y and thereby cancel Y from three places in which it appears. We can cancel the K in the top and bottom of the first term on the right-hand side, and the L in the top and bottom of the second term on the right-hand side. These algebraic manipulations turn this equation into the previous one.

This form of the equation relates the growth rate of output, $\Delta Y/Y$, to the growth rate of capital, $\Delta K/K$, and the growth rate of labour, $\Delta L/L$.

Next, we need to find some way to measure the terms in parentheses in the last equation. In Chapter 3 we showed that the marginal product of capital equals its real rental price. Therefore, $MPK \times K$ is the total return to capital, and $(MPK \times K)/Y$ is capital's share of output. Similarly, the marginal product of labour equals the real wage. Therefore, $MPL \times L$ is the total compensation that labour receives, and $(MPL \times L)/Y$ is labour's share of output. Under the assumption that the production function has constant returns to scale, Euler's theorem (which we discussed in Chapter 3) tells us that these two shares sum to 1. In this case, we can write

$$\frac{\Delta Y}{Y} = \alpha\frac{\Delta K}{K} + (1 - \alpha)\frac{\Delta L}{L},$$

where α is capital's share and $(1 - \alpha)$ is labour's share.

This last equation gives us a simple formula for showing how changes in inputs lead to changes in output. In particular, we must weight the growth rates of the inputs by the factor shares. As we discussed in Chapter 3, capital's share in the most developed economies is about 30 per cent, that is, $\alpha = 0.30$. Therefore, a 10 per cent increase in the amount of capital ($\Delta K/K = 0.10$) leads to a 3 per cent increase in the amount of output ($\Delta Y/Y = 0.03$). Similarly, a 10 per cent increase in the amount of labour ($\Delta L/L = 0.10$) leads to a 7 per cent increase in the amount of output ($\Delta Y/Y = 0.07$).

Technological Progress

So far in our analysis of the sources of growth, we have been assuming that the production function does not change over time. In practice, of course, technological progress improves the production function. For any given amount of inputs, we get more output today than we did in the past. We now extend the analysis to allow for technological progress.

We include the effects of the changing technology by writing the production function as

$$Y = AF(K, L),$$

where A is a measure of the current level of technology called *total factor productivity*. Output now increases not only because of increases in capital and labour, but also because of increases in total factor productivity. If total factor productivity increases by 1 per cent, and if the inputs are unchanged, then output increases by 1 per cent.

Allowing for a changing technology adds another term to our equation accounting for economic growth:

$$\frac{\Delta Y}{Y} = \alpha\frac{\Delta K}{K} + (1 - \alpha)\frac{\Delta L}{L} + \frac{\Delta A}{A}$$

| Growth in Output | = | Contribution of Capital | + | Contribution of Labour | + | Growth in Total Factor Productivity. |

This is the key equation of growth accounting. It identifies and allows us to measure the three sources of growth: changes in the amount of capital, changes in the amount of labour and changes in total factor productivity.

Because total factor productivity is not observable directly, it is measured indirectly. We have data on the growth in output, capital and labour; we also have data on capital's share of output. From these data and the growth-accounting equation, we can compute the growth in total factor productivity to make sure that everything adds up:

$$\frac{\Delta A}{A} = \frac{\Delta Y}{Y} - \alpha\frac{\Delta K}{K} - (1 - \alpha)\frac{\Delta L}{L}$$

or

$$\frac{\Delta A}{A} = \left(\frac{\Delta Y}{Y} - \frac{\Delta L}{L}\right) - \alpha\left(\frac{\Delta K}{K} - \frac{\Delta L}{L}\right).$$

$\Delta A/A$ is the change in output that cannot be explained by changes in inputs. Thus, the growth in total factor productivity is computed as a residual – that is, as the amount of output growth that remains after we have accounted for the determinants of growth that we can measure directly. Indeed, $\Delta A/A$ is sometimes called the *Solow residual*, after Robert Solow, who first showed how to compute it.[18]

Total factor productivity can change for many reasons. Changes most often arise because of increased knowledge about production methods, and the Solow residual is often used as a measure of technological progress. Yet other factors, such as education and government regulation, can affect total factor productivity as well. For example, if higher public spending raises the quality of education, then workers may become more productive and output may rise, which implies higher total factor productivity. As another example, if government regulations require firms to purchase capital to reduce pollution or increase worker safety, then the capital stock may rise without any increase in measured output, which implies lower total factor productivity. Still another example might be an adverse supply shock arising from a dramatic increase in oil prices. If the economy is dependent on oil in many of its production processes, and oil is largely imported, then because a larger amount of resources have to be extracted from the economy to pay the increased oil bill, the net effect is that less is produced for any given level of inputs. In brief: *total factor productivity captures anything that changes the relation between measured inputs and measured output.*

---

[18] Robert M. Solow, 'Technical Change and the Aggregate Production Function', *Review of Economics and Statistics*, 1957, vol. 39, pp. 312–320. It is natural to ask how growth in labour efficiency E relates to growth in total factor productivity. One can show that $\Delta A/A = (1 - \alpha)\Delta E/E$, where α is capital's share. Thus, technological change as measured by growth in the efficiency of labour is proportional to technological change as measured by the Solow residual.

The Sources of Growth

Having learned how to measure the sources of economic growth, we now look at the data for a group of countries – the UK, France, Italy, the US and Japan – for selected historical periods, to assess the contribution of growth in total factor productivity to overall growth in real GDP per capita. We obtained data on the non-residential capital stock per worker (K/L) and on real GDP per worker (Y/L), from which we computed the growth in real GDP per worker $\left(\frac{\Delta Y}{Y} - \frac{\Delta L}{L}\right)$ and the growth in the capital stock per worker $\left(\frac{\Delta K}{K} - \frac{\Delta L}{L}\right)$. Finally, we computed the growth in total factor productivity (TFP), using the equation

$$\frac{\Delta A}{A} = \left(\frac{\Delta Y}{Y} - \frac{\Delta L}{L}\right) - \alpha\left(\frac{\Delta K}{K} - \frac{\Delta L}{L}\right),$$

assuming a value of α of 1/3 (as capital income is in fact stable at around one-third or so of output for most advanced economies).

Table 9-3 shows that TFP growth generally represents a large contribution to per capita growth, the major exception being in the period 1971–1975, when measured TFP growth was very small, and indeed negative for four of the five countries. In 1973–1974, however, there was a substantial oil price shock, which, as we noted earlier, would be expected to reduce TFP. Apart from this period, TFP has accounted for a large proportion of per capita growth in these countries – often the major proportion. For example, over the period 1986–1990, TFP growth accounted for nearly two-thirds of growth in real GDP per worker in the UK, and around half or more of real per capita growth in all the other countries.

CASE STUDY

Growth in the East Asian Tigers

Perhaps the most spectacular growth experiences in recent history have been those of the 'Tigers' of East Asia: Hong Kong, Singapore, South Korea and Taiwan. From 1966 to 1990, while real income per person was growing at about 2 to 2.5 per cent or so per year in Europe and the United States, it grew more than 7 per cent per year in each of these countries. In the course of a single generation, real income per person increased fivefold, moving the Tigers from among the world's poorest countries to among the richest. (In the late 1990s, a period of pronounced financial turmoil tarnished the reputation of some of these economies. But this short-run problem, which we examine in a case study in Chapter 13, does not come close to reversing the spectacular long-run growth performance that the Asian Tigers have experienced.)

What accounts for these growth miracles? Some commentators have argued that the success of these four countries is hard to reconcile with basic growth theory, such as the Solow growth model, which takes technology as growing at a constant, exogenous rate. They have suggested that these countries' rapid growth is explained by their ability to imitate foreign technologies. By adopting technology developed abroad, the argument goes, these countries managed to improve their production functions substantially in a relatively short period of time. If this

TABLE 9-3

The Contribution of Total Factor Productivity Growth to Growth in Real GDP per Worker

	UNITED KINGDOM		FRANCE		ITALY		UNITED STATES		JAPAN	
	Output growth per worker	Growth in TFP	Output growth per worker	Growth in TFP	Output growth per worker	Growth in TFP	Output growth per worker	Growth in TFP	Output growth per worker	Growth in TFP
1966–1970	2.2	0.2	4.9	2.3	6.4	4.4	1.7	−0.3	9.5	5.4
1971–1975	1.4	−0.1	2.0	−0.1	2.1	0.2	−0.2	−0.9	3.1	−0.8
1976–1980	1.4	0.6	2.4	1.2	4.7	3.6	1.0	0.7	4.0	2.0
1981–1985	1.6	1.2	0.2	−0.4	0.3	−0.4	1.3	0.8	2.9	1.3
1986–1990	3.1	1.9	2.3	1.6	2.5	1.7	1.7	0.7	3.8	2.0

Source: Authors' calculations and Penn World Tables (Alan Heston, Robert Summers and Bettina Aten, Penn World Tables, Center for International Comparisons of Production, Income and Prices, University of Pennsylvania).

argument is correct, these countries should have experienced unusually rapid growth in total factor productivity.

One recent study shed light on this issue by examining in detail the data from these four countries. The study found that their exceptional growth can be traced to large increases in measured factor inputs: increases in labour-force participation, increases in the capital stock and increases in educational attainment. In South Korea, for example, the investment–GDP ratio rose from about 5 per cent in the 1950s to about 30 per cent in the 1980s; the percentage of the working population with at least a high-school education went from 26 per cent in 1966 to 75 per cent in 1991.

Once we account for growth in labour, capital and human capital, little of the growth in output is left to explain. None of these four countries experienced unusually rapid growth in total factor productivity. Indeed, the average growth in total factor productivity in the East Asian Tigers was almost exactly the same as in the United States and Europe. Thus, although these countries' rapid growth has been truly impressive, it is easy to explain using the tools of basic growth theory.[19] ∎

MORE PROBLEMS AND APPLICATIONS

1. In the economy of Solovia, the owners of capital get two-thirds of national income, and the workers receive one-third.

a. The men of Solovia stay at home performing household chores, while the women work in factories. If some of the men started working

[19] Alwyn Young, 'The Tyranny of Numbers: Confronting the Statistical Realities of the East Asian Growth Experience', *Quarterly Journal of Economics*, 1995, vol. 101, pp. 641–680.

outside the home so that the labour force increased by 5 per cent, what would happen to the measured output of the economy? Does labour productivity – defined as output per worker – increase, decrease or stay the same? Does total factor productivity increase, decrease or stay the same?

b. In year 1, the capital stock was 6, the labour input was 3 and output was 12. In year 2, the capital stock was 7, the labour input was 4 and output was 14. What happened to total factor productivity between the two years?

2. Labour productivity is defined as Y/L, the amount of output divided by the amount of labour input. Start with the growth-accounting equation and show that the growth in labour productivity depends on growth in total factor productivity and growth in the capital–labour ratio. In particular, show that

$$\frac{\Delta(Y/L)}{Y/L} = \frac{\Delta A}{A} + \alpha \frac{\Delta(K/L)}{K/L}.$$

(*Hint:* You may find the following mathematical trick helpful. If $z = wx$, then the growth rate of z is approximately the growth rate of w plus the growth rate of x. That is,

$$\Delta z/z \approx \Delta w/w + \Delta x/x.)$$

3. Suppose an economy described by the Solow model is in a steady state, with population growth n of 1.2 per cent per year, and technological progress g of 2.4 per cent per year. Total output and total capital grow at 3.6 per cent per year. Suppose further that the capital share of output is 1/3. If you used the growth-accounting equation to divide output growth into three sources – capital, labour and total factor productivity – how much would you attribute to each source? Compare your results to the figures we found for the contributions of TFP growth to per capita growth in Table 9-3.

PART 4

Business Cycle Theory: The Economy in the Short Run

CHAPTER 10

Introduction to Economic Fluctuations

> *The modern world regards business cycles much as the ancient Egyptians*
> *regarded the overflowing of the Nile. The phenomenon recurs at intervals, it is*
> *of great importance to everyone, and natural causes of it are not in sight.*
>
> — *John Bates Clark, 1898*

Economic fluctuations present a recurring problem for economists and policy makers. In the mature economies of Western Europe, for example, real GDP grows about 2 to 3 per cent per year on average. But this long-run average hides the fact that the economy's output of goods and services does not grow smoothly. Growth is higher in some years than in others; sometimes the economy loses ground and growth turns negative. These fluctuations in the economy's output are closely associated with fluctuations in employment. When the economy experiences a period of falling output and rising unemployment, the economy is said to be in *recession*.

Economists call these short-run fluctuations in output and employment the *business cycle*. Although this term suggests that economic fluctuations are regular and predictable, they are not – they vary greatly in terms of both their frequency and their severity, and are usually extremely difficult to predict. Consider, for example, Figure 10-1, which shows the quarterly growth of real GDP (compared with four quarters earlier) in the United Kingdom and France since 1972. If we define a recession as occurring when real GDP falls for two successive quarters, then we can discern five recessions in the UK since the early 1970s: one in the first half of 1974 (when output fell by just over 3 per cent from peak to trough), one in the second and third quarters of 1975 (when output fell about 2.5 per cent), one from the second quarter of 1980 until the third quarter of 1981 (a particularly severe recession, with a fall in output of more than 4 per cent), one from about the fourth quarter of 1990 until the second quarter of 1992 (a contraction of just over 2 per cent), and the most recent one from the third quarter of 2008 until the fourth quarter of 2009 (with contraction in output reaching its highest in early 2009 at more than 6 per cent). For France, there are three discernible recessions on this definition: one in the first three-quarters of 1975 (when real GDP fell by about 0.75 per cent), one during the whole of 1993 (a 1 per cent contraction), and, similarly to the UK, one from the third quarter of 2008 until the last quarter

FIGURE 10-1

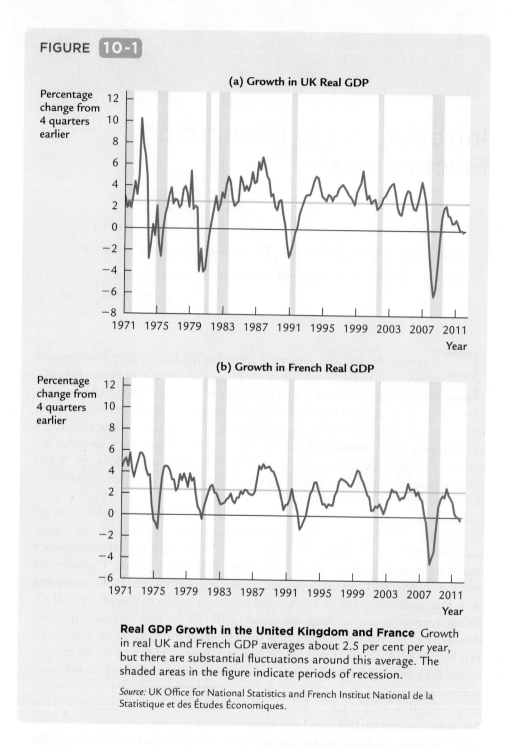

(a) Growth in UK Real GDP

Percentage change from 4 quarters earlier

(b) Growth in French Real GDP

Percentage change from 4 quarters earlier

Real GDP Growth in the United Kingdom and France Growth in real UK and French GDP averages about 2.5 per cent per year, but there are substantial fluctuations around this average. The shaded areas in the figure indicate periods of recession.

Source: UK Office for National Statistics and French Institut National de la Statistique et des Études Économiques.

of 2009 (with an average contraction of 2.5 per cent). The period from the last quarter of 1980 through to the second quarter of 1981, however, was something akin to a period of recession in France, with annualized GDP growth below 1 per cent in each quarter and virtually zero in the second quarter of 1981.

Sometimes the recessions are close together, as in the UK in the 1970s. Sometimes the economy goes many years without a recession. From the the early

1990s until late 2008, neither France nor the UK had suffered a recession at all, whereas in 2008, an EU-wide financial crisis erupted, with severe repercussions on economic growth for all European countries.

These historical events raise a variety of related questions: What causes short-run fluctuations? What model should we use to explain them? Can policy makers avoid recessions? If so, what policy levers should they use?

In Parts II and III of this book, we developed theories to explain how the economy behaves in the long run. Here, in Part IV, we see how economists explain these short-run fluctuations. We begin in this chapter with three tasks. First, we examine the data that describe short-run economic fluctuations. Second, we discuss the key differences between how the economy behaves in the long run and how it behaves in the short run. Third, we introduce the model of aggregate supply and aggregate demand, which most economists use to explain short-run fluctuations. Developing this model in more detail will be our primary job in the chapters that follow.

Just as Egypt now controls the flooding of the Nile Valley with the Aswan Dam, modern society tries to control the business cycle with appropriate economic policies. The model we develop over the next several chapters shows how monetary and fiscal policies influence the business cycle. We will see that these policies can potentially stabilize the economy or, if poorly conducted, make the problem of economic instability even worse.

10-1 The Facts about the Business Cycle

Before thinking about the theory of business cycles, let's look at some of the facts that describe short-run fluctuations in economic activity.

GDP and Its Components

The economy's gross domestic product measures total income and total expenditure in the economy. Because GDP is the broadest gauge of overall economic conditions, it is the natural place to start when analysing the business cycle. In Figure 10-1, as well as the growth of real GDP in the United Kingdom and France since 1971, the horizontal line in each case shows the average growth rate over the whole period; for both countries it is close to 2.5 per cent per year (the actual figures are 2.41 per cent for the UK and 2.22 per cent for France). You can see, however, that economic growth is not at all steady around this average level and that, occasionally, it turns negative.

The shaded areas in Figure 10-2 indicate periods of recession. What determines whether a downturn in the economy is sufficiently severe to be deemed a recession? There is no simple answer. According to an old rule of thumb, a recession is a period of at least two consecutive quarters of declining real GDP. As this book was going to press, there were some signs that these and many other European economies were beginning to recover from the 2008–2009 recession, but recovery has been slow and weak by historical standards.

Figure 10-2 shows the growth in two major components of GDP – consumption in panels (a) and (b) and investment in panels (c) and (d). Growth in both these

FIGURE 10-2

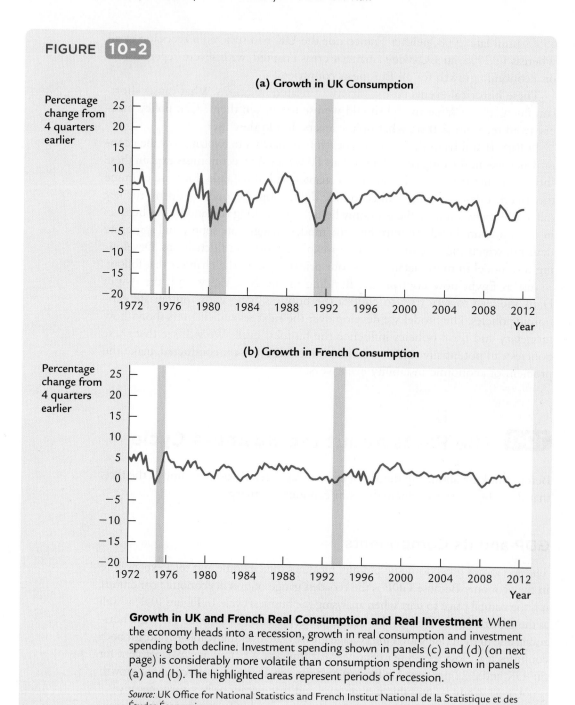

Growth in UK and French Real Consumption and Real Investment When the economy heads into a recession, growth in real consumption and investment spending both decline. Investment spending shown in panels (c) and (d) (on next page) is considerably more volatile than consumption spending shown in panels (a) and (b). The highlighted areas represent periods of recession.

Source: UK Office for National Statistics and French Institut National de la Statistique et des Études Économiques.

variables declines during recessions. Note that investment is far more volatile than consumption over the business cycle. When the economy heads into a recession, households respond to the fall in their incomes by consuming less, but the decline in spending on business equipment, structures, new housing and inventories is even

FIGURE 10-2 *Continued*

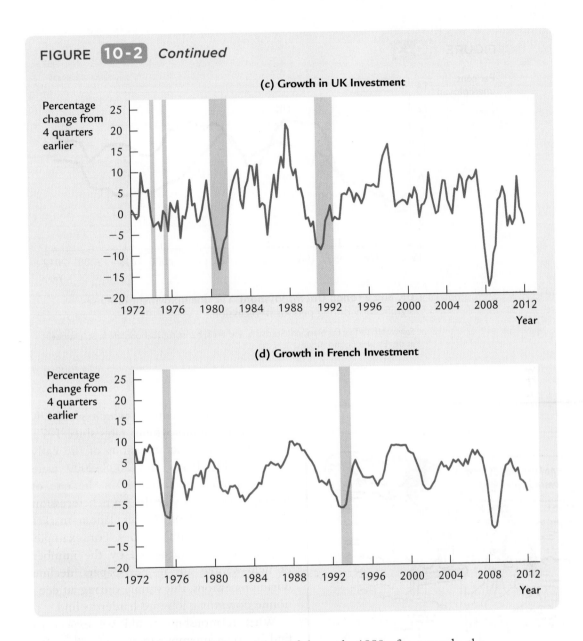

(c) Growth in UK Investment

(d) Growth in French Investment

more substantial. In the severe UK recession of the early 1980s, for example, the maximum decline in consumption expenditure compared with four quarters earlier was around 3.65 per cent, whereas the maximum annual decline in investment expenditure was around 13.5 per cent. Similarly, looking at the recent recession, the consumption level contracted by 4.6 per cent in the first quarter of 2009, whereas investment, during the same period, reduced by 18.3 per cent.

Unemployment and Okun's Law

The business cycle is apparent not only in data from the national income accounts but also in data that describe conditions in the labour market. In

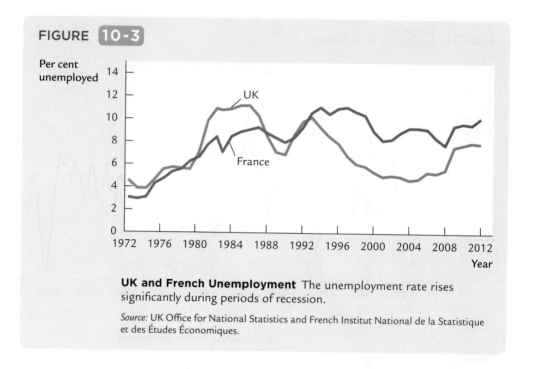

FIGURE 10-3

UK and French Unemployment The unemployment rate rises significantly during periods of recession.

Source: UK Office for National Statistics and French Institut National de la Statistique et des Études Économiques.

Figure 10-3, for example, which plots UK and French unemployment rates since 1972, we can see that the recessions of the early 1970s, 1980s, 1990s and 2008–2009 were indeed marked by increases in the rate of unemployment, as was the French recession of the early 1990s. Other labour-market measures tell a similar story. For example, job vacancies, as measured by the number of help-wanted ads in newspapers, decline during recessions. Put simply, during an economic downturn, jobs are harder to find.

What relationship should we expect to find between unemployment and real GDP? Because employed workers help to produce goods and services and unemployed workers do not, increases in the unemployment rate should be associated with decreases in real GDP. This negative relationship between unemployment and GDP is called **Okun's law**, after Arthur Okun, the economist who first studied it.

Figure 10-4 uses annual data for the United Kingdom to illustrate Okun's law. In this scatterplot, each point represents the data for one year. The horizontal axis represents the change in the unemployment rate from the previous year, and the vertical axis represents the percentage change in GDP. This figure shows clearly that year-to-year changes in the unemployment rate are closely associated with year-to-year changes in real GDP.

FIGURE 10-4

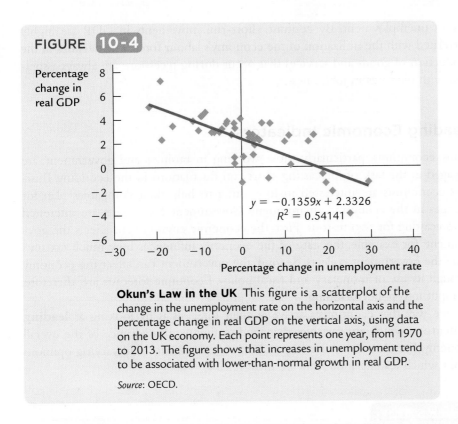

Okun's Law in the UK This figure is a scatterplot of the change in the unemployment rate on the horizontal axis and the percentage change in real GDP on the vertical axis, using data on the UK economy. Each point represents one year, from 1970 to 2013. The figure shows that increases in unemployment tend to be associated with lower-than-normal growth in real GDP.

Source: OECD.

We can be more precise about the magnitude of the Okun's law relationship. The line drawn through the scatter of points tells us that

Percentage Change in Real GDP = 3% − 2 × Change in Unemployment Rate.

If the unemployment rate remains the same, real GDP grows by about 3 per cent; this normal growth in the production of goods and services is due to growth in the labour force, capital accumulation and technological progress. In addition, for every percentage point the unemployment rate rises, real GDP growth typically falls by 2 per cent. Hence, if the unemployment rate rises from 5 to 7 per cent, then real GDP growth would be

Percentage Change in Real GDP = 3% − 2 × (7% − 5%)

= −1%.

In this case, Okun's law says that GDP would fall by 1 per cent, indicating that the economy is in a recession.

Okun's law is a reminder that the forces that govern the short-run business cycle are very different from those that shape long-run economic growth. As we saw in Chapters 8 and 9, long-run growth in GDP is determined primarily by technological progress. The long-run trend leading to higher standards of living from generation to generation is not associated with any long-run trend in the rate of unemployment. By contrast, short-run movements in GDP are highly correlated with the utilization of the economy's labour force. The declines in the production of goods and services that occur during recessions are always associated with increases in joblessness.

Leading Economic Indicators

Many economists, particularly those working in business and government, are engaged in the task of forecasting short-run fluctuations in the economy. Business economists are interested in forecasting to help their companies plan for changes in the economic environment. Government economists are interested in forecasting for two reasons. First, the economic environment affects the government; for example, the state of the economy influences how much tax revenue the government collects. Second, the government can affect the economy through its use of monetary and fiscal policy. Economic forecasts are, therefore, an input into policy planning.

One way that economists arrive at their forecasts is by looking at **leading indicators**, which are variables that tend to fluctuate in advance of the overall economy. Forecasts can differ in part because economists hold varying opinions about which leading indicators are most reliable.

CASE STUDY

The Conference Board Index of Leading Economic Indicators

Each month in the US the Conference Board, a private economics research group, announces the *index of leading economic indicators*. This index includes ten data series that are often used to forecast changes in economic activity about six to nine months into the future. Here is a list of the series.

- *Average workweek of production workers in manufacturing.* Because businesses often adjust the work hours of existing employees before making new hires or laying off workers, average weekly hours is a leading indicator of employment changes. A longer working week indicates that firms are asking their employees to work long hours because they are experiencing strong demand for their products; thus, it indicates that firms are likely to increase hiring and production in the future. A shorter working week indicates weak demand, suggesting that firms are more likely to lay off workers and cut back production.

- *Average initial weekly claims for unemployment insurance.* The number of people making new claims on the unemployment-insurance system is one of the most quickly available indicators of conditions in the labour market. This series is inverted in computing the index of leading indicators, so that an increase in the series lowers the index. An increase in the number of people making new claims for unemployment insurance indicates that firms are laying off workers and cutting back production; these layoffs and cutbacks will soon show up in data on employment and production.

- *New orders for consumer goods and materials, adjusted for inflation.* This indicator is a direct measure of the demand that firms are experiencing. Because an increase in orders depletes a firm's inventories, this statistic typically predicts subsequent increases in production and employment.

- *New orders for non-defence capital goods.* This series is the counterpart to the previous one, but for investment goods rather than consumer goods.

- *Index of supplier deliveries.* This variable, sometimes called *vendor performance,* is a measure of the number of companies receiving slower deliveries from suppliers. Vendor performance is a leading indicator because deliveries slow down when companies are experiencing increased demand for their products. Slower deliveries therefore indicate a future increase in economic activity.

- *New building permits issued.* Construction of new buildings is part of investment – a particularly volatile component of GDP. An increase in building permits means that planned construction is increasing, which indicates a rise in overall economic activity.

- *Index of stock prices.* The stock market reflects expectations about future economic conditions because stock market investors bid up prices when they expect companies to be profitable. An increase in stock prices indicates that investors expect the economy to grow rapidly; a decrease in stock prices indicates that investors expect an economic slowdown.

- *Money supply (M2), adjusted for inflation.* Because the money supply is related to total spending, more money predicts increased spending, which in turn means higher production and employment.

- *Interest rate spread: the yield spread between ten-year Treasury notes and three-month Treasury bills.* This spread, sometimes called the slope of the yield curve, reflects the market's expectation about future interest rates, which in turn reflect the condition of the economy. A large spread means that interest rates are expected to rise, which typically occurs when economic activity increases.

- *Index of consumer expectations.* This is a direct measure of expectations, based on a survey conducted by the University of Michigan's Survey Research Center. Increased optimism about future economic conditions among consumers suggests increased consumer demand for goods and services, which in turn will encourage businesses to expand production and employment to meet the demand.

The index of leading indicators is far from a precise forecast of the future, as short-run economic fluctuations are largely unpredictable. Nonetheless, the index is a useful input into planning by both businesses and the US government. ■

10-2 Time Horizons in Macroeconomics

Now that we have some sense about the facts that describe short-run economic fluctuations, we turn to our basic task in this part of the book: building a theory to explain these fluctuations. That job, it turns out, is not a simple one. It will take us not only the rest of this chapter, but also the next four chapters to develop the model of short-run fluctuations in its entirety.

Before we start building the model, however, let's step back and ask a fundamental question: Why do economists need different models for different time horizons? Why can we not stop the course here and be content with the classical models developed in Chapters 3 to 9? The answer, as this book has consistently reminded its reader, is that classical macroeconomic theory applies to the long run, but not to the short run. But why is this so?

How the Short Run and Long Run Differ

Most macroeconomists believe that the key difference between the short run and the long run is the behaviour of prices. *In the long run, prices are flexible and can respond to changes in supply or demand. In the short run, many prices are 'sticky' at some predetermined level.* Because prices behave differently in the short run from in the long run, various economic events and policies have different effects over different time horizons.

To see how the short run and the long run differ, consider the effects of a change in monetary policy. Suppose that the central bank suddenly reduces the money supply by 5 per cent. According to the classical model, which almost all economists agree describes the economy in the long run, the money supply affects nominal variables – variables measured in terms of money – but not real variables. As you may recall from Chapter 5, the theoretical separation of real and nominal variables is called the classical dichotomy, and the irrelevance of the money supply for the determination of real variables is called monetary neutrality. Most economists believe that these classical ideas describe how the economy works in the long run: a 5 per cent reduction in the money supply lowers all prices (including nominal wages) by 5 per cent, while output, employment and other real variables remain the same. Thus, in the long run, changes in the money supply do not cause fluctuations in output and employment.

In the short run, however, many prices do not respond to changes in monetary policy. A reduction in the money supply does not immediately cause all firms to cut the wages they pay, all shops to change the price tags on their goods, all mail-order firms to issue new catalogues, and all restaurants to print new menus. Instead, there is little immediate change in many prices; that is, many prices are sticky. This short-run price stickiness implies that the short-run impact of a change in the money supply is not the same as the long-run impact.

A model of economic fluctuations must take into account this short-run price stickiness. We will see that the failure of prices to adjust quickly and completely means that, in the short run, real variables such as output and employment must do some of the adjusting instead. In other words, during the time horizon over which prices are sticky, the classical dichotomy no longer holds: nominal variables can influence real variables, and the economy can deviate from the equilibrium predicted by the classical model.

CASE STUDY

Why Are Prices Sticky?

How sticky are prices? The answer to this question depends on what price we consider. Some commodities, such as wheat, copper and oil, are traded on organized exchanges, and their prices change every minute. No one would call these prices sticky. Yet the prices of most goods and services change much less frequently. Price stickiness seems particularly evident in Europe. For example, an empirical study has shown that the average frequency of retail price changes is only about once a year in Europe, while it is about twice a year in the US. In any given year, only about 15 per cent of European products have price changes.

The reasons for price stickiness are not always apparent, and there are various theories that have been advanced to explain it. However, the researchers found that European firms often justify not changing prices too fast as a means of building up long-term relationships with their customers, so that they will continue to shop with them instead of constantly looking for goods at lower prices elsewhere. This can benefit both the firm and the customer, since the firm gets predictable sales and the customer gets the benefit of not worrying about price changes or having to shop around for the best price. Although this reason was the most popular among the firms surveyed, not all firms gave the same answer.[1]

The cause of price stickiness is, in fact, an active area of research, but in this chapter, we simply assume that prices are sticky so we can start developing the link between sticky prices and the business cycle. Although not yet fully explained, short-run price stickiness is widely believed to be crucial for understanding short-run economic fluctuations. ■

The Model of Aggregate Supply and Aggregate Demand

How does the introduction of sticky prices change our view of how the economy works? We can answer this question by considering economists' two favourite words – supply and demand.

In classical macroeconomic theory, the amount of output depends on the economy's ability to *supply* goods and services, which in turn depends on the

[1] Luis J. Álvarez, Emmanuel Dhyne, Marco M. Hoeberichts, Claudia Kwapil, Hervé Le Bihan, Patrick Lünnemann, Fernando Martins, Roberto Sabbatini, Harald Stahl, Philip Vermeulen and Jouko Vilmen, *Sticky Prices in the Euro Area: A Summary of New Micro Evidence*, European Central Bank Discussion paper No. 563, December 2005. This study actually looked at prices in the Euro Area rather in the whole of Europe.

supplies of capital and labour and on the available production technology. This is the essence of the basic classical model in Chapter 3, as well as the Solow growth model in Chapters 8 and 9. Flexible prices are a crucial assumption of classical theory. The theory posits, sometimes implicitly, that prices adjust to ensure that the quantity of output demanded equals the quantity supplied.

The economy works quite differently when prices are sticky. In this case, as we will see, output also depends on the economy's *demand* for goods and services. Demand, in turn, depends on a variety of factors: consumers' confidence about their economic prospects, firms' perceptions about the profitability of new investments, and monetary and fiscal policy. Because monetary and fiscal policy can influence demand, and demand, in turn, can influence the economy's output over the time horizon when prices are sticky, price stickiness provides a rationale for why these policies may be useful in stabilizing the economy in the short run.

In the rest of this chapter, we start developing a model that makes these ideas more precise. The model of supply and demand, which we used in Chapter 1 to discuss the market for pizza, offers some of the most fundamental insights in economics. This model shows how the supply and demand for any good jointly determine the good's price and the quantity sold, and how shifts in supply and demand affect the price and quantity. We now introduce the 'economy-size' version of this model – *the model of aggregate supply and aggregate demand*. This macroeconomic model allows us to study how the aggregate price level and the quantity of aggregate output are determined in the short run. It also provides a way to contrast how the economy behaves in the long run and how it behaves in the short run.

Although the model of aggregate supply and aggregate demand resembles the model of supply and demand for a single good, the analogy is not exact. The model of supply and demand for a single good considers only one good within a large economy. By contrast, as we will see in the coming chapters, the model of aggregate supply and aggregate demand is a sophisticated model that incorporates the interactions among many markets. In the remainder of this chapter, we get a first glimpse at those interactions by examining the model in its most simplified form. Our goal here is not to explain the model fully, but, instead, to introduce the model's key elements and illustrate how it can help explain short-run economic fluctuations.

10-3 Aggregate Demand

Aggregate demand (*AD*) is the relationship between the quantity of output demanded and the aggregate price level. In other words, the aggregate demand curve tells us the quantity of goods and services people want to buy at any given level of prices. We examine the theory of aggregate demand in detail in Chapters 11 to 13. Here we use the quantity theory of money to provide a simple, although incomplete, derivation of the aggregate demand curve.

The Quantity Equation as Aggregate Demand

Recall from Chapter 5 that the quantity theory says that

$$MV = PY,$$

where M is the money supply, V is the velocity of money, P is the price level and Y is the amount of output. If the velocity of money is constant, then this equation states that the money supply determines the nominal value of output, which in turn is the product of the price level and the amount of output.

When interpreting this equation, it is useful to recall that the quantity equation can be rewritten in terms of the supply and demand for real money balances:

$$M/P = (M/P)^d = kY,$$

where $k = 1/V$ is a parameter determining how much money people want to hold for every euro of income. In this form, the quantity equation states that the supply of real money balances M/P equals the demand for real money balances $(M/P)^d$, and that the demand is proportional to output Y. The velocity of money V is the 'flip side' of the money demand parameter k. The assumption of constant velocity is equivalent to the assumption of a constant demand for real money balances per unit of output.

If we assume that velocity V is constant and the money supply M is fixed by the central bank, then the quantity equation yields a negative relationship between the price level P and output Y. Figure 10-5 graphs the combinations of P and Y that satisfy the quantity equation holding M and V constant. This downward-sloping curve is called the aggregate demand curve.

Why the Aggregate Demand Curve Slopes Downward

As a strictly mathematical matter, the quantity equation explains the downward slope of the aggregate demand curve very simply. The money supply M and the

---

FIGURE 10-5

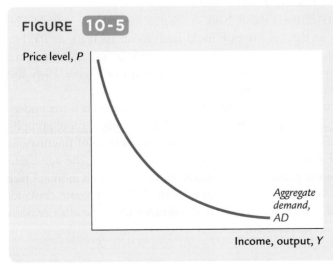

Price level, P

Income, output, Y

Aggregate demand, AD

The Aggregate Demand Curve The aggregate demand curve AD shows the relationship between the price level P and the quantity of goods and services demanded Y. It is drawn for a given value of the money supply M. The aggregate demand curve slopes downward: the higher the price level P, the lower the level of real balances M/P, and therefore the lower the quantity of goods and services demanded Y.

velocity of money V determine the nominal value of output PY. Once PY is fixed, if P goes up, Y must go down.

What is the economics that lies behind this mathematical relationship? For a complete explanation of the downward slope of the aggregate demand curve, we have to wait a couple of chapters. For now, however, consider the following logic: Because we have assumed the velocity of money is fixed, the money supply determines the euro value of all transactions in the economy. (This conclusion should be familiar from Chapter 5.) If the price level rises, each transaction requires more euros, so the number of transactions, and thus the quantity of goods and services purchased, must fall.

We can also explain the downward slope of the aggregate demand curve by thinking about the supply and demand for real money balances. If output is higher, people engage in more transactions and need higher real balances M/P. For a fixed money supply M, higher real balances imply a lower price level. Conversely, if the price level is lower, real money balances are higher; the higher level of real balances allows a greater volume of transactions, which means a greater quantity of output is demanded.

Shifts in the Aggregate Demand Curve

The aggregate demand curve is drawn for a fixed value of the money supply. In other words, it tells us the possible combinations of P and Y for a given value of M. If the central bank changes the money supply, then the possible combinations of P and Y change, which means the aggregate demand curve shifts.

For example, consider what happens if the central bank reduces the money supply. The quantity equation, $MV = PY$, tells us that the reduction in the money supply leads to a proportionate reduction in the nominal value of output PY. For any given price level, the amount of output is lower, and for any given amount of output, the price level is lower. As in panel (a) of Figure 10-6, the aggregate demand curve relating P and Y shifts inward.

The opposite occurs if the central bank increases the money supply. The quantity equation tells us that an increase in M leads to an increase in PY. For any given price level, the amount of output is higher, and for any given amount of output, the price level is higher. As shown in panel (b) of Figure 10-6, the aggregate demand curve shifts outward.

Although the quantity theory of money gives a very simple basis for understanding the aggregate demand curve, be forewarned that reality is more complicated. Fluctuations in the money supply are not the only source of fluctuations in aggregate demand. Even if the money supply is held constant, the aggregate demand curve shifts if some event causes a change in the velocity of money. Over the next two chapters, we develop a more general model of aggregate demand, called the *IS-LM model,* which will allow us to consider many possible reasons for shifts in the aggregate demand curve.

FIGURE 10-6

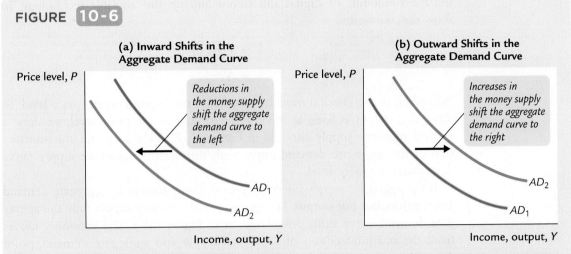

(a) Inward Shifts in the Aggregate Demand Curve

Price level, P

Reductions in the money supply shift the aggregate demand curve to the left

AD_1

AD_2

Income, output, Y

(b) Outward Shifts in the Aggregate Demand Curve

Price level, P

Increases in the money supply shift the aggregate demand curve to the right

AD_2

AD_1

Income, output, Y

Shifts in the Aggregate Demand Curve Changes in the money supply shift the aggregate demand curve. In panel (a), a decrease in the money supply M reduces the nominal value of output PY. For any given price level P, output Y is lower. Thus, a decrease in the money supply shifts the aggregate demand curve inward from AD_1 to AD_2. In panel (b), an increase in the money supply M raises the nominal value of output PY. For any given price level P, output Y is higher. Thus, an increase in the money supply shifts the aggregate demand curve outward from AD_1 to AD_2.

10-4 Aggregate Supply

By itself, the aggregate demand curve does not tell us the price level or the amount of output that will prevail in the economy; it merely gives a relationship between these two variables. To accompany the aggregate demand curve, we need another relationship between P and Y that crosses the aggregate demand curve — an aggregate supply curve. The aggregate demand and aggregate supply curves together pin down the economy's price level and quantity of output.

Aggregate supply (*AS*) is the relationship between the quantity of goods and services supplied and the price level. Because the firms that supply goods and services have flexible prices in the long run, but sticky prices in the short run, the aggregate supply relationship depends on the time horizon. We need to discuss two different aggregate supply curves: the long-run aggregate supply curve *LRAS* and the short-run aggregate supply curve *SRAS*. We also need to discuss how the economy makes the transition from the short run to the long run.

The Long Run: The Vertical Aggregate Supply Curve

Because the classical model describes how the economy behaves in the long run, we derive the long-run aggregate supply curve from the classical model. Recall from Chapter 3 that the amount of output produced depends on the fixed amounts of capital and labour and on the available technology. To show this, we write

$$Y = F(\overline{K}, \overline{L})$$
$$= \overline{Y}.$$

According to the classical model, output does not depend on the price level. To show that output is fixed at this level, regardless of the price level, we draw a vertical aggregate supply curve, as in Figure 10-7. In the long run, the intersection of the aggregate demand curve with this vertical aggregate supply curve determines the price level.

If the aggregate supply curve is vertical, then changes in aggregate demand affect prices, but not output. For example, if the money supply falls, the aggregate demand curve shifts downward, as in Figure 10-8. The economy moves from the old intersection of aggregate supply and aggregate demand, point A, to the new intersection, point B. The shift in aggregate demand affects only prices.

The vertical aggregate supply curve satisfies the classical dichotomy, because it implies that the level of output is independent of the money supply. This long-run level of output, $\overline{Y}$, is called the *full-employment*, or *natural*, level of output. It is the level of output at which the economy's resources are fully employed or, more realistically, at which unemployment is at its natural rate.

The Short Run: The Horizontal Aggregate Supply Curve

The classical model and the vertical aggregate supply curve apply only in the long run. In the short run, some prices are sticky and, therefore, do not adjust

---

FIGURE 10-7

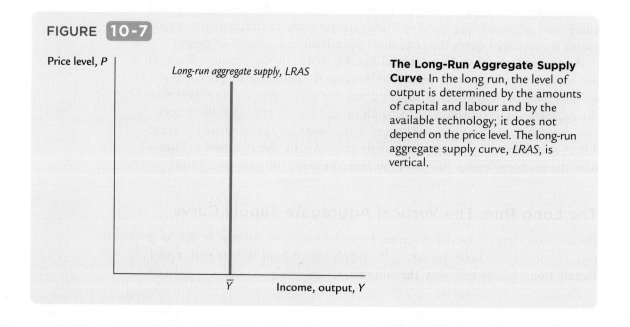

Price level, P

Long-run aggregate supply, LRAS

$\overline{Y}$ Income, output, Y

The Long-Run Aggregate Supply Curve In the long run, the level of output is determined by the amounts of capital and labour and by the available technology; it does not depend on the price level. The long-run aggregate supply curve, *LRAS*, is vertical.

FIGURE 10-8

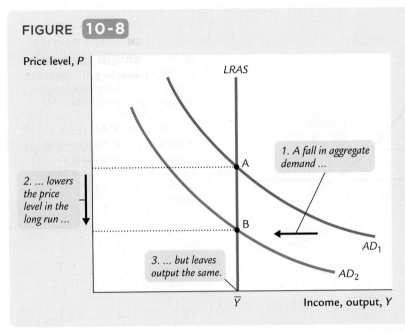

Shifts in Aggregate Demand in the Long Run A reduction in the money supply shifts the aggregate demand curve downward from AD_1 to AD_2. The equilibrium for the economy moves from point A to point B. Because the aggregate supply curve is vertical in the long run, the reduction in aggregate demand affects the price level but not the level of output.

to changes in demand. Because of this price stickiness, the short-run aggregate supply curve is not vertical.

In this chapter, we will simplify things by assuming an extreme example. Suppose that all firms have issued price catalogues and that it is too costly for them to issue new ones. Thus, all prices are stuck at predetermined levels. At these prices, firms are willing to sell as much as their customers are willing to buy, and they hire just enough labour to produce the amount demanded. Because the price level is fixed, we represent this situation in Figure 10-9 with a horizontal aggregate supply curve.

The short-run equilibrium of the economy is the intersection of the aggregate demand curve and this horizontal short-run aggregate supply curve. In this case, changes in aggregate demand do affect the level of output. For example,

FIGURE 10-9

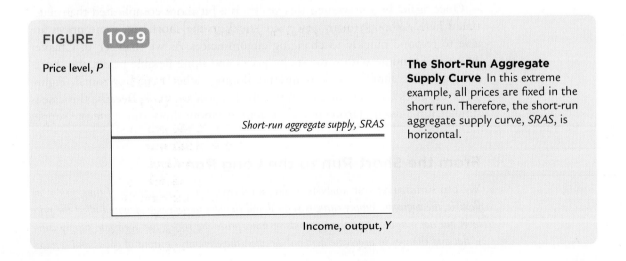

The Short-Run Aggregate Supply Curve In this extreme example, all prices are fixed in the short run. Therefore, the short-run aggregate supply curve, SRAS, is horizontal.

FIGURE 10-10

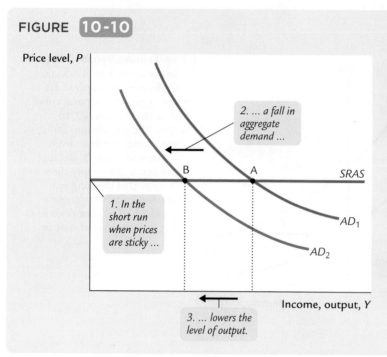

Shifts in Aggregate Demand in the Short Run A reduction in the money supply shifts the aggregate demand curve inward from AD_1 to AD_2. The equilibrium for the economy moves from point A to point B. Because the aggregate supply curve is horizontal in the short run, the reduction in aggregate demand reduces the level of output.

if the central bank suddenly reduces the money supply, the aggregate demand curve shifts inward, as in Figure 10-10. The economy moves from the old intersection of aggregate demand and aggregate supply, point A, to the new intersection, point B. The movement from point A to point B represents a decline in output at a fixed price level.

Thus, a fall in aggregate demand reduces output in the short run because prices do not adjust instantly. After the sudden fall in aggregate demand, firms are stuck with prices that are too high. With demand low and prices high, firms sell less of their product, so they reduce production and lay off workers. The economy experiences a recession.

Once again, be forewarned that reality is a bit more complicated than illustrated here. Although many prices are sticky in the short run, some prices are able to respond quickly to changing circumstances. As we shall see in Chapter 14, in an economy with some sticky prices and some flexible prices, the short-run aggregate supply curve is upward sloping rather than horizontal. Figure 10-9 illustrates the extreme case in which all prices are stuck. Because this case is simpler, it is a useful starting point for thinking about short-run aggregate supply.

From the Short Run to the Long Run

We can summarize our analysis so far as follows: *Over long periods of time, prices are flexible, the aggregate supply curve is vertical and changes in aggregate demand affect the price level but not output. Over short periods of time, prices are sticky, the aggregate supply curve is flat and changes in aggregate demand do affect the economy's output of goods and services.*

FIGURE 10-11

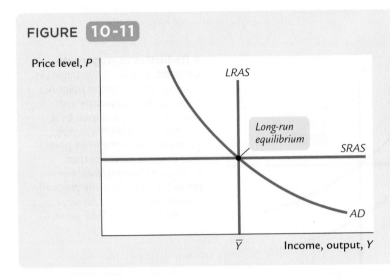

Long-Run Equilibrium In the long run, the economy finds itself at the intersection of the long-run aggregate supply curve and the aggregate demand curve. Because prices have adjusted to this level, the short-run aggregate supply curve crosses this point as well.

How does the economy make the transition from the short run to the long run? Let's trace the effects over time of a fall in aggregate demand. Suppose that the economy is initially in long-run equilibrium, as shown in Figure 10-11. In this figure, there are three curves: the aggregate demand curve, the long-run aggregate supply curve and the short-run aggregate supply curve. The long-run equilibrium is the point at which aggregate demand crosses the long-run aggregate supply curve. Prices have adjusted to reach this equilibrium. Therefore, when the economy is in its long-run equilibrium, the short-run aggregate supply curve must cross this point as well.

Now suppose that the central bank reduces the money supply and the aggregate demand curve shifts inward, as in Figure 10-12. In the short run, prices are sticky, so the economy moves from point A to point B. Output and employment fall below their natural levels, which means the economy is in a recession. Over time, in response to the low demand, wages and prices fall. The gradual reduction in the price level moves the economy downward along the aggregate demand curve to point C, which is the new long-run equilibrium. In the new long-run equilibrium (point C), output and employment are back to their natural levels, but prices are lower than in the old long-run equilibrium (point A). Thus, a shift in aggregate demand affects output in the short run, but this effect dissipates over time as firms adjust their prices.

CASE STUDY

Gold, the Pound Sterling and the UK Contraction of the 1920s

Before World War I, the United Kingdom was on a gold standard. Paper pounds were readily convertible into gold. Under this policy, the quantity of gold determined the money supply and the price level.

FIGURE 10-12

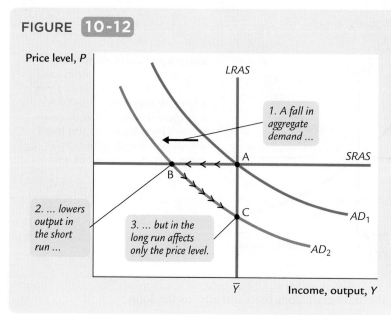

Price level, *P*

LRAS

1. *A fall in aggregate demand ...*

A

SRAS

B

2. *... lowers output in the short run ...*

3. *... but in the long run affects only the price level.*

C

AD_1

AD_2

$\overline{Y}$

Income, output, *Y*

A Reduction in Aggregate Demand The economy begins in long-run equilibrium at point A. A reduction in aggregate demand, perhaps caused by a decrease in the money supply, moves the economy from point A to point B, where output is below its natural level. As prices fall, the economy gradually recovers from the recession, moving from point B to point C.

In 1914, soon after World War I broke out, the UK authorities announced that they would no longer redeem British pounds for gold. In essence, this act replaced the gold standard with a system of fiat money. Over the next few years, the UK government printed large quantities of paper currency and used the seigniorage to finance wartime expenditure. Because of this increase in the money supply, the price level increased dramatically during the war. In 1914, the inflation rate had been around 2.5 per cent per year; over the next four years it averaged around 18.5 per cent per year.

When the war was over, much political debate centred on the question of whether or not to return to the gold standard, and, if so, at what rate. Eventually, the pound sterling was returned to the gold standard in 1925, by the Chancellor of the Exchequer Winston Churchill, on the advice of conservative economists at the time (although against the advice of John Maynard Keynes, who wrote a pamphlet attacking the decision, entitled *The Economic Consequences of Mr Churchill*).

Although a higher gold price and significant inflation had followed the ending of the gold standard, Churchill returned to the standard at the pre-war gold price. Returning to the gold standard in this way required reversing the wartime rise in prices, which meant aggregate demand had to fall. (To be more precise, the growth in aggregate demand needed to fall short of the growth in the natural level of output.) In fact, the British authorities began to prepare for this from 1920 onwards, and prices fell by around 30 per cent over the period 1921–1925. As the price level fell, the economy experienced a severe recession. In 1920 and 1921, for example, UK GDP fell by around 20 per cent. In addition, the British deflation reached across the remnants of the British Empire where the pound sterling was still used as the primary unit of account. ∎

10-5 Stabilization Policy

Fluctuations in the economy as a whole come from changes in aggregate supply or aggregate demand. Economists call exogenous events that shift these curves **shocks** to the economy. A shock that shifts the aggregate demand curve is called a **demand shock**, and a shock that shifts the aggregate supply curve is called a **supply shock**. These shocks disrupt the economy by pushing output and employment away from their natural levels. One goal of the model of aggregate supply and aggregate demand is to show how shocks cause economic fluctuations.

Another goal of the model is to evaluate how macroeconomic policy can respond to these shocks. Economists use the term **stabilization policy** to refer to policy actions aimed at reducing the severity of short-run economic fluctuations. Because output and employment fluctuate around their long-run natural levels, stabilization policy dampens the business cycle by keeping output and employment as close to their natural levels as possible.

In the coming chapters, we examine in detail how stabilization policy works and what practical problems arise in its use. Here we begin our analysis of stabilization policy using our simplified version of the model of aggregate demand and aggregate supply. In particular, we examine how monetary policy might respond to shocks. Monetary policy is an important component of stabilization policy because, as we have seen, the money supply has a powerful impact on aggregate demand.

Shocks to Aggregate Demand

Consider an example of a demand shock: the introduction and expanded availability of credit cards. Because credit cards are often a more convenient way to make purchases than using cash, they reduce the quantity of money that people choose to hold. This reduction in money demand is equivalent to an increase in the velocity of money. When each person holds less money, the money demand parameter k falls. This means that each euro moves from hand to hand more quickly, so velocity $V (= 1/k)$ rises.

If the money supply is held constant, the increase in velocity causes nominal spending to rise and the aggregate demand curve to shift outward, as in Figure 10-13. In the short run, the increase in demand raises the output of the economy – it causes an economic boom. At the old prices, firms now sell more output. Therefore, they hire more workers, ask their existing workers to work longer hours, and make greater use of their factories and equipment.

Over time, the high level of aggregate demand pulls up wages and prices. As the price level rises, the quantity of output demanded declines, and the economy gradually approaches the natural level of production. But during the transition to the higher price level, the economy's output is higher than its natural level.

What can the central bank do to dampen this boom and keep output closer to the natural level? The central bank might reduce the money supply to offset the increase in velocity. Offsetting the change in velocity would stabilize aggregate demand. Thus, the central bank can reduce or even eliminate the impact of

FIGURE 10-13

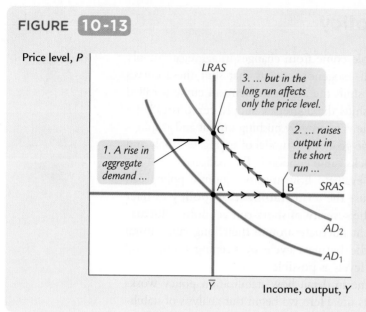

Price level, *P*

LRAS

3. ... but in the long run affects only the price level.

2. ... raises output in the short run ...

1. A rise in aggregate demand ...

C

A

B

SRAS

AD₂

AD₁

$\overline{Y}$

Income, output, *Y*

An Increase in Aggregate Demand The economy begins in long-run equilibrium at point A. An increase in aggregate demand, perhaps due to an increase in the velocity of money, moves the economy from point A to point B, where output is above its natural level. As prices rise, output gradually returns to its natural level, and the economy moves from point B to point C.

demand shocks on output and employment if it can skilfully control the money supply. Whether the central bank in fact has the necessary skill is a more difficult question, which we take up in Chapter 15.

Shocks to Aggregate Supply

Shocks to aggregate supply, as well as shocks to aggregate demand, can cause economic fluctuations. A supply shock is a shock to the economy that alters the cost of producing goods and services, and, as a result, the prices that firms charge. Because supply shocks have a direct impact on the price level, they are sometimes called *price shocks*. Here are some examples:

■ A drought that destroys crops. The reduction in food supply pushes up food prices.

■ A new environmental protection law that requires firms to reduce their emissions of pollutants. Firms pass on the added costs to customers in the form of higher prices.

■ An increase in union aggressiveness. This pushes up wages and the prices of the goods produced by union workers.

■ The organization of an international oil cartel. By curtailing competition, the major oil producers can raise the world price of oil.

All these events are *adverse* supply shocks, which means they push costs and prices upward. A *favourable* supply shock, such as the break-up of an international oil cartel, reduces costs and prices.

FIGURE 10-14

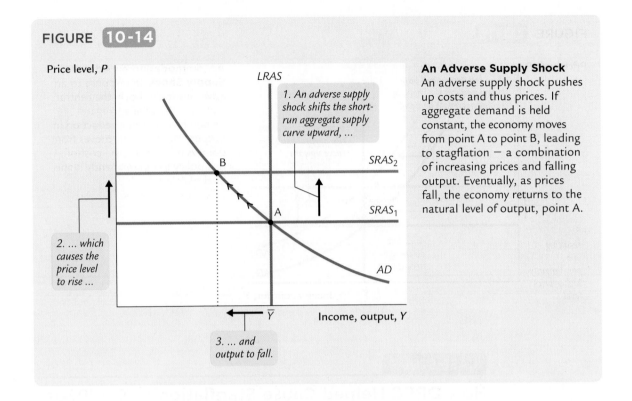

FIGURE 10-14

Price level, *P*

LRAS

1. An adverse supply shock shifts the short-run aggregate supply curve upward, ...

B

SRAS₂

A

SRAS₁

2. ... which causes the price level to rise ...

AD

Ȳ

Income, output, *Y*

3. ... and output to fall.

An Adverse Supply Shock An adverse supply shock pushes up costs and thus prices. If aggregate demand is held constant, the economy moves from point A to point B, leading to stagflation — a combination of increasing prices and falling output. Eventually, as prices fall, the economy returns to the natural level of output, point A.

Figure 10-14 shows how an adverse supply shock affects the economy. The short-run aggregate supply curve shifts upward. (The supply shock may also lower the natural level of output and thus shift the long-run aggregate supply curve to the left, but we ignore that effect here.) If aggregate demand is held constant, the economy moves from point A to point B: the price level rises and the amount of output falls below its natural level. An experience like this is called *stagflation,* because it combines stagnation (falling output) with inflation (rising prices).

Faced with an adverse supply shock, a policy maker controlling aggregate demand, such as the central bank, has a difficult choice between two options. The first option, implicit in Figure 10-14, is to hold aggregate demand constant. In this case, output and employment are lower than the natural level. Eventually, prices will fall to restore full employment at the old price level (point A), but the cost of this adjustment process is a painful recession.

The second option, illustrated in Figure 10-15, is to expand aggregate demand to bring the economy towards the natural level of output more quickly. If the increase in aggregate demand coincides with the shock to aggregate supply, the economy goes immediately from point A to point C. In this case, the central bank is said to *accommodate* the supply shock. The drawback of this option, of course, is that the price level is permanently higher. There is no way to adjust aggregate demand to maintain full employment and keep the price level stable.

FIGURE 10-15

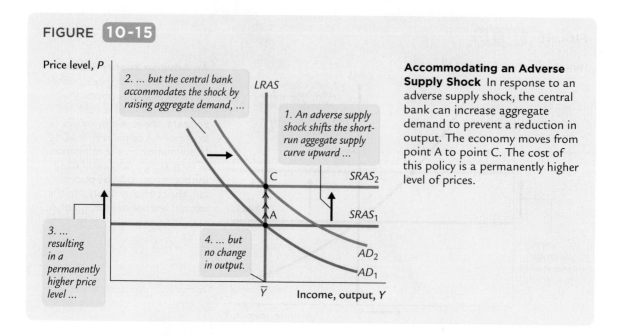

Price level, *P*

2. ... but the central bank accommodates the shock by raising aggregate demand, ...

LRAS

1. An adverse supply shock shifts the short-run aggegate supply curve upward ...

C

SRAS₂

A

SRAS₁

3. ... resulting in a permanently higher price level ...

4. ... but no change in output.

AD₂

AD₁

Ȳ

Income, output, *Y*

Accommodating an Adverse Supply Shock In response to an adverse supply shock, the central bank can increase aggregate demand to prevent a reduction in output. The economy moves from point A to point C. The cost of this policy is a permanently higher level of prices.

CASE STUDY

How OPEC Helped Cause Stagflation in the 1970s and Euphoria in the 1980s

The most disruptive supply shocks in recent history were caused by OPEC, the Organization of Petroleum Exporting Countries. OPEC is a cartel, which is an organization of suppliers that coordinate production levels and prices. In the early 1970s, OPEC's reduction in the supply of oil nearly doubled the world price. This increase in oil prices caused stagflation in most industrial countries. The statistics in Table 10-1 show what happened in the UK and France.

TABLE 10-1

Year	Change in Oil Price (%)	UK Inflation Rate (%)	UK Unemployment Rate (%)	French Inflation Rate (%)	French Unemployment Rate (%)
1973	11.0	7.3	2.6	7.4	2.8
1974	68.0	14.7	2.6	13.6	2.9
1975	16.0	27.1	4.1	11.7	4.2
1976	3.3	15.2	5.6	9.6	4.6
1977	8.1	13.5	5.7	9.5	5.2

The 68 per cent increase in the price of oil in 1974 was an adverse supply shock of major proportions. As one would have expected, this shock led to both higher inflation and higher unemployment.

A few years later, when the world economy had nearly recovered from the first OPEC recession, almost the same thing happened again. OPEC raised oil prices, causing further stagflation. Table 10-2 presents the statistics for the UK and France.

TABLE 10-2

Year	Change in Oil Price (%)	UK Inflation Rate (%)	UK Unemployment Rate (%)	French Inflation Rate (%)	French Unemployment Rate (%)
1978	9.4	11.7	5.6	9.3	6.1
1979	25.4	14.5	5.2	10.6	6.5
1980	47.8	19.4	6.7	13.5	7.6
1981	44.4	11.3	10.2	13.3	8.3
1982	−8.7	7.5	11.9	12.0	8.3

The increases in oil prices in 1979, 1980 and 1981 again led to double-digit inflation and higher unemployment.

In the mid-1980s, political turmoil among the Arab countries weakened OPEC's ability to restrain supplies of oil. Oil prices fell, reversing the stagflation of the 1970s and the early 1980s. Table 10-3 shows what happened.

TABLE 10-3

Year	Change in Oil Price (%)	UK Inflation Rate (%)	UK Unemployment Rate (%)	French Inflation Rate (%)	French Unemployment Rate (%)
1983	−7.1	5.5	13.0	9.5	8.6
1984	−1.7	4.5	14.1	7.7	10.0
1985	−7.5	5.7	14.5	5.8	10.5
1986	−44.5	3.3	14.8	2.5	10.6
1987	18.3	6.3	13.3	3.3	10.8

In 1986 oil prices fell by nearly half. This favourable supply shock led to a dramatic fall in the inflation rate. The positive oil shock did not feed through to unemployment immediately, despite the fact that the oil price had rebounded by about 18 per cent.

Since this period, OPEC has not been a major cause of economic fluctuations. There are two reasons for the cartel's diminished macroeconomic influence.

First, OPEC has been less successful at raising the price of oil. Although world oil prices have fluctuated, the changes have not been as large as those experienced during the 1970s, and the real price of oil has only recently returned to the peaks reached in the early 1980s. Measured in 2013 dollars, oil reached about

$100 a barrel in the early 1980s. By comparison, from 2003 to 2005, oil prices were a source of much concern, as the Iraq war and other events pushed oil prices higher. But oil prices during this time period stayed below $70 a barrel. Recently, prices have again broken the $100 a barrel threshold, first in 2008 as a result of strengthening demand from China and a lack of spare capacity. Following a decline after the financial crisis, from early 2011 onwards prices have hovered around the $100 a barrel mark. This may be due to demand and supply factors, but also increased trading in oil futures and a decline in the dollar, as well as tensions in the Middle East.

Second, conservation efforts and technological changes have made the advanced industrialized economies less susceptible to oil shocks. The economies of Europe and the US in the early 21st century are more service based and less manufacturing based, and services typically use less energy to produce than manufactured goods. The amount of oil consumed per unit of real GDP has fallen about 50 per cent in Europe and the US since the mid-1970s. This fact suggests that even with oil prices at $100 per barrel, the macroeconomic impact is much smaller. In other words, it would take a much larger oil price change to have the impact on the economy that we observed in the 1970s and 1980s.

But we should not be too sanguine. Events in the Middle East are still a potential source of shocks to economies around the world. If the rise in oil prices were ever large enough, the economic result could well resemble the stagflation of the 1970s.[2] ■

10-6 Conclusion

This chapter introduced a framework to study economic fluctuations: the model of aggregate supply and aggregate demand. The model is built on the assumption that prices are sticky in the short run and flexible in the long run. It shows how shocks to the economy cause output to deviate temporarily from the level implied by the classical model.

The model also highlights the role of monetary policy. On the one hand, poor monetary policy can be a source of destabilizing shocks to the economy. On the other hand, a well-run monetary policy can respond to shocks and stabilize the economy.

In the chapters that follow, we refine our understanding of this model and our analysis of stabilization policy. Chapters 11 to 13 go beyond the quantity equation to refine our theory of aggregate demand. Chapter 14 examines aggregate supply in more detail. Chapter 15 examines the debate over the virtues and limits of stabilization policy.

---

[2] Some economists have suggested that changes in oil prices played a major role in economic fluctuations even before the 1970s. See James D. Hamilton, 'Oil and the Macroeconomy since World War II', *Journal of Political Economy*, April 1983, vol. 91, pp. 228–248.

Summary

1. Economies experience short-run fluctuations in economic activity, measured most broadly by real GDP. These fluctuations are associated with movement in many macroeconomic variables. In particular, when GDP growth declines, consumption growth falls (typically by a smaller amount), investment growth falls (typically by a larger amount) and unemployment rises. Although economists look at various leading indicators to predict these fluctuations, they are largely unpredictable.

2. The crucial difference between how the economy works in the long run and how it works in the short run is that prices are flexible in the long run, but sticky in the short run. The model of aggregate supply and aggregate demand provides a framework to analyse economic fluctuations and see how the impact of policies and events varies over different time horizons.

3. The aggregate demand curve slopes downward. It tells us that the lower the price level, the greater the aggregate quantity of goods and services demanded.

4. In the long run, the aggregate supply curve is vertical because output is determined by the amounts of capital and labour and by the available technology, but not by the level of prices. Therefore, shifts in aggregate demand affect the price level, but not output or employment.

5. In the short run, the aggregate supply curve is horizontal, because wages and prices are sticky at predetermined levels. Therefore, shifts in aggregate demand affect output and employment.

6. Shocks to aggregate demand and aggregate supply cause economic fluctuations. Because the central bank can shift the aggregate demand curve, it can attempt to offset these shocks to maintain output and employment at their natural levels.

KEY CONCEPTS

Aggregate demand	Shocks	Stabilization policy
Aggregate supply	Demand shocks	Okun's law
Leading indicators	Supply shocks	

QUESTIONS FOR REVIEW

1. When real GDP declines during a recession, what typically happens to consumption, investment and the unemployment rate?

2. Give an example of a price that is sticky in the short run and flexible in the long run.

3. Why does the aggregate demand curve slope downward?

4. Explain the impact of an increase in the money supply in the short run and in the long run.

5. Why is it easier for the central bank to deal with demand shocks than with supply shocks?

PROBLEMS AND APPLICATIONS

1. Suppose that a change in government regulations allows banks to start paying interest on current accounts. Recall that the money stock is the sum of currency and demand deposits, including current accounts, so this regulatory change makes holding money more attractive.

   a. How does this change affect the demand for money?

   b. What happens to the velocity of money?

   c. If the central bank keeps the money supply constant, what will happen to output and prices in the short run and in the long run?

   d. Should the central bank keep the money supply constant in response to this regulatory change? Why, or why not?

2. Suppose the central bank reduces the money supply by 5 per cent.

   a. What happens to the aggregate demand curve?

   b. What happens to the level of output and the price level in the short run and in the long run?

   c. What happens to the real interest rate in the short run and in the long run? (*Hint:* Use the model of the real interest rate in Chapter 3 to see what happens when output changes.)

3. Let's examine how the goals of the central bank influence its response to shocks. Suppose Central Bank A cares only about keeping the price level stable, and Central Bank B cares only about keeping output and employment at their natural levels. Explain how each central bank would respond to each of the following:

   a. An exogenous decrease in the velocity of money.

   b. An exogenous increase in the price of oil.

CHAPTER 11

Aggregate Demand I: Building the *IS-LM* Model

I shall argue that the postulates of the classical theory are applicable to a special case only and not to the general case . . . Moreover, the characteristics of the special case assumed by the classical theory happen not to be those of the economic society in which we actually live, with the result that its teaching is misleading and disastrous if we attempt to apply it to the facts of experience.

— *John Maynard Keynes,* The General Theory

Of all the economic fluctuations in world history, the one that stands out as particularly large, painful and intellectually significant is the Great Depression of the 1930s. During this time, many countries experienced massive unemployment and greatly reduced incomes.

This devastating episode caused many economists to question the validity of classical economic theory – the theory we examined in Chapters 3 to 7. Classical theory seemed incapable of explaining the Great Depression. According to that theory, national income depends on factor supplies and the available technology, neither of which changed substantially from 1929 to 1933. After the onset of the Great Depression, many economists believed that a new model was needed to explain such a large and sudden economic downturn and to suggest government policies that might reduce the economic hardship so many people faced.

In 1936, the British economist John Maynard Keynes revolutionized economics with his book *The General Theory of Employment, Interest and Money*. Keynes proposed a new way to analyse the economy, which he presented as an alternative to classical theory. His vision of how the economy works quickly became a centre of controversy. Yet, as economists debated *The General Theory*, a new understanding of economic fluctuations gradually developed.

Keynes proposed that low aggregate demand is responsible for the low income and high unemployment that characterize economic downturns. He criticized classical theory for assuming that aggregate supply alone – capital, labour and technology – determines national income. Economists today reconcile these two views with the model of aggregate demand and aggregate supply introduced in Chapter 10. In the long run, prices are flexible and aggregate supply determines income. But, in the short run, prices are sticky, so changes in aggregate demand influence income.

In this chapter and the next, we continue our study of economic fluctuations by looking more closely at aggregate demand. Our goal is to identify the variables that shift the aggregate demand curve, causing fluctuations in national income. We also examine more fully the tools policy makers can use to influence aggregate demand. In Chapter 10 we derived the aggregate demand curve from the quantity theory of money, and we showed that monetary policy can shift the aggregate demand curve. In this chapter we see that the government can influence aggregate demand with both monetary and fiscal policy.

The model of aggregate demand developed in this chapter, called the **IS-LM model**, is the leading interpretation of Keynes's theory. The goal of the model is to show what determines national income for a given price level. There are two ways to view this exercise. We can view the *IS-LM* model as showing what causes income to change in the short run when the price level is fixed because all prices are sticky. Or we can view the model as showing what causes the aggregate demand curve to shift. These two views of the model are equivalent: as Figure 11-1 shows, in the short run when the price level is fixed, shifts in the aggregate demand curve lead to changes in the equilibrium level of national income.

The two parts of the *IS-LM* model are, not surprisingly, the **IS curve** and the **LM curve**. *IS* stands for 'investment' and 'saving', and the *IS* curve represents what is going on in the market for goods and services (which we first discussed

FIGURE 11-1

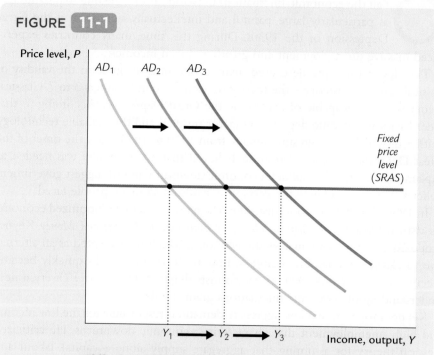

Shifts in Aggregate Demand For a given price level, national income fluctuates because of shifts in the aggregate demand curve. The *IS-LM* model takes the price level as given and shows what causes income to change. The model therefore shows what causes aggregate demand to shift.

in Chapter 3). *LM* stands for 'liquidity' and 'money', and the *LM* curve represents what is happening to the supply and demand for money (which we first discussed in Chapter 5). Because the interest rate influences both investment and money demand, it is the variable that links the two halves of the *IS-LM* model. The model shows how interactions between the goods and money markets determine the position and slope of the aggregate demand curve and, therefore, the level of national income in the short run.[1]

11-1 The Goods Market and the *IS* Curve

The *IS* curve plots the relationship between the interest rate and the level of income that arises in the market for goods and services. To develop this relationship, we start with a basic model called the **Keynesian cross**. This model is the simplest interpretation of Keynes's theory of national income and is a building block for the more complex and realistic *IS-LM* model.

The Keynesian Cross

In *The General Theory* Keynes proposed that an economy's total income was, in the short run, determined largely by the spending plans of households, businesses and government. The more people want to spend, the more goods and services firms can sell. The more firms can sell, the more output they will choose to produce and the more workers they will choose to hire. Keynes believed that the problem during recessions and depressions was inadequate spending. The Keynesian cross is an attempt to model this insight.

Planned Expenditure We begin our derivation of the Keynesian cross by drawing a distinction between actual and planned expenditure. *Actual expenditure* is the amount households, firms and the government spend on goods and services, and, as we first saw in Chapter 2, it equals the economy's gross domestic product (GDP). *Planned expenditure* is the amount households, firms and the government would like to spend on goods and services.

Why would actual expenditure ever differ from planned expenditure? The answer is that firms might engage in unplanned inventory investment because their sales do not meet their expectations. When firms sell less of their product than they planned, their stock of inventories automatically rises; conversely, when firms sell more than planned, their stock of inventories falls. Because these unplanned changes in inventory are counted as investment spending by firms, actual expenditure can be either above or below planned expenditure.

Now consider the determinants of planned expenditure. Assuming that the economy is closed, so that net exports are zero, we write planned expenditure *E* as the sum of consumption *C*, planned investment *I* and government purchases *G*:

$$E = C + I + G.$$

---

[1] The *IS-LM* model was introduced in a classic article by the Nobel Prize–winning economist John R. Hicks, 'Mr. Keynes and the Classics: A Suggested Interpretation', *Econometrica*, 1937, vol. 5, pp. 147–159.

To this equation, we add the consumption function

$$C = C(Y - T).$$

This equation states that consumption depends on disposable income $(Y - T)$, which is total income Y minus taxes T. To keep things simple, for now we take planned investment as exogenously fixed:

$$I = \bar{I}.$$

Finally, as in Chapter 3, we assume that fiscal policy – the levels of government purchases and taxes – is fixed:

$$G = \bar{G},$$

$$T = \bar{T}.$$

Combining these five equations, we obtain

$$E = C(Y - \bar{T}) + \bar{I} + \bar{G}.$$

This equation shows that planned expenditure is a function of income Y, the level of planned investment $\bar{I}$ and the fiscal policy variables $\bar{G}$ and $\bar{T}$.

Figure 11-2 graphs planned expenditure as a function of the level of income. This line slopes upward because higher income leads to higher consumption and thus higher planned expenditure. The slope of this line is the marginal propensity to consume, the *MPC*: it shows how much planned expenditure increases when income rises by one unit of income. This planned-expenditure function is the first piece of the model called the Keynesian cross.

FIGURE 11-2

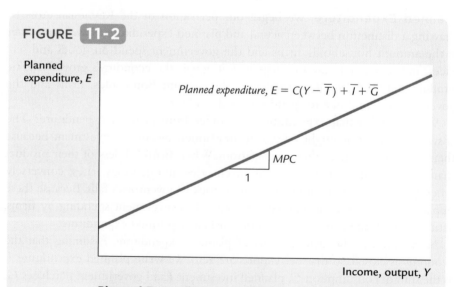

Planned expenditure, E

Planned expenditure, $E = C(Y - \bar{T}) + \bar{I} + \bar{G}$

MPC

1

Income, output, Y

Planned Expenditure as a Function of Income Planned expenditure depends on income because higher income leads to higher consumption, which is part of planned expenditure. The slope of the planned-expenditure function is the marginal propensity to consume, *MPC*.

The Economy in Equilibrium The next piece of the Keynesian cross is the assumption that the economy is in equilibrium when actual expenditure equals planned expenditure. This assumption is based on the idea that when people's plans have been realized, they have no reason to change what they are doing. Recalling that Y as GDP equals not only total income but also total actual expenditure on goods and services, we can write this equilibrium condition as

$$\text{Actual Expenditure} = \text{Planned Expenditure}$$

$$Y = E.$$

The 45-degree line in Figure 11-3 plots the points where this condition holds. With the addition of the planned-expenditure function, this diagram becomes the Keynesian cross. The equilibrium of this economy is at point A, where the planned-expenditure function crosses the 45-degree line.

How does the economy get to equilibrium? In this model, inventories play an important role in the adjustment process. Whenever an economy is not in equilibrium, firms experience unplanned changes in inventories, and this induces them to change production levels. Changes in production, in turn, influence total income and expenditure, moving the economy towards equilibrium.

For example, suppose the economy finds itself with GDP at a level greater than the equilibrium level, such as the level Y_1 in Figure 11-4. In this case, planned expenditure E_1 is less than production Y_1, so firms are selling less than they are producing. Firms add the unsold goods to their stock of inventories. This unplanned rise in inventories induces firms to lay off workers and reduce

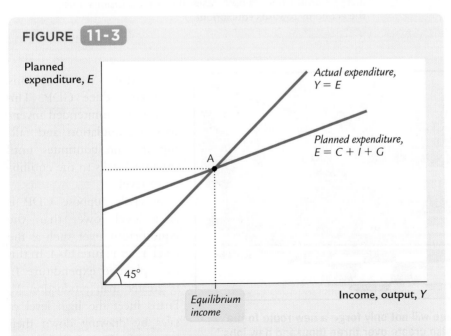

FIGURE 11-3

Planned expenditure, *E*

Actual expenditure, $Y = E$

Planned expenditure, $E = C + I + G$

A

45°

Equilibrium income

Income, output, *Y*

The Keynesian Cross The equilibrium in the Keynesian cross is the point at which income (actual expenditure) equals planned expenditure (point A).

FIGURE 11-4

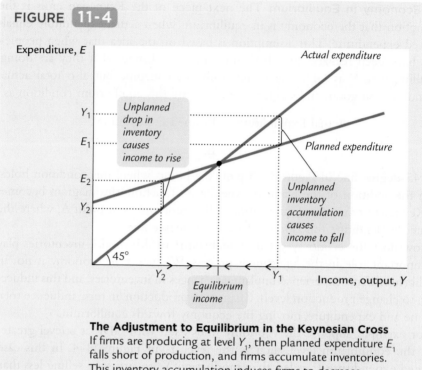

The Adjustment to Equilibrium in the Keynesian Cross
If firms are producing at level Y_1, then planned expenditure E_1 falls short of production, and firms accumulate inventories. This inventory accumulation induces firms to decrease production. Similarly, if firms are producing at level Y_2, then planned expenditure E_2 exceeds production, and firms run down their inventories. This fall in inventories induces firms to increase production. In both cases, the firms' decisions drive the economy towards equilibrium.

'Your Majesty, my voyage will not only forge a new route to the spices of the East but also create over three thousand new jobs.'

production; these actions, in turn, reduce GDP. This process of unintended inventory accumulation and falling income continues until income Y falls to the equilibrium level.

Similarly, suppose GDP is at a level lower than the equilibrium level, such as the level Y_2 in Figure 11-4. In this case, planned expenditure E_2 is greater than production Y_2. Firms meet the high level of sales by drawing down their inventories. But when firms see their stock of inventories dwindle, they hire more workers and increase production. GDP rises and the economy approaches the equilibrium.

In summary, the Keynesian cross shows how income Y is determined for given levels of planned investment I and fiscal policy G and T. We can use this model to show how income changes when one of these exogenous variables changes.

Fiscal Policy and the Multiplier: Government Purchases Consider how changes in government purchases affect the economy. Because government purchases are one component of expenditure, higher government purchases result in higher planned expenditure for any given level of income. If government purchases rise by ΔG, then the planned-expenditure schedule shifts upward by ΔG, as in Figure 11-5. The equilibrium of the economy moves from point A to point B.

This graph shows that an increase in government purchases leads to an even greater increase in income. That is, ΔY is larger than ΔG. The ratio $\Delta Y/\Delta G$ is called the **government-purchases multiplier**; it tells us how much income rises in response to a €1 increase in government purchases. An implication of the Keynesian cross is that the government-purchases multiplier is larger than 1.

Why does fiscal policy have a multiplied effect on income? The reason is that, according to the consumption function $C = C(Y - T)$, higher income causes higher consumption. When an increase in government purchases raises income,

FIGURE 11-5

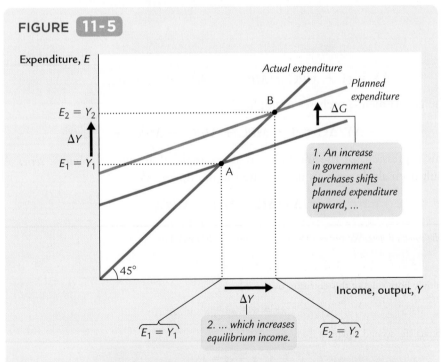

An Increase in Government Purchases in the Keynesian Cross An increase in government purchases of ΔG raises planned expenditure by that amount for any given level of income. The equilibrium moves from point A to point B, and income rises from Y_1 to Y_2. Note that the increase in income ΔY exceeds the increase in government purchases ΔG. Thus, fiscal policy has a multiplied effect on income.

it also raises consumption, which further raises income, which further raises consumption, and so on. Therefore, in this model, an increase in government purchases causes a greater increase in income.

How big is the multiplier? To answer this question, we trace through each step of the change in income. The process begins when expenditure rises by ΔG, which implies that income rises by ΔG as well. This increase in income, in turn, raises consumption by $MPC \times \Delta G$, where MPC is the marginal propensity to consume. This increase in consumption raises expenditure and income once again. This second increase in income of $MPC \times \Delta G$ again raises consumption, this time by $MPC \times (MPC \times \Delta G)$, which again raises expenditure and income, and so on. This feedback from consumption to income to consumption continues indefinitely. The total effect on income is

Initial Change in Government Purchases $= \Delta G$

First Change in Consumption $\qquad = MPC \times \Delta G$

Second Change in Consumption $\qquad = MPC^2 \times \Delta G$

Third Change in Consumption $\qquad = MPC^3 \times \Delta G$

.

.

.

$$\Delta Y = (1 + MPC + MPC^2 + MPC^3 + \ldots)\, \Delta G.$$

The government-purchases multiplier is

$$\Delta Y/\Delta G = 1 + MPC + MPC^2 + MPC^3 + \ldots$$

This expression for the multiplier is an example of an *infinite geometric series*. A result from algebra allows us to write the multiplier as[2]

$$\Delta Y/\Delta G = 1/(1 - MPC).$$

---

[2] *Mathematical note:* We prove this algebraic result as follows. For $|x| < 1$, let

$$z = 1 + x + x^2 + \ldots$$

Multiply both sides of this equation by x:

$$xz = x + x^2 + x^3 + \ldots$$

Subtract the second equation from the first:

$$z - xz = 1.$$

Rearrange this last equation to obtain

$$z(1 - x) = 1,$$

which implies

$$z = 1/(1 - x).$$

This completes the proof.

For example, if the marginal propensity to consume is 0.6, the multiplier is

$$\Delta Y/\Delta G = 1 + 0.6 + 0.6^2 + 0.6^3 + \ldots$$

$$= 1/(1 - 0.6)$$

$$= 2.5.$$

In this case, a €1 increase in government purchases raises equilibrium income by €2.50.[3]

Fiscal Policy and the Multiplier: Taxes Consider now how changes in taxes affect equilibrium income. A decrease in taxes of ΔT immediately raises disposable income $Y - T$ by ΔT and, therefore, increases consumption by $MPC \times \Delta T$. For any given level of income Y, planned expenditure is now higher. As Figure 11-6 shows, the planned-expenditure schedule shifts upward by $MPC \times \Delta T$. The equilibrium of the economy moves from point A to point B.

Just as an increase in government purchases has a multiplied effect on income, so does a decrease in taxes. As before, the initial change in expenditure, now $MPC \times \Delta T$, is multiplied by $1/(1 - MPC)$. The overall effect on income of the change in taxes is

$$\Delta Y/\Delta T = -MPC/(1 - MPC).$$

This expression is the **tax multiplier**, the amount income changes in response to a €1 change in taxes. (The negative sign indicates that income moves in the opposite direction to taxes.) For example, if the marginal propensity to consume is 0.6, then the tax multiplier is

$$\Delta Y/\Delta T = -0.6/(1 - 0.6) = -1.5.$$

In this example, a €1 cut in taxes raises equilibrium income by €1.50.[4]

---

[3] *Mathematical note*: The government-purchases multiplier is most easily derived using a little calculus. Begin with the equation

$$Y = C(Y - T) + I + G.$$

Holding T and I fixed, totally differentiate to obtain

$$dY = C'dY + dG,$$

and then rearrange to find

$$dY/dG = 1/(1 - C').$$

This is the same as the equation in the text.

[4] *Mathematical note*: As before, the multiplier is most easily derived using a little calculus. Begin with the equation

$$Y = C(Y - T) + I + G.$$

Holding I and G fixed, differentiate to obtain

$$dY = C'(dY - dT),$$

and then rearrange to find

$$dY/dT = -C'/(1 - C').$$

This is the same as the equation in the text.

FIGURE 11-6

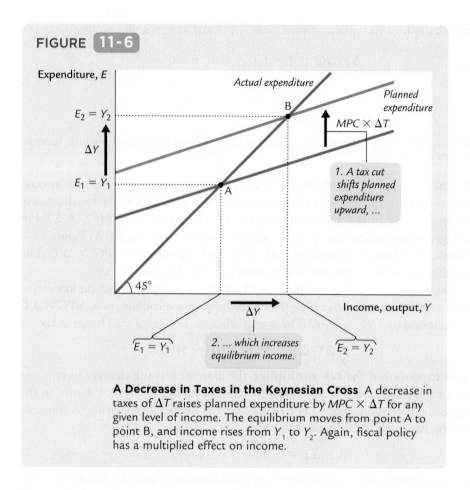

A Decrease in Taxes in the Keynesian Cross A decrease in taxes of ΔT raises planned expenditure by $MPC \times \Delta T$ for any given level of income. The equilibrium moves from point A to point B, and income rises from Y_1 to Y_2. Again, fiscal policy has a multiplied effect on income.

CASE STUDY

The Dwindling Popularity of Fiscal Policy as a Means to Fine-Tune the Economy

Although the model of the macroeconomy that we have developed describes how the level of output may be affected by taxes and government expenditure (i.e. through fiscal policy), via the expenditure and tax multipliers, the use of fiscal policy as a means by which to iron out the business cycle diminished greatly in many advanced economies over the last 30 years, only to find favour again more recently during the repercussions of the financial crisis of 2008–2009. One reason that may explain its decline in popularity may be that fiscal policy, especially through government expenditure, is in practice hard to enact in a timely and accurate fashion. This is because considerable time may pass between the decision to increase public expenditure in a certain area and the actual implementation of the programme. Suppose, for example, the government decides to spend more on hospitals in a recession in order to generate an increase in output through the expenditure multiplier. It then needs to decide where and how the extra money should be spent, draw up a plan for implementing the new programme – including what new buildings and new staff are required – and then implement the plan. This is likely to take a few years, by which time the economy will most likely have moved into a different phase of the business cycle and the economy may be overheating, requiring cuts in government expenditure. In fact, governments often undershoot their expenditure plans, largely because of problems in attracting sufficient extra staff into key public services such as transport, education and health.

To some extent, the problem can be mitigated by basing the spending decisions on forecasts of future business cycle movements, but, as we have already noted, forecasting the business cycle is notoriously difficult.

The same is less true, of course, with taxes – if the finance minister decides to cut income tax or increase the tax on petrol, the rate changes happen very quickly (in fact, increases in direct taxes on goods often take effect overnight following their announcement, in order to stop people trying to stock up on them before the tax change takes effect). However, although tax rates may change quickly, the effect on tax revenues may take some time to work through and may be offset by government spending on benefits. For example, an increase in taxes may reduce consumer spending, but the reduction in spending, in turn, may lead to higher unemployment as firms find that their sales have fallen, and then the government will have to increase its own spending on unemployment benefit – offsetting some or all of the initial reduction in consumer spending. In addition, constantly changing direct and indirect taxes from year to year may cause more confusion in the economy than the fine-tuning is worth.

In an open economy, moreover, fiscal policy will also have an effect on the trade balance, as we saw in Chapter 6, through the induced change in national saving. In the UK during the 1950s, 1960s and the first half of the 1970s, fiscal policy was used largely as an instrument to fine-tune the economy (i.e. iron out relatively small variations in output over the business cycle). The result was a series of 'stop-go' cycles whereby expansionary fiscal policy was used to boost aggregate demand, which then led to strong increases in the demand for imports and a widening of the trade deficit, which was followed by contractionary fiscal policy in an attempt to cure the trade deficit. While the stop-go syndrome appears to have been a largely UK phenomenon, many macroeconomists now argue that, if anything, the use of fiscal policy for fine-tuning may also have exacerbated rather than ameliorated the business cycle in other advanced economies. For these reasons, during a time of relative stability, fiscal policy was used increasingly less by governments in the advanced economies of Europe and North America as a means by which to fine-tune the economy. Economists often sum up this view by referring to fiscal policy as a 'blunt instrument'.

Does this mean that Keynes was wrong in his advocacy of fiscal policy? Not necessarily. Keynes was writing during the Great Depression – a time of massive unemployment throughout many countries of the world. His policy prescriptions were meant not so much as means of fine-tuning the economy, but as a means of shocking it out of deep recession. To use another analogy, Keynes was proposing emergency surgery, not a day-to-day health regime.

This may explain why fiscal stimulus packages have increasingly featured in policy responses to the current recession following the financial crisis of 2008–2009 when again the advanced economies faced deep recession. Advocates of such policies argue that increased government spending is likely to have a greater effect on output than reducing taxes. As we have shown above, the government spending multiplier exceeds the tax multiplier. Clearly, when the government spends a euro, that euro gets spent, whereas some of a tax cut of a euro might be saved by households. This argument has supported calls for increased public spending on infrastructure projects such as roads, high-speed rail links, schools and hospitals. Indeed, many economists argue that the reason for the recovery from recession being so weak is that such stimulus packages have not been large enough. These economists have also criticized those policy makers who advocate cuts in government spending as a means of deficit reduction. They argue that cutting public spending will set in train a negative multiplier effect, thus further reducing output and increasing unemployment, which will in turn reduce tax revenues, increase the welfare bill, and in fact ultimately worsen the deficit. ■

CASE STUDY

Increasing Government Purchases to Stimulate the Economy: The Obama Spending Plan

When President Barack Obama took office in January 2009, the US economy was suffering from a significant recession. Even before he was inaugurated, the president and his advisers proposed a sizable stimulus package to increase aggregate demand. As it was proposed, the package would cost the federal government about $800 billion, or about 5 per cent of annual GDP. The package included some tax cuts and higher transfer payments, but much of it was made up of increases in government purchases of goods and services.

Professional economists debated the merits of the plan. Advocates of the Obama plan argued that increased spending was better than reduced taxes because, according to standard Keynesian theory, the government-purchases multiplier exceeds the tax multiplier. As we said above, one reason for this difference is simple: when the government spends a dollar, that dollar gets spent, whereas when the government gives households a tax cut of a dollar, some of that dollar might be saved. According to an analysis by Obama administration economists, the government-purchases multiplier is 1.57, whereas the tax multiplier is only 0.99. Thus, they argued that increased government spending on roads, schools and other infrastructure was the better route to increase aggregate demand and create jobs. The logic here is quintessentially Keynesian: as the economy sinks into recession, the government is acting as the demander of last resort.

The Obama stimulus proposal was controversial among economists for various reasons. One criticism was that the stimulus was not large enough given the apparent depth of the economic downturn. In March 2008, economist Paul Krugman wrote in the *New York Times*:

> The plan was too small and too cautious. . . . Employment has already fallen
> more in this recession than in the 1981–82 slump, considered the worst since
> the Great Depression. As a result, Mr. Obama's promise that his plan will create

or save 3.5 million jobs by the end of 2010 looks underwhelming, to say the least. It's a credible promise – his economists used solidly mainstream estimates of the impacts of tax and spending policies. But 3.5 million jobs almost two years from now isn't enough in the face of an economy that has already lost 4.4 million jobs, and is losing 600,000 more each month.

Other economists argued that despite the predictions of conventional Keynesian models, spending-based fiscal stimulus is not as effective as tax-based initiatives. A recent study of fiscal policy in OECD countries since 1970 examined which kinds of fiscal stimulus have historically been most successful at promoting growth in economic activity. It found that successful fiscal stimulus relies almost entirely on cuts in business and income taxes, whereas failed fiscal stimulus relies primarily on increases in government spending.[5]

In addition, some economists thought that using infrastructure spending to promote employment might conflict with the goal of obtaining the infrastructure that was most needed. Here is how economist Gary Becker explained the concern on his blog:

> Putting new infrastructure spending in depressed areas like Detroit might have a big stimulating effect since infrastructure building projects in these areas can utilize some of the considerable unemployed resources there. However, many of these areas are also declining because they have been producing goods and services that are not in great demand, and will not be in demand in the future. Therefore, the overall value added by improving their roads and other infrastructure is likely to be a lot less than if the new infrastructure were located in growing areas that might have relatively little unemployment, but do have great demand for more roads, schools, and other types of long-term infrastructure.

In the end, Congress went ahead with President Obama's proposed stimulus plans with relatively minor modifications. The president signed the $787 billion bill on 17 February 2009. Did it work? The economy did recover from the recession, but much more slowly than the Obama administration economists initially forecast. Whether the slow recovery reflects the failure of stimulus policy or a sicker economy than the economists first appreciated is a question of continuing debate. ■

The Interest Rate, Investment and the *IS* Curve

The Keynesian cross is only a stepping stone on our path to the *IS-LM* model, which explains the economy's aggregate demand curve. The Keynesian cross is useful because it shows how the spending plans of households, firms and the government determine the economy's income. Yet it makes the simplifying assumption that the level of planned investment I is fixed. As we discussed in Chapter 3, an important macroeconomic relationship is that planned investment depends on the interest rate r.

---

[5] Alberto Alesina and Silvia Ardagna, 'Large Changes in Fiscal Policy: Taxes Versus Spending', in *Tax Policy and the Economy*, Chicago: Chicago University Press, 2010, vol. 24, pp. 35–68.

FIGURE 11-7

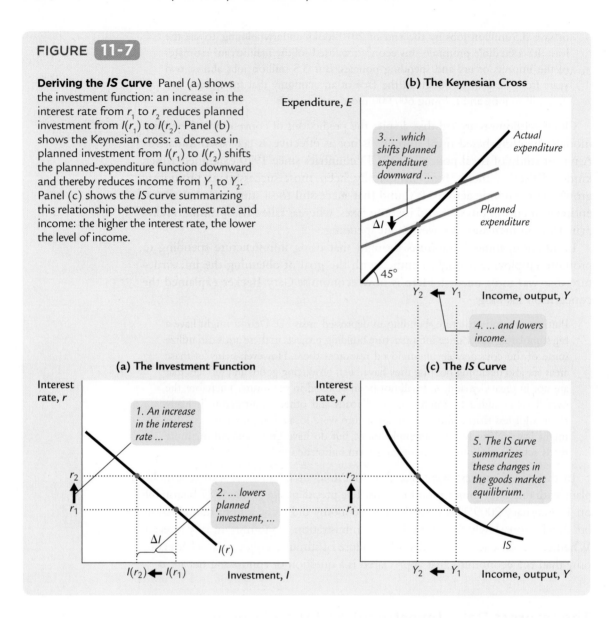

FIGURE 11-7

Deriving the *IS* Curve Panel (a) shows the investment function: an increase in the interest rate from r_1 to r_2 reduces planned investment from $I(r_1)$ to $I(r_2)$. Panel (b) shows the Keynesian cross: a decrease in planned investment from $I(r_1)$ to $I(r_2)$ shifts the planned-expenditure function downward and thereby reduces income from Y_1 to Y_2. Panel (c) shows the *IS* curve summarizing this relationship between the interest rate and income: the higher the interest rate, the lower the level of income.

To add this relationship between the interest rate and investment to our model, we write the level of planned investment as

$$I = I(r).$$

This investment function is graphed in panel (a) of Figure 11-7. Because the interest rate is the cost of borrowing to finance investment projects, an increase in the interest rate reduces planned investment. As a result, the investment function slopes downward.

To determine how income changes when the interest rate changes, we can combine the investment function with the Keynesian cross diagram. Because investment is inversely related to the interest rate, an increase in the interest rate from r_1 to r_2 reduces the quantity of investment from $I(r_1)$ to $I(r_2)$. The reduction in planned investment, in turn, shifts the planned-expenditure function downward, as in panel (b) of Figure 11-7. The shift in the planned-expenditure function causes the level of income to fall from Y_1 to Y_2. Hence, an increase in the interest rate lowers income.

The *IS* curve, shown in panel (c) of Figure 11-7, summarizes this relationship between the interest rate and the level of income. In essence, the *IS* curve combines the interaction between r and I expressed by the investment function, and the interaction between I and Y demonstrated by the Keynesian cross. Each point on the *IS* curve represents equilibrium in the goods market, and the curve illustrates how the equilibrium level of income depends on the interest rate. Because an increase in the interest rate causes planned investment to fall, which in turn causes equilibrium income to fall, the *IS* curve slopes downward.

How Fiscal Policy Shifts the *IS* Curve

The *IS* curve shows us, for any given interest rate, the level of income that brings the goods market into equilibrium. As we learned from the Keynesian cross, the equilibrium level of income also depends on government spending G and taxes T. The *IS* curve is drawn for a given fiscal policy; that is, when we construct the *IS* curve, we hold G and T fixed. When fiscal policy changes, the *IS* curve shifts.

Figure 11-8 uses the Keynesian cross to show how an increase in government purchases ΔG shifts the *IS* curve. This figure is drawn for a given interest rate $\bar{r}$, and thus for a given level of planned investment. The Keynesian cross shows that this change in fiscal policy raises planned expenditure and thereby increases equilibrium income from Y_1 to Y_2. Therefore, an increase in government purchases shifts the *IS* curve outward.

We can use the Keynesian cross to see how other changes in fiscal policy shift the *IS* curve. Because a decrease in taxes also expands expenditure and income, it too shifts the *IS* curve outward. A decrease in government purchases or an increase in taxes reduces income; therefore, such a change in fiscal policy shifts the *IS* curve inward.

In summary, the IS curve shows the combinations of the interest rate and the level of income that are consistent with equilibrium in the market for goods and services. The IS curve is drawn for a given fiscal policy. Changes in fiscal policy that raise the demand for goods and services shift the IS curve to the right. Changes in fiscal policy that reduce the demand for goods and services shift the IS curve to the left.

A Loanable-Funds Interpretation of the *IS* Curve

When we first studied the market for goods and services in Chapter 3, we noted an equivalence between the supply and demand for goods and services and the supply and demand for loanable funds. This equivalence provides another way to interpret the *IS* curve.

FIGURE 11-8

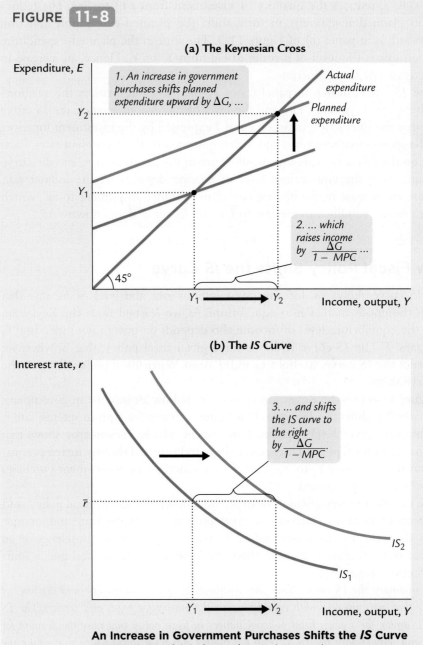

(a) The Keynesian Cross

Expenditure, E

1. An increase in government purchases shifts planned expenditure upward by ΔG, ...

Y_2

Actual expenditure

Planned expenditure

Y_1

2. ... which raises income by $\dfrac{\Delta G}{1 - MPC}$ ...

45°

Y_1 ⟶ Y_2 Income, output, Y

(b) The IS Curve

Interest rate, r

3. ... and shifts the IS curve to the right by $\dfrac{\Delta G}{1 - MPC}$.

$\bar{r}$

IS_2

IS_1

Y_1 ⟶ Y_2 Income, output, Y

An Increase in Government Purchases Shifts the IS Curve Outward Panel (a) shows that an increase in government purchases raises planned expenditure. For any given interest rate, the upward shift in planned expenditure of ΔG leads to an increase in income Y of $\Delta G/(1 - MPC)$. Therefore, in panel (b), the IS curve shifts to the right by this amount.

Recall that the national income accounts identity can be written as

$$Y - C - G = I,$$
$$S = I.$$

The left-hand side of this equation is national saving S, and the right-hand side is investment I. National saving represents the supply of loanable funds, and investment represents the demand for these funds.

To see how the market for loanable funds produces the *IS* curve, substitute the consumption function for C and the investment function for I:

$$Y - C(Y - T) - G = I(r).$$

The left-hand side of this equation shows that the supply of loanable funds depends on income and fiscal policy. The right-hand side shows that the demand for loanable funds depends on the interest rate. The interest rate adjusts to equilibrate the supply and demand for loans.

As Figure 11-9 illustrates, we can interpret the *IS* curve as showing the interest rate that equilibrates the market for loanable funds for any given level of income. When income rises from Y_1 to Y_2, national saving, which equals $Y - C - G$, increases. (Consumption rises by less than income, because the marginal propensity to consume is less than 1.) As panel (a) shows, the increased supply of loanable funds drives down the interest rate from r_1 to r_2. The *IS* curve in panel (b) summarizes this relationship: higher income implies higher saving, which in turn implies a lower equilibrium interest rate. For this reason, the *IS* curve slopes downward.

FIGURE 11-9

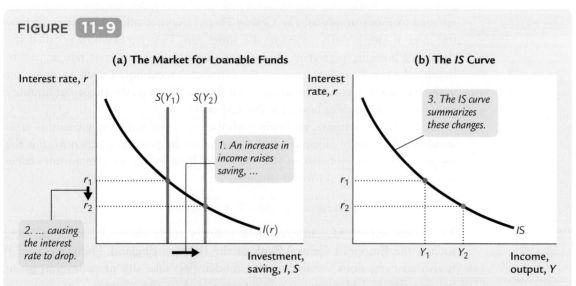

A Loanable-Funds Interpretation of the *IS* Curve Panel (a) shows that an increase in income from Y_1 to Y_2 raises saving and thus lowers the interest rate that equilibrates the supply and demand for loanable funds. The *IS* curve in panel (b) expresses this negative relationship between income and the interest rate.

This alternative interpretation of the *IS* curve also explains why a change in fiscal policy shifts the *IS* curve. An increase in government purchases or a decrease in taxes reduces national saving for any given level of income. The reduced supply of loanable funds raises the interest rate that equilibrates the market. Because the interest rate is now higher for any given level of income, the *IS* curve shifts upward in response to the expansionary change in fiscal policy.

Finally, note that the *IS* curve does not determine either income Y or the interest rate r − it describes only the relationship between Y and r that arises in the market for goods and services (or, equivalently, the market for loanable funds). Recall that our goal in this chapter is to understand aggregate demand; that is, we want to find what determines equilibrium income Y for a given price level P. The *IS* curve is just half the story. To complete the story, we need another relationship between Y and r, to which we now turn.

11-2 The Money Market and the *LM* Curve

The *LM* curve plots the relationship between the interest rate and the level of income that arises in the market for money balances. To understand this relationship, we begin by looking at a theory of the interest rate, called the **theory of liquidity preference**.

The Theory of Liquidity Preference

In his classic work *The General Theory of Employment, Interest and Money* (often referred to more simply as *The General Theory*), Keynes offered his view of how the interest rate is determined in the short run. That explanation is called the theory of liquidity preference, because it posits that the interest rate adjusts to balance the supply and demand for the economy's most liquid asset − money. Just as the Keynesian cross is a building block for the *IS* curve, the theory of liquidity preference is a building block for the *LM* curve.

To develop this theory, we begin with the supply of real money balances. If M stands for the supply of money and P stands for the price level, then M/P is the supply of real money balances. The theory of liquidity preference assumes there is a fixed supply of real money balances. That is,

$$(M/P)^s = \overline{M}/\overline{P}.$$

The money supply M is an exogenous policy variable chosen by a central bank, such as the European Central Bank or the Bank of England. The price level P is also an exogenous variable in this model. (We take the price level as given because the *IS-LM* model − our ultimate goal in this chapter − explains the short run when the price level is fixed.) These assumptions imply that the supply of real money balances is fixed and, in particular, does not depend on the interest rate. Thus, when we plot the supply of real money balances against the interest rate in Figure 11-10, we obtain a vertical supply curve.

FIGURE 11-10

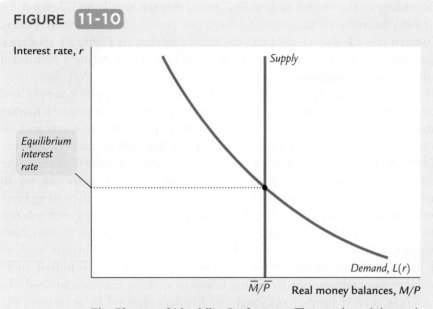

The Theory of Liquidity Preference The supply and demand for real money balances determine the interest rate. The supply curve for real money balances is vertical because the supply does not depend on the interest rate. The demand curve is downward-sloping because a higher interest rate raises the cost of holding money and thus lowers the quantity demanded. At the equilibrium interest rate, the quantity of real money balances demanded equals the quantity supplied.

Next, consider the demand for real money balances. The theory of liquidity preference posits that the interest rate is one determinant of how much money people choose to hold. The reason is that the interest rate is the opportunity cost of holding money: it is what you forgo by holding some of your assets as money, which does not bear interest, instead of as interest–bearing bank deposits or bonds. When the interest rate rises, people want to hold less of their wealth in the form of money. We can write the demand for real money balances as

$$(M/P)^{\text{d}} = L(r),$$

where the function $L(\ )$ shows that the quantity of money demanded depends on the interest rate. The demand curve in Figure 11–10 slopes downward because higher interest rates reduce the quantity of real money balances demanded.[6]

---

[6] Note that r is being used to denote the interest rate here, as it was in our discussion of the *IS* curve. More accurately, it is the nominal interest rate that determines money demand and the real interest rate that determines investment. To keep things simple, we are ignoring expected inflation, which creates the difference between the real and nominal interest rates. For short-run analysis, it is often realistic to assume that expected inflation is constant, in which case real and nominal interest rates move together. The role of expected inflation in the *IS-LM* model is explored in Chapter 12.

According to the theory of liquidity preference, the supply and demand for real money balances determine what interest rate prevails in the economy. That is, the interest rate adjusts to equilibrate the money market. As Figure 11-10 shows, at the equilibrium interest rate, the quantity of real money balances demanded equals the quantity supplied.

How does the interest rate get to this equilibrium of money supply and money demand? The adjustment occurs because whenever the money market is not in equilibrium, people try to adjust their portfolios of assets and, in the process, alter the interest rate. For instance, if the interest rate is above the equilibrium level, the quantity of real money balances supplied exceeds the quantity demanded. Individuals holding the excess supply of money try to convert some of their non-interest-bearing money into interest-bearing bank deposits or bonds. Banks and bond issuers, who prefer to pay lower interest rates, respond to this excess supply of money by lowering the interest rates they offer. Conversely, if the interest rate is below the equilibrium level, so that the quantity of money demanded exceeds the quantity supplied, individuals try to obtain money by selling bonds or making bank withdrawals. To attract now scarcer funds, banks and bond issuers respond by increasing the interest rates they offer. Eventually, the interest rate reaches the equilibrium level, at which people are content with their portfolios of monetary and non-monetary assets.

Now that we have seen how the interest rate is determined, we can use the theory of liquidity preference to show how the interest rate responds to changes in the supply of money. Suppose, for instance, that the central bank suddenly decreases the money supply. A fall in M reduces M/P, because P is fixed in the model. The supply of real money balances shifts to the left, as in Figure 11-11. The equilibrium interest rate rises from r_1 to r_2, and the higher interest rate makes people satisfied to hold the smaller quantity of real money balances. The opposite would occur if the central bank had suddenly increased the money supply. Thus, according to the theory of liquidity preference, a decrease in the money supply raises the interest rate, and an increase in the money supply lowers the interest rate.

CASE STUDY

Does a Monetary Tightening Raise or Lower Interest Rates?

How does a tightening of monetary policy influence nominal interest rates? According to the theories we have been developing, the answer depends on the time horizon. Our analysis of the Fisher effect in Chapter 5 suggests that, in the long run when prices are flexible, a reduction in money growth would lower inflation, and this in turn would lead to lower nominal interest rates. Yet the theory of liquidity preference predicts that, in the short run when prices are sticky, anti-inflationary monetary policy would lead to falling real money balances and higher interest rates. Both conclusions are consistent with experience.

FIGURE 11-11

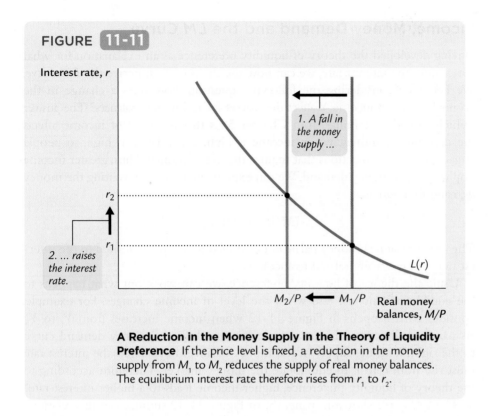

A Reduction in the Money Supply in the Theory of Liquidity Preference If the price level is fixed, a reduction in the money supply from M_1 to M_2 reduces the supply of real money balances. The equilibrium interest rate therefore rises from r_1 to r_2.

A good illustration occurred during the early 1980s, when the UK economy saw the largest and quickest reduction in inflation in recent history.

Here is the background: by the late 1970s inflation in the UK economy had reached the double-digit range and was a major national problem. In 1980 consumer prices were rising at a rate of nearly 20 per cent per year. In early 1980, the newly elected Conservative government, led by Prime Minister Margaret Thatcher, announced that monetary policy would aim to reduce the rate of inflation. This announcement began a period of tight money, which, by 1983, brought the inflation rate down to about 5 per cent.

Let's look at what happened to UK nominal interest rates. During the early years of the Thatcher administration's attempts to rein in the money supply, interest rates rose sharply – just as the theory of liquidity preference predicts. Nominal interest rates on three-month Treasury bills rose from about 12 per cent when the Thatcher government came to power in May 1979, to around 17 per cent in mid-1980. Yet these high interest rates were only temporary. As the Thatcher policy lowered inflation and expectations of inflation, nominal interest rates gradually fell, reaching 9 per cent by autumn 1982.

The lesson is that to understand the link between monetary policy and nominal interest rates, we need to keep in mind both the theory of liquidity preference and the Fisher effect. A monetary tightening leads to higher nominal interest rates in the short run and lower nominal interest rates in the long run. ∎

Income, Money Demand and the *LM* Curve

Having developed the theory of liquidity preference as an explanation for what determines the interest rate, we can now use the theory to derive the *LM* curve. We begin by considering the following question: how does a change in the economy's level of income *Y* affect the market for real money balances? The answer (which should be familiar from Chapter 5) is that the level of income affects the demand for money. When income is high, expenditure is high, so people engage in more transactions that require the use of money. Thus, greater income implies greater money demand. We can express these ideas by writing the money demand function as

$$(M/P)^{\mathrm{d}} = L(r, Y).$$

The quantity of real money balances demanded is negatively related to the interest rate and positively related to income.

Using the theory of liquidity preference, we can work out what happens to the equilibrium interest rate when the level of income changes. For example, consider what happens in Figure 11-12 when income increases from Y_1 to Y_2. As panel (a) illustrates, this increase in income shifts the money demand curve to the right. With the supply of real money balances unchanged, the interest rate must rise from r_1 to r_2 to equilibrate the money market. Therefore, according to the theory of liquidity preference, higher income leads to a higher interest rate.

The *LM* curve shown in panel (b) of Figure 11-12 summarizes this relationship between the level of income and the interest rate. Each point on the *LM* curve represents equilibrium in the money market, and the curve illustrates how

FIGURE 11-12

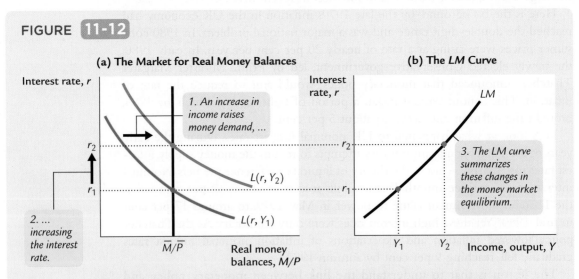

(a) The Market for Real Money Balances

Interest rate, *r*

1. An increase in income raises money demand, ...

r_2

r_1

$L(r, Y_2)$

$L(r, Y_1)$

2. ... increasing the interest rate.

$\overline{M/P}$

Real money balances, *M/P*

(b) The *LM* Curve

Interest rate, *r*

LM

r_2

3. The LM curve summarizes these changes in the money market equilibrium.

r_1

Y_1 Y_2 Income, output, *Y*

Deriving the *LM* Curve Panel (a) shows the market for real money balances: an increase in income from Y_1 to Y_2 raises the demand for money and thus raises the interest rate from r_1 to r_2. Panel (b) shows the *LM* curve summarizing this relationship between the interest rate and income: the higher the level of income, the higher the interest rate.

the equilibrium interest rate depends on the level of income. The higher the level of income, the higher the demand for real money balances, and the higher the equilibrium interest rate. For this reason, the *LM* curve slopes upward.

How Monetary Policy Shifts the *LM* Curve

The *LM* curve tells us the interest rate that equilibrates the money market at any level of income. Yet, as we saw earlier, the equilibrium interest rate also depends on the supply of real money balances, *M/P.* This means that the *LM* curve is drawn for a *given* supply of real money balances. If real money balances change – for example, if the central bank alters the money supply – the *LM* curve shifts.

We can use the theory of liquidity preference to understand how monetary policy shifts the *LM* curve. Suppose that the central bank decreases the money supply from M_1 to M_2, which causes the supply of real money balances to fall from M_1/P to M_2/P. Figure 11-13 shows what happens. Holding constant the amount of income and thus the demand curve for real money balances, we see that a reduction in the supply of real money balances raises the interest rate that equilibrates the money market. Hence, a decrease in the money supply shifts the *LM* curve upward.

In summary, the LM curve shows the combinations of the interest rate and the level of income that are consistent with equilibrium in the market for real money balances. The LM

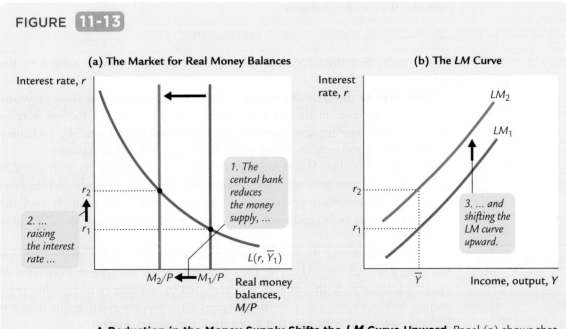

FIGURE 11-13

(a) The Market for Real Money Balances

(b) The *LM* Curve

A Reduction in the Money Supply Shifts the *LM* Curve Upward Panel (a) shows that for any given level of income $\overline{Y}$, a reduction in the money supply raises the interest rate that equilibrates the money market. Therefore, the *LM* curve in panel (b) shifts upward.

curve is drawn for a given supply of real money balances. Decreases in the supply of real money balances shift the LM curve upward. Increases in the supply of real money balances shift the LM curve downward.

A Quantity-Equation Interpretation of the *LM* Curve

When we first discussed aggregate demand and the short-run determination of income in Chapter 10, we derived the aggregate demand curve from the quantity theory of money. We described the money market with the quantity equation,

$$MV = PY,$$

and assumed that velocity V is constant. This assumption implies that, for any given price level P, the supply of money M by itself determines the level of income Y. Because the level of income does not depend on the interest rate, the quantity theory is equivalent to a vertical *LM* curve.

We can derive the more realistic upward-sloping *LM* curve from the quantity equation by relaxing the assumption that velocity is constant. The assumption of constant velocity is based on the assumption that the demand for real money balances depends only on the level of income. Yet, as we have noted in our discussion of the liquidity-preference model, the demand for real money balances also depends on the interest rate: a higher interest rate raises the cost of holding money and reduces money demand. When people respond to a higher interest rate by holding less money, each euro they do hold must be used more often to support a given volume of transactions – that is, the velocity of money must increase. We can write this as

$$MV(r) = PY.$$

The velocity function $V(r)$ indicates that velocity is positively related to the interest rate.

This form of the quantity equation yields an *LM* curve that slopes upward. Because an increase in the interest rate raises the velocity of money, it raises the level of income for any given money supply and price level. The *LM* curve expresses this positive relationship between the interest rate and income.

This equation also shows why changes in the money supply shift the *LM* curve. For any given interest rate and price level, the money supply and the level of income must move together. Thus, increases in the money supply shift the *LM* curve to the right, and decreases in the money supply shift the *LM* curve to the left.

Keep in mind that the quantity equation is merely another way to express the theory behind the *LM* curve. This quantity-theory interpretation of the *LM* curve is substantively the same as that provided by the theory of liquidity preference. In both cases, the *LM* curve represents a positive relationship between income and the interest rate that arises from the money market.

Finally, remember that the *LM* curve by itself does not determine either income Y or the interest rate r that will prevail in the economy. Like the *IS* curve, the *LM* curve is only a relationship between these two endogenous variables.

To understand the economy's overall equilibrium for a given price level, we must consider both equilibrium in the goods market and equilibrium in the money market. That is, we need to use the *IS* and *LM* curves together.

11-3 Conclusion: The Short-Run Equilibrium

We now have all the pieces of the *IS-LM* model. The two equations of this model are

$$Y = C(Y - T) + I(r) + G, \qquad\qquad IS$$

$$M/P = L(r, Y). \qquad\qquad LM$$

The model takes fiscal policy, G and T, monetary policy M, and the price level P as exogenous. Given these exogenous variables, the *IS* curve provides the combinations of r and Y that satisfy the equation representing the goods market, and the *LM* curve provides the combinations of r and Y that satisfy the equation representing the money market. These two curves are shown together in Figure 11-14.

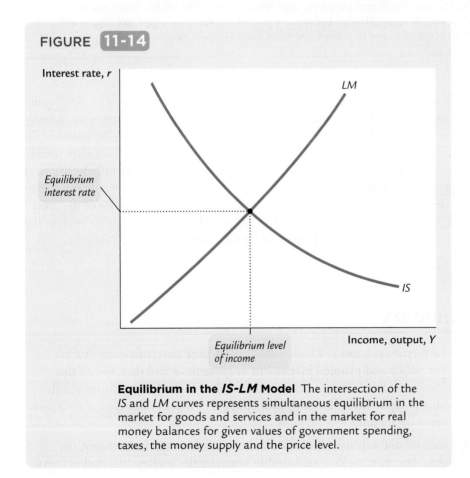

FIGURE 11-14

Equilibrium in the *IS-LM* Model The intersection of the *IS* and *LM* curves represents simultaneous equilibrium in the market for goods and services and in the market for real money balances for given values of government spending, taxes, the money supply and the price level.

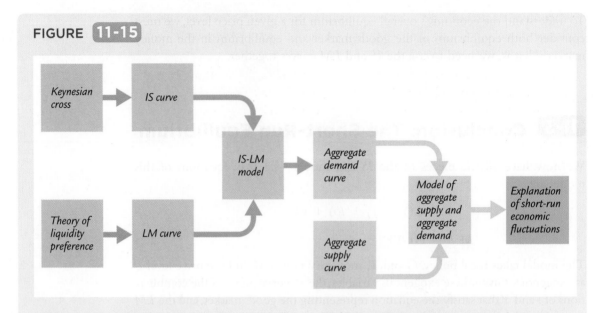

FIGURE 11-15

The Theory of Short-Run Fluctuations This schematic diagram shows how the different pieces of the theory of short-run fluctuations fit together. The Keynesian cross explains the *IS* curve, and the theory of liquidity preference explains the *LM* curve. The *IS* and *LM* curves together yield the *IS-LM* model, which explains the aggregate demand curve. The aggregate demand curve is part of the model of aggregate supply and aggregate demand, which economists use to explain short-run fluctuations in economic activity.

As we conclude this chapter, let's recall that our ultimate goal in developing the *IS-LM* model is to analyse short-run fluctuations in economic activity. Figure 11–15 illustrates how the different pieces of our theory fit together. In this chapter we developed the Keynesian cross and the theory of liquidity preference as building blocks for the *IS-LM* model. As we see more fully in the next chapter, the *IS-LM* model helps to explain the position and slope of the aggregate demand curve. The aggregate demand curve, in turn, is a piece of the model of aggregate supply and aggregate demand, which economists use to explain the short-run effects of policy changes and other events on national income.

Summary

1. The Keynesian cross is a basic model of income determination. It takes fiscal policy and planned investment as exogenous and then shows that there is one level of national income at which actual expenditure equals planned expenditure. It shows that changes in fiscal policy have a multiplied impact on income.

2. Once we allow planned investment to depend on the interest rate, the Keynesian cross yields a relationship between the interest rate and national

income. A higher interest rate lowers planned investment, and this in turn lowers national income. The downward-sloping *IS* curve summarizes this negative relationship between the interest rate and income.

3. The theory of liquidity preference is a basic model of the determination of the interest rate. It takes the money supply and the price level as exogenous and assumes that the interest rate adjusts to equilibrate the supply and demand for real money balances. The theory implies that increases in the money supply lower the interest rate.

4. Once we allow the demand for real money balances to depend on national income, the theory of liquidity preference yields a relationship between income and the interest rate. A higher level of income raises the demand for real money balances, and this in turn raises the interest rate. The upward-sloping *LM* curve summarizes this positive relationship between income and the interest rate.

5. The *IS-LM* model combines the elements of the Keynesian cross and the elements of the theory of liquidity preference. The *IS* curve shows the points that satisfy equilibrium in the goods market, and the *LM* curve shows the points that satisfy equilibrium in the money market. The intersection of the *IS* and *LM* curves shows the interest rate and income that satisfy equilibrium in both markets for a given price level.

KEY CONCEPTS

IS-LM model	Keynesian cross	Theory of liquidity preference
IS curve	Government-purchases multiplier	
LM curve	Tax multiplier	

QUESTIONS FOR REVIEW

1. Use the Keynesian cross to explain why fiscal policy has a multiplied effect on national income.

2. Use the theory of liquidity preference to explain why an increase in the money supply lowers the interest rate. What does this explanation assume about the price level?

3. Why does the *IS* curve slope downward?

4. Why does the *LM* curve slope upward?

PROBLEMS AND APPLICATIONS

1. Use the Keynesian cross to predict the impact of the following:

    a. An increase in government purchases.

    b. An increase in taxes.

    c. An equal increase in government purchases and taxes.

2. In the Keynesian cross, assume that the consumption function is given by

$$C = 200 + 0.75(Y - T).$$

Planned investment is 100; government purchases and taxes are both 100.

a. Graph planned expenditure as a function of income.

b. What is the equilibrium level of income?

c. If government purchases increase to 125, what is the new equilibrium income?

d. What level of government purchases is needed to achieve an income of 1600?

3. Although our development of the Keynesian cross in this chapter assumes that taxes are a fixed amount, in many countries taxes depend on income. Let's represent the tax system by writing tax revenue as

$$T = \overline{T} + tY,$$

where $\overline{T}$ and t are parameters of the tax code. The parameter t is the marginal tax rate: if income rises by €1, taxes rise by $t \times$ €1.

a. How does this tax system change the way consumption responds to changes in GDP?

b. In the Keynesian cross, how does this tax system alter the government-purchases multiplier?

c. In the *IS-LM* model, how does this tax system alter the slope of the *IS* curve?

4. Consider the impact of an increase in thriftiness in the Keynesian cross. Suppose the consumption function is

$$C = \overline{C} + c(Y - T),$$

where $\overline{C}$ is a parameter called *autonomous consumption* and c is the marginal propensity to consume.

a. What happens to equilibrium income when the society becomes more thrifty, as represented by a decline in $\overline{C}$?

b. What happens to equilibrium saving?

c. Why do you suppose this result is called the paradox of thrift?

d. Does this paradox arise in the classical model of Chapter 3? Why, or why not?

5. Although our development of the Keynesian cross in this chapter assumes that taxes are a fixed amount, most countries levy some taxes that rise automatically with national income (for example, income tax). Let's represent the tax system by writing tax revenue as

$$T = tY,$$

where the parameter t is the marginal tax rate: if income rises by €1, taxes rise by $t \times$ €1.

a. How does this tax system change the way consumption responds to changes in GDP?

b. In the Keynesian cross, how does this tax system alter the government-purchases multiplier?

c. In the *IS–LM* model, how does this tax system alter the slope of the *IS* curve?

6. Suppose that the money demand function is $(M/P)^d = 1000 - 100r$, where r is the interest rate in per cent. The money supply M is 1000 and the price level P is 2.

a. Graph the supply and demand for real money balances.

b. What is the equilibrium interest rate?

c. Assume that the price level is fixed. What happens to the equilibrium interest rate if the supply of money is raised from 1000 to 1200?

d. If the monetary authorities wish to raise the interest rate to 7 per cent, what money supply should it set?

Aggregate Demand II: Applying the *IS-LM* Model

Science is a parasite: the greater the patient population the better the advance
in physiology and pathology; and out of pathology arises therapy. The year
1932 was the trough of the great depression, and from its rotten soil was
belatedly begot a new subject that today we call macroeconomics.

— Paul Samuelson

In Chapter 11 we assembled the pieces of the *IS-LM* model as a step towards
understanding short-run economic fluctuations. We saw that the *IS* curve represents the equilibrium in the market for goods and services, that the *LM* curve
represents the equilibrium in the market for real money balances, and that the *IS*
and *LM* curves together determine the interest rate and national income in the
short run when the price level is fixed. Now we turn our attention to applying
the *IS-LM* model to analyse three issues.

First, we examine the potential causes of fluctuations in national income. We
use the *IS-LM* model to see how changes in the exogenous variables (government purchases, taxes and the money supply) influence the endogenous variables
(the interest rate and national income) for a given price level. We also examine
how various shocks to the goods market (the *IS* curve) and the money market
(the *LM* curve) affect the interest rate and national income in the short run.

Second, we discuss how the *IS-LM* model fits into the model of aggregate
supply and aggregate demand we introduced in Chapter 10. In particular, we
examine how the *IS-LM* model provides a theory to explain the slope and position of the aggregate demand curve. Here we relax the assumption that the price
level is fixed and show that the *IS-LM* model implies a negative relationship
between the price level and national income. The model can also tell us what
events shift the aggregate demand curve and in what direction.

Third, we examine the Great Depression of the 1930s. As this chapter's opening quotation indicates, this episode gave birth to short-run macroeconomic
theory, for it led Keynes and his many followers to think that aggregate demand
was the key to understanding fluctuations in national income. With the benefit
of hindsight, we can use the *IS-LM* model to discuss the various explanations of
this traumatic economic downturn.

12-1 Explaining Fluctuations with the *IS-LM* Model

The intersection of the *IS* curve and the *LM* curve determines the level of national income. When one of these curves shifts, the short-run equilibrium of the economy changes and national income fluctuates. In this section we examine how changes in policy and shocks to the economy can cause these curves to shift.

How Fiscal Policy Shifts the *IS* Curve and Changes the Short-Run Equilibrium

We begin by examining how changes in fiscal policy (government purchases and taxes) alter the economy's short-run equilibrium. Recall that changes in fiscal policy influence planned expenditure and thereby shift the *IS* curve. The *IS-LM* model shows how these shifts in the *IS* curve affect income and the interest rate.

Changes in Government Purchases Consider an increase in government purchases of ΔG. The government-purchases multiplier in the Keynesian cross tells us that this change in fiscal policy raises the level of income at any given interest rate by $\Delta G/(1 - MPC)$. Therefore, as Figure 12-1 shows, the *IS* curve shifts to the right by this amount. The equilibrium of the economy moves from point A to point B. The increase in government purchases raises both income and the interest rate.

To understand fully what is happening in Figure 12-1, it helps to keep in mind the building blocks for the *IS-LM* model from the preceding chapter – the Keynesian cross and the theory of liquidity preference. Here is the story. When the government increases its purchases of goods and services, the economy's planned expenditure rises. The increase in planned expenditure stimulates the production of goods and services, which causes total income Y to rise. These effects should be familiar from the Keynesian cross.

Now consider the money market, as described by the theory of liquidity preference. Because the economy's demand for money depends on income, the rise in total income increases the quantity of money demanded at every interest rate. The supply of money has not changed, however, so higher money demand causes the equilibrium interest rate r to rise.

The higher interest rate arising in the money market, in turn, has ramifications back in the goods market. When the interest rate rises, firms cut back on their investment plans. This fall in investment partially offsets the expansionary effect of the increase in government purchases. Thus, the increase in income in response to a fiscal expansion is smaller in the *IS-LM* model than it is in the Keynesian cross (where investment is assumed to be fixed). You can see this in Figure 12-1. The horizontal shift in the *IS* curve equals the rise in equilibrium income in the Keynesian cross. This amount is larger than the increase in equilibrium income here in the *IS-LM* model. The difference is explained by the crowding out of investment due to a higher interest rate.

Changes in Taxes In the *IS-LM* model, changes in taxes affect the economy much the same as changes in government purchases do, except that taxes affect

FIGURE 12-1

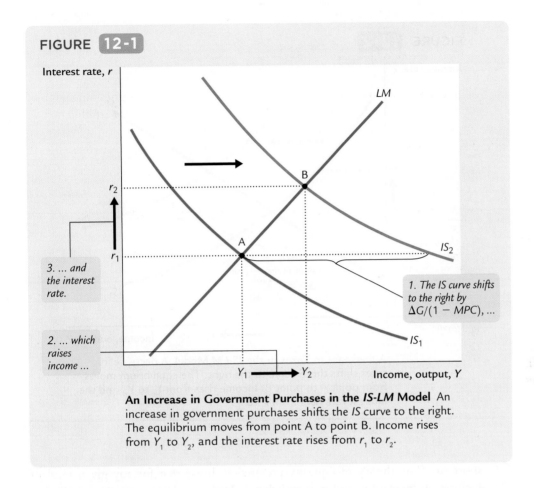

An Increase in Government Purchases in the *IS-LM* Model An increase in government purchases shifts the *IS* curve to the right. The equilibrium moves from point A to point B. Income rises from Y_1 to Y_2, and the interest rate rises from r_1 to r_2.

expenditure through consumption. Consider, for instance, a decrease in taxes of ΔT. The tax cut encourages consumers to spend more and, therefore, increases planned expenditure. The tax multiplier in the Keynesian cross tells us that this change in policy raises the level of income at any given interest rate by $\Delta T \times MPC/(1 - MPC)$. Therefore, as Figure 12-2 illustrates, the *IS* curve shifts to the right by this amount. The equilibrium of the economy moves from point A to point B. The tax cut raises both income and the interest rate. Once again, because the higher interest rate depresses investment, the increase in income is smaller in the *IS-LM* model than it is in the Keynesian cross.

How Monetary Policy Shifts the *LM* Curve and Changes the Short-Run Equilibrium

We now examine the effects of monetary policy. Recall that a change in the money supply alters the interest rate that equilibrates the money market for any given level of income, and thereby shifts the *LM* curve. The *IS-LM* model shows how a shift in the *LM* curve affects income and the interest rate.

Consider an increase in the money supply. An increase in M leads to an increase in real money balances M/P, because the price level P is fixed in the

FIGURE 12-2

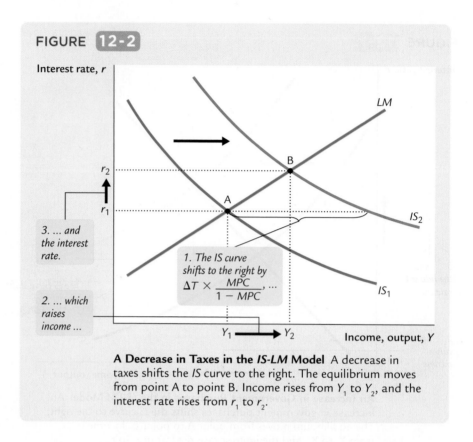

A Decrease in Taxes in the *IS-LM* Model A decrease in taxes shifts the *IS* curve to the right. The equilibrium moves from point A to point B. Income rises from Y_1 to Y_2, and the interest rate rises from r_1 to r_2.

short run. The theory of liquidity preference shows that for any given level of income, an increase in real money balances leads to a lower interest rate. Therefore, the *LM* curve shifts downward, as in Figure 12-3. The equilibrium moves from point A to point B. The increase in the money supply lowers the interest rate and raises the level of income.

Once again, to tell the story that explains the economy's adjustment from point A to point B, we rely on the building blocks of the *IS-LM* model – the Keynesian cross and the theory of liquidity preference. This time, we begin with the money market, where the monetary policy action occurs. When the central bank increases the supply of money, people have more money than they want to hold at the prevailing interest rate. As a result, they start depositing this extra money in banks or use it to buy bonds. The interest rate *r* then falls until people are willing to hold all the extra money that the central bank has created; this brings the money market to a new equilibrium. The lower interest rate, in turn, has ramifications for the goods market. A lower interest rate stimulates planned investment, which increases planned expenditure, production and income *Y*.

Thus, the *IS-LM* model shows that monetary policy influences income by changing the interest rate. This conclusion sheds light on our analysis of monetary policy in Chapter 10. In that chapter we showed that in the short run, when prices are sticky, an expansion in the money supply raises income. But we did not discuss *how* a monetary expansion induces greater spending on goods and services – a process called the **monetary transmission mechanism**. The *IS-LM* model shows

FIGURE 12-3

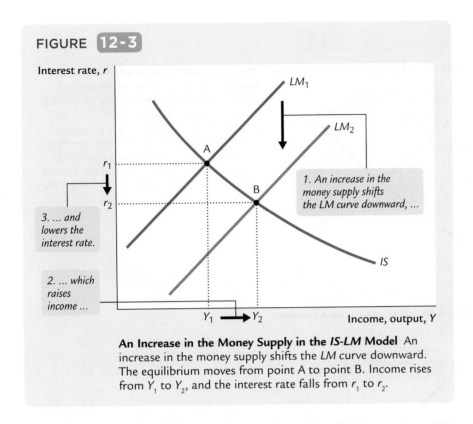

Interest rate, *r*

LM_1

LM_2

A

r_1

B

r_2

1. *An increase in the money supply shifts the LM curve downward, ...*

3. *... and lowers the interest rate.*

2. *... which raises income ...*

Y_1 Y_2

IS

Income, output, *Y*

An Increase in the Money Supply in the *IS-LM* Model An increase in the money supply shifts the *LM* curve downward. The equilibrium moves from point A to point B. Income rises from Y_1 to Y_2, and the interest rate falls from r_1 to r_2.

an important part of that mechanism: *an increase in the money supply lowers the interest rate, which stimulates investment and thereby expands the demand for goods and services.* The next chapter shows that in open economies, such as those in Europe, the exchange rate also has an important role in the monetary transmission mechanism.

The Interaction between Monetary and Fiscal Policy

When analysing any change in monetary or fiscal policy, it is important to keep in mind that the policy makers who control these policy tools are aware of what the other policy makers are doing. A change in one policy, therefore, may influence the other, and this interdependence may alter the impact of a policy change.

For example, suppose the government raises taxes. What effect will this policy have on the economy? According to the *IS-LM* model, the answer depends on how the central bank responds to the tax increase. Figure 12-4 shows just three of the many possible outcomes. In panel (a) the central bank holds the money supply constant. The tax increase shifts the *IS* curve to the left. Income falls (because higher taxes reduce consumer spending), and the interest rate falls (because lower income reduces the demand for money). The fall in income indicates that the tax hike causes a recession.

In panel (b) the central bank wants to hold the interest rate constant. In this case, when the tax increase shifts the *IS* curve to the left, the central bank must decrease the money supply to keep the interest rate at its original level. This fall in the money supply shifts the *LM* curve upward. The interest rate does not fall,

FIGURE 12-4

(a) Central Bank Holds Money Supply Constant

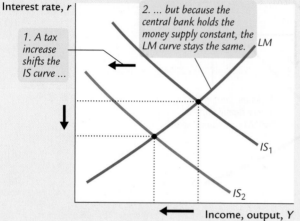

Interest rate, r

1. A tax increase shifts the IS curve ...

2. ... but because the central bank holds the money supply constant, the LM curve stays the same.

LM

IS_1

IS_2

Income, output, Y

The Response of the Economy to a Tax Increase How the economy responds to a tax increase depends on how the central bank responds. In panel (a) the central bank holds the money supply constant. In panel (b) the central bank holds the interest rate constant by reducing the money supply. In panel (c) the central bank holds the level of income constant by raising the money supply.

(b) Central Bank Holds Interest Rate Constant

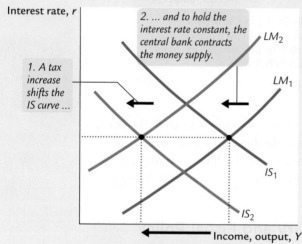

Interest rate, r

1. A tax increase shifts the IS curve ...

2. ... and to hold the interest rate constant, the central bank contracts the money supply.

LM_2

LM_1

IS_1

IS_2

Income, output, Y

(c) Central Bank Holds Income Constant

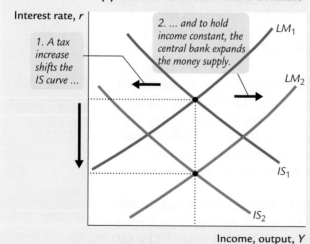

Interest rate, r

1. A tax increase shifts the IS curve ...

2. ... and to hold income constant, the central bank expands the money supply.

LM_1

LM_2

IS_1

IS_2

Income, output, Y

but income falls by a larger amount than if the central bank had held the money supply constant. Whereas in panel (a) the lower interest rate stimulated investment and partially offset the contractionary effect of the tax hike, in panel (b) the central bank deepens the recession by keeping the interest rate high.

In panel (c) the central bank wants to prevent the tax increase from lowering income. It must, therefore, raise the money supply and shift the *LM* curve downward enough to offset the shift in the *IS* curve. In this case, the tax increase does not cause a recession, but it does cause a large fall in the interest rate. Although the level of income is not changed, the combination of a tax increase and a monetary expansion does change the allocation of the economy's resources. The higher taxes depress consumption, while the lower interest rate stimulates investment. Income is not affected because these two effects balance exactly.

From this example we can see that the impact of a change in fiscal policy depends on the policy the central bank pursues – that is, on whether it holds the money supply, the interest rate or the level of income constant. More generally, whenever analysing a change in one policy, we must make an assumption about its effect on the other policy. The most appropriate assumption depends on the case at hand and the many political considerations that lie behind economic policy making.

Shocks in the *IS-LM* Model

Because the *IS-LM* model shows how national income is determined in the short run, we can use the model to examine how various economic disturbances affect income. So far we have seen how changes in fiscal policy shift the *IS* curve and how changes in monetary policy shift the *LM* curve. Similarly, we can group other disturbances into two categories: shocks to the *IS* curve and shocks to the *LM* curve.

Shocks to the *IS* curve are exogenous changes in the demand for goods and services. Some economists, including Keynes, have emphasized that such changes in demand can arise from investors' *animal spirits* – exogenous and perhaps self-fulfilling waves of optimism and pessimism. For example, suppose that firms become pessimistic about the future of the economy and that this pessimism causes them to build fewer new factories. This reduction in the demand for investment goods causes a contractionary shift in the investment function: at every interest rate, firms want to invest less. The fall in investment reduces planned expenditure and shifts the *IS* curve to the left, reducing income and employment. This fall in equilibrium income in part validates the firms' initial pessimism.

Shocks to the *IS* curve may also arise from changes in the demand for consumer goods. Suppose, for instance, that the election of a popular president increases consumer confidence in the economy. This induces consumers to save less for the future and consume more today. We can interpret this change as an upward shift in the consumption function. This shift in the consumption function increases planned expenditure and shifts the *IS* curve to the right, and this raises income.

Shocks to the *LM* curve arise from exogenous changes in the demand for money. For example, suppose that new restrictions on credit card availability increase the amount of money people choose to hold. According to the theory of liquidity preference, when money demand rises, the interest rate necessary to

equilibrate the money market is higher (for any given level of income and money supply). Hence, an increase in money demand shifts the *LM* curve upward, which tends to raise the interest rate and depress income.

In summary, several kinds of events can cause economic fluctuations by shifting the *IS* curve or the *LM* curve. Remember, however, that such fluctuations are not inevitable. Policy makers can try to use the tools of monetary and fiscal policy to offset exogenous shocks. If policy makers are sufficiently quick and skillful (admittedly, a big if), shocks to the *IS* or *LM* curves need not lead to fluctuations in income or employment.

CASE STUDY

The International Decline in GDP Growth in 2001

In Table 12-1 we show annual growth rates for a range of European countries, as well as the US, the UK and the whole Euro Area (Eurozone), over the period 1996–2005. Note that all the countries listed (as well as the Euro Area) register a marked decline in GDP growth in 2001.

This co-movement in GDP growth across Europe and the United States in 2001 is at least partly attributable to two notable shocks that occurred at this time. The first was a decline in European and American stock markets. During the 1990s, Western stock markets experienced a boom of historic proportions, as investors became optimistic about the prospects of the new information technology. Some economists viewed the optimism as excessive at the time, and in hindsight this proved to be the case. When the optimism faded, average stock prices fell. Although the falls were most dramatic in the US, European stock markets also experienced severe declines from late 2000 to late 2001. The fall in the stock market reduced household wealth and thus consumer spending. In addition, the declining perceptions of the profitability of the new technologies led to a fall in investment spending. In the language of the *IS-LM* model, the *IS* curve shifted to the left.

The second shock came in the form of the terrorist attacks on New York and Washington, DC, on 11 September 2001. Again, although it was the US that was most directly affected, the attacks increased uncertainty about what the future would hold among all Western nations. Uncertainty can reduce spending

TABLE 12-1

Annual GDP Growth Rates for the Euro Area, the UK, the US and a Range of European Countries 1996–2005

	1996	1997	1998	1999	2000	2001	2002	2003	2004	2005
Euro Area	1.4	2.5	2.8	3.0	3.9	1.9	0.9	0.8	2.1	1.3
Belgium	1.2	3.3	1.9	3.1	3.9	1.0	1.5	0.9	2.6	1.2
Denmark	2.8	3.2	2.2	2.6	3.5	0.7	0.5	0.7	1.9	3.1
Germany	1.0	1.8	2.0	2.0	3.2	1.2	0.1	−0.2	1.6	1.0
France	1.1	2.2	3.5	3.2	4.0	1.9	1.0	1.1	2.3	1.2
Italy	0.7	1.9	1.4	1.9	3.6	1.8	0.3	0	1.1	0
Netherlands	3.4	4.3	3.9	4.7	3.9	1.9	0.1	−0.1	1.7	1.1
Switzerland	0.5	1.9	2.8	1.3	3.6	1.0	0.3	−0.3	2.1	1.9
United Kingdom	2.7	3.2	3.2	3.0	4.0	2.2	2.0	2.5	3.1	1.8
United States	3.7	4.5	4.2	4.4	3.7	0.8	1.6	2.7	4.2	3.5

Source: Eurostat.

because households and firms postpone some of their plans until the uncertainty is resolved. Thus, the terrorist attacks shifted the *IS* curve further to the left.

In many European countries the effects of this reduction in growth persisted for many years. Indeed many countries had not recovered when their economies were hit by the next recession of 2008, which is examined in another case study later in this chapter. ■

What Is the Central Bank's Policy Instrument: The Money Supply or the Interest Rate?

Our analysis of monetary policy has been based on the assumption that the central bank influences the economy by controlling the money supply. However, when the media report on changes in central bank policy, they often just say that the central bank has raised or lowered interest rates. Which is right? Even though these two views may seem different, both are correct, and it is important to understand why.

The central bank of an economy will set an interest rate at which it is willing to lend to commercial banks on a short-term basis. The term for this interest rate differs across central banks – in the UK it is the Official Bank Rate; in the US it is the federal funds rate; and at the European Central Bank (ECB) it is the refinancing rate. We will refer to this rate as the policy rate or the official rate. The major central banks have an interest rate-setting committee that meets every few weeks – the ECB's committee is called the Governing Council; at the Bank of England it is the Monetary Policy Committee; and in the US Federal Reserve it is the Open Market Committee. At this meeting, the committee votes on a target for the policy rate that will apply until the next meeting. After the meeting, the central bank's bond traders are told to conduct the open-market operations necessary to hit that target. These open-market operations change the money supply and shift the *LM* curve so that the equilibrium interest rate (determined by the intersection of the *IS* and *LM* curves) equals the target interest rate that the central bank's interest rate-setting committee has chosen.

As a result of this operating procedure, central bank policy is often discussed in terms of changing interest rates. Keep in mind, however, that behind these changes in interest rates are the necessary changes in the money supply. A newspaper might report, for instance, that 'the central bank has lowered interest rates'. To be more precise, we can interpret this statement as meaning that 'the central bank's interest rate-setting committee has instructed the central bank's bond traders to buy bonds in open-market operations so as to increase the money supply, shift the *LM* curve and reduce the equilibrium interest rate to hit a new lower target'.

Why do the major central banks choose to use an interest rate, rather than the money supply, as the short-term monetary policy instrument? One possible answer is that shocks to the *LM* curve are more prevalent than shocks to the *IS* curve. When the central bank targets interest rates, it automatically offsets *LM* shocks by adjusting the money supply, although this policy exacerbates *IS* shocks. If *LM* shocks are the more prevalent type, then a policy of targeting the interest rate leads to greater economic stability than a policy of targeting the money supply. (Problem 7 at the end of this chapter asks you to analyse this issue more fully.)

Another possible reason for using the interest rate as the short-term policy instrument is that interest rates are easier to measure than the money supply. As we saw in Chapter 4, the central bank has various measures of money, and these sometimes move in different directions. Rather than deciding which measure is best, the central bank avoids the question by using the policy interest rate (the refinancing rate at the ECB; the repo rate at the Bank of England) as its policy instrument.

12-2 *IS-LM* as a Theory of Aggregate Demand

We have been using the *IS-LM* model to explain national income in the short run when the price level is fixed. To see how the *IS-LM* model fits into the model of aggregate supply and aggregate demand introduced in Chapter 10, we now examine what happens in the *IS-LM* model if the price level is allowed to change. By examining the effects of changing the price level, we can finally deliver what was promised when we began our study of the *IS-LM* model: a theory to explain the position and slope of the aggregate demand curve.

From the *IS-LM* Model to the Aggregate Demand Curve

Recall from Chapter 10 that the aggregate demand curve describes a relationship between the price level and the level of national income. In Chapter 10 this relationship was derived from the quantity theory of money. The analysis showed that for a given money supply, a higher price level implies a lower level of income. Increases in the money supply shift the aggregate demand curve to the right, and decreases in the money supply shift the aggregate demand curve to the left.

To understand the determinants of aggregate demand more fully, we now use the *IS-LM* model, rather than the quantity theory, to derive the aggregate demand curve. First, we use the *IS-LM* model to show why national income falls as the price level rises — that is, why the aggregate demand curve is downward sloping. Second, we examine what causes the aggregate demand curve to shift.

To explain why the aggregate demand curve slopes downward, we examine what happens in the *IS-LM* model when the price level changes (as shown in Figure 12-5). For any given money supply M, a higher price level P reduces the supply of real money balances M/P. A lower supply of real money balances shifts the *LM* curve upward, which raises the equilibrium interest rate and lowers the equilibrium level of income, as shown in panel (a). Here the price level rises from P_1 to P_2,

FIGURE 12-5

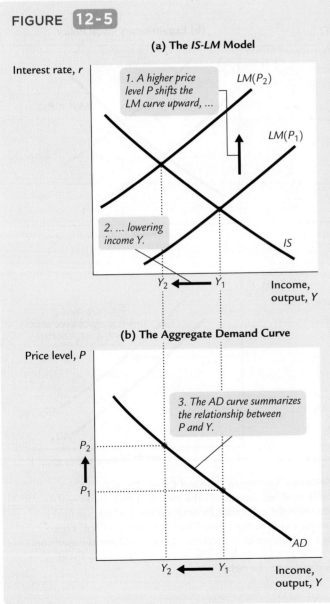

(a) The *IS-LM* Model

Interest rate, r

1. A higher price level P shifts the LM curve upward, ...

$LM(P_2)$

$LM(P_1)$

2. ... lowering income Y.

IS

$Y_2 \leftarrow Y_1$ Income, output, Y

(b) The Aggregate Demand Curve

Price level, P

3. The AD curve summarizes the relationship between P and Y.

P_2

P_1

AD

$Y_2 \leftarrow Y_1$ Income, output, Y

Deriving the Aggregate Demand Curve with the *IS-LM* Model Panel (a) shows the *IS-LM* model: an increase in the price level from P_1 to P_2 lowers real money balances and thus shifts the *LM* curve upward. The shift in the *LM* curve lowers income from Y_1 to Y_2. Panel (b) shows the aggregate demand curve summarizing this relationship between the price level and income: the higher the price level, the lower the level of income.

and income falls from Y_1 to Y_2. The aggregate demand curve in panel (b) plots this negative relationship between national income and the price level. In other words, the aggregate demand curve shows the set of equilibrium points that arise in the *IS-LM* model as we vary the price level and see what happens to income.

What causes the aggregate demand curve to shift? Because the aggregate demand curve is merely a summary of results from the *IS-LM* model, events that shift the *IS* curve or the *LM* curve (for a given price level) cause the aggregate demand curve to shift. For instance, an increase in the money supply raises income in the *IS-LM* model for any given price level; it thus shifts the aggregate demand curve to the right, as shown in panel (a) of Figure 12-6.

FIGURE 12-6

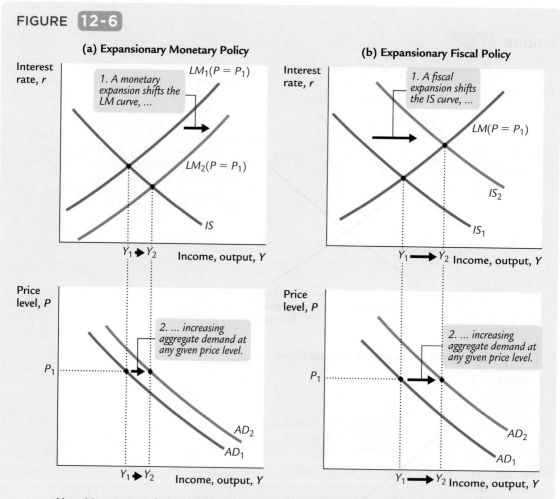

How Monetary and Fiscal Policies Shift the Aggregate Demand Curve Panel (a) shows a monetary expansion. For any given price level, an increase in the money supply raises real money balances, shifts the *LM* curve to the right and raises income. Hence, an increase in the money supply shifts the aggregate demand curve to the right. Panel (b) shows a fiscal expansion, such as an increase in government purchases or a decrease in taxes. The fiscal expansion shifts the *IS* curve to the right and, for any given price level, raises income. Hence, a fiscal expansion shifts the aggregate demand curve to the right.

Similarly, an increase in government purchases or a decrease in taxes raises income in the *ISLM* model for a given price level; it also shifts the aggregate demand curve to the right, as shown in panel (b) of Figure 12-6. Conversely, a decrease in the money supply, a decrease in government purchases or an increase in taxes lowers income in the *IS-LM* model and shifts the aggregate demand curve to the left. Anything that changes income in the *IS-LM* model other than a change in the price level causes a shift in the aggregate demand curve. The factors shifting aggregate demand include not only monetary and fiscal policy, but also shocks to the goods market (the *IS* curve) and shocks to the money market (the *LM* curve).

We can summarize these results as follows: *A change in income in the IS-LM model resulting from a change in the price level represents a movement along the aggregate demand curve. A change in income in the IS-LM model for a given price level represents a shift in the aggregate demand curve.*

The *IS-LM* Model in the Short Run and Long Run

The *IS-LM* model is designed to explain the economy in the short run when the price level is fixed. Yet, now that we have seen how a change in the price level influences the equilibrium in the *IS-LM* model, we can also use the model to describe the economy in the long run, when the price level adjusts to ensure that the economy produces at its natural rate. By using the *IS-LM* model to describe the long run, we can show clearly how the Keynesian model of income determination differs from the classical model of Chapter 3.

Panel (a) of Figure 12-7 shows the three curves that are necessary for understanding the short-run and long-run equilibria: the *IS* curve, the *LM* curve and the vertical line representing the natural level of output $\overline{Y}$. The *LM* curve is, as always, drawn for a fixed price level P_1. The short-run equilibrium of the economy is point K, where the *IS* curve crosses the *LM* curve. Notice that in this short-run equilibrium, the economy's income is less than its natural level.

Panel (b) of Figure 12-7 shows the same situation in the diagram of aggregate supply and aggregate demand. At the price level P_1, the quantity of output demanded is below the natural level. In other words, at the existing price level, there is insufficient demand for goods and services to keep the economy producing at its potential.

In these two diagrams we can examine the short-run equilibrium at which the economy finds itself and the long-run equilibrium towards which the economy gravitates. Point K describes the short-run equilibrium because it assumes that the price level is stuck at P_1. Eventually, the low demand for goods and services causes prices to fall, and the economy moves back towards its natural rate. When the price level reaches P_2, the economy is at point C, the long-run equilibrium. The diagram of aggregate supply and aggregate demand shows that at point C, the quantity of goods and services demanded equals the natural level of output. This long-run equilibrium is achieved in the *IS-LM* diagram by a shift in the *LM* curve: the fall in the price level raises real money balances and therefore shifts the *LM* curve to the right.

FIGURE 12-7

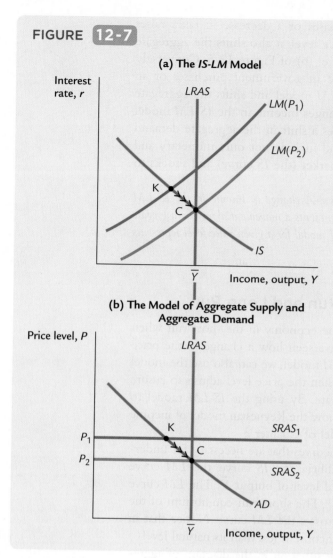

(a) The IS-LM Model

Interest rate, r

LRAS

$LM(P_1)$

$LM(P_2)$

K

C

IS

$\overline{Y}$ Income, output, Y

(b) The Model of Aggregate Supply and Aggregate Demand

Price level, P

LRAS

K

P_1

C

$SRAS_1$

P_2

$SRAS_2$

AD

$\overline{Y}$ Income, output, Y

The Short-Run and Long-Run Equilibria We can compare the short-run and long-run equilibria using either the IS-LM diagram in panel (a) or the aggregate supply and aggregate demand diagram in panel (b). In the short run, the price level is stuck at P_1. The short-run equilibrium of the economy is therefore point K. In the long run, the price level adjusts so that the economy is at the natural level of output. The long-run equilibrium is therefore point C.

We can now see the key difference between Keynesian and classical approaches to the determination of national income. The Keynesian assumption (represented by point K) is that the price level is stuck. Depending on monetary policy, fiscal policy and the other determinants of aggregate demand, output may deviate from its natural level. The classical assumption (represented by point C) is that the price level is fully flexible. The price level adjusts to ensure that national income is always at its natural level.

To make the same point somewhat differently, we can think of the economy as being described by three equations. The first two are the IS and LM equations:

$$Y = C(Y - T) + I(r) + G, \qquad\qquad IS$$

$$M/P = L(r, Y). \qquad\qquad LM$$

The *IS* equation describes the equilibrium in the goods market, and the *LM* equation describes the equilibrium in the money market. These *two* equations contain *three* endogenous variables: *Y*, *P* and *r*. To complete the system, we need a third equation. The Keynesian approach completes the model with the assumption of fixed prices, so the Keynesian third equation is

$$P = P_1.$$

This assumption implies that the remaining two variables *r* and *Y* must adjust to satisfy the remaining two equations *IS* and *LM*. The classical approach completes the model with the assumption that output reaches its natural level, so the classical third equation is

$$Y = \overline{Y}.$$

This assumption implies that the remaining two variables *r* and *P* must adjust to satisfy the remaining two equations *IS* and *LM*. Thus the classical approach fixes output and allows the price level to adjust to satisfy the goods and money market equilibrium conditions, whereas the Keynesian approach fixes the price level and lets output move to satisfy the equilibrium conditions.

Which assumption is most appropriate? The answer depends on the time horizon. The classical assumption best describes the long run. Hence, our long-run analysis of national income in Chapter 3 and prices in Chapter 5 assumes that output equals its natural level. The Keynesian assumption best describes the short run. Therefore, our analysis of economic fluctuations relies on the assumption of a fixed price level.

12-3 The Great Depression

Now that we have developed the model of aggregate demand, let's use it to address the question that originally motivated Keynes: what caused the Great Depression? Almost a century after the event, economists continue to debate the cause of this major economic downturn. The Great Depression provides an extended case study to show how economists use the *IS-LM* model to analyse economic fluctuations.[1]

As we discussed in a case study in Chapter 10, the UK's return to the gold standard in 1925 at the rate which had held before World War I required a substantial deflation of the economy, which resulted in strong falls in UK output in the early 1920s. Starting in 1929, however, the US economy went into a severe recession that lasted several years and quickly spread to Europe, particularly

---

[1] For a flavour of the debate, see Milton Friedman and Anna J. Schwartz, *A Monetary History of the United States, 1867–1960*, 1963, Princeton, NJ: Princeton University Press; Peter Temin, *Did Monetary Forces Cause the Great Depression?*, New York: W.W. Norton, 1976; the essays in Karl Brunner, ed., *The Great Depression Revisited*, 1981, Boston, MA: Martinus Nijhoff; and the symposium on the Great Depression, *Journal of Economic Perspectives*, spring 1993.

TABLE 12-2

What Happened in the US During the Great Depression?

Year	Unemployment Rate (1)	Real GNP (2)	Consumption (2)	Investment (2)	Government Purchases (2)
1929	3.2	203.6	139.6	40.4	22.0
1930	8.9	183.5	130.4	27.4	24.3
1931	16.3	169.5	126.1	16.8	25.4
1932	24.1	144.2	114.8	4.7	24.2
1933	25.2	141.5	112.8	5.3	23.3
1934	22.0	154.3	118.1	9.4	26.6
1935	20.3	169.5	125.5	18.0	27.0
1936	17.0	193.2	138.4	24.0	31.8
1937	14.3	203.2	143.1	29.9	30.8
1938	19.1	192.9	140.2	17.0	33.9
1939	17.2	209.4	148.2	24.7	35.2
1940	14.6	227.2	155.7	33.0	36.4

Source: Historical Statistics of the United States, Colonial Times to 1970, Parts I and II (Washington, DC: US Department of Commerce, Bureau of Census, 1975).
Notes: (1) The unemployment rate is series D9. (2) Real GNP, consumption, investment and government purchases are series F3, F48, F52 and F66, and are measured in billions of 1958 dollars.

Germany and, subsequently, France. This recession is known as the Great Depression, and economists continue to debate its causes and the reasons why it spread to Europe. The Great Depression therefore provides an interesting piece of economic history to which we can apply our *IS-LM* apparatus to see if it can provide us with some clues.

Before turning to the explanations economists have proposed, look at Table 12-2, which presents some statistics regarding the Great Depression in the country in which it originated, the United States. These statistics are the battlefield on which debate about the Great Depression takes place. What do you think happened? An *IS* shift? An *LM* shift? Or something else?

The Spending Hypothesis: Shocks to the *IS* Curve

Table 12-2 shows that the decline in US income in the early 1930s coincided with falling interest rates. This fact has led some economists to suggest that the cause of the decline may have been a contractionary shift in the *IS* curve. This view is sometimes called the *spending hypothesis,* because it places primary blame for the Great Depression on an exogenous fall in spending on goods and services.

Economists have attempted to explain this decline in spending in several ways. Some argue that a downward shift in the consumption function caused the contractionary shift in the *IS* curve. The US stock market crash of 1929 may have been partly responsible for this shift: by reducing wealth and increasing

TABLE 12-2 *Continued*

Year	Nominal Interest Rate (3)	Money Supply (4)	Price Level (5)	Inflation (6)	Real Money Balances (7)
1929	5.9	26.6	50.6	–	52.6
1930	3.6	25.8	49.3	−2.6	52.3
1931	2.6	24.1	44.8	−10.1	54.5
1932	2.7	21.1	40.2	−9.3	52.5
1933	1.7	19.9	39.3	−2.2	50.7
1934	1.0	21.9	42.2	7.4	51.8
1935	0.8	25.9	42.6	0.9	60.8
1936	0.8	29.6	42.7	0.2	62.9
1937	0.9	30.9	44.5	4.2	69.5
1938	0.8	30.5	43.9	−1.3	69.5
1939	0.6	34.2	43.2	−1.6	79.1
1940	0.6	39.7	43.9	1.6	90.3

(3) The interest rate is the prime Commercial Paper rate, 4–6 months, series x445. (4) The money supply is series x414, currency plus demand deposits, measured in billions of dollars. (5) The price level is the GNP deflator (1958 = 100), series E1. (6) The inflation rate is the percentage change in the price level series. (7) Real money balances, calculated by dividing the money supply by the price level and multiplying by 100, are in billions of 1958 dollars.

uncertainty about the future prospects of the US economy, the crash may have induced consumers to save more of their income rather than spend it.

Others explain the decline in spending by pointing to the large drop in investment in housing. Some economists believe that the US residential investment boom of the 1920s was excessive, and that once this 'overbuilding' became apparent, the demand for residential investment declined drastically. Another possible explanation for the fall in residential investment is the reduction in immigration into the US in the 1930s: a more slowly growing population demands less new housing.

Once the Depression began, several events occurred that could have reduced spending further. First, many US banks failed in the early 1930s, in part because of inadequate bank regulation; and these bank failures may have exacerbated the fall in investment spending. Banks play the crucial role of getting the funds available for investment to those households and firms that can best use them. The closing of many banks in the early 1930s may have prevented some businesses from getting the funds they needed for capital investment and, therefore, may have led to a further contractionary shift in the investment function.[2]

In addition, US fiscal policy of the 1930s caused a contractionary shift in the *IS* curve. Politicians at that time were more concerned with balancing the budget than with using fiscal policy to keep production and employment at their natural levels. The US Revenue Act of 1932 increased various taxes, especially

---

[2] Ben Bernanke, 'Non-Monetary Effects of the Financial Crisis in the Propagation of the Great Depression', *American Economic Review*, June 1983, vol. 73, pp. 257–276.

those falling on lower- and middle-income consumers.[3] The Democratic platform of that year expressed concern about the budget deficit and advocated an 'immediate and drastic reduction of governmental expenditures'. In the midst of historically high unemployment, policy makers searched for ways to raise taxes and reduce government spending.

There are, therefore, several ways to explain a contractionary shift in the *IS* curve. Keep in mind that these different views may all be true. There may be no single explanation for the decline in spending. It is possible that all these changes coincided and that together they led to a massive reduction in spending.

The Money Hypothesis: A Shock to the *LM* Curve

Table 12-2 shows that the US money supply fell 25 per cent from 1929 to 1933, during which time the unemployment rate rose from 3.2 per cent to 25.2 per cent. This fact provides the motivation and support for what is called the *money hypothesis*, which places primary blame for the Great Depression on the US central bank – the Federal Reserve – for allowing the money supply to fall by such a large amount.[4] The best-known advocates of this interpretation are Milton Friedman and Anna Schwartz, who defend it in their treatise on US monetary history. Friedman and Schwartz argue that contractions in the money supply have caused most economic downturns and that the Great Depression is a particularly vivid example.

Using the *IS-LM* model, we might interpret the money hypothesis as explaining the Depression by a contractionary shift in the *LM* curve. Seen in this way, however, the money hypothesis runs into two problems.

The first problem is the behaviour of *real* money balances. Monetary policy leads to a contractionary shift in the *LM* curve only if real money balances fall. Yet from 1929 to 1931, US real money balances rose slightly, because the fall in the money supply was accompanied by an even greater fall in the price level. Although the monetary contraction may be responsible for the rise in US unemployment from 1931 to 1933, when real money balances did fall, it cannot easily explain the initial downturn from 1929 to 1931.

The second problem for the money hypothesis is the behaviour of interest rates. If a contractionary shift in the *LM* curve triggered the Great Depression, we should have observed higher interest rates. Yet US nominal interest rates fell continuously from 1929 to 1933.

These two reasons appear sufficient to reject the view that the Great Depression was instigated by a contractionary shift in the *LM* curve. But was the fall in the money stock irrelevant? Next, we turn to another mechanism through which monetary policy might have been responsible for the severity of the Great Depression – the deflation of the 1930s.

[3] E. Cary Brown, 'Fiscal Policy in the Thirties: A Reappraisal', *American Economic Review*, December 1956, vol. 46, pp. 857–879.
[4] We discuss the reasons for this large decrease in the US money supply in Chapter 4, where we examine the money supply process in more detail. In particular, see the case study 'Bank Failures and the Money Supply in the 1930s'.

The Money Hypothesis Again: The Effects of Falling Prices

From 1929 to 1933, the US price level fell 25 per cent. Many economists blame this deflation for the severity of the Great Depression. They argue that the deflation may have turned what in 1931 was a typical economic downturn into an unprecedented period of high unemployment and depressed income. If correct, this argument gives new life to the money hypothesis. Because the falling money supply was, plausibly, responsible for the falling price level, it could have been responsible for the severity of the Depression. To evaluate this argument, we must discuss how changes in the price level affect income in the *IS-LM* model.

The Stabilizing Effects of Deflation In the *IS-LM* model we have developed so far, falling prices raise income. For any given supply of money M, a lower price level implies higher real money balances M/P. An increase in real money balances causes an expansionary shift in the *LM* curve, which leads to higher income.

Another channel through which falling prices expand income is called the **Pigou effect**. Arthur Pigou, a prominent British classical economist in the 1930s, pointed out that real money balances are part of households' wealth. As prices fall and real money balances rise, consumers should feel wealthier and spend more. This increase in consumer spending should cause an expansionary shift in the *IS* curve, also leading to higher income.

These two reasons led some economists in the 1930s to believe that falling prices would help to stabilize the economy. That is, they thought that a decline in the price level would automatically push the economy back towards full employment. Yet other economists were less confident in the economy's ability to correct itself. They pointed to other effects of falling prices, to which we now turn.

The Destabilizing Effects of Deflation Economists have proposed two theories to explain how falling prices could depress income rather than raise it. The first, called the **debt-deflation theory**, describes the effects of unexpected falls in the price level. The second explains the effects of expected deflation.

The debt-deflation theory begins with an observation from Chapter 5: unanticipated changes in the price level redistribute wealth between debtors and creditors. If a debtor owes a creditor €1000, then the real amount of this debt is €1000/P, where P is the price level. A fall in the price level raises the real amount of this debt – the amount of purchasing power the debtor must repay the creditor. Therefore, an unexpected deflation enriches creditors and impoverishes debtors.

The debt-deflation theory then posits that this redistribution of wealth affects spending on goods and services. In response to the redistribution from debtors to creditors, debtors spend less and creditors spend more. If these two groups have equal spending propensities, there is no aggregate impact. But it seems reasonable to assume that debtors have higher propensities to spend than creditors – perhaps that is why the debtors are in debt in the first place. In this case, debtors reduce their spending by more than creditors raise theirs. The net effect is a reduction in spending, a contractionary shift in the *IS* curve and lower national income.

To understand how *expected* changes in prices can affect income, we need to add a new variable to the *IS-LM* model. Our discussion of the model so far has not distinguished between nominal and real interest rates. Yet we know from previous chapters that investment depends on the real interest rate and that money demand depends on the nominal interest rate. If i is the nominal interest rate and π^e is expected inflation, then the *ex ante* real interest rate is $i - \pi^e$. We can now write the *IS-LM* model as

$$Y = C(Y - T) + I(i - \pi^e) + G, \qquad\qquad IS$$

$$M/P = L(i, Y). \qquad\qquad LM$$

Expected inflation enters as a variable in the *IS* curve. Thus, changes in expected inflation shift the *IS* curve.

Let's use this extended *IS-LM* model to examine how changes in expected inflation influence the level of income. We begin by assuming that everyone expects the price level to remain the same. In this case, there is no expected inflation ($\pi^e = 0$) and these two equations produce the familiar *IS-LM* model. Figure 12-8 depicts this initial situation with the *LM* curve and the *IS* curve labelled IS_1. The intersection of these two curves determines the nominal and real interest rates, which for now are the same.

Now suppose that everyone suddenly expects that the price level will fall in the future, so that π^e becomes negative. The real interest rate is now higher at

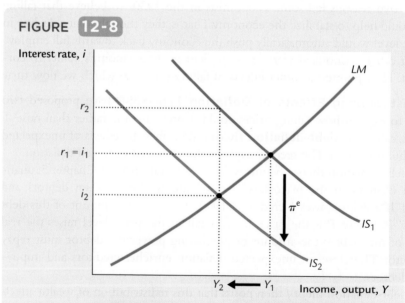

FIGURE 12-8

Expected Deflation in the *IS-LM* Model An expected deflation (a negative value of π^e) raises the real interest rate for any given nominal interest rate, and this depresses investment spending. The reduction in investment shifts the *IS* curve downward. The level of income falls from Y_1 to Y_2. The nominal interest rate falls from i_1 to i_2, and the real interest rate rises from r_1 to r_2.

any given nominal interest rate. This increase in the real interest rate depresses planned investment spending, shifting the *IS* curve from IS_1 to IS_2. (The vertical distance of the downward shift exactly equals the expected deflation.) Thus, an expected deflation leads to a reduction in national income from Y_1 to Y_2. The nominal interest rate falls from i_1 to i_2, while the real interest rate rises from r_1 to r_2.

Here is the story behind this figure. When firms come to expect deflation, they become reluctant to borrow to buy investment goods because they believe they will have to repay these loans later in more valuable dollars. The fall in investment depresses planned expenditure, which in turn depresses income. The fall in income reduces the demand for money, and this reduces the nominal interest rate that equilibrates the money market. The nominal interest rate falls by less than the expected deflation, so the real interest rate rises.

Note that there is a common thread in these two stories of destabilizing deflation. In both, falling prices depress national income by causing a contractionary shift in the *IS* curve. Because a deflation of the size observed in the US from 1929 to 1933 is unlikely, except in the presence of a major contraction in the money supply, these two explanations give some of the responsibility for the Great Depression – especially its severity – to the US central bank. In other words, if falling prices are destabilizing, a contraction in the money supply can lead to a fall in income, even without a decrease in real money balances or a rise in nominal interest rates.

Could the Depression Happen Again?

Economists study the Great Depression both because of its intrinsic interest as a major economic event and to provide guidance to policy makers so that it will not happen again. To state with confidence whether or not this event could recur, we would need to know why it happened. Because there is not yet agreement on the causes of the Great Depression, it is impossible to rule out with certainty another depression of this magnitude.

Yet most economists believe that a repetition of the mistakes that led to the Great Depression is improbable. Central banks today seem unlikely to allow the money supply to fall by a quarter. Many economists believe that the deflation of the early 1930s was responsible for the depth and length of the Great Depression. And it seems likely that such a prolonged deflation was possible only in the presence of a falling money supply.

The fiscal policy mistakes of the Depression are also unlikely to be repeated. US fiscal policy in the 1930s not only failed to help, but actually further depressed aggregate demand. Few economists today would advocate such a rigid adherence to a balanced budget in the face of massive unemployment.

In addition, there are many institutions today that would help prevent the events of the 1930s from recurring. Modern banking systems have systems of insurance that make widespread bank failures less likely. Income tax causes an automatic reduction in taxes when income falls, which stabilizes the economy. Finally, economists know more today than they did in the 1930s. Our knowledge of how the economy works, limited as it still is, should help policy makers formulate better policies to combat such widespread unemployment.

CASE STUDY

The Japanese Slump of the 1990s

After many years of rapid growth and enviable prosperity, the Japanese economy experienced a prolonged downturn during the 1990s. Real GDP grew at an average rate of only 1.3 per cent over the decade, compared with 4.3 per cent over the previous 20 years. Industrial production stagnated: having risen by 50 per cent from 1980 to 1991, it fell by 8 per cent from 1991 to 2002. The unemployment rate, which had historically been very low in Japan, rose from 2.1 per cent in 1991 to 5.4 per cent in 2002 – the highest rate since the government began compiling the statistic in 1953. After 2002, the Japanese economy started to recover, but only slowly. By the end of 2006, the unemployment rate had fallen to a little over 4 per cent.

Although the Japanese slump of the 1990s is not even close in magnitude to the Great Depression of the 1930s, the episodes are similar in several ways. First, both episodes are traced in part to a large decline in stock prices. In Japan, stock prices at the end of the 1990s were less than half the peak level they had reached about a decade earlier. Like the stock market, Japanese land prices had also sky-rocketed in the 1980s before crashing in the 1990s. (At the peak of Japan's land bubble, it was said that the land under the Imperial Palace was worth more than the entire state of California.) When stock and land prices collapsed, Japanese citizens saw their wealth plummet. This decline in wealth, like that during the Great Depression, depressed consumer spending.

Second, during both episodes, banks ran into trouble and exacerbated the slump in economic activity. Japanese banks in the 1980s had made many loans that were backed by stock or land. When the value of this collateral fell, borrowers started defaulting on their loans. These defaults on the old loans reduced the banks' ability to make new loans. The resulting 'credit crunch' made it harder for firms to finance investment projects, and thus depressed investment spending.

Third, both episodes saw a fall in economic activity coincide with very low interest rates. In Japan in the 1990s, as in the United States in the 1930s, short-term nominal interest rates were less than 1 per cent. This fact suggests that the cause of the slump was primarily a contractionary shift in the *IS* curve, because such a shift reduces both income and the interest rate. The obvious suspects to explain the *IS* shift are the crashes in stock and land prices and the problems in the banking system.

Finally, the policy debate in Japan mirrored the debate over the Great Depression. Some economists recommended that the Japanese government pass large tax cuts to encourage more consumer spending. Although this advice was followed to some extent, Japanese policy makers were reluctant to enact very large tax cuts because, like the US policy makers in the 1930s, they wanted to avoid budget deficits. In Japan, this reluctance to increase government debt arose in part because the government was facing a large unfunded pension liability and a rapidly ageing population.

Other economists recommended that the Bank of Japan expand the money supply more rapidly. Even if nominal interest rates could not go much lower, perhaps more rapid money growth could raise expected inflation, lower real interest rates and stimulate investment spending. Thus, although economists differed about whether fiscal or monetary policy was more likely to be effective, there was wide agreement that the solution to Japan's slump, like the solution to the Great Depression, rested in more aggressive expansion of aggregate demand.[5] ■

CASE STUDY

The Financial Crisis and Economic Downturn of 2008 and 2009

In 2008, the US economy experienced a financial crisis, followed by a deep recession. Several developments at this time were reminiscent of events during the 1930s, causing many observers to fear that the economy might experience a second Great Depression. This crisis then spread to other economies around the world, which we explore in greater detail in Chapter 20.

The story of the 2008 crisis begins a few years earlier with a substantial boom in the housing market in the US. The boom had several sources. In part, it was fuelled by low interest rates. The Federal Reserve lowered interest rates to historically low levels in the aftermath of the recession of 2001, which we looked at in a case study earlier in this chapter. Low interest rates helped the economy recover, but by making it less expensive to get a mortgage and buy a home, they also contributed to a rise in housing prices.

In addition, developments in the mortgage market made it easier for *subprime borrowers* – those borrowers whose income and credit history indicated a higher risk of default – to get mortgages to buy homes. One of these developments was *securitization*, the process by which a mortgage originator makes loans and then sells them to an investment bank, which in turn bundles them together into a variety of 'mortgage-backed securities' and then sells them to a third financial institution (such as a bank, pension fund, or insurance company). These securities pay a return as long as homeowners continue to repay their loans, but they lose value if homeowners default. Unfortunately, it seems that

---

[5] To learn more about this episode, see Kenneth N. Kuttner and Adam S. Posen, 'The Great Recession: Lessons for Macroeconomic Policy from Japan', *Brookings Papers on Economic Activity*, 2001, vol. 2, pp. 93–160. Readers of this book will find Kuttner and Posen's conclusions reassuring: 'despite the persistent stagnation, and despite the seeming ineffectiveness of several well publicised announcements of policy changes (which proved to be more noise than action), the Japanese economy has behaved much as the textbooks would have predicted . . . In short, the basic lesson of Japan's Great Recession for policy makers is to trust what you learned in intermediate macroeconomics class: even under difficult economic circumstances, and even in institutional contexts far removed from those in which they were developed, the stabilization policy framework of the mainstream textbooks still applies.'

FYI

The Liquidity Trap

In Japan in the 1990s and the United States in the 1930s, interest rates reached very low levels. As Table 12-2 shows, US interest rates were well under 1 per cent throughout the second half of the 1930s. The same was true in Japan during the second half of the 1990s. In 1999, Japanese short-term interest rates fell to about one-tenth of 1 per cent. In December of 2008, the Federal Reserve cut its target for the federal funds rate to the range of zero to 0.25 per cent, and it kept the rate at that level for the next several years. On 9 August 2011, the Fed released a statement pledging to keep interest rates low 'at least through mid-2013'. Meanwhile, the UK Monetary Policy Committee (MPC) has held UK base rates at their record low of 0.5 per cent since March 2009. Recently, the MPC has provided some explicit guidance regarding the future conduct of monetary policy. This is known as 'forward guidance'. This involves the maintenance of the 'highly stimulative stance of monetary policy until economic slack has been substantially reduced, provided this does not entail material risks to price stability or financial stability'. Specifically, the intention is not to raise the Official Bank Rate from its current level of 0.5 per cent at least until the Labour Force Survey headline measure of the unemployment rate has fallen to a threshold of 7 per cent, unless medium-term inflation is expected to be 0.5 percentage points or more above the 2 per cent target or the stance of monetary policy poses a significant threat to financial stability.

Some economists describe this situation as a *liquidity trap*. According to the *IS-LM* model, expansionary monetary policy works by reducing interest rates and stimulating investment spending. But if interest rates have already fallen almost to zero, then perhaps monetary policy is no longer effective. Nominal interest rates cannot fall below zero: rather than making a loan at a negative nominal interest rate, a person would just hold cash. In this environment, expansionary monetary policy raises the supply of money, making the public more liquid, but because interest rates cannot fall any further, the extra liquidity might not have any effect. Aggregate demand, production and employment may be 'trapped' at low levels.

Other economists are sceptical about this argument. One response is that expansionary monetary policy might raise inflation expectations. Even if nominal interest rates cannot fall any further, higher expected inflation can lower real interest rates by making them negative, which would stimulate investment spending. A second response is that monetary expansion would cause the currency to lose value in the market for foreign-currency exchange. This depreciation would make the nation's goods cheaper abroad, stimulating export demand. This second argument goes beyond the closed-economy *IS-LM* model we have used in this chapter, but it has merit in the open-economy version of the model developed in the next chapter. A third possibility is that the central bank could conduct expansionary open-market operations in a larger variety of financial instruments than it normally does. For example, it could buy mortgages and corporate debt and thereby lower the interest rates on these kinds of loans. Many central banks, including the US Federal Reserve, actively pursued this last option in response to the downturn of 2008 and 2009, a policy sometimes called *quantitative easing*. In the UK, since March 2009, the MPC has authorized several tranches of asset purchases under its quantitative easing policy, mostly of UK Government debt or 'gilts', totalling £375 billion by June 2013.

How much do monetary policy makers need to worry about the liquidity trap? Might the tools of monetary policy at times lose their power to influence the economy? There is no consensus about the answers. Sceptics say we should not worry about the liquidity trap. But others say the possibility of a liquidity trap argues for a target rate of inflation greater than zero. Under zero inflation, the real interest rate, like the nominal interest, can never fall below zero. But if the normal rate of inflation is, say, 4 per cent, then the central bank can easily push the real interest rate to negative 4 per cent by lowering the nominal interest rate towards zero. Thus moderate inflation gives monetary policy makers more room to stimulate the economy when needed, reducing the risk of falling into a liquidity trap.[6]

---

[6] To read more about the liquidity trap, see Paul R. Krugman, 'It's Baaack: Japan's Slump and the Return of the Liquidity Trap', *Brookings Panel on Economic Activity*, 1998, vol. 2, pp. 137–205.

the ultimate holders of these mortgage-backed securities sometimes failed to fully appreciate the risks they were taking. Some economists blame insufficient regulation for these high-risk loans. Others believe the problem was not too little regulation but the wrong kind: some government policies encouraged this high-risk lending to make the goal of homeownership more attainable for low-income families.

Together, these forces drove up housing demand and housing prices. From 1995 to 2006, average housing prices in the United States more than doubled. Some observers view this rise in housing prices as a speculative bubble, as more people bought homes in the hope and expectation that the prices would continue to rise.

The high price of housing, however, proved unsustainable. From 2006 to 2009, housing prices in the US fell by about 30 per cent. Such price fluctuations should not necessarily be a problem in a market economy. After all, price movements are how markets equilibrate supply and demand. But, in this case, the price decline led to a series of problematic repercussions.

The first of these repercussions was a substantial rise in mortgage defaults and home foreclosures. During the housing boom, many homeowners had bought their homes largely with borrowed money and minimal down payments. When housing prices declined, these homeowners were in *negative equity*: they owed more on their mortgages than their homes were worth. Many of these homeowners stopped paying their loans. The banks servicing the mortgages responded to the defaults by taking the houses away in foreclosure procedures and then selling them off. The banks' goal was to recoup whatever they could. The increase in the number of homes for sale, however, exacerbated the downward spiral of housing prices.

A second repercussion was large losses at the various financial institutions that owned mortgage-backed securities. In essence, by borrowing large sums to buy high-risk mortgages, these companies had bet that housing prices would keep rising; when this bet turned bad, they found themselves at or near the point of bankruptcy. Even healthy banks stopped trusting one another and avoided interbank lending, as it was hard to discern which institution would be the next to go out of business. Because of these large losses at financial institutions and the widespread fear and distrust, the ability of the financial system to make loans even to creditworthy customers was impaired. Chapter 20 discusses financial crises, including this one, in more detail.

A third repercussion was a substantial rise in stock market volatility. Many companies rely on the financial system to get the resources they need for business expansion or to help them manage their short-term cash flows. With the financial system less able to perform its normal operations, the profitability of many companies was called into question. Because it was hard to know how bad things would get, stock market volatility reached levels not seen since the 1930s.

Higher volatility, in turn, led to a fourth repercussion: a decline in consumer confidence. In the midst of all the uncertainty, households started putting off spending plans. Expenditure on durable goods, in particular, plummeted. As a result of all these events, the US economy experienced a large contractionary shift in the *IS* curve.

The US government responded vigorously as the crisis unfolded. First, the Federal Reserve cut its target for the federal funds rate from 5.25 per cent in September 2007 to about zero in December 2008. Second, in an even more unusual move in October 2008, the US Congress appropriated $700 billion for the Treasury to use to rescue the financial system. Much of these funds were used for equity injections into banks. That is, the Treasury put funds into the banking system, which the banks could use to make loans; in exchange for these funds, the US government became a part owner of these banks, at least temporarily. The goal of the rescue (or 'bailout', as it was sometimes called) was to stem the financial crisis on Wall Street and prevent it from causing a depression on every other street in America. This picture was repeated in the UK and many European countries as the effects of the financial crisis spread.

Recovery from this recession has been slow in many countries. Economic growth has been weak, and many economies have experienced 'double dip' recessions – a second recession before the economy had fully recovered from the previous one. Although policy makers could take some credit for having averted another Great Depression, there is no doubt that the financial crisis of 2008–2009 and its aftermath was a painful event for many families. ∎

12-4 Conclusion

The purpose of this chapter and the previous one has been to deepen our understanding of aggregate demand. We now have the tools to analyse the effects of monetary and fiscal policy in the long run and in the short run. In the long run, prices are flexible, and we use the classical analysis of Parts II and III of this book. In the short run, prices are sticky, and we use the *IS-LM* model to examine how changes in policy influence the economy.

Although the model in this chapter provides the basic framework for analysing the economy in the short run, it is not the whole story. In Chapter 13 we examine how international interactions affect our theory of aggregate demand; in Chapter 14 we examine the theory behind short-run aggregate supply; and in Chapter 15 we consider how this theoretical framework should be applied to the making of stabilization policy. In addition, in later chapters, we examine in more detail the elements of the *IS-LM* model, thereby refining our understanding of aggregate demand. In Chapter 18, for example, we study theories of consumption. Because the consumption function is a crucial piece of the *IS-LM* model, a deeper analysis of consumption may modify our view of the impact of monetary and fiscal policy on the economy. The simple *IS-LM* model presented in Chapters 11 and 12 provides the starting point for this further analysis.

Summary

1. The *IS-LM* model is a general theory of the aggregate demand for goods and services. The exogenous variables in the model are fiscal policy, monetary policy and the price level. The model explains two endogenous variables: the interest rate and the level of national income.

2. The *IS* curve represents the negative relationship between the interest rate and the level of income that arises from equilibrium in the market for goods and services. The *LM* curve represents the positive relationship between the interest rate and the level of income that arises from equilibrium in the market for real money balances. Equilibrium in the *IS-LM* model – the intersection of the *IS* and *LM* curves – represents simultaneous equilibrium in the market for goods and services and in the market for real money balances.

3. The aggregate demand curve summarizes the results from the *IS-LM* model by showing equilibrium income at any given price level. The aggregate demand curve slopes downward because a lower price level increases real money balances, lowers the interest rate, stimulates investment spending and thereby raises equilibrium income.

4. Expansionary fiscal policy – an increase in government purchases or a decrease in taxes – shifts the *IS* curve to the right. This shift in the *IS* curve increases the interest rate and income. The increase in income represents a rightward shift in the aggregate demand curve. Similarly, contractionary fiscal policy shifts the *IS* curve to the left, lowers the interest rate and income, and shifts the aggregate demand curve to the left.

5. Expansionary monetary policy shifts the *LM* curve downward. This shift in the *LM* curve lowers the interest rate and raises income. The increase in income represents a rightward shift of the aggregate demand curve. Similarly, contractionary monetary policy shifts the *LM* curve upward, raises the interest rate, lowers income and shifts the aggregate demand curve to the left.

KEY CONCEPTS

Monetary transmission mechanism	Pigou effect	Debt–deflation theory

QUESTIONS FOR REVIEW

1. Explain why the aggregate demand curve slopes downward.

2. What is the impact of an increase in taxes on the interest rate, income, consumption and investment?

3. What is the impact of a decrease in the money supply on the interest rate, income, consumption and investment?

4. Describe the possible effects of falling prices on equilibrium income.

PROBLEMS AND APPLICATIONS

1. According to the *IS-LM* model, what happens to the interest rate, income, consumption and investment under the following circumstances?

   a. The central bank increases the money supply.

   b. The government increases government purchases.

   c. The government increases taxes.

   d. The government increases government purchases and taxes by equal amounts.

2. Use the *IS-LM* model to predict the effects of each of the following shocks on income, the interest rate, consumption and investment. In each case, explain what the central bank should do to keep income at its initial level.

   a. After the invention of a new high-speed computer chip, many firms decide to upgrade their computer systems.

   b. A wave of credit card fraud increases the frequency with which people make transactions in cash.

   c. A bestseller titled *Retire Rich* convinces the public to increase the percentage of their income devoted to saving.

3. Consider the economy of Hicksonia.

   a. The consumption function is given by

   $$C = 200 + 0.75(Y - T).$$

   The investment function is

   $$I = 200 - 25r.$$

   Government purchases and taxes are both 100. For this economy, graph the *IS* curve for *r* ranging from 0 to 8.

   b. The money demand function in Hicksonia is

   $$(M/P)^d = Y - 100r.$$

   The money supply *M* is 1000 and the price level *P* is 2. For this economy, graph the *LM* curve for *r* ranging from 0 to 8.

   c. Find the equilibrium interest rate *r* and the equilibrium level of income *Y*.

   d. Suppose that government purchases are raised from 100 to 150. How much does the *IS* curve shift? What are the new equilibrium interest rate and level of income?

   e. Suppose instead that the money supply is raised from 1000 to 1200. How much does the *LM* curve shift? What are the new equilibrium interest rate and level of income?

   f. With the initial values for monetary and fiscal policy, suppose that the price level rises from 2 to 4. What happens? What are the new equilibrium interest rate and level of income?

   g. Derive and graph an equation for the aggregate demand curve. What happens to this aggregate demand curve if fiscal or monetary policy changes, as in parts (d) and (e)?

4. Explain why each of the following statements is true. Discuss the impact of monetary and fiscal policy in each of these special cases.

   a. If investment does not depend on the interest rate, the *IS* curve is vertical.

   b. If money demand does not depend on the interest rate, the *LM* curve is vertical.

   c. If money demand does not depend on income, the *LM* curve is horizontal.

   d. If money demand is extremely sensitive to the interest rate, the *LM* curve is horizontal.

5. Suppose that the government wants to raise investment but keep output constant. In the

ISLM model, what mix of monetary and fiscal policy will achieve this goal? Suppose the government cuts taxes and runs a budget deficit while the central bank pursues a tight monetary policy. What effect should this policy mix have?

6. Use the *IS-LM* diagram to describe the short-run and long-run effects of the following changes on national income, the interest rate, the price level, consumption, investment and real money balances.

   a. An increase in the money supply.

   b. An increase in government purchases.

   c. An increase in taxes.

7. The central bank is considering two alternative monetary policies:

   • holding the money supply constant and letting the interest rate adjust, or

   • adjusting the money supply to hold the interest rate constant.

In the *IS-LM* model, which policy will better stabilize output under the following conditions?

   a. All shocks to the economy arise from exogenous changes in the demand for goods and services.

   b. All shocks to the economy arise from exogenous changes in the demand for money.

8. Suppose that the demand for real money balances depends on disposable income. That is, the money demand function is

$$M/P = L(r, Y - T).$$

Using the *IS-LM* model, discuss whether this change in the money demand function alters the following:

   a. The analysis of changes in government purchases.

   b. The analysis of changes in taxes.

The Simple Algebra of the *IS-LM* Model and the Aggregate Demand Curve

The chapter analyses the *IS-LM* model with graphs of the *IS* and *LM* curves. Here we analyse the model with algebra. This alternative presentation offers additional insight into how monetary and fiscal policy influence aggregate demand.

The *IS* Curve

One way to think about the *IS* curve is that it describes the combinations of income Y and the interest rate r that satisfy an equation we first saw in Chapter 3:

$$Y = C(Y - T) + I(r) + G.$$

This equation combines the national income accounts identity, the consumption function and the investment function. It states that the quantity of goods produced, Y, must equal the quantity of goods demanded, $C + I + G$.

We can learn more about the *IS* curve by considering the special case in which the consumption function and investment function are linear. That is, suppose that the consumption function is

$$C(Y - T) = a + b(Y - T),$$

where a and b are numbers greater than zero. The parameter b is the marginal propensity to consume, so we expect b to be between zero and one. The parameter a influences the level of consumption; it captures everything that affects consumer spending other than disposable income. Similarly, suppose the investment function is

$$I(r) = c - dr,$$

where c and d are also numbers greater than zero. The parameter d determines how much investment responds to the interest rate; because investment rises when the interest rate falls, there is a minus sign in front of d. The parameter c influences the level of investment; it captures everything that affects investment spending other than the interest rate.

We can now derive an algebraic expression for the *IS* curve and see what influences the *IS* curve's position and slope. If we substitute the consumption and investment functions into the goods market equilibrium condition, we obtain

$$Y = [a + b(Y - T)] + (c - dr) + G.$$

Note that Y shows up on both sides of this equation. We can simplify this equation by bringing all the Y terms to the left-hand side and rearranging the terms on the right-hand side:

$$Y - bY = (a + c) + (G - bT) - dr.$$

We solve for Y to get

$$Y = \frac{a + c}{1 - b} + \frac{1}{1 - b} G + \frac{-b}{1 - b} T + \frac{-d}{1 - b} r.$$

This equation expresses the *IS* curve algebraically. It tells us the level of income Y for any given interest rate r and fiscal policy G and T. Holding fiscal policy fixed, the equation gives us a relationship between the interest rate and the level of income: the higher the interest rate, the lower the level of income. The *IS* curve graphs this equation for different values of Y and r given fixed values of G and T.

Using this last equation, we can verify our previous conclusions about the *IS* curve. First, because the coefficient of the interest rate is negative, the *IS* curve slopes downward: higher interest rates reduce income. Second, because the coefficient of government purchases is positive, an increase in government purchases shifts the *IS* curve to the right. Third, because the coefficient of taxes is negative, an increase in taxes shifts the *IS* curve to the left.

The coefficient of the interest rate, $-d/(1 - b)$, tells us what determines whether the *IS* curve is steep or flat. If investment is highly sensitive to the interest rate, then d is large, and income is highly sensitive to the interest rate as well. In this case, small changes in the interest rate lead to large changes in income: the *IS* curve is relatively flat. Conversely, if investment is not very sensitive to the interest rate, then d is small, and income is not very sensitive to the interest rate either. In this case, large changes in interest rates lead to small changes in income: the *IS* curve is relatively steep.

Similarly, the slope of the *IS* curve depends on the marginal propensity to consume b. The larger the marginal propensity to consume, the larger the change in income resulting from a given change in the interest rate. The reason is that a large marginal propensity to consume leads to a large multiplier for changes in investment. The larger the multiplier, the larger the impact of a change in investment on income, and the flatter the *IS* curve.

The marginal propensity to consume b also determines how much changes in fiscal policy shift the *IS* curve. The coefficient of G, $1/(1 - b)$, is the government-purchases multiplier in the Keynesian cross. Similarly, the coefficient of T, $-b/(1 - b)$, is the tax multiplier in the Keynesian cross. The larger the marginal propensity to consume, the greater the multiplier, and thus the greater the shift in the *IS* curve that arises from a change in fiscal policy.

The *LM* Curve

The *LM* curve describes the combinations of income Y and the interest rate r that satisfy the money market equilibrium condition

$$M/P = L(r, Y).$$

This equation simply equates money supply and money demand.

We can learn more about the *LM* curve by considering the case in which the money demand function is linear — that is,

$$L(r, Y) = eY - fr,$$

where e and f are numbers greater than zero. The value of e determines how much the demand for money rises when income rises. The value of f determines how much the demand for money falls when the interest rate rises. There is a minus sign in front of the interest rate term because money demand is inversely related to the interest rate.

The equilibrium in the money market is now described by

$$M/P = eY - fr.$$

To see what this equation implies, rearrange the terms so that r is on the left-hand side. We obtain

$$r = (e/f)Y - (1/f)M/P.$$

This equation gives us the interest rate that equilibrates the money market for any values of income and real money balances. The *LM* curve graphs this equation for different values of Y and r given a fixed value of M/P.

From this last equation, we can verify some of our conclusions about the *LM* curve. First, because the coefficient of income is positive, the *LM* curve slopes upward: higher income requires a higher interest rate to equilibrate the money market. Second, because the coefficient of real money balances is negative, decreases in real balances shift the *LM* curve upward, and increases in real balances shift the *LM* curve downward.

From the coefficient of income, e/f, we can see what determines whether the *LM* curve is steep or flat. If money demand is not very sensitive to the level of income, then e is small. In this case, only a small change in the interest rate is necessary to offset the small increase in money demand caused by a change in income: the *LM* curve is relatively flat. Similarly, if the quantity of money demanded is not very sensitive to the interest rate, then f is small. In this case, a shift in money demand due to a change in income leads to a large change in the equilibrium interest rate: the *LM* curve is relatively steep.

The Aggregate Demand Curve

To find the aggregate demand equation, we must find the level of income that satisfies both the *IS* equation and the *LM* equation. To do this, substitute the *LM* equation for the interest rate r into the *IS* equation to obtain

$$Y = \frac{a + c}{1 - b} + \frac{1}{1 - b}G + \frac{-b}{1 - b}T + \frac{-d}{1 - b}[(e/f)Y - (1/f)M/P].$$

With some algebraic manipulation, we can solve for Y. The final equation for Y is

$$Y = \frac{z(a + c)}{1 - b} + \frac{z}{1 - b}G + \frac{-zb}{1 - b}T + \frac{d}{(1 - b)[f + de/(1 - b)]}M/P,$$

where $z = f/[f + de/(1 - b)]$ is a composite of some of the parameters and is between zero and one.

This last equation expresses the aggregate demand curve algebraically. It says that income depends on fiscal policy, G and T, monetary policy M and the price level P. The aggregate demand curve graphs this equation for different values of Y and P given fixed values of G, T and M.

We can explain the slope and position of the aggregate demand curve with this equation. First, the aggregate demand curve slopes downward because an increase in P lowers M/P and thus lowers Y. Second, increases in the money supply raise income and shift the aggregate demand curve to the right. Third, increases in government purchases or decreases in taxes also raise income and shift the aggregate demand curve to the right. Note that, because z is less than 1, the multipliers for fiscal policy are smaller in the *IS-LM* model than in the Keynesian cross. Hence, the parameter z reflects the crowding out of investment discussed earlier.

Finally, this equation shows the relationship between the aggregate demand curve derived in this chapter from the *IS-LM* model and the aggregate demand curve derived in Chapter 10 from the quantity theory of money. The quantity theory assumes that the interest rate does not influence the quantity of real money balances demanded. Put differently, the quantity theory assumes that the parameter f equals zero. If f equals zero, then the composite parameter z also equals zero, so fiscal policy does not influence aggregate demand. Thus, the aggregate demand curve derived in Chapter 10 is a special case of the aggregate demand curve derived here.

CASE STUDY

The Effectiveness of Monetary and Fiscal Policy

Economists have long debated whether monetary or fiscal policy exerts a more powerful influence on aggregate demand. According to the *IS-LM* model, the answer to this question depends on the parameters of the *IS* and *LM* curves. Therefore, economists have spent much energy arguing about the size of these parameters. The most hotly contested parameters are those that describe the influence of the interest rate on economic decisions.

Those economists who believe that fiscal policy is more potent than monetary policy argue that the responsiveness of investment to the interest rate – measured by the parameter d – is small. If you look at the algebraic equation for aggregate demand, you will see that a small value of d implies a small effect of the money supply on income. The reason is that when d is small, the *IS* curve is nearly vertical, and shifts in the *LM* curve do not cause much of a change in income. In addition, a small value of d implies a large value of z, which in turn implies that fiscal policy has a large effect on income. The reason for this large effect is that when investment is not very responsive to the interest rate, there is little crowding out.

Those economists who believe that monetary policy is more potent than fiscal policy argue that the responsiveness of money demand to the interest rate –

measured by the parameter f – is small. When f is small, z is small, and fiscal policy has a small effect on income; in this case, the LM curve is nearly vertical. In addition, when f is small, changes in the money supply have a large effect on income.

Few economists in the early 21st century endorse either of these extreme views. The evidence indicates that the interest rate affects both investment and money demand. This finding implies that both monetary and fiscal policy are important determinants of aggregate demand. ■

MORE PROBLEMS AND APPLICATIONS

1. Give an algebraic answer to each of the following questions. Then explain in words the economics that underlies your answer.

   a. How does the sensitivity of investment to the interest rate affect the slope of the aggregate demand curve?

   b. How does the sensitivity of money demand to the interest rate affect the slope of the aggregate demand curve?

   c. How does the marginal propensity to consume affect the response of aggregate demand to changes in government purchases?

The Open Economy Revisited: The Mundell–Fleming Model and the Exchange-Rate Regime

The world is still a closed economy, but its regions and countries are becoming increasingly open . . . The international economic climate has changed in the direction of financial integration, and this has important implications for economic policy.

– Robert Mundell, 1963

When conducting monetary and fiscal policy, policy makers often look beyond their own country's borders. Even if domestic prosperity is their sole objective, it is necessary for them to consider the rest of the world. The international flow of goods and services and the international flow of capital can affect an economy in profound ways. Policy makers ignore these effects at their peril. This is especially true of European economies, where exports and imports typically account for a large proportion of GDP.

In this chapter we extend our analysis of aggregate demand to include international trade and finance. The model developed in this chapter is called the **Mundell–Fleming model**. This model has been described as 'the dominant policy paradigm for studying open-economy monetary and fiscal policy'. In 1999, Robert Mundell was awarded the Nobel Prize for his work in open-economy macroeconomics, including this model.[1]

The Mundell–Fleming model is a close relative of the *IS-LM* model. Both models stress the interaction between the goods market and the money market. Both models assume that the price level is fixed and then show what causes short-run fluctuations in aggregate income (or, equivalently, shifts in the aggregate demand curve). The key difference is that the *IS-LM* model assumes a closed economy, whereas the

---

[1] The quotation is from Maurice Obstfeld and Kenneth Rogoff, *Foundations of International Finance*, Cambridge, MA: The MIT Press, 1996 – a leading graduate-level textbook in open-economy macroeconomics. The Mundell–Fleming model was developed in the early 1960s. Mundell's contributions are collected in Robert A. Mundell, *International Economics*, 1968, New York: Macmillan. For Fleming's contribution, see J. Marcus Fleming, 'Domestic Financial Policies under Fixed and under Floating Exchange Rates', *IMF Staff Papers*, November 1962, vol. 9, pp. 369–379. Fleming died in 1976, so was not eligible to share in the Nobel award.

Mundell–Fleming model assumes an open economy. The Mundell–Fleming model extends the short-run model of national income from Chapters 11 and 12 by including the effects of international trade and finance discussed in Chapter 6.

The Mundell–Fleming model makes one important and extreme assumption: it assumes that the economy being studied is a small open economy with perfect capital mobility. That is, the economy can borrow or lend as much as it wants in world financial markets and, as a result, the economy's interest rate is determined by the world interest rate. Here is how Mundell himself motivated this assumption in his original 1963 article:

> In order to present my conclusions in the simplest possible way and to bring the implications for policy into sharpest relief, I assume the extreme degree of mobility that prevails when a country cannot maintain an interest rate different from the general level prevailing abroad. This assumption will overstate the case but it has the merit of posing a stereotype towards which international financial relations seem to be heading. At the same time it might be argued that the assumption is not far from the truth in those financial centres, of which Zurich, Amsterdam, and Brussels may be taken as examples, where the authorities already recognize their lessening ability to dominate money market conditions and insulate them from foreign influences. It should also have a high degree of relevance to a country like Canada whose financial markets are dominated to a great degree by the vast New York market.

As we will see, Mundell's assumption of a small open economy with perfect capital mobility will prove useful in developing a tractable and illuminating model.

One lesson from the Mundell–Fleming model is that the behaviour of an economy depends on the exchange-rate system it has adopted. Indeed, the model was first developed in large part to understand how alternative exchange-rate regimes work, and how the choice of exchange-rate regime impinges on monetary and fiscal policy. We begin by assuming that the economy operates with a floating exchange rate. That is, we assume that the central bank allows the exchange rate to adjust to changing economic conditions. We then examine how the economy operates under a fixed exchange rate. After developing the model, we will be in a position to address an important policy question: What exchange rate system should a nation adopt?

These issues of open-economy macroeconomics have been very much in the news in recent years. As various European nations, most notably Greece, experienced severe financial difficulties, many observers wondered whether it was wise for much of the continent to adopt a common currency – the most extreme form of a fixed exchange rate. If each nation had its own currency, monetary policy and the exchange rate could have more easily adjusted to the changing individual circumstances and needs of each nation. Meanwhile, many American policy makers, including both President George W. Bush and President Barack Obama, were objecting that China did not allow the value of its currency to float freely against the US dollar. They argued that China kept its currency artificially cheap, making its goods more competitive on world markets. As we will see, the Mundell–Fleming model offers a useful starting point for understanding and evaluating these often heated international policy debates.

13-1 The Mundell–Fleming Model

In this section we construct the Mundell–Fleming model, and in the following sections we use the model to examine the impact of various policies. As you will see, the Mundell–Fleming model is built from components we have used in previous chapters. But these pieces are put together in a new way to address a new set of questions.

The Key Assumption: Small Open Economy with Perfect Capital Mobility

Let's begin with the assumption of a small open economy with perfect capital mobility. As we saw in Chapter 6, this assumption means that the interest rate in this economy r is determined by the world interest rate r^*. Mathematically, we can write this assumption as

$$r = r^*.$$

This world interest rate is assumed to be exogenously fixed because the economy is small enough, relative to the world economy, to enable it to borrow or lend as much as it wants in world financial markets, without affecting the world interest rate.

Although the idea of perfect capital mobility is expressed with a simple equation, it is important not to lose sight of the sophisticated process that this equation represents. Imagine that some event were to occur that would normally raise the interest rate (such as a decline in domestic saving). In a small open economy, the domestic interest rate might rise a little for a short time, but as soon as it did foreigners would see the higher interest rate and start lending to this country (by, for instance, buying this country's bonds). The capital inflow would drive the domestic interest rate back towards r^*. Similarly, if any event were ever to start driving the domestic interest rate downward, capital would flow out of the country to earn a higher return abroad, and this capital outflow would drive the domestic interest rate back up to r^*. Hence, the $r = r^*$ equation represents the assumption that the international flow of capital is rapid enough to keep the domestic interest rate equal to the world interest rate.

The Goods Market and the *IS** Curve

The Mundell–Fleming model describes the market for goods and services much as the *IS-LM* model does, but it adds a new term for net exports. In particular, the goods market is represented with the following equation:

$$Y = C(Y - T) + I(r) + G + NX(e).$$

This equation states that aggregate income Y is the sum of consumption C, investment I, government purchases G and net exports NX. Consumption depends positively on disposable income $Y - T$. Investment depends negatively on the interest rate. Net exports depend negatively on the exchange rate e. As before, we define the exchange rate e as the amount of foreign currency per unit of domestic currency – for example, e might be 100 yen per euro.

You may recall that in Chapter 6 we related net exports to the real exchange rate (the relative price of goods at home and abroad) rather than the nominal exchange rate (the relative price of domestic and foreign currencies). If e is the nominal exchange rate, then the real exchange rate ε equals eP/P^*, where P is the domestic price level and P^* is the foreign price level. The Mundell–Fleming model, however, assumes that the price levels at home and abroad are fixed, so the real exchange rate is proportional to the nominal exchange rate. That is, when the nominal exchange rate appreciates (say, from 100 to 120 yen per euro), foreign goods become cheaper compared to domestic goods, and this causes exports to fall and imports to rise.

The goods market equilibrium condition above has two financial variables affecting expenditure on goods and services (the interest rate and the exchange rate), but the situation can be simplified using the assumption of perfect capital mobility, so $r = r^*$. We obtain

$$Y = C(Y - T) + I(r^*) + G + NX(e). \qquad IS^*$$

Let's call this the IS^* equation. (The asterisk reminds us that the equation holds the interest rate constant at the world interest rate r^*.) We can illustrate this equation on a graph in which income is on the horizontal axis and the exchange rate is on the vertical axis. This curve is shown in panel (c) of Figure 13-1.

The IS^* curve slopes downward because a higher exchange rate reduces net exports, which in turn lowers aggregate income. To show how this works, the other panels of Figure 13-1 combine the net-exports schedule and the Keynesian cross to derive the IS^* curve. In panel (a) an increase in the exchange rate from e_1 to e_2 lowers net exports from $NX(e_1)$ to $NX(e_2)$. In panel (b) the reduction in net exports shifts the planned-expenditure schedule downward and thus lowers income from Y_1 to Y_2. The IS^* curves summarizes this relationship between the exchange rate e and income Y.

The Money Market and the *LM** Curve

The Mundell–Fleming model represents the money market with an equation that should be familiar from the *IS-LM* model:

$$M/P = L(r, Y).$$

This equation states that the supply of real money balances, M/P, equals the demand, $L(r, Y)$. The demand for real balances depends negatively on the interest rate and positively on income Y. The money supply M is an exogenous variable controlled by the central bank, and because the Mundell–Fleming model is designed to analyse short-run fluctuations, the price level P is also assumed to be exogenously fixed.

Once again, we add the assumption that the domestic interest rate equals the world interest rate, so $r = r^*$:

$$M/P = L(r^*, Y). \qquad LM^*$$

FIGURE 13-1

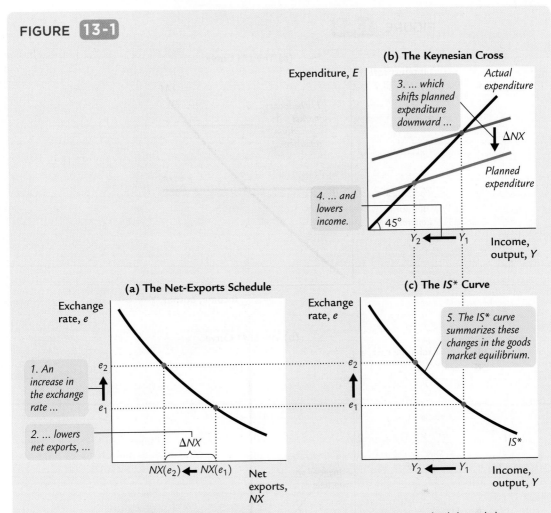

The _IS*_ Curve The _IS*_ curve is derived from the net-exports schedule and the Keynesian cross. Panel (a) shows the net-exports schedule: an increase in the exchange rate from e_1 to e_2 lowers net exports from $NX(e_1)$ to $NX(e_2)$. Panel (b) shows the Keynesian cross: a decrease in net exports from $NX(e_1)$ to $NX(e_2)$ shifts the planned-expenditure schedule downward and reduces income from Y_1 to Y_2. Panel (c) shows the _IS*_ curve summarizing this relationship between the exchange rate and income: the higher the exchange rate, the lower the level of income.

Let's call this the _LM*_ equation. We can represent it graphically with a vertical curve, as in panel (b) of Figure 13-2. The _LM*_ curve is vertical because the exchange rate does not enter into the _LM*_ equation. Given the world interest rate, the _LM*_ equation determines aggregate income, regardless of the exchange rate. Figure 13-2 shows how the _LM*_ curve arises from the world interest rate and the _LM_ curve, which relates the interest rate and income.

FIGURE 13-2

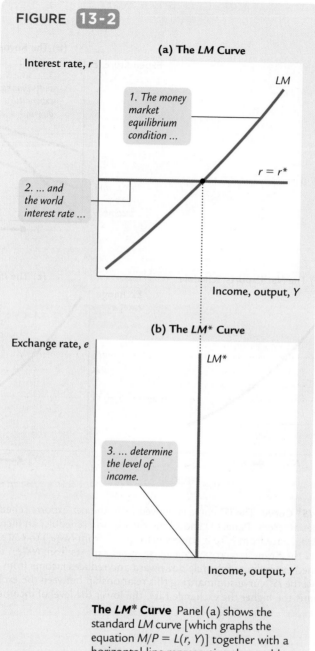

(a) The LM Curve

Interest rate, r

LM

1. The money market equilibrium condition ...

2. ... and the world interest rate ...

r = r*

Income, output, Y

(b) The LM* Curve

Exchange rate, e

LM*

3. ... determine the level of income.

Income, output, Y

The LM* Curve Panel (a) shows the standard *LM* curve [which graphs the equation $M/P = L(r, Y)$] together with a horizontal line representing the world interest rate r^*. The intersection of these two curves determines the level of income, regardless of the exchange rate. Therefore, as panel (b) shows, the *LM** curve is vertical.

FIGURE 13-3

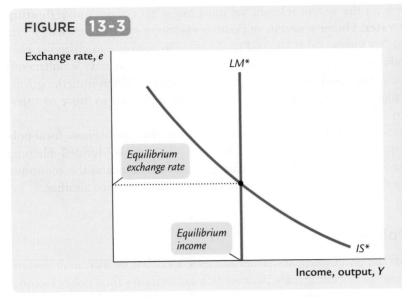

Exchange rate, *e*

LM*

Equilibrium
exchange rate

Equilibrium
income

IS*

Income, output, *Y*

**The Mundell–Fleming
Model** This graph of the
Mundell-Fleming model plots
the goods market equilibrium
condition *IS** and the money
market equilibrium condition
*LM**. Both curves are drawn
holding the interest rate
constant at the world interest
rate. The intersection of these
two curves shows the level of
income and the exchange rate
that satisfy equilibrium both in
the goods market and in the
money market.

Putting the Pieces Together

According to the Mundell–Fleming model, a small open economy with perfect
capital mobility can be described by two equations:

$$Y = C(Y - T) + I(r^*) + G + NX(e), \qquad IS^*$$

$$M/P = L(r^*, Y). \qquad LM^*$$

The first equation describes equilibrium in the goods market, and the second
equation describes equilibrium in the money market. The exogenous variables
are fiscal policy *G* and *T*, monetary policy *M*, the price level *P* and the world
interest rate r^*. The endogenous variables are income *Y* and the exchange rate *e*.

Figure 13-3 illustrates these two relationships. The equilibrium for the economy is found where the *IS** curve and the *LM** curve intersect. This intersection
shows the exchange rate and the level of income at which the goods market and
the money market are in equilibrium. With this diagram, we can use the
Mundell–Fleming model to show how aggregate income *Y* and the exchange
rate *e* respond to changes in policy.

13-2 The Small Open Economy under Floating Exchange Rates

Analysing the impact of policies in an open economy, we must specify the international monetary system in which the country has chosen to operate. That is,
we must consider how people engaged in international trade and finance can
convert the currency of one country into the currency of another.

We start with the system relevant for most major economies today: **floating exchange rates**. Under a system of floating exchange rates, the exchange rate is set by market forces and is allowed to fluctuate in response to changing economic conditions. In this case, the exchange rate adjusts to achieve simultaneous equilibrium in the goods market and the money market. When something happens to change that equilibrium, the exchange rate is allowed to move to a new equilibrium value.

Let's now consider three policies that can change the equilibrium: fiscal policy, monetary policy and trade policy. Our goal is to use the Mundell–Fleming model to show the impact of policy changes and to understand the economic forces at work as the economy moves from one equilibrium to another.

Fiscal Policy

Suppose that the government stimulates domestic spending by increasing government purchases or by cutting taxes. Because such expansionary fiscal policy increases planned expenditure, it shifts the IS^* curve to the right, as in Figure 13-4. As a result, the exchange rate appreciates, while the level of income remains the same.

Notice that fiscal policy has very different effects in a small open economy compared to a closed economy. In the closed-economy $IS\text{-}LM$ model, a fiscal expansion raises income, whereas in a small open economy with a floating exchange rate, a fiscal expansion leaves income at the same level. Mechanically,

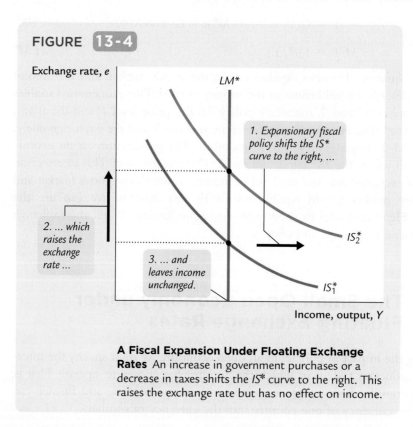

FIGURE 13-4

Exchange rate, e

LM*

1. Expansionary fiscal policy shifts the IS^* curve to the right, ...

2. ... which raises the exchange rate ...

3. ... and leaves income unchanged.

IS_2^*

IS_1^*

Income, output, Y

A Fiscal Expansion Under Floating Exchange Rates An increase in government purchases or a decrease in taxes shifts the IS^* curve to the right. This raises the exchange rate but has no effect on income.

the difference arises because the LM^* curve is vertical, while the LM curve we used to study a closed economy is upward sloping. But this explanation is not very satisfying. What are the economic forces that lie behind the different outcomes? To answer this question, we must think through what is happening to the international flow of capital and the implications of these capital flows for the domestic economy.

The interest rate and the exchange rate are the key variables in the story. When income rises in a closed economy, the interest rate rises, because higher income increases the demand for money. That is not possible in a small open economy because, as soon as the interest rate starts to rise above the world interest rate r^*, capital quickly flows in from abroad to take advantage of the higher return. This capital inflow not only pushes the interest rate back to r^*, but it also has another effect: because foreign investors need to buy the domestic currency to invest in the domestic economy, the capital inflow increases the demand for the domestic currency in the market for foreign-currency exchange, bidding up the value of the domestic currency. The appreciation of the domestic currency makes domestic goods expensive relative to foreign goods, reducing net exports. The fall in net exports exactly offsets the effects of the expansionary fiscal policy on income.

Why is the fall in net exports so great that it renders fiscal policy powerless to influence income? To answer this question, consider the equation that describes the money market:

$$M/P = L(r, Y).$$

In both closed and open economies, the quantity of real money balances supplied M/P is fixed by the central bank (which sets M) and the assumption of sticky prices (which fixes P). The quantity demanded (determined by r and Y) must equal this fixed supply. In a closed economy, a fiscal expansion causes the equilibrium interest rate to rise. This increase in the interest rate (which reduces the quantity of money demanded) allows equilibrium income to rise (which increases the quantity of money demanded). By contrast, in a small open economy, r is fixed at r^*, so there is only one level of income that can satisfy this equation, and this level of income does not change when fiscal policy changes. Thus, when the government increases spending or cuts taxes, the appreciation of the exchange rate and the fall in net exports must be large enough to offset fully the expansionary effect of the policy on income.

Monetary Policy

Suppose now that the central bank increases the money supply. Because the price level is assumed to be fixed, the increase in the money supply means an increase in real money balances. The increase in real balances shifts the LM^* curve to the right, as in Figure 13-5. Hence, an increase in the money supply raises income and lowers the exchange rate.

Although monetary policy influences income in an open economy, as it does in a closed economy, the monetary transmission mechanism is different. Recall that in a closed economy an increase in the money supply increases

FIGURE 13-5

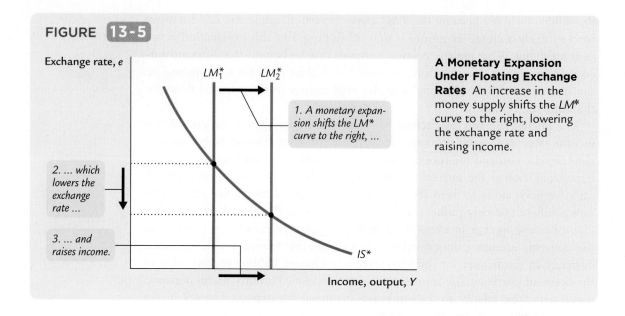

Exchange rate, e

LM_1^* LM_2^*

1. A monetary expansion shifts the LM* curve to the right, ...

2. ... which lowers the exchange rate ...

3. ... and raises income.

IS^*

Income, output, Y

A Monetary Expansion Under Floating Exchange Rates An increase in the money supply shifts the LM^* curve to the right, lowering the exchange rate and raising income.

spending, because it lowers the interest rate and stimulates investment. In a small open economy, this channel of monetary transmission is not available, because the interest rate is fixed by the world interest rate. So how does monetary policy influence spending? To answer this question, once again we need to think about the international flow of capital and its implications for the domestic economy.

The interest rate and the exchange rate are again the key variables. As soon as an increase in the money supply starts putting downward pressure on the domestic interest rate, capital flows out of the economy, as investors seek a higher return elsewhere. This capital outflow prevents the domestic interest rate from falling below the world interest rate r^*. It also has another effect: because investing abroad requires converting domestic currency into foreign currency, the capital outflow increases the supply of the domestic currency in the market for foreign-currency exchange, causing the domestic currency to depreciate in value. This depreciation makes domestic goods inexpensive relative to foreign goods, stimulating net exports. Hence, in a small open economy, monetary policy influences income by altering the exchange rate rather than the interest rate.

Trade Policy

Suppose that the government reduces the demand for imported goods by imposing an import quota or a tariff. What happens to aggregate income and the exchange rate? How does the economy reach its new equilibrium?

Because net exports equal exports minus imports, a reduction in imports means an increase in net exports. That is, the net-exports schedule shifts to the

FIGURE 13-6

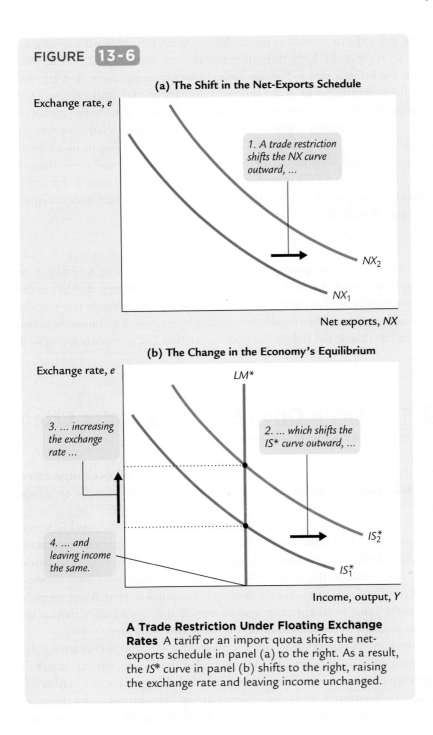

(a) The Shift in the Net-Exports Schedule

Exchange rate, e

1. A trade restriction shifts the NX curve outward, ...

NX_2

NX_1

Net exports, NX

(b) The Change in the Economy's Equilibrium

Exchange rate, e

LM^*

3. ... increasing the exchange rate ...

2. ... which shifts the IS^* curve outward, ...

4. ... and leaving income the same.

IS_2^*

IS_1^*

Income, output, Y

A Trade Restriction Under Floating Exchange Rates A tariff or an import quota shifts the net-exports schedule in panel (a) to the right. As a result, the IS^* curve in panel (b) shifts to the right, raising the exchange rate and leaving income unchanged.

right, as in Figure 13-6. This shift in the net-exports schedule increases planned expenditure and thus moves the IS^* curve to the right. Because the LM^* curve is vertical, the trade restriction raises the exchange rate but does not affect income.

The economic forces behind this transition are similar to the case of expansionary fiscal policy. Because net exports are a component of GDP, the rightward shift in the net-exports schedule, other things equal, puts upward pressure on income Y; an increase in Y, in turn, increases money demand and puts upward pressure on the interest rate r. Foreign capital quickly responds by flowing into the domestic economy, pushing the interest rate back to the world interest rate r^* and causing the domestic currency to appreciate in value. Finally, the appreciation of the currency makes domestic goods more expensive relative to foreign goods, which decreases net exports NX and returns income Y to its initial level.

Often a stated goal of policies to restrict trade is to alter the trade balance NX. Yet, as we first saw in Chapter 6, such policies do not necessarily have that effect. The same conclusion holds in the Mundell–Fleming model under floating exchange rates. Recall that

$$NX(e) = Y - C(Y - T) - I(r^*) - G.$$

Because a trade restriction does not affect income, consumption, investment or government purchases, it does not affect the trade balance. Although the shift in the net-exports schedule tends to raise NX, the increase in the exchange rate reduces NX by the same amount. The overall effect is simply *less trade*. The domestic economy imports less than it did before the trade restriction, but it exports less as well.

13-3 The Small Open Economy under Fixed Exchange Rates

We now turn to the second type of exchange-rate system: **fixed exchange rates**. Under a fixed exchange rate, the central bank announces a value for the exchange rate and stands ready to buy and sell the domestic currency to keep the exchange rate at its announced level. In the 1950s and 1960s, most of the world's major economies operated within the Bretton Woods system – an international monetary system under which most governments agreed to fix exchange rates. The world abandoned this system in the early 1970s, and most exchange rates were allowed to float. Yet fixed exchange rates are not merely of historical interest. More recently, China fixed the value of its currency against the US dollar – a policy that, as we will see, was a source of some tension between the two countries.

In this section we discuss how such a system works, and we examine the impact of economic policies on an economy with a fixed exchange rate. Later in the chapter we examine the pros and cons of fixed exchange rates. In Chapter 17, we shall discuss the more radical case where a group of countries adopt the same currency (form a monetary union) and so effectively fix their exchange rates between one another at 1.

How a Fixed-Exchange-Rate System Works

Under a system of fixed exchange rates, a central bank stands ready to buy or sell the domestic currency for foreign currencies at a predetermined price.

For example, suppose the central bank announced that it was going to fix the exchange rate at 100 yen per euro. It would then stand ready to give €1 in exchange for 100 yen, or to give 100 yen in exchange for €1. To carry out this policy, the central bank would need a reserve of euros (which it can print) and a reserve of yen (which it must have purchased previously).

A fixed exchange rate dedicates a country's monetary policy to the single goal of keeping the exchange rate at the announced level. In other words, the essence of a fixed-exchange-rate system is the commitment of the central bank to allow the money supply to adjust to whatever level will ensure that the equilibrium exchange rate in the market for foreign-currency exchange equals the announced exchange rate. Moreover, as long as the central bank stands ready to buy or sell foreign currency at the fixed exchange rate, the money supply adjusts automatically to the necessary level.

To see how fixing the exchange rate determines the money supply, consider the following example. Suppose the central bank announces that it will fix the exchange rate at 100 yen per euro, but, in the current equilibrium with the current money supply, the market exchange rate is 150 yen per euro. This situation is illustrated in panel (a) of Figure 13-7. Notice that there is a profit opportunity: an arbitrageur could buy 300 yen in the foreign exchange market for €2, and then sell the yen to the central bank for €3, making a €1 profit. When the central bank buys these yen from the arbitrageur, the euros it pays for them automatically

FIGURE 13-7

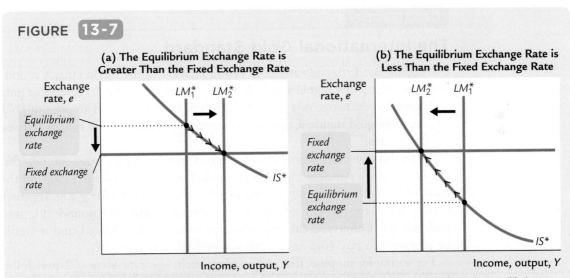

(a) The Equilibrium Exchange Rate is Greater Than the Fixed Exchange Rate

(b) The Equilibrium Exchange Rate is Less Than the Fixed Exchange Rate

How a Fixed Exchange Rate Governs the Money Supply In panel (a) the equilibrium exchange rate initially exceeds the fixed level. Arbitrageurs will buy foreign currency in foreign-exchange markets and sell it to the central bank for a profit. This process automatically increases the money supply, shifting the LM^* curve to the right and lowering the exchange rate. In panel (b) the equilibrium exchange rate is initially below the fixed level. Arbitrageurs will buy domestic currency in foreign-exchange markets and use this to buy foreign currency from the central bank. This process automatically reduces the money supply, shifting the LM^* curve to the left and raising the exchange rate.

increase the money supply. The rise in the money supply shifts the LM^* curve to the right, lowering the equilibrium exchange rate. In this way, the money supply continues to rise until the equilibrium exchange rate falls to the announced level.

Conversely, suppose that when the central bank announces that it will fix the exchange rate at 100 yen per euro, the equilibrium has a market exchange rate of 50 yen per euro. Panel (b) of Figure 13-7 illustrates this situation. In this case, an arbitrageur could make a profit by buying 100 yen from the central bank for €1 and then selling the yen in the marketplace for €2. When the central bank sells these yen, the €1 it receives automatically reduces the money supply. The fall in the money supply shifts the LM^* curve to the left, raising the equilibrium exchange rate. The money supply continues to fall until the equilibrium exchange rate rises to the announced level.

It is important to understand that this exchange-rate system fixes the *nominal* exchange rate. Whether it also fixes the real exchange rate depends on the time horizon under consideration. If prices are flexible, as they are in the long run, then the real exchange rate can change even while the nominal exchange rate is fixed. Therefore, in the long run described in Chapter 6, a policy to fix the nominal exchange rate would not influence any real variable, including the real exchange rate. A fixed nominal exchange rate would influence only the money supply and the price level. Yet in the short run described by the Mundell–Fleming model, prices are fixed, so a fixed nominal exchange rate implies a fixed real exchange rate as well.

CASE STUDY

The International Gold Standard

During the late 19th and early 20th centuries, most of the world's major economies operated under a gold standard. Each country maintained a reserve of gold and agreed to exchange one unit of its currency for a specified amount of gold. Through the gold standard, the world's economies maintained a system of fixed exchange rates.

To see how an international gold standard fixes exchange rates, suppose that the US Treasury stands ready to buy or sell 1 ounce of gold for $100, and the Bank of England stands ready to buy or sell 1 ounce of gold for £100. Together, these policies fix the rate of exchange between dollars and pounds: $1 must trade for £1. Otherwise, the law of one price would be violated, and it would be profitable to buy gold in one country and sell it in the other.

For example, suppose that the market exchange rate were £2 per dollar. In this case, an arbitrageur could buy £200 for $100, use the pounds to buy 2 ounces of gold from the Bank of England, take the gold to the United States, and sell it to the US Treasury for $200 – making a $100 profit. Moreover, by taking the gold to the United States from the United Kingdom, the arbitrageur would increase the money supply in the US and decrease the money supply in the UK.

Thus, during the era of the gold standard, the international transport of gold by arbitrageurs was an automatic mechanism adjusting the money supply and

FIGURE 13-8

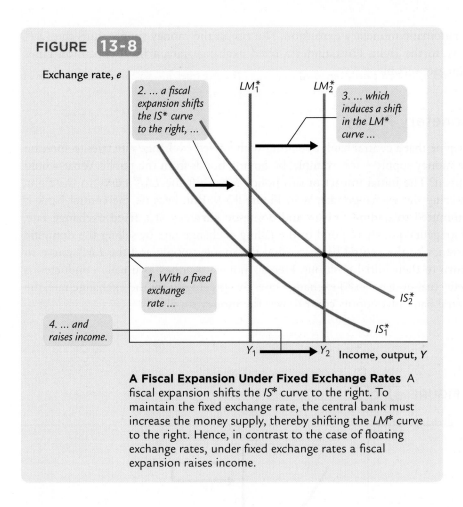

Exchange rate, e

2. ... a fiscal expansion shifts the IS^* curve to the right, ...

LM_1^*

LM_2^*

3. ... which induces a shift in the LM^* curve ...

1. With a fixed exchange rate ...

4. ... and raises income.

IS_2^*

IS_1^*

Y_1 Y_2 Income, output, Y

A Fiscal Expansion Under Fixed Exchange Rates A fiscal expansion shifts the IS^* curve to the right. To maintain the fixed exchange rate, the central bank must increase the money supply, thereby shifting the LM^* curve to the right. Hence, in contrast to the case of floating exchange rates, under fixed exchange rates a fiscal expansion raises income.

stabilizing exchange rates. This system did not completely fix exchange rates, because shipping gold across the Atlantic was costly. Yet the international gold standard did keep the exchange rate within a range dictated by transportation costs. It thereby prevented large and persistent movements in exchange rates.[2] ∎

Fiscal Policy

Let's now examine how economic policies affect a small open economy with a fixed exchange rate. Suppose that the government stimulates domestic spending by increasing government purchases or by cutting taxes. This policy shifts the IS^* curve to the right, as in Figure 13-8, putting upward pressure on the market exchange rate. But because the central bank stands ready to trade foreign and domestic currency at the fixed exchange rate, arbitrageurs quickly respond to the rising exchange rate by selling foreign currency to the central bank, leading to

[2] For more on how the gold standard worked, see the essays in Barry Eichengreen, ed., *The Gold Standard in Theory and History*, New York: Methuen, 1985.

an automatic monetary expansion. The rise in the money supply shifts the *LM** curve to the right. Thus, under a fixed exchange rate, a fiscal expansion raises aggregate income.

Monetary Policy

Imagine that a central bank operating with a fixed exchange rate tries to increase the money supply – for example, by buying bonds from the public. What would happen? The initial impact of this policy is to shift the *LM** curve to the right, lowering the exchange rate, as in Figure 13-9. But, because the central bank is committed to trading foreign and domestic currency at a fixed exchange rate, arbitrageurs quickly respond to the falling exchange rate by selling the domestic currency to the central bank, causing the money supply and the *LM** curve to return to their initial positions. Hence, monetary policy as usually conducted is ineffectual under a fixed exchange rate. By agreeing to fix the exchange rate, the central bank gives up its control over the money supply.

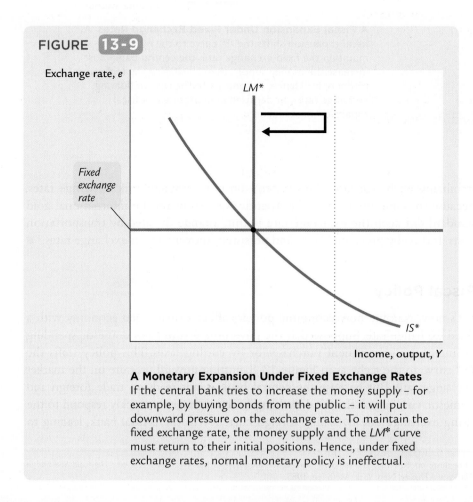

FIGURE 13-9

A Monetary Expansion Under Fixed Exchange Rates
If the central bank tries to increase the money supply – for example, by buying bonds from the public – it will put downward pressure on the exchange rate. To maintain the fixed exchange rate, the money supply and the *LM** curve must return to their initial positions. Hence, under fixed exchange rates, normal monetary policy is ineffectual.

A country with a fixed exchange rate, however, can conduct a type of monetary policy: it can decide to change the level at which the exchange rate is fixed. A reduction in the official value of the currency is called a **devaluation**, and an increase in its official value is called a **revaluation**. In the Mundell–Fleming model, a devaluation shifts the LM^* curve to the right; it acts like an increase in the money supply under a floating exchange rate. A devaluation thus expands net exports and raises aggregate income. Conversely, a revaluation shifts the LM^* curve to the left, reduces net exports and lowers aggregate income.

CASE STUDY

Devaluation and European Recovery from the Great Depression

The Great Depression of the 1930s was a global problem. Although events in the United States may have precipitated the downturn, all of the world's major economies experienced huge declines in production and employment. Yet not all governments responded to this calamity in the same way, and this was especially evident in Europe.

One key difference among governments was how committed they were to the fixed exchange rate set by the international gold standard. Some countries, such as France, Germany, Italy and the Netherlands, maintained the old rate of exchange between gold and currency. Other countries, such as Denmark, Finland, Norway, Sweden and the United Kingdom, reduced the amount of gold they would pay for each unit of currency by about 50 per cent. By reducing the gold content of their currencies, these governments devalued their currencies relative to those of other countries.

The subsequent experience of these two groups of countries conforms to the prediction of the Mundell–Fleming model. Those countries that pursued a policy of devaluation recovered quickly from the Great Depression. The lower value of the currency raised the money supply, stimulated exports and expanded production. By contrast, those countries that maintained the old exchange rate suffered longer with a depressed level of economic activity.[3] ■

Trade Policy

Suppose that the government reduces imports by imposing an import quota or a tariff. This policy shifts the net-exports schedule to the right and thus shifts the IS^* curve to the right, as in Figure 13-10. The shift in the IS^* curve tends to raise the exchange rate. To keep the exchange rate at the fixed level, the money supply must rise, shifting the LM^* curve to the right.

The result of a trade restriction under a fixed exchange rate is very different from that under a floating exchange rate. In both cases, a trade restriction shifts

---

[3] Barry Eichengreen and Jeffrey Sachs, 'Exchange Rates and Economic Recovery in the 1930s', *Journal of Economic History*, December 1985, vol. 45, pp. 925–946.

FIGURE 13-10

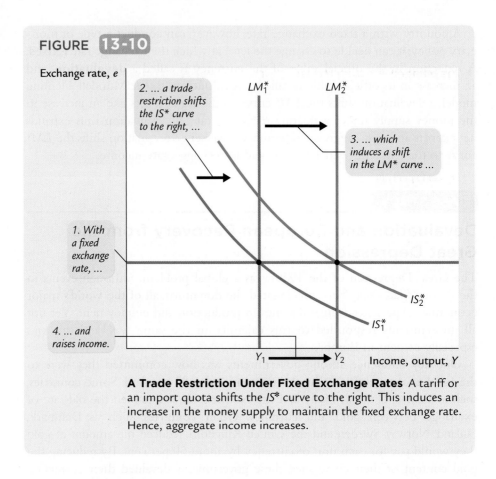

A Trade Restriction Under Fixed Exchange Rates A tariff or an import quota shifts the *IS** curve to the right. This induces an increase in the money supply to maintain the fixed exchange rate. Hence, aggregate income increases.

the net-exports schedule to the right, but only under a fixed exchange rate does a trade restriction increase net exports *NX*. The reason is that a trade restriction under a fixed exchange rate induces monetary expansion rather than an appreciation of the exchange rate. The monetary expansion, in turn, raises aggregate income. Recall the accounting identity

$$NX = S - I.$$

When income rises, saving also rises, and this implies an increase in net exports.

Policy in the Mundell–Fleming Model: A Summary

The Mundell–Fleming model shows that the effect of almost any economic policy on a small open economy depends on whether the exchange rate is floating or fixed. Table 13-1 summarizes our analysis of the short-run effects of fiscal, monetary and trade policies on income, the exchange rate and the trade balance. What is most striking is that all the results are different under floating and fixed exchange rates.

To be more specific, the Mundell–Fleming model shows that the power of monetary and fiscal policy to influence aggregate income depends on the

TABLE 13-1

The Mundell–Fleming Model: Summary of Policy Effects

	EXCHANGE-RATE REGIME					
	Floating			Fixed		
	impact on:					
Policy	Y	e	NX	Y	e	NX
Fiscal Expansion	0	↑	↓	↑	0	0
Monetary Expansion	↑	↓	↑	0	0	0
Import Restriction	0	↑	0	↑	0	↑

Note: This table shows the direction of impact of various economic policies on income *Y*, the exchange rate *e* and the trade balance *NX*. A '↑' indicates that the variable increases; a '↓' indicates that it decreases; a '0' indicates no effect. Remember that the exchange rate is defined as the amount of foreign currency per unit of domestic currency (for example, 150 yen per euro).

exchange-rate regime. Under floating exchange rates, only monetary policy can affect income. The usual expansionary impact of fiscal policy is offset by a rise in the value of the currency and a decrease in net exports. Under fixed exchange rates, only fiscal policy can affect income. The normal potency of monetary policy is lost because the money supply is dedicated to maintaining the exchange rate at the announced level.

13-4 Interest-Rate Differentials

So far, our analysis has assumed that the interest rate in a small open economy is equal to the world interest rate: $r = r^*$. To some extent, however, interest rates differ around the world. We now extend our analysis by considering the causes and effects of international interest-rate differentials.

Country Risk and Exchange-Rate Expectations

When we assumed earlier that the interest rate in our small open economy is determined by the world interest rate, we were applying the law of one price. We reasoned that if the domestic interest rate were above the world interest rate, people from abroad would lend to that country, driving the domestic interest rate down. And if the domestic interest rate were below the world interest rate, domestic residents would lend abroad to earn a higher return, driving the domestic interest rate up. In the end, the domestic interest rate would equal the world interest rate.

Why does this logic not always apply? There are two reasons.

One reason is country risk. When investors buy bonds issued by a European government or make loans to European corporations, they are fairly confident that they will be repaid with interest (though this confidence was shaken somewhat during the euro crisis of 2011–2012). By contrast, in some less developed countries, it is plausible to fear that a revolution or other political upheaval might lead to a default on loan repayments. Borrowers in such countries often have to pay higher interest rates to compensate lenders for this risk.

Another reason interest rates differ across countries is expected changes in the exchange rate. For example, suppose that people expect the Mexican peso to fall in value relative to the euro. Loans made in pesos will be repaid in a less valuable currency than loans made in euros. To compensate for this expected fall in the Mexican currency, the interest rate in Mexico will be higher than the interest rate in the Euro Area (Eurozone).

Thus, because of both country risk and expectations of future exchange-rate changes, the interest rate of a small open economy can differ from interest rates in other economies around the world. Let's now see how this fact affects our analysis.

Differentials in the Mundell–Fleming Model

To incorporate interest-rate differentials into the Mundell–Fleming model, we assume that the interest rate in our small open economy is determined by the world interest rate plus a risk premium θ:

$$r = r^* + \theta.$$

The risk premium is determined by the perceived political risk of making loans in a country and the expected change in the real exchange rate. For our purposes here, we can take the risk premium as exogenous in order to examine how changes in the risk premium affect the economy.

The model is largely the same as before. The two equations are

$$Y = C(Y - T) + I(r^* + \theta) + G + NX(e), \qquad\qquad IS^*$$

$$M/P = L(r^* + \theta, Y). \qquad\qquad LM^*$$

For any given fiscal policy, monetary policy, price level and risk premium, these two equations determine the level of income and exchange rate that equilibrate the goods market and the money market. Holding constant the risk premium, the tools of monetary, fiscal and trade policy work as we have already seen.

Now suppose that political turmoil causes the country's risk premium θ to rise. Because $r = r^* + \theta$, the most direct effect is that the domestic interest rate r rises. The higher interest rate, in turn, has two effects. First, the IS^* curve shifts to the left, because the higher interest rate reduces investment. Second, the LM^* curve shifts to the right, because the higher interest rate reduces the demand for money, and this allows a higher level of income for any given money supply. [Recall that Y must satisfy the equation $M/P = L(r^* + \theta, Y)$.] As Figure 13-11 shows, these two shifts cause income to rise and the currency to depreciate.

This analysis has an important implication: expectations about the exchange rate are partially self-fulfilling. For example, suppose that people come to believe

FIGURE 13-11

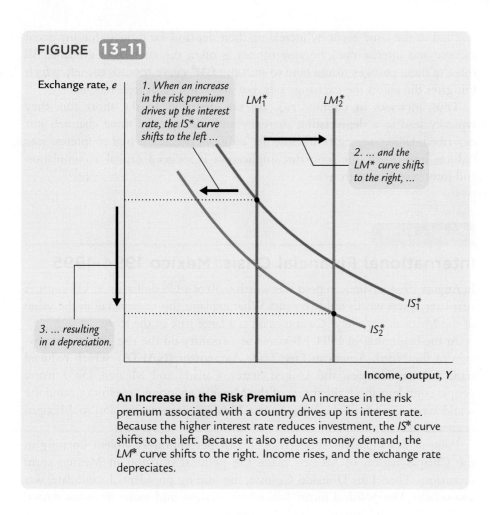

Exchange rate, e

1. *When an increase in the risk premium drives up the interest rate, the IS* curve shifts to the left …*

LM_1^* LM_2^*

2. *… and the LM* curve shifts to the right, …*

3. *… resulting in a depreciation.*

IS_1^*

IS_2^*

Income, output, Y

An Increase in the Risk Premium An increase in the risk premium associated with a country drives up its interest rate. Because the higher interest rate reduces investment, the *IS** curve shifts to the left. Because it also reduces money demand, the *LM** curve shifts to the right. Income rises, and the exchange rate depreciates.

that the Mexican peso will not be valuable in the future. Investors will place a larger risk premium on Mexican assets: θ will rise in Mexico. This expectation will drive up Mexican interest rates and, as we have just seen, will drive down the value of the Mexican currency. *Thus, the expectation that a currency will lose value in the future causes it to lose value today.*

One surprising — and perhaps inaccurate — prediction of this analysis is that an increase in country risk as measured by θ will cause the economy's income to increase. This occurs in Figure 13-11 because of the rightward shift in the *LM** curve. Although higher interest rates depress investment, the depreciation of the currency stimulates net exports by an even greater amount. As a result, aggregate income rises.

There are three reasons why, in practice, such a boom in income does not occur. First, the central bank might want to avoid the large depreciation of the domestic currency and, therefore, may respond by decreasing the money supply *M*. Second, the depreciation of the domestic currency may suddenly increase the price of imported goods, causing an increase in the price level *P*. Third, when some event increases the country risk premium θ, residents of the country might respond to the same event by increasing their demand for money (for any given income and interest rate), because money is often the safest asset available. All three of these changes would tend to shift the LM^* curve towards the left, which mitigates the fall in the exchange rate, but also tends to depress income.

Thus, increases in country risk are not desirable. In the short run, they typically lead to a depreciating currency and, through the three channels just described, falling aggregate income. In addition, because a higher interest rate reduces investment, the long-run implication is reduced capital accumulation and lower economic growth.

CASE STUDY

International Financial Crisis: Mexico 1994–1995

In August 1994, a Mexican peso was worth 0.30 of a US dollar, or 30 US cents. A year later, it was worth only 16 cents. What explains this massive fall in the value of the Mexican currency? Country risk is a large part of the story.

At the beginning of 1994, Mexico was a country on the rise. The recent passage of the North American Free Trade Agreement (NAFTA), which reduced trade barriers between the United States, Canada and Mexico, made many people confident about the future of the Mexican economy. Investors around the world were eager to make loans to the Mexican government and to Mexican corporations.

Political developments soon changed that perception. A violent uprising in the Chiapas region of Mexico made the political situation in Mexico seem precarious. Then Luis Donaldo Colosio, the leading presidential candidate, was assassinated. The political future looked less certain, and many investors started placing a larger risk premium on Mexican assets.

At first, the rising risk premium did not affect the value of the peso, because Mexico was operating with a fixed exchange rate. As we have seen, under a fixed exchange rate, the central bank agrees to trade the domestic currency (pesos) for a foreign currency (US dollars) at a predetermined rate Thus, when an increase in the country risk premium put downward pressure on the value of the peso, the Mexican central bank had to accept pesos and pay out dollars. This automatic exchange-market intervention contracted the Mexican money supply (shifting the LM^* curve to the left) when the currency might otherwise have depreciated.

Yet Mexico's foreign-currency reserves were too small to maintain its fixed exchange rate. When Mexico ran out of dollars at the end of 1994, the Mexican government announced a devaluation of the peso. This decision had repercussions, however, because the government had repeatedly promised that it would not devalue. Investors became even more distrustful of Mexican policy makers and feared further Mexican devaluations.

Investors around the world (including those in Mexico) avoided buying Mexican assets. The country risk premium rose once again, adding to the upward pressure on interest rates and the downward pressure on the peso. The Mexican stock market plummeted. When the Mexican government needed to roll over some of its debt that was coming due, investors were unwilling to buy the new debt. Default appeared to be the government's only option. In just a few months, Mexico had gone from being a promising emerging economy to being a risky economy with a government on the verge of bankruptcy.

Then the United States stepped in. The US government had three motives: to help its neighbour to the south, to prevent the massive illegal immigration that might follow government default and economic collapse, and to prevent the investor pessimism regarding Mexico from spreading to other developing countries. The US government, together with the International Monetary Fund (IMF), led an international effort to bail out the Mexican government. In particular, the United States provided loan guarantees for Mexican government debt, which allowed the Mexican government to refinance the debt that was coming due. These loan guarantees helped restore confidence in the Mexican economy, thereby reducing to some extent the country risk premium.

Although the US loan guarantees may well have stopped a bad situation from getting worse, they did not prevent the Mexican meltdown of 1994–1995 from being a painful experience for the Mexican people. Not only did the Mexican currency lose much of its value, but Mexico also went through a deep recession. Fortunately, by the late 1990s, the worst was over, and aggregate income was growing again. But the lesson from this experience is clear and could well apply again in the future: changes in perceived country risk, often attributable to political instability, are an important determinant of interest rates and exchange rates in small open economies. ■

CASE STUDY

International Financial Crisis: East Asia 1997–1998

In 1997, as the Mexican economy was recovering from its financial crisis, a similar story started to unfold in several Asian economies, including in Thailand, South Korea and, especially, Indonesia. The symptoms were familiar: high interest rates, falling asset values and a depreciating currency. In Indonesia, for instance, short-term nominal interest rates rose above 50 per cent; the stock market lost about 90 per cent of its value (measured in US dollars); and the rupiah fell against the dollar by more than 80 per cent. The crisis led to rising inflation in these countries (because the depreciating currency made imports more expensive) and to falling GDP (because high interest rates and reduced confidence depressed spending). Real GDP in Indonesia fell about 13 per cent in 1998 – a scale of contraction not seen in advanced economies since the 1920s and 1930s.

What sparked this firestorm? The problem began in the East Asian banking systems. For many years, the governments in the East Asian nations had been more involved in managing the allocation of resources – in particular, financial resources – than is true in the advanced economies of Europe or North America. Some commentators had applauded this 'partnership' between government and private enterprise, and had even suggested that Europe and the US should follow the example. Over time, however, it became clear that many Asian banks had been extending loans to those with the most political clout rather than to those with the most profitable investment projects. Once rising default rates started to expose this 'crony capitalism', as it was then called, international investors started to lose confidence in the future of these economies. The risk premiums for Asian assets rose, causing interest rates to skyrocket and currencies to collapse.

International crises of confidence often involve a vicious circle that can amplify the problem. Here is one story about what happened in Asia:

1. Problems in the banking system eroded international confidence in these economies.

2. Loss of confidence raised risk premiums and interest rates.

3. Rising interest rates, together with the loss of confidence, depressed the prices of stock and other assets.

4. Falling asset prices reduced the value of collateral being used for bank loans.

5. Reduced collateral increased default rates on bank loans.

6. Greater defaults exacerbated problems in the banking system. Now return to step 1 to complete and continue the vicious cycle.

Some economists have used this vicious-cycle argument to suggest that the East Asian crisis was a self-fulfilling prophecy: bad things happened merely because people expected bad things to happen. Most economists, however, thought the political corruption of the banking system was a real problem, which was then compounded by this vicious cycle of reduced confidence.

As the Asian crisis developed, the IMF tried to restore confidence, much as they had with Mexico a few years earlier. In particular, the IMF made loans to the Asian countries to help them over the crisis; in exchange for these loans, it exacted promises that the governments would reform their banking systems and eliminate crony capitalism. The IMF's hope was that the short-term loans and longer-term reforms would restore confidence, lower the risk premium and turn the vicious cycle into a virtuous cycle. This policy seems to have worked: the Asian economies recovered quickly from their crisis. ■

13-5 Should Exchange Rates Be Floating or Fixed?

Having analysed how an economy works under floating and fixed exchange rates, let's consider which exchange-rate regime is better.

Pros and Cons of Different Exchange-Rate Systems

The primary argument for a floating exchange rate is that it allows monetary policy to be used for other purposes. Under fixed rates, monetary policy is committed to the single goal of maintaining the exchange rate at its announced level. Yet the exchange rate is only one of many macro-economic variables that monetary policy can influence. A system of floating exchange rates leaves monetary policy makers free to pursue other goals, such as stabilizing employment or prices.

Advocates of fixed exchange rates argue that exchange-rate uncertainty makes international trade more difficult. After the world abandoned the Bretton Woods system of fixed exchange rates in the early 1970s, both real and nominal exchange rates became (and have remained) much more volatile than anyone had expected. Some economists attribute this volatility to irrational and destabilizing speculation by international investors. Business executives often claim that this volatility is harmful because it increases the uncertainty that accompanies international business transactions. Despite this exchange-rate volatility, however, the amount of world trade has continued to rise under floating exchange rates.

'Then it's agreed. Until the dollar firms up, we let the clamshell float.'

Advocates of fixed exchange rates sometimes argue that a commitment to a fixed exchange rate is one way to discipline a nation's monetary authority and prevent excessive growth in the money supply. Yet there are many other policy rules to which the central bank could be committed. In Chapter 15, for instance, we discuss policy rules such as targets for nominal GDP or the inflation rate. Fixing the exchange rate has the advantage of being simpler to implement than these other policy rules, because the money supply adjusts automatically, but this policy may lead to greater volatility in income and employment.

In practice, the choice between floating and fixed rates is not as stark as it may seem at first. Under systems of fixed exchange rates, countries can change the value of their currency if maintaining the exchange rate conflicts too severely with other goals. Under systems of floating exchange rates, countries often use formal or informal targets for the exchange rate when deciding whether to expand or contract the money supply. We rarely observe exchange rates that are completely fixed or completely floating. Instead, under both systems, stability of the exchange rate is usually one among many of the central bank's objectives.

The Debate over the Euro

If you were ever to drive the 3000 miles from New York City to San Francisco you would find that you never needed to change your money from one form of currency to another. In all 50 US states, local residents are happy to accept the

US dollar for the items you buy. Such a monetary union is the most extreme form of a fixed exchange rate. The exchange rate between New York dollars and San Francisco dollars is so irrevocably fixed that you may not even know that there is a difference between the two. (What is the difference? Each dollar bill is issued by one of the dozen local Federal Reserve Banks. Although the bank of origin can be identified from the bill's markings, you don't care which type of dollar you hold because everyone else, including the Federal Reserve system, is ready to trade any dollar from one bank for a dollar from another.)

If you had made a similar 3000-mile trip across Europe during the 1990s, however, your experience would have been very different. You would not have to travel far before needing to exchange your French francs for German marks, Dutch guilders, Spanish pesetas, or Italian lira. The large number of currencies in Europe made travelling less convenient and more expensive than in the US. Every time you crossed a border, you had to go to a bank to get the local money, and you had to pay the bank a fee for the service.

Today, however, the situation in Europe is more like that in the United States. Many European countries have given up having their own currencies and have formed a monetary union that uses a common currency called the euro. As a result, the exchange rate between France and Germany is now as fixed as the exchange rate between New York and California.

The introduction of a common currency has had its costs. The most important is that those nations of Europe that are part of the Euro Area are no longer able to conduct their own monetary policies. Instead, the European Central Bank, with the participation of all member countries, sets a single monetary policy for the whole of Europe. The central banks of the individual countries play a role similar to that of regional Federal Reserve Banks in the US: they monitor local conditions but they have no control over the money supply or interest rates. Critics of the move towards a common currency argue that the cost of losing national monetary policy is large. When a recession hits one country but not others in Europe, that country does not have the tool of monetary policy to combat the downturn. This argument is one reason that some European nations, such as the United Kingdom and Sweden, have chosen not to give up their own currency in favour of the euro.

Why, according to the euro critics, is monetary union a bad idea for Europe if it works so well in the United States? These economists argue that the United States is different from Europe in two important ways. First, labour is more mobile among US states than among European countries. This is in part because the United States has a common language and in part because most Americans are descended from immigrants who have shown a willingness to move. Therefore, when a regional recession occurs, US workers are more likely to move from high-unemployment states to low-unemployment states. Second, the United States has a strong central government that can use fiscal policy – such as the federal income tax – to redistribute resources among regions. Because Europe does not have these two advantages, it bears a larger cost when it restricts itself to a single monetary policy.

Advocates of a common currency believe that the loss of national monetary policy is more than offset by other gains. With a single currency across Europe, travellers and businesses no longer need to worry about exchange rates, and this encourages more international trade. In addition, a common currency may have the political advantage of making Europeans feel more connected to one another. The 20th century was marked by two world wars, both of which were sparked by European discord. If a common currency makes the nations of Europe more harmonious, euro advocates argue, it benefits the entire world.

In recent years, the debate over the euro has become particularly fervent. In 2011, the government of Greece ran into severe financial difficulties. For years, the Greek government had spent much more than it had received in tax revenue, financing the substantial budget deficits by borrowing. Moreover, some of these fiscal problems were hidden by dubious accounting. When the magnitude of the problem came to light, interest rates on Greek government debt skyrocketed, as investors around the world began to fear default. The government then had little choice but to alter its fiscal policy – that is, to cut spending and raise taxes – despite widespread protests within the country. We will examine these events more thoroughly in Chapter 17, but one aspect of the situation is relevant here: if Greece had had its own currency, rather than being part of the Euro Area, it could have offset its contractionary fiscal policy with expansionary monetary policy. An expansionary monetary policy would have weakened the Greek currency and made Greek exports less expensive on world markets; the increase in net exports would have helped maintain aggregate demand and soften the recession that resulted from the fiscal contraction.

The future of the euro remains uncertain. Many European policy makers remained committed to a common currency as part of a broader agenda of strong political and economic ties within Europe. Some commentators, however, suggested that Europe should reconsider its decision to form a monetary union. ■

Speculative Attacks, Currency Boards, 'Dollarization' and 'Euroization'

Imagine that you are a central banker of a small country. You and your fellow policy makers decide to fix your currency – let's call it the lev – against the euro. From now on, one lev will sell for one euro.

As we discussed earlier, you now have to stand ready to buy and sell levs for one euro each. The money supply will adjust automatically to make the equilibrium exchange rate equal your target. There is, however, one potential problem with this plan: you might run out of euros. If people come to the central bank to sell large quantities of levs, the central bank's euro reserves might dwindle to zero. In this case, the central bank has no choice but to abandon the fixed exchange rate and let the lev depreciate.

This fact raises the possibility of a *speculative attack* – a change in investors' perceptions that makes the fixed exchange rate untenable. Suppose that, for no good reason, a rumour spreads that the central bank is going to abandon the exchange rate peg. People would respond by rushing to the central bank to convert levs into euros before the levs lose value. This rush would drain the central bank's reserves and could force the central bank to abandon the peg. In this case, the rumour would prove self-fulfilling.

To avoid this possibility, some economists argue that a fixed exchange rate should be supported by a *currency board,* such as that used by Bulgaria, Estonia and Lithuania. A currency board is an arrangement by which the central bank holds enough foreign currency to back each unit of the domestic currency. In our example, the central bank would hold one euro (or one euro invested in a euro-denominated government bond) for every lev. No matter how many levs turned up at the central bank to be exchanged, the central bank would never run out of euros because the lev is backed one-for-one with euros.

Once a central bank has adopted a currency board, it might consider the natural next step: it can abandon the lev altogether and let its country use the euro. In fact, this is probably the long-term aim of Bulgaria and Lithuania, as part of their integration into the European Union.

As we shall discuss in a later chapter, however, members of a monetary union such as the European monetary union typically share in the seigniorage revenue from printing the common currency. If a country unilaterally decides to adopt another country's currency – as Panama did in adopting the US dollar – then the issuing country gets the revenue that is generated from printing money. The advantage to the adopting currency is that it effectively imports price and currency stability from the issuing country. This is the reason why adoption of the US dollar – either officially, as in Panama, or unofficially, because local residents have more faith in the US dollar as a store of value than they do in their local currency – has often occurred in high-inflation countries in Latin America. So much so, in fact, that the process has earned itself the name of *dollarization*.

In Europe, there is some debate as to whether the 'accession countries' of Central and Eastern Europe – which are in the process of integrating into Europe by applying for membership of the European monetary union – should unilaterally 'euroize' and adopt the euro as their currency, accepting the loss of seigniorage in favour of closer European integration. As we shall discuss later, the European Union has laid down various criteria for a country to be eligible to join the European monetary union, and unilateral adoption of the euro would effectively sidestep these. Apart from the loss in seigniorage, the euroized country would also have no say in interest-rate setting in the Euro Area. More importantly, however, the political costs would be very high – if an accession country were seen as forcing its way into the European monetary union without the full consent of the other members, it may reduce the likelihood of its ever being accepted as a full member of the club.

CASE STUDY

International Financial Crisis: The Speculative Attack on the European Exchange Rate Mechanism, 1992

Before the introduction of the euro (which we shall study in Chapter 17), most of the European Union countries that now make up the Euro Area, plus several others, such as the UK and the Scandinavian countries of Denmark, Norway and Sweden, participated in the European Exchange Rate Mechanism (ERM).[4] At the beginning of the 1990s, the ERM was a 'semi-fixed' exchange rate system in which exchange rates between currencies of participating countries were only allowed to fluctuate within small bands of ±2.25 around an agreed parity (with the exception of the Italian lira, which was allowed a ±6 per cent band), while their value against non-member currencies (such as the US dollar) was allowed to be determined in the markets (i.e. to float freely). If there was a tendency for an ERM currency to move out of the agreed band against another ERM currency, then the government in question was obliged to take action to keep it inside. One rationale for the ERM was that it reduced the uncertainty caused by fluctuating exchange rates while allowing countries to have their own currencies.

However, as we have discussed, fixed-exchange-rate arrangements like this always run the risk of a speculative attack: international speculators start selling a currency heavily in the belief that they can force the government to let the value of the currency fall, so that the speculators can buy back the currency they have sold at a lower price and so make a profit. The initial reaction of the government to a speculative attack will be to raise interest rates, but if the speculators continue to sell the currency, then in order to stop its value falling, the government will have to intervene in the foreign exchange market and buy its own currency, using up its reserves of foreign currency to do so. If the speculators carry on selling the currency, the government will eventually run out of reserves and will have to let the value of their currency fall in the foreign-currency exchange market. The speculators will then be able to buy back all the currency that they sold and will make a huge profit. Of course, the government will make a huge loss because they used up their reserves of foreign currency to defend their domestic currency, at a high rate of exchange; the domestic currency is now worth much less against the foreign currencies, so the government may let the domestic currency depreciate before they have completely exhausted their reserves if they judge that they will eventually run out anyway.

This is exactly what happened to the ERM in 1992. From mid-1992, speculators began selling several ERM currencies against the German mark, focusing initially on the pound sterling, the French franc and the Italian lira, and then on other currencies, including the Scandinavian currencies. On 'Black Wednesday', 16 September 1992, led by Hungarian-born international financier George Soros, the speculators increased the ferocity of their selling and launched a massive speculative attack on the ERM. In desperate attempts to shore up the British pound, the UK government raised interest rates no less than three times over the course of the day, from 10 per cent to 12, and then finally to 15 per cent. At the same time, it ordered the Bank of England to intervene in the foreign exchange

---

[4] In fact, strictly speaking, neither Norway nor Sweden were members of the ERM, since neither was a member of the European Union (Sweden joined the EU in 1995; Norway was still not a member in 2013). However, the Norwegian and Swedish central banks did pursue a policy of pegging their exchange rates against ERM currencies very much as if they were formal members of the ERM.

market and buy sterling heavily. But with foreign exchange reserves perilously low and the tide of speculative sales of sterling still strong, the UK government was eventually forced to let sterling devalue and drop out of the ERM.

The Italian lira was also forced out of the ERM on Black Wednesday, and with speculators keeping up the pressure on the other currencies, before the end of the year both Sweden and Norway had also been forced to let their currencies devalue, drop out of the fixed-rate system and float freely. In Sweden, even a marginal rate of 500 per cent was insufficient to prevent speculative sales of the Swedish krona and eventual devaluation. In mid-1993, the ERM was reconstituted to allow much wider bands of fluctuation of ±15 per cent, but the UK, Norway and Sweden did not participate.

In figures released by the UK government in 2005, it was revealed that the cost to the UK government of the failed foreign-exchange intervention operations on Black Wednesday amounted to £3.3 billion. George Soros himself was rumoured to have made a personal profit of £1 billion from the successful speculative attack. ■

The Impossible Trinity

The analysis of exchange-rate regimes leads to a simple conclusion: you can't have it all. To be more precise, it is impossible for a nation to have free capital flows, a fixed exchange rate, and independent monetary policy. This fact, often called the impossible trinity (or sometimes the trilemma of international finance), is illustrated in Figure 13-12. A nation must choose one side of this triangle, giving up the institutional feature at the opposite corner.

The first option is to allow free flows of capital and to conduct an independent monetary policy, as the United Kingdom, Sweden and Norway have done in the late 20th and early 21st centuries. In this case, it is impossible to have a fixed exchange rate. Instead, the exchange rate must float to equilibrate the market for foreign-currency exchange.

The second option is to allow free flows of capital and to fix the exchange rate, as Hong Kong has done during the same period. In this case, the nation loses the ability to run an independent monetary policy. The money supply must adjust to keep the exchange rate at its predetermined level. In a sense, when a nation fixes its currency to that of another nation, it is adopting that other nation's monetary policy.

The third option is to restrict the international flow of capital in and out of the country, as has been the case in China. Here, the interest rate is no longer fixed by world interest rates, but is determined by domestic forces, much as is the case in a completely closed economy. Thus it is possible to both fix the exchange rate and conduct an independent monetary policy.

History has shown that nations can, and do, choose different sides of the triangle. Every nation must ask itself the following question: Does it want to live with exchange-rate volatility (option 1), give up the use of monetary policy for purposes of domestic stabilization (option 2), or restrict its citizens from participating in world financial markets (option 3)? The impossible trinity says that no nation can avoid making one of these choices.

FIGURE 13-12

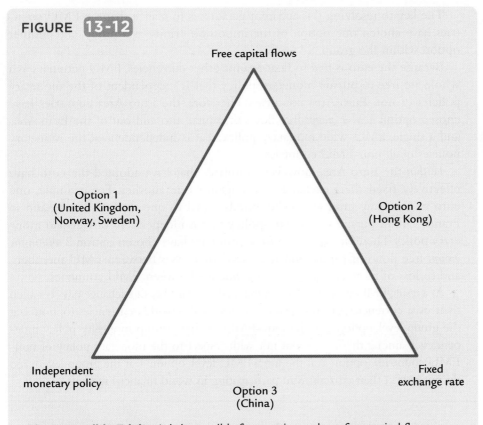

The Impossible Trinity It is impossible for a nation to have free capital flows, a fixed exchange rate and independent monetary policy. A nation must choose one side of this triangle, giving up the opposite corner.

CASE STUDY

European Monetary Union: Squaring the Triangle?

In Chapter 17, we shall study the economics behind the decision of a group of countries to have the same currency among themselves and form a so-called 'common currency area'. A major example of a common currency area is the Euro Area, which is composed of the European countries that form the European Economic and Monetary Union (EMU) and have adopted the euro as their common currency. In some ways, the EMU may not seem to fall into any of the three options in the impossible trinity triangle. EMU members do not restrict the international flow of capital into or out of the Euro Area. They do not fix the exchange rate between the euro and non-EMU currencies (such as the British pound, the Swedish krona or the US dollar). And yet, because EMU countries all have the same currency (the euro), they all have to have the same interest rates and cannot pursue an independent monetary policy.

The key to resolving this apparent paradox is to realize that the EMU countries have chosen one option of the impossible trinity as a group, and another option within the group.

Because the euro is free to float against other currencies, EMU countries as a whole are free to pursue monetary policy that is independent of the monetary policies of non–Euro Area countries. Therefore, the Euro Area countries have chosen option 1 *as a group*: free flows of capital into and out of the Euro Area, and a single, EMU-wide monetary policy that is independent of the monetary policies of all non-EMU countries.

Within the Euro Area, however, countries that have adopted the euro have effectively fixed their exchange rates against one another. For example, one euro in Germany must always be exactly equal to one euro in France, and so France cannot pursue a monetary policy that is independent of German monetary policy. Therefore, the Euro Area countries have chosen option 2 *within the group*: free flows of capital and fixed exchange rates between EMU members, and so loss of monetary policy independence between EMU countries.

As a result, EMU members have eliminated the volatility of exchange rates between their own currencies, but not against the rest of the world's currencies (option 1 at the group level, option 2 at the intra-EMU level); given up monetary policy independence among themselves, but not with respect to the monetary policy of non-EMU countries (option 2 at the intra-EMU level, option 1 at the group level); and do not restrict their citizens from participating in world financial markets. ∎

The Chinese Currency Controversy

From 1995 to 2005 the Chinese currency, the yuan, was pegged to the dollar at an exchange rate of 8.28 yuan per US dollar. In other words, the Chinese central bank stood ready to buy and sell yuan at this price. This policy of fixing the exchange rate was combined with a policy of restricting international capital flows. Chinese citizens were not allowed to convert their savings into dollars or euros and invest abroad.

By the early 2000s, many observers believed that the yuan was significantly undervalued. They suggested that if the yuan were allowed to float it would increase in value relative to the dollar. The evidence in favour of this hypothesis was that China was accumulating large dollar reserves in its efforts to maintain the fixed exchange rate. That is, the Chinese central bank had to supply yuan and demand dollars in foreign-exchange markets to keep the yuan at the pegged level. If this intervention in the currency market ceased, the yuan would rise in value compared with the dollar.

The pegged yuan became a contentious political issue in the United States. US producers that competed against Chinese imports complained that the undervalued yuan made Chinese goods cheaper, putting the US producers at a disadvantage. (Of course, US consumers benefited from inexpensive imports, but in the politics of international trade, producers usually shout louder than consumers.) In response to these concerns, President George W. Bush called on

China to let its currency float. Several senators proposed a more drastic step – a steep tariff on Chinese imports until China adjusted the value of its currency.

China no longer completely fixes the exchange rate. In July 2005 China announced a new policy: it would still intervene in foreign-exchange markets to prevent large and sudden movements in the exchange rate, but it would permit gradual changes. Moreover, it would judge the value of the yuan not just relative to the dollar but also relative to a broad basket of currencies. By October 2011, the exchange rate had moved to 6.38 yuan per dollar – a 30 per cent appreciation of the yuan. Despite this large change in the exchange rate, China's critics, including President Barack Obama, continue to complain about that nation's intervention in foreign-exchange markets. ■

13-6 From the Short Run to the Long Run: The Mundell–Fleming Model with a Changing Price Level

So far we have used the Mundell–Fleming model to study the small open economy in the short run when the price level is fixed. We now consider what happens when the price level changes. Doing so will show how the Mundell–Fleming model provides a theory of the aggregate demand curve in a small open economy. It will also show how this short-run model relates to the long-run model of the open economy we examined in Chapter 6.

Because we now want to consider changes in the price level, the nominal and real exchange rate in the economy will no longer be moving in tandem. Thus, we must distinguish between these two variables. The nominal exchange rate is e and the real exchange rate is ε, which equals eP/P^*, as you should recall from Chapter 6. We can write the Mundell–Fleming model as

$$Y = C(Y - T) + I(r^*) + G + NX(\varepsilon), \qquad IS^*$$

$$M/P = L(r^*, Y). \qquad LM^*$$

These equations should be familiar by now. The first equation describes the IS^* curve, and the second equation describes the LM^* curve. Note that net exports depend on the real exchange rate.

Figure 13-13 shows what happens when the price level falls. Because a lower price level raises the level of real money balances, the LM^* curve shifts to the right, as in panel (a) of Figure 13-13. The real exchange rate depreciates, and the equilibrium level of income rises. The aggregate demand curve summarizes this negative relationship between the price level and the level of income, as shown in panel (b) of Figure 13-13.

Thus, just as the IS-LM model explains the aggregate demand curve in a closed economy, the Mundell–Fleming model explains the aggregate demand curve for a small open economy. In both cases, the aggregate demand curve shows the set of equilibria in the goods and money markets that arise as the price level varies. And in both cases, anything that changes equilibrium income, other than a change in the price level, shifts the aggregate demand curve. Policies and

FIGURE 13-13

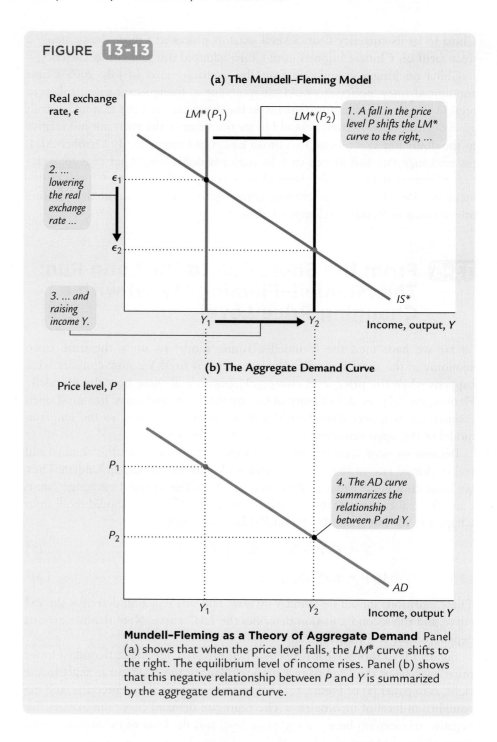

(a) The Mundell–Fleming Model

Real exchange rate, ϵ

$LM^*(P_1)$

$LM^*(P_2)$

1. *A fall in the price level P shifts the LM* curve to the right, …*

2. *… lowering the real exchange rate …*

ϵ_1

ϵ_2

3. *… and raising income Y.*

IS^*

Y_1

Y_2

Income, output, Y

(b) The Aggregate Demand Curve

Price level, P

P_1

P_2

4. *The AD curve summarizes the relationship between P and Y.*

AD

Y_1

Y_2

Income, output Y

Mundell–Fleming as a Theory of Aggregate Demand Panel (a) shows that when the price level falls, the LM^* curve shifts to the right. The equilibrium level of income rises. Panel (b) shows that this negative relationship between P and Y is summarized by the aggregate demand curve.

events that raise income for a given price level shift the aggregate demand curve to the right; policies and events that lower income for a given price level shift the aggregate demand curve to the left.

We can use this diagram to show how the short-run model in this chapter is related to the long-run model in Chapter 6. Figure 13-14 shows the short-run

FIGURE 13-14

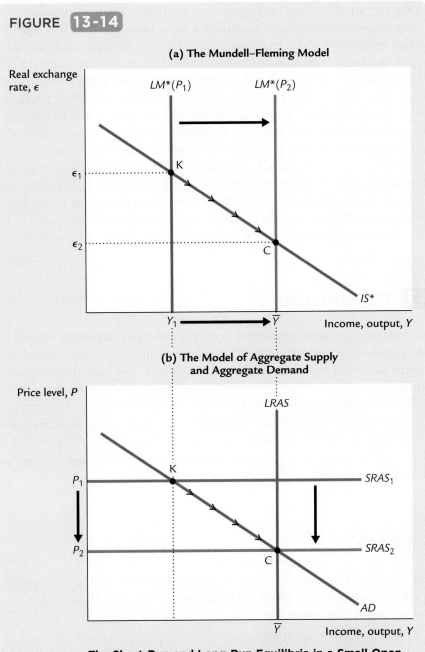

(a) The Mundell–Fleming Model

(b) The Model of Aggregate Supply and Aggregate Demand

The Short-Run and Long-Run Equilibria in a Small Open Economy Point K in both panels shows the equilibrium under the Keynesian assumption that the price level is fixed at P_1. Point C in both panels shows the equilibrium under the classical assumption that the price level adjusts to maintain income at its natural level $\overline{Y}$.

and long-run equilibria. In both panels of the figure, point K describes the short-run equilibrium, because it assumes a fixed price level. At this equilibrium, the demand for goods and services is too low to keep the economy producing at its natural level. Over time, low demand causes the price level to fall. The fall in the price level raises real money balances, shifting the LM^* curve to the right. The real exchange rate depreciates, so net exports rise. Eventually, the economy reaches point C, the long-run equilibrium. The speed of transition between the short-run and long-run equilibria depends on how quickly the price level adjusts to restore the economy to the natural level of output.

The levels of income at point K and point C are both of interest. Our central concern in this chapter has been how policy influences point K, the short-run equilibrium. In Chapter 6 we examined the determinants of point C, the long-run equilibrium. Whenever policy makers consider any change in policy, they need to consider both the short-run and the long-run effects of their decision.

13-7 Conclusion

In this chapter we have examined how a small open economy works in the short run when prices are sticky. We have seen how monetary and fiscal policy influence income and the exchange rate, and how the behaviour of the economy depends on whether the exchange rate is floating or fixed. The open economy model is probably a reasonable short-run approximation for the UK and most other European economies, and not such a good approximation to the US economy. In fact, the Mundell–Fleming model is probably still the most useful and important macroeconomic model that has been developed to date.

Summary

1. The Mundell–Fleming model is the *IS-LM* model for a small open economy. It takes the price level as given and then shows what causes fluctuations in income and the exchange rate.

2. The Mundell–Fleming model shows that fiscal policy does not influence aggregate income under floating exchange rates. A fiscal expansion causes the currency to appreciate, reducing net exports and offsetting the usual expansionary impact on aggregate income. Fiscal policy does influence aggregate income under fixed exchange rates.

3. The Mundell–Fleming model shows that monetary policy does not influence aggregate income under fixed exchange rates. Any attempt to expand the money supply is futile, because the money supply must adjust to ensure that the exchange rate stays at its announced level. Monetary policy does influence aggregate income under floating exchange rates.

4. If investors are wary of holding assets in a country, the interest rate in that country may exceed the world interest rate by some risk premium. According to the Mundell–Fleming model, an increase in the risk premium causes the interest rate to rise and the currency of that country to depreciate.

5. There are advantages to both floating and fixed exchange rates. Floating exchange rates leave monetary policy makers free to pursue objectives other than exchange-rate stability. Fixed exchange rates reduce some of the uncertainty in international business transactions. When deciding on an exchange-rate regime, policy makers are constrained by the fact that it is impossible for a nation to have free capital flows, a fixed exchange rate and independent monetary policy.

KEY CONCEPTS

Mundell–Fleming model

Floating exchange rates

Fixed exchange rates

Devaluation

Revaluation

Impossible trinity

QUESTIONS FOR REVIEW

1. In the Mundell–Fleming model with floating exchange rates, explain what happens to aggregate income, the exchange rate and the trade balance when taxes are raised. What would happen if exchange rates were fixed rather than floating?

2. In the Mundell–Fleming model with floating exchange rates, explain what happens to aggregate income, the exchange rate and the trade balance when the money supply is reduced. What would happen if exchange rates were fixed rather than floating?

3. In the Mundell–Fleming model with floating exchange rates, explain what happens to aggregate income, the exchange rate and the trade balance when a quota on imported cars is removed. What would happen if exchange rates were fixed rather than floating?

4. What are the advantages of floating exchange rates and fixed exchange rates?

5. Describe the impossible trinity.

PROBLEMS AND APPLICATIONS

1. A small open economy with a floating exchange rate is in recession with balanced trade. If policy makers want to reach full employment while maintaining balanced trade, what combination of monetary and fiscal policy should they choose? Use a graph, and be sure to identify the effects of each policy.

2. Business executives and policy makers are often concerned about the 'competitiveness' of industry (the ability of domestic industries to sell their goods profitably in world markets).

   a. How would a change in the exchange rate affect competitiveness?

b. Suppose you wanted to make domestic industries more competitive, but did not want to alter aggregate income. According to the Mundell–Fleming model, what combination of monetary and fiscal policies should you pursue?

3. Use the Mundell–Fleming model to predict what would happen to aggregate income, the exchange rate and the trade balance, under both floating and fixed exchange rates, in response to each of the following shocks:

   a. A fall in consumer confidence about the future induces consumers to spend less and save more.

   b. The introduction of a stylish line of Toyotas makes some consumers prefer foreign cars over domestic cars.

   c. The introduction of automated teller machines reduces the demand for money.

4. The Mundell–Fleming model takes the world interest rate r^* as an exogenous variable. Let's consider what happens when this variable changes.

   a. What might cause the world interest rate to rise?

   b. In the Mundell–Fleming model with a floating exchange rate, what happens to aggregate income, the exchange rate and the trade balance when the world interest rate rises?

   c. In the Mundell–Fleming model with a fixed exchange rate, what happens to aggregate income, the exchange rate and the trade balance when the world interest rate rises?

5. Suppose that the price level relevant for money demand includes the price of imported goods and that the price of imported goods depends on the exchange rate. That is, the money market is described by

$$M/P = L(r, Y),$$

   where

$$P = \lambda P_d + (1 - \lambda)P_f /e.$$

The parameter λ is the share of domestic goods in the price index P. Assume that the price of domestic goods P_d and the price of foreign goods measured in foreign currency P_f are fixed.

   a. Suppose we graph the LM^* curve for given values of P_d and P_f (instead of the usual P). Explain why in this model the LM^* curve is upward sloping rather than vertical.

   b. What is the effect of expansionary fiscal policy under floating exchange rates in this model? Explain. Contrast with the standard Mundell–Fleming model.

   c. Suppose that political instability increases the country risk premium and, thereby, the interest rate. What is the effect on the exchange rate, the price level and aggregate income in this model? Contrast with the standard Mundell–Fleming model.

6. Suppose that higher income implies higher imports and thus lower net exports. That is, the net exports function is

$$NX = NX(e, Y).$$

Examine the effects in a small open economy of a fiscal expansion on income and the trade balance under the following conditions:

   a. A floating exchange rate.

   b. A fixed exchange rate.

How does your answer compare to the results in Table 13-1?

7. Suppose that money demand depends on disposable income, so that the equation for the money market becomes

$$M/P = L(r, Y - T).$$

Analyse the impact of a tax cut in a small open economy on the exchange rate and income under both floating and fixed exchange rates.

A Short-Run Model of the Large Open Economy

When analysing policies in an economy such as that of the United States, or a group of countries under monetary union such as the Euro Area (Eurozone), we need to combine the closed-economy logic of the *IS-LM* model and the small-open-economy logic of the Mundell–Fleming model. This appendix presents a model for the intermediate case of a large open economy.

As we discussed in the appendix to Chapter 6, a large open economy differs from a small open economy because its interest rate is not fixed by world financial markets. In a large open economy, we must consider the relationship between the interest rate and the flow of capital abroad. The net capital outflow is the amount that domestic investors lend abroad minus the amount that foreign investors lend here. As the domestic interest rate falls, domestic investors find foreign lending more attractive, and foreign investors find lending here less attractive. Thus, the net capital outflow is negatively related to the interest rate. Here we add this relationship to our short-run model of national income.

The three equations of the model are

$$Y = C(Y - T) + I(r) + G + NX(e),$$

$$M/P = L(r, Y),$$

$$NX(e) = CF(r).$$

The first two equations are the same as those used in the Mundell–Fleming model of this chapter. The third equation, taken from the appendix to Chapter 6, states that the trade balance NX equals the net capital outflow CF, which in turn depends on the domestic interest rate.

To see what this model implies, substitute the third equation into the first, so the model becomes

$$Y = C(Y - T) + I(r) + G + CF(r), \qquad\qquad IS$$

$$M/P = L(r, Y) \qquad\qquad LM.$$

These two equations are much like the two equations of the closed-economy *IS-LM* model. The only difference is that expenditure now depends on the interest rate for two reasons. As before, a higher interest rate reduces investment. But now, a higher interest rate also reduces the net capital outflow and thus lowers net exports.

To analyse this model, we can use the three graphs in Figure 13-15. Panel (a) shows the *IS-LM* diagram. As in the closed-economy model in Chapters 11 and 12, the interest rate r is on the vertical axis, and income Y is on the horizontal

FIGURE 13-15

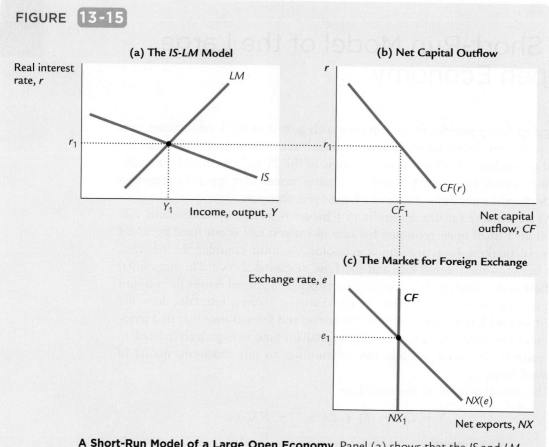

A Short-Run Model of a Large Open Economy Panel (a) shows that the *IS* and *LM* curves determine the interest rate r_1 and income Y_1. Panel (b) shows that r_1 determines the net capital outflow CF_1. Panel (c) shows that CF_1 and the net-exports schedule determine the exchange rate e_1.

axis. The *IS* and *LM* curves together determine the equilibrium level of income and the equilibrium interest rate.

The new net–capital–outflow term in the *IS* equation, $CF(r)$, makes this *IS* curve flatter than it would be in a closed economy. The more responsive international capital flows are to the interest rate, the flatter the *IS* curve is. You might recall from the Chapter 6 appendix that the small open economy represents the extreme case in which the net capital outflow is infinitely elastic at the world interest rate. In this extreme case, the *IS* curve is completely flat. Hence, a small open economy would be depicted in this figure with a horizontal *IS* curve.

Panels (b) and (c) show how the equilibrium from the *IS–LM* model determines the net capital outflow, the trade balance, and the exchange rate. In panel (b) we see that the interest rate determines the net capital outflow. This curve slopes downward because a higher interest rate discourages domestic investors from lending abroad and encourages foreign investors to lend here, thereby reducing the net capital outflow. In panel (c) we see that the exchange rate adjusts to ensure that net exports of goods and services equal the net capital outflow.

Now let's use this model to examine the impact of various policies. We assume that the economy has a floating exchange rate, because this assumption is correct for most large open economies.

Fiscal Policy

Figure 13-16 examines the impact of a fiscal expansion. An increase in government purchases or a cut in taxes shifts the *IS* curve to the right. As panel (a) illustrates, this shift in the *IS* curve leads to an increase in the level of income

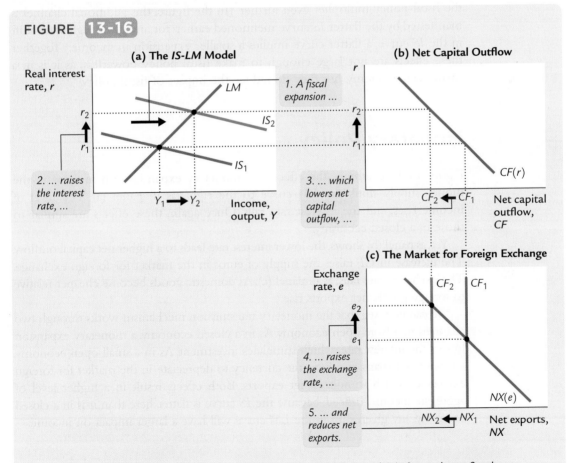

FIGURE 13-16

(a) The *IS-LM* Model

Real interest rate, *r*

r_2

r_1

LM

IS₂

IS₁

2. ... raises the interest rate, ...

$Y_1 \rightarrow Y_2$ Income, output, *Y*

1. A fiscal expansion ...

(b) Net Capital Outflow

r

r_2

r_1

$CF(r)$

3. ... which lowers net capital outflow, ...

$CF_2 \leftarrow CF_1$ Net capital outflow, *CF*

(c) The Market for Foreign Exchange

Exchange rate, *e*

CF_2 CF_1

e_2

e_1

4. ... raises the exchange rate, ...

$NX(e)$

5. ... and reduces net exports.

$NX_2 \leftarrow NX_1$ Net exports, *NX*

A Fiscal Expansion in a Large Open Economy Panel (a) shows that a fiscal expansion shifts the *IS* curve to the right. Income rises from Y_1 to Y_2, and the interest rate rises from r_1 to r_2. Panel (b) shows that the increase in the interest rate causes the net capital outflow to fall from CF_1 to CF_2. Panel (c) shows that the fall in the net capital outflow reduces the net supply of euros, causing the exchange rate to rise from e_1 to e_2.

and an increase in the interest rate. These two effects are similar to those in a closed economy.

Yet, in the large open economy, the higher interest rate reduces the net capital outflow, as in panel (b). The fall in the net capital outflow reduces the supply of dollars in the market for foreign exchange. The exchange rate appreciates, as in panel (c). Because domestic goods become more expensive relative to foreign goods, net exports fall.

Figure 13-16 shows that a fiscal expansion does raise income in the large open economy, unlike in a small open economy under a floating exchange rate. The impact on income, however, is smaller than in a closed economy. In a closed economy, the expansionary impact of fiscal policy is partially offset by the crowding out of investment: as the interest rate rises, investment falls, reducing the fiscal-policy multipliers. In a large open economy, there is yet another offsetting factor: as the interest rate rises, the net capital outflow falls, the currency appreciates in the foreign-exchange market, and net exports fall. This reduces the fiscal-policy multiplier even further. (In the figure, this additional channel is manifested by the flatter *IS* curve mentioned earlier: for any given rightward shift in the *IS* curve, a flatter curve implies a smaller expansion in income.) Together these effects are not large enough to make fiscal policy powerless, as it is in a small open economy, but they do reduce the impact of fiscal policy.

Monetary Policy

Figure 13-17 examines the effect of a monetary expansion. An increase in the money supply shifts the *LM* curve to the right, as in panel (a). The level of income rises, and the interest rate falls. Once again, these effects are similar to those in a closed economy.

Yet, as panel (b) shows, the lower interest rate leads to a higher net capital outflow. The increase in *CF* raises the supply of euros in the market for foreign exchange. The exchange rate falls, as in panel (c). As domestic goods become cheaper relative to foreign goods, net exports rise.

We can now see that the monetary transmission mechanism works through two channels in a large open economy. As in a closed economy, a monetary expansion lowers the interest rate, which stimulates investment. As in a small open economy, a monetary expansion causes the currency to depreciate in the market for foreign exchange, which stimulates net exports. Both effects result in a higher level of aggregate income. Indeed, because the *IS* curve is flatter here than it is in a closed economy, any given shift in the *LM* curve will have a larger impact on income.

A Rule of Thumb

Fortunately, there is a useful rule of thumb to help you determine how policies influence a large open economy without remembering all the details of the

FIGURE 13-17

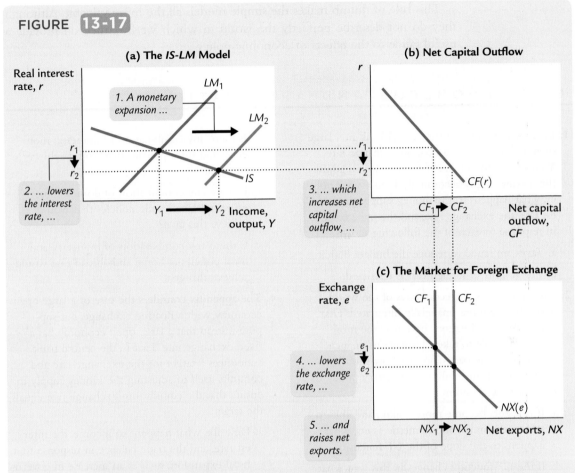

(a) The *IS-LM* Model

Real interest rate, r

1. A monetary expansion ...

LM_1

LM_2

r_1

r_2

IS

2. ... lowers the interest rate, ...

$Y_1 \longrightarrow Y_2$ Income, output, Y

(b) Net Capital Outflow

r

r_1

r_2

$CF(r)$

3. ... which increases net capital outflow, ...

$CF_1 \to CF_2$ Net capital outflow, CF

(c) The Market for Foreign Exchange

Exchange rate, e

CF_1 CF_2

e_1

e_2

4. ... lowers the exchange rate, ...

$NX(e)$

5. ... and raises net exports.

$NX_1 \to NX_2$ Net exports, NX

A Monetary Expansion in a Large Open Economy Panel (a) shows that a monetary expansion shifts the *LM* curve to the right. Income rises from Y_1 to Y_2, and the interest rate falls from r_1 to r_2. Panel (b) shows that the decrease in the interest rate causes the net capital outflow to increase from CF_1 to CF_2. Panel (c) shows that the increase in the net capital outflow raises the net supply of euros, which causes the exchange rate to fall from e_1 to e_2.

model: *The large open economy is an average of the closed economy and the small open economy. To find how any policy will affect any variable, find the answer in the two extreme cases and take an average.*

For example, how does a monetary contraction affect the interest rate and investment in the short run? In a closed economy, the interest rate rises, and investment falls. In a small open economy, neither the interest rate nor the investment changes. The effect in the large open economy is an average of these two cases: a monetary contraction raises the interest rate and reduces investment, but only somewhat. The fall in the net capital outflow mitigates the rise in the interest rate and the fall in investment that would occur in a closed economy. But unlike in a small open economy, the international flow of capital is not so strong as to negate fully these effects.

This rule of thumb makes the simple models all the more valuable. Although they do not describe perfectly the world in which we live, they do provide a useful guide to the effects of economic policy.

MORE PROBLEMS AND APPLICATIONS

1. Imagine that you run the central bank in a large open economy with a floating exchange rate. Your goal is to stabilize income, and you adjust the money supply accordingly. Under your policy, what happens to the money supply, the interest rate, the exchange rate, and the trade balance in response to each of the following shocks?

   a. Taxes are raised to reduce the budget deficit.

   b. The import of foreign cars is restricted.

2. Since the 1980s, the economies of the world have become more financially integrated. That is, investors in all nations have become more willing and able to take advantage of financial opportunities abroad. Consider how this development affects the ability of monetary policy to influence the economy.

   a. If investors become more willing and able to substitute foreign and domestic assets, what happens to the slope of the *CF* function?

   b. If the *CF* function changes in this way, what happens to the slope of the *IS* curve?

   c. How does this change in the *IS* curve affect the Fed's ability to control the interest rate?

   d. How does this change in the *IS* curve affect the Fed's ability to control national income?

3. Suppose that policy makers in a large open economy want to raise the level of investment without changing aggregate income or the exchange rate.

   a. Is there any combination of domestic monetary and fiscal policies that would achieve this goal?

   b. Is there any combination of domestic monetary, fiscal, and trade policies that would achieve this goal?

   c. Is there any combination of monetary and fiscal policies at home and abroad that would achieve this goal?

4. The appendix considers the case of a large open economy with a floating exchange, but suppose instead that a large open economy has a fixed exchange rate. That is, the central bank announces a target for the exchange rate and commits itself to adjusting the money supply to ensure that the equilibrium exchange rate equals the target.

   a. Describe what happens to income, the interest rate, and the trade balance in response to a fiscal expansion, such as an increase in government purchases. Compare your answer with the case of a small open economy with a fixed exchange rate.

   b. Describe what happens to income, the interest rate, and the trade balance if the central bank expands the money supply by buying bonds from the public. Compare your answer with the case of a small open economy with a fixed exchange rate.

CHAPTER 14

Aggregate Supply and the Short-Run Trade-Off between Inflation and Unemployment

Probably the single most important macroeconomic relationship is the Phillips Curve.

— *George Akerlof*

There is always a temporary trade-off between inflation and unemployment; there is no permanent trade-off. The temporary trade-off comes not from inflation per se, but from unanticipated inflation, which generally means, from a rising rate of inflation.

— *Milton Friedman*

Most economists analyse short-run fluctuations in aggregate income and the price level using the model of aggregate demand and aggregate supply. In the previous three chapters, we examined aggregate demand in some detail. The *IS-LM* model – together with its open-economy cousin, the Mundell–Fleming model – shows how changes in monetary and fiscal policy and shocks to the money and goods markets shift the aggregate demand curve. In this chapter, we turn our attention to aggregate supply and develop theories that explain the position and slope of the aggregate supply curve.

When we introduced the aggregate supply curve in Chapter 10, we established that aggregate supply behaves differently in the short run to how it does in the long run. In the long run, prices are flexible, and the aggregate supply curve is vertical. When the aggregate supply curve is vertical, shifts in the aggregate demand curve affect the price level, but the output of the economy remains at its natural level. By contrast, in the short run, prices are sticky and the aggregate supply curve is not vertical. In this case, shifts in aggregate demand do cause fluctuations in output. In Chapter 10 we took a simplified view of price stickiness by drawing the short-run aggregate supply curve as a horizontal line, representing the extreme situation in which all prices are fixed. Our task now is to refine this understanding of short-run aggregate supply to better reflect the real world in which some prices are sticky and others are not.

Unfortunately, one fact makes our task more difficult: economists disagree about how best to explain aggregate supply. As a result, this chapter begins by presenting three models of the short-run aggregate supply curve. Among economists, each of these models has some prominent adherents (as well as some prominent critics), and you can decide for yourself which you find most plausible. Although these models differ in some significant details, they are related in an important way: they share a common theme about what makes the short-run and long-run aggregate supply curves differ, and a common conclusion that the short-run aggregate supply curve is upward sloping.

After examining the models, we examine an implication of the short-run aggregate supply curve. We show that this curve implies a trade-off between two measures of economic performance – inflation and unemployment. This trade-off, called the *Phillips curve,* tells us that to reduce the rate of inflation, policy makers must temporarily raise unemployment, and to reduce unemployment, they must accept higher inflation. As the quotation from Milton Friedman at the beginning of the chapter suggests, the trade-off between inflation and unemployment is only temporary. One goal of this chapter is to explain why policy makers face such a trade-off in the short run and, just as important, why they do not face it in the long run.

14-1 Three Models of Aggregate Supply

When classes in physics study balls rolling down inclined planes, they often begin by assuming away the existence of friction. This assumption makes the problem simpler and is useful in many circumstances, but no good engineer would ever take this assumption as a literal description of how the world works. Similarly, this book began with classical macroeconomic theory, but it would be a mistake to assume that this model is always true. Our job now is to look more deeply into the 'frictions' of macroeconomics.

We do this by examining three prominent models of aggregate supply. In all the models, some market imperfection (that is, some type of friction) causes the output of the economy to deviate from its natural level. As a result, the short-run aggregate supply curve is upward sloping, rather than vertical, and shifts in the aggregate demand curve cause output to fluctuate. These temporary deviations of output from its natural level represent the booms and busts of the business cycle.

Although each of the three models takes us down a different theoretical route, each route ends up in the same place. That final destination is a short-run aggregate supply equation of the form

$$Y = \overline{Y} + \alpha(P - P^e), \quad \alpha > 0,$$

where Y is output, $\overline{Y}$ is the natural level of output, P is the price level and P^e is the expected price level. This equation states that output deviates from its natural level when the price level deviates from the expected price level. The parameter α indicates how much output responds to unexpected changes in the price level; $1/\alpha$ is the slope of the aggregate supply curve.

Each of the three models tells a different story about what lies behind this short-run aggregate supply equation. In other words, each model highlights a particular reason why unexpected movements in the price level are associated with fluctuations in aggregate output.

The Sticky-Price Model

Our first explanation for the upward-sloping short-run aggregate supply curve is called the **sticky-price model**. This model emphasizes that firms do not instantly adjust the prices they charge in response to changes in demand. Sometimes prices are set by long-term contracts between firms and customers. Even without formal agreements, firms may hold prices steady in order not to annoy their regular customers with frequent price changes. Some prices are sticky because of the way markets are structured: once a firm has printed and distributed its catalogue or price list, it is costly to alter prices.

To see how sticky prices can help explain an upward-sloping aggregate supply curve, we first consider the pricing decisions of individual firms, and then add together the decisions of many firms to explain the behaviour of the economy as a whole. Notice that this model encourages us to depart from the assumption of perfect competition, which we have used since Chapter 3. Perfectly competitive firms are price takers rather than price setters. If we want to consider how firms set prices, it is natural to assume that these firms have at least some monopoly control over the prices they charge.

Consider the pricing decision facing a typical firm. The firm's desired price p depends on two macroeconomic variables:

- The overall level of prices P: a higher price level implies that the firm's costs are higher – hence, the higher the overall price level, the more the firm would like to charge for its product.
- The level of aggregate income Y: a higher level of income raises the demand for the firm's product – because marginal cost increases at higher levels of production, the greater the demand, the higher the firm's desired price.

$$p = P + a(Y - \overline{Y}).$$

This equation says that the desired price p depends on the overall level of prices P and on the level of aggregate output relative to the natural level $Y - \overline{Y}$. The parameter a (which is greater than zero) measures how much the firm's desired price responds to the level of aggregate output.[1]

Now assume that there are two types of firms. Some have flexible prices: they always set their prices according to this equation. Others have sticky prices: they announce their prices in advance, based on what they expect economic conditions to be. Firms with sticky prices set prices according to

$$p = P^e + a(Y^e - \overline{Y}^e),$$

where, as before, a superscript 'e' represents the expected value of a variable. For simplicity, assume that these firms expect output to be at its natural level, so that the last term, $a(Y^e - \overline{Y}^e)$, is zero. Then these firms set the price

$$p = P^e.$$

---

[1] *Mathematical note*: The firm cares most about its relative price, which is the ratio of its nominal price to the overall price level. If we interpret p and P as the logarithms of the firm's price and the price level, then this equation states that the desired relative price depends on the deviation of output from its natural level.

That is, firms with sticky prices set their prices based on what they expect other firms to charge.

We can use the pricing rules of the two groups of firms to derive the aggregate supply equation. To do this, we find the overall price level in the economy, which is the weighted average of the prices set by the two groups. If s is the fraction of firms with sticky prices, and $1 - s$ is the fraction with flexible prices, then the overall price level is

$$P = sP^e + (1 - s)[P + a(Y - \overline{Y})].$$

The first term is the price of the sticky-price firms weighted by their fraction in the economy, and the second term is the price of the flexible-price firms weighted by their fraction. Now subtract $(1 - s)P$ from both sides of this equation to obtain

$$sP = sP^e + (1 - s)[a(Y - \overline{Y})].$$

Divide both sides by s to solve for the overall price level:

$$P = P^e + [(1 - s)a/s](Y - \overline{Y}).$$

The two terms in this equation are explained as follows:

- When firms expect a high price level, they expect high costs. Those firms that fix prices in advance set their prices high. These high prices cause the other firms to set high prices also. Hence, a high expected price level P^e leads to a high actual price level P.

- When output is high, the demand for goods is high. Those firms with flexible prices set their prices high, which leads to a high price level. The effect of output on the price level depends on the proportion of firms with flexible prices.

Hence, the overall price level depends on the expected price level and on the level of output.

Algebraic rearrangement puts this aggregate pricing equation into a more familiar form:

$$Y = \overline{Y} + \alpha(P - P^e),$$

where $\alpha = s/[(1 - s)a]$. The sticky-price model says that the deviation of output from the natural level is positively associated with the deviation of the price level from the expected price level.[2]

The Sticky-Wage Model

To explain why the short-run aggregate supply curve is upward sloping, many economists stress the sluggish adjustment of nominal wages. In many industries, nominal wages are set by long-term contracts, so wages cannot adjust quickly

---

[2] For a more advanced development of the sticky-price model, see Julio Rotemberg, 'Monopolistic Price Adjustment and Aggregate Output', *Review of Economic Studies*, 1982, vol. 49, pp. 517–531.

when economic conditions change. Even in industries not covered by formal contracts, implicit agreements between workers and firms may limit wage changes. Wages may also depend on social norms and notions of fairness that evolve slowly. For these reasons, many economists believe that nominal wages are sticky in the short run.

The **sticky-wage model** shows what a sticky nominal wage implies for aggregate supply. To preview the model, consider what happens to the amount of output produced when the price level rises:

1. When the nominal wage is stuck, a rise in the price level lowers the real wage, making labour cheaper.

2. The lower real wage induces firms to hire more labour.

3. The additional labour hired produces more output.

This positive relationship between the price level and the amount of output means that the aggregate supply curve slopes upward during the time when the nominal wage cannot adjust to a change in the price level.

To develop this story of aggregate supply more formally, assume that workers and firms bargain over and agree on the nominal wage before they know what the price level will be when their agreement takes effect. The bargaining parties – the workers and the firms – have in mind a target real wage. The target may be the real wage that equilibrates labour supply and demand. More likely, the target real wage is higher than the equilibrium real wage: as discussed in Chapter 7, union power and efficiency-wage considerations tend to keep real wages above the level that brings labour supply and labour demand into balance.

The workers and firms set the nominal wage W based on the target real wage ω and on their expectation of the price level P^e. The nominal wage they set is

$$W \quad = \quad \omega \quad \times \quad P^e,$$

Nominal Wage = Target Real Wage × Expected Price Level.

After the nominal wage has been set and before labour has been hired, firms learn the actual price level P. The real wage turns out to be

$$W/P \quad = \quad \omega \quad \times \quad (P^e/P),$$

$$\text{Real Wage} = \text{Target Real Wage} \times \frac{\text{Expected Price Level}}{\text{Actual Price Level}}.$$

This equation shows that the real wage deviates from its target if the actual price level differs from the expected price level. When the actual price level is greater than expected, the real wage is less than its target; when the actual price level is less than expected, the real wage is greater than its target.

The final assumption of the sticky-wage model is that employment is determined by the quantity of labour that firms demand. In other words, the bargain between the workers and the firms does not determine the level of employment in advance; instead, the workers agree to provide as much labour as the firms wish to buy at the predetermined wage. We describe the firms' hiring decisions by the labour demand function

$$L = L^d(W/P),$$

which states that the lower the real wage, the more labour firms hire. The labour demand curve is shown in panel (a) of Figure 14-1. Output is determined by the production function

$$Y = F(L),$$

FIGURE 14-1

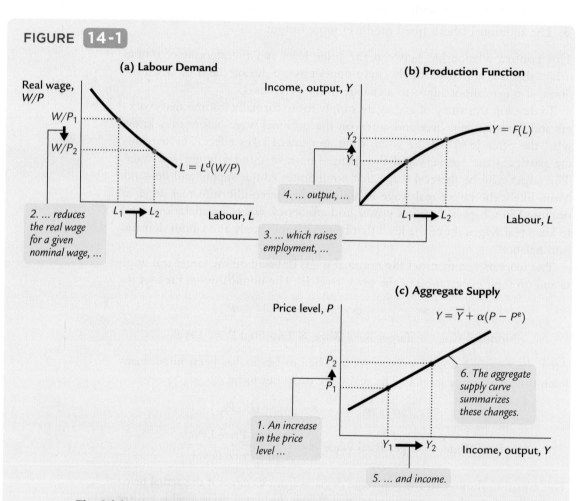

The Sticky-Wage Model Panel (a) shows the labour demand curve. Because the nominal wage W is stuck, an increase in the price level from P_1 to P_2 reduces the real wage from W/P_1 to W/P_2. The lower real wage raises the quantity of labour demanded from L_1 to L_2. Panel (b) shows the production function. An increase in the quantity of labour from L_1 to L_2 raises output from Y_1 to Y_2. Panel (c) shows the aggregate supply curve summarizing this relationship between the price level and output. An increase in the price level from P_1 to P_2 raises output from Y_1 to Y_2.

which states that the more labour is hired, the more output is produced. This is shown in panel (b) of Figure 14-1.

Panel (c) of Figure 14-1 shows the resulting aggregate supply curve. Because the nominal wage is sticky, an unexpected change in the price level moves the real wage away from the target real wage, and this change in the real wage influences the amounts of labour hired and output produced. The aggregate supply curve can be written as

$$Y = \overline{Y} + \alpha(P - P^e).$$

Output deviates from its natural level when the price level deviates from the expected price level.[3]

CASE STUDY

The Cyclical Behaviour of the Real Wage

In any model with an unchanging labour demand curve, such as the model we just discussed, employment rises when the real wage falls. In the sticky-wage model, an unexpected rise in the price level lowers the real wage and thereby raises the quantity of labour hired and the amount of output produced. Thus, the real wage should be *counter-cyclical:* it should fluctuate in the opposite direction from employment and output. Keynes himself wrote in *The General Theory* that 'an increase in employment can only occur to the accompaniment of a decline in the rate of real wages'.

The earliest attacks on *The General Theory* came from economists challenging Keynes's prediction. Figure 14-2 is a scatterplot of the percentage change in average real earnings and the percentage change in real GDP, using annual data for the UK economy from 1960 to 2011. If Keynes's prediction were correct, the dots in this figure would show a downward-sloping pattern, indicating a negative relationship. Yet the figure shows only a weak correlation between real earnings and output, and it is the opposite of what Keynes predicted. That is, if the real wage is cyclical at all, it is slightly *pro-cyclical:* the real wage tends to rise when output rises. Abnormally high labour costs cannot explain the low employment and output observed in recessions.

How should we interpret this evidence? Most economists conclude that the sticky-wage model cannot fully explain aggregate supply. They advocate models in which the labour demand curve shifts over the business cycle. These shifts may arise because firms have sticky prices: when prices are stuck too high, firms sell less of their output and reduce their demand for labour. Alternatively, the labour demand curve may shift because shocks to technology alter labour productivity. Economists have developed this idea, known as the theory of real

---

[3] For more on the sticky-wage model, see Jo Anna Gray, 'Wage Indexation: A Macroeconomic Approach', *Journal of Monetary Economics*, April 1976, vol. 2, pp. 221–235; and Stanley Fischer, 'Long-term Contracts, Rational Expectations, and the Optimal Money Supply Rule', *Journal of Political Economy*, February 1977, vol. 85, pp. 191–205.

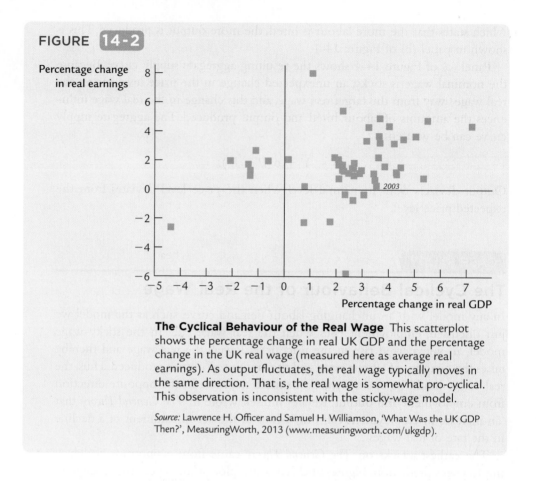

FIGURE 14-2

Percentage change in real earnings (y-axis) vs Percentage change in real GDP (x-axis)

2003

The Cyclical Behaviour of the Real Wage This scatterplot shows the percentage change in real UK GDP and the percentage change in the UK real wage (measured here as average real earnings). As output fluctuates, the real wage typically moves in the same direction. That is, the real wage is somewhat pro-cyclical. This observation is inconsistent with the sticky-wage model.

Source: Lawrence H. Officer and Samuel H. Williamson, 'What Was the UK GDP Then?', MeasuringWorth, 2013 (www.measuringworth.com/ukgdp).

business cycles, which gives a prominent role to technology shocks as a source of economic fluctuations.[4] ■

The Imperfect-Information Model

The third explanation for the upward slope of the short-run aggregate supply curve is called the **imperfect-information model**. Unlike the previous two models, this model assumes that markets clear — that is, all wages and prices are free to adjust to balance supply and demand. In this model, the short-run and long-run aggregate supply curves differ because of temporary misperceptions about prices.

The imperfect-information model assumes that each supplier in the economy produces a single good and consumes many goods. Because the number of goods is so large, suppliers cannot observe all prices at all times. They monitor closely the prices of what they produce, but less closely the prices of all the goods they

---

[4] For some of the recent work on the cyclical behaviour of the real wage, see Scott Sumner and Stephen Silver, 'Real Wages, Employment, and the Phillips Curve', *Journal of Political Economy*, June 1989, vol. 97, pp. 706–720; and Gary Solon, Robert Barsky and Jonathan A. Parker, 'Measuring the Cyclicality of Real Wages: How Important is Composition Bias?', *Quarterly Journal of Economics*, February 1994, vol. 109, pp. 1–25.

consume. Because of imperfect information, they sometimes confuse changes in the overall level of prices with changes in relative prices. This confusion influences decisions about how much to supply, and it leads to a positive relationship between the price level and output in the short run.

Consider the decision facing a single supplier – a wheat farmer, for instance. Because the farmer earns income from selling wheat, and uses this income to buy goods and services, the amount of wheat she chooses to produce depends on the price of wheat relative to the prices of other goods and services in the economy. If the relative price of wheat is high, the farmer is motivated to work hard and produce more wheat, because the reward is great. If the relative price of wheat is low, she prefers to enjoy more leisure and produce less wheat.

Unfortunately, when the farmer makes her production decision, she does not know the relative price of wheat. As a wheat producer, she monitors the wheat market closely and always knows the nominal price of wheat. But she does not know the prices of all the other goods in the economy. She must therefore estimate the relative price of wheat using the nominal price of wheat and her expectation of the overall price level.

Consider how the farmer responds if all prices in the economy, including the price of wheat, increase. One possibility is that she expected this change in prices. When she observes an increase in the price of wheat, her estimate of its relative price is unchanged. She does not work any harder.

The other possibility is that the farmer did not expect the price level to increase (or to increase by this much). When she observes the increase in the price of wheat, she is not sure whether other prices have risen (in which case wheat's relative price is unchanged) or whether only the price of wheat has risen (in which case its relative price is higher). The rational inference is that both have increased to some degree. In other words, the farmer infers from the increase in the nominal price of wheat that its relative price has risen somewhat. She works harder and produces more.

Our wheat farmer is not unique. When the price level rises unexpectedly, all suppliers in the economy observe increases in the prices of the goods they produce. They all infer, rationally but mistakenly, that the relative prices of the goods they produce have risen. They work harder and produce more.

To sum up, the imperfect-information model says that when actual prices exceed expected prices, suppliers raise their output. The model implies an aggregate supply curve with the familiar form:

$$Y = \overline{Y} + \alpha(P - P^e).$$

Output deviates from the natural level when the price level deviates from the expected price level.[5]

---

[5] Two economists who have emphasized the role of imperfect information for understanding the short-run effects of monetary policy are the Nobel Prize winners Milton Friedman and Robert Lucas. See Milton Friedman, 'The Role of Monetary Policy', *American Economic Review*, March 1968, vol. 58, pp. 1–17; and Robert E. Lucas, Jr., 'Understanding Business Cycles', *Carnegie-Rochester Conference on Public Policy*, vol. 5: *Stabilization of the Domestic and International Economy*, Amsterdam: North-Holland, 1999, pp. 7–29.

International Differences in the Aggregate Supply Curve

Although all countries experience economic fluctuations, these fluctuations are not exactly the same everywhere. International differences are intriguing puzzles in themselves, and they often provide a way to test alternative economic theories. Examining international differences has been especially fruitful in research on aggregate supply.

When economist Robert Lucas proposed the imperfect-information model, he derived a surprising interaction between aggregate demand and aggregate supply: according to his model, the slope of the aggregate supply curve should depend on the volatility of aggregate demand. In countries where aggregate demand fluctuates widely, the aggregate price level fluctuates widely as well. Because most movements in prices in these countries do not represent movements in relative prices, suppliers should have learned not to respond much to unexpected changes in the price level. Therefore, the aggregate supply curve should be relatively steep (that is, α will be small). Conversely, in countries where aggregate demand is relatively stable, suppliers should have learned that most price changes are relative price changes. Accordingly, in these countries, suppliers should be more responsive to unexpected price changes, making the aggregate supply curve relatively flat (that is, α will be large).

Lucas tested this prediction by examining international data on output and prices. He found that changes in aggregate demand have the biggest effect on output in those countries where aggregate demand and prices are most stable. Lucas concluded that the evidence supports the imperfect-information model.[6]

The sticky-price model also makes predictions about the slope of the short-run aggregate supply curve. In particular, it predicts that the average rate of inflation should influence the slope of the short-run aggregate supply curve. When the average rate of inflation is high, it is very costly for firms to keep prices fixed for long intervals. Thus, firms adjust prices more frequently. More frequent price adjustment, in turn, allows the overall price level to respond more quickly to shocks to aggregate demand. Hence, a high rate of inflation should make the short-run aggregate supply curve steeper.

International data support this prediction of the sticky-price model. In countries with low average inflation, the short-run aggregate supply curve is relatively flat: fluctuations in aggregate demand have large effects on output and are slowly reflected in prices. High-inflation countries have steep short-run aggregate supply curves. In other words, high inflation appears to erode the frictions that cause prices to be sticky.[7]

Note that the sticky-price model can also explain Lucas's finding that countries with variable aggregate demand have steep aggregate supply curves. If the

---

[6] Robert E. Lucas, Jr., 'Some International Evidence on Output–Inflation Tradeoffs', *American Economic Review*, June 1973, vol. 63, pp. 326–334.

[7] Laurence Ball, N. Gregory Mankiw and David Romer, 'The New Keynesian Economics and the Output–Inflation Trade-off ', *Brookings Papers on Economic Activity*, 1988, vol. 1, pp. 1–65.

price level is highly variable, few firms will commit to prices in advance (s will be small). Hence the aggregate supply curve will be steep (α will be small). ■

Summary and Implications

We have seen three models of aggregate supply and the market imperfection that each uses to explain why the short-run aggregate supply curve is upward sloping. One model assumes that the prices of some goods are sticky; the second assumes that nominal wages are sticky; the third assumes that information about prices is imperfect. Keep in mind that these models are not incompatible with one another. We need not accept one model and reject the others. The world may contain all three of these market imperfections, and all may contribute to the behaviour of short-run aggregate supply.

Although the three models of aggregate supply differ in their assumptions and emphases, their implications for aggregate output are similar. All can be summarized by the equation

$$Y = \overline{Y} + \alpha(P - P^e).$$

This equation states that deviations of output from the natural level are related to deviations of the price level from the expected price level. *If the price level is higher than the expected price level, output exceeds its natural level. If the price level is lower than the expected price level, output falls short of its natural level.* Figure 14-3 graphs this equation. Notice that the short-run aggregate supply curve is drawn for a given expectation P^e and that a change in P^e would shift the curve.

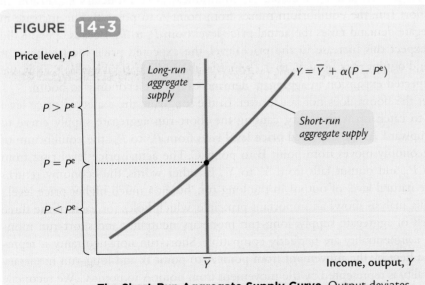

FIGURE 14-3

The Short-Run Aggregate Supply Curve Output deviates from its natural level $\overline{Y}$ if the price level P deviates from the expected price level P^e.

FIGURE 14-4

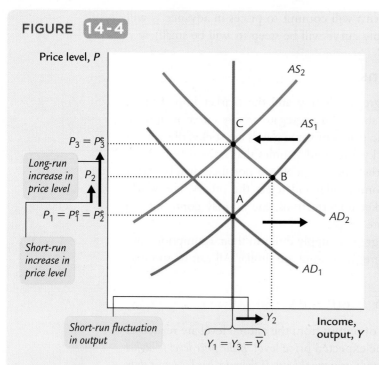

FIGURE 14-4

How Shifts in Aggregate Demand Lead to Short-Run Fluctuations Here the economy begins in a long-run equilibrium, point A. When aggregate demand increases unexpectedly, the price level rises from P_1 to P_2. Because the price level P_2 is above the expected price level P_2^e, output rises temporarily above the natural level, as the economy moves along the short-run aggregate supply curve from point A to point B. In the long run, the expected price level rises to P_3^e, causing the short-run aggregate supply curve to shift upward. The economy returns to a new long-run equilibrium, point C, where output is back at its natural level.

Now that we have a better understanding of aggregate supply, let's put aggregate supply and aggregate demand back together. Figure 14-4 uses our aggregate supply equation to show how the economy responds to an unexpected increase in aggregate demand attributable, say, to an unexpected monetary expansion. In the short run, the equilibrium moves from point A to point B. The increase in aggregate demand raises the actual price level from P_1 to P_2. Because people did not expect this increase in the price level, the expected price level remains at P_2^e, and output rises from Y_1 to Y_2, which is above the natural level $\overline{Y}$. Thus, the unexpected expansion in aggregate demand causes the economy to boom.

Yet the boom does not last forever. In the long run, the expected price level rises to catch up with reality, causing the short-run aggregate supply curve to shift upward. As the expected price level rises from P_2^e to P_3^e, the equilibrium of the economy moves from point B to point C. The actual price level rises from P_2 to P_3, and output falls from Y_2 to Y_3. In other words, the economy returns to the natural level of output in the long run, but at a much higher price level.

This analysis shows an important principle, which holds for each of the three models of aggregate supply: long-run monetary neutrality and short-run monetary *non*-neutrality are perfectly compatible. Short-run non-neutrality is represented here by the movement from point A to point B, and long-run monetary neutrality is represented by the movement from point A to point C. We reconcile the short-run and long-run effects of money by emphasizing the adjustment of expectations about the price level.

14-2 Inflation, Unemployment and the Phillips Curve

Two goals of economic policy makers are low inflation and low unemployment, but often these goals conflict. Suppose, for instance, that policy makers were to use monetary or fiscal policy to expand aggregate demand. This policy would move the economy along the short-run aggregate supply curve to a point of higher output and a higher price level. (Figure 14-4 shows this as the change from point A to point B.) Higher output means lower unemployment, because firms employ more workers when they produce more. A higher price level, given the previous year's price level, means higher inflation. Thus, when policy makers move the economy up along the short-run aggregate supply curve, they reduce the unemployment rate and raise the inflation rate. Conversely, when they contract aggregate demand and move the economy down the short-run aggregate supply curve, unemployment rises and inflation falls.

This trade-off between inflation and unemployment, called the *Phillips curve,* is our topic in this section. As we have just seen (and will derive more formally in a moment), the Phillips curve is a reflection of the short-run aggregate supply curve: as policy makers move the economy along the short-run aggregate supply curve, unemployment and inflation move in opposite directions. The Phillips curve is a useful way to express aggregate supply because inflation and unemployment are such important measures of economic performance.

Deriving the Phillips Curve from the Aggregate Supply Curve

The **Phillips curve** in its modern form states that the inflation rate depends on three forces:

- expected inflation;
- the deviation of unemployment from the natural rate, called *cyclical unemployment;*
- supply shocks.

These three forces are expressed in the following equation:

$$\pi \quad = \quad \pi^e \quad - \quad \beta(u - u^n) \quad + \quad v,$$

Inflation = Expected Inflation − (β × Cyclical Unemployment) + Supply Shock,

where β is a parameter measuring the response of inflation to cyclical unemployment. Notice that there is a minus sign before the cyclical unemployment term: other things equal, higher unemployment is associated with lower inflation.

Where does this equation for the Phillips curve come from? Although it may not seem familiar, we can derive it from our equation for aggregate supply. To see how, write the aggregate supply equation as

$$P = P^e + (1/\alpha)(Y - \overline{Y}).$$

With one addition, one subtraction and one substitution, we can transform this equation into the Phillips curve relationship between inflation and unemployment.

Here are the three steps. First, add to the right-hand side of the equation a supply shock v to represent exogenous events (such as a change in world oil prices) that alter the price level and shift the short-run aggregate supply curve:

$$P = P^e + (1/\overline{Y})(Y - \overline{Y}) + v.$$

Next, to go from the price level to inflation rates, subtract last year's price level P_{-1} from both sides of the equation to obtain

$$(P - P_{-1}) = (P^e - P_{-1}) + (1/\overline{Y})(Y - \overline{Y}) + v.$$

The term on the left-hand side, $P - P_{-1}$, is the difference between the current price level and last year's price level, which is inflation π.[8] The term on the right-hand side, $P^e - P_{-1}$, is the difference between the expected price level and last year's price level, which is expected inflation π^e. Therefore, we can replace $P - P_{-1}$ with π, and $P^e - P_{-1}$ with π^e:

$$\pi = \pi^e + (1/\overline{Y})(Y - \overline{Y}) + v.$$

Third, to go from output to unemployment, we simply note that output will be a positive function of the number of people employed, through the aggregate production function. But if output is positively related to the level of employment, it must in general be negatively related to the level of unemployment. In particular, the deviation of output from its natural level will tend to be inversely related to the deviation of unemployment from its natural rate; that is, when output is higher than the natural level of output, unemployment is lower than the natural rate of unemployment. We can write this as

$$(1/\alpha)(Y - \overline{Y}) = -\beta(u - u^n).$$

Using this relationship, we can substitute $-\beta(u - u^n)$ for $(1/\alpha)(Y - \overline{Y})$ in the previous equation to obtain

$$\pi = \pi^e - \beta(u - u^n) + v.$$

Thus, we can derive the Phillips curve equation from the aggregate supply equation.

All this algebra is meant to show one thing: the Phillips curve equation and the short-run aggregate supply equation represent essentially the same macroeconomic ideas. In particular, both equations show a link between real and

---

[8] *Mathematical note:* This statement is not precise, because inflation is really the *percentage* change in the price level. To make the statement more precise, interpret P as the logarithm of the price level. By the properties of logarithms, the change in P is roughly the inflation rate. The reason is that $dP = d$ (log price level) $= d$ (price level)/price level.

F Y I

The History of the Modern Phillips Curve

The Phillips curve is named after New Zealand-born economist A. W. Phillips, who worked at the London School of Economics. In 1958, Phillips observed a negative relationship between the unemployment rate and the rate of wage inflation in data for the United Kingdom.[9] The Phillips curve that economists use today differs in three ways from the relationship Phillips examined.

First, the modern Phillips curve substitutes price inflation for wage inflation. This difference is not crucial, because price inflation and wage inflation are closely related. In periods when wages are rising quickly, prices are rising quickly as well.

Second, the modern Phillips curve includes expected inflation. This addition is due to the work of Nobel Prize winners Milton Friedman and Edmund Phelps. In developing early versions of the imperfect-information model in the 1960s, these two economists emphasized the importance of expectations for aggregate supply.

Third, the modern Phillips curve includes supply shocks. Credit for this addition goes to OPEC, the Organization of Petroleum Exporting Countries. In the 1970s, OPEC caused large increases in the world price of oil, which made economists more aware of the importance of shocks to aggregate supply.

[9] A. W. Phillips, 'The Relationship between Unemployment and the Rate of Change of Money Wages in the United Kingdom, 1861–1957', *Economica*, November 1958, vol. 25, pp. 283–299.

nominal variables which causes the classical dichotomy (the theoretical separation of real and nominal variables) to break down in the short run. According to the short-run aggregate supply equation, output is related to unexpected movements in the price level. According to the Phillips curve equation, unemployment is related to unexpected movements in the inflation rate. The aggregate supply curve is more convenient when we are studying output and the price level, whereas the Phillips curve is more convenient when we are studying unemployment and inflation. But we should not lose sight of the fact that the Phillips curve and the aggregate supply curve are two sides of the same coin.

Adaptive Expectations and Inflation Inertia

To make the Phillips curve useful for analysing the choices facing policy makers, we need to say what determines expected inflation. A simple and often plausible assumption is that people form their expectations of inflation based on recently observed inflation. This assumption is called **adaptive expectations**. For example, suppose that people expect prices to rise this year at the same rate as they did last year. Then expected inflation π^e equals last year's inflation π_{-1}:

$$\pi^e = \pi_{-1}.$$

In this case, we can write the Phillips curve as

$$\pi = \pi_{-1} - \beta(u - u^n) + v,$$

which states that inflation depends on past inflation, cyclical unemployment and a supply shock. When the Phillips curve is written in this form, the natural rate of unemployment is sometimes called the Non-Accelerating Inflation Rate of Unemployment, or *NAIRU*.

The first term in this form of the Phillips curve, π_{-1}, implies that inflation has inertia. That is, like an object moving through space, inflation keeps going unless something acts to stop it. In particular, if unemployment is at the NAIRU and if there are no supply shocks, the continued rise in price level neither speeds up nor slows down. This inertia arises because past inflation influences expectations of future inflation, and because these expectations influence the wages and prices that people set. Robert Solow captured the concept of inflation inertia well when, during the high inflation of the 1970s, he wrote: 'Why is our money ever less valuable? Perhaps it is simply that we have inflation because we expect inflation, and we expect inflation because we've had it.'

In the model of aggregate supply and aggregate demand, inflation inertia is interpreted as persistent upward shifts in both the aggregate supply curve and the aggregate demand curve. Consider, first, aggregate supply. If prices have been rising quickly, people will expect them to continue to rise quickly. Because the position of the short-run aggregate supply curve depends on the expected price level, the short-run aggregate supply curve will shift upward over time. It will continue to shift upward until some event, such as a recession or a supply shock, changes inflation and thereby changes expectations of inflation.

The aggregate demand curve must also shift upward to confirm the expectations of inflation. Most often, the continued rise in aggregate demand is due to persistent growth in the money supply. If the central bank suddenly halted money growth, aggregate demand would stabilize, and the upward shift in aggregate supply would cause a recession. The high unemployment in the recession would reduce inflation and expected inflation, causing inflation inertia to subside.

Two Causes of Rising and Falling Inflation

The second and third terms in the Phillips curve equation show the two forces that can change the rate of inflation.

The second term, $\beta(u - u^n)$, shows that cyclical unemployment – the deviation of unemployment from its natural rate – exerts upward or downward pressure on inflation. Low unemployment pulls the inflation rate up. This is called **demand-pull inflation** because high aggregate demand is responsible for this type of inflation. High unemployment pulls the inflation rate down. The parameter β measures how responsive inflation is to cyclical unemployment.

The third term, v, shows that inflation also rises and falls because of supply shocks. An adverse supply shock, such as the rise in world oil prices in the 1970s, implies a positive value of v and causes inflation to rise. This is called **cost-push inflation** because adverse supply shocks are typically events that push up the costs of production. A beneficial supply shock, such as the oil glut that led to a fall in oil prices in the 1980s, makes v negative and causes inflation to fall.

Inflation and Unemployment in the United Kingdom

Because inflation and unemployment are such important measures of economic performance, macroeconomic developments are often viewed through the lens of the Phillips curve. Figure 14-5 displays the history of inflation and unemployment in the United Kingdom since 1971. These four decades of data illustrate some of the causes of rising or falling inflation in terms of the demand-pull and cost-push influences that operate through the Phillips curve.

The 1970s was a period of economic turmoil. Inflation, as measured by the RPI, rose from 7.1 per cent in 1972 to 24.2 per cent in 1975. At the same time, unemployment rose from 4 per cent to just over 5 per cent. In part, this was due to the large negative supply shocks caused by the Organization of Petroleum Exporting Countries (OPEC), in the form of a quadrupling of oil prices in 1973–1974, a form of cost-push inflation. However, during the early 1970s, expansionary fiscal policy had strongly stimulated aggregate demand, pushing unemployment below its natural rate, so that unemployment was already set to rise back towards the natural rate. When the oil shock was piled on top of this, the combination led to simultaneously rising inflation and rising unemployment –

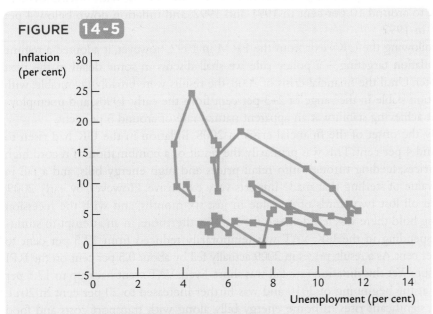

FIGURE 14-5

Inflation and Unemployment in the United Kingdom Since 1971 This figure uses annual data on the unemployment rate and the inflation rate (percentage change in the GDP deflator) to illustrate macroeconomic developments in almost a half-century of UK history.

Source: Lawrence H. Officer and Samuel H. Williamson, 'What Was the UK GDP Then?', MeasuringWorth, 2013 (www.measuringworth.com/ukgdp) and UK Office for National Statistics.

so-called stagflation. High unemployment during the ensuing recession reduced inflation somewhat, but further OPEC price hikes pushed inflation up again in the late 1970s.

The 1980s began with high inflation and high expectations of inflation. The newly elected Conservative government, led by Margaret Thatcher, doggedly pursued monetary policies aimed at reducing inflation. In 1983, the unemployment rate reached its highest level in 50 years. High unemployment and a consequent contraction in aggregate demand, aided by a fall in oil prices in 1980, pulled the inflation rate down from about 18 per cent in 1980 to about 5 per cent by 1984. By 1987, the unemployment rate of about 9.5 per cent was close to most estimates of the natural rate, and inflation was stable at a little over 4 per cent.

In the late 1980s, a combination of measures raised inflation again: tax cuts in 1987 and 1988, some relaxation of monetary policy, and rising asset prices all boosted aggregate demand and meant that the UK ended the decade with unemployment around 8 per cent and inflation around 10 per cent.

In the early 1990s, the UK tried to keep its exchange rate pegged against the German mark and other European currencies when it joined the European Exchange Rate Mechanism (ERM), but the UK had arguably set its rate against the mark at too high a level, making its exports uncompetitive and requiring high levels of interest rates. The result was a contraction in aggregate demand that ushered in the recession of the early 1990s, with unemployment back to around 10 per cent in 1991 and 1992, and inflation down below 4 per cent in 1992.

Following the UK's exit from the ERM in 1992, however, it adopted a regime of inflation targeting – a policy rule we shall discuss in some detail in the next chapter. Until the financial crisis of 2008, the results were broadly favourable, with inflation stable in the range of 2–3 per cent from the early 1990s, and unemployment achieving stability at an apparent natural rate of around 5 per cent.

By the onset of the financial crisis in 2008, inflation in the UK had risen to around 4 per cent. This was primarily the result of a combination of record high oil prices, feeding through into retail prices and high energy bills, and a fall in the value of sterling that made imports very expensive. However, by early 2009, crude oil lost two-thirds of its value in just six months, and with the recession taking hold there was less demand for fuel. Furthermore, in an attempt to stimulate spending in the UK, VAT was temporarily reduced from 17.5 per cent to 15 per cent. As a result, prices in 2009 actually fell by about 0.5 per cent on the RPI measure. Yet this inflation rate fall was short-lived: VAT went back up to 17.5 per cent at the beginning of 2010 and was further increased to 20 per cent in 2011. Also, significant rises in home energy bills, along with transport costs and food prices, pushed up prices even further. By 2011, inflation was at 5.2 per cent, the highest since 1991. Over the same period, unemployment rose steadily. When the financial crisis hit in 2008, the unemployment rate was a little over 5 per cent. Towards the end of 2009, with the UK struggling to recover from its severest recession since the 1930s, unemployment was up by two percentage points, and peaked at just over 8 per cent in mid-2012. The main driving force behind the increase in unemployment was reduced private and public spending. The austerity measures, a lack of market confidence and increased financial uncertainty weakened aggregate demand and consequently the demand for labour as well. The latest figures for 2013 suggest that 7.7 per cent of the labour force are jobless. The fall in the jobless figures suggest that the UK economy has finally begun to emerge from the recession.

Thus, macroeconomic history illustrates the many forces working on the inflation rate, as described in the Phillips curve equation. The 1960s and 1980s show the two sides of demand–pull inflation: in the 1960s low unemployment pulled inflation up, and in the 1980s high unemployment pulled inflation down. The oil-price hikes of the 1970s show the effects of cost-push inflation. And the 2000s show that inflation sometimes surprises us, in part because changing expectations are not always easy to predict. ■

The Short-Run Trade-Off between Inflation and Unemployment

Consider the options the Phillips curve gives to a policy maker who can influence aggregate demand with monetary or fiscal policy. At any moment, expected inflation and supply shocks are beyond the policy maker's immediate control. Yet by changing aggregate demand, the policy maker can alter output, unemployment and inflation. The policy maker can expand aggregate demand to lower unemployment and raise inflation. Or the policy maker can depress aggregate demand to raise unemployment and lower inflation.

Figure 14-6 plots the Phillips curve equation and shows the short-run trade-off between inflation and unemployment. When unemployment is at its natural rate ($u = u^n$), inflation depends on expected inflation and the supply

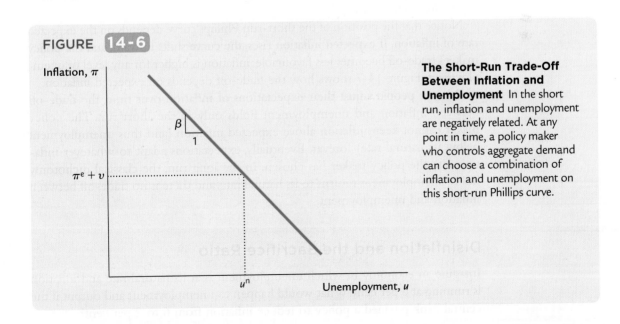

FIGURE 14-6

Inflation, π

β

1

$\pi^e + \upsilon$

u^n

Unemployment, u

The Short-Run Trade-Off Between Inflation and Unemployment In the short run, inflation and unemployment are negatively related. At any point in time, a policy maker who controls aggregate demand can choose a combination of inflation and unemployment on this short-run Phillips curve.

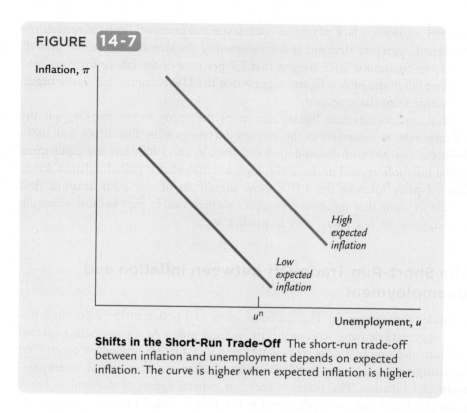

FIGURE 14-7

Shifts in the Short-Run Trade-Off The short-run trade-off between inflation and unemployment depends on expected inflation. The curve is higher when expected inflation is higher.

shock ($\pi = \pi^e + \nu$). The parameter β determines the slope of the trade-off between inflation and unemployment. In the short run, for a given level of expected inflation, policy makers can manipulate aggregate demand to choose any combination of inflation and unemployment on this curve, called the *short-run Phillips curve*.

Notice that the position of the short-run Phillips curve depends on the expected rate of inflation. If expected inflation rises, the curve shifts upward, and the policy maker's trade-off becomes less favourable: inflation is higher for any level of unemployment. Figure 14-7 shows how the trade-off depends on expected inflation.

Because people adjust their expectations of inflation over time, the trade-off between inflation and unemployment holds only in the short run. The policy maker cannot keep inflation above expected inflation (and thus unemployment below its natural rate) forever. Eventually, expectations adapt to whatever inflation rate the policy maker has chosen. In the long run, the classical dichotomy holds, unemployment returns to its natural rate, and there is no trade-off between inflation and unemployment.

Disinflation and the Sacrifice Ratio

Imagine an economy in which unemployment is at its natural rate and inflation is running at 6 per cent. What would happen to unemployment and output if the central bank pursued a policy to reduce inflation from 6 to 2 per cent?

F Y I

How Precise Are Estimates of the Natural Rate of Unemployment?

If you ask an astronomer how far a particular star is from our sun, he will give you a number, but it will not be accurate. Man's ability to measure astronomical distances is still limited. An astronomer might well take better measurements and conclude that a star is really twice or half as far away as he previously thought.

Estimates of the natural rate of unemployment, or NAIRU, are also far from precise. One problem is supply shocks. Shocks to oil supplies, farm harvests or technological progress can cause inflation to rise or fall in the short run. When we observe rising inflation, therefore, we cannot be sure if it is evidence that the unemployment rate is below the natural rate or

evidence that the economy is experiencing an adverse supply shock.

A second problem is that the natural rate changes over time. Demographic changes (such as the ageing of the baby-boom generation), policy changes (such as minimum-wage laws) and institutional changes (such as the declining role of unions) all influence the economy's normal level of unemployment. Estimating the natural rate is like hitting a moving target.

This conclusion has profound implications. Policy makers may want to keep unemployment close to its natural rate, but their ability to do so is limited by the fact that they cannot be sure what that natural rate is.

The Phillips curve shows that in the absence of a beneficial supply shock, lowering inflation requires a period of high unemployment and reduced output. But by how much and for how long would unemployment need to rise above the natural rate? Before deciding whether to reduce inflation, policy makers must know how much output would be lost during the transition to lower inflation. This cost can then be compared with the benefits of lower inflation.

Much research has used the available data to examine the Phillips curve quantitatively. The results of these studies are often summarized in a number called the **sacrifice ratio**, the percentage of a year's real GDP that must be forgone to reduce inflation by 1 percentage point. Estimates of the sacrifice ratio vary widely from country to country. For example, the economist Laurence Ball, using data on 25 disinflation episodes for 19 countries during the 1960s, 1970s and 1980s, estimated the average sacrifice ratio at around 2 for Austria, Denmark, the Netherlands and Sweden, at around 3 for the UK, Belgium, Ireland and Spain, at around 6 for Italy and at about 10 for the US and Germany.[10]

These estimates are not comforting. Even if we take the lower end of the estimated range, the implication is that for every percentage point that inflation is to fall, at least 2 per cent of one year's GDP must be sacrificed.

We can also express the sacrifice ratio in terms of unemployment. When we move along the short-run Phillips curve, we trade off inflation against unemployment. A typical estimate of this trade-off says that a change of 1 percentage

---

[10] Laurence Ball, 'What Determines the Sacrifice Ratio?', in N. Gregory Mankiw, ed., *Monetary Policy*, Chicago: University of Chicago Press, 1994, pp. 153–193..

point in the unemployment rate translates into a change of 1.5 percentage points in GDP. Therefore, assuming an output–inflation sacrifice ratio of 2, reducing inflation by 1 percentage point requires about 3 percentage points of cyclical unemployment.[11]

We can use the sacrifice ratio to estimate by how much and for how long unemployment must rise to reduce inflation. If reducing inflation by 1 percentage point requires a sacrifice of 2 per cent of a year's GDP, reducing inflation by 4 percentage points requires a sacrifice of 8 per cent of a year's GDP. Equivalently, this reduction in inflation requires a sacrifice of about 12 percentage points of cyclical unemployment.

This disinflation could take various forms, each totalling the same sacrifice of 8 per cent of a year's GDP. For example, a rapid disinflation would lower output by 4 per cent for two years: this is sometimes called the *cold-turkey* solution to inflation. A moderate disinflation would lower output by 2 per cent for four years. An even more gradual disinflation would depress output by just under 1 per cent for a decade.

Rational Expectations and the Possibility of Painless Disinflation

Because the expectation of inflation influences the short-run trade-off between inflation and unemployment, it is crucial to understand how people form expectations. So far, we have been assuming that expected inflation depends on recently observed inflation. Although this assumption of adaptive expectations is plausible, it is probably too simple to apply in all circumstances.

An alternative approach is to assume that people have **rational expectations**. That is, we might assume that people optimally use all the available information, including information about current government policies, to forecast the future. Because monetary and fiscal policies influence inflation, expected inflation should also depend on the monetary and fiscal policies in effect. According to the theory of rational expectations, a change in monetary or fiscal policy will change expectations, and an evaluation of any policy change must incorporate this effect on expectations. If people do form their expectations rationally, then inflation may have less inertia than it first appears.

---

[11] A simple estimate of this trade-off can be derived from the Cobb-Douglas production function, $Y = AK^\alpha L^{1-\alpha}$. As we discussed in Chapter 3, the Cobb–Douglas production function is not a bad description of aggregate production in many advanced economies. Moreover, α, capital's share in income, is fairly constant at around 0.3 for advanced economies, and labour's share, $1 - \alpha$, is fairly constant at around 0.7. But note that $1 - \alpha$ can also be interpreted as an elasticity – it tells us the percentage change in output that results from a 1 per cent change in labour input, holding the capital stock and total factor productivity constant. Hence, a good rule of thumb is that a 1 per cent reduction in employment leads to a 0.7 per cent reduction in output. If employment and unemployment are closely linked so that, to a first approximation, increases in unemployment are equal to reductions in employment, this means that a 1 per cent increase in unemployment will be associated with a 0.7 per cent fall in output, or, alternatively expressed, that a 1 per cent fall in output will be associated with a $1/0.7 \approx 1.5$ per cent increase in unemployment.

Here is how Thomas Sargent, a prominent advocate of rational expectations and a 2011 Nobel laureate in economics, describes its implications for the Phillips curve:

> An alternative 'rational expectations' view denies that there is any inherent momentum to the present process of inflation. This view maintains that firms and workers have now come to expect high rates of inflation in the future and that they strike inflationary bargains in light of these expectations. However, it is held that people expect high rates of inflation in the future precisely because the government's current and prospective monetary and fiscal policies warrant those expectations . . . Thus inflation only seems to have a momentum of its own; it is actually the long-term government policy of persistently running large deficits and creating money at high rates which imparts the momentum to the inflation rate. An implication of this view is that inflation can be stopped much more quickly than advocates of the 'momentum' view have indicated and that their estimates of the length of time and the costs of stopping inflation in terms of foregone output are erroneous . . . [Stopping inflation] would require a change in the policy regime: there must be an abrupt change in the continuing government policy, or strategy, for setting deficits now and in the future that is sufficiently binding as to be widely believed . . . How costly such a move would be in terms of foregone output and how long it would be in taking effect would depend partly on how resolute and evident the government's commitment was.[12]

Thus, advocates of rational expectations argue that the short-run Phillips curve does not accurately represent the options that policy makers have available. They believe that if policy makers are credibly committed to reducing inflation, rational people will understand the commitment and will quickly lower their expectations of inflation. Inflation can then come down without a rise in unemployment and fall in output. According to the theory of rational expectations, traditional estimates of the sacrifice ratio are not useful for evaluating the impact of alternative policies. Under a credible policy, the costs of reducing inflation may be much lower than estimates of the sacrifice ratio suggest.

In the most extreme case, one can imagine reducing the rate of inflation without causing any recession at all. A painless disinflation has two requirements. First, the plan to reduce inflation must be announced before the workers and firms who set wages and prices have formed their expectations. Second, the workers and firms must believe the announcement; otherwise, they will not reduce their expectations of inflation. If both requirements are met, the announcement will immediately shift the short-run trade-off between inflation and unemployment downward, permitting a lower rate of inflation without higher unemployment.

Although the rational-expectations approach remains controversial, almost all economists agree that expectations of inflation influence the short-run trade-off between inflation and unemployment. The credibility of a policy to reduce inflation is therefore one determinant of how costly the policy will be. Unfortunately, it is often difficult to predict whether the public will view the announcement of

---

[12] Thomas J. Sargent, 'The Ends of Four Big Inflations', in Robert E. Hall, ed., *Inflation: Causes and Effects*, Chicago: University of Chicago Press, 1982, pp. 41–98.

a new policy as credible. The central role of expectations makes forecasting the results of alternative policies far more difficult.

The Sacrifice Ratio in Practice: The Thatcher Disinflation

The Phillips curve with adaptive expectations implies that reducing inflation requires a period of high unemployment and low output. By contrast, the rational-expectations approach suggests that reducing inflation can be much less costly. What happens during actual disinflations?

Consider the UK disinflation in the early 1980s. This decade began with some of the highest rates of inflation in UK history. Yet because of the tight monetary policies the government pursued under Prime Minister Margaret Thatcher, the rate of inflation fell substantially in the first few years of the decade. This episode provides a natural experiment with which to estimate how much output is lost during the process of disinflation.

The first question is: How much did inflation fall? As measured by the GDP deflator, inflation reached a peak of about 18 per cent in 1980. It is natural to end the episode in 1985 because oil prices plunged in 1986 – a large, beneficial supply shock unrelated to government policy. In 1985, UK inflation was about 6 per cent, so we can estimate that the Thatcher administration engineered a reduction in inflation of 12 percentage points over five years.

The second question is: How much output was lost during this period? Table 14-1 shows the unemployment rate from 1981 to 1985. Assuming that the natural rate of unemployment was 9.5 per cent over this period, we can compute the amount of cyclical unemployment in each year. In total over this period, there were 8.7 percentage points of cyclical unemployment.

Now we can compute the sacrifice ratio for this episode. We know that about 9 percentage points of cyclical unemployment were generated and that inflation fell by about 12 points. Hence, 9/12 or about 0.75 percentage points of cyclical

TABLE 14-1

UK Unemployment During the Thatcher Disinflation

Year	Unemployment Rate u (%)	Natural Rate u^n (%)	Cyclical Unemployment $u - u^n$ (%)
1981	10.4	9.5	0.9
1982	11.2	9.5	1.7
1983	11.8	9.5	2.3
1984	11.5	9.5	2.0
1985	11.3	9.5	1.8
		Total	**8.7%**

unemployment were generated for each percentage-point reduction in inflation. Alternatively, if we use the rule of thumb that each 1.5 per cent increase in cyclical unemployment reduces output by 1 per cent, then the 9 percentage points of cyclical unemployment translate into 9/1.5 = 6 percentage points of GDP, and the sacrifice ratio is estimated as 6/12, or 0.5.

This estimate of the sacrifice ratio is actually very much smaller than had been expected – as we discussed earlier, estimates of the UK sacrifice ratio tended to put it at around 3. Thus, Thatcher reduced inflation at a smaller cost than many economists had predicted. One explanation is that Thatcher's tough stand, both on monetary policy and on labour market reform, was credible enough to influence expectations of inflation directly. Yet the change in expectations was not large enough to make the disinflation painless: the UK unemployment rates of the early 1980s were at their highest levels since the Great Depression of the 1930s.

Although the Thatcher disinflation is only one historical episode, this kind of analysis can be applied to other disinflations. Laurence Ball's study of the sacrifice ratio and disinflation episodes, which we discussed earlier, found that in almost all cases the reduction in inflation came at the cost of temporarily lower output. Yet the size of the output loss varied from episode to episode. Rapid disinflations usually had smaller sacrifice ratios than slower ones. That is, in contrast to what the Phillips curve with adaptive expectations suggests, a cold-turkey approach appears less costly than a gradual one. Moreover, countries with more flexible wage-setting institutions, such as shorter labour contracts, had smaller sacrifice ratios. These findings indicate that reducing inflation always has some cost, but that policies and institutions can affect its magnitude. ■

Hysteresis and the Challenge to the Natural-Rate Hypothesis

Our discussion of the cost of disinflation – and indeed our entire discussion of economic fluctuations in the past four chapters – has been based on an assumption called the **natural-rate hypothesis**. This hypothesis is summarized in the following statement: *Fluctuations in aggregate demand affect output and employment only in the short run. In the long run, the economy returns to the levels of output, employment and unemployment described by the classical model.*

The natural-rate hypothesis allows macroeconomists to study separately short-run and long-run developments in the economy. It is one expression of the classical dichotomy.

Some economists have challenged the natural-rate hypothesis by suggesting that aggregate demand may affect output and employment even in the long run. They have pointed out a number of mechanisms through which recessions might leave permanent scars on the economy by altering the natural rate of unemployment. **Hysteresis** is the term used to describe the long-lasting influence of history on the natural rate.

A recession can have permanent effects if it changes the people who become unemployed. For instance, workers might lose valuable job skills when unemployed, lowering their ability to find a job even after the recession ends. Alternatively, a long period of unemployment may change an individual's attitude towards work and reduce his or her desire to find employment. In either case, the recession permanently inhibits the process of job search and raises the amount of frictional unemployment.

Another way in which a recession can permanently affect the economy is by changing the process that determines wages. Those who become unemployed may lose their influence on the wage-setting process. Unemployed workers may lose their status as union members, for example. More generally, some of the *insiders* in the wage-setting process become *outsiders*. If the smaller group of insiders cares more about high real wages and less about high employment, then the recession may permanently push real wages further above the equilibrium level and raise the amount of structural unemployment.

Hysteresis remains a controversial theory. Some economists believe the theory helps explain persistently high unemployment in Europe, because the rise in European unemployment starting in the early 1980s coincided with disinflation but continued after inflation stabilized. Moreover, the increase in unemployment tended to be larger for those countries that experienced the greatest reductions in inflations, such as Ireland, Italy and Spain. Yet there is still no consensus on whether the hysteresis phenomenon is significant, or why it might be more pronounced in some countries than in others. (Other explanations of high European unemployment, discussed in Chapter 7, give little role to disinflation.) If it is true, however, the theory is important, because hysteresis greatly increases the cost of recessions. Put another way, hysteresis raises the sacrifice ratio, because output is lost even after the period of disinflation is over.

This issue rose to prominence once again in the aftermath of the great recession of 2008–2009. Many economists wondered whether or not the extraordinarily high levels of long-term unemployment (discussed in Chapter 7) would increase the natural rate of unemployemnt for years to come. If so, it would mean that, as the economy recovered and unemployment fell, inflation might start rising more quickly than one might have otherwise expected. It would also mean that the cost of recession in terms of reduced incomes and human suffering would be long-lasting. These issues were not resolved as this book was going to press.[13]

14-3 Conclusion

We began this chapter by discussing three models of aggregate supply, each of which focuses on a different reason why, in the short run, output rises above its natural level when the price level rises above the level that people had expected.

---

[13] Olivier J. Blanchard and Lawrence H. Summers, 'Beyond the Natural Rate Hypothesis', *American Economic Review*, May 1988, vol. 78, pp. 182–187; Laurence Ball, 'Disinflation and the NAIRU', in Christina D. Romer and David H. Romer, eds, *Reducing Inflation: Motivation and Strategy*, Chicago: University of Chicago Press, 1997, pp. 167–185.

All three models explain why the short-run aggregate supply curve is upward sloping, and all of them yield a short-run trade-off between inflation and unemployment. A convenient way to express and analyse that trade-off is with the Phillips-curve equation, according to which inflation depends on expected inflation, cyclical unemployment and supply shocks.

Keep in mind that not all economists endorse all the ideas discussed here. There is widespread disagreement, for instance, about the practical importance of rational expectations and the relevance of hysteresis. If you find it difficult to fit all the pieces together, you are not alone. The study of aggregate supply remains one of the most unsettled – and therefore one of the most exciting – research areas in macroeconomics.

Summary

1. The three theories of aggregate supply – the sticky-price, sticky-wage and imperfect-information models – attribute deviations of output and employment from their natural levels to various market imperfections. According to all three theories, output rises above its natural level when the price level exceeds the expected price level, and output falls below its natural level when the price level is less than the expected price level.

2. Economists often express aggregate supply in a relationship called the Phillips curve. The Phillips curve says that inflation depends on expected inflation, the deviation of unemployment from its natural rate and supply shocks. According to the Phillips curve, policy makers who control aggregate demand face a short-run trade-off between inflation and unemployment.

3. If expected inflation depends on recently observed inflation, then inflation has inertia, which means that reducing inflation requires either a beneficial supply shock or a period of high unemployment and reduced output. If people have rational expectations, however, then a credible announcement of a change in policy might be able to influence expectations directly, and therefore reduce inflation without causing a recession.

4. Most economists accept the natural-rate hypothesis, according to which fluctuations in aggregate demand have only short-run effects on output and unemployment. Yet some economists have suggested ways in which recessions can leave permanent scars on the economy by raising the natural rate of unemployment.

KEY CONCEPTS

Sticky-price model

Sticky-wage model

Imperfect-information model

Phillips curve

Adaptive expectations

Demand-pull inflation

Cost-push inflation

Sacrifice ratio

Rational expectations

Natural-rate hypothesis

Hysteresis

QUESTIONS FOR REVIEW

1. Explain the three theories of aggregate supply. On what market imperfection does each theory rely? What do the theories have in common?

2. How is the Phillips curve related to aggregate supply?

3. Why might inflation be inertial?

4. Explain the differences between demand-pull inflation and cost-push inflation.

5. Under what circumstances might it be possible to reduce inflation without causing a recession?

6. Explain two ways in which a recession might raise the natural rate of unemployment.

PROBLEMS AND APPLICATIONS

1. In the sticky-price model, describe the aggregate supply curve in the following special cases. How do these cases compare to the short-run aggregate supply curve we discussed in Chapter 10?

a. No firms have flexible prices ($s = 1$).

b. The desired price does not depend on aggregate output ($a = 0$).

2. Consider the following changes in the sticky-wage model.

a. Suppose that labour contracts specify that the nominal wage be fully indexed for inflation. That is, the nominal wage is to be adjusted to fully compensate for changes in the consumer price index. How does full indexation alter the aggregate supply curve in this model?

b. Suppose now that indexation is only partial. That is, for every increase in the CPI, the nominal wage rises, but by a smaller percentage. How does partial indexation alter the aggregate supply curve in this model?

3. Suppose that an economy has the Phillips curve

$$\pi = \pi_{-1} - 0.5(u - 0.06).$$

a. What is the natural rate of unemployment?

b. Graph the short-run and long-run relationships between inflation and unemployment.

c. How much cyclical unemployment is necessary to reduce inflation by 5 percentage points?

d. Inflation is running at 10 per cent. The central bank wants to reduce it to 5 per cent. Give two scenarios that will achieve that goal.

4. According to the rational-expectations approach, if everyone believes that policy makers are committed to reducing inflation, the cost of reducing inflation – the sacrifice ratio – will be lower than if the public is sceptical about the policy makers' intentions. Why might this be true? How might credibility be achieved?

5. Assume that people have rational expectations and that the economy is described by the sticky-wage or sticky-price model. Explain why each of the following propositions is true:

a. Only unanticipated changes in the money supply affect real GDP. Changes in the money supply that were anticipated when wages and prices were set do not have any real effects.

b. If the central bank chooses the money supply at the same time as people are setting wages and prices, so that everyone has the same information about the state of the economy, then monetary policy cannot be used systematically to stabilize output. Hence, a policy of keeping the money supply constant will have the same real effects as a policy of adjusting the money supply in response to the state of the economy. (This is called the *policy irrelevance proposition*.)

c. If the central bank sets the money supply well after people have set wages and prices, so that the central bank has collected more information about the state of the economy, then monetary policy can be used systematically to stabilize output.

6. Suppose that an economy has the Phillips curve

$$\pi = \pi_{-1} - 0.5(u - u^n),$$

and that the natural rate of unemployment is given by an average of the past two years' unemployment:

$$u^n = 0.5(u_{-1} + u_{-2}).$$

a. Why might the natural rate of unemployment depend on recent unemployment (as is assumed in the preceding equation)?

b. Suppose that the central bank follows a policy to reduce permanently the inflation rate by 1 percentage point. What effect will that policy have on the unemployment rate over time?

c. What is the sacrifice ratio in this economy? Explain.

d. What do these equations imply about the short-run and long-run trade-offs between inflation and unemployment?

7. Some economists believe that taxes have an important effect on labour supply. They argue that higher taxes cause people to want to work less, and that lower taxes cause them to want to work more. Consider how this effect alters the macroeconomic analysis of tax changes.

a. If this view is correct, how does a tax cut affect the natural level of output?

b. How does a tax cut affect the aggregate demand curve? The long-run aggregate supply curve? The short-run aggregate supply curve?

c. What is the short-run impact of a tax cut on output and the price level? How does your answer differ from the case without the labour-supply effect?

d. What is the long-run impact of a tax cut on output and the price level? How does your answer differ from the case without the labour-supply effect?

A Big, Comprehensive Model

In the previous chapters, we have seen many models of how the economy works. When learning these models, it can be hard to see how they are related. Now that we have finished developing the model of aggregate demand and aggregate supply, this is a good time to look back at what we have learned. This appendix sketches a large model that incorporates much of the theory we have already seen, including the classical theory presented in Part II and the business cycle theory presented in Part IV. The notation and equations should be familiar from previous chapters.

The model has seven equations:

$Y = C(Y - T) + I(r) + G + NX(\varepsilon)$	*IS:* Goods Market Equilibrium
$M/P = L(i, Y)$	*LM:* Money Market Equilibrium
$NX(\varepsilon) = CF(r - r^*)$	Foreign Exchange Market Equilibrium
$i = r + \pi^e$	Relationship between Real and Nominal Interest Rates
$\varepsilon = eP/P^*$	Relationship between Real and Nominal Exchange Rates
$Y = \overline{Y} + \alpha\,(P - P^e)$	Aggregate Supply
$Y = F(K, L)$	Natural Level of Output.

These seven equations determine the equilibrium values of seven endogenous variables: output Y, the natural level of output $\overline{Y}$, the real interest rate r, the nominal interest rate i, the real exchange rate ε, the nominal exchange rate e and the price level P.

There are many exogenous variables that influence these endogenous variables. They include the money supply M, government purchases G, taxes T, the capital stock K, the labour force L, the world price level P^* and the world real interest rate r^*. In addition, there are two expectation variables: the expectation of future inflation π^e and the expectation of the current price level formed in the past P^e. As written, the model takes these expectations as exogenous, although additional equations could be added to make them endogenous.

Although mathematical techniques are available to analyse this seven-equation model, they are beyond the scope of this book. But this large model is still useful, because we can use it to see how the smaller models we have examined are related to one another. In particular, *many of the models we have been studying are special cases of this large model.* Let's consider six special cases.

Special Case 1: The Classical Closed Economy Suppose that $P^e = P$, $L(i, Y) = (1/V)Y$, and $CF(r - r^*) = 0$. In words, this means that expectations of the price level adjust so that expectations are correct, money demand is proportional to income and there are no international capital flows. In this case, output is always at its natural level, the real interest rate adjusts to equilibrate the goods market, the price level moves parallel with the money supply, and the nominal interest rate adjusts one-for-one with expected inflation. This special case corresponds to the economy analysed in Chapters 3 and 4.

Special Case 2: The Classical Small Open Economy Suppose that $P^e = P$, $L(i, Y) = (1/V)Y$, and $CF(r - r^*)$ is infinitely elastic. Now we are examining the special case when international capital flows respond greatly to any differences between the domestic and world interest rates. This means that $r = r^*$ and that the trade balance NX equals the difference between saving and investment at the world interest rate. This special case corresponds to the economy analysed in Chapter 6.

Special Case 3: The Basic Model of Aggregate Demand and Aggregate Supply Suppose that α is infinite and $L(i, Y) = (1/V)Y$. In this case, the short-run aggregate-supply curve is horizontal, and the aggregate demand curve is determined only by the quantity equation. This special case corresponds to the economy analysed in Chapter 10.

Special Case 4: The *IS-LM* Model Suppose that α is infinite and $CF(r - r^*) = 0$. In this case, the short-run aggregate-supply curve is horizontal, and there are no international capital flows. For any given level of expected inflation π^e, the level of income and interest rate must adjust to equilibrate the goods market and the money market. This special case corresponds to the economy analysed in Chapters 11 and 12.

Special Case 5: The Mundell-Fleming Model with a Floating Exchange Rate Suppose that α is infinite and $CF(r - r^*)$ is infinitely elastic. In this case, the short-run aggregate-supply curve is horizontal, and international capital flows are so great as to ensure that $r = r^*$. The exchange rate floats freely to reach its equilibrium level. This special case corresponds to the first economy analysed in Chapter 13.

Special Case 6: The Mundell-Fleming Model with a Fixed Exchange Rate Suppose that α is infinite, $CF(r - r^*)$ is infinitely elastic and e is fixed. In this case, the short-run aggregate-supply curve is horizontal, huge international capital flows ensure that $r = r^*$, but the exchange rate is set by the central bank. The exchange rate is now an exogenous policy variable, but the money supply M is an endogenous variable that must adjust to ensure the exchange rate hits the fixed level. This special case corresponds to the second economy analysed in Chapter 13.

You should now see the value in this big model. Even though the model is too large to be useful in developing an intuitive understanding of how the economy works, it shows that the different models we have been studying are closely related. Each model shows a different facet of the larger and more realistic model presented here. In each chapter, we made some simplifying assumptions to make the big model smaller and easier to understand. When thinking about the real world, it is important to keep the simplifying assumptions in mind and to draw on the insights learned in each of the chapters.

PART 5

Macroeconomic Policy Debates

CHAPTER 15

Stabilization Policy

What we need is not a skilled monetary driver of the economic vehicle continuously turning the steering wheel to adjust to the unexpected irregularities of the route, but some means of keeping the monetary passenger who is in the back seat as ballast from occasionally leaning over and giving the steering wheel a jerk that threatens to send the car off the road.

— *Milton Friedman*

The financial crisis of 2008–2009 has revived a long-standing debate that has for many years occupied a central place in economics literature: how should government policy makers respond to the business cycle? The answer depends on one's beliefs and viewpoint. Some economists view the economy as inherently unstable. They argue that the economy experiences frequent shocks to aggregate demand and aggregate supply. Unless policy makers use monetary and fiscal policy to stabilize the economy, these shocks will lead to unnecessary and inefficient fluctuations in output, unemployment and inflation. According to the popular saying, macroeconomic policy should 'lean against the wind', stimulating the economy when it is depressed and slowing the economy when it is overheated.

Other economists (such as Milton Friedman) view the economy as naturally stable. They blame bad economic policies for the large and inefficient fluctuations we have sometimes experienced. They argue that economic policy should not try to 'fine-tune' the economy. Instead, economic policy makers should admit their limited abilities and be satisfied if they do no harm.

This debate has persisted for decades, with numerous protagonists advancing various arguments for their positions, and became especially relevant as economies around the world sank into recession in 2008. The fundamental issue is how policy makers should use the theory of short-run economic fluctuations developed in the preceding chapters. In this chapter we ask two questions that arise in this debate. First, should monetary and fiscal policy take an active role in trying to stabilize the economy, or should policy remain passive? Second, should policy makers be free to use their discretion in responding to changing economic conditions, or should they be committed to following a fixed policy rule?

15-1 Should Policy Be Active or Passive?

As we have seen in the preceding chapters, monetary and fiscal policy can exert a powerful impact on aggregate demand and, thereby, on inflation and unemployment. When the government is considering a major change in fiscal policy, or when the central bank is considering a major change in monetary policy, foremost in the discussion are how the change will influence inflation and unemployment, and whether aggregate demand needs to be stimulated or restrained.

Although the governments of advanced industrialized economies have long conducted monetary and fiscal policy, the view that they should use these policy instruments to try to stabilize the economy is more recent, dating from the immediate post-World War II period, when the memory of the Great Depression and its political repercussions were still fresh in the minds of policy makers. In the immediate post-war period, it seemed that in the absence of an active government role in the economy, events like the Great Depression could occur regularly. The financial crisis that erupted in 2008 across Europe brought to the epicentre of the debate the role that governments and policy makers should have played in order to prevent such economic turmoil and how they should now respond in order to minimize the repercussions of recession and to facilitate the process of economic recovery.

To many economists, the case for active government policy is clear and simple. Recessions are periods of high unemployment, low incomes and increased economic hardship. The model of aggregate demand and aggregate supply shows how shocks to the economy can cause recessions. It also shows how monetary and fiscal policy can prevent (or at least soften) recessions by responding to these shocks. These economists consider it wasteful not to use these policy instruments to stabilize the economy.

Other economists are critical of the government's attempts to stabilize the economy. These critics argue that the government should take a hands-off approach to macroeconomic policy. At first, this view might seem surprising. If our model shows how to prevent or reduce the severity of recessions, why do these critics want the government to refrain from using monetary and fiscal policy for economic stabilization? To find out, let's consider some of their arguments.

Lags in the Implementation and Effects of Policies

Economic stabilization would be easy if the effects of policy were immediate. Making policy would be like driving a car: policy makers would simply adjust their instruments to keep the economy on the desired path.

Making economic policy, however, is less like driving a car than it is like piloting a large ship. A car changes direction almost immediately after the steering wheel is turned. By contrast, a ship changes course long after the pilot adjusts the rudder, and once the ship starts to turn, it continues turning long after the rudder is set back to normal. A novice pilot is likely to over-steer and, after noticing the mistake, overreact by steering too much in the opposite direction. The ship's path could become unstable, as the novice responds to previous mistakes by making larger and larger corrections.

Like a ship's pilot, economic policy makers face the problem of long lags. Indeed, the problem for policy makers is even more difficult, because the lengths of the lags are hard to predict. These long and variable lags greatly complicate the conduct of monetary and fiscal policy.

Economists distinguish between two lags that are relevant for the conduct of stabilization policy: the inside lag and the outside lag. The **inside lag** is the time between a shock to the economy and the policy action responding to that shock. This lag arises because it takes time for policy makers first to recognize that a shock has occurred and then to put appropriate policies into effect. The **outside lag** is the time between a policy action and its influence on the economy. This lag arises because policies do not immediately influence spending, income and employment.

The inside lag of tax policy in the economies of European countries that have a parliamentary system of government is generally quite short, because once the government announces a tax change, it can become law and be implemented very quickly. On the other hand, a considerable amount of time may still pass between the decision to increase public spending in a certain area and the actual implementation of the spending programme, due to the planning, staffing and general administration that the programme may require.

Matters become more complex when there are no existing practices, and intervention procedures need to be designed from the beginning. The EU was caught unprepared in the recent crisis because it did not have in place a crisis management mechanism that could be utilized to ease the pressure primarily on the peripheral countries. As a result, in 2010 the European Financial Stability Facility (EFSF) and the European Financial Stabilisation Mechanism (EFSM) were set up in order to address the immediate difficulties faced by the most exposed Euro Area (Eurozone) economies. In late 2012 the Euro Area finance ministers introduced a permanent crisis management mechanism, the European Stability Mechanism (ESM), which provides access to financial assistance for Euro Area members in financial difficulty. It replaced the two earlier temporary EU funding programmes, though the previously approved bailout loans to Ireland, Portugal and Greece are still operated within the two earlier schemes. All new bailouts for any Euro Area member state will now be operated under the ESM, with a lending ceiling of €500 billion. ESM member states can apply for a bailout if they are in financial difficulty or if their financial sector is in need of recapitalization. These bailouts are conditional on member states having first ratified the European Fiscal Compact and then agreeing to the necessary reforms or fiscal consolidation required to restore financial stability as determined by the European Commission, ECB and IMF. To date, the ESM has assigned up to €100 billion for recapitalization of Spanish banks and €9 billion for a sovereign state bailout and financial sector recapitalization programme for Cyprus.

In the United States, which does not have a parliamentary government system, the inside lag of fiscal policy is much longer for both tax and spending, compared to most European economies. This is because of the US system of government: changes in spending or taxes require the approval of the president and both houses of Congress and generally involve a slow and cumbersome legislative process.

However, even though the inside lag of tax policy in Europe may be relatively short, the outside lag – the time taken for the effect on tax revenues to work through – may still be long.

Overall, therefore, fiscal policy is nowadays seen as a somewhat imprecise tool for stabilizing the economy.

Monetary policy has a much shorter inside lag than fiscal policy, because a central bank can decide on and implement a policy change in less than a day, but monetary policy has a substantial outside lag. Monetary policy works by changing the money supply and interest rates, which in turn influence investment and aggregate demand. Many firms make investment plans far in advance, however, so a change in monetary policy is thought not to affect economic activity until about six months after it is made.

The long and variable lags associated with monetary and fiscal policy certainly make stabilizing the economy more difficult. Advocates of passive policy argue that, because of these lags, successful stabilization policy is almost impossible. Indeed, attempts to stabilize the economy can be *destabilizing*. Monetary policy interventions in fact become pro-cyclical, pushing the economy even further away from steady state and destabilizing it more. Suppose that the economy's condition changes between the beginning of a policy action and its impact on the economy. In this case, active policy may end up stimulating the economy when it is heating up, or depressing the economy when it is cooling off. Advocates of active policy admit that such lags do require policy makers to be cautious. But, they argue, these lags do not necessarily mean that policy should be completely passive, especially in the face of a severe and protracted economic downturn, such as the recession that began in 2008.

Some fiscal policies, called **automatic stabilizers**, are designed to reduce the lags associated with stabilization policy. Automatic stabilizers are policies that stimulate or depress the economy when necessary, without any deliberate policy change. For example, the system of income taxes automatically reduces taxes when the economy goes into a recession, without any change in the tax laws, because individuals and corporations pay less tax when their incomes fall. Similarly, the unemployment-insurance and welfare systems automatically raise transfer payments when the economy moves into a recession, because more people apply for benefits. One can view these automatic stabilizers as a type of fiscal policy without any inside lag.

The Difficult Job of Economic Forecasting

Because policy influences the economy only after a long lag, successful stabilization policy requires the ability to predict accurately future economic conditions. If we cannot predict whether the economy will be in a boom or a recession in six months or a year, we cannot evaluate whether monetary and fiscal policy should now be trying to expand or contract aggregate demand. Unfortunately, economic developments are often unpredictable, at least given our current understanding of the economy.

One way forecasters try to look ahead is with macroeconometric models, which have been developed both by government agencies and by private firms for forecasting and policy analysis. These large-scale computer models are made up of many equations, each representing a part of the economy. After making assumptions about the path of the exogenous variables, such as monetary policy, fiscal policy and oil prices, these models yield predictions about unemployment, inflation and other endogenous variables. Keep in mind, however, that the validity of these predictions is only as good as the model and the forecasters' assumptions about the exogenous variables.

CASE STUDY

Mistakes in Forecasting

'Light showers, bright intervals, and moderate winds.' This was the forecast offered by the renowned British national weather service on 14 October 1987. The next day Britain was hit by its worst storm in more than two centuries.

Like weather forecasts, economic forecasts are a crucial input to private and public decision making. Business executives rely on economic forecasts when deciding how much to produce and how much to invest in plant and equipment. Government policy makers also rely on forecasts when developing economic policies. Unfortunately, like weather forecasts, economic forecasts are far from precise.

The most severe economic downturn in US history, the Great Depression of the 1930s, caught economic forecasters completely by surprise. Even after the stock market crash of 1929, they remained confident that the economy would not suffer a substantial setback. In late 1931, when the economy was clearly in bad shape, the eminent economist Irving Fisher predicted that it would recover quickly. Subsequent events showed that these forecasts were much too optimistic: the unemployment rate continued to rise until 1933, and it remained elevated for the rest of the decade.[1]

Figure 15-1 shows how economic forecasters did during the recession of 1982, one of the most severe economic downturns in the United States since the Great Depression. This figure shows the actual unemployment rate (in red) and six attempts to predict it for the following five quarters (in green). You can see that the forecasters did well when predicting unemployment one quarter ahead. The more distant forecasts, however, were often inaccurate. For example, in the second quarter of 1981, forecasters were predicting little change in the unemployment rate over the next five quarters; yet only two quarters later unemployment began to rise sharply. The rise in unemployment to almost 11 per cent in the fourth quarter of 1982 caught the forecasters by surprise. After the depth of

---

[1] Kathryn M. Dominguez, Ray C. Fair and Matthew D. Shapiro, 'Forecasting the Depression: Harvard Versus Yale', *American Economic Review*, September 1988, vol. 78, pp. 595–612. This article shows how badly economic forecasters did during the Great Depression, and it argues that they could not have done any better with the modern forecasting techniques available today.

FIGURE 15-1

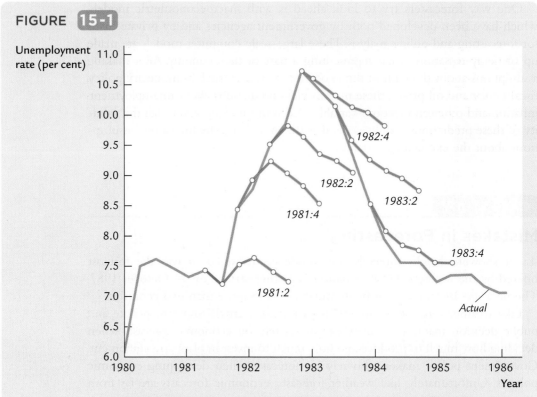

Forecasting the Recession of 1982 The red line shows the actual unemployment rate from the first quarter of 1980 to the first quarter of 1986. The green lines show the unemployment rate predicted as six points in time: the second quarter of 1981, the fourth quarter of 1981, the second quarter of 1982, and so on. For each forecast, the symbols mark the current unemployment rate and the forecast for the subsequent five quarters. Notice that the forecasters failed to predict both the rapid rise in the unemployment rate and the subsequent rapid decline.

Source: The unemployment rate is from the US Department of Labor. The predicted unemployment rate is the median forecast of about 20 forecasters by the American Statistical Association and the National Bureau of Economic Research.

the recession became apparent, the forecasters failed to predict how rapid the subsequent decline in unemployment would be.

The story was much the same for the economic downturn of 2008. The November 2007 Survey of Professional Forecasters predicted a slowdown, but only a modest one: the US unemployment rate was projected to increase from 4.7 per cent in the fourth quarter of 2007 to 5.0 per cent in the fourth quarter of 2008. By the May 2008 survey, the forecasters had raised their predictions for unemployment at the end of the year, but only to 5.5 per cent. In fact, the unemployment rate was 6.9 per cent in the last quarter of 2008. The forecasters became more pessimistic as the recession unfolded, but still not pessimistic enough. In November 2008, they predicted that the unemployment would rise to 7.7 per cent in the fourth quarter of 2009. In fact, it was 10.0 per cent. At that point, the professional forecasters predicted a meagre recovery from the recession, with only a slight fall in the unemployment rate over the following year. Unfortunately, this time they proved correct.

These episodes – the Great Depression, the recession and recovery of 1982 and the 2008 economic downturn – show that many of the most dramatic economic events are unpredictable. Although private and public decision makers have little choice but to rely on economic forecasts, they must always keep in mind that these forecasts come with a large margin of error. ■

Ignorance, Expectations and the Lucas Critique

The prominent economist Robert Lucas once wrote: 'As an advice-giving profession we are in way over our heads.' Even many of those who advise policy makers would agree with this assessment. Economics is a young science, and there is still much that we do not know. Economists cannot be completely confident when they assess the effects of alternative policies. This ignorance suggests that economists should be cautious when offering policy advice.

In his writings on macroeconomic policy making, Lucas has emphasized that economists need to pay more attention to the issue of how people form expectations of the future. Expectations play a crucial role in the economy because they influence all sorts of behaviour. For instance, households decide how much to consume based on how much they

'**It's true, Caesar. Rome is declining, but I expect it to pick up in the next quarter.**'

expect to earn in the future, and firms decide how much to invest based on their expectations of future profitability. These expectations depend on many things, but one factor, according to Lucas, is especially important: the policies being pursued by the government. When policy makers estimate the effect of any policy change, therefore, they need to know how people's expectations will respond to the policy change. Lucas has argued that traditional methods of policy evaluation – such as those that rely on standard macroeconometric models – do not adequately take into account the impact of policy on expectations. This criticism of traditional policy evaluation is known as the **Lucas critique**.[2]

An important example of the Lucas critique arises in the analysis of disinflation. As you may recall from Chapter 14, the cost of reducing inflation is often measured by the sacrifice ratio, which is the number of percentage points of GDP that must be forgone to reduce inflation by 1 percentage point. Because estimates of the sacrifice ratio are often large, they have led some economists to

---

[2] Robert E. Lucas, Jr., 'Econometric Policy Evaluation: A Critique', *Carnegie Rochester Conference on Public Policy*, vol. 1, Amsterdam: North-Holland, 1976, pp. 19–46. Lucas won the Nobel Prize for this and other work in 1995.

argue that policy makers should learn to live with inflation, rather than incur the large cost of reducing it.

According to advocates of the 'rational expectations' approach, however, these estimates of the sacrifice ratio are unreliable because they are subject to the Lucas critique. Traditional estimates of the sacrifice ratio are based on adaptive expectations, that is, on the assumption that expected inflation depends on past inflation. Adaptive expectations may be a reasonable premise in some circumstances, but if the policy makers make a credible change in policy, workers and firms setting wages and prices will rationally respond by adjusting their expectations of inflation appropriately. This change in inflation expectations will quickly alter the short-run trade-off between inflation and unemployment. As a result, reducing inflation can potentially be much less costly than is suggested by traditional estimates of the sacrifice ratio.

The Lucas critique leaves us with two lessons. The narrow lesson is that economists evaluating alternative policies need to consider how policy affects expectations and, thereby, behaviour. The broad lesson is that policy evaluation is hard, so economists engaged in this task should be sure to show the requisite humility.

The Historical Record

In judging whether government policy should play an active or passive role in the economy, we must give some weight to the historical record. If the economy has experienced many large shocks to aggregate supply and aggregate demand, and if policy has successfully insulated the economy from these shocks, then the case for active policy should be clear. Conversely, if the economy has experienced few large shocks, and if the fluctuations we have observed can be traced to inept economic policy, then the case for passive policy should be clear. In other words, our view of stabilization policy should be influenced by whether policy has historically been stabilizing or destabilizing. For this reason, the debate over macroeconomic policy frequently turns into a debate over macroeconomic history.

Yet history does not settle the debate over stabilization policy. Disagreements over history arise because it is not easy to identify the sources of economic fluctuations. The historical record often permits more than one interpretation.

CASE STUDY

The Remarkable Stability of the Modern Economy

Although economists who take a long historical view debate how much the economy has stabilized over time, there is less controversy about the more recent experience. Everyone agrees that the 1990s and early 2000s stand out as a period of remarkable stability for the advanced economies of the UK, Continental Europe and the US.

Figure 15-2 shows the volatility of annual growth in real GDP and the volatility of annual inflation for the UK, France and the US, for ten-year periods from 1900 to 1990, and for six-year periods from 2000 to 2011. The standard

FIGURE 15-2

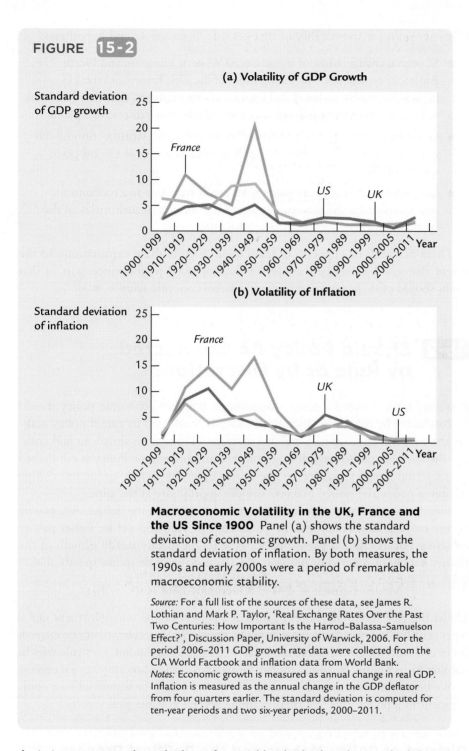

(a) Volatility of GDP Growth

Standard deviation of GDP growth

France

US

UK

Year

(b) Volatility of Inflation

Standard deviation of inflation

France

UK

US

Year

Macroeconomic Volatility in the UK, France and the US Since 1900 Panel (a) shows the standard deviation of economic growth. Panel (b) shows the standard deviation of inflation. By both measures, the 1990s and early 2000s were a period of remarkable macroeconomic stability.

Source: For a full list of the sources of these data, see James R. Lothian and Mark P. Taylor, 'Real Exchange Rates Over the Past Two Centuries: How Important Is the Harrod–Balassa–Samuelson Effect?', Discussion Paper, University of Warwick, 2006. For the period 2006–2011 GDP growth rate data were collected from the CIA World Factbook and inflation data from World Bank.
Notes: Economic growth is measured as annual change in real GDP. Inflation is measured as the annual change in the GDP deflator from four quarters earlier. The standard deviation is computed for ten-year periods and two six-year periods, 2000–2011.

deviation measures the volatility of a variable: the higher the standard deviation, the more volatile the variable is. One striking result from this figure is the low volatility in both variables during the 1990s and early 2000s: in all three countries, both inflation and growth were more stable during this period than they have been at any time during the past century.

What accounts for the stability of that period? There are several hypotheses:

- Structural change. Most of the advanced Western European and North American economies – including those of the UK, France and the US – became more service-based and less manufacturing-based than they had been in the past, and service industries are less volatile than manufacturing industries.

- Good luck. During that period and until 2008, the world economy did not have to deal with adverse supply shocks as severe as the oil price shocks of the 1970s.

- Good policy. Many economists gave credit to better macroeconomic management by the governments and the monetary authorities of the world's major economies during that time.

There may well be elements of truth to all three of these explanations. To the extent that good policy gets credit for the improved performance, part of that credit should perhaps go to advances in macroeconomic science. ■

15-2 Should Policy Be Conducted by Rule or by Discretion?

A second topic debated among economists is whether economic policy should be conducted by rule or by discretion. Policy is conducted by rule if policy makers announce in advance how policy will respond to various situations and commit themselves to following through on this announcement. Policy is conducted by discretion if policy makers are free to size up events as they occur and choose whatever policy the policy makers consider appropriate at the time.

The debate over rules versus discretion is distinct from the debate over passive versus active policy. Policy can be conducted by rule and yet be either passive or active. For example, a passive policy rule might specify steady growth in the money supply of 3 per cent per year. An active policy rule might specify that

$$\text{Money Growth} = 2\% + (\text{Unemployment Rate} - 5\%).$$

Under this rule, the money supply grows at 2 per cent if the unemployment rate is 5 per cent, but for every percentage point by which the unemployment rate exceeds 5 per cent, money growth increases by an extra percentage point. This rule tries to stabilize the economy by raising money growth when the economy is in a recession.

We begin this section by discussing why policy might be improved by a commitment to a policy rule. We then examine several possible policy rules.

Distrust of Policy Makers and the Political Process

'You can fool all the people some of the time, and some of the people all the time, but you cannot fool all the people all the time.'

Abraham Lincoln

Some economists believe that economic policy is too important to be left to the discretion of policy makers. Although this view is more political than economic, evaluating it is central to how we judge the role of economic policy. If politicians are incompetent or opportunistic, then we may not want to give them the discretion to use the powerful tools of monetary and fiscal policy.

Incompetence in economic policy arises for several reasons. Some economists view the political process as erratic, perhaps because it reflects the shifting power of special interest groups. In addition, macroeconomics is complicated, and politicians often do not have sufficient knowledge of it to make informed judgements. This ignorance allows charlatans to propose incorrect but superficially appealing solutions to complex problems. The political process often cannot weed out the advice of charlatans from that of competent economists.

Opportunism in economic policy arises when the objectives of policy makers conflict with the well-being of the public. Some economists fear that politicians use macroeconomic policy to further their own electoral ends. If citizens vote on the basis of economic conditions prevailing at the time of the election, then politicians have an incentive to pursue policies that will make the economy look good during election years. A government might cause a recession soon after coming into office in order to lower inflation, and then stimulate the economy as the next election approaches to lower unemployment; this would ensure that both inflation and unemployment are low on election day. Manipulation of the economy for electoral gain, called the **political business cycle**, has been the subject of extensive research by economists and political scientists.[3]

Distrust of the political process leads some economists to advocate placing economic policy outside the realm of politics.

The Time Inconsistency of Discretionary Policy

If we assume that we can trust our policy makers, discretion at first glance appears superior to a fixed policy rule. Discretionary policy is, by its nature, flexible. As long as policy makers are intelligent and benevolent, there might appear to be little reason to deny them flexibility in responding to changing conditions.

Yet a case for rules over discretion arises from the problem of **time inconsistency** of policy. In some situations, policy makers may want to announce in advance the policy they will follow to influence the expectations of private decision makers. But later, after the private decision makers have acted on the basis of their expectations, these policy makers may be tempted to renege on their announcement. Understanding that policy makers may be inconsistent over time, private decision makers are led to distrust policy announcements. In this situation, to make their announcements credible, policy makers may want to make a commitment to a fixed policy rule.

---

[3] William Nordhaus, 'The Political Business Cycle', *Review of Economic Studies*, 1975, vol. 42, pp. 169–190; and Edward Tufte, *Political Control of the Economy*, Princeton, NJ: Princeton University Press, 1978.

Time inconsistency is illustrated most simply in a political rather than an economic example – specifically, public policy about negotiating with terrorists over the release of hostages. The announced policy of many nations is that they will not negotiate over hostages. Such an announcement is intended to deter terrorists: if there is nothing to be gained from kidnapping hostages, rational terrorists will not kidnap any. In other words, the purpose of the announcement is to influence the expectations of terrorists and, thereby, their behaviour.

In fact, unless the policy makers are credibly committed to the policy, the announcement has little effect. Terrorists know that once hostages are taken, policy makers face an overwhelming temptation to make some concession to obtain the hostages' release. The only way to deter rational terrorists is to take away the discretion of policy makers and commit them to a rule of never negotiating. If policy makers were truly unable to make concessions, the incentive for terrorists to take hostages would be largely eliminated.

The same problem arises less dramatically in the conduct of monetary policy. Consider the dilemma of a central bank that cares about both inflation and unemployment. According to the Phillips curve, the trade-off between inflation and unemployment depends on expected inflation. The central bank would prefer everyone to expect low inflation so that it will face a favourable trade-off. To reduce expected inflation, the central bank might announce that low inflation is the paramount goal of monetary policy.

But an announcement of a policy of low inflation is by itself not credible. Once households and firms have formed their expectations of inflation and set wages and prices accordingly, the central bank has an incentive to renege on its announcement and implement expansionary monetary policy to reduce unemployment. People understand the central bank's incentive to renege and therefore do not believe the announcement in the first place. Just as a government facing a hostage crisis is sorely tempted to negotiate their release, a central bank with discretion is sorely tempted to inflate in order to reduce unemployment. And just as terrorists discount announced policies of never negotiating, households and firms discount announced policies of low inflation.

The surprising outcome of this analysis is that policy makers can sometimes better achieve their goals by having their discretion taken away from them. In the case of rational terrorists, fewer hostages will be taken and killed if policy makers are committed to following the seemingly harsh rule of refusing to negotiate for hostages' freedom. In the case of monetary policy, there will be lower inflation without higher unemployment if the central bank is committed to a policy of low inflation. (This conclusion about monetary policy is modelled more explicitly in the appendix to this chapter.)

The time inconsistency of policy arises in many other contexts. Here are some examples:

- To encourage investment, the government announces that it will not tax income from capital. But after factories have been built, the government is tempted to renege on its promise to raise more tax revenue from them.

- To encourage research, the government announces that it will give a temporary monopoly (a patent) to companies that discover new drugs. But after a drug has been discovered, the government is tempted to revoke the patent or to regulate the price to make the drug more affordable.

- To encourage good behaviour, a parent announces that he or she will punish a child whenever the child breaks a rule. But after the child has misbehaved, the parent is tempted to forgive the transgression, because punishment is unpleasant for the parent as well as for the child.

- To encourage you to work hard, your professor announces that this course will end with an examination. But after you have studied and learned all the material, the professor is tempted to cancel the exam so that he or she will not have to mark it.

In each case, rational agents understand the incentive for the policy maker to renege, and this expectation affects their behaviour. And in each case, the solution is to take away the policy maker's discretion with a credible commitment to a fixed policy rule.

Rules for Monetary Policy

Even if we are convinced that policy rules are superior to discretion, the debate over macroeconomic policy is not over. If the central bank were to commit to a rule for monetary policy, what rule should it choose? Let's discuss briefly three policy rules that various economists advocate.

Some economists, called **monetarists**, advocate that the central bank should keep the money supply growing at a steady rate. The quotation at the beginning of this chapter from Milton Friedman – the most famous monetarist – exemplifies this view of monetary policy. Monetarists believe that fluctuations in the money supply are responsible for most large fluctuations in the economy. They argue that slow and steady growth in the money supply would yield stable output, employment and prices.

Although a monetarist policy rule might have prevented many of the economic fluctuations we have experienced historically, most economists believe that it is not the best possible policy rule. Steady growth in the money supply stabilizes aggregate demand only if the velocity of money is stable. But sometimes the economy experiences shocks, such as shifts in money demand, which cause velocity to be unstable. Most economists believe that a policy rule needs to allow the money supply to adjust to various shocks to the economy.

A second policy rule that economists widely advocate is nominal GDP targeting. Under this rule, the central bank announces a planned path for nominal GDP. If nominal GDP rises above the target, the central bank reduces money growth to dampen aggregate demand. If it falls below the target, the central bank raises money growth to stimulate aggregate demand. Because a nominal GDP target allows monetary policy to adjust to changes in the velocity of money, most economists believe it would lead to greater stability in output and prices than a monetarist policy rule.

A third policy rule that is often advocated is **inflation targeting**. Under this rule, the central bank would announce a target for the inflation rate (usually a low one) and then adjust the money supply when the actual inflation deviates from the target. Like nominal GDP targeting, inflation targeting insulates the economy from changes in the velocity of money. In addition, an inflation target has the political advantage that it is easy to explain to the public.

Notice that all these rules are expressed in terms of some nominal variable – the money supply, nominal GDP or the price level. One can also imagine policy rules expressed in terms of real variables. For example, the central bank might try to target the unemployment rate at 5 per cent. The problem with such a rule is that no one knows exactly what the natural rate of unemployment is. If the central bank chose a target for the unemployment rate below the natural rate, the result would be accelerating inflation. Conversely, if the central bank chose a target for the unemployment rate above the natural rate, the result would be accelerating deflation. For this reason, economists rarely advocate rules for monetary policy expressed solely in terms of real variables, even though real variables such as unemployment and real GDP are the best measures of economic performance.

The Taylor Rule of Monetary Policy

If you wanted to set interest rates to achieve stable prices, while avoiding large fluctuations in output and employment, how would you do it? This is exactly the question that central bank policy makers must ask themselves every day. As we discussed in Chapter 12, the short-term policy instrument that many central banks use is a short-term interest rate at which they will make short-term loans to the banking system – in other words, the 'official rate' or 'policy rate'. Whenever the central bank's interest rate-setting committee meets, it chooses a level for the policy rate. As we also saw in Chapter 12, the central bank's bond traders are then told to conduct open-market operations in line with the official rate. In terms of an *IS-LM* model, we can think of the central bank as choosing a point on the *IS* curve corresponding to a particular interest rate, and then expanding or contracting the money supply through open-market operations so that the *LM* curve intersects the *IS* curve at the interest rate chosen.

The hard part of the central bank's job is choosing the target for the official interest rate. Two general guidelines are clear. First, when inflation heats up, the official interest rate should rise. An increase in the interest rate will mean a smaller money supply and, eventually, lower investment, lower output, higher unemployment and reduced inflation. Second, when real economic activity slows – as reflected in real GDP or unemployment – the official interest rate should fall. A decrease in the interest rate will mean a larger money supply and, eventually, higher investment, higher output and lower unemployment.

The central bank needs to go beyond these general guidelines, however, and decide exactly how much to respond to changes in inflation and real economic activity. To help it make this decision, economist John Taylor proposed a simple rule for the official interest rate of the form:

Nominal Official Interest Rate =
Inflation + 2.0 + 0.5 (Inflation − 2.0) − 0.5 (GDP gap).

The GDP gap is the percentage shortfall of real GDP from an estimate of its natural level.

The **Taylor rule** has the real official interest rate – the nominal rate minus inflation – responding to inflation and the GDP gap. According to this rule, the real official interest rate equals 2 per cent when inflation is 2 per cent and GDP is at its natural level. For each percentage point by which inflation rises above 2 per cent, the real official interest rate rises by 0.5 per cent. For each percentage point by which real GDP falls below its natural level, the real official interest rate falls by 0.5 per cent. If GDP rises above its natural level, so that the GDP gap is negative, the real official interest rate rises accordingly.

One way of interpreting the Taylor rule is as a complement to (or a tool of) inflation targeting, which we discuss in the next section.

15-3 Inflation Targeting: Rule or Constrained Discretion?

Since the late 1980s, many of the world's central banks – including those of Australia, Canada, Israel, New Zealand, Spain, Sweden and the United Kingdom, as well as the European Central Bank – have adopted some form of **inflation targeting**. Inflation targeting involves setting a target for inflation and changing interest rates from time to time in order to achieve that target. Clearly, it is not appropriate to change interest rates in response to *current* inflation – it is already too late to change today's prices. Instead, inflation targets are usually based on forecasts of inflation: if the central bank forecasts that inflation will rise in, say, a year or 18 months from now, because of inflationary pressures that are building up in the economy, then it may wish to raise short-term interest rates in an attempt to dampen those inflationary pressures.

Should we interpret inflation targeting as a type of pre-commitment to a policy rule? Not completely. In all the countries that have adopted inflation targeting, central banks are left with a fair amount of discretion. In particular, there is no explicit formula that dictates how much interest rates should be changed for a given deviation of inflation from its target. In addition, the central banks are sometimes allowed to adjust their targets for inflation, at least temporarily, if some exogenous event (such as an easily identified supply shock) pushes inflation outside the range that was previously announced.

In light of this flexibility, what is the purpose of inflation targeting? Although inflation targeting leaves the central bank with some discretion, the policy does constrain how this discretion is used. When a central bank is told simply to 'do the right thing', it is hard to hold the central bank accountable, because people can argue for ever about what the right thing is in any specific circumstance. By contrast, when a central bank has announced a specific inflation target, or even a target range, the public can judge more easily whether the central bank is meeting its objectives. Thus, although inflation targeting does not completely tie the hands of the central bank, it does increase the transparency of monetary policy and, by doing so, makes central bankers more accountable for their actions. In that sense, inflation targeting may be viewed as a framework for constrained discretion on the part of the central bank.

The Taylor Rule and Inflation Targeting

One way to view the Taylor rule of monetary policy, which we discussed earlier, is as a complement to inflation targeting. Inflation targeting offers a plan for the central bank in the medium run, but it does not tightly constrain its month-to-month policy decisions. The Taylor rule may be a good short-run operating procedure for hitting a medium-run inflation target. According to the Taylor rule, monetary policy responds directly to inflation – as any inflation-targeting central bank must. But it also responds to the output gap, which can be viewed as a measure of inflationary pressures.[4]

However, because inflation targeting depends on setting interest rates according to *forecasts* of inflation, it might be argued that a Taylor rule consistent with such a policy should include *forecast* rather than current inflation, resulting in a **forward-looking Taylor rule** of the form:

$$\text{Nominal Official Interest Rate} = \text{Current Inflation} + 2.0$$
$$+ \ 0.5 \ (\text{Medium-Term Inflation Forecast} - \text{Inflation Target}) - 0.5 \ (\text{GDP gap}).$$

According to this forward-looking Taylor rule, the central bank should raise the short-term real interest rate if inflation is forecast to exceed its target over the medium term.

A question now arises, however, as to whether the output gap should be included in the forward-looking Taylor rule. We suggested earlier that the output gap can be interpreted as a measure of inflationary pressures. However, if the central bank has already taken into account the size of the output gap in forming its inflation forecast, and it is committed to hitting that target regardless of the output gap, then it could be argued that the output gap should not appear at all in the interest rate-setting equation of an inflation-targeting central bank.

Of course, in practice, no central bank in the world actually sets interest rates slavishly according to a Taylor rule. As we have discussed, inflation targeting is best viewed as a framework for constrained discretion, rather than a rigid policy rule, so this question is to some extent academic. However, a number of economists have estimated Taylor rules for major central banks, such as the European Central Bank and the Bank of England, by looking at the pattern of their interest rate decisions and the size of the output gap and forecasts of inflation, and estimating the weights given to the forecast deviation of inflation from its target and the output gap econometrically (instead of just assuming that they are each 0.5). In other words, they attempt to see if the central bank's interest rate-setting behaviour is tantamount to following a forward-looking Taylor rule. Invariably,

---

[4] John B. Taylor, 'Discretion versus Policy Rules in Practice', *Carnegie-Rochester Conference Series on Public Policy*, 1993, vol. 39, pp. 195–214.

these studies find a non-zero weight attached to the output gap in the estimated forward-looking Taylor rule, even where the central bank in question is explicitly pursuing inflation targeting.

One possible interpretation of this evidence is that the central bank does to some extent take into account the effect of its interest rate decisions on the output gap and employment, even though its primary objective is to maintain low and stable inflation. For example, for a given deviation of forecast inflation from its target, if the economy is operating well above the natural rate, with a large negative output gap, the central bank may feel happier raising interest rates sharply, compared to a situation where the output is only a small way above its natural rate.

Indeed, central banks typically have a secondary duty to maintain stability of the economy more generally, even if their primary duty is to maintain price stability. For example, in the UK, the 1998 Bank of England Act states that the monetary policy objectives of the Bank of England are: 'a) to maintain price stability, and b) subject to that, to support the economic objectives of the government in relation to growth and employment'. Similarly, the official mandate of the European Central Bank lists the maintenance of price stability in the Euro Area as its 'primary objective', but adds that, 'without prejudice to the objective of price stability', it should support the 'general economic policies' of EMU member governments, 'with a view to contributing to the achievement of a high level of employment and sustainable and non-inflationary growth'.

Supporting the economic objectives of the government in relation to growth and employment may be interpreted as keeping one eye on the size of the output gap when setting interest rates.

15-4 Central Bank Independence

Suppose you were put in charge of writing the constitution and laws for a country. Would you give the government of the country authority over the policies of the central bank? Or would you allow the central bank to make decisions free from such political influence? In other words, assuming that monetary policy is made by discretion rather than by rule, who should exercise that discretion?

Countries vary greatly in how they choose to answer this question. In some countries, the central bank is a branch of the government; in others, the central bank is largely independent. Many researchers have investigated the effects of constitutional design on monetary policy. They have examined the laws of different countries to construct an index of central bank independence. This index is based on various characteristics, such as the length of bankers' terms, the role of government officials on the interest rate-setting committee, and the frequency of contact between the government and the central bank. The researchers then examined the correlation between central bank independence and macro-economic performance.

The results of these studies are striking: more independent central banks are strongly associated with lower and more stable inflation. Figure 15-3 shows a

FIGURE 15-3

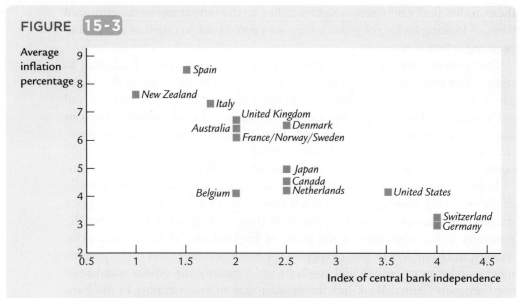

Inflation and Central Bank Independence This scatterplot presents the international experience with central bank independence. The evidence shows that more independent central banks tend to produce lower rates of inflation.

Source: Figure 1a, p. 155, of Alberto Alesina and Lawrence H. Summers, 'Central Bank Independence and Macroeconomic Performance: Some Comparative Evidence', *Journal of Money, Credit, and Banking,* May 1993, vol. 25, pp. 151–162. Average inflation is for the period 1955-1988.

scatterplot of central bank independence and average inflation for the period 1955 to 1988. Countries that had an independent central bank, such as Germany, Switzerland and the United States, tended to have low average inflation. Countries that had central banks with less independence, such as New Zealand and Spain, tended to have higher average inflation.

Researchers have also found there is no relationship between central bank independence and real economic activity. In particular, central bank independence is not correlated with average unemployment, the volatility of unemployment, the average growth of real GDP or the volatility of real GDP. Central bank independence appears to offer countries a free lunch: it has the benefit of lower inflation without any apparent cost. This finding has led some countries, such as the UK in 1997 and Sweden in 1999, to rewrite their laws to give their central banks greater independence.[5]

---

[5] For a more complete presentation of these findings and references to the large literature on central bank independence, see Alberto Alesina and Lawrence H. Summers, 'Central Bank Independence and Macroeconomic Performance: Some Comparative Evidence', *Journal of Money, Credit, and Banking,* May 1993, vol. 25, pp. 151–162. For a study that questions the link between inflation and central bank independence, see Marta Campillo and Jeffrey A. Miron, 'Why Does Inflation Differ Across Countries?' in Christina D. Romer and David H. Romer, eds, *Reducing Inflation: Motivation and Strategy,* Chicago: University of Chicago Press, 1997, pp. 335–362.

15-5 Inflation Targeting and Central Bank Independence

In recent years, a number of countries have given their central banks greater independence in the setting of interest rates, as well as instructing them to pursue an explicit policy of inflation targeting. Four important central banks that have done this are the European Central Bank, the Bank of England, the Riksbank (Sweden's central bank) and the Norges Bank (Norway's central bank). The US Federal Reserve has always enjoyed independence in setting interest rates, although it has not explicitly adopted inflation targeting until recently (January 2012). Let's take a closer look at each of these central banks and how they set monetary policy.

The European Central Bank

The European Central Bank (ECB), located in Frankfurt, Germany, was officially created on 1 June 1998, as a number of European countries had decided that they wished to enter European monetary union and have the same currency – the euro – circulating among them. We will discuss the pros and cons of monetary union in Chapter 17. For now, though, we just note that if a group of countries has the same currency, then the countries in the group must have a common monetary policy, and the ECB was set up for precisely this purpose. The primary objective of the ECB is to promote price stability throughout the Euro Area, and to design and implement monetary policy that is consistent with this objective. Monetary policy at the ECB is both designed and set by its Governing Council. The Governing Council, which meets every two weeks in Frankfurt and includes a representative of each of the 17 member countries, as well as other ECB officials, is the most important decision-making body of the ECB, and decides, for example, on the level of the ECB's official interest rate, the refinancing rate. The Governing Council also decides how to interpret its duty to achieve price stability.

Formally, the ECB follows a 'two-pillar strategy' of monetary policy, where the first pillar is based on monitoring the growth rate of the money supply, while the second pillar is based on maintaining stable inflation over the medium term.[6] However, a number of economists have argued that, in practice, the ECB appears to have concentrated on the 'second pillar' and has effectively pursued inflation targeting.

In October 1998, the ECB agreed that price stability should be defined as a year-on-year increase in prices of less than 2 per cent, as measured by the annual change in a Harmonized Index of Consumer Prices throughout the Euro Area. A problem with this definition of price stability, however, is that 'less than 2 per cent' is a little vague – an annual inflation rate of 1 per cent and an annual

---

[6] See ECB, *The Monetary Policy of the ECB*, 2nd edn, Frankfurt: European Central Bank, 2004.

inflation rate of 0 per cent are both less than 2 per cent. In fact, some people were worried that the ECB might even aim for falling prices or negative inflation in order to achieve its target of less than 2 per cent. As we discuss more fully in the coming chapters, this would tend to reduce sharply output and employment in the economy, especially in the short to medium run. In May 2003, therefore, the Governing Council confirmed its official definition of price stability as less than 2 per cent per annum, but clarified that it would seek to maintain inflation rates close to 2 per cent over the medium term.

An important feature of the ECB is its independence. In setting monetary policy, the ECB is not allowed to seek or take instructions from any external body, including any member governments or any European Union institutions. The members of the Governing Council are all appointed for non-renewable terms of office, ranging from five to eight years, so that their decisions cannot be influenced by a desire to be reappointed.

The Bank of England

The Bank of England was founded in 1694, although it is not the oldest European central bank (the Swedish Riksbank was founded in 1668). Despite its name, the Bank of England is in fact the central bank for the whole of the United Kingdom. Arguably the most significant event in the Bank's 300-year history was when the UK government granted it independence in the setting of interest rates in 1997, which was formalized in an Act of Parliament in 1998. The important body within the Bank that makes the decision on the level at which to set the Bank's key interest rate, the Official Bank Rate (previously the repo rate), is the Monetary Policy Committee (MPC). The MPC consists of the Governor and two Deputy Governors of the Bank of England, each of whom is appointed by the Chancellor of the Exchequer (the UK Finance Minister), two other members appointed by the Bank after consultation with the Chancellor, and four other members appointed by the Chancellor. The Governor and the two Deputy Governors serve five-year renewable terms of office, while other MPC members serve three-year renewable terms. The MPC meets monthly and its interest-rate decision is announced immediately after the meeting.

Like the ECB, one of the Bank of England's primary duties is to deliver price stability. Also in common with the ECB, it enjoys independence in the setting of monetary policy – and in particular interest rates – in order to achieve the objective of price stability. *Unlike* the ECB, however, the Bank of England does not have the freedom to define for itself precisely what 'price stability' means in this context. This is done by the UK government and, in particular, by the Chancellor of the Exchequer. In fact, the 1998 Bank of England Act requires that the Chancellor write to the Governor of the Bank of England once a year to specify what price stability is to be defined as. Currently, the inflation target of 2 per cent is expressed in terms of an annual rate of inflation based on the consumer price index (CPI). If the target is missed by more than 1 percentage point on either side (i.e. if the annual rate of CPI inflation is more than 3 per cent or less than 1 per cent) the Governor of the Bank of England must write an open letter to the Chancellor explaining the reasons why inflation has increased or fallen to such an extent, and what the Bank proposes to do to ensure that inflation comes back to the target.

Since the ECB is free to choose its own objectives in its interpretation of price stability (e.g. an inflation target of 2 per cent), as well as the instruments it wishes to use in order to achieve those objectives (e.g. the setting of short-term interest rates), the ECB is said to have *objective independence* as well as *instrument independence*. In contrast, while the Bank of England is free to choose its instruments of monetary policy (and it chooses to set short-term interest rates), its objectives (e.g. a 2 per cent inflation target) are set by the UK Chancellor of the Exchequer, so that the Bank has *instrument independence* but not *objective independence*. Observers have also argued that the Bank of England is less independent of government than the ECB because the UK Chancellor directly appoints or is consulted on the appointment of the MPC members.

The Riksbank

In November 1992, the Swedish central bank, the Riksbank, abandoned its policy of pegging the value of the Swedish krona following speculative attacks on this and other European currencies (as we discussed in a case study in Chapter 13). After a brief period, the Riksbank declared, in January 1993, that the new flexible exchange rate policy would be combined with an explicit target for inflation. This decision was based partly on the recent positive experiences of inflation targeting in other countries. Sweden thus became the fourth country to introduce a formal inflation targeting regime (New Zealand had been the first, followed by Canada and the UK), and announced a CPI annual inflation target of 2 per cent.

It was decided, however, to have a transitional period, 1993–1994, because large initial inflationary impulses were expected from the depreciation of the krona and increases in indirect taxes that would have made the 2 per cent target infeasible in the short term.

Although it took several years, the Riksbank's independence and legal mandate to maintain price stability was put into law in 1999. Interest rate decisions at the Riksbank are taken by its Executive Board, which is composed of six members, who are also full-time employees of the Riksbank – the Governor and five Deputy Governors. These are appointed by a General Council, which in turn is elected by the Swedish Parliament and consists of 11 members. The six members of the Executive Board are appointed for six-year terms, with overlapping mandates, so that normally one appointment is made each year.

Like the ECB, the Riksbank, as well as being free to set the official interest rate, is also free to interpret its legal objective to maintain price stability and to set its inflation target. It thus has objective independence as well as instrument independence.

The Riksbank Executive Board meets to discuss and set monetary policy around eight times a year. These monetary policy meetings, at which interest rate decisions are taken and released to the press shortly afterwards, are announced four to six months in advance, and edited minutes of the meetings are published with a delay of around two weeks.

The Norges Bank

Norway adopted inflation targeting in 2001, and its government gave the Norwegian central bank, the Norges Bank, instrument independence in setting its official rate to achieve a target of CPI inflation of 2.5 per cent over time. The Norges Bank's Executive Board sets the official rate at regular times, normally every eighth week, and the interest rate decision is published shortly afterwards. The dates of monetary policy meetings are announced in advance, although the minutes of the meetings are not published. The Executive Board consists of two internal members – the Governor and Deputy Governor – and five external members drawn from the private sector and academia (at the time of writing this chapter, the Executive Board included two professors of economics).

The US Federal Reserve System

The US Federal Reserve System, commonly referred to as 'the Fed', was created in 1914. The Fed is run by its Board of Governors, which has seven members appointed by the US President. Six of the governors have 14-year terms to give them independence from short-term political pressures when they formulate monetary policy, although the Chairman has a four-year term. The Federal Reserve System is made up of the Federal Reserve Board in Washington, DC, and 12 regional Federal Reserve Banks located in major cities around the US.

At the Federal Reserve, monetary policy is made by the Federal Open Market Committee (FOMC). The FOMC meets about every six weeks in Washington, DC, to discuss the condition of the economy and consider changes in monetary policy, including the setting of its official interest rate, the discount rate. It is made up of the seven members of the Board of Governors and five of the twelve regional bank presidents.

The US Federal Reserve up until 2012 had not adopted an explicit policy of inflation targeting (although some commentators had suggested that it was, implicitly, targeting inflation between 1.7 and 2 per cent). However, in a historic shift, the Federal Reserve in January 2012 formally announced the setting of an inflation target at 2 per cent. For many this was regarded as a personal victory for the Chairman of the Federal Reserve and former professor of economics Ben Bernanke, who has been a very prominent advocate of inflation targeting.[7]

---

[7] See Ben S. Bernanke and Frederic S. Mishkin, 'Inflation Targeting: A New Framework for Monetary Policy?' *Journal of Economic Perspectives*, spring 1997, vol. 11, pp. 97–116.

15-6 Conclusion: Making Policy in an Uncertain World

In this chapter we have examined whether policy should take an active or passive role in responding to economic fluctuations, and whether policy should be conducted by rule or by discretion. There are many arguments on both sides of these questions. Perhaps the only clear conclusion is that there is no simple and compelling case for any particular view of macroeconomic policy. In the end, you must weigh the various arguments, both economic and political, and decide for yourself what kind of role the government should play in trying to stabilize the economy.

For better or worse, economists play a key role in the formulation of economic policy. Because the economy is complex, this role is often difficult. Yet it is also inevitable. Economists cannot sit back and wait until our knowledge of the economy has been perfected before giving advice. In the meantime, someone must advise economic policy makers. That job, difficult as it sometimes is, falls to economists.

The role of economists in the policy making process goes beyond giving advice to policy makers. Even economists cloistered in academia influence policy indirectly through their research and writing. In the conclusion of *The General Theory*, John Maynard Keynes wrote that

> the ideas of economists and political philosophers, both when they are right and when they are wrong, are more powerful than is commonly understood. Indeed, the world is ruled by little else. Practical men, who believe themselves to be quite exempt from intellectual influences, are usually the slaves of some defunct economist. Madmen in authority, who hear voices in the air, are distilling their frenzy from some academic scribbler of a few years back.

This is as true today as it was when Keynes wrote it in 1936.

Summary

1. Advocates of active policy view the economy as subject to frequent shocks that will lead to unnecessary fluctuations in output and employment unless monetary or fiscal policy responds. Many believe that economic policy has been successful in stabilizing the economy.

2. Advocates of passive policy argue that because monetary and fiscal policies work with long and variable lags, attempts to stabilize the economy are likely to end up being destabilizing. In addition, they believe that our present understanding of the economy is too limited to be useful in formulating successful stabilization policy and that inept policy is a frequent source of economic fluctuations.

3. Advocates of discretionary policy argue that discretion gives more flexibility to policy makers in responding to various unforeseen situations.

4. Advocates of policy rules argue that the political process cannot be trusted. They believe that politicians make frequent mistakes in conducting economic policy and sometimes use economic policy for their own political ends. In addition, advocates of policy rules argue that a commitment to a fixed policy rule is necessary to solve the problem of time inconsistency.

5. Since the late 1980s, many of the world's central banks have adopted inflation targeting. Inflation targeting involves setting a target for inflation and changing interest rates from time to time in order to achieve that target over the medium term of one to two years.

KEY CONCEPTS

Inside and outside lags

Automatic stabilizers

Lucas critique

Political business cycle

Time inconsistency

Monetarists

Taylor rule

Inflation targeting

Forward-looking Taylor rule

QUESTIONS FOR REVIEW

1. What are the inside lag and the outside lag? Which has the longer inside lag – monetary or fiscal policy? Which has the longer outside lag? Why?

2. Why would more accurate economic forecasting make it easier for policy makers to stabilize the economy? Describe two ways economists try to forecast developments in the economy.

3. Describe the Lucas critique.

4. How does a person's interpretation of macroeconomic history affect his or her view of macroeconomic policy?

5. What is meant by the 'time inconsistency' of economic policy? Why might policy makers be tempted to renege on an announcement they made earlier? In this situation, what is the advantage of a policy rule?

6. List three policy rules that the central bank might follow. Which of these would you advocate? Why?

7. Should a policy of inflation targeting be viewed as a policy rule or as a framework for constrained discretion on the part of the central bank?

PROBLEMS AND APPLICATIONS

1. Suppose that the trade-off between unemployment and inflation is determined by the Phillips curve:

$$u = u^n - \alpha (\pi - \pi^e),$$

where u denotes the unemployment rate, u^n the natural rate, π the rate of inflation and π^e the expected rate of inflation. In addition, suppose that one political party always follows a policy of

high money growth and the other political party (assume that there are only two) always follows a policy of low money growth. What 'political business cycle' pattern of inflation and unemployment would you predict under the following conditions?

a. Every four years, one of the parties takes control based on a random flip of a coin.

(*Hint:* What will expected inflation be prior to the election?)

b. The two parties take turns.

2. When cities pass laws limiting the rent landlords can charge on apartments, the laws usually apply to existing buildings and exempt any buildings not yet built. Advocates of rent control argue that this exemption ensures that rent control does not discourage the construction of new housing. Evaluate this argument in light of the time-inconsistency problem.

3. Go to the website of the European Central Bank (www.ecb.int) and find and download the press release of the President of the ECB, explaining the last three monetary policy decisions. What kind of economic considerations underlay each of these decisions. What do you think of the ECB's policy?

4. Go to the website of the Bank of England (www.bankofengland.co.uk). Follow the link to 'Monetary Policy' and then download the Bank's latest *Inflation Report*. Summarize what it says. What is the outlook for inflation over the next two years? How did the Monetary Policy Committee respond to this outlook at its last meeting?

Time Inconsistency and the Trade-Off between Inflation and Unemployment

In this appendix, we examine more formally the time-inconsistency argument for rules rather than discretion. This analysis is relegated to an appendix because we need to use some calculus.[8]

Suppose that the Phillips curve describes the relationship between inflation and unemployment. Letting u denote the unemployment rate, u^n the natural rate of unemployment, π the rate of inflation and π^e the expected rate of inflation, unemployment is determined by

$$u = u^n - \alpha(\pi - \pi^e).$$

Unemployment is low when inflation exceeds expected inflation, and high when inflation falls below expected inflation. The parameter α determines how much unemployment responds to surprise inflation.

For simplicity, suppose also that the central bank chooses the rate of inflation. Of course, more realistically, the central bank controls inflation only imperfectly through its control of the money supply. But for purposes of illustration, it is useful to assume that the central bank can control inflation perfectly.

The central bank likes low unemployment and low inflation. Suppose that the cost of unemployment and inflation, as perceived by the central bank, can be represented as

$$L(u, \pi) = u + \gamma\pi^2,$$

where the parameter γ represents how much the central bank dislikes inflation relative to unemployment. $L(u, \pi)$ is called the *loss function*. The central bank's objective is to make the loss as small as possible.

Having specified how the economy works and the central bank's objective, let's compare monetary policy made under a fixed rule and under discretion.

We begin by considering policy under a fixed rule. A rule commits the central bank to a particular level of inflation. As long as private agents understand that the central bank is committed to this rule, the expected level of inflation will be the level the central bank is committed to produce. Because expected inflation equals actual inflation ($\pi^e = \pi$), unemployment will be at its natural rate ($u = u^n$).

---

[8] The material in this appendix is derived from Finn E. Kydland and Edward C. Prescott, 'Rules Rather Than Discretion: The Inconsistency of Optimal Plans', *Journal of Political Economy*, June 1977, vol. 85, pp. 473–492; and Robert J. Barro and David Gordon, 'A Positive Theory of Monetary Policy in a Natural Rate Model', *Journal of Political Economy*, August 1983, vol. 91, pp. 589–610. Kydland and Prescott won the Nobel Prize for this and other work in 2004.

What is the optimal rule? Because unemployment is at its natural rate regardless of the level of inflation legislated by the rule, there is no benefit to having any inflation at all. Therefore, the optimal fixed rule requires that the central bank produce zero inflation.

Now let's consider discretionary monetary policy. Under discretion, the economy works as follows:

1. Private agents form their expectations of inflation π^e.

2. The central bank chooses the actual level of inflation π.

3. Based on expected and actual inflation, unemployment is determined.

Under this arrangement, the central bank minimizes its loss $L(u, \pi)$, subject to the constraint that the Phillips curve imposes. When making its decision about the rate of inflation, the central bank takes expected inflation as already determined.

To find what outcome we would obtain under discretionary policy, we must examine what level of inflation the central bank would choose. By substituting the Phillips curve into the central bank's loss function, we obtain

$$L(u, \pi) = u^n - \alpha(\pi - \pi^e) + \gamma\pi^2.$$

Notice that the central bank's loss is negatively related to unexpected inflation (the second term in the equation) and positively related to actual inflation (the third term). To find the level of inflation that minimizes this loss, differentiate with respect to π to obtain

$$dL/d\pi = -\alpha + 2\gamma\pi.$$

The loss is minimized when this derivative equals zero.[9] Solving for π, we get

$$\pi = \alpha/(2\gamma).$$

Whatever level of inflation private agents expected, this is the 'optimal' level of inflation for the central bank to choose. Of course, rational private agents understand the objective of the central bank and the constraint that the Phillips curve imposes. They therefore expect that the central bank will choose this level of inflation. Expected inflation equals actual inflation $\pi^e = \pi = \alpha/(2\gamma)$, and unemployment equals its natural rate ($u = u^n$).

Now compare the outcome under optimal discretion to the outcome under the optimal rule. In both cases, unemployment is at its natural rate. Yet discretionary policy produces more inflation than does policy under the rule. *Thus, optimal discretion is worse than the optimal rule.* This is true even though the central bank under discretion was attempting to minimize its loss, $L(u, \pi)$.

At first it may seem strange that the central bank can achieve a better outcome by being committed to a fixed rule. Why can the central bank with discretion

---

[9] The second derivative, $d^2L/d\pi^2 = 2\gamma$, is positive, ensuring that we are solving for a minimum of the loss function rather than a maximum!

not mimic the central bank committed to a zero-inflation rule? The answer is that the central bank is playing a game against private decision makers who have rational expectations. Unless it is committed to a fixed rule of zero inflation, the central bank cannot get private agents to expect zero inflation.

Suppose, for example, that the central bank simply announces that it will follow a zero-inflation policy. Such an announcement by itself cannot be credible. After private agents have formed their expectations of inflation, the central bank has the incentive to renege on its announcement in order to decrease unemployment. (As we have just seen, once expectations are given, the central bank's optimal policy is to set inflation at $\pi = \alpha/(2\gamma)$, regardless of π^e.) Private agents understand the incentive to renege and therefore do not believe the announcement in the first place.

This theory of monetary policy has an important corollary. Under one circumstance, the central bank with discretion achieves the same outcome as the central bank committed to a fixed rule of zero inflation. If the central bank dislikes inflation much more than it dislikes unemployment (so that γ is very large), inflation under discretion is near zero, because the central bank has little incentive to inflate. This finding provides some guidance to those who have the job of appointing central bankers. An alternative to imposing a fixed rule is to appoint an individual with a fervent distaste for inflation. Perhaps this is why even politicians who are more concerned about unemployment than inflation sometimes appoint conservative central bankers who are more concerned about inflation.

MORE PROBLEMS AND APPLICATIONS

1. In the 1970s, the inflation rate and the natural rate of unemployment both rose in many countries. Let's use the model of time inconsistency to examine this phenomenon. Assume that policy is discretionary.

   a. In the model as developed so far, what happens to the inflation rate when the natural rate of unemployment rises?

   b. Let's now change the model slightly by supposing that the central bank's loss function is quadratic in both inflation and unemployment. That is,

   $$L(u, \pi) = u^2 + \gamma\pi^2.$$

   Follow steps similar to those in the text to solve for the inflation rate under discretionary policy.

   c. Now what happens to the inflation rate when the natural rate of unemployment rises?

   d. Now suppose that the government appoints a conservative central banker to head the central bank. According to this model, what will happen to inflation and unemployment?

CHAPTER 16

Government Debt

The budget should be balanced, the treasury refilled, public debt reduced, the arrogance of officialdom tempered and controlled, and the assistance to foreign lands curtailed, lest Rome become bankrupt.

— Quintus Tullius Cicero (102–43 BCE)

When a government spends more than it collects in taxes, it runs a budget deficit, which it finances by borrowing from the private sector or from foreign governments. The accumulation of past borrowing is the government debt (which is also referred to as public debt or the national debt). Government debt differs from the private debt of individuals. For individuals, there are periods of their lives when they need to borrow, and other periods when they can afford to pay off their debts, and perhaps save a little. When individuals are young their income is usually insufficient to cover, for example, the cost of buying a house, and many people therefore take out a mortgage to cover this shortfall. Later in life, as income rises, people tend to pay off this debt — repay their mortgages — and perhaps save some money for retirement. Thus, you would expect that over the course of a lifetime the individual's budget would broadly balance. However, economies as a whole differ from individuals in that they essentially have infinite lives, so there is no reason why they should ever have to pay off their debts entirely. Nevertheless, there are very important economic principles that a government should follow in managing the public debt. For example, many economists argue that governments should aim to balance their budget over the economic cycle. That is, during good times governments should seek to run a surplus and pay off some debt, so that in bad times they can afford to run a deficit — spend more (say, on unemployment benefits) than they collect in tax revenue (which tends to fall during a recession). Another difference between government debt and an individual's debt is the effect it has on other people. If you spend more than your income and run up debt, this has very little impact on anyone except you. When a government's spending exceeds its tax revenue, this can have major effects on the macroeconomy and affect the lives of a great many people.

The debate over government debt has been particularly fervent in recent years. In the aftermath of the financial crisis of 2008–2009, the governments of many European countries ran very large budget deficits. These deficits were in part attributable to automatic stabilizers: tax revenue falls and government spending on programmes such as unemployment benefit rise when the economy goes into recession. In addition, various discretionary changes in fiscal policy aimed at stimulating their economies further increased budget deficits. Government deficits in the Euro Area (Eurozone) countries had risen from around 2 per cent of GDP before the crisis to over 6 per cent of GDP in 2009. While this fell back by 2012 to a little less than 4 per cent, some countries in the Euro Area with particular problems, such as Greece and Spain, still had government deficits over 10 per cent of GDP.

In this chapter we consider various aspects of the debate over the economic effects of government debt and rules by which such debt should be managed. We begin by looking at the numbers. Section 16-1 examines the size of the government debt in a number of European countries, and also looks at the history of the UK national debt. Section 16-2 discusses why measuring changes in government indebtedness is not as straightforward as it might seem. Indeed, some economists argue that traditional measures are so misleading that they should be ignored completely.

We then look at how government debt affects the economy. Section 16-3 describes the traditional view of government debt, according to which government borrowing reduces national saving and crowds out capital accumulation. This view is held by most economists and has been implicit in the discussion of fiscal policy throughout this book. Section 16-4 discusses an alternative view, called *Ricardian equivalence,* which is held by a small but influential minority of economists. According to the Ricardian view, government debt does not influence national saving and capital accumulation. As we will see, the debate between the traditional and Ricardian views of government debt arises from disagreements over how consumers respond to the government's debt policy.

Section 16-5 then looks at other facets of the debate over government debt. It begins by discussing whether the government should always try to balance its budget (i.e. exactly match government spending and tax revenue) and, if not, when a budget deficit or surplus is desirable. It also examines the effects of government debt on monetary policy and its possible effects on a nation's role in the world economy. Finally, in Section 16-6, we look at the issue of fiscal sustainability – the ability of an economy to service its public debt in terms of meeting the interest payments on it and any capital repayments that fall due. As we shall see, this implies a close relationship between the level of public debt as a percentage of GDP, the inflation rate, the rate of growth of real GDP and the budget deficit.

In Chapter 17 we shall examine the economics of adopting a single currency among a group of countries – a monetary union – and, in particular, the European Economic and Monetary Union (EMU), which has adopted the euro as the single currency among 17 European countries. Monetary union has a number of implications for the management of public debt and for fiscal policy more generally, and we shall discuss them in the next chapter, using some of the tools and insights that we will develop in this chapter. Then, in Chapter 20, we will examine the financial system more broadly, including the causes of financial crises. As we will see, excessive government debt can be at the centre of such crises – a lesson that several European nations have recently been learning, all too painfully.

16-1 The Size of the Government Debt

Table 16-1 shows the amount of general government debt for the EU-27 countries, expressed as a percentage of each country's GDP.[1] At the top of the list are the four heavily indebted countries of Greece, Italy, Portugal and Ireland, each of which has accumulated a government debt that exceeds annual GDP. Belgium,

TABLE 16-1

How Indebted Are the EU-27 Governments?

Country	Government Debt as a Percentage of GDP (2012)
Greece	156.9
Italy	127.0
Portugal	123.6
Ireland	117.6
Belgium	99.6
France	90.2
United Kingdom	90.0
Cyprus	85.8
EU (27 countries)	85.3
Spain	84.2
Germany	81.9
Hungary	79.2
Austria	73.4
Malta	72.1
Netherlands	71.2
Poland	55.6
Slovenia	54.1
Finland	53.0
Slovakia	52.1
Denmark	45.8
Czech Republic	45.8
Lithuania	40.7
Latvia	40.7
Sweden	38.2
Romania	37.8
Luxembourg	20.8
Bulgaria	18.5
Estonia	10.1

Source: Eurostat.
Note: Data are based on estimates of general government gross debt and nominal GDP for 2012.

---

[1] By 'general government' we mean local and central government together. The figures in Table 16-1 are for general government gross debt.

FIGURE 16-1

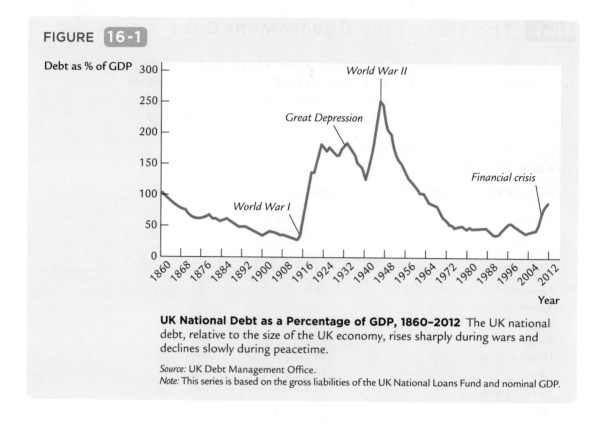

UK National Debt as a Percentage of GDP, 1860–2012 The UK national debt, relative to the size of the UK economy, rises sharply during wars and declines slowly during peacetime.

Source: UK Debt Management Office.
Note: This series is based on the gross liabilities of the UK National Loans Fund and nominal GDP.

France and the United Kingdom, are next, with public debt over 90 per cent of GDP. Cyprus, Spain and Germany also have relatively high debt levels (between 80 and 85 per cent of GDP). At the bottom of the table is Estonia, with a debt level of just over 10 per cent of GDP.

Over the course of history, government indebtedness has varied substantially for most countries. Figure 16-1 shows the ratio of the UK national debt to GDP since 1860. The UK national debt, relative to the size of the economy, varies from around 100 per cent of GDP in 1860, to a minimum of a quarter of GDP in 1914, to a maximum of two and a half times GDP in 1946.[2] In the period since the 2008 financial crisis, debt has increased from an average level of around 40 per cent in the previous decade to 90 per cent in 2012. These trends led to a significant event in February 2013 when ratings agency Moody's reduced its credit rating on UK government debt to one notch below the top AAA grade. Moody's was concerned about the UK government's fiscal policy, but their stance has not been followed by other ratings agencies. Standard and Poors, which had downgraded US debt in 2011, reaffirmed the UK's AAA rating in April 2013, although it did place the

---

[2] The historical series shown in Figure 16-1 is based on the gross liabilities of the UK National Loans Fund, and is defined very slightly differently from the figures presented in Table 16-1, which is based on general government gross debt. (The figures in Table 16-1, however, are consistent across countries, and the historical figures in Figure 16-1 are consistent through time.) These accounting differences are small and unimportant for our purposes, however, especially when we are looking at historical movements in national debt.

UK under 'negative watch' in a warning about possible downgrading if economic growth faltered or there was any weakening of the UK government's deficit reduction policies.

Historically, the primary cause of increases in the government debt is war. The debt-to-GDP ratio rises sharply during major wars and falls slowly during peacetime. The effects of World War I (1914–1918) and World War II (1939–1945) on UK public debt can be seen clearly in Figure 16-1. Many economists think that this historical pattern is the appropriate way to run fiscal policy. As we will discuss more fully later in this chapter, deficit financing of wars appears optimal for reasons of both tax smoothing and generational equity.

Even in peacetime, however, similar issues may arise. For example, if the government builds a new motorway system that will benefit future generations, is it fair to make the current generation of taxpayers foot the entire bill, or should some of it be met by issuing debt that future generations can pay off? We will return to this question below.

16-2 Problems in Measurement

The government budget deficit equals government spending minus government revenue, which in turn equals the amount of new debt the government needs to issue to finance its operations. This definition may sound simple enough, but in fact debates over fiscal policy sometimes arise over how the budget deficit should be measured. Some economists believe that the standard measure of the deficit is not a good indicator of the stance of fiscal policy. That is, they believe that the budget deficit does not accurately gauge either the impact of fiscal policy on today's economy or the burden being placed on future generations of taxpayers. In this section we discuss four problems with the usual measure of the budget deficit.

Measurement Problem 1: Inflation

The least controversial of the measurement issues is the correction for inflation. Almost all economists agree that the government's indebtedness should be measured in real terms, not in nominal terms. The measured deficit should equal the change in the government's real debt, not the change in its nominal debt.

The budget deficit as commonly measured, however, does not correct for inflation. To see how large an error this induces, consider the following example. Suppose that the real government debt is not changing; in other words, in real terms, the budget is balanced. In this case, the nominal debt must be rising at the rate of inflation. That is,

$$\Delta D/D = \pi,$$

where π is the inflation rate and D is the stock of government debt. This implies

$$\Delta D = \pi D.$$

The government would look at the change in the nominal debt ΔD and would report a budget deficit of πD. Hence, most economists believe that the reported budget deficit is overstated by the amount πD.

We can make the same argument in another way. The deficit is government expenditure minus government revenue. Part of expenditure is the interest paid on the government debt. Recall from Chapter 3, however, that in the presence of inflation, we need to distinguish between the nominal interest rate (the rate of interest paid to borrow money) and the real interest rate (the nominal interest rate corrected for the effects of inflation). Expenditure should include only the real interest paid on the debt rD, not the nominal interest paid iD. Because the difference between the nominal interest rate i and the real interest rate r is the inflation rate π, we can see that $iD - rD = (i - r)D = [i - (i - \pi)] D = \pi D$. Hence, the budget deficit is overstated by πD.

Measurement Problem 2: Capital Assets

Many economists believe that an accurate assessment of the government's budget deficit requires taking into account the government's assets as well as its liabilities. In particular, when measuring the government's overall indebtedness, we should subtract government assets from government debt. Therefore, the budget deficit should be measured as the change in debt minus the change in assets.

Certainly, individuals and firms treat assets and liabilities symmetrically. When a person borrows to buy a house, we do not say that he is running a budget deficit. Instead, we offset the increase in assets (the house) against the increase in debt (the mortgage) and record no change in net wealth. Perhaps we should treat the government's finances in the same way.

A budget procedure that accounts for assets as well as liabilities is called **capital budgeting**, because it takes into account changes in capital. For example, suppose that the government sells one of its office buildings or some of its land, and uses the proceeds to reduce the government debt. Under standard budget procedures, the reported deficit would be lower. Under capital budgeting, the revenue received from the sale would not lower the deficit, because the reduction in debt would be offset by a reduction in assets. Similarly, under capital budgeting, government borrowing to finance the purchase of a capital good would not raise the deficit.

A clear advantage of capital budgeting is that it prevents a government from financing a deficit by selling off government-owned capital assets. This would not be sustainable behaviour because, sooner or later, the stock of assets to sell off will have been exhausted. Conversely, if a government spends on a capital asset like a new school building, there ought to be some allowance for the fact that this will yield benefits to the economy in the future (better educated and more economically productive citizens) that may largely repay the cost of the asset.

The major difficulty with capital budgeting is that it is hard to decide which government expenditures should count as capital expenditures. For example, should the motorway system be counted as an asset of the government? If so, what is its value? What about the stockpile of military hardware, such as missiles? Should spending on education services (e.g. teachers' salaries) be treated as expenditure on human capital? These difficult questions must be answered if the government is to adopt a capital budget.

Economists and policy makers disagree about whether governments should use capital budgeting. Opponents of capital budgeting argue that, although the system is superior in principle to the standard system, it is too difficult to implement in practice. Proponents of capital budgeting argue that even an imperfect treatment of capital assets would be better than ignoring them altogether.

Measurement Problem 3: Uncounted Liabilities

Some economists argue that the measured budget deficit is misleading because it excludes some important government liabilities. For example, consider the pensions of government workers. These workers provide labour services to the government today, but part of their compensation is deferred to the future. In essence, these workers are providing a loan to the government. Their future pension benefits represent a government liability not very different from government debt. Yet this liability is not included as part of the government debt, and the accumulation of this liability is not included as part of the budget deficit. According to some estimates, this implicit liability is almost as large as the official government debt.

Similarly, consider the social security system. In some ways, the system is like a personal pension plan. People pay some of their income into the system when young and expect to receive benefits when old. Perhaps accumulated future social security benefits should be included in the government's liabilities.

One might argue that social security liabilities are different from government debt because the government can change the laws determining social security benefits. Yet in principle, the government could always choose not to repay all of its debt: the government honours its debt only because it chooses to do so. Promises to pay the holders of government debt may not be fundamentally different from promises to pay the future recipients of social security.

Measurement Problem 4: The Business Cycle

Many changes in the government's budget deficit occur automatically in response to a fluctuating economy. For example, when the economy goes into a recession, incomes fall, so people pay less in personal income taxes. Profits fall, so corporations pay less in corporate income taxes. More people become eligible for government assistance, such as social security and unemployment benefits, so government spending rises. Even without any change in the laws governing taxation and spending, the budget deficit increases.

These automatic changes in the deficit are not errors in measurement, because the government truly borrows more when a recession depresses tax revenue and boosts government spending. But these changes do make it more difficult to use the deficit to monitor changes in fiscal policy. That is, the deficit can rise or fall either because the government has changed policy or because the economy has changed direction. For some purposes, it would be good to know which is occurring.

FYI

Measuring National Indebtedness: General Government Gross Debt or Public Sector Net Debt?

The figures on the government debt of the EU-27 countries that we discussed earlier, in Table 16–1, relate to the total indebtedness of local and central government taken together, for each of the countries concerned, and are termed 'general government gross debt'. This is a standard measure of national indebtedness that is used, for example, by the European Commission in assessing a country's public debt. However, in some countries – notably the UK – policy makers often refer to an alternative measure of government indebtedness, namely 'public sector net debt'. Public sector net debt includes, in addition to general government debt, the debt of public sector corporations (i.e. publicly owned corporations, such as the Post Office or the British Broadcasting Corporation (BBC) in the UK). It also nets out (i.e. offsets) any public sector liquid financial assets against gross indebtedness. Liquid financial assets are assets that are held by the public sector and are either already in cash or could be quickly turned in cash, and include holdings of cash, bank and building society deposits, short-term commercial bonds and the official reserves, which include gold, foreign currencies and foreign government bonds.

It is not immediately clear which of the two measures of indebtedness is better. Certainly, public sector net debt includes the debt of all organizations that are nationally owned, so it may be said to be a better measure of *national* indebtedness than general government gross debt. On the other hand, spending by some public corporations (e.g. the BBC) may not be directly under the control of the government. Hence, general government gross indebtedness is probably closer to our theoretical discussions of the debt that arises when government spends more than it receives in tax revenue and has to sell bonds.

What about offsetting liquid financial assets against gross debt? Imagine that you take out a mortgage with a bank for £100,000 to buy a flat, but you still have savings of, say, £20,000 in your bank account, which you keep for emergencies (incidentally, you probably worry too much). Which is a better measure of how much you are in debt – £100,000 or £80,000? Most people would probably say that your *gross debt* (i.e. the £100,000 mortgage) is the true measure, since it is, after all, how much you owe the bank. On the other hand, you are in much better financial shape than someone with a £100,000 and nothing in the bank, and this is only reflected in your *net indebtedness* (i.e. the £100,000 you owe the bank, less the £20,000 you have in your account). Similarly, public sector *net* debt may be a better indicator of the health of the public sector finances than general government *gross* debt.

Overall, general government gross debt is probably closer to the concept of public debt that we have been analysing in our theoretical discussions in this chapter. On the other hand, public sector net debt may give a better picture of national indebtedness (because it refers to the whole public sector, not just government) and may better reflect national financial health (because it refers to net rather than gross indebtedness).

Figure 16-2 graphs the two measures of public debt for the UK, as a percentage of GDP, over the period 2000–2012. As the figure makes clear, the two measures tend to move together over time, although general government gross debt has been persistently higher than public sector net debt. The difference narrowed during the middle part of this period, but has since widened again.

The important point to remember is that, as a macroeconomist, when you read or listen to policy debates about public debt, you need to avoid confusion between these two measures.

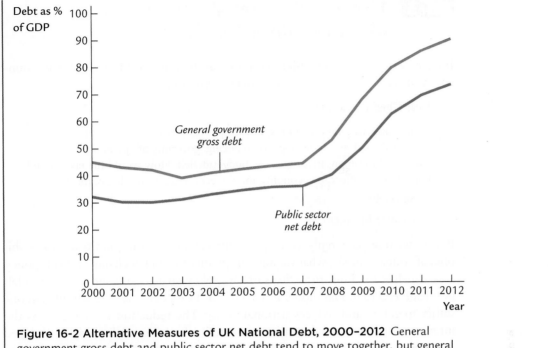

Figure 16-2 Alternative Measures of UK National Debt, 2000–2012 General government gross debt and public sector net debt tend to move together, but general government gross debt is persistently greater.

Source: UK Debt Management Office.

To solve this problem, some countries calculate a **cyclically adjusted budget deficit** (sometimes called the *full-employment budget deficit*). The cyclically adjusted deficit is based on estimates of what government spending and tax revenue would be if the economy were operating at its natural level of output and employment. The cyclically adjusted deficit is a useful measure because it reflects policy changes but not the current stage of the business cycle. Alternatively viewed, given that the economy must on average be at the natural rates of output and unemployment over the economic cycle, the cyclically adjusted deficit can be thought of as an average over the cycle.

Summing Up

Economists differ in the importance they place on these measurement problems. Some believe that the problems are so severe that the budget deficit as normally measured is almost meaningless. Most take these measurement problems seriously, but still view the measured budget deficit as a useful indicator of fiscal policy.

The undisputed lesson is that to evaluate fully what fiscal policy is doing, economists and policy makers must look at more than just the measured budget deficit. No economic statistic is perfect. Whenever we see a number reported in the media, we need to know what it is measuring and what it is leaving out. This is especially true for data on government debt and budget deficits.

16-3 The Traditional View of Government Debt

Imagine that you are the Chief Economist at the Finance Ministry of your country.[3] You receive a letter from the Finance Minister:

Dear Chief Economist:

I am considering cutting all taxes by 20 per cent. Before doing so, I would like your analysis. I see little hope of reducing government spending, so the tax cut would mean an increase in the budget deficit. How would the tax cut and budget deficit affect the economy and the economic well-being of the country?

Sincerely,

Finance Minister

Before writing your reply, you open your favourite economics textbook – this one, of course – to see what the models predict for such a change in fiscal policy.

To analyse the long-run effects of this policy change, you turn to the models in Chapters 3 to 9. The model in Chapter 3 shows that a tax cut stimulates consumer spending and reduces national saving. The reduction in saving raises the interest rate, which crowds out investment. The Solow growth model introduced in Chapter 8 shows that lower investment eventually leads to a lower steady-state capital stock and a lower level of output. Because we concluded in Chapter 9 that most advanced economies have less capital than in the Golden Rule steady state (the steady state with maximum consumption), the fall in steady-state capital means lower consumption and reduced economic well-being.

To analyse the short-run effects of the policy change, you turn to the *IS-LM* model in Chapters 11 and 12. This model shows that a tax cut stimulates consumer spending, which implies an expansionary shift in the *IS* curve. If there is no change in monetary policy, the shift in the *IS* curve leads to an expansionary shift in the aggregate demand curve. In the short run, when prices are sticky, the expansion in aggregate demand leads to higher output and lower unemployment. Over time, as prices adjust, the economy returns to the natural rate of output, and the higher aggregate demand results in a higher price level.

To see how international trade affects your analysis, you turn to the open-economy models in Chapters 6 and 13. The model in Chapter 6 shows that when national saving falls, people start financing investment by borrowing from abroad, causing a trade deficit. Although the inflow of capital from abroad lessens the effect of the fiscal policy change on the economy's capital accumulation, the economy becomes indebted to foreign countries. The fiscal policy change also causes the external value of the currency to appreciate in the foreign exchange market, which makes foreign goods cheaper in the domestic economy and domestic goods more expensive abroad. The Mundell–Fleming model in Chapter 13 shows that the appreciation of the exchange rate and the resulting fall in net exports reduce the short-run expansionary impact of the fiscal change on output and employment.

---

[3] In the UK and the US, the Finance Ministry is known as the Treasury and the Finance Minister is known as the Chancellor of the Exchequer (in the UK) or the Treasury Secretary (in the US).

With all these models in mind, you sit down to write your report:

Dear Finance Minister:

A tax cut financed by government borrowing would have many effects on the economy. The immediate impact of the tax cut would be to stimulate consumer spending. Higher consumer spending affects the economy in both the short run and the long run.

In the short run, higher consumer spending would raise the demand for goods and services and thus raise output and employment. Interest rates would also rise, however, as investors competed for a smaller flow of saving. Higher interest rates would discourage investment and would encourage capital to flow in from abroad. The value of the currency would rise in value against foreign currencies, and domestic firms would become less competitive in world markets.

In the long run, the smaller national saving caused by the tax cut would mean a smaller capital stock and a greater foreign debt. Therefore, the output of the nation would be smaller, and a greater share of that output would be owed to foreigners. The overall effect of the tax cut on economic well-being is hard to judge. Current generations would benefit from higher consumption and higher employment, although inflation would likely be higher as well. Future generations would bear much of the burden of today's budget deficits: they would be born into a nation with a smaller capital stock and a larger foreign debt.

Your faithful servant,

Chief Economist

The Finance Minister replies:

Dear Chief Economist:

Thank you for your letter. It made sense to me. But yesterday I spoke to a prominent economist who called herself a 'Ricardian' and who reached quite a different conclusion. She said that a tax cut by itself would not stimulate consumer spending. She concluded that the budget deficit would therefore not have all the effects you listed. What's going on here?

Sincerely,

Finance Minister

After studying the next section, you write back to the Finance Minister, explaining in detail the debate over Ricardian equivalence.

CASE STUDY

The Laffer Curve and Supply-Side Economics

Figure 16-3 depicts the so-called Laffer curve, and shows the relationship between income tax rates and the total amount of tax revenue. On the horizontal axis is the average rate of income tax payable in the economy – that is, what percentage of a person's total income, on average, the government would require to be paid in tax. On the vertical axis is total government income tax revenue. The Laffer curve suggests that, while increasing income tax rates may

F Y I

Taxes and Incentives

Throughout this book we have summarized the tax system with a single variable T. In our models, the policy instrument is the level of taxation that the government chooses; we have ignored the issue of how the government raises this tax revenue. In practice, however, taxes are not lump-sum payments, but are levied on some type of economic activity. Governments raise tax revenue in various ways, including taxing personal income, payrolls and corporate profits.

Courses in public finance spend much time studying the pros and cons of alternative types of taxes. One lesson emphasized in such courses is that taxes affect incentives. When people are taxed on their labour earnings, they have less incentive to work hard. When people are taxed on the income from owning capital, they have less incen-

tive to save and invest in capital. As a result, when taxes change, incentives change, and this can have macroeconomic effects. If lower tax rates encourage increased work and investment, the aggregate supply of goods and services increases.

Some economists, called *supply-siders*, believe that the incentive effects of taxes are large. Some supply-siders go so far as to suggest that tax cuts can be self-financing: a cut in tax rates induces such a large increase in aggregate supply that tax revenue increases, despite the fall in tax rates. Although all economists agree that taxes affect incentives and that incentives affect aggregate supply to some degree, most believe that the incentive effects are not large enough to make tax cuts self-financing in most circumstances.

increase tax revenue at first, there comes a point where tax rates are so high that people's incentive to work is severely diminished and tax revenue falls as tax rates are raised further.

The existence of a Laffer curve is uncontentious — no one would disagree that average income tax rates of zero and 100 per cent would each raise no revenue. The issue, therefore, is whether the Laffer curve is relevant. More specifically, at what income tax rate would the Laffer curve change its slope from positive to negative? On the other hand, as economists, we know that people make decisions at the margin, so that it is the marginal rate of income tax — the tax paid on an extra final unit of income — that may be more relevant for determining behaviour. However, since all developed countries have progressive tax systems in which the marginal tax rate increases as income rises, not everyone in the economy faces the same marginal rate of income tax. Nevertheless, the same supply-side principles apply: would raising the marginal rate of income tax for people within a certain income band actually reduce tax revenue because it gives them an incentive to work less?

The Laffer curve is named after the American supply-side economist Arthur Laffer, who famously drew the curve on the back of a napkin in a Washington restaurant in 1974. Laffer suggested to journalists lunching with him that the United States was on the downward-sloping side of this curve. Tax rates were so high, he argued, that reducing them would actually raise tax revenue by increasing the incentives for people to work.

Most economists were sceptical of Laffer's suggestion. The idea that a cut in tax rates could raise tax revenue was correct as a matter of economic theory, but

FIGURE 16-3

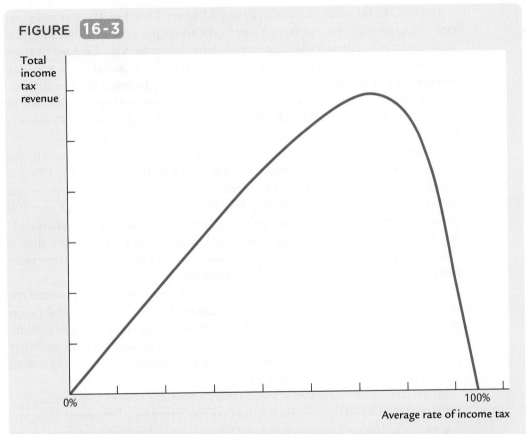

The Laffer Curve The Laffer curve traces out the relationship between the average rate of income tax in the economy and the amount of income tax revenue raised by the government. At an income tax rate of either zero or 100 per cent, income tax revenue must be zero (at zero per cent there is no tax at all, and at 100 per cent there is no incentive whatsoever to work). Also, raising the tax rate slightly above zero per cent clearly raises tax revenue from zero to a positive amount, so that the slope of the Laffer curve must initially be positive. At some point between zero and 100 per cent, therefore, total tax revenue must achieve a maximum and the slope becomes negative: the disincentive to work as a result of higher income tax rates means that people work a lot less and so the total amount of income tax paid begins to fall.

there was more doubt about whether it would do so in practice. There was little evidence for Laffer's view that tax rates – in the US or elsewhere – had in fact reached such extreme levels.

Nevertheless, the thinking underlying the Laffer curve (as it became known) became very influential in policy circles during the 1980s, particularly in the US during the years of President Ronald Reagan's administration, and in the UK during Prime Minister Margaret Thatcher's government during the 1980s. Tax rates – particularly income tax rates – were cut aggressively in both the US and the UK during the 1980s.

In the UK, for example, under Prime Minister Thatcher, the top marginal rate of income tax was cut from 83 per cent to 60 per cent in 1980, and then again to 40 per cent in 1988. Economists have, however, found it hard to trace any strong incentive effects of these tax cuts leading to increases in total tax revenue, as the Laffer curve would suggest. The UK Institute for Fiscal Studies, for example, concluded that, at most, about 3 per cent of the increase in tax revenue between 1980 and 1986 could be attributed to the 1980 income tax cut.

In the US, President Reagan also cut taxes aggressively, but the result was less tax revenue, not more. Revenue from personal income taxes in the US (per person, adjusted for inflation) fell by 9 per cent from 1980 to 1984, even though average income (per person, adjusted for inflation) grew by 4 per cent over this period. The tax cut, together with policy makers' unwillingness to restrain spending, began a long period during which the US government spent more than it collected in taxes. Throughout Reagan's two terms in office, and for many years thereafter, the US government ran large budget deficits.

Yet Laffer's argument is not completely without merit. Although an overall cut in tax rates normally reduces revenue, some taxpayers at some times may be on the wrong side of the Laffer curve. The idea that cutting taxes can raise revenue may be correct if applied to those taxpayers facing the highest tax rates, but most people face lower marginal rates. Where the typical worker is on the top end of the Laffer curve, it may be more appropriate.

In Sweden in the early 1980s, for instance, the typical worker faced a marginal tax rate of about 80 per cent. Such a high tax rate provides a substantial disincentive to work. Studies have suggested that Sweden would indeed have raised more tax revenue if it had lowered its tax rates.

Policy makers and economists still debate these issues. There is no debate, however, about the general lesson that how much revenue the government gains or loses from a tax change cannot be computed just by looking at tax rates. It also depends on how the tax change affects people's behaviour. ∎

16-4 The Ricardian View of Government Debt

The traditional view of government debt presumes that when the government cuts taxes and runs a budget deficit, consumers respond to their higher after-tax income by spending more. An alternative view, called **Ricardian equivalence**, questions this presumption. According to the Ricardian view, consumers are forward-looking and, therefore, base their spending decisions not only on their current income, but also on their expected future income. As we explore more fully in Chapter 18, the forward-looking consumer is at the heart of many modern theories of consumption. The Ricardian view of government debt applies the logic of the forward-looking consumer to analyse the effects of fiscal policy.

The Basic Logic of Ricardian Equivalence

Consider the response of a forward-looking consumer to the tax cut that the Finance Minister is considering. The consumer might reason as follows:

> The government is cutting taxes without any plans to reduce government spending. Does this policy alter my set of opportunities? Am I richer because of this tax cut? Should I consume more? Perhaps not. The government is financing the tax cut by running a budget deficit. At some point in the future, the government will have to raise taxes to pay off the debt and accumulated interest. So the policy really represents a tax cut today coupled with a tax hike in the future. The tax cut merely gives me transitory income that eventually will be taken back. I am not any better off, so I will leave my consumption unchanged.

The forward-looking consumer understands that government borrowing today means higher taxes in the future. A tax cut financed by government debt does not reduce the tax burden; it merely reschedules it. Thus it should not encourage the consumer to spend more.

One can view this argument another way. Suppose that the government borrows €1000 from the typical citizen to give that citizen a €1000 tax cut. In essence, this policy is the same as giving the citizen a €1000 government bond as a gift. One side of the bond says, 'The government owes you, the bondholder, €1000 plus interest.' The other side says, 'You, the taxpayer, owe the government €1000 plus interest.' Overall, the gift of a bond from the government to the typical citizen does not make the citizen richer or poorer, because the value of the bond is offset by the value of the future tax liability.

The general principle is that government debt is equivalent to future taxes, and if consumers are sufficiently forward-looking, future taxes are equivalent to current taxes. Hence, financing the government by debt is equivalent to financing it by taxes. This view is called *Ricardian equivalence,* after the famous 19th-century British economist David Ricardo, because he first noted the theoretical argument.

The implication of Ricardian equivalence is that a debt-financed tax cut leaves consumption unaffected. Households save the extra disposable income to pay the future tax liability that the tax cut implies. This increase in private saving exactly offsets the decrease in public saving. National saving – the sum of private and public saving – remains the same. The tax cut therefore has none of the effects that the traditional analysis predicts.

The logic of Ricardian equivalence does not mean that all changes in fiscal policy are irrelevant. Changes in fiscal policy do influence consumer spending if they influence present or future government purchases. For example, suppose that the government cuts taxes today because it plans to reduce government purchases in the future. If the consumer understands that this tax cut does not require an increase in future taxes, he feels richer and raises his consumption. But note that it is the reduction in government purchases, rather than the reduction in taxes, that stimulates consumption: the announcement of a future reduction in government purchases would raise consumption today even if current taxes were unchanged, because it would imply lower taxes at some time in the future.

Consumers and Future Taxes

The essence of the Ricardian view is that when people choose their consumption, they rationally look ahead to the future taxes implied by government debt. But how forward-looking are consumers? Defenders of the traditional view of government debt believe that the prospect of future taxes does not have as large an influence on current consumption as the Ricardian view assumes. Here are some of their arguments.[4]

Myopia Proponents of the Ricardian view of fiscal policy assume that people are rational when making decisions such as choosing how much of their income to consume and how much to save. When the government borrows to pay for current spending, rational consumers look ahead to the future taxes required to support this debt. Thus, the Ricardian view presumes that people have substantial knowledge and foresight.

One possible argument for the traditional view of tax cuts is that people are short-sighted, perhaps because they do not fully comprehend the implications of government budget deficits. It is possible that some people follow simple and not fully rational rules of thumb when choosing how much to save. Suppose, for example, that a person acts on the assumption that future taxes will be the same as current taxes. This person will fail to take account of future changes in taxes required by current government policies. A debt-financed tax cut will lead this person to believe that his lifetime income has increased, even if it has not done so. The tax cut will therefore lead to higher consumption and lower national saving.

Borrowing Constraints The Ricardian view of government debt assumes that consumers base their spending not on their current income but on their lifetime income, which includes both current and expected future income. According to the Ricardian view, a debt-financed tax cut increases current income, but it does not alter lifetime income or consumption. Advocates of the traditional view of government debt argue that current income is more important than lifetime income for those consumers who face binding borrowing constraints. A *borrowing constraint* is a limit on how much an individual can borrow from banks or other financial institutions.

A person who would like to consume more than his current income – perhaps because he expects higher income in the future – has to do so by borrowing. If he cannot borrow to finance current consumption, or can borrow only a limited amount, his current income determines his spending, regardless of what his lifetime income might be. In this case, a debt-financed tax cut raises current income and thus consumption, even though future income is lower. In essence, when the government cuts current taxes and raises future taxes, it is giving taxpayers a loan. For a person who wanted to obtain a loan but was unable to, the tax cut expands his opportunities and stimulates consumption.

Future Generations Besides myopia and borrowing constraints, a third argument for the traditional view of government debt is that consumers expect the implied

---

[4] For a survey of the debate over Ricardian equivalence, see Douglas Bernheim, 'Ricardian Equivalence: An Evaluation of Theory and Evidence', *NBER Macroeconomics Annual*, 1987, pp. 263–303. See also the symposium on budget deficits in the *Journal of Economic Perspectives*, spring 1989.

future taxes to fall not on them but on future generations. Suppose, for example, that the government cuts taxes today, issues 30-year bonds to finance the budget deficit, and then raises taxes in 30 years to repay the loan. In this case, the government debt represents a transfer of wealth from the next generation of taxpayers (which faces the tax hike) to the current generation of taxpayers (which gets the tax cut). This transfer raises the lifetime resources of the current generation, so it raises their consumption. In essence, a debt-financed tax cut stimulates consumption because it gives the current generation the opportunity to consume at the expense of the next generation.

Economist Robert Barro has provided a clever rejoinder to this argument to support the Ricardian view. Barro argues that because future generations are the children and grandchildren of the current generation, we should not view them as independent economic actors. Instead, he argues, the appropriate assumption is that current generations care about future generations. This altruism between generations is evidenced by the gifts that many people give their children, often in the form of bequests at the time of their deaths. The existence of bequests suggests that many people are not eager to take advantage of the opportunity to consume at their children's expense.

'What's this I hear about you adults mortgaging my future?'

According to Barro's analysis, the relevant decision-making unit is not the individual, whose life is finite, but the family, which continues forever. In other words, an individual decides how much to consume based not only on his own income but also on the income of future members of his family. A debt-financed tax cut may raise the income an individual receives in his lifetime, but it does not raise his family's overall resources. Instead of consuming the extra income from the tax cut, the individual saves it and leaves it as a bequest to his children, who will bear the future tax liability.

We can see now that the debate over government debt is really a debate over consumer behaviour. The Ricardian view assumes that consumers have a long time horizon. Barro's analysis of the family implies that the consumer's time horizon, like the government's, is effectively infinite. Yet it is possible that consumers do not look ahead to the tax liabilities of future generations. Perhaps they expect their children to be richer than they are and therefore welcome the opportunity to consume at their children's expense. The fact that many people leave zero or minimal bequests to their children is consistent with this hypothesis. For these zero-bequest families, a debt-financed tax cut alters consumption by redistributing wealth among generations.[5]

---

[5] Robert J. Barro, 'Are Government Bonds Net Wealth?', *Journal of Political Economy*, 1974, vol. 81, pp. 1095–1117.

CASE STUDY

Why Do Parents Leave Bequests?

The debate over Ricardian equivalence is partly a debate over how different generations are linked to one another. Robert Barro's defence of the Ricardian view is based on the assumption that parents leave their children bequests because they care about them. But is altruism really the reason that parents leave bequests?

One group of economists has suggested that parents use bequests to control their children. Parents often want their children to do certain things for them, such as phoning home regularly and visiting on holidays. Perhaps parents use the implicit threat of disinheritance to induce their children to be more attentive.

To test this 'strategic bequest motive', these economists examined data on how often children visit their parents. They found that the more wealthy the parent, the more often the children visit. Even more striking was another result: only wealth that can be left as a bequest induces more frequent visits. Wealth that cannot be bequeathed, such as pension wealth which reverts to the pension company in the event of an early death, does not encourage children to visit. These findings suggest that there may be more to the relationships among generations than mere altruism.[6] ∎

Making a Choice

Having seen the traditional and Ricardian views of government debt, you should ask yourself two sets of questions.

First, with which view do you agree? If the government cuts taxes today, runs a budget deficit and raises taxes in the future, how will the policy affect the economy? Will it stimulate consumption, as the traditional view holds? Or will consumers understand that their lifetime income is unchanged and, therefore, offset the budget deficit with higher private saving?

Second, why do you hold the view that you do? If you agree with the traditional view of government debt, what is the reason? Do consumers fail to understand that higher government borrowing today means higher taxes tomorrow? Or do they ignore future taxes, either because they are borrowing-constrained or because future taxes fall on future generations with which they do not feel an economic link? If you hold the Ricardian view, do you believe that consumers have the foresight to see that government borrowing today will result in future taxes levied on them or their descendants? Do you believe that consumers will save the extra income to offset that future tax liability?

We might hope that the evidence could help us decide between these two views of government debt. Yet when economists have examined macroeconomic data in order to analyse these issues, the results have been largely inconclusive. Nevertheless, it is probably true to say that most macroeconomists would not adhere to the proposition of Ricardian equivalence, strictly interpreted. The

---

[6] B. Douglas Bernheim, Andrei Shleifer and Lawrence H. Summers, 'The Strategic Bequest Motive', *Journal of Political Economy*, 1985, vol. 93, pp. 1045–1076.

FYI

Ricardo on Ricardian Equivalence

David Ricardo was a millionaire stockbroker and one of the great economists of all time. His most important contribution to the field was his 1817 book, *Principles of Political Economy and Taxation,* in which he developed the theory of comparative advantage, which economists still use to explain the gains from international trade. Ricardo was also a member of the British Parliament, where he put his own theories to work and opposed the Corn Laws, which restricted international trade in grain.

Ricardo was interested in the alternative ways in which a government might pay for its expenditure. In an 1820 article called 'Essay on the Funding System', he considered an example of a war that cost £20 million. He noted that if the interest rate were 5 per cent, this expense could be financed with a one-time tax of £20 million, a perpetual tax of £1 million or a tax of £1.2 million for 45 years. He wrote:

> In point of economy, there is no real difference in either of the modes; for twenty million in one payment, one million per annum forever, or 1,200,0000 pounds for 45 years, are precisely of the same value.

Ricardo was aware that the issue involved the linkages among generations:

> It would be difficult to convince a man possessed of 20,000 pounds, or any other sum, that a perpetual payment of 50 pounds per annum was equally burdensome with a single tax of 1000 pounds. He

would have some vague notion that the 50 pounds per annum would be paid by posterity, and would not be paid by him; but if he leaves his fortune to his son, and leaves it charged with this perpetual tax, where is the difference whether he leaves him 20,000 pounds with the tax, or 19,000 pounds without it?

Although Ricardo viewed these alternative methods of government finance as equivalent, he did not think other people would view them as such:

> The people who pay taxes . . . do not manage their private affairs accordingly. We are apt to think that the war is burdensome only in proportion to what we are at the moment called to pay for it in taxes, without reflecting on the probable duration of such taxes.

Thus, Ricardo doubted that people were rational and far-sighted enough to look ahead fully to their future tax liabilities.

As a policy maker, Ricardo took seriously the government debt. Before the British Parliament, he once declared:

> This would be the happiest country in the world, and its progress in prosperity would go beyond the powers of imagination to conceive, if we got rid of two great evils – the national debt and the corn laws.

It is one of the great ironies in the history of economic thought that Ricardo rejected the theory that now bears his name!

consensus view is probably that, while there may be *some* offsetting effects of tax changes due to the perceived effect on future tax liabilities, a combination of myopia and borrowing constraints is likely to prohibit full Ricardian equivalence.

16-5 Other Perspectives on Government Debt

The policy debates over government debt have many facets. So far we have considered the traditional and Ricardian views of government debt. According to the traditional view, a government budget deficit expands aggregate demand

and stimulates output in the short run, but crowds out capital and depresses economic growth in the long run. According to the Ricardian view, a government budget deficit has none of these effects, because consumers understand that a budget deficit represents merely the postponement of a tax burden. With these two theories as background, we now consider several other perspectives on government debt.

Balanced Budgets versus Optimal Fiscal Policy

Sometimes politicians argue that the government should run a balanced budget. Most economists, however, oppose a strict rule requiring the government to balance its budget. There are three reasons why optimal fiscal policy may at times call for a budget deficit or surplus.

Stabilization A budget deficit or surplus can help to stabilize the economy. In essence, a balanced-budget rule would revoke the automatic stabilizing powers of the system of taxes and transfers. When the economy goes into a recession, taxes automatically fall and transfers automatically rise. Although these automatic responses help to stabilize the economy, they push the budget into deficit. A strict balanced-budget rule would require that the government raise taxes or reduce spending in a recession, but these actions would further depress aggregate demand. Discretionary fiscal policy is more likely to move in the opposite direction over the course of the business cycle. In 2009, for example, US President Barack Obama signed a stimulus bill authorizing a large increase in spending to try to reduce the severity of the recession, even though it led to the largest budget deficit in more than half a century.

Tax Smoothing A budget deficit or surplus can be used to reduce the distortion of incentives caused by the tax system. As we discussed earlier, high tax rates impose a cost on society by discouraging economic activity. A tax on labour earnings, for instance, reduces the incentive that people have to work long hours. Because this disincentive becomes particularly large at very high tax rates, the total social cost of taxes is minimized by keeping tax rates relatively stable, rather than making them high in some years and low in others. Economists call this policy *tax smoothing*. To keep tax rates smooth, a deficit is necessary in years of unusually low income (recessions) or unusually high expenditure (wars).

Intergenerational Redistribution A budget deficit can be used to shift a tax burden from current to future generations. For example, some economists argue that if the current generation fights a war to preserve freedom, future generations benefit as well and should bear some of the burden. To pass on some of the war's costs, the current generation can finance the war with a budget deficit. The government can later retire the debt by levying taxes on the next generation.

Given that it is now more than 60 years since European countries were engaged in a major war, perhaps a more compelling argument for shifting tax burdens over time is connected with public investment. If the government enhances the economy's infrastructure by building new roads, hospitals and schools, this is investment that will benefit future generations as well as the current generation of taxpayers, since the investments will last many years. Why, then, should the current generation foot the entire bill? Surely future generations should pay their share too? Also, since public investments may raise the future growth rate of the economy, future generations may be richer as a result, and so better able to pay their share of the investment. Hence, the government may wish to pass on some of the costs of public investment to future generations by using debt finance.

These considerations lead most economists to reject a strict balanced-budget rule. At the very least, a rule for fiscal policy needs to take account of the recurring episodes, such as recessions and wars, during which it is reasonable for the government to run a budget deficit; and may also distinguish between government expenditure on current goods and services, and expenditure on public investment, when analysing the budget deficit.

Fiscal Effects on Monetary Policy

We first discussed the possibility of a link between fiscal policy and monetary policy in Chapter 5. As we saw, one way for a government to finance a budget deficit is simply to print money – a policy that leads to higher inflation. Indeed, when countries experience hyperinflation, the typical reason is that fiscal policy makers are relying on the inflation tax to pay for some of their spending. The ends of hyperinflations almost always coincide with fiscal reforms that include large cuts in government spending, and therefore a reduced need for seigniorage.

In addition to this link between the budget deficit and inflation, some economists have suggested that a high level of debt might also encourage the government to create inflation. Because most government debt is specified in nominal terms, the real value of the debt falls when the price level rises. This is the usual redistribution between creditors and debtors caused by unexpected inflation – here the debtor is the government and the creditor is the private sector. But this debtor, unlike others, has access to the monetary printing press. A high level of debt might encourage the government to print money, thereby raising the price level and reducing the real value of its debts.

Despite these concerns about a possible link between government debt and monetary policy, there is little evidence that this link is important in most developed countries. Thus, although monetary policy might be driven by fiscal policy in some situations, such as during the classic hyperinflations, this situation appears not to be the norm in most countries today. There are several reasons for this. First, most governments can finance deficits by selling debt and do not need to rely on seigniorage. Second, central banks often have enough independence to resist political pressure for more expansionary monetary policy. Third, and most important, policy makers in all parts of government know that inflation is a poor solution to fiscal problems.

International Dimensions

Government debt may affect a nation's role in the world economy. As we first saw in Chapter 6, when a government budget deficit reduces national saving, it often leads to a trade deficit, which in turn is financed by borrowing from abroad. For instance, many observers have blamed US fiscal policy for the relatively recent switch of the United States from a major creditor in the world economy to a major debtor. This link between the budget deficit and the trade deficit leads to two further effects of government debt.

First, high levels of government debt may increase the risk that an economy will experience capital flight – an abrupt decline in the demand for a country's assets in world financial markets. International investors are aware that a government can always deal with its debt simply by defaulting. This approach was used as far back as 1335, when England's King Edward III defaulted on his debt to Italian bankers. More recently, several Latin American countries defaulted on their debts in the 1980s, and Russia did the same in 1998. In 2011, it seemed likely that Greece was heading towards that outcome as well (a topic we discuss in Chapter 20). The higher the level of the government debt, the greater the temptation of default. Thus, as government debt increases, international investors may come to fear default and curtail their lending. If this loss of confidence occurs suddenly, the result could be the classic symptoms of capital flight: a collapse in the value of the currency and an increase in interest rates. As we discussed in Chapter 13, this is precisely what happened to Mexico in the early 1990s when default appeared likely.

Second, high levels of government debt financed by foreign borrowing may reduce a nation's political clout in world affairs. This fear was emphasized by economist Ben Friedman in his 1988 book, *Day of Reckoning*. He wrote: 'World power and influence have historically accrued to creditor countries. It is not coincidental that America emerged as a world power simultaneously with our transition from a debtor nation . . . to a creditor supplying investment capital to the rest of the world.' Friedman suggests that if the United States continues to run large trade deficits, it will eventually lose some of its international influence. So far, the record has not been kind to this hypothesis: the United States has run trade deficits throughout the 1980s, 1990s and the first decade of the 2000s and, nonetheless, remains a leading superpower. But perhaps other events – such as the collapse of the Soviet Union – offset the fall in political clout that the United States would have experienced because of its increased indebtedness.

CASE STUDY

Indexed Bonds

In a number of countries – including nine European countries – the government issues bonds that pay a return based on the consumer price index (CPI). These bonds pay a rate of interest linked to the overall price level as measured by the CPI. In addition, when the principal (the price of the bond when it is issued) is repaid, that amount is also adjusted for changes in the CPI. The interest paid on the bonds, therefore, is a real interest rate. No longer do professors of macro-economics need to define the real interest rate as an abstract construct. They can just look up the interest rate paid on indexed bonds. Looked at another way, indexed bonds also provide data on expected inflation: since the real interest rate is the nominal rate plus expected inflation, one way to measure the bond market's expected inflation rate is to look at the difference between the yield on nominal bonds and the yield on real bonds. This variable can also be useful for macroeconomic analysis, since many macroeconomic theories point to expected inflation as a key variable to explain the relationship between inflation and unemployment.

Table 16-2 lists the nine European countries that currently issue indexed bonds, as well as the year they first started issuing them and the price indices to which the bonds are linked.

TABLE 16-2

The European Countries that Issue Indexed Government Bonds

Country	Year of First Issue	Index
France	1998	Domestic CPI minus tobacco
	2001	Euro Area CPI minus tobacco
Greece	1997	Domestic CPI
Germany	2003	Euro Area CPI minus tobacco
	2006	Euro Area CPI minus tobacco
Hungary	1995	CPI
Iceland	1964	CPI
Italy	2003	Euro Area CPI minus tobacco
Poland	1992	CPI
Romania	2003	CPI
Sweden	1994	CPI
UK	1981	RPI

Source: UK Debt Management Office.

Iceland has been issuing indexed bonds since 1964. The UK government began issuing them 17 years later, in 1981. Among the Euro Area countries, Germany and Italy currently issue bonds indexed to the Euro Area CPI (minus tobacco), while France and Greece issue bonds linked to this measure of Euro Area inflation and also bonds indexed to their national CPIs.

Note that indexed bonds are not confined to Europe, however: over 20 countries around the world issue indexed government bonds. The US began issuing them in 1997.

Indexed bonds benefit bondholder and taxpayer alike. They insulate both sides of the transaction from inflation risk. Bondholders should care about the real interest rate they earn, and taxpayers should care about the real interest rate they pay. When government bonds are specified in nominal terms, both sides take on risk that is neither productive nor necessary. Indexed bonds eliminate this inflation risk.

Other reasons why issuing indexed bonds may be beneficial to government macroeconomic policy include the following. First, indexed bonds reduce the government's incentive to produce surprise inflation in order to reduce the real value of its debt. In contrast to other debtors, governments can print the money they need. The greater the government's nominal debts, the more incentive the government has to inflate away its debt. Issuing indexed debt reduces this potentially problematic incentive.

Second, investors may be willing to accept a lower average real interest rate on indexed debt because they are effectively being insured against inflation. Put another way, if there is a large risk of high inflation eroding the value of nominal debt, investors may demand very high interest rates in order to compensate them for this risk. The effect of issuing indexed bonds, which eliminates the inflation risk for the investor, may therefore be to lower the overall real borrowing costs of the government.

In effect, therefore, issuing indexed bonds allows a government the opportunity to send a message that they intend to stem the tide of inflation — an action that may also result in lower borrowing costs and potentially lower nominal interest rates. It is reasoning like this that made Iceland one of first issuers of indexed bonds: although Iceland has enjoyed low and fairly stable inflation rates that have compared well to those of other European countries since the 1990s, it had relatively high inflation during much of the 1960s, 1970s and 1980s. Similar reasoning underlay the issuance of indexed bonds in Hungary, Poland and Romania, when those countries were experiencing high inflation, as well as Brazil, Chile and Colombia, which began issuing them in the 1960s, and Israel, which began issuing them in 1955.

In the past, economists have proposed a variety of rules that could be used to conduct monetary policy, as we discussed in the preceding chapter. While the issuance of indexed bonds is typically not the major proportion of debt issued by European governments (in the UK, indexed bonds account for about 20 per cent of debt issued by central government), they do nevertheless expand the number of possible monetary policy rules. Here is one idea: the central bank announces a target for the inflation rate. Then, every day, the central bank measures expected inflation as the spread between the yield on nominal debt and the yield on indexed debt. If expected inflation is above the target, the central bank contracts the money supply. If expected inflation is below the target, the central bank expands the money supply. In this way, the central bank can use the bond market's inflation forecast to ensure that the money supply is growing at the rate needed to keep inflation close to its target.[7] ▪

---

[7] To read more about indexed bonds, see John Y. Campbell and Robert J. Shiller, 'A Scorecard for Indexed Government Debt', *NBER Macroeconomics Annual*, 1996, pp. 155–197; and David W. Wilcox, 'Policy Watch: The Introduction of Indexed Government Debt in the United States', *The Journal of Economic Perspectives*, winter 1998, vol. 12, pp. 219–227.

16-6 Fiscal Sustainability, Budget Deficits and the Debt-to-GDP Ratio

From an economic point of view, a country is in some ways like a household or an individual, and in other ways it is quite different. One way in which individuals and countries differ is in the analysis of their debt. An individual's debt might be thought of as sustainable if it is feasible for the individual to repay the debt over his or her lifetime. This is why large loans to individuals, such as mortgage loans with which to purchase a house or a flat, are always backed by a claim on the property and based on an analysis of the individual's (or the household's) income, and are usually worked out so that the final payment on the mortgage can be made before the individual retires. An economy is slightly different in this respect. Since an economy in some sense lives forever and never retires, there is no reason why it should ever have to pay off its debts entirely. What is important for an economy is **fiscal sustainability**, which means that the government is able to service its debt (i.e. pay interest on the debt and honour capital repayments when they fall due). For this to be the case, the ratio of government debt to GDP must settle down at some constant level; in other words, government debt and GDP must grow at the same rate. If this is not the case, government debt will become a larger and larger multiple of GDP, and there must come a point at which the government is no longer able to service the debt.

We can formalize our analysis of fiscal sustainability with the help of a little algebra. If the nominal value of government debt is D, we can write an equation for changes in D as follows:

$$\Delta D = iD + G - T,$$

where i, G and T are the nominal interest rate on the debt, and the level of government purchases and tax revenue (expressed in nominal terms), respectively. This equation says that changes in government debt will be equal to interest paid on the debt (iD), plus the increase in debt arising from the excess of government purchases over tax revenue (we assume that the budget deficit is financed entirely by borrowing — as we discussed earlier, very little government spending in developed economies is financed by the seigniorage revenue from printing money).

Now the total budget deficit that a government runs is equal to the excess of government spending on goods and services over tax revenue, $G - T$, plus the interest payment that the government has to make on its debt, iD. Hence, the **total budget deficit** is defined as $B = iD + G - T$. Up until now, we have been referring to the simple excess of government expenditure over tax revenue, $G - T$, as the budget deficit. While this is standard usage, if we want to be more precise, we refer to the excess of government expenditure on goods and services over tax revenue as the **primary budget deficit**. Thus, the total budget deficit is equal to the primary budget deficit plus interest payments on the debt outstanding. Using this definition, our equation for the movements in government debt becomes simply $\Delta D = B$, and so growth in nominal debt must be given by

$$\frac{\Delta D}{D} = \frac{B}{D}.$$

For the level of debt to be sustainable, the ratio of nominal debt to nominal GDP, D/Y, must settle down at some long-run constant value (note that we are thinking of GDP, Y, *in nominal or money terms here, since D* is also in nominal terms). But if D/Y is a constant in equilibrium, then the numerator (D) and the denominator (Y) must be growing at the same rate. Long-run growth in *nominal* GDP, Y, will be equal to long-run growth in real GDP (which we analysed in detail in Chapters 8 and 9) plus the long-run rate of inflation. Suppose long-run real GDP growth is g (in Chapters 8 and 9, we determined that the long-run real GDP growth was $g + n$, which we are redefining here as g to keep the notation simple) and the long-run inflation rate is π. For long-run fiscal sustainability, we would need to set the growth in nominal debt equal to the sum of real GDP growth plus inflation:

$$\frac{\Delta D}{D} = g + \pi.$$

Thus, using the previous equation,

$$\frac{B}{D} = g + \pi,$$

and dividing both sides of this last equation by Y and rearranging, we then have

$$\frac{D}{Y} = \frac{1}{(g + \pi)}\frac{B}{Y}.$$

The term on the left-hand side of this equation is the equilibrium **debt-to-GDP ratio**. The equation tells us the stable equilibrium level towards which the debt-to-GDP ratio will head for a given level of nominal GDP growth (i.e. $g + \pi$) and a given total budget deficit as a proportion of GDP.

Note that having a constant equilibrium debt-to-GDP ratio is a necessary but not a sufficient condition for fiscal sustainability. This is because the formula is worked out assuming stable long-run growth, and does not allow for short-run shocks. Thus, an economy may have a constant equilibrium debt-to-GDP ratio according to this formula, and yet this debt-to-GDP ratio may be so large that when a sudden shock occurs — for example a negative supply shock that greatly reduces national income — the government may suddenly find itself unable to service the debt. For this reason, it is necessary to set the equilibrium debt-to-GDP ratio at a level that is thought to be prudent. This then allows us to solve for the appropriate budget deficit for which to aim. Suppose, for example, that a long-run debt-to-GDP ratio of d was thought to be prudent. Then we could solve our equation for the level of the budget deficit that will deliver this in the long run, given the long-run growth rate of GDP and the long-run inflation rate:

$$\frac{B}{Y} = (g + \pi)d.$$

This equation gives us the condition for fiscal sustainability in terms of the *total* budget deficit (including interest payments) as a proportion of GDP. It tells us that, for a given target long-run debt-to-GDP ratio d, the total budget deficit may be higher for higher rates of nominal GDP growth, since this will tend to increase the denominator of the debt-to-GDP ratio, and so allow a higher accumulation of debt for a given debt-to-GDP ratio.

We can also get some insight into fiscal sustainability by looking at the *primary* budget deficit (remember that this is just the excess of government spending over tax revenue, $G - T$, and excludes interest payments on government debt). Rewriting our expression for fiscal sustainability using the definition of the total budget deficit (i.e. $B = iD + G - T$),

$$\frac{iD + G - T}{Y} = (g + \pi)\frac{D}{Y},$$

or, rearranging slightly,

$$\frac{G - T}{Y} = (g + \pi - i)\frac{D}{Y}.$$

But $(g + \pi - i) = (g - r)$, where r is the real interest rate, so this last expression can be written as

$$\frac{G - T}{Y} = (g - r)\frac{D}{Y}.$$

Again, suppose that we choose a 'prudent' level, d, for the equilibrium debt-to-GDP ratio. Then we have

$$\frac{G - T}{Y} = (g - r)d.$$

This equation gives us the condition for fiscal sustainability in terms of the *primary* budget deficit. In words, it says that, for fiscal sustainability, the primary deficit as a proportion of GDP must be equal to the excess of real GDP growth over the real interest rate times the equilibrium debt-to-GDP ratio.

Suppose, for example, that $g = r$. Then $g - r = 0$, implying that $G - T = 0$, and the expression implies that fiscal sustainability requires the primary budget to balance. This means that the government is not adding to the stock of debt through its expenditure, and the government can 'roll over' its debt interest without the debt-to-GDP ratio growing, because the real value of government debt will then grow exactly in line with real national income.[8]

---

[8] Note that, when we analysed fiscal sustainability in terms of the total budget deficit, we found it convenient to think of the debt-to-GDP ratio as the ratio of *nominal* government debt to nominal GDP, while when analysing sustainability in terms of the primary deficit, we are implicitly thinking of the debt-to-GDP ratio as the ratio of the *real* value of government debt (which grows at the real rate of interest, r) to the *real* value of national income (which grows at the real rate of GDP growth, g). In fact, the ratio of two variables expressed in nominal terms is exactly the same as the ratio of the two corresponding real terms, because the price level cancels out. For example, if X and Z are two macroeconomic quantities expressed in nominal terms, then we can convert them to real terms by dividing them by the price level P, to get X/P and Z/P. But when we take the ratio of the real terms, $[X/P]/[Z/P]$, the Ps cancel and so $[X/P]/[Z/P] = (X/Z)$. Thus, the ratio of nominal government debt to nominal GDP is the same as the ratio of real government debt to real GDP.

What if $g < r$? In that case, $g - r < 0$, and so fiscal sustainability requires $G - T < 0$, and the government must run a primary surplus for fiscal sustainability (i.e. $G < T$). This is because the real interest rate is greater than the rate of real GDP growth, and so the real value of the debt will rise faster than real income unless the government uses some of its tax revenue to pay the debt service, rather than spending it.

The third possible case is $g > r$, or $g - r > 0$, so that fiscal sustainability can be achieved with a primary budget deficit, $G - T > 0$. This is because the real value of national income is growing faster than the real value of public debt, so the government can afford to increase debt a little (by running a primary deficit) while still keeping the equilibrium debt-to-GDP ratio constant, so long as the resulting increase does not exceed the amount by which real growth exceeds the real interest rate.

You may wonder why we have set out two conditions for fiscal sustainability, one in terms of the total budget deficit and the other in terms of the primary budget deficit. If the two conditions are equivalent, you might reasonably point out, why not just use one of them and make everyone's life easier?

The simple answer is that, in practice, some policy makers talk about fiscal sustainability in terms of primary deficits and others talk about it in terms of total budget deficits. As a macroeconomist, you need to understand both these equivalent ways of viewing fiscal sustainability – and why they are equivalent.

CASE STUDY

The Stability and Growth Pact: A Sneak Preview

In the next chapter, we shall discuss the economics of monetary union (i.e. adopting a single currency among a group of countries), including the implications for fiscal policy and the management of government debt. For now, however, we can get a sneak preview of what is to come, and at the same time see an application of our rules for fiscal sustainability.

At the outset of the European Economic and Monetary Union (EMU), a set of fiscal rules was drawn up and agreed to by EMU members. This set of rules was known as the Stability and Growth Pact (SGP). We will discuss the economic rationale for the SGP in the next chapter, but it is sufficient to note for now that the SGP laid down a rule that the *total* budget deficit of EMU member countries should not exceed 3 per cent of GDP per year. Where did this 3 per cent rule come from? It is in fact governed by our rule for fiscal sustainability.

According to the Treaty of Maastricht, candidates for entry into EMU should have a level of general government gross debt that is no more than 60 per cent of GDP.[9] Effectively, therefore, the Maastricht Treaty set the 'prudent' debt-to-GDP ratio at 60 per cent. Given long-run European growth rates of the order of 2.5–3 per cent per year, and allowing for long-run inflation of 2–2.5 per cent per

---

[9] Note the use of general government gross debt as the measure of public debt. In the event, at the outset of the EMU, several countries did not meet the 60 per cent debt-to-GDP ratio criterion (in Italy and Belgium the ratio exceeded 120 per cent), but they were still allowed to join on the grounds that they had taken significant steps to reduce their government debt.

year (as we discussed in Chapter 15, the European Central Bank has an inflation target of 2 per cent per year), the average Euro Area (Eurozone) country could presumably expect long-run nominal GDP growth of about 5 per cent a year. In terms of our fiscal arithmetic that we developed above, therefore, we have $x + \pi = 0.05$ and the equilibrium debt-to-GDP ratio, $d = 0.6$. Using the formula for fiscal sustainability in terms of the total budget deficit, $(B/Y) = (x + \pi)\,d$, we therefore have

$$\frac{B}{Y} = 0.05 \times 0.6,$$

which implies a maximum total budget deficit of 0.03, or 3 per cent – exactly as laid down in the Stability and Growth Pact. ∎

CASE STUDY

The 'Golden Rule' of UK Public Finance

The UK government announced in 1998 that, according to the guidelines of its *Code for Fiscal Stability,* it would adhere to two fiscal rules on its spending, the first of which it referred to as the *Golden Rule.* (Beware! The Golden Rule of public finance has nothing to do with the Golden Rule level of capital that we analysed in Chapter 8. The similarity in names is purely coincidental.)

The Golden Rule states that over the economic cycle, the government will borrow only to invest. This means that the cyclically adjusted budget deficit on current expenditure (i.e. the excess over tax revenue of government spending on current goods and services, not taking into account public investment) must balance or be in surplus.

On its own, however, the Golden Rule would allow the government to undertake huge amounts of public investment and run up correspondingly huge amounts of public debt. Hence, the Golden Rule is coupled with another rule, the *Sustainable Investment Rule,* which states that public sector net debt as a proportion of GDP will be held over the economic cycle at a stable and prudent level, which the government has defined as 'below 40 per cent of GDP over the economic cycle'.[10]

The Golden Rule and its twin, the Sustainable Investment Rule, seem to be good fiscal rules. The Golden Rule allows for the current budget deficit (i.e. excluding investment) to vary over the business cycle, so that it can be used for macroeconomic stabilization, but it allows the costs of public investment to be spread over current and future generations, who will be the beneficiaries of the investment, rather than simply requiring the current generation to foot the bill. The Sustainable Investment Rule, meanwhile, ensures that the public debt does not get out of hand as a result of public investments financed by issuing government bonds.

Critics of these fiscal rules have argued that they are not as rigid as they seem, for two reasons. First, the Chancellor is free to define the economic or business

---

[10] Note the use of public sector net debt as the measure of public debt by the UK authorities.

FYI

Ponzi Finance

Have you ever received an email or Facebook post that asked you to forward that message to several of your friends? These so-called *chain-letter schemes* may be a bit of a nuisance or just harmless fun. But you might receive one that asks you to send money, with the promise that within a few weeks you will receive large amounts of money from the ever-multiplying friends of the friends of the friends to whom the email has since been forwarded. As an economist, you should recognize that instances of getting something for nothing are rare, and this is no exception.

A chain-letter scheme is an example of a *Ponzi game*. It works by recruiting larger and larger numbers of people to send the cheques (or emails). Eventually, there will not be enough recruits and the process will stop. The losers will be the (by now large) number of people who sent the last set of cheques, but received nothing back.

Ponzi games are named after an Italian, Charles Ponzi, who carried out a similar set of investment swindles, also known as *pyramid investment schemes*, in Boston in the US, in the 1920s. The typical pyramid investment scheme is a Ponzi game that asks you to invest in the scheme by putting some money up front, and then to recruit other investors to do the same. The scheme only pays out dividends so long as more and more investors are recruited. The recruitment process eventually stops and the last group of people to put money in lose their money.

In the late 1990s, a number of pyramid investment schemes were started in some of the former communist countries of Eastern Europe; they were able to do so because of the lack of appropriate financial regulation, and perhaps also because of the lack of experience of the general public of those countries at that time with the capitalist system. This problem became particularly acute in Albania in 1997, where the government, remarkably, had appeared to approve a series of pyramid investment schemes. When the schemes inevitably collapsed, the citizens of Albania, who collectively had lost about 1 billion, took their protest to the streets in a revolt that toppled the government. Even as recently as 2009 Bernard Madoff, a US financier, was sentenced to 150 years in prison for masterminding what was in effect a large-scale Ponzi scheme, thought to be the largest in history.

Another reason why a constant equilibrium debt-to-GDP ratio is a sound rule of public finance is that it rules out Ponzi finance. Ponzi finance is a Ponzi game applied to the public debt, whereby the government issues public debt in order to service its debt (i.e. to pay the interest on its debt and repay capital when bonds mature). This requires greater and greater amounts of debt to be issued (and consequently higher and higher debt-to-GDP ratios), and eventually investors get worried about the size of the total public debt outstanding and stop buying government bonds. At this point, the government has no option but to default on its debt. Ponzi finance, like all Ponzi games, ends in tears.

cycle, since there is no official business cycle–dating committee in the UK (as there is, for example, in the US). Second, the government may define some of its spending as investment expenditure and therefore allow itself to borrow in order to finance this expenditure, when others might define it as current expenditure. For example, government expenditure on physical infrastructure such as school buildings is clearly investment, since it leads to an accumulation of physical capital. But what about an increase in spending on teachers' salaries? It could be argued that this is expenditure on a current service – teaching – and so is not investment. On the other hand, it might be argued that by using the money to pay for more teachers (or better qualified teachers), the government has helped school students to learn more and to accumulate more human capital. According to that argument, spending more on teachers is investment. ▪

16-7 Conclusion

Fiscal policy and government debt are central to macroeconomic policy. This chapter has discussed some of the economic issues that lie behind fiscal policy decisions. As we have seen, economists are not in complete agreement about the measurement or effects of government indebtedness. Nor are economists in agreement about the best budget policy. Given the profound importance of this topic, there seems little doubt that the debates will continue in the years to come.

Summary

1. The size of the government debt as a proportion of GDP varies greatly across European countries. The government debt of the United Kingdom – around 90 per cent of GDP – is just above the EU-27 median level of around 85 per cent.

2. Standard measures of the budget deficit are imperfect measures of fiscal policy because they do not correct for the effects of inflation, do not offset changes in government liabilities with changes in government assets, omit some liabilities altogether, and do not correct for the effects of the business cycle.

3. According to the traditional view of government debt, a debt-financed tax cut stimulates consumer spending and lowers national saving. This increase in consumer spending leads to greater aggregate demand and higher income in the short run, but it leads to a lower capital stock and lower income in the long run.

4. According to the Ricardian view of government debt, a debt-financed tax cut does not stimulate consumer spending because it does not raise consumers' overall resources – it merely reschedules taxes from the present to the future. The debate between the traditional and Ricardian views of government debt is ultimately a debate over how consumers behave. Are consumers rational or short-sighted? Do they face binding borrowing constraints? Are they economically linked to future generations through altruistic bequests? Economists' views of government debt hinge on their answers to these questions, but the consensus is probably that full Ricardian equivalence does not hold.

5. Most economists oppose a strict rule requiring a balanced budget. A budget deficit can sometimes be justified on the basis of short-run stabilization, tax smoothing or intergenerational redistribution of the tax burden.

6. Government debt can potentially have other effects. Large government debt or budget deficits may encourage excessive monetary expansion and, therefore, lead to greater inflation. The possibility of running budget deficits may encourage politicians to unduly burden future generations when setting government spending and taxes. A high level of government debt may risk capital flight and diminish a nation's influence around the world. Economists differ in which of these effects they consider most important.

7. Fiscal sustainability – the ability of a government to service its debt – requires that the debt-to-GDP ratio settle down at a constant equilibrium level, and that this equilibrium level be set at a 'prudent level', in order to allow for short-term shocks. The equilibrium level of the debt-to-GDP ratio multiplied by the rate of growth of nominal GDP gives the maximum total budget deficit (including interest payments), as a percentage of GDP, with which it is consistent.

KEY CONCEPTS

Capital budgeting	Fiscal sustainability	Debt-to-GDP ratio
Cyclically adjusted budget deficit	Total budget deficit	
Ricardian equivalence	Primary budget deficit	

QUESTIONS FOR REVIEW

1. What is the range of public debt-to-GDP ratios among developed countries?

2. Describe four problems affecting measurement of the government budget deficit.

3. According to the traditional view of government debt, how does a debt-financed tax cut affect public saving, private saving and national saving?

4. According to the Ricardian view of government debt, how does a debt-financed tax cut affect public saving, private saving and national saving?

5. Do you believe the traditional or the Ricardian view of government debt? Why?

6. Give three reasons why a budget deficit might be a good policy choice.

7. Why might the level of government debt affect the government's incentives regarding money creation?

8. Give two conditions for fiscal sustainability, one in terms of the primary budget deficit and one in terms of the total budget deficit.

PROBLEMS AND APPLICATIONS

1. In the 1990s, Italy underwent a massive privatization of its public-sector corporations, including its public utility and telecom companies. As a result, its debt-to-GDP ratio fell by around 10 percentage points in the mid to late 1990s. Would this reduction in national debt have been effected if Italy had adopted capital budgeting?

2. Draft a letter to the Finance Minister as described in Section 16-3, explaining and evaluating the Ricardian view of government debt.

3. Social security systems levy a tax on workers and pay benefits to the elderly. Suppose that the government increases both the tax and the benefits. For simplicity, assume that the government announces that the increases will last for one year only.

   a. How do you suppose this change would affect the economy? (*Hint:* Think about the marginal propensities to consume of the young and the old.)

   b. Does your answer depend on whether generations are altruistically linked?

4. Some economists have proposed the rule that the cyclically adjusted budget deficit always be balanced. Compare this proposal to a strict balanced-budget rule. Which is preferable? What problems do you see with the rule requiring a balanced cyclically adjusted budget?

5. Using the library or the Internet, find some recent projections for the future path of government debt in your country as a percentage of GDP. What assumptions are made about government spending, taxes and economic growth? Do you think these assumptions are reasonable? If the country experiences a productivity slowdown, how will reality differ from this projection?

Common Currency Areas and European Economic and Monetary Union

Or, supposing that the Common Market countries proceed with their plans for economic union, should these countries allow each national currency to fluctuate, or would a single currency area be preferable?

— *Robert Mundell, 1961*

The crisis in the Euro Area (the Eurozone) since 2010 has led many to question the very viability of a single European currency. From there being almost a consensus within Europe not too many years ago to push ahead with the euro project, there is now widespread doubt as to whether a single currency offers sufficient flexibility for member countries to withstand and mitigate the effects of financial crisis and recession. In countries outside the Euro Area, such as the UK, where there had been consideration by some to join the euro, such a prospect is now firmly off the agenda. In this chapter we look at why the Euro Area was set up and then examine the problems it now faces.

In the late 1990s, a number of European countries decided to give up their national currencies and use a new, common currency called the euro, by forming the European Economic and Monetary Union (EMU). This was one of the most radical steps ever taken in the field of national economic policy in the modern era. Most of the currencies concerned had been legal tender in their respective countries for hundreds of years, and they ceased to exist overnight. Further, in adopting a single currency, each country gave up control over its own monetary policy (since if a group of countries have the same money, clearly they must have the same monetary policy). Why did these countries enter into EMU? The answer to this question is in part political and in part economic, and in this chapter we focus on the economics of EMU.

The underlying economic rationale for a group of countries to adopt a single, common currency was analysed in detail more than 40 years ago by Robert Mundell in his theory of 'optimum currency areas', and we will spend some time discussing this theory,[1] as well as the costs and benefits of common currencies more generally, and some of the issues regarding fiscal policy that arise in this connection. However, rather than discuss these issues in an abstract way, throughout our discussion we will focus on the Euro Area in order to illustrate the analysis, and we will analyse whether or not Europe is indeed an optimum currency area.

17-1 Common Currency Areas

A **common currency area** is a geographical area through which one currency circulates and is accepted as the medium of exchange. A common currency area is also referred to as a **currency union** or a **monetary union**.[2]

The common currency area that is formed by 17 European countries that have adopted the **euro** as their currency is the **European Economic and Monetary Union**, or **EMU**.[3] The 17 members of EMU (at the time of writing, 2013) are: Belgium, Germany, Spain, France, Ireland, Italy, Luxembourg, the Netherlands, Austria, Portugal, Finland, Greece, Slovenia, Cyprus, Malta, Slovakia and Estonia.[4] These countries make up the **Euro Area**. Figure 17-1 shows a map of the Euro Area.

The single European currency – the euro – officially came into existence on 1 January 1999.[5] On this date, exchange rates between the old national currencies of Euro Area countries were irrevocably locked, and a few days later the financial markets began to trade the euro against other currencies, such as the dollar, as well as trading securities denominated in euros.

Since the EMU countries have a single currency, they also have a single monetary policy. The monetary policy of the Euro Area is formulated and implemented by the **European Central Bank** (ECB), based in Frankfurt, which, together with the national central banks of the countries making up the common currency area, forms the European System of Central Banks (ESCB).

From an economic point of view, monetary union brings with it a number of costs and benefits that can be large or small according to the characteristics of the countries concerned. Let's take a look at the costs and benefits.

---

[1] Robert A. Mundell, 'A Theory of Optimum Currency Areas', *American Economic Review*, 1961, vol. 51, no. 4, pp. 657–665. This is the same Robert Mundell who gave us the Mundell–Fleming model that we discussed at length in Chapter 12. In 1999, Professor Mundell was awarded the Nobel Prize in economics 'for his analysis of monetary and fiscal policy under different exchange rate regimes and his analysis of optimum currency areas'.

[2] Strictly speaking, a monetary union is a group of countries, all of which have adopted permanently and irrevocably fixed exchange rates among their various currencies. Nevertheless, the terms 'common currency area', 'currency union' and 'monetary union' are now used more or less interchangeably, and in this book we will follow this practice.

[3] Note that 'EMU' stands for 'Economic and Monetary Union', not 'European Monetary Union'.

[4] In January 2014 Latvia will be joining the Euro Area, bringing the number of member countries up to 18.

[5] Greece did not join EMU until 1 January 2001. Slovenia joined the Euro Area on 1 January 2007, Cyprus and Malta on 1 January 2008, Slovakia on 1 January 2009 and Estonia on 1 January 2011.

FIGURE 17-1

1999 2001 2007 2008 2009 2011

2011

■ EU ■ Euro Area ⌐ New member

A Map of the Euro Area

Source: European Central Bank.

17-2 The Benefits of a Single Currency

Reduction in Transactions Costs in Trade

One direct benefit of a common currency is that there is a reduction in the transactions costs involved in trade between members of the common currency area. When a Belgian company imports French wine, it no longer has to pay a charge to a bank for converting Belgian francs into French francs with which to pay the wine producer – it can just pay in euros. Of course, the banking sector loses out on the commission it used to charge for converting currencies, but this does not affect the fact that the reduction in transactions costs is a net gain. This is because paying a cost to convert currencies is in fact a *deadweight loss*, in the sense that companies pay the transaction cost but get nothing tangible in return. If the resources formerly used in banking services for this purpose were transferred elsewhere, it would result in a net increase in welfare.

How large have been the gains from the elimination of transactions costs as a result of the introduction of the euro? The European Commission estimates them to be of the order of about 0.25 to 0.5 per cent of Euro Area GDP. While this may seem quite small, recall that this is not a one-off gain, but one that accrues every year and so is cumulative.

It should be noted, however, that these gains could be larger if the inter-bank payments systems across countries were better integrated: at present, when a payment is made from one Euro Area country to another, the recipient bank still makes a charge for the receipt of the payment from another country, even though it is denominated in euros. While this charge is generally less than would have been charged before EMU, it is still a charge that is not made to payments within a particular EMU country.

Reduction in Price Discrimination

It is sometimes argued that a second gain to the members of a common currency area results from the reduction in price discrimination that should ensue when there is a single currency. If goods are priced in a single currency, it should be much harder to disguise price differences across countries. This argument assumes that the transparency in prices that results from a common currency will lead to arbitrage in goods across the common currency area, so that people will buy goods where they are cheaper (tending to raise their price in that location) and reduce their demand for goods where they are more expensive (tending to reduce the price in that location).

Overall, however, EMU does not seem to have brought an end to price discrimination across Euro Area countries. In fact, differences in the prices of goods are still much greater across Euro Area countries than they are across the regions of any particular country. This is especially true of supermarket goods like groceries, but is also true (to a lesser extent) of consumer durables like televisions. On reflection, this is perhaps not very surprising. For items like groceries, having a single currency is unlikely to be much of an impetus to price convergence across the common currency area because of the large transactions costs (mainly involving travelling) involved in arbitraging, relative to the prices of the goods themselves: unless you live near a border, it is clearly not feasible to shop for groceries in another country, even if they use the same currency. Big-ticket items like household appliances and electronic goods, where the transactions costs may be lower as a percentage of the price of the good in question, are also unlikely to be arbitraged heavily across national borders by consumers because of their durable nature and the consequent need for confidence in after-sales service.

Reduction in Foreign-Exchange-Rate Variability

A third argument relates to the reduction in exchange-rate variability and the consequent reduction in uncertainty that results from having a single currency. Exchange rates can fluctuate substantially on a day-to-day basis. Before EMU, when a Dutch supermarket imported wine from France to be delivered, say, a month later, it had to worry about how much a French franc would be worth in terms of Dutch guilders a month later, and therefore what the total cost of the wine would be in guilders. This uncertainty might deter the supermarket company from importing wine at all, and lead them to concentrate on selling Dutch beer instead, thereby forgoing the gains from trade and reducing economic welfare. The supermarket could have eliminated the uncertainty by getting a bank to agree to sell the francs at an agreed rate against guilders, to be delivered a month later (an example of a forward foreign exchange contract). But the bank would charge for this service, and this charge would be equivalent to a tariff on the imported wine and would again represent a deadweight loss to society.

The reduction in uncertainty arising from the removal of exchange-rate fluctuations may also affect investment in the economy. This would clearly be the case for companies that export a large amount of their output to other Euro Area countries, since less uncertainty concerning the receipts from its exports mean that it is able to plan for the future with less risk, so that investment projects, such as building new factories, appear less risky. An increase in investment will benefit the whole economy because it is likely to lead to higher economic growth.

17-3 The Costs of a Single Currency

Loss of Monetary Policy Sovereignty

When a country joins a monetary union, it gives up its national currency and thereby gives up its freedom to set its own monetary policy and the possibility of macroeconomic adjustment coming about through movements in the external value of its currency. This is the major cost to an economy in joining a common currency. Below, we investigate two key reasons why this is a potential problem.

Asymmetric Demand Shocks

Suppose, for example, that there is a shift in consumer preferences across the common currency area, away from goods and services produced in one country (e.g. Germany) and towards goods and services produced in another country (e.g. France). This situation is depicted in Figure 17-2, which shows a rightward shift in the French aggregate demand curve (panel (a)) and a leftward shift in the German aggregate demand curve (panel (b)). In France, the economy was initially in equilibrium at the natural rate of output $\overline{Y}_1^F$ at point A in panel (a) of Figure 17-2. The rightward shift of the aggregate demand function from AD_1^F

FIGURE 17-2

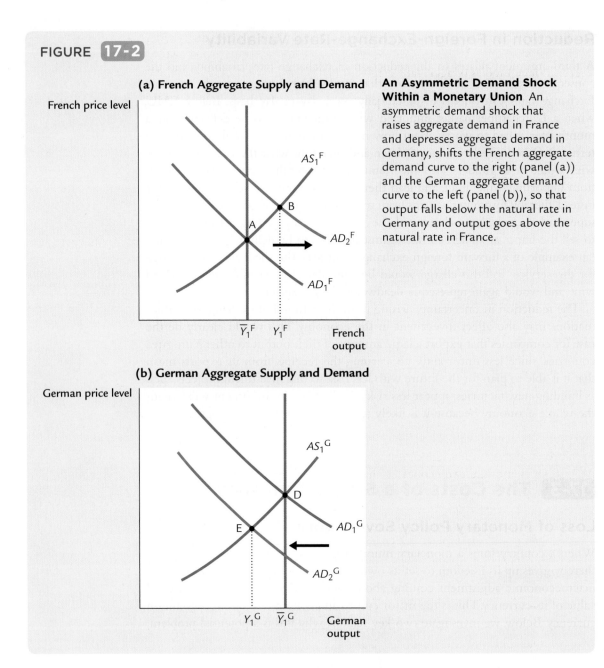

(a) French Aggregate Supply and Demand

French price level

AS_1^F

B

A

AD_2^F

AD_1^F

$\overline{Y}_1^F$ Y_1^F French output

An Asymmetric Demand Shock Within a Monetary Union An asymmetric demand shock that raises aggregate demand in France and depresses aggregate demand in Germany, shifts the French aggregate demand curve to the right (panel (a)) and the German aggregate demand curve to the left (panel (b)), so that output falls below the natural rate in Germany and output goes above the natural rate in France.

(b) German Aggregate Supply and Demand

German price level

AS_1^G

D

E

AD_1^G

AD_2^G

Y_1^G $\overline{Y}_1^G$ German output

to AD_2^F moves the economy to a short-run equilibrium at point B, where AD_2^F intersects with the short-run aggregate supply curve AD_1^F and output moves above its natural rate to Y_1^F.

In Germany, the opposite occurs, because aggregate demand has contracted. In panel (b) of Figure 17-2, the leftward shift of the German aggregate demand function from AD_1^G to AD_2^G moves the economy from the initial equilibrium at point D to a short-run equilibrium at point E, with output equal to Y_1^G, below the German natural rate of $\overline{Y}_1^G$.

Thus, Germany moves into recession and France moves into a boom. What should policy makers in France and Germany do about this? In Chapter 14 we discussed three models of aggregate supply: the sticky-wage model, the imperfect-information model and the sticky-price model. Although the three models differ in their assumptions and emphasis, their implications for the behaviour of aggregate supply are similar and can be summarized by the equation

$$Y = \overline{Y} + \alpha(P - P^e),$$

where $\overline{Y}$ is the natural rate and P^e denotes the expected price level. In words: the short-run aggregate supply curve tells us that output can only be above the natural rate of output if the price level is above its expected level, and, conversely, output can only be below the natural rate if the price level is below its expected level.

At point B in Figure 17-2, the increase in aggregate demand raises French prices, but we remain at point B so long as people do not perceive the price rise and price expectations are lower than the actual price level. But this cannot persist for ever; once people notice that the price level has risen, the gap between expected and actual prices disappears, the short-run aggregate supply curve shifts to the left and we move to a new equilibrium, depicted by point C in panel (a) of Figure 17-3, where French output is back at the natural rate.

In Germany, the converse happens. At point E in Figure 17-2, prices have fallen because of the fall in aggregate demand, but price expectations have not yet adjusted. Once German residents revise downward their expectations of the price level to match the actual price level, the short-run aggregate supply curve shifts rightward, as in panel (b) of Figure 17-3, and the economy moves back to equilibrium at the natural rate of output at point F.

Because each of the two economies has a long-run vertical supply curve, output will eventually return to the natural rate in response to demand shocks. The only cost to the two economies is therefore in terms of the short-term fluctuations in output. While this may not seem problematic in theory, in practice the resulting fluctuations in output and unemployment in each country will tend to create tensions within the monetary union, as unemployment rises in Germany and inflation rises in France. German policy makers, dismayed at the rise in unemployment, will favour a cut in interest rates in order to boost aggregate demand in their country, while their French counterparts, worried about rising inflation, will be calling for an increase in interest rates in order to curtail French aggregate demand. The European Central Bank, which sets interest rates for the whole of the Euro Area, will not be able to keep both countries happy. Most likely, it will set interest rates higher than the German desired level and lower than the French desired level. All that is possible is a 'one-size-fits-all' monetary policy.

Note, however, that if Germany and France had maintained their own currencies and a flexible foreign exchange rate between them, the short-term fluctuations in aggregate demand would be alleviated by a movement in the exchange rate. In fact, as we know from previous chapters, net exports are a component of aggregate demand and are a function of the real exchange rate:

$$Y = C + I + G + NX(\varepsilon).$$

FIGURE 17-3

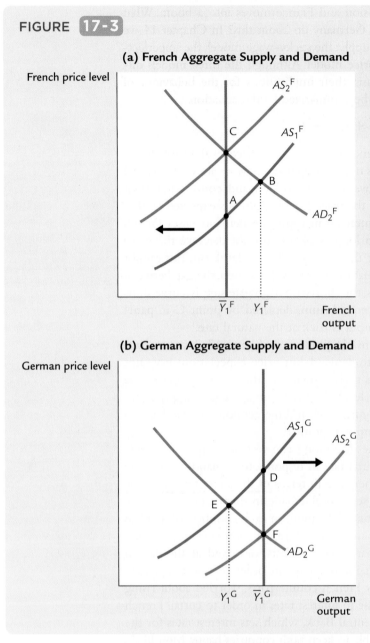

(a) French Aggregate Supply and Demand

French price level

AS_2^F

C

AS_1^F

B

A

AD_2^F

$\overline{Y}_1^F$ Y_1^F French output

(b) German Aggregate Supply and Demand

German price level

AS_1^G

AS_2^G

D

E

F

AD_2^G

Y_1^G $\overline{Y}_1^G$ German output

The Long-Run Supply Response to an Asymmetric Demand Shock Within a Monetary Union The positive demand shock in France leads to rising prices and, as expected prices catch up with actual prices, the short-run aggregate supply curve shifts leftward and French output returns to the natural rate (panel (a)). In Germany (panel (b)), the converse happens: the negative demand shock leads to falling prices and, as price expectations catch up, the short-run aggregate supply curve shifts to the right and output returns to the natural rate.

As the demand for French goods rises and the demand for German goods falls, the demand for French francs would increase and the demand for German marks would be depressed, making the value of francs rise in terms of marks in the foreign-currency exchange market. Assuming that the prices of goods and services are sticky, this would affect the real exchange rate, making French goods more expensive to German residents and German goods less expensive to French residents. Therefore, French net exports would fall, leading to a fall in aggregate demand. In fact, if the response of net exports is fast enough, this effect will stop the aggregate demand curve from shifting altogether: the appreciation of the real exchange rate in France will lead to a fall in net exports which exactly offsets the initial demand shock that raised French aggregate demand. In terms of Figure 17-2, therefore, having a flexible exchange rate means that the French economy never moves away from point A. Similarly, in Germany, the real exchange-rate depreciation stimulates net exports so that they offset exactly the initial negative demand shock and Germany stays at point D in Figure 17-2, with output at the natural rate. In practice, of course, the effect of a real depreciation may take a little while to affect net exports, but the principle remains the same: a flexible exchange rate can insulate an open economy from asymmetric aggregate demand shocks.

(In terms of the Mundell–Fleming model that we examined in Chapter 13, the effect of a shock to aggregate demand is formally similar to the effect of fiscal policy – that is, there is no effect on output in a small open economy with sticky prices and a floating exchange rate.)

In a currency union, however, this automatic adjustment mechanism through the exchange rate is not available, since, of course, France and Germany have the same currency (the euro). The best that can be done is to wait for French and German wages and prices to adjust fully to the asymmetric demand shocks so that the aggregate supply curve shifts in each country, as in Figure 17-3.

Asymmetric Supply Shocks

Countries within a monetary union may also be subject to asymmetric supply shocks. A good example of this would be as a result of increased oil prices, or more generally, energy prices, often because of political instability in regions where such energy is produced. These supply shocks can also lead to a divergence in GDP and unemployment between member states. However, the response by a central bank can also have important consequences. Suppose that France is hit by an adverse supply shock. This shifts the French aggregate supply curve leftwards on Figure 17-4 from AS_1^F to AD_2^F. The short-run equilibrium will move from point A to point B. The adverse supply shock has increased the French price level and reduced output. If the European Central Bank responds by loosening monetary policy in order to mitigate the output effect, then the aggregate demand curve will move rightwards to AS_2^F, moving the equilibrium point from B to C, restoring output back to the original level. However, if the Central Bank responds by tightening monetary policy in order to control inflation, then aggregate demand will move leftwards to AD_3^F, moving the equilibrium point from B to D, bringing inflation down but at the cost of an even greater fall in output. This is a good example of when an independent central bank with a sole anti-inflation objective may not always be desirable. Taking cognisance of this, it is notable that the Bank of England and the European Central Bank have not increased interest rates during the recent recession period, despite inflation being above target levels.

Loss of Fiscal Policy Sovereignty

We can use the demand shocks example from earlier in this chapter to analyse the effect of fiscal policy. If France operates an expansionary fiscal policy there is

FIGURE 17-4

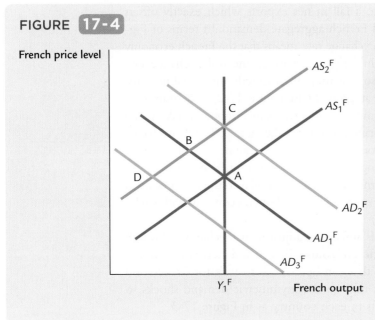

French price level

AS_2^F

AS_1^F

C

B

D   A

AD_2^F

AD_1^F

AD_3^F

Y_1^F French output

An Asymmetric Supply Shock Within a Monetary Union An adverse supply shock in France shifts the French aggregate supply curve leftwards, increasing the French price level and reducing output. If the European Central Bank responds by loosening monetary policy in order to mitigate the output effect, then the aggregate demand curve will move rightwards, restoring output back to the original level. However, if the ECB responds by tightening monetary policy in order to control inflation, then aggregate demand will move leftwards, bringing inflation down but at the cost of an even greater fall in output.

a rightward shift in the French aggregate demand curve, taking us to the short-run equilibrium point B in panel (a) of Figure 17-2. This leads to a rise in French output, and the French price level. Point B in Figure 17-2 cannot persist for ever since as soon as people notice that the price level has risen, the short-run aggregate supply curve shifts to the left and we move to a new equilibrium, depicted by point C in panel (a) of Figure 17-3, where French output is back at the natural rate, but at a higher price level. If exchange rates had been flexible, the short-term fluctuations in aggregate demand would have been alleviated by a movement in the exchange rate − in this case a real appreciation, making French goods less competitive in comparison with German goods. With a fixed exchange rate, the exchange rate can no longer insulate the economy from aggregate demand fluctuations. Thus, differences in output and unemployment will exist between member states until wages and prices adjust. Moreover, rising prices in France will increase pressure on the ECB to increase interest rates in order to curtail French aggregate demand and control inflation. Any increase in interest rates would not be welcome in Germany. Such a monetary contraction would decrease German aggregate demand to the short-run equilibrium point E in panel (b) of Figure 17-2, and eventually to long-run equilibrium, point F in panel (b) of Figure 17-3. Thus the expansionary fiscal policy in France, and the response of the ECB to control inflation, has had an adverse impact on Germany − depressing output and increasing unemployment in the short run. The output gap between the two countries has widened. This is often referred to as a 'beggar thy neighbour' policy and has clear political and social implications in terms of cohesion between nations. For this reason, and to limit the potential of member states to run up levels of debt that may be ultimately unsustainable, monetary union in practice normally implies some degree of fiscal coordination. The Maastricht criteria are the most obvious evidence of this in the practical implementation of the Euro Area. These state that government budget deficits should not exceed 3 per cent of GDP, and government debt relative to GDP should not exceed 60 per cent. Thus, while it may seem obvious that when two countries join in monetary union they lose control of their own monetary policy, it is also the case that countries effectively lose fiscal policy sovereignty too.

We know from recent experience following the financial crisis of 2008 that some countries have been especially hard hit by recession, in particular by high levels of unemployment. Some countries in the Euro Area are less economically developed than others and as such are more vulnerable to economic crises. Suppose we have a country hit by just such a recession. Normally this could be mitigated by a loosening of fiscal stance – borrowing more to invest in job creation or cutting taxes to encourage spending – and allowing the exchange rate to depreciate so as to boost exports and reduce imports in favour of domestic goods. With a single currency these are no longer options. So, GDP falls and unemployment rises. Thus the GDP and unemployment gap between the countries in the single currency area will widen. In other words, living standards diverge. As we saw in the previous section, in the long run this will lead to prices falling and pressure for interest rate cuts. Such interest rate cuts may, however, not be welcome by more economically developed nations within the Euro Area. In other words, the common monetary policy will be put under strain. In the absence of high degrees of labour mobility, the only solution to these tensions is fiscal transfers between states – from those who are doing well to those who are not. In other words, monetary union implies some degree of fiscal union. Within the EU, such fiscal transfers do exist, but they are dwarfed in comparison with, say, federal transfers between US states. Whereas these transfers have been accepted within the US over a long period of time, such large-scale transfers are politically contentious between Euro Area members, as evidenced recently by the relationship between Germany and Greece. We discuss issues surrounding fiscal federalism in further detail in section 17-6.

Loss of monetary policy sovereignty may be a major problem for one further reason – if it becomes less certain that the central bank will bail out a high-debt country by supplying more money and thus deflating the real value of public debt. This makes public debt more risky.

17-4 The Theory of Optimum Currency Areas

Optimum currency area theory attempts to set down a set of criteria for a group of countries, such that, if the criteria were satisfied, it would in some sense be 'optimal' for the countries to adopt a common currency. The qualifier 'optimal' here refers to the ability of each of the countries to limit the costs of monetary union and enhance the benefits. It is generally used loosely, since there is no way of ensuring whether it is indeed optimal for a group of countries to form a currency union, and, more often than not, countries will fulfil some but not all of the optimum currency area criteria. An **optimum currency area** is therefore best thought of as group of countries for which the benefits of adopting a single currency heavily outweigh the costs.

Characteristics that Reduce the Costs of a Single Currency

Consider first the characteristics of a group of countries that would reduce the costs of adopting a common currency. As we have discussed, the main cost to participating in a monetary union is the loss of monetary policy autonomy for the individual countries concerned, as well as ruling out the possibility of macroeconomic adjustment through exchange-rate movements. One way in which the economic (and political) tensions arising from the loss of the exchange-rate instrument and the imposition of a one-size-fits-all monetary policy will be alleviated is if the economies in question move rapidly to long-run equilibrium following a macroeconomic shock. Since we know there is only a short-run trade-off between inflation and unemployment, the faster the economies concerned can get to the long run – in other words, return to their natural rates of output and unemployment – the better. This speed of adjustment to long-run equilibrium will be high if there is a high degree of wage flexibility in the common currency area, and/or if there is a high degree of labour mobility.

Another way in which tensions across the common currency area would be alleviated would be if all countries in the currency union were prone to the same kind of demand shocks (e.g. if aggregate demand fell in all countries simultaneously), since each would then favour similar macroeconomic policy decisions (e.g. a reduction in interest rates).

We consider each of these types of characteristics in turn.

Real Wage Flexibility Suppose there is a high degree of wage flexibility in each of the member countries, so that wages respond strongly to rises and falls in unemployment. This means that the adjustment to long-run equilibrium, as shown in Figure 17-3, occurs very quickly. In our example, the shift in aggregate demand in Germany leads to falling wages, so that firms make more profit for any given level of prices, the aggregate supply curve shifts to the right and Germany returns to the natural rate of output. If wages are very flexible, this adjustment may be very rapid, so that the short run is very short indeed. Similarly for France: the rightward shift in aggregate demand leads to rapidly rising wages and firms find it less profitable to produce any given level of output, so that the supply curve shifts leftward and a new long-run equilibrium is established at the natural rate of output. Hence, by compressing the short-run, tensions across the monetary union are ironed out very quickly.

Note that it is the real wage that is of importance here: it is real wages that must adjust in order to affect the aggregate supply curve by making it more (or less) profitable for firms to produce a given level of output at any given level of prices.

It is also worth noting that, in terms of our discussion of the determination of the short-run aggregate supply curve in Chapter 14, we are implicitly assuming the *sticky-wage model* of aggregate supply in this discussion. Greater wage flexibility simply means less wage stickiness and, if the sticky-wage model of short-run aggregate supply is correct, a faster adjustment towards long-run equilibrium.

Labour Mobility Alternatively, suppose that labour is highly mobile between the member countries of the currency union: unemployed workers in Germany simply migrate to France and find a job. Again, the macroeconomic imbalance is alleviated, since unemployment in Germany will fall as many of the unemployed have left the country, and inflationary wage pressures in France decline as the labour force expands with the migrants from France. Therefore, it is clear that labour mobility may in some measure cushion a currency union from asymmetric shocks.

Note that labour mobility does not affect the speed of adjustment of short-run aggregate supply, as in the case of wage flexibility. Instead, it actually shifts the natural rate of output. Consider an example. Suppose the size of the labour force in France is 28 million and the natural rate of unemployment is 10 per cent. In long-run equilibrium there will be 2.8 (= 10 per cent of 28) million people unemployed and 25.2 (= 28 − 2.8) million people in employment. Now suppose that the recession in Germany causes 2 million workers to migrate to France to find a job (this is, admittedly, an extreme example). The labour force in France has now grown to 30 million and, in long-run equilibrium at the natural rate of unemployment of 10 per cent, there will be 27 million people in work. But we know that aggregate output is determined by the production function

$$Y = F(L, K),$$

which states that the more labour that is hired, the more output is produced. Hence, increasing employment in long-run equilibrium from 25.2 million to 27 million workers will increase the natural rate of output (while keeping the natural rate of unemployment unchanged). The converse happens in Germany, where the exodus of 2 million workers shrinks the labour force and so reduces the natural rate of output.

In terms of our diagrams, the rightward shift of the natural rate of output in France and its leftward shift in Germany, as in Figure 17-5, narrows the gap between the short-run levels of output and the natural rate. The migration of labour from depressed Germany to booming France leads to the natural rate of output falling from $\overline{Y}_1^G$ to $\overline{Y}_2^G$ in Germany, and rising from $\overline{Y}_1^F$ to $\overline{Y}_2^F$ in France. Thus, the absolute size of the output gaps (the gap between the natural level of output and the actual level of output) arising from the asymmetric demand shocks are reduced from $(\overline{Y}_1^G - Y_1^G)$ to $(\overline{Y}_2^G - Y_1^G)$ in Germany, and from $(Y_1^F - \overline{Y}_1^F)$ to $(Y_1^F - \overline{Y}_2^F)$ in France. Because the output gaps are smaller in absolute size, this means that there is less fluctuation in output and unemployment in each country, and the adjustment to the long-run equilibrium will be faster.

Capital Mobility Sometimes economists argue that capital mobility can also compensate for the loss of monetary autonomy and the absence of exchange-rate adjustment among the members of a common currency area. A distinction should be made here between physical capital (plant and machinery) and financial capital (bonds, company shares and bank loans).

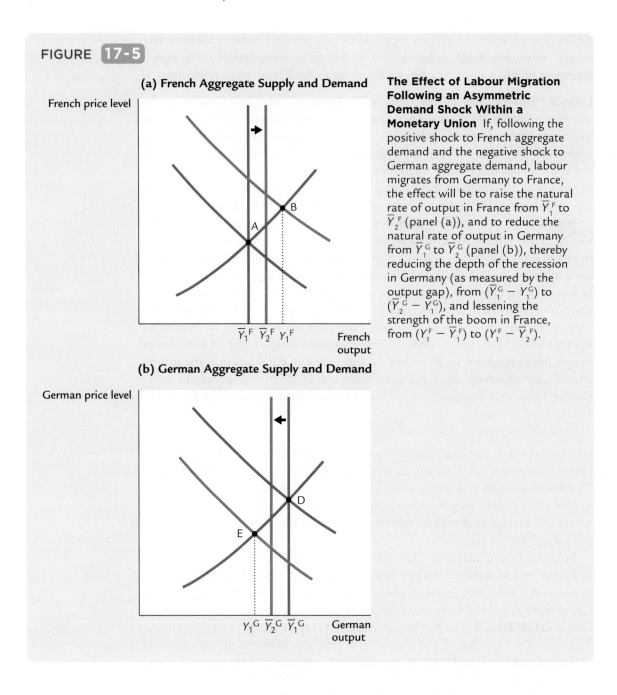

FIGURE **17-5**

(a) French Aggregate Supply and Demand

French price level

$\overline{Y}_1^F$ $\overline{Y}_2^F$ Y_1^F French output

(b) German Aggregate Supply and Demand

German price level

Y_1^G $\overline{Y}_2^G$ $\overline{Y}_1^G$ German output

The Effect of Labour Migration Following an Asymmetric Demand Shock Within a Monetary Union If, following the positive shock to French aggregate demand and the negative shock to German aggregate demand, labour migrates from Germany to France, the effect will be to raise the natural rate of output in France from $\overline{Y}_1^F$ to $\overline{Y}_2^F$ (panel (a)), and to reduce the natural rate of output in Germany from $\overline{Y}_1^G$ to $\overline{Y}_2^G$ (panel (b)), thereby reducing the depth of the recession in Germany (as measured by the output gap), from $(\overline{Y}_1^G - Y_1^G)$ to $(\overline{Y}_2^G - Y_1^G)$, and lessening the strength of the boom in France, from $(Y_1^F - \overline{Y}_1^F)$ to $(Y_1^F - \overline{Y}_2^F)$.

In terms of cushioning a currency union from asymmetric shocks, movements in *physical capital* can help by expanding productive capacity in countries experiencing a boom as firms in other member countries build factories there. Increasing the amount of capital stock in a country means that labour would become more productive and the natural rate of output would increase. However, given the long lags involved in the installation of plant and equipment, physical capital mobility is likely to be helpful mainly for narrowing persistent regional disparities rather than offsetting short-term shocks.

The mobility of *financial capital* may be more useful in cushioning economies from short-term output shocks. For example, residents of a country experiencing a recession may wish to borrow money from the residents of a country experiencing a boom in order to overcome their short-term difficulties. In our two-country example, German residents would effectively borrow money from French residents in order to make up for their temporary fall in income. Clearly, this would require that German residents can easily borrow from French residents through the capital markets, so that financial capital mobility will be highest between countries whose capital markets are highly integrated with one another. For example, if a bank has branches in more than one country of a currency union, then borrowing and lending between boom and recession countries will be more or less automatic, as residents in the booming country increase the money they are holding in the bank as their income goes up and residents of the country in recession increase their overdrafts (or reduce their money holdings) as their income goes down.

Of course, although we have discussed only bank loans, there are other forms of financial capital, such as bonds and company shares, but the principle of the recessionary economy being able to obtain funds from the booming economy remains the same. In effect, therefore, financial capital market integration across countries allows households to insure one another against asymmetric shocks so that the variability of consumption over the economic cycle can be reduced.

Symmetric Macroeconomic Shocks Note that, in describing the costs of belonging to a monetary union, we have used the example of a positive demand shock in one country and a simultaneous negative demand shock in another. A similar analysis would have followed if we had simply allowed either a positive or a negative demand shock in one country and no shock at all in the other country. The central point was that the demand shock was asymmetric in the sense that it impacted differently on different members of the currency union, requiring different short-run policy responses. Clearly, if the shock were symmetric (the same in both countries) there would be no policy problem across the monetary union. If, for example, aggregate demand rose simultaneously in all member countries, increasing expected future inflation, then a policy of raising interest rates would be welcomed by all members of the monetary union. This would be the case if the economic cycles of each of the countries making up the currency were synchronized in the sense that the various economies tended to enter recession at the same time and enter the recovery phase of the cycle at the same time, so that disagreements about the best interest-rate policy are less likely to occur.

Characteristics that Increase the Benefits of a Single Currency

High Degree of Trade Integration The greater the amount of trade that is done between a group of countries (i.e. the greater the degree of trade integration), the more they will benefit from adopting a common currency. One of the principal benefits of a currency union (and the most direct benefit) is the reduction in transactions costs that are incurred in trade transactions between the various countries when there is a constant need to switch one national currency into another on the foreign-currency exchange market. Clearly, therefore, the greater the amount of international trade that is carried out between member countries – and the greater the amount of foreign currency transactions – the greater the reduction in transactions costs that having a common currency entails.

The reduction in exchange-rate volatility – another benefit of a currency union – will also clearly be greater with a higher degree of intra-union trade, since more firms will benefit from knowing with certainty exactly the revenue generated from their sales to other currency union members, rather than having to bear the uncertainty associated with exchange-rate fluctuations.

17-5 Is Europe an Optimum Currency Area?

Having determined what characteristics of a group of countries would make the benefits of a single currency stronger and the costs weaker, we can take a closer look to see whether Europe – and in particular the group of 17 countries that form the Euro Area – forms an optimum currency area in the sense of the benefits of having a single currency heavily outweighing the costs.

Trade Integration To get a measure of the openness of the Euro Area countries to trade with the rest of Europe, we will adapt the measure of openness that we used in Chapter 6. Recall that (as in Figure 6-1 of Chapter 6), we measured the degree of openness of an economy to trade by taking an average of exports and imports (i.e. adding exports and imports together and dividing by 2), and then expressed the resulting figure as a percentage of GDP. To measure the degree of trade integration with other EU countries, we can do something similar. Table 17-1 shows the average of intra-union imports and exports of goods (i.e. the sum of imports from and exports of goods to other European Union countries, divided by 2) for the EU-27 countries (i.e. the 17 countries that make up the Euro Area plus the other European Union countries that are not members of Euro Area) for each year from 2003 to 2012, expressed as a percentage of GDP. Taking an average of intra-union imports and exports is appropriate here because transactions costs in trade between countries are incurred on both imports and exports. Thus we can think of this percentage as an index of trade integration of each of the countries with the rest of Europe and a measure of the gains to the reduction of transactions costs in trade.

Martin Gut/Cartoonstock.com

TABLE 17-1

Average of Imports and Exports of the EU-27 Countries from and to Other European Union Countries as a Percentage of GDP (Euro Area countries are highlighted)

	2003	2004	2005	2006	2007	2008	2009	2010	2011	2012
EU (27 countries)	18.5	19.2	19.7	21.0	21.2	21.5	18.4	20.4	21.9	21.6
Belgium	59.2	61.3	64.4	66.4	67.2	67.6	55.8	60.5	64.0	63.0
Bulgaria	26.6	28.4	28.7	31.3	34.1	32.9	25.4	28.7	34.4	34.1
Czech Republic	41.6	50.9	49.6	52.6	55.1	51.5	44.8	52.0	57.5	59.3
Denmark	20.8	21.0	22.1	23.2	23.0	23.1	19.5	19.8	21.0	21.0
Germany	18.3	19.4	20.3	22.1	23.1	22.9	19.6	21.5	23.1	22.7
Estonia	40.2	45.3	49.8	48.7	45.5	45.1	37.6	46.7	56.1	56.8
Ireland	28.8	28.5	28.5	26.6	26.2	26.2	24.9	26.1	26.5	26.4
Greece	8.9	9.0	8.8	9.5	9.7	9.9	8.1	7.8	8.2	8.4
Spain	14.8	14.9	14.4	14.3	14.7	13.9	11.7	13.2	14.1	13.7
France	15.1	15.2	14.8	15.5	15.6	15.5	13.1	14.3	15.2	15.1
Italy	12.4	12.6	12.8	13.6	14.1	13.5	11.2	12.7	13.5	13.0
Cyprus	10.4	14.2	16.1	15.4	15.9	16.6	13.8	15.0	14.4	13.3
Latvia	27.8	30.5	32.6	33.1	31.0	28.4	24.4	32.0	37.9	38.7
Lithuania	26.1	31.1	32.6	35.0	35.3	33.7	28.8	35.4	41.1	42.9
Luxembourg	41.8	43.8	44.4	46.6	39.7	42.5	36.5	34.7	35.2	32.3
Hungary	40.1	42.9	44.1	50.9	52.0	51.3	46.6	52.1	56.2	58.0
Malta	31.4	33.7	33.1	34.4	33.2	31.1	27.0	30.0	35.2	34.5
Netherlands	35.5	37.3	39.5	42.3	43.2	44.8	37.7	43.8	47.2	49.6
Austria	30.4	31.9	31.5	31.9	33.0	33.0	27.2	30.5	32.5	31.4
Poland	21.1	25.2	24.2	26.4	27.2	26.5	25.1	26.8	28.6	27.6
Portugal	19.5	19.1	21.0	22.1	22.3	22.4	19.1	20.5	22.1	21.9
Romania	24.9	25.8	22.6	22.5	23.2	22.7	21.2	24.5	27.5	27.2
Slovenia	33.0	37.8	40.9	44.4	46.5	45.3	37.2	43.6	48.4	47.9
Slovakia	53.3	56.3	57.2	62.8	63.9	60.6	51.3	58.0	65.5	68.6
Finland	18.5	18.6	19.5	21.3	21.0	20.3	15.5	17.3	18.2	17.4
Sweden	19.0	20.0	21.0	22.2	22.9	23.1	19.3	20.5	20.9	19.7
United Kingdom	11.0	10.6	11.1	12.8	10.6	11.3	10.3	11.2	11.9	11.3

Source: Eurostat.

Consider first the Euro Area countries. In 2012, Belgium's intra-EU exports and imports were around two-thirds of its GDP, while the Netherlands, Estonia, Slovenia and Slovakia appear to also have benefited greatly from the reduction in transactions costs associated with the single currency, since the average of intra-union exports and imports for these countries ranged from about 50 per cent to about two-thirds of their GDP. Next in the list come Malta, Latvia and Bulgaria, with indices of trade integration between a third and a half of GDP, while for France, Germany, Portugal and Finland, the corresponding figure is between around 15 per cent and 25 per cent. The trade-integration indices for Italy and Spain, however, amounted to only a little over 13 per cent, while Greece appeared to gain least from monetary union on this criterion, with the average of EU exports and imports amounting to only 8 per cent of GDP in 2012.

Among the three non-Euro Area countries for which we have figures, Denmark and Sweden actually had average intra-European Union exports and imports as a percentage of GDP, around 20 per cent – a higher figure than many countries that have adopted the euro as their common currency. On the other hand, the UK's European trade integration index came to just over 11 per cent in 2012 – the lowest figure of any country in the table, with the single exception of Greece.

What does all this tell us? First, the degree of trade integration across Europe is quite variable, but nevertheless quite high on average – with the notable exception of Greece.

Second, however, we can see from Table 17-1 that the degree of European trade integration appears to have been rising over time in nearly every country: comparing the index of trade integration in 2003 to its value in 2012, it has increased for the vast majority of countries in the table. For some countries, such as Czech Republic and Hungary, this growth in European trade integration is very marked (an increase of around 18 percentage points), while for others, such as Italy and the UK, the increase over the ten-year period is only slight.

In the period immediately prior to that described in the table, many countries, such as Germany and Ireland, experienced high increases in trade integration. This has led some economists to argue that some of the criteria for an optimum currency area – such as a high degree of trade integration – may actually be endogenous: actually being a member of a currency union may enhance the degree of trade between members of the union, precisely because of the decline in transactions costs in carrying out such trade.[6]

Overall, the figures presented in Table 17-1 suggest that many European countries have gained from the reduction in transactions costs in international trade as a result of the single currency. Indeed, these gains have been estimated at about one-quarter to one-half of 1 per cent of Euro Area GDP. This may not sound massive, but remember that transactions costs are a deadweight loss. Moreover, the gains are not one-off: they accrue continuously so long as the single currency persists, since they would have to be paid in the absence of the currency union. They therefore become cumulative. In addition, if the degree of Euro Area trade integration tends to rise over time as a result of the single currency, as some economists have suggested, then the implicit gain from not having to pay transactions costs also rises over time.

The other, indirect benefit of a single currency when there is a high degree of trade integration follows from the reduction in uncertainty associated with doing away with the volatility in the exchange rates between members' national currencies (since those currencies are replaced with a common currency). These gains are hard to quantify, but the figures presented in Table 17-1, again, do suggest that they are not negligible for the Euro Area.

---

[6] See Jeffrey A. Frankel and Andrew K. Rose, 'The Endogeneity of the Optimum Currency Area Criteria', *The Economic Journal*, 1998, vol. 108, pp. 1009–1025.

Real Wage Flexibility A great deal of research has been undertaken on real wage flexibility in Europe, and virtually all of it concludes that Continental European labour markets are among the most rigid in the world, while the UK labour market, at least since the 1980s, has become one of the most flexible. We discussed both the UK and Continental European labour markets at some length in Chapter 7, and concluded that major reasons for inflexibility in Continental European labour markets included high levels of union coverage and the more generous unemployment benefit systems of many European countries, combined with various laws that reduce labour market flexibility.

In addition, the introduction of the single European currency may have had a negative effect on European wage flexibility, since many European collective wage agreements between workers and a firm in one country will also often extend to the firm's workforce in other European countries, and a single currency brings transparency in wage differences across countries, as well as price transparency. To return again to our example of a negative demand shock in Germany and a positive shock in France, a company with employees in both countries would find it hard to reduce real wages in Germany while raising them in France.

Furthermore, because of the high non-wage costs of employing workers in many European countries, even if there were movements in the real wage, firms would be slow to expand or contract their output in response, so that shifts in aggregate supply will be slow to come about.

On the whole, therefore, movements in real wages are unlikely to make a significant contribution to the macroeconomic adjustment of Euro Area countries to asymmetric shocks.

Labour Mobility Labour is notoriously immobile across European countries, at least if one rules out migration from the Eastern European members of the EU such as Poland. In part, this might be attributed to differences in language, culture and other social institutions across Europe that make it difficult for workers to migrate. However, it seems that European workers are also very loath to move location even within their own countries. Indeed, the degree of labour mobility as measured by the percentage of the workforce that moves geographical location over any given period, is much lower within any particular European country than it is within the United States, and is even lower between the Euro Area countries. Europe therefore scores very low on this optimum currency area criterion.

Financial Capital Mobility In discussing financial capital mobility, a distinction must be made between the wholesale and the retail capital markets. The wholesale financial markets are the capital markets in which only financial institutions such as banks and investment trusts operate, as well as very large corporations, while the retail financial markets (such as high street banks) are those open to individual households and to small and medium-sized corporations. Prior to the introduction of the euro, financial integration among Euro Area countries was probably quite low, in both the wholesale and retail sectors. Following the introduction of the euro, however, integration of the wholesale financial markets has increased dramatically. In particular, a liquid euro money market with single inter-bank market interest rates was established, so that a bank in Luxembourg, for example, can now borrow euros just as easily and at the same rate of interest from another bank in Frankfurt as it can from a bank located in the same street. In the government bond market, the degree of market integration is also high, and this is shown by the fact that the interest rates on government bonds of the different Euro Area countries are very close to one another and tend to move very closely together. On the other hand, the integration of retail market products, such as loans to households and small and medium-sized enterprises, is lagging behind compared with the wholesale market products. This becomes evident from persistent cross-country differences in bank lending rates and the rather limited cross-border retail banking activity. Indeed, national banking sectors have remained largely segregated, with only marginal cross-border penetration: only around 5 per cent of total bank loans are granted across borders to customers in other Euro Area countries.

Symmetric Demand Shocks The economic cycle across the countries of the Euro Area does seem to be positively correlated, in the sense that the timing of booms and recessions appear to be very close. In Figure 17-6, we have graphed data on annual growth rates in real GDP for Belgium, France, Germany, Italy, Greece, Ireland and Austria, for the ten years 2003–2012. Clearly, the movements in growth rates over this period for this group of countries tend to have similar turning points: the generally improving position until 2004, the dip in growth

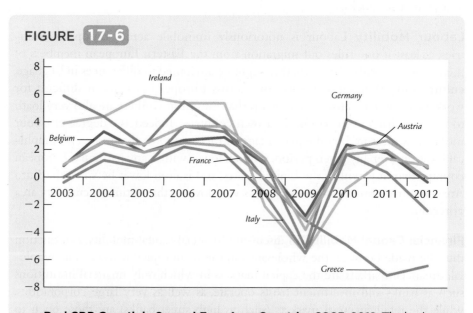

FIGURE 17-6

Real GDP Growth in Several Euro Area Countries 2003–2012 The business cycle appears to be largely synchronized across the economies of these Euro Area countries.

Source: Eurostat.

in 2005, subsequent recovery 2005–2007, and the sharp dip during the recession of 2008–2009 are features that all the growth paths share. We can also see how Ireland's growth rate outstripped the performance of the other countries during the period up to 2007, indicating that ECB monetary policy was initially somewhat loose for the Irish economy in this early period. On the other hand, while the Irish economy has recovered relatively well from the 2008 recession, we can see that Greece has not fared so well, continuing to contract. Other countries, such as Italy, also dipped into negative growth towards the end of the period, and growth across these countries overall is at best weak.

Overall, therefore, the evidence is somewhat mixed, although, on the whole, it suggests that the problem of asymmetric demand shocks is not a great one for the current member countries of EMU. The fact that there is not strong evidence of asymmetric demand shocks at the aggregate level, however, does not rule out the possibility that there may be asymmetric shocks at other levels in the economy. In fact, researchers have found that many of the shocks that impact on European countries asymmetrically tend to be specific to a region or to an industry rather than to a country as a whole. This is not a problem made worse by joining a monetary union, however, since a country that experienced, say, a negative shock to one of its industries or regions, would not in any case be able to deal with this using monetary or exchange-rate policy without generating imbalances in its other regions or industries.

Summing Up: Is Europe an Optimum Currency Area?

As in many policy debates in economics, there is no clear-cut answer to this question. Certainly, many European countries have a high degree of intra-union trade and have economic cycles that are more or less synchronized. Labour mobility and wage flexibility (and labour market flexibility in general), however, is low in Europe, and while the euro has increased financial market integration in the Euro Area's wholesale financial markets, the retail financial markets remain highly segregated at the national level.

Overall, therefore, if very strong differences in the economic cycle were to emerge across the Euro Area, the lack of independent monetary and exchange-rate policy would be felt acutely. For that reason, many economists argue that Europe – meaning the current Euro Area – is not an optimum currency area. Nevertheless, as we have noted in our discussion, it is possible that some of the optimum currency area criteria may be endogenous. In particular, the single currency is likely to generate even greater trade among EMU members. Given this, it is likely that the economic cycles of member currencies will become even more closely synchronized as aggregate demand shifts in one country have increasingly strong spillover effects in other Euro Area countries. Moreover, the single currency may raise labour mobility across Europe in the long run, since being paid in the same currency as in one's home country is one less issue to come to terms with when moving location to find a job. Also, with time, one would expect financial market integration to spread to the retail capital markets.

17-6 Fiscal Policy and Common Currency Areas

Our discussion so far has tended to centre on the loss of autonomy in monetary policy that is entailed in adopting a single currency among a group of countries. However, it is obvious that there is nothing in the adoption of a common currency that implies that members of the currency union should not still retain independence in fiscal policy. For example, in our example of an asymmetric demand shock that expands demand in France and contracts aggregate demand in Germany, the French government could reduce government spending in order to offset the demand shock, while the German government could expand government spending. In fact, even if France and Germany did not make up an optimal currency area because wages were sticky and labour mobility was low between the countries, national fiscal policy could, in principle, still be used to compensate for the loss of monetary policy autonomy.

Fiscal Federalism

Suppose that a currency union had a common fiscal policy in the sense of having a single, common fiscal budget covering tax and spending decisions across the common currency area. This means that fiscal policy in the currency union would work much as fiscal policy in a single national economy works, with a surplus of government tax revenue over government spending in one region used to pay for a budget deficit in another region. Return again to our example of an asymmetric demand shock that expands aggregate demand in France and contracts aggregate demand in Germany, as in Figure 17-2. Now, the fiscal policy of an economy will generally have built in to it stabilizers that automatically stimulate aggregate demand when the economy goes into recession, without policy makers having to take any deliberate action. For example, since almost all taxes are closely related to the level of economic activity in the economy, tax revenue will automatically decline in Germany as a result of the negative aggregate demand shock that shifts it into recession. At the same time, transfer payments in the form of unemployment benefit and other social security benefits will also rise in Germany. The opposite will be true in France, where the automatic stabilizers will be operating in reverse, as transfer payments fall and tax receipts rise with the level of economic activity. These changes will tend to expand aggregate demand in Germany and contract it in France, to some extent offsetting the asymmetric demand shock.

If the governments of France and Germany have a common fiscal budget, then the increased net government revenue in France can be used to offset the reduction in net government revenue in Germany. If the resulting movements in aggregate are not enough to offset the demand shock, the French and German governments may even go further and decide to increase government expenditure further in Germany and pay for it by reducing spending and perhaps raising taxes in France.

This kind of arrangement — a fiscal system for a group of countries involving a common fiscal budget and a system of taxes and fiscal transfers across countries — is known as **fiscal federalism.** The problem with it is that the taxpayers of one country (here, France) may not be happy about paying for government spending and transfer payments in another country (in this example, Germany).

National Fiscal Policies in a Currency Union: The Free-Rider Problem

Assuming that, for political reasons, fiscal federalism is not an option open to the currency union, we still need to explore the possibility of individual members of the union using fiscal policy in order to offset asymmetric macroeconomic shocks that cannot be dealt with by the common monetary policy. In particular, in our example, what is wrong with Germany running a big government budget deficit in order to counteract the fall in aggregate demand, and borrowing heavily in order to finance the deficit? One answer may lie in the effect on other members of the currency union of a rise in the debt of a member country.

Whenever a government raises its debt to very high levels, there is always the possibility that the government may default on the debt. In general, this can be done in one of two ways. Where a country is not a member of a currency union and controls its own monetary policy, it can engineer a surprise inflation by a sudden increase in the money supply, so that the real value of the debt shrinks. In addition, as we discussed in Chapter 6, when there is a sharp rise in the price level, this will usually be accompanied by a sharp fall in the foreign-currency value of the domestic currency. This means that, valued in foreign currency, the stock of government debt will now be worth far less. Thus, the government has in effect defaulted on a large portion of its debt by reducing its value both internally and externally.

If this is not possible — for example, because, as in a currency union, the country no longer enjoys monetary policy autonomy and is not able to devalue the external value of its currency (since it uses the common currency) — the only other way of reneging on the debt is through an outright default (e.g. stopping interest payments and/or failing to honour capital repayments when they fall due). Generally, the financial markets are good at disciplining governments that run up large debts, by charging them high rates of interest on the debt that the government issues — after all, if you thought there was even a slight possibility that you might not get your money back if you lent it, you would want to be paid a higher rate of interest in order to compensate for that risk. In the case of a monetary union, however, this means that excessive debt issuance by one member country (e.g. Germany) will tend to force up interest rates throughout the common currency area. Although the ECB controls very short-term interest rates in the Euro Area through its open-market operations, it does not control longer-term interest rates, such as those paid on 10- or 20-year government bonds. Hence, fiscal profligacy by the German government will tend to push up the cost of borrowing for all members of the currency union.

On the other hand, interest rates may not be raised enough to discipline properly the high-borrowing German government. This is because the markets feel that the other members of the monetary union would not allow the country concerned actually to default, and that if it threatened to do so, the other members would probably rush in and buy up its government debt and 'bail out' the country concerned. If the markets believe in this possibility, then German debt will not be considered as risky, so the interest rates charged to Germany on its debt will not be as high as they otherwise might be. The net effect is for Germany to pay interest rates on its large stock of debt that are lower because of the implicit belief that it will be bailed out if it has problems servicing the debt, and for all other members of the currency union to pay higher interest rates on their government debt because Germany has flooded the financial markets with euro-denominated government bonds. In essence, this is an example of a free-rider problem: Germany is enjoying the benefits of a fiscal expansion without paying the full costs. We can also think of this problem as another example of *moral hazard,* which we first encountered in Chapter 7 in our discussion of labour markets. In that discussion, we defined moral hazard as the tendency of people to behave inappropriately when their behaviour is imperfectly monitored. The same is true here, except that now we have the possibility of a national government behaving inappropriately.

In addition, if Germany is using the proceeds of its borrowing to fund a strong fiscal expansion, this may undo or work against the anti-inflationary monetary policy of the ECB by stoking up aggregate demand throughout the Euro Area.

In order to circumvent some of these problems, the currency union members can enter into a 'no bail-out' agreement, which states that member countries cannot expect other members to come to their rescue if their debt levels become unsustainable, in an attempt to convince the markets to charge profligate spend-and-borrow countries higher interest rates on their debt. In fact, exactly such a no bail-out agreement exists among members of EMU. Unfortunately, however, it seems clear that the no bail-out clause is not credible: if Germany (or any other EMU member) were to default on its debt, this would have strong repercussions throughout the Euro Area, as it would probably lead to the financial markets losing confidence in debt issued by other members and to strong selling of the euro in the foreign-currency exchange market. In order to avoid this, it is likely that EMU members would in fact bail out a member country that was threatening to default on its debt. Indeed, bailouts have been made to Greece, Portugal, Ireland and Cyprus during the period 2010–2013, albeit with strings attached, for example agreements to substantial cuts in public spending.

For these reasons, the members of the currency union may wish to impose rules on one another concerning the conduct of national fiscal policies in order to avoid fiscal profligacy by any one member. At the outset of EMU, a set of fiscal rules was indeed drawn up and agreed to by members of the European monetary union. This set of rules was known as the Stability and Growth Pact (SGP). The SGP not only laid down strict rules on the maximum permissible budget deficit and debt-to-GDP ratio for EMU members, but it also stipulated harsh punishments – fines amounting to as much as 0.5 per cent of GDP – for offenders. Let's take a closer look at the SGP.

The Stability and Growth Pact

The SGP was a set of formal rules by which members of EMU were supposed to be bound in their conduct of national fiscal policy. Its two main components were as follows:

- Members should aim to achieve balanced budgets.
- Members with a total budget deficit of more than 3 per cent of GDP will be subject to fines that may be as high 0.5 per cent of GDP unless the country experiences exceptional circumstances (such as a natural disaster) or a very sharp recession in which GDP declines by 2 per cent or more in a single year.

The rationale for imposing the SGP among EMU members is clear, since it would rule out any free-rider or moral hazard problems associated with excessive spending and borrowing in any one member country, by simply limiting the amount of spending that can be done that is not financed by taxation.

The Treaty on Stability, Coordination and Governance was signed in March 2012 by all Euro Area members and eight other EU member states, and came into force on 1 January 2013. Signatories to the treaty agreed to implement a balanced budget rule in their national legislation through permanent, binding provisions, preferably of a constitutional character, by the end of 2013. Under the treaty, the annual structural government deficit (that part of the budget deficit not related to the ups and downs of the economic cycle) of signatories must not exceed 0.5% of GDP. Signatories must additionally implement a correction mechanism whereby measures to reduce the budget deficit kick in automatically if there is a significant deviation from the agreed country-specific minimum benchmark figure for long-term sustainability.

How does the SGP square with our discussion of government debt in Chapter 16? First of all, as we discussed in the previous chapter, there is nothing particularly optimal about achieving a balanced budget. A balanced budget – even a budget balanced on average over the business cycle – is consistent with an equilibrium debt-to-GDP ratio of zero. This must be true because a balanced budget means that debt cannot be growing, and if GDP is growing, at least on average, then the debt-to-GDP ratio must be shrinking and will eventually reach zero. If there is a positive long-run rate of growth of real GDP that exceeds the real interest rate, however, there seems to be no economic rationale for a balanced budget.

Second, what is the basis for the maximum 3 per cent budget deficit rule? It is related to the rules for entry into EMU which were laid down in the Maastricht Treaty in 1992. According to the Treaty, candidates for entry into EMU should have a debt-to-GDP ratio of no more than 60 per cent of GDP and a budget deficit of no more than 3 per cent of GDP. Effectively (and perhaps in implied contradiction of the requirement that governments should aim to balance the budget), therefore, the Maastricht Treaty sets the 'prudent' debt-to-GDP ratio at 60 per cent. Although largely arbitrary, this ratio does not seem unreasonable (it certainly sounds more prudent than a debt-to-GDP ratio of 200 per cent or even 100 per cent of GDP).

Suppose, therefore, that a country was unable to balance its budget, even on average, as prescribed in the first part of the SGP. It could, nevertheless, avoid triggering any fines by keeping its total budget deficit at 3 per cent of GDP. However, given long-run European growth rates of the order of 2.5–3 per cent per year, and allowing for long-run inflation of 2–2.5 per cent per year (as we discussed in Chapter 15, the ECB inflation target is in fact 2 per cent per year), the average Euro Area country could presumably expect long-run nominal GDP growth of about 5 per cent a year. In Chapter 16, we showed that a condition for fiscal sustainability of a country (in the sense that its government is able to service the government debt) is that

$$\frac{B}{Y} = (x + \pi)d,$$

where B is the total budget deficit (including interest payments on government debt), Y is GDP, x is the rate of growth of real GDP, π is the inflation rate and d is the equilibrium debt-to-GDP ratio. If, therefore, $x + \pi = 0.05$ (the rate of growth of nominal GDP) and the target debt-to-GDP ratio $d = 0.6$, we can work out the maximum consistent budget deficit, as a percentage of GDP, as

$$\frac{B}{Y} = 0.05 \times 0.6 = 0.03$$

In words, the government should aim to run a total budget deficit of no more than 3 per cent of GDP per year if it wants an equilibrium debt-to-GDP ratio of 60 per cent. This is the rationale for the maximum of 3 per cent of GDP imposed on total budget deficits by the SGP.

Overall, while the budgetary arithmetic underlying the SGP is clearly related to the notion of fiscal sustainability, it nevertheless seems flawed as a viable and reasonable constraint on the behaviour of EMU member governments – on at least two counts. First, the first component of the SGP, although apparently unenforceable, encourages balanced government budgets, for which there is no economic rationale.

Second, however, having given up sovereignty over monetary policy (or, at the very least, having 'pooled' sovereignty with the other members of EMU), an EMU member is left with only fiscal policy with which to attempt to counter any asymmetric shocks that it may encounter, and the SGP effectively limits the ability of EMU members to avail themselves of this. This straitjacketing of national fiscal policy that the SGP implied may have reflected a desire among the architects of EMU for the ECB to maintain an effective monopoly on demand management, so that its polices could not be countered by national fiscal policies.

The crucial question for the SGP, however, was whether or not the maximum allowable budget deficit would be enough for a country to let its automatic fiscal stabilizers come into play if it were to go into recession. This is crucial in a monetary union because member countries will have already given up their right to pursue an independent monetary policy and they cannot use the exchange rate as an instrument of policy.

In practice, the SGP proved to be something of a toothless watchdog. As the Euro Area experienced sluggish growth in the early years of EMU, several member countries – in particular, France and Germany, two of the largest member countries – found themselves in breach of the SGP excessive deficit criteria. However, both France and Germany managed to persuade other EMU members not to impose fines and, in 2004, the European Commission drew up guidelines for softening the SGP. These guidelines included considering more widely the sustainability of countries' public finances on an individual basis, paying more attention to overall debt burdens and to long-term liabilities such as pensions, rather than to a single year's deficit.

Some critics of the new SGP guidelines argued that they were subjective and somewhat fuzzy. Yet perhaps fuzziness is the best solution. In effect, the commitment of an EMU member to maintaining fiscal prudence and not becoming a free-rider now relies on peer pressure and national prestige: no country wants to have fingers wagged at them for spending and borrowing excessively. Most importantly, currency unions are, by definition, short on policy instruments – they require flexibility rather than rigidity in the conduct of fiscal policy. Having a system of rigid rules and draconian punishments and no credible way of enforcing the sanctions was not the correct way to ensure fiscal stability in the Euro Area.

CASE STUDY

The Euro Area Crisis

The recent crisis in the Euro Area has led many to question the very viability of a single European currency. This case study looks at how the crisis unfolded. The jubilant scenes witnessed at the beginning of the Euro project are now a distant memory, replaced by a widespread doubt as to whether the Euro offers sufficient flexibility for member countries to withstand and mitigate the effects of financial crisis and recession. In recent years, the financial markets have begun to question the ability of some European governments to honour their sovereign debt repayment obligations. The debt issued by these countries is no longer perceived as being risk-free, reducing the price of these government bonds and pushing up interest rates.

The problems began with Greece. From 2008, Greek debt increased steadily from 113 per cent GDP, almost double the European average, and subsequently peaking at over 170 per cent. The Greek budget deficit for 2009 was revised upwards from 3.9 per cent of GDP to 12.7 per cent. These are well above the SGP guidelines discussed in the previous section. This cast doubt on the ability of the Greek authorities to collect tax or cut spending. Greek state and bank debt was then downgraded by rating agencies on account of its poor perceived credit risk. To head off the immediate risk of default, in the spring of 2010 Greece received a series of emergency loans from Euro Area countries. These, however, had strings attached. Greece had to agree to substantial cuts in public spending and rises in taxes, leading to widespread public unrest. We examine the case of Greece further in Chapter 20.

As the full extent of the problems in Greece began to be uncovered, concerns were raised about other countries: Portugal, Italy, Ireland and Spain were placed under the spotlight. There was a fear that the European banking system may not be able to cope if this larger group of countries went the same way as Greece. Over the following year bailouts were received by Ireland and Portugal. The Euro Area countries established the European Financial Stability Mechanism (EFSM) in February 2011, initially backed by €500 billion, but increased just eight months later. In October 2011, 50 per cent of Greek debt was written off (a so-called 'haircut') and €130 billion provided to the Greek government to recapitalize their banks.

During 2012, the effects of fiscal reform in the countries most at risk appear to have improved financial stability in the Euro Area. In Spain, for example, substantial fiscal tightening has reduced the budget deficit from over 10 per cent of GDP in 2009 to around 7 per cent in 2013. Labour market reforms have also began to pay dividends, with more inward investment attracted by lower unit labour costs and more flexible working practices, accompanied by an improvement in the current account. However, unemployment remains stubbornly high, particularly among the youth, and per-capita incomes are back where they were ten years ago.

In Ireland, the austerity programme and banking reform promised at the time of their 2010 bailout has taken its toll on output per head, which still languishes at its 2003 level and shows little sign of speedy recovery. The budget deficit, at over 8 per cent of GDP in 2013, still remains uncomfortably high from the perspective of investor confidence.

Negative growth has been a major worry in Portugal, despite the country's progress in reducing their government deficit to just under 5 per cent in 2013.

So, while the euro crisis has receded somewhat, events in Cyprus in 2013 show that there is still cause for vigilance. Moreover, the cuts in public spending required by these bailouts are proving politically unpopular, resulting in changes in government and record low approval ratings for politicians in many European countries. ∎

17-7 Conclusion

In this chapter we have examined some of the main issues concerned with common currency areas, focusing in particular on the EMU. Where there is a high degree of trade among a group of countries, there are benefits to be had from forming a currency union, largely arising from the reduction in transactions costs in international trade and reductions in exchange-rate uncertainty. There are also costs associated with joining a monetary union, however, largely related to the loss of monetary autonomy (member countries are no longer free to set their own interest rates) and the loss of exchange-rate movements as a means of achieving macroeconomic adjustment. Any decision to form a currency union must weigh these costs and benefits against one another to see if there is an overall net benefit. Although, in the long run, the loss of exchange-rate adjustment and monetary autonomy may have little effect on the equilibrium levels of output and unemployment in the economies involved, there may be substantial short-term economic fluctuations in these macroeconomic variables as a result of joining the currency union. This is particularly the case if there are asymmetric demand shocks impacting on the currency union so that it is impossible to design a one-size-fits-all monetary policy to suit every country. Short-run adjustment will also be long and painful when wages do not adjust very quickly, although this problem may be overcome by labour mobility across the member countries.

A group of countries for which the benefits of monetary union are high and the costs are relatively low is termed an optimum currency area. Even though there is quite a high degree of trade integration among the member countries of the current European monetary union (with the notable exception of Greece), and their economic cycles do seem more or less synchronized and of a similar amplitude (with the notable exception of Ireland), labour mobility and wage flexibility in Europe are both notoriously low, and integration of Euro Area financial markets, although high in the wholesale sector, has so far been disappointing in the retail financial markets. Overall, therefore, the Euro Area is probably not an optimum currency area. Nevertheless, it is possible that some of these criteria may be endogenous: EMU may lead to increasing economic integration in the Euro Area that will in turn significantly raise the benefits and reduce the costs to each country of remaining in the monetary union.

Summary

1. A common currency area (or currency union or monetary union) is a geographical area through which one currency circulates and is accepted as the medium of exchange.

2. The formation of a common currency area can bring significant benefits to the members of the currency union, particularly if there is already a high level of trade integration, primarily because of the reductions in transactions costs and in exchange-rate uncertainty.

3. The costs of joining a currency union include the loss of an independent monetary policy and the loss of the exchange rate as a means of macro-economic adjustment. Given a long-run vertical supply curve, this will affect mainly short-run macroeconomic adjustment.

4. Short-run adjustment problems will be reduced by greater degrees of real-wage flexibility, labour mobility and capital market integration across the currency union. They will also be less important, the fewer members of the currency union suffering from asymmetric demand shocks.

5. A group of countries with a high level of trade integration, high labour mobility and real-wage flexibility, a high level of capital market integration and that does not suffer asymmetric demand shocks across the different members of the group, is termed an optimum currency area. An optimum currency area is most likely to benefit from currency union.

6. It is possible that a group of countries may become an optimum currency area after forming a currency union, since this may enhance trade integration and help to synchronize members' economic cycles, and a single currency may also encourage labour mobility and capital market integration.

7. While the current Euro Area displays, overall, a high degree of trade integration and does not appear to be plagued by asymmetric demand shocks, real-wage flexibility and labour mobility both appear to be low. And while the introduction of the euro has led to a high degree of Euro Area financial market integration at the wholesale level, retail financial markets remain nationally segregated. Overall, therefore, the Euro Area is probably not at present an optimum currency area, although it may eventually become one.

8. The problems of adjustment within a currency union that is not an optimum currency area may be alleviated by fiscal federalism – a common fiscal budget and a system of taxes and fiscal transfers across member countries. In practice, however, fiscal federalism may be difficult to implement for political reasons.

9. The national fiscal policies of the countries making up a currency union may be subject to a free-rider problem, with one member country issuing a large amount of government debt at a lower interest rate than it might otherwise have paid, leading to other member countries having to pay higher interest rates. A currency union may therefore wish to impose rules on the national fiscal policies of its members.

KEY CONCEPTS

Common currency area (or currency union or monetary union)

Euro

European Economic and Monetary Union (EMU)

Euro Area

European Central Bank (ECB)

Optimum currency area

Fiscal federalism

QUESTIONS FOR REVIEW

1. What are the main advantages of forming a currency union? What are the main disadvantages?

2. Is a reduction in price discrimination across countries likely to be an important benefit of forming a currency union?

3. What is an optimum currency area? List the criteria that an optimum currency area must satisfy.

4. Is EMU an optimum currency area?

5. What is fiscal federalism? How might the problems of macroeconomic adjustment in a currency union be alleviated by fiscal federalism?

6. Why might the members of a currency union wish to impose rules on the conduct of national fiscal policies?

PROBLEMS AND APPLICATIONS

1. Consider two countries that trade heavily with one another, Ruritania and Circuitania. The output of Ruritania is mainly agricultural, while the output of Circuitania is mainly high-technology electronic goods. Suppose that each economy is initially in a long-run macroeconomic equilibrium. The national currency of Ruritania is the cob, while the Circuitania national currency is the byte.

   a. Use aggregate supply–aggregate demand diagrams to illustrate the state of each economy. Be sure to show aggregate demand, short-run aggregate supply and long-run aggregate supply.

   b. Now suppose that there is an increase in demand for electronic goods in both countries, and a simultaneous decline in demand for agricultural goods. Use your diagrams to show what happens to output and the price level in the short run in each country. What happens to the unemployment rate in each country?

   c. Using your diagrams, show how each country could use monetary policy to reduce the short-run fluctuation in output.

   d. What do you think will happen to the cob–byte exchange rate? Show diagrammatically how this could reduce short-run fluctuations in output in each country.

2. Suppose Circuitania and Ruritania form a currency union and adopt the electrocarrot as their common currency. Now suppose that there is an increase in demand for electronic goods in both countries, and a simultaneous decline in demand for agricultural goods. As president of the central bank for the currency union, would you raise or lower the electrocarrot interest rate, or keep it the same? Explain. (*Hint:* You are charged with maintaining low and stable inflation across the Electrocarrot Area.)

3. Suppose that Circuitania and Ruritania decide to engage in fiscal federalism and adopt a common fiscal budget.

   a. Show, again using aggregate demand–aggregate supply diagrams, how fiscal policy can be used to alleviate the short-run fluctuations generated by the asymmetric demand shock.

   b. Given the typical lags in the implementation of fiscal policy, would you advise the use of federal fiscal policy to alleviate short-run macroeconomic fluctuations? (*Hint:* Distinguish between automatic stabilizers and discretionary fiscal policy.)

4. The United States can be thought of as a nontrivial currency union since, although it is a single country, it encompasses many states that have economies comparable in size to those of some European countries. Given that the US has had a single currency for 200 years, it may be thought of as a *successful* currency union. Yet many of the American states produce very different products and services, so that they are likely to be impacted by different kinds of macroeconomic shocks (expansionary and recessionary) over time. For example, Texas produces oil, while Kansas produces agricultural goods. How do you explain the long-term success of the US currency union given this diversity? Are there any lessons or predictions for Europe that can be drawn from the US experience? (*Hint:* Think about taxes and transfers.)

5. Explain, giving reasons, whether the following statements are true or false.

   a. A high degree of trade among a group of countries implies that there would be benefits from them adopting a common currency and forming a currency union.

   b. A high degree of trade among a group of countries implies that they should definitely adopt a common currency and form a currency union.

6. Do you think that the free-rider or moral hazard problem associated with national fiscal policies in a currency union, as we discussed in this chapter, is likely to be a problem in actual practice? Justify your answer.

PART 6

More on the Microeconomics behind Macroeconomics

CHAPTER 18

Consumption

Consumption is the sole end and purpose of all production.

— Adam Smith

How do households decide how much of their income to consume today and how much to save for the future? This is a microeconomic question because it addresses the behaviour of individual decision makers. Yet its answer has important macroeconomic consequences. As we have seen in previous chapters, households' consumption decisions affect the way the economy as a whole behaves, both in the long run and in the short run.

The consumption decision is crucial for long-run analysis because of its role in economic growth. The Solow growth model of Chapters 8 and 9 shows that the saving rate is a key determinant of the steady-state capital stock and thus of the level of economic well-being. The saving rate measures how much of its income the present generation is not consuming, but is instead putting aside for its own future and for future generations.

The consumption decision is crucial for short-run analysis because of its role in determining aggregate demand. In most advanced economies, consumption is about two-thirds of GDP, so fluctuations in consumption are a key element of booms and recessions. The *IS-LM* model of Chapters 11 and 12 shows that changes in consumers' spending plans can be a source of shocks to the economy, and that the marginal propensity to consume is a determinant of the fiscal-policy multipliers.

In previous chapters we explained consumption with a function that relates consumption to disposable income: $C = C(Y - T)$. This approximation allowed us to develop simple models for long-run and short-run analysis, but it is too simple to provide a complete explanation of consumer behaviour. In this chapter we examine the consumption function in greater detail and develop a more thorough explanation of what determines aggregate consumption.

Since macroeconomics began as a field of study, many economists have written about the theory of consumer behaviour and suggested alternative ways of interpreting the data on consumption and income. This chapter presents the views of six prominent economists to show the diverse approaches to explaining consumption.

18-1 John Maynard Keynes and the Consumption Function

We begin our study of consumption with John Maynard Keynes's *General Theory*, which was published in 1936. Keynes made the consumption function central to his theory of economic fluctuations, and it has played a key role in macroeconomic analysis ever since. Let's consider what Keynes thought about the consumption function, and then see what puzzles arose when his ideas were confronted with the data.

Keynes's Conjectures

Today, economists who study consumption rely on sophisticated techniques of data analysis. With the help of computers, they analyse aggregate data on the behaviour of the overall economy from the national income accounts and detailed data on the behaviour of individual households from surveys. Because Keynes wrote in the 1930s, however, he had neither the advantage of these data nor the computers necessary to analyse such large data sets. Instead of relying on statistical analysis, Keynes made conjectures about the consumption function based on introspection and casual observation.

First, and most importantly, Keynes conjectured that the **marginal propensity to consume** – the amount consumed out of an additional unit of income – is between zero and one. He wrote that the 'fundamental psychological law, on which we are entitled to depend with great confidence, . . . is that men are disposed, as a rule and on the average, to increase their consumption as their income increases, but not by as much as the increase in their income.' That is, when a person earns an extra unit of income – a euro or a pound – he typically spends some of it and saves some of it. As we saw in Chapter 11 when we developed the Keynesian cross, the marginal propensity to consume was crucial to Keynes's policy recommendations for how to reduce widespread unemployment. The power of fiscal policy to influence the economy – as expressed by the fiscal-policy multipliers – arises from the feedback between income and consumption.

Second, Keynes posited that the ratio of consumption to income, called the **average propensity to consume**, falls as income rises. He believed that saving was a luxury, so he expected the rich to save a higher proportion of their income than the poor. Although not essential for Keynes's own analysis, the postulate that the average propensity to consume falls as income rises became a central part of early Keynesian economics.

Third, Keynes thought that income is the primary determinant of consumption and that the interest rate does not have an important role. This conjecture stood in stark contrast to the beliefs of the classical economists who preceded him. The classical economists held that a higher interest rate encourages saving and discourages consumption. Keynes admitted that the interest rate could influence consumption as a matter of theory. Yet he wrote: 'the main conclusion suggested by experience, I think, is that the short-period influence of the rate of interest on individual spending out of a given income is secondary and relatively unimportant.'

On the basis of these three conjectures, the Keynesian consumption function is often written as

$$C = \overline{C} + cY, \quad \overline{C} > 0, \quad 0 < c < 1,$$

where C is consumption, Y is disposable income, $\overline{C}$ is a constant and c is the marginal propensity to consume. This consumption function, shown in Figure 18-1, is graphed as a straight line. $\overline{C}$ determines the intercept on the vertical axis, and c determines the slope.

Notice that this consumption function exhibits the three properties that Keynes posited. It satisfies Keynes's first property because the marginal propensity to consume c is between zero and one, so that higher income leads to higher consumption and also to higher saving. This consumption function satisfies Keynes's second property because the average propensity to consume, APC, is

$$APC = C/Y = \overline{C}/Y + c.$$

As Y rises, $\overline{C}/Y$ falls, so the average propensity to consume C/Y falls. Finally, this consumption function satisfies Keynes's third property because the interest rate is not included in this equation as a determinant of consumption.

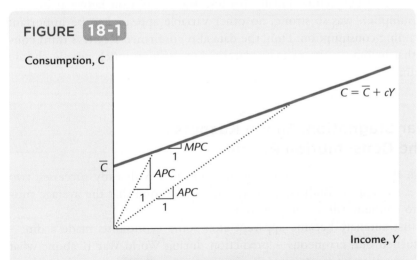

FIGURE 18-1

The Keynesian Consumption Function This figure graphs a consumption function with the three properties that Keynes conjectured. First, the marginal propensity to consume c is between zero and one. Second, the average propensity to consume falls as income rises. Third, consumption is determined by current income.

Note: The marginal propensity to consume, *MPC*, is the slope of the consumption function. The average propensity to consume, *APC* = *C/Y*, equals the slope of a line drawn from the origin to a point on the consumption function.

The Early Empirical Successes

Soon after Keynes proposed the consumption function, economists began collecting and examining data to test his conjectures. The earliest studies indicated that the Keynesian consumption function is a good approximation of how consumers behave.

In some of these studies, researchers surveyed households and collected data on consumption and income. They found that households with higher income consumed more, which confirms that the marginal propensity to consume is greater than zero. They also found that households with higher income saved more, which confirms that the marginal propensity to consume is less than one. In addition, these researchers found that higher-income households saved a larger fraction of their income, which confirms that the average propensity to consume falls as income rises. Thus, these data verified Keynes's conjectures about the marginal and average propensities to consume.

In other studies, researchers examined aggregate data on consumption and income for the period between the two world wars for the US and the UK. These data also supported the Keynesian consumption function. In years when income was unusually low, such as during the depths of the Great Depression, both consumption and saving were low, indicating that the marginal propensity to consume is between zero and one. In addition, during those years of low income, the ratio of consumption to income was high, confirming Keynes's second conjecture. Finally, because the correlation between income and consumption was so strong, no other variable appeared to be important for explaining consumption. Thus, the data also confirmed Keynes's third conjecture that income is the primary determinant of how much people choose to consume.

Secular Stagnation, Simon Kuznets and the Consumption Puzzle

Although the Keynesian consumption function met with early successes, two anomalies soon arose. Both concern Keynes's conjecture that the average propensity to consume falls as income rises.

The first anomaly became apparent after some economists made a dire — and, it turned out, erroneous — prediction during World War II about what would happen to aggregate economic activity in the major industrialized economies after the war. On the basis of the Keynesian consumption function, these economists reasoned that, as incomes in the economy grew over time, households would consume an increasingly smaller proportion of their incomes. They feared that there might not be enough profitable investment projects to absorb all this saving. If so, the low consumption would lead to an inadequate demand for goods and services, resulting in a depression once the wartime demand from the government ceased. In other words, on the basis of the Keynesian consumption function, these economists predicted that the mature economies would experience what they called *secular stagnation* – a long depression of indefinite duration – unless the government used fiscal policy to expand aggregate demand.

Fortunately for the global economy, but unfortunately for the Keynesian consumption function, the years following the end of World War II did not see the advanced economies sinking into another major depression. Although incomes in the post-war period were much higher than before the war, these higher incomes did not lead to large increases in the rate of saving. Keynes's conjecture that the average propensity to consume would fall as income rose appeared not to hold.

The second anomaly arose when economist Simon Kuznets constructed new aggregate data on US consumption and income dating back to 1869. Kuznets assembled these data in the 1940s and would later receive the Nobel Prize for this work. He discovered that the ratio of consumption to income was remarkably stable from decade to decade, despite large increases in income over the period he studied. Again, Keynes's conjecture that the average propensity to consume would fall as income rose appeared not to hold.

The failure of the secular-stagnation hypothesis and the findings of Kuznets both indicated that the average propensity to consume is fairly constant over long periods of time in advanced economies. This fact presented a puzzle that motivated much of the subsequent research on consumption. Economists wanted to know why some studies confirmed Keynes's conjectures and others refuted them. That is, why did Keynes's conjectures hold up well in the studies of household data and in the studies of short time-series, but fail when long time-series were examined?

Figure 18-2 illustrates the puzzle. The evidence suggested that there were two consumption functions. For the household data or for the short time-series, the

FIGURE 18-2

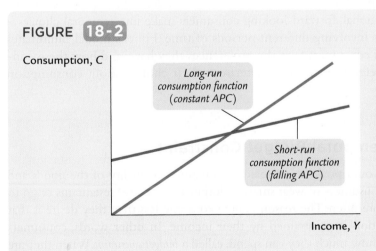

The Consumption Puzzle Studies of household data and short time-series found a relationship between consumption and income similar to the one Keynes conjectured. In the figure, this relationship is called the short-run consumption function. But studies of long time-series found that the average propensity to consume did not vary systematically with income. This relationship is called the long-run consumption function. Notice that the short-run consumption function has a falling average propensity to consume, whereas the long-run consumption function has a constant average propensity to consume.

Keynesian consumption function appeared to work well. Yet for the long time-series, the consumption function appeared to have a constant average propensity to consume. In Figure 18-2, these two relationships between consumption and income are called the short-run and long-run consumption functions. Economists needed to explain how these two consumption functions could be consistent with each other.

In the 1950s, Franco Modigliani and Milton Friedman each proposed explanations of these seemingly contradictory findings. Both economists later won Nobel Prizes, in part because of their work on consumption. But before we see how Modigliani and Friedman tried to solve the consumption puzzle, we must discuss Irving Fisher's contribution to consumption theory. Both Modigliani's life-cycle hypothesis and Friedman's permanent-income hypothesis rely on the theory of consumer behaviour proposed much earlier by Irving Fisher.

18-2 Irving Fisher and Intertemporal Choice

The consumption function introduced by Keynes relates current consumption to current income. This relationship, however, is at best incomplete. When people decide how much to consume and how much to save, they consider both the present and the future. The more consumption they enjoy today, the less they will be able to enjoy tomorrow. In making this trade-off, households must look ahead to the income they expect to receive in the future, and to the consumption of goods and services they hope to be able to afford.

The economist Irving Fisher developed the model with which economists analyse how rational, forward-looking consumers make intertemporal choices – that is, choices involving different periods of time. Fisher's model illuminates the constraints consumers face, the preferences they have, and how these constraints and preferences together determine their choices about consumption and saving.

The Intertemporal Budget Constraint

Most people would prefer to increase the quantity or quality of the goods and services they consume – to wear smarter clothes, eat at better restaurants or go to the cinema more often. The reason people consume less than they desire is that their consumption is constrained by their income. In other words, consumers face a limit on how much they can spend, called a *budget constraint*. When they are deciding how much to consume today versus how much to save for the future, they face an **intertemporal budget constraint**, which measures the total resources available for consumption today and in the future. Our first step in developing Fisher's model is to examine this constraint in some detail.

To keep things simple, we examine the decision facing a consumer who lives during two periods. Period one represents the consumer's youth, and period two represents the consumer's old age. The consumer earns income Y_1 and consumes C_1 in period one, and earns income Y_2 and consumes C_2 in period two. (All variables are real — that is, adjusted for inflation.) Because the consumer has the opportunity to borrow and save, consumption in any single period can be either greater or less than income in that period.

Consider how the consumer's income in the two periods constrains consumption in the two periods. In the first period, saving equals income minus consumption. That is,

$$S = Y_1 - C_1,$$

where S is saving. In the second period, consumption equals the accumulated saving, including the interest earned on that saving, plus second-period income. That is,

$$C_2 = (1 + r)S + Y_2,$$

where r is the real interest rate. For example, if the real interest rate is 5 per cent, then for every €1 of saving in period one, the consumer enjoys an extra €1.05 of consumption in period two. Because there is no third period, the consumer does not save in the second period.

Note that the variable S can represent either saving or borrowing and that these equations hold in both cases. If first-period consumption is less than first-period income, the consumer is saving, and S is greater than zero. If first-period consumption exceeds first-period income, the consumer is borrowing, and S is less than zero. For simplicity, we assume that the interest rate for borrowing is the same as the interest rate for saving.

To derive the consumer's budget constraint, combine the two preceding equations. Substitute the first equation for S into the second equation to obtain

$$C_2 = (1 + r)(Y_1 + C_1) + Y_2.$$

To make the equation easier to interpret, we must rearrange terms. To place all the consumption terms together, bring $(1 + r)C_1$ from the right-hand side to the left-hand side of the equation to obtain

$$(1 + r)C_1 + C_2 = (1 + r)Y_1 + Y_2.$$

Now divide both sides by $1 + r$ to obtain

$$C_1 + \frac{C_2}{1 + r} = Y_1 + \frac{Y_2}{1 + r}.$$

This equation relates consumption in the two periods to income in the two periods. It is the standard way of expressing the consumer's intertemporal budget constraint.

The consumer's budget constraint is easily interpreted. If the interest rate is zero, the budget constraint shows that total consumption in the two periods equals total income in the two periods. In the usual case in which

FIGURE 18-3

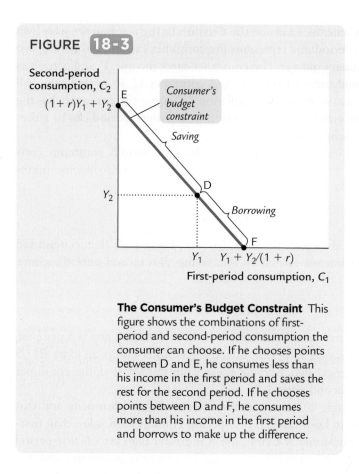

The Consumer's Budget Constraint This figure shows the combinations of first-period and second-period consumption the consumer can choose. If he chooses points between D and E, he consumes less than his income in the first period and saves the rest for the second period. If he chooses points between D and F, he consumes more than his income in the first period and borrows to make up the difference.

the interest rate is greater than zero, future consumption and future income are discounted by a factor $1 + r$. This **discounting** arises from the interest earned on savings. In essence, because the consumer earns interest on current income that is saved, future income is worth less than current income. Similarly, because future consumption is paid for out of savings that have earned interest, future consumption costs less than current consumption. The factor $1/(1 + r)$ is the price of second-period consumption measured in terms of first-period consumption: it is the amount of first-period consumption that the consumer must forgo to obtain one unit of second-period consumption.

Figure 18-3 graphs the consumer's budget constraint. Three points are marked on this figure. At point D, the consumer consumes exactly his income in each period ($C_1 = Y_1$ and $C_2 = Y_2$), so there is neither saving nor borrowing between the two periods. At point E, the consumer consumes nothing in the first period ($C_1 = 0$) and saves all income, so second-period consumption C_2 is $(1 + r)Y_1 + Y_2$. At point F, the consumer plans to consume nothing in the second period ($C_2 = 0$) and borrows as much as possible against second-period income, so first-period consumption C_1 is $Y_1 + Y_2/(1 + r)$. Of course, these are only three of the many combinations of first- and second-period consumption that the consumer can afford: all the points on the line from E to F are available to the consumer.

FYI

Present Value, or Why European Lottery Prizes Are Worth More than US Lottery Prizes

The use of discounting in the consumer's budget constraint illustrates an important fact of economic life: cash in the future is less valuable than cash today. This is true because €1 today can be deposited in an interest-bearing bank account and produce more than €1 in the future. If the interest rate is 5 per cent, for instance, then €1 today can be turned to €1.05 next year, €1.1025 in two years', €1.1576 in three years' – or €2.65 in 20 years' time.

Economists use a concept called *present value* to compare amounts of money from different times. The present value of any amount in the future is the amount that would be needed today, given available interest rates, to produce that future amount. Thus, if you are going to be paid X euros in T years and the interest rate is r, the present value of that payment is

Present Value = $X/(1 + r)^T$.

In light of this definition, we can see a new interpretation of the consumer's budget constraint in our two-period consumption problem. The intertemporal budget constraint states that the present value of consumption must equal the present value of income.

The concept of present value has many applications. Here is one of them: the value of a lottery prize.

The EuroMillions lottery is a pan-European lottery operated by the British firm Camelot. In February 2006, after 11 successive rollovers (weeks in which no one won the top prize and it was rolled over and added to the following week's top prize), one Portuguese and two French lottery winners picked the right numbers and shared a jackpot of €183 million. The

operators of the lottery, Camelot, claimed at the time that this was the biggest lottery prize ever paid out anywhere in the world.

However, many bigger lottery prizes had apparently been recorded in the United States. For example, in July 2004, the US Mega Millions lottery awarded a jackpot prize of $294 million to a single winner, Geraldine Williams of Lowell, Massachusetts. The dollar–euro exchange rate at that time was about 1.24 dollars per euro, so $294 million was equivalent to about €237. So was that not a bigger payout than the EuroMillions payout of €183 million?

The answer lies in compounding. In Europe, lottery prizes are generally paid as a lump-sum prize. In the US, however, they are paid out over time. For example, if you won a $1 million prize in a US lottery, you would not receive $1 million, but, say, $50,000 a year for 20 years. What is the present value of such a delayed prize? By applying the above formula for each of the 20 payments and adding up the result, we learn that the $1 million prize, discounted at an interest rate of 5 per cent, has a present value of only $623,000. (If the prize were paid out as a dollar a year for a million years, the present value would be a mere $20!) If a US lottery winner wants all the prize money now as a lump sum, they have to accept the present value of the delayed prize.

In fact, Mega Millions Lottery winner Ms Williams did opt for a lump-sum cash payment (as most US lottery winners do) and received a 'mere' $168 million (about €135.5 million) – somewhat less than the EuroMillions payout of €183 million (although at least she did not have to share her prize with two other winners).[1]

---

[1] Ms Williams did, however, have to pay tax on her prize, whereas lottery prizes are exempt from tax in the UK and most other European countries. After tax, her lump-sum prize was further reduced to $117.6 million, or about €94.8 million – less than half the announced value of the prize of $294 (or €237) million.

Consumer Preferences

The consumer's preferences regarding consumption in the two periods can be represented by **indifference curves**. An indifference curve shows the combinations of first-period and second-period consumption that make the consumer equally happy.

Figure 18-4 shows two of the consumer's many indifference curves. The consumer is indifferent among combinations W, X and Y, because they are all on the same curve. Not surprisingly, if the consumer's first-period consumption is reduced, say from point W to point X, second-period consumption must increase to keep him equally happy. If first-period consumption is reduced again, from point X to point Y, the amount of extra second-period consumption he requires for compensation is greater.

The slope at any point on the indifference curve shows how much second-period consumption the consumer requires in order to be compensated for a one-unit reduction in first-period consumption. This slope is the **marginal rate of substitution** between first-period consumption and second-period consumption. It tells us the rate at which the consumer is willing to substitute second-period consumption for first-period consumption.

Notice that the indifference curves in Figure 18-4 are not straight lines and, as a result, the marginal rate of substitution depends on the levels of consumption in the two periods. When first-period consumption is high and second-period

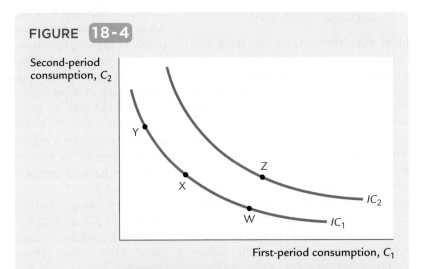

FIGURE 18-4

Second-period consumption, C_2

First-period consumption, C_1

The Consumer's Preferences Indifference curves represent the consumer's preferences over first-period and second-period consumption. An indifference curve gives the combinations of consumption in the two periods that make the consumer equally happy. This figure shows two of many indifference curves. Higher indifference curves such as IC_2 are preferred to lower curves such as IC_1. The consumer is equally happy at points W, X and Y, but prefers point Z to points W, X or Y.

consumption is low, as at point W, the marginal rate of substitution is low: the consumer requires only a little extra second-period consumption to give up one unit of first-period consumption. When first-period consumption is low and second-period consumption is high, as at point Y, the marginal rate of substitution is high: the consumer requires much additional second-period consumption to give up one unit of first-period consumption.

The consumer is equally happy at all points on a given indifference curve, but he prefers some indifference curves to others. Because he prefers more consumption to less, he prefers higher indifference curves to lower ones. In Figure 18-4, the consumer prefers any of the points on curve IC_2 to any of the points on curve IC_1.

The set of indifference curves gives a complete ranking of the consumer's preferences. It tells us that the consumer prefers point Z to point W, but that may be obvious because point Z has more consumption in both periods. Yet compare point Z and point Y: point Z has more consumption in period one and less in period two. Which is preferred – Z or Y? Because Z is on a higher indifference curve than Y, we know that the consumer prefers point Z to point Y. Hence we can use the set of indifference curves to rank any combinations of first-period and second-period consumption.

Optimization

Having discussed the consumer's budget constraint and preferences, we can consider the decision about how much to consume in each period of time. The consumer would like to end up with the best possible combination of consumption in the two periods – that is, on the highest possible indifference curve. But the budget constraint requires that the consumer also ends up on or below the budget line, because the budget line measures the total resources available to him.

Figure 18-5 shows that many indifference curves cross the budget line. The highest indifference curve that the consumer can obtain without violating the budget constraint is the indifference curve that barely touches the budget line, which is curve IC_3 in Figure 18-5. The point at which the curve and line touch – point O for 'optimum' – is the best combination of consumption in the two periods that the consumer can afford.

Notice that, at the optimum, the slope of the indifference curve equals the slope of the budget line. The indifference curve is *tangent* to the budget line. The slope of the indifference curve is the marginal rate of substitution *MRS*, and the slope of the budget line is 1 plus the real interest rate. We conclude that at point O

$$MRS = 1 + r.$$

The consumer chooses consumption in the two periods so that the marginal rate of substitution equals 1 plus the real interest rate.

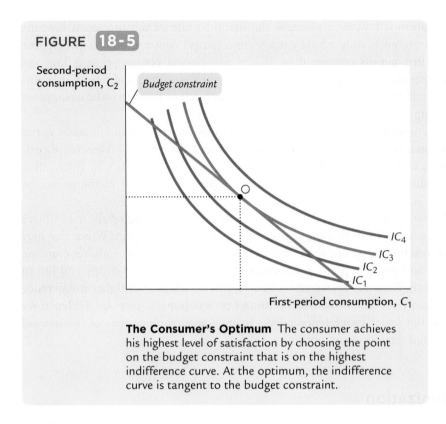

FIGURE 18-5

The Consumer's Optimum The consumer achieves his highest level of satisfaction by choosing the point on the budget constraint that is on the highest indifference curve. At the optimum, the indifference curve is tangent to the budget constraint.

How Changes in Income Affect Consumption

Now that we have seen how the consumer makes the consumption decision, let's examine how consumption responds to an increase in income. An increase in either Y_1 or Y_2 shifts the budget constraint outward, as in Figure 18-6. The higher budget constraint allows the consumer to choose a better combination of first- and second-period consumption – that is, the consumer can now reach a higher indifference curve.

In Figure 18-6, the consumer responds to the shift in his budget constraint by choosing more consumption in both periods. Although it is not implied by the logic of the model alone, this situation is the most usual. Since the utility of an additional unit of consumption is decreasing in both periods, starting from an initial optimum, it will usually not be optimal to increase consumption in just one period by the full increase in lifetime income. If a consumer wants more of a good when his or her income rises, economists call it a **normal good**. The indifference curves in Figure 18-6 are drawn under the assumption that consumption in period one and consumption in period two are both normal goods.

The key conclusion from Figure 18-6 is that, regardless of whether the increase in income occurs in the first period or the second period, the consumer spreads it over consumption in both periods. This behaviour is sometimes called *consumption smoothing*. Because the consumer can borrow and lend between periods, the timing of the income is irrelevant to how much is consumed today

FIGURE 18-6

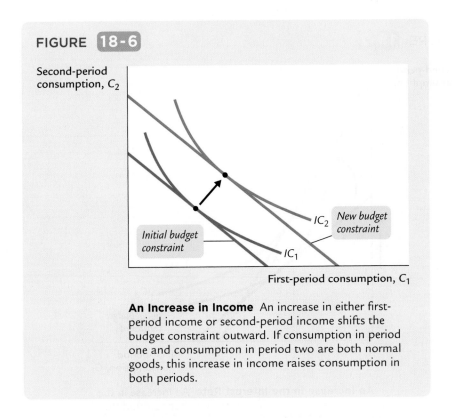

An Increase in Income An increase in either first-period income or second-period income shifts the budget constraint outward. If consumption in period one and consumption in period two are both normal goods, this increase in income raises consumption in both periods.

(except that future income is discounted by the interest rate). The lesson of this analysis is that consumption depends on the present value of current and future income, which can be written as

$$\text{Present Value of Income} = Y_1 + \frac{Y_2}{1 + r}.$$

Notice that this conclusion is quite different from that reached by Keynes. *Keynes posited that a person's current consumption depends largely on his current income. Fisher's model says, instead, that consumption is based on the income the consumer expects over his entire lifetime.*

How Changes in the Real Interest Rate Affect Consumption

Let's now use Fisher's model to consider how a change in the real interest rate alters the consumer's choices. There are two cases to consider: the case in which the consumer is initially saving and the case in which he is initially borrowing. Here we discuss the saving case; Problem 1 at the end of the chapter asks you to analyse the borrowing case.

Figure 18-7 shows that an increase in the real interest rate rotates the consumer's budget line around the point (Y_1, Y_2) and, thereby, alters the amount of consumption he chooses in both periods. Here, the consumer moves from point A

FIGURE 18-7

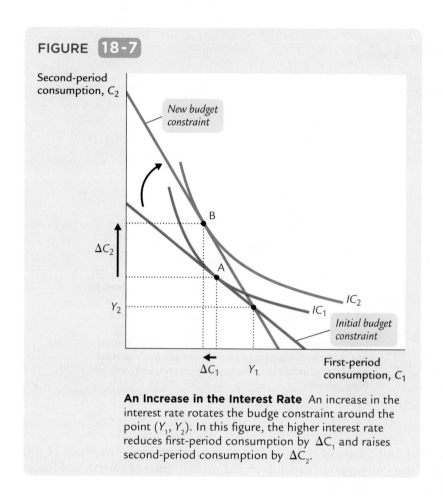

An Increase in the Interest Rate An increase in the interest rate rotates the budge constraint around the point (Y_1, Y_2). In this figure, the higher interest rate reduces first-period consumption by ΔC_1 and raises second-period consumption by ΔC_2.

to point B. You can see that for the indifference curves drawn in this figure, first-period consumption falls and second-period consumption rises.

Economists decompose the impact of an increase in the real interest rate on consumption into two effects: an **income effect** and a **substitution effect**. Textbooks in microeconomics discuss these effects in detail. We summarize them briefly here.

The *income effect* is the change in consumption that results from the movement to a higher indifference curve. Because the consumer is a saver rather than a borrower (as indicated by the fact that first-period consumption is less than first-period income), the increase in the interest rate makes him better off (as reflected by the movement to a higher indifference curve). If consumption in period one and consumption in period two are both normal goods, the consumer will want to spread this improvement in his welfare over both periods. This income effect tends to make the consumer want more consumption in both periods.

The *substitution effect* is the change in consumption that results from the change in the relative price of consumption in the two periods. In particular, consumption in period two becomes less expensive relative to consumption in period one when the interest rate rises. That is, because the real interest rate earned on saving is higher, the consumer must now give up less first-period consumption to obtain an extra unit of second-period consumption. This substitution effect tends to make the consumer choose more consumption in period two and less consumption in period one.

The consumer's choice depends on both the income effect and the substitution effect. Because both effects act to increase the amount of second-period consumption, we can conclude that an increase in the real interest rate raises second-period consumption. But the two effects have opposite impacts on first-period consumption, so the increase in the interest rate could either lower or raise it. *Hence, depending on the relative size of income and substitution effects, an increase in the interest rate could either stimulate or depress saving.*

Constraints on Borrowing

Fisher's model assumes that the consumer can borrow as well as save. The ability to borrow allows current consumption to exceed current income. In essence, when the consumer borrows, he consumes some of his future income today. Yet for many people such borrowing is impossible. For example, a student wishing to enjoy a summer holiday in St Tropez would probably be unable to finance this holiday with a bank loan. Let's examine how Fisher's analysis changes if the consumer cannot borrow.

The inability to borrow prevents current consumption from exceeding current income. A constraint on borrowing can therefore be expressed as

'What I'd like, basically, is a temporary line of credit just to tide me over the rest of my life.'

$$C_1 \leq Y_1.$$

This inequality states that consumption in period one must be less than or equal to income in period one. This additional constraint on the consumer is called a **borrowing constraint** or, sometimes, a *liquidity constraint*.

Figure 18-8 shows how this borrowing constraint restricts the consumer's set of choices. The consumer's choice must satisfy both the intertemporal budget constraint and the borrowing constraint. The shaded area represents the combinations of first-period consumption and second-period consumption that satisfy both constraints.

Figure 18-9 shows how this borrowing constraint affects the consumption decision. There are two possibilities. In panel (a), the consumer wishes to consume less in period one than he earns. The borrowing constraint is not binding and, therefore, does not affect consumption. In panel (b), the consumer would like to choose point D, where he consumes more in period one than he earns, but the borrowing constraint prevents this outcome. The best the consumer can do is to consume his first-period income, represented by point E.

The analysis of borrowing constraints leads us to conclude that there are two consumption functions. For some consumers, the borrowing constraint is not binding, and consumption in both periods depends on the present value of lifetime income, $Y_1 + [Y_2/(1 + r)]$. For other consumers, the borrowing constraint binds, and the consumption function is $C_1 = Y_1$ and $C_2 = Y_2$. *Hence, for those consumers who would like to borrow but cannot, consumption depends only on current income.*

FIGURE 18-8

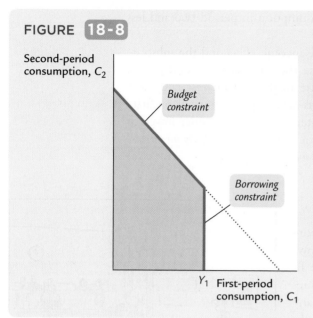

Second-period consumption, C_2

Budget constraint

Borrowing constraint

Y_1 First-period consumption, C_1

A Borrowing Constraint If the consumer cannot borrow, he faces the additional constraint that first-period consumption cannot exceed first-period income. The shaded area represents the combination of first-period and second-period consumption the consumer can choose.

FIGURE 18-9

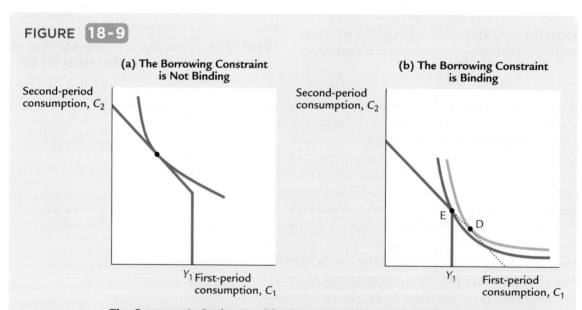

(a) The Borrowing Constraint is Not Binding

Second-period consumption, C_2

Y_1 First-period consumption, C_1

(b) The Borrowing Constraint is Binding

Second-period consumption, C_2

E

D

Y_1 First-period consumption, C_1

The Consumer's Optimum with a Borrowing Constraint When the consumer faces a borrowing constraint, there are two possible situations. In panel (a), the consumer chooses first-period consumption to be less than first-period income, so the borrowing constraint is not binding and does not affect consumption in either period. In panel (b), the borrowing constraint is binding. The consumer would like to borrow and choose point D. But because borrowing is not allowed, the best available choice is point E. When the borrowing constraint is binding, first-period consumption equals first-period income.

The High Japanese Saving Rate

In Figure 18-10 we have graphed national savings rates for Europe, Japan and the United States since the 1980s. As the figure reflects, historically, Japan has had one of the world's highest saving rates. In 2011, for example, the savings rate in Japan, at around 22.5 per cent of national income, was more than double the US savings rate of 11.7 per cent. Over the last few decades the Japanese savings rate has declined from being more than 1.5 times the European level to being only 1.1 times the European level in 2011.

The high Japanese saving rate is important for understanding both the long-run and short-run performance of its economy. On the one hand, many economists believe that the high Japanese saving rate is a key to the rapid growth Japan experienced in the decades after World War II. The Solow growth model developed in Chapters 8 and 9 shows that the saving rate is a primary determinant of a country's steady-state level of income. On the other hand, some economists have argued that the high Japanese saving rate contributed to Japan's slump during the 1990s. High saving means low consumer spending, which, according to the *IS-LM* model of Chapters 11 and 12, translates into low aggregate demand and reduced income.

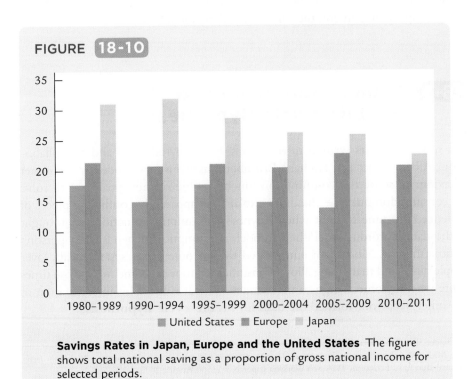

FIGURE 18-10

Savings Rates in Japan, Europe and the United States The figure shows total national saving as a proportion of gross national income for selected periods.

Source: OECD, IMF, Eurostat.
Note: The European savings rate was constructed using figures for the following countries: Austria, Belgium, Switzerland, Germany, Denmark, Spain, Finland, France, Greece, Ireland, Italy, Netherlands, Norway, Portugal, Sweden and the United Kingdom.

Why have the Japanese consumed a much smaller fraction of their income than Europeans or Americans? One reason is that it is harder for households to borrow in Japan.[2] For example, in Europe or the US, it is not uncommon to borrow 90 or even 95 per cent of the purchase price of a house or a flat, whereas Japanese households will typically find it difficult to borrow more than 60 per cent of the purchase price, and so will have to save longer to get a bigger deposit if they want to buy a home. In addition, property prices are on average much higher in Japan than in the US and Europe, requiring even higher saving for potential homebuyers.

As Fisher's model shows, a household facing a binding borrowing constraint consumes less than it would without the borrowing constraint. Hence, societies in which borrowing constraints are common will tend to have higher rates of saving.

Although constraints on borrowing are part of the explanation of high Japanese saving, there are many other differences between Japan and Europe and the United States that contribute to the difference in the saving rates. The Japanese tax system encourages saving by taxing capital income very lightly. In addition, cultural differences may lead to differences in consumer preferences regarding present and future consumption.

Although the rate of investment in Japan has also been very high, it has generally not been as high as the saving rate, so that the Japanese economy has typically experienced trade surpluses (since net exports must be equal to saving minus investments, $NX = S - I$) and capital outflows (since if savings are not being mopped up by investment, the funds must flow abroad). ∎

18-3 Franco Modigliani and the Life-Cycle Hypothesis

In a series of papers written in the 1950s, Franco Modigliani and his collaborators, Albert Ando and Richard Brumberg, used Fisher's model of consumer behaviour to study the consumption function. One of their goals was to solve the consumption puzzle – that is, to explain the apparently conflicting pieces of evidence that came to light when Keynes's consumption function was brought to the data. According to Fisher's model, consumption depends on a person's lifetime income. Modigliani emphasized that income varies systematically over people's lives and that saving allows consumers to move income from those times in life when income is high to those times when it is low. This interpretation of consumer behaviour formed the basis for his **life–cycle hypothesis**.[3]

---

[2] See Midori Wakabayashi and Charles Yuji Horioka, *Borrowing Constraints and Consumption Behavior in Japan*, National Bureau of Economic Research Working paper No. 11560, August 2005.

[3] For references to the large body of work on the life-cycle hypothesis, a good place to start is the lecture Modigliani gave when he won the Nobel Prize. Franco Modigliani, 'Life Cycle, Individual Thrift, and the Wealth of Nations', *American Economic Review*, June 1986, vol. 76, pp. 297–313. For an example of more recent research in this tradition, see Pierre-Olivier Gourinchas and Jonathan A. Parker, 'Consumption over the Life Cycle', *Econometrica*, January 2002, vol. 70, pp. 47–89.

The Hypothesis

One important reason that income varies over a person's life is retirement. Most people plan to stop working at about age 65, and they expect their incomes to fall when they retire. Yet they do not want a large drop in their standard of living, as measured by their consumption. To maintain their level of consumption after retirement, people must save during their working years. Let's see what this motive for saving implies for the consumption function.

Consider a consumer who expects to live another T years, has wealth W and expects to earn income Y until she retires R years from now. What level of consumption will the consumer choose if she wishes to maintain a smooth level of consumption over her life?

The consumer's lifetime resources are composed of initial wealth W and lifetime earnings of $R \times Y$. (For simplicity, we are assuming an interest rate of zero; if the interest rate were greater than zero, we would need to take into account the interest earned on savings as well.) The consumer can divide up her lifetime resources among her T remaining years of life. We assume that she wishes to achieve the smoothest possible path of consumption over her lifetime. Therefore, she divides this total of $W + RY$ equally among the T years and each year consumes

$$C = (W + RY)/T.$$

We can write this person's consumption function as

$$C = (1/T)W + (R/T)Y.$$

For example, if the consumer expects to live for 50 more years and work for 30 of them, then $T = 50$ and $R = 30$, so her consumption function is

$$C = 0.02W + 0.6Y.$$

This equation says that consumption depends on both income and wealth. An extra €1 of income per year raises consumption by €0.60 per year, and an extra €1 of wealth raises consumption by €0.02 per year.

If every individual in the economy plans consumption like this, then the aggregate consumption function is much the same as the individual one. In particular, aggregate consumption depends on both wealth and income. That is, the economy's consumption function is

$$C = \alpha W + \beta Y,$$

where the parameter α is the marginal propensity to consume out of wealth, and the parameter β is the marginal propensity to consume out of income.

Implications

Figure 18-11 graphs the relationship between consumption and income predicted by the life-cycle model. For any given level of wealth W, the model yields a conventional consumption function similar to the one shown in Figure 18-1. Notice, however, that the intercept of the consumption function, which shows

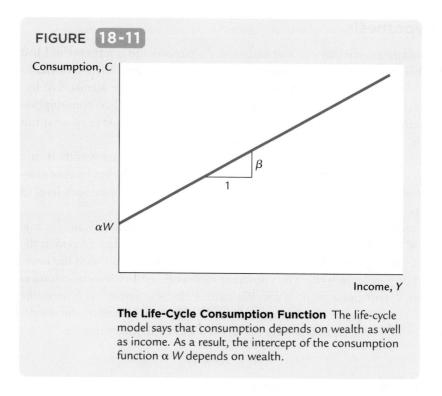

FIGURE 18-11

The Life-Cycle Consumption Function The life-cycle model says that consumption depends on wealth as well as income. As a result, the intercept of the consumption function α *W* depends on wealth.

what would happen to consumption if income ever fell to zero, is not a fixed value, as it is in Figure 18-1. Instead, the intercept here is α*W,* and thus depends on the level of wealth.

This life-cycle model of consumer behaviour can solve the consumption puzzle. According to the life-cycle consumption function, the average propensity to consume is

$$C/Y = \alpha(W/Y) + \beta.$$

Because wealth does not vary proportionately with income from person to person or from year to year, we should find that high income corresponds to a low average propensity to consume when looking at data across individuals or over short periods of time. Over long periods of time, however, wealth and income grow together, resulting in a constant ratio W/Y, and thus a constant average propensity to consume.

To make the same point somewhat differently, consider how the consumption function changes over time. As Figure 18-11 shows, for any given level of wealth, the life-cycle consumption function looks like the one Keynes suggested. But this function holds only in the short run when wealth is constant. In the long run, as wealth increases, the consumption function shifts upward, as in Figure 18-12. This upward shift prevents the average propensity to consume from falling as income increases. In this way, Modigliani resolved the consumption puzzle posed by Simon Kuznets's data.

The life-cycle model makes many other predictions as well. Most importantly, it predicts that saving varies over a person's lifetime. If a person begins adulthood

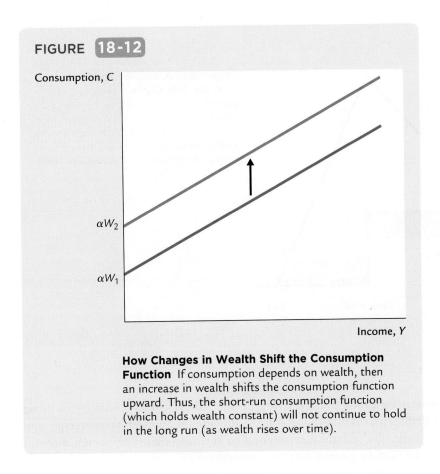

FIGURE 18-12

How Changes in Wealth Shift the Consumption Function If consumption depends on wealth, then an increase in wealth shifts the consumption function upward. Thus, the short-run consumption function (which holds wealth constant) will not continue to hold in the long run (as wealth rises over time).

with no wealth, she will accumulate wealth during her working years and then run down her wealth during her retirement years. Figure 18-13 illustrates the consumer's income, consumption and wealth over her adult life. According to the life-cycle hypothesis, because people want to smooth consumption over their lives, the young who are working save, while the old who are retired dissave (i.e. spend more than they earn).

CASE STUDY

The Consumption and Saving of the Elderly

Many economists have studied the consumption and saving of the elderly. Their findings present a problem for the life-cycle model. It appears that the elderly do not dissave as much as the model predicts. In other words, the elderly do not run down their wealth as quickly as one would expect if they were trying to smooth their consumption over their remaining years of life.

There are two chief explanations for why the elderly do not dissave to the extent that the model predicts. Each suggests a direction for further research on consumption.

The first explanation is that the elderly are concerned about unpredictable expenses. Additional saving that arises from uncertainty is called **precautionary saving**.

FIGURE 18-13

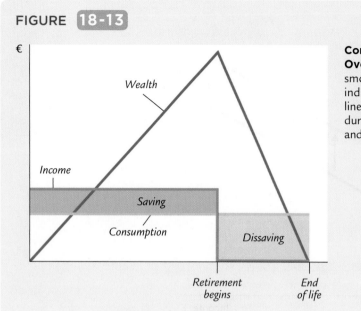

€

Wealth

Income

Saving

Consumption

Dissaving

Retirement
begins

End
of life

Consumption, Income and Wealth Over the Life Cycle If the consumer smooths consumption over her life (as indicated by the horizontal consumption line), she will save and accumulate wealth during her working years and then dissave and run down her wealth during retirement.

One reason for precautionary saving by the elderly is the possibility of living longer than expected and thus having to provide for a longer-than-average span of retirement. The elderly may respond to this uncertainty by saving more in order to be better prepared for these contingencies.

The precautionary-saving explanation is not completely persuasive, because the elderly can largely insure against these risks. To protect against uncertainty regarding lifespan, they can buy *annuities* from insurance companies. For a fixed fee, annuities offer a stream of income that lasts as long as the recipient lives.

The second explanation for the failure of the elderly to dissave is that they may want to leave bequests to their children. Economists have proposed various theories of the parent–child relationship and the bequest motive. In Chapter 16 we discussed some of these theories and their implications for consumption and fiscal policy.

Overall, research on the elderly suggests that the simplest life-cycle model cannot fully explain consumer behaviour. There is no doubt that providing for retirement is an important motive for saving, but other motives, such as precautionary saving and bequests, appear to be important as well.[4] ∎

---

[4] To read more about the consumption and saving of the elderly, see Albert Ando and Arthur Kennickell, 'How Much (or Little) Life Cycle Saving Is There in Micro Data?', in Rudiger Dornbusch, Stanley Fischer and John Bossons, eds, *Macroeconomics and Finance: Essays in Honor of Franco Modigliani*, Cambridge, MA: The MIT Press, 1986, pp. 159–228.; and Michael Hurd, 'Research on the Elderly: Economic Status, Retirement, and Consumption and Saving', *Journal of Economic Literature*, June 1990, vol. 28, pp. 565–589.

18-4 Milton Friedman and the Permanent-Income Hypothesis

In a book published in 1957, Milton Friedman proposed the permanent-income hypothesis to explain consumer behaviour. Friedman's **permanent-income hypothesis** complements Modigliani's life-cycle hypothesis: both use Irving Fisher's theory of the consumer to argue that consumption should not depend on current income alone. Unlike the life-cycle hypothesis, however, which emphasizes that income follows a regular pattern over a person's lifetime, the permanent-income hypothesis emphasizes that people experience random and temporary changes in their incomes from year to year.[5]

The Hypothesis

Friedman suggested that we view current income Y as the sum of two components, **permanent income** Y^P and **transitory income** Y^T. That is,

$$Y = Y^P + Y^T.$$

Permanent income is the part of income that people expect to persist into the future. Transitory income is the part of income that people do not expect to persist. Put differently, permanent income is average income, and transitory income is the random deviation from that average.

To see how we might separate income into these two parts, consider these examples:

- Maria, who has a law degree, earned more this year than John, who left school with no qualifications. Maria's higher income resulted from higher permanent income, because her education will continue to provide her with a higher salary.

- Vito, an Italian olive grower, earned less than usual this year because freak bad weather destroyed much of his crop. George, a Greek olive grower, earned more than usual because the bad Italian weather drove up the price of European olives. George's higher income resulted from higher transitory income, because he is no more likely than Vito to have good weather next year.

These examples show that different forms of income have different degrees of persistence. A good education provides a permanently higher income, whereas good weather provides only transitorily higher income. Although one can imagine intermediate cases, it is useful to keep things simple by supposing that there are only two kinds of income: permanent and transitory.

Friedman reasoned that consumption should depend primarily on permanent income, because consumers use saving and borrowing to smooth

---

[5] Milton Friedman, *A Theory of the Consumption Function*, Princeton, NJ: Princeton University Press, 1957.

consumption in response to transitory changes in income. For example, if a person received a permanent raise of €10,000 per year, his consumption would rise by about as much. Yet if a person won a lump-sum prize of €10,000 in a lottery, he would not consume the full amount in one year. Instead, he would spread the extra consumption over the rest of his life. Assuming an interest rate of zero and a remaining lifespan of 50 years, consumption would rise by only €200 per year in response to the €10,000 prize. Thus, consumers spend their permanent income, but they save rather than spend most of their transitory income. Friedman concluded that we should view the consumption function as approximately

$$C = \alpha\, Y^{P},$$

where α is a constant that measures the fraction of permanent income consumed. The permanent-income hypothesis, as expressed by this equation, states that consumption is proportional to permanent income.

Implications

The permanent-income hypothesis solves the consumption puzzle by suggesting that the standard Keynesian consumption function uses the wrong variable. According to the permanent-income hypothesis, consumption depends on permanent income Y^{P}; yet many studies of the consumption function try to relate consumption to current income Y. Friedman argued that this *errors-in-variables problem* explains the seemingly contradictory findings.

Let's see what Friedman's hypothesis implies for the average propensity to consume. Divide both sides of his consumption function by Y to obtain

$$APC = C/Y = \alpha\, Y^{P}/Y.$$

According to the permanent-income hypothesis, the average propensity to consume depends on the ratio of permanent income to current income. When current income temporarily rises above permanent income, the average propensity to consume temporarily falls; when current income temporarily falls below permanent income, the average propensity to consume temporarily rises.

Now consider the studies of household data. Friedman reasoned that these data reflect a combination of permanent and transitory income. Households with high permanent income have proportionately higher consumption. If all variation in current income came from the permanent component, the average propensity to consume would be the same in all households. But some of the variation in income comes from the transitory component, and households with high transitory income do not have higher consumption. Therefore, researchers find that high-income households have, on average, lower average propensities to consume.

Similarly, consider the studies of time-series data. Friedman reasoned that year-to-year fluctuations in income are dominated by transitory income.

Therefore, years of high income should be years of low average propensities to consume. But over long periods of time – say, from decade to decade – the variation in income comes from the permanent component. Hence, in long time-series, one should observe a constant average propensity to consume, as in fact Kuznets found.

The Contrasting Effects of Permanent and Temporary Tax Changes

The permanent-income hypothesis can help us to interpret how the economy responds to changes in fiscal policy. According to the *IS-LM* model of Chapters 11 and 12, tax cuts stimulate consumption and raise aggregate demand, and tax increases depress consumption and reduce aggregate demand. The permanent-income hypothesis, however, predicts that consumption responds only to changes in permanent income. Therefore, transitory changes in taxes will have only a negligible effect on consumption and aggregate demand. If a change in taxes is to have a large effect on aggregate demand, it must be permanent.

Is this what we observe in the real world? Unfortunately, tax changes that are announced as temporary are rare in the real world, so the hypothesis that temporary or transitory changes in taxes will have relatively small effects is hard to test. However, something like this did occur in the US in the 1960s, when a permanent tax cut was followed within a few years by a temporary tax rise.

In 1964, the US government announced a major and permanent reduction in tax rates. As we discussed in Chapter 11, this policy change had the intended effect of stimulating the economy.

Four years later, however, in 1968, the government decided to raise taxes. At that time, the US was heavily engaged in the Vietnam War, and the government's economic advisors believed that the resulting increase in government spending had stimulated aggregate demand excessively. To offset this effect, they recommended a tax increase. But President Johnson, aware that the Vietnam War was already unpopular, feared the political repercussions of higher taxes. He finally agreed to a temporary tax surcharge – in essence, a one-year increase in taxes. The tax surcharge did not have the desired effect of reducing aggregate demand. US unemployment continued to fall and inflation continued to rise. This is precisely what the permanent income hypothesis would lead us to predict: the tax increase only affected transitory income, so consumption behaviour and aggregate demand were not greatly affected.

The lesson to be learned from these episodes is that a full analysis of tax policy must go beyond the simple Keynesian consumption function; it must take into account the distinction between permanent and transitory income. If consumers expect a tax change to be temporary, it will have a smaller impact on consumption and aggregate demand. ■

18-5 Robert Hall and the Random-Walk Hypothesis

The permanent-income hypothesis is based on Fisher's model of intertemporal choice. It builds on the idea that forward-looking consumers base their consumption decisions not only on their current income, but also on the income they expect to receive in the future. Thus, the permanent-income hypothesis highlights that consumption depends on people's expectations.

Recent research on consumption has combined this view of the consumer with the assumption of rational expectations. The rational-expectations assumption states that people use all available information to make optimal forecasts about the future. As we saw in Chapter 14, this assumption can have profound implications for the costs of stopping inflation. It can also have profound implications for the study of consumer behaviour.

The Hypothesis

The economist Robert Hall was the first to derive the implications of rational expectations for consumption. He showed that if the permanent-income hypothesis is correct, and if consumers have rational expectations, then changes in consumption over time should be unpredictable. When changes in a variable are unpredictable, the variable is said to follow a **random walk**. According to Hall, the combination of the permanent-income hypothesis and rational expectations implies that consumption follows a random walk.

Hall reasoned as follows. According to the permanent-income hypothesis, consumers face fluctuating income and try their best to smooth their consumption over time. At any moment, consumers choose consumption based on their current expectations of their lifetime incomes. Over time, they change their consumption because they receive news that causes them to revise their expectations. For example, a person getting an unexpected promotion increases consumption, whereas a person getting an unexpected demotion decreases consumption. In other words, changes in consumption reflect 'surprises' about lifetime income. If consumers are optimally using all available information, then they should be surprised only by events that were entirely unpredictable. Therefore, changes in their consumption should be unpredictable as well.[6]

Implications

The rational-expectations approach to consumption has implications not only for forecasting, but also for the analysis of economic policies. *If consumers obey the permanent-income hypothesis and have rational expectations, then only unexpected policy changes influence consumption. These policy changes take effect when they change expectations.*

---

[6] Robert E. Hall, 'Stochastic Implications of the Life Cycle-Permanent Income Hypothesis: Theory and Evidence', *Journal of Political Economy*, April 1978, vol. 86, pp. 971–987.

For example, suppose that today the government passes a tax increase to be effective next year. In this case, consumers receive the news about their lifetime incomes when the government passes the law (or even earlier if the law's passage was predictable). The arrival of this news causes consumers to revise their expectations and reduce their consumption. The following year, when the tax hike goes into effect, consumption is unchanged because no news has arrived.

Hence, if consumers have rational expectations, policy makers influence the economy not only through their actions, but also through the public's expectation of their actions. Expectations, however, cannot be observed directly. Therefore, it is often hard to know how and when changes in fiscal policy alter aggregate demand.

CASE STUDY

Do Predictable Changes in Income Lead to Predictable Changes in Consumption?

Of the many facts about consumer behaviour, one is impossible to dispute: income and consumption fluctuate together over the business cycle. When the economy goes into a recession, both income and consumption fall, and when the economy booms, both income and consumption rise rapidly.

By itself, this fact does not say much about the rational-expectations version of the permanent-income hypothesis. Most short-run fluctuations are unpredictable. Thus, when the economy goes into a recession, the typical consumer is receiving bad news about his lifetime income, so consumption naturally falls. And when the economy booms, the typical consumer is receiving good news, so consumption rises. This behaviour does not necessarily violate the random-walk theory that changes in consumption are impossible to forecast.

Yet suppose we could identify some *predictable* changes in income. According to the random-walk theory, these changes in income should not cause consumers to revise their spending plans. If consumers expected income to rise or fall, they should have adjusted their consumption already in response to that information. Thus, predictable changes in income should not lead to predictable changes in consumption.

Data on consumption and income, however, appear not to satisfy this implication of the random-walk theory. When income is expected to fall by €1, consumption will on average fall at the same time by about €0.50. In other words, predictable changes in income lead to predictable changes in consumption of roughly half the amount.

Why is this so? One possible explanation of this behaviour is that some consumers may fail to have rational expectations. Instead, they may base their expectations of future income excessively on current income. Thus, when income rises or falls (even predictably), they act as if they received news about their lifetime resources and change their consumption accordingly. Another possible explanation is that some consumers are borrowing-constrained and, therefore, base their consumption on current income alone. Regardless of which explanation is correct, Keynes's original consumption function starts to look more attractive. That is, current income has a larger role in determining consumer spending than the random-walk hypothesis suggests.[7] ■

18-6 David Laibson and the Pull of Instant Gratification

Keynes called the consumption function a 'fundamental psychological law'. Yet, as we have seen, psychology has played little role in the subsequent study of consumption. Most economists assume that consumers are rational maximizers of utility, who are always evaluating their opportunities and plans in order to obtain the highest lifetime satisfaction. This model of human behaviour was the basis for all the work on consumption theory, from Irving Fisher to Robert Hall.

More recently, economists have started to return to psychology. They have suggested that consumption decisions are not made by the ultra-rational *homo economicus,* but by real human beings whose behaviour can be far from rational. This new subfield infusing psychology into economics is called *behavioural economics.* The most prominent behavioural economist studying consumption is Harvard professor David Laibson.

Laibson notes that many consumers judge themselves to be imperfect decision makers. In one survey of the American public, 76 per cent said they were not saving enough for retirement. In another survey of the baby-boom generation, respondents were asked the percentage of income that they save and the percentage that they thought they should save. The saving shortfall averaged 11 percentage points.

According to Laibson, the insufficiency of saving is related to another phenomenon: the pull of instant gratification. Consider the following two questions:

- Question 1: Would you prefer (A) a chocolate bar today or (B) two chocolate bars tomorrow?

- Question 2: Would you prefer (A) a chocolate bar in 100 days or (B) two chocolate bars in 101 days?

Many people confronted with such choices will answer A to the first question and B to the second. In a sense, they are more patient in the long run than they are in the short run.

This raises the possibility that consumers' preferences may be *time-inconsistent:* they may alter their decisions simply because time passes. A person confronting

---

[7] John Y. Campbell and N. Gregory Mankiw, 'Consumption, Income, and Interest Rates: Reinterpreting the Time-Series Evidence', *NBER Macroeconomics Annual,* 1989, pp. 185–216; Jonathan Parker, 'The Response of Household Consumption to Predictable Changes in Social Security Taxes', *American Economic Review,* September 1999, vol. 89, pp. 959–973; Nicholas S. Souleles, 'The Response of Household Consumption to Income Tax Refunds', *American Economic Review,* September 1999, vol. 89, pp. 947–958.

question 2 may choose B and wait the extra day for the extra chocolate bar. But after 100 days pass, he finds himself in a new short run, confronting question 1. The pull of instant gratification may induce him to change his mind.

We see this kind of behaviour in many situations in life. A person on a diet may have a second helping at dinner, while promising himself that he will eat less tomorrow. A person may smoke one more cigarette, while promising herself that this is the last one. And a consumer may splurge at the shopping centre, while promising himself that tomorrow he will cut back his spending and start saving more for retirement. But when tomorrow arrives, the promises are in the past, and a new self takes control of the decision making, with its own desire for instant gratification.

These observations raise as many questions as they answer. Will the renewed focus on psychology among economists offer a better understanding of consumer behaviour? Will it offer new and better prescriptions regarding tax policy towards saving, for instance? It is too early to give a full evaluation, but, without doubt, these questions are at the forefront of the research agenda.[8]

CASE STUDY

How to Encourage People to Save More: A Proposal from the Field of Behavioural Economics

Many economists believe that it would be desirable for people to increase the fraction of their income that they save. There are several reasons for this conclusion. From a microeconomic perspective, greater saving would mean that people would be better prepared for retirement; this goal is especially important, since a 'pension crisis' is projected in many countries, whereby the state pension scheme will run into financial difficulties as the population ages. From a macroeconomic perspective, greater saving would increase the supply of loanable funds available to finance investment; the Solow growth model shows that increased capital accumulation leads to higher income. From an open-economy perspective, greater saving would mean that less domestic investment would be financed by capital flows from abroad; a smaller capital inflow pushes the trade balance from deficit towards surplus.

The difficult issue is how to get people to save more. The burgeoning field of behavioural economics offers some answers. For example, one intriguing possibility is the 'Save More Tomorrow' scheme proposed by behavioural economist Richard Thaler, which is designed to give people the opportunity to control their desires for instant gratification. The essence of this scheme is that people commit in advance to putting a portion of their future salary increases into a retirement savings account. When a worker signs up, he or she makes no sacrifice

---

[8] For more on this topic, see David Laibson, 'Golden Eggs and Hyperbolic Discounting', *Quarterly Journal of Economics*, May 1997, vol. 62, pp. 443–477; George-Marios Angeletos, David Laibson, Andrea Repetto, Jeremy Tobacman and Stephen Weinberg, 'The Hyperbolic Buffer Stock Model: Calibration, Simulation, and Empirical Evidence', *Journal of Economic Perspectives*, summer 2001, vol. 15, pp. 47–68.

of lower consumption today, but instead commits to reducing consumption growth in the future.

When this plan was implemented in several firms in the US, it had a significant impact. A high proportion (78 per cent) of those offered the plan joined. In addition, of those enrolled, the vast majority (80 per cent) stayed with the programme through at least the fourth annual pay raise. The average saving rates for those in the programme increased from 3.5 per cent to 13.6 per cent over the course of 40 months.

How successful would more widespread applications of these ideas be in increasing national saving rates? It is impossible to say for sure, but given the importance of saving to both personal and national economic prosperity, many economists believe these proposals are worth a try.[9] ■

18-7 Conclusion

In the work of six prominent economists, we have seen a progression of views on consumer behaviour. Keynes proposed that consumption depends largely on current income.

$$\text{Consumption} = f\,(\text{Current Income}).$$

Since then, economists have argued that consumers understand that they face an intertemporal decision. Consumers look ahead to their future resources and needs, implying a more complex consumption function than the one that Keynes proposed.

$$\text{Consumption} = f\,(\text{Current Income, Wealth, Expected}$$
$$\text{Future Income, Interest Rates}).$$

He suggested a consumption function of the form. In other words, current income is only one determinant of aggregate consumption.

Economists continue to debate the importance of these determinants of consumption. There remains disagreement, for example, about the influence of interest rates on consumer spending, the prevalence of borrowing constraints, and the importance of psychological effects. Economists sometimes disagree about economic policy because they assume different consumption functions. For instance, as we saw in Chapter 16, the debate over the effects of government debt is in part a debate over the determinants of consumer spending. The key role of consumption in policy evaluation is certain to sustain economists' interest in studying consumer behaviour for many years to come.

---

[9] James J. Choi, David I. Laibson, Brigitte Madrian and Andrew Metrick, 'Defined Contribution Pensions: Plan Rules, Participant Decisions, and the Path of Least Resistance', in James Poterba, ed., *Tax Policy and the Economy*, vol. 16, 2002, pp. 67–113; Richard H. Thaler and Shlomo Benartzi, 'Save More Tomorrow: Using Behavioral Economics to Increase Employee Saving', *Journal of Political Economy*, 2004, vol. 112, pp. S164–S187.

Summary

1. Keynes conjectured that the marginal propensity to consume is between zero and one, that the average propensity to consume falls as income rises, and that current income is the primary determinant of consumption. Studies of household data and short time-series confirmed Keynes's conjectures. Yet studies of long time-series found no tendency for the average propensity to consume to fall as income rises over time.

2. Recent work on consumption builds on Irving Fisher's model of the consumer. In this model, the consumer faces an intertemporal budget constraint and chooses consumption for the present and the future to achieve the highest level of lifetime satisfaction. As long as the consumer can save and borrow, consumption depends on the consumer's lifetime resources.

3. Modigliani's life-cycle hypothesis emphasizes that income varies somewhat predictably over a person's life and that consumers use saving and borrowing to smooth their consumption over their lifetimes. According to this hypothesis, consumption depends on both income and wealth.

4. Friedman's permanent-income hypothesis emphasizes that individuals experience both permanent and transitory fluctuations in their income. Because consumers can save and borrow, and because they want to smooth their consumption, consumption does not respond much to transitory income. Consumption depends primarily on permanent income.

5. Hall's random-walk hypothesis combines the permanent-income hypothesis with the assumption that consumers have rational expectations about future income. It implies that changes in consumption are unpredictable, because consumers change their consumption only when they receive news about their lifetime resources.

6. Laibson has suggested that psychological effects are important for understanding consumer behaviour. In particular, because people have a strong desire for instant gratification, they may exhibit time-inconsistent behaviour and may end up saving less than they would like.

KEY CONCEPTS

Marginal propensity to consume	Normal good	Permanent-income hypothesis
Average propensity to consume	Income effect	Permanent income
Intertemporal budget constraint	Substitution effect	Transitory income
Discounting	Borrowing constraint	Random walk
Indifference curves	Life-cycle hypothesis	
Marginal rate of substitution	Precautionary saving	

QUESTIONS FOR REVIEW

1. What were Keynes's three conjectures about the consumption function?

2. Describe the evidence that was consistent with Keynes's conjectures and the evidence that was inconsistent with them.

3. How do the life-cycle and permanent-income hypotheses resolve the seemingly contradictory pieces of evidence regarding consumption behaviour?

4. Use Fisher's model of consumption to analyse an increase in second-period income. Compare the case in which the consumer faces a binding borrowing constraint and the case in which he does not.

5. Explain why changes in consumption are unpredictable if consumers obey the permanent-income hypothesis and have rational expectations.

6. Give an example in which someone might exhibit time-inconsistent preferences.

PROBLEMS AND APPLICATIONS

1. This chapter uses the Fisher model to discuss a change in the interest rate for a consumer who saves some of his first-period income. Suppose, instead, that the consumer is a borrower. How does that alter the analysis? Discuss the income and substitution effects on consumption in both periods.

2. Jack and Jill both obey the two-period Fisher model of consumption. Jack earns €100 in the first period and €100 in the second period. Jill earns nothing in the first period and €210 in the second period. Both of them can borrow or lend at the interest rate r.

   a. You observe both Jack and Jill consuming €100 in the first period and €100 in the second period. What is the interest rate r?

   b. Suppose the interest rate increases. What will happen to Jack's consumption in the first period? Is Jack better off or worse off than before the interest rate rise?

   c. What will happen to Jill's consumption in the first period when the interest rate increases? Is Jill better off or worse off than before the interest rate increase?

3. The chapter analyses Fisher's model for the case in which the consumer can save or borrow at an interest rate of r, and for the case in which the consumer can save at this rate but cannot borrow at all. Consider now the intermediate case in which the consumer can save at rate r_s and borrow at rate r_b, where $r_s < r_b$.

   a. What is the consumer's budget constraint in the case in which he consumes less than his income in period one?

   b. What is the consumer's budget constraint when he consumes more than his income in period one?

   c. Graph the two budget constraints and shade the area that represents the combination of first-period and second-period consumption the consumer can choose.

   d. Now add to your graph the consumer's indifference curves. Show three possible outcomes: one in which the consumer saves, one in which he borrows, and one in which he neither saves nor borrows.

   e. What determines first-period consumption in each of the three cases?

4. Explain whether borrowing constraints increase or decrease the potency of fiscal policy to influence aggregate demand in each of the following cases:

   a. A temporary tax cut.

   b. An announced future tax cut.

5. In the discussion of the life-cycle hypothesis in the text, income is assumed to be constant during the period before retirement. For most people, however, income grows over their lifetime. How does this growth in income influence the lifetime pattern of consumption and

wealth accumulation shown in Figure 18-13 under the following conditions?

a. Consumers can borrow, so their wealth can be negative.

b. Consumers face borrowing constraints that prevent their wealth from falling below zero.

Do you consider case (a) or case (b) to be more realistic? Why?

6. In many European countries, demographers predict that the proportion of the population that is elderly will increase significantly over the next 20 years. What does the life-cycle model predict for the influence of this demographic change on the national saving rate?

7. One study found that the elderly who do not have children dissave at about the same rate as the elderly who do have children. What might this finding imply about the reason the elderly do not dissave as much as the life-cycle model predicts?

8. Consider two savings accounts that pay the same interest rate. One account lets you take your money out on demand. The second requires that you give 30 days' advance notification before withdrawals. Which account would you prefer? Why? Can you imagine a person who might make the opposite choice? What do these choices say about the theory of the consumption function?

CHAPTER 19

Investment

The social object of skilled investment should be to defeat the dark forces of time and ignorance which envelop our future.

— *John Maynard Keynes*

While spending on consumption goods provides utility to households today, spending on investment goods is aimed at providing a higher standard of living at a later date. Investment is the component of GDP that links the present and the future.

Investment spending plays a key role not only in long-run growth, but also in the short-run business cycle, because it is the most volatile component of GDP. When expenditure on goods and services falls during a recession, much of the decline is usually due to a drop in investment. In the severe UK recession of 2008–2009, for example, real GDP fell by almost £24 billion from its peak in the first quarter of 2008 to the trough in the third quarter of 2009. Investment spending fell by just over £26 billion, accounting for more than the entire fall in spending.

Economists study investment to understand better the fluctuations in the economy's output of goods and services. The models of GDP we saw in previous chapters, such as the *IS-LM* model in Chapters 11 and 12, were based on a simple investment function relating investment to the real interest rate: $I = I(r)$. That function states that an increase in the real interest rate reduces investment. In this chapter we look more closely at the theory behind this investment function.

There are three types of investment spending. **Business fixed investment** includes the equipment and structures that businesses buy to use in production. **Residential investment** includes the new housing that people buy to live in and that landlords buy to rent out. **Inventory investment** includes those goods that businesses put aside in storage, including materials and supplies, work in process and finished goods. Figure 19-1 illustrates total investment and its three components in the UK over the last ten years. You can see that all types of investment fell during the 2008-2009 recession.

In this chapter we build models of each type of investment to explain these fluctuations. The models will shed light on the following questions:

- Why is investment negatively related to the interest rate?
- What causes the investment function to shift?
- Why does investment rise during booms and fall during recessions?

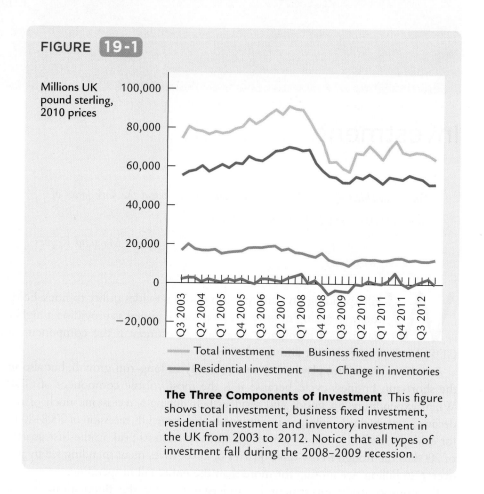

FIGURE 19-1

The Three Components of Investment This figure shows total investment, business fixed investment, residential investment and inventory investment in the UK from 2003 to 2012. Notice that all types of investment fall during the 2008–2009 recession.

At the end of the chapter, we return to these questions and summarize the answers that the models offer.

19-1 Business Fixed Investment

The largest piece of investment spending, accounting for about three-quarters of the total, is business fixed investment. The term 'business' means that these investment goods are bought by firms for use in future production. The term 'fixed' means that this spending is for capital that will stay put for a while, as opposed to inventory investment, which will be used or sold within a short time. Business fixed investment includes everything from fax machines to factories, computers to company cars.

The standard model of business fixed investment is called the **neoclassical model of investment**. The neoclassical model examines the benefits and costs to firms of owning capital goods. The model shows how the level of investment – the addition to the stock of capital – is related to the marginal product of capital, the interest rate and the tax rules affecting firms.

To develop the model, imagine that there are two kinds of firms in the economy. *Production firms* produce goods and services using capital that they rent. *Rental firms* make all the investments in the economy; they buy capital and rent it out to the production firms. Most firms in the real world perform both functions: they produce goods and services, and they invest in capital for future production. We can simplify our analysis and clarify our thinking, however, if we separate these two activities by imagining that they take place in different firms.

The Rental Price of Capital

Let's first consider the typical production firm. As we discussed in Chapter 3, this firm decides how much capital to rent by comparing the cost and benefit of each unit of capital. The firm rents capital at a rental rate R and sells its output at a price P; the real cost to the production firm of renting one unit of capital for one period is R/P. The real benefit of a unit of capital is the marginal product of capital MPK – the extra output produced with one more unit of capital. The marginal product of capital declines as the amount of capital rises: the more capital the firm has, the less an additional unit of capital will add to its output. Chapter 3 concluded that, to maximize profit, the firm rents capital until the marginal product of capital falls to equal the real rental price.

Figure 19-2 shows the equilibrium in the rental market for capital. For the reasons just discussed, the marginal product of capital determines the demand

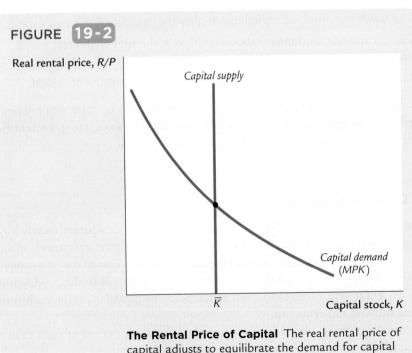

FIGURE 19-2

The Rental Price of Capital The real rental price of capital adjusts to equilibrate the demand for capital (determined by the marginal product of capital) and the fixed supply.

curve. The demand curve slopes downward because the marginal product of capital is low when the level of capital is high. At any point in time, the amount of capital in the economy is fixed, so the supply curve is vertical. The real rental price of capital adjusts to equilibrate supply and demand.

To see what variables influence the equilibrium rental price, let's consider a particular production function. As we saw in Chapter 3, many economists consider the Cobb–Douglas production function a good approximation of how the actual economy turns capital and labour into goods and services. The Cobb–Douglas production function is

$$Y = AK^\alpha L^{1-\alpha},$$

where Y is output, K is capital, L is labour, A is a parameter measuring the level of technology and α is a parameter between zero and one that measures capital's share of output. The marginal product of capital for the Cobb–Douglas production function is

$$MPK = \alpha A(L/K)^{1-\alpha}.$$

Because the real rental price R/P equals the marginal product of capital in equilibrium, we can write

$$R/P = \alpha A(L/K)^{1-\alpha}.$$

This expression identifies the variables that determine the real rental price. It shows the following:

- The lower the stock of capital, the higher the real rental price of capital.
- The greater the amount of labour employed, the higher the real rental price of capital.
- The better the technology, the higher the real rental price of capital.

Events that reduce the capital stock (e.g. an earthquake), or raise employment (an expansion in aggregate demand), or improve the technology (e.g. a scientific discovery), raise the equilibrium real rental price of capital.

The Cost of Capital

Next consider the rental firms. These firms, such as car-rental companies, merely buy capital goods and rent them out. Because our goal is to explain the investments made by the rental firms, we begin by considering the benefit and cost of owning capital.

The benefit of owning capital is the revenue from renting it to the production firms. The rental firm receives the real rental price of capital R/P for each unit of capital it owns and rents out.

The cost of owning capital is more complex. For each period of time that it rents out a unit of capital, the rental firm bears three costs:

1. When a rental firm borrows to buy a unit of capital, which it intends to rent out, it must pay interest on the loan. If P_K is the purchase price of a

unit of capital and i is the nominal interest rate, then iP_K is the interest cost. Notice that this interest cost would be the same even if the rental firm did not have to borrow: if the rental firm buys a unit of capital using cash on hand, it loses out on the interest it could have earned by depositing this cash in the bank. In either case, the interest cost equals iP_K.

2. While the rental firm is renting out the capital, the price of capital can change. If the price of capital falls, the firm loses, because the firm's asset has fallen in value. If the price of capital rises, the firm gains, because the firm's asset has risen in value. The cost of this loss or gain is $-\Delta P_K$. (The minus sign is here because we are measuring costs, not benefits.)

3. While the capital is rented out, it suffers wear and tear, called **depreciation**. If δ is the rate of depreciation – the fraction of capital's value lost per period because of wear and tear – then the cost of depreciation is δP_K.

The total cost of renting out a unit of capital for one period is therefore

$$\text{Cost of Capital} = iP_K - \Delta P_K + \delta P_K$$
$$= P_K(i - \Delta P_K/P_K + \delta).$$

The cost of capital depends on the price of capital, the interest rate, the rate at which capital prices are changing and the depreciation rate.

For example, consider the cost of capital to a car-rental company. The company buys cars for €10,000 each and rents them out to other businesses. The company faces an interest rate i of 10 per cent per year, so the interest cost iP_K is €1000 per year for each car the company owns. Car prices are rising at 6 per cent per year, so, excluding wear and tear, the firm gets a capital gain ΔP_K of €600 per year. Cars depreciate at 20 per cent per year, so the loss due to wear and tear δP_K is €2000 per year. Therefore, the company's cost of capital is

$$\text{Cost of Capital} = €1000 - €600 + €2000$$
$$= €2400.$$

The cost to the car-rental company of keeping a car in its capital stock is €2400 per year.

To make the expression for the cost of capital simpler and easier to interpret, we assume that the price of capital goods rises with the prices of other goods. In this case, $\Delta P_K/P_K$ equals the overall rate of inflation π. Because $i - \pi$ equals the real interest rate r, we can write the cost of capital as

$$\text{Cost of Capital} = P_K(r + \delta).$$

This equation states that the cost of capital depends on the price of capital, the real interest rate and the depreciation rate.

Finally, we want to express the cost of capital relative to other goods in the economy. The **real cost of capital** – the cost of buying and renting out a unit of capital measured in units of the economy's output – is

$$\text{Real Cost of Capital} = (P_K/P)(r + \delta).$$

This equation states that the real cost of capital depends on the relative price of a capital good P_K/P, the real interest rate r and the depreciation rate δ.

The Determinants of Investment

Now consider a rental firm's decision about whether to increase or decrease its capital stock. For each unit of capital, the firm earns real revenue R/P and bears the real cost $(P_K/P)(r + \delta)$. The real profit per unit of capital is

$$\text{Profit Rate} = \text{Revenue} - \text{Cost}$$
$$= R/P - (P_K/P)(r + \delta).$$

Because the real rental price in equilibrium equals the marginal product of capital, we can write the profit rate as

$$\text{Profit Rate} = MPK - (P_K/P)(r + \delta).$$

The rental firm makes a profit if the marginal product of capital is greater than the cost of capital. It incurs a loss if the marginal product is less than the cost of capital.

We can now see the economic incentives that lie behind the rental firm's investment decision. The firm's decision regarding its capital stock – that is, whether to add to it or to let it depreciate – depends on whether owning and renting out capital is profitable. The change in the capital stock, called **net investment**, depends on the difference between the marginal product of capital and the cost of capital. *If the marginal product of capital exceeds the cost of capital, firms find it profitable to add to their capital stock. If the marginal product of capital falls short of the cost of capital, they let their capital stock shrink.*

We can also see now that the separation of economic activity between production and rental firms, although useful for clarifying our thinking, is not necessary for our conclusion regarding how firms choose how much to invest. For a firm that both uses and owns capital, the benefit of an extra unit of capital is the marginal product of capital, and the cost is the cost of capital. Like a firm that owns and rents out capital, this firm adds to its capital stock if the marginal product exceeds the cost of capital. Thus, we can write

$$\Delta K = I_n[MPK - (P_K/P)(r + \delta)],$$

where $I_n(\ )$ is the function showing how much net investment responds to the incentive to invest.

We can now derive the investment function. Total spending on business fixed investment is the sum of net investment and the replacement of depreciated capital. The investment function is

$$I = I_n[MPK - (P_K/P)(r + \delta)] + \delta K.$$

Business fixed investment depends on the marginal product of capital, the cost of capital and the amount of depreciation.

This model shows why investment depends on the interest rate. A decrease in the real interest rate lowers the cost of capital. It therefore raises the amount of profit from owning capital and increases the incentive to accumulate more capital. Similarly, an increase in the real interest rate raises the cost of capital and leads firms to reduce their investment. For this reason, the investment schedule relating investment to the interest rate slopes downward, as in panel (a) of Figure 19-3.

The model also shows what causes the investment schedule to shift. Any event that raises the marginal product of capital increases the profitability of investment and causes the investment schedule to shift outward, as in panel (b) of Figure 19-3. For example, a technological innovation that increases the production function parameter A raises the marginal product of capital and, for any given interest rate, increases the amount of capital goods that rental firms wish to buy.

Finally, consider what happens as this adjustment of the capital stock continues over time. If the marginal product begins above the cost of capital, the capital stock will rise and the marginal product will fall. If the marginal product of capital begins below the cost of capital, the capital stock will fall and the marginal product will rise. Eventually, as the capital stock adjusts, the marginal product of capital approaches the cost of capital. When the capital stock reaches a steady-state level, we can write

$$MPK = (P_K/P)(r + \delta).$$

Thus, in the long run, the marginal product of capital equals the real cost of capital. The speed of adjustment towards the steady state depends on how quickly

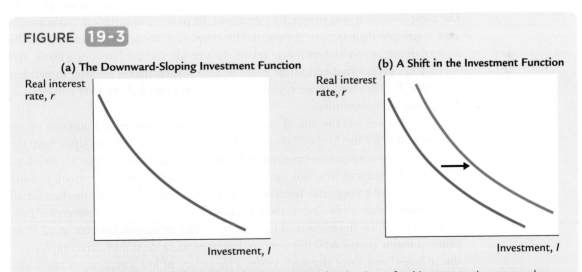

FIGURE 19-3

(a) The Downward-Sloping Investment Function

Real interest rate, r

Investment, I

(b) A Shift in the Investment Function

Real interest rate, r

Investment, I

The Investment Function Panel (a) shows that business fixed investment increases when the interest rate falls. This is because a lower interest rate reduces the cost of capital and therefore makes owning capital more profitable. Panel (b) shows an outward shift in the investment function, which might be due to an increase in the marginal product of capital.

firms adjust their capital stock, which in turn depends on how costly it is to build, deliver and install new capital.[1]

Taxes and Investment

Tax laws influence firms' incentives to accumulate capital in many ways. Sometimes policy makers change the tax system to shift the investment function and influence aggregate demand. Two ways in which governments can do this is through the corporate income tax (also known as corporation tax) and investment tax breaks.

Corporation tax is a tax on corporate profits. The effect of corporation tax on investment depends on how the law defines 'profit' for the purpose of taxation. Suppose, first, that the law defined profit as we did previously – the rental price of capital minus the cost of capital. In this case, even though firms would be sharing a fraction of their profits with the government, it would still be rational for them to invest if the rental price of capital exceeded the cost of capital, and to disinvest if the rental price fell short of the cost of capital. A tax on profit, measured in this way, would not alter investment incentives.

Yet, because of the way profit is defined in the tax law of most countries, corporation tax does affect investment decisions. There are many differences between the typical definition of profit in tax law and our definition. For example, one difference is the treatment of depreciation. Our definition of profit deducts the *current* value of depreciation as a cost. That is, it bases depreciation on how much it would cost today to replace worn-out capital. By contrast, under the corporate tax laws of European and North American countries, firms deduct depreciation using *historical* cost. That is, the depreciation deduction is based on the price of the capital when it was originally purchased. In periods of inflation, replacement cost is greater than historical cost, so the corporate tax tends to understate the cost of depreciation and overstate profit. As a result, the tax law sees a profit and levies a tax even when economic profit is zero, which makes owning capital less attractive. For this and other reasons, many economists believe that corporation tax discourages investment.

Figure 19-4 shows the rate of corporation tax for a number of European countries as well as for the United States and Japan in 2013. The US and Japan have the highest rates of corporation tax (just under 40 per cent), although they are followed closely by France and Belgium (just below 35 per cent). Austria, Denmark and the Netherlands have corporate income tax rates of 25 per cent – the median for all the countries in the table – while the UK rate of corporation tax is 23 per cent. At the bottom end of the figure, Ireland has the lowest rate of corporation tax, at 12.5 per cent – a major reason why this country has been so successful in attracting foreign direct investment since the mid-1990s. This policy of low corporation tax is also

---

[1] Economists often measure capital goods in units such that the price of one unit of capital equals the price of one unit of other goods and services ($P_K = P$). This was the approach taken implicitly in Chapters 7 and 8, for example. In this case, the steady-state condition says that the marginal product of capital net of depreciation, $MPK - \delta$, equals the real interest rate r.

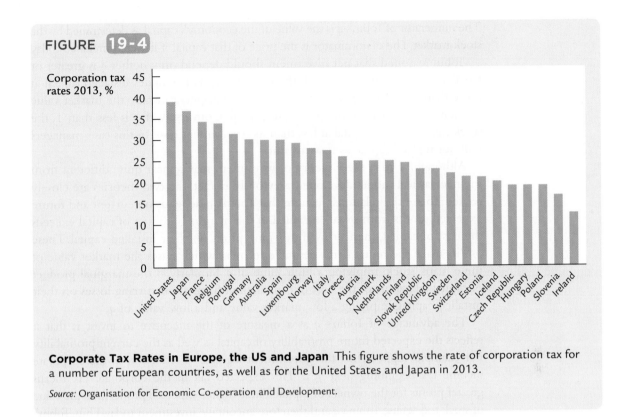

Corporate Tax Rates in Europe, the US and Japan This figure shows the rate of corporation tax for a number of European countries, as well as for the United States and Japan in 2013.

Source: Organisation for Economic Co-operation and Development.

followed by the European Union accession countries of Czech Republic, Hungary, Poland and Slovenia (all with rates below 20 per cent).

Policy makers often change the rules governing corporation tax in an attempt to encourage investment, or at least mitigate the disincentive the tax provides. One example is the **investment tax credit**, a tax provision that reduces a firm's taxes by a certain amount for each euro spent on capital goods. Because a firm recoups part of its expenditure on new capital in lower taxes, the credit reduces the effective purchase price of a unit of capital P_K. Thus, the investment tax credit reduces the cost of capital and raises investment.

The Stock Market and Tobin's *q*

Many economists see a link between fluctuations in investment and fluctuations in the stock market. The term **stock** refers to the shares in the ownership of corporations, and the **stock market** is the market in which these shares are traded. Stock prices tend to be high when firms have opportunities for profitable investment, because these profit opportunities mean higher future income for the shareholders. Thus, stock prices reflect the incentives to invest.

The Nobel Prize-winning economist James Tobin proposed that firms base their investment decisions on the following ratio, which is now called **Tobin's *q***:

$$q = \frac{\text{Market Value of Installed Capital}}{\text{Replacement Cost of Installed Capital}}.$$

The numerator of Tobin's q is the value of the economy's capital as determined by the stock market. The denominator is the price of that capital if it were purchased today.

Tobin reasoned that net investment should depend on whether q is greater or less than 1. If q is greater than 1, then the stock market values installed capital at more than its replacement cost. In this case, managers can raise the market value of their firms' stock by buying more capital. Conversely, if q is less than 1, the stock market values capital at less than its replacement cost. In this case, managers will not replace capital as it wears out.

Although, at first, the q theory of investment may appear quite different from the neoclassical model developed previously, in fact, the two theories are closely related. To see the relationship, note that Tobin's q depends on current and future expected profits from installed capital. If the marginal product of capital exceeds the cost of capital, then firms are earning profit on their installed capital. These profits make the rental firms desirable to own, which raises the market value of these firms' stock, implying a high value of q. Similarly, if the marginal product of capital falls short of the cost of capital, then firms are incurring losses on their installed capital, implying a low market value and a low value of q.

The advantage of Tobin's q as a measure of the incentive to invest is that it reflects the expected future profitability of capital as well as the current profitability. For example, suppose that the government legislates a reduction in the corporate income tax beginning next year. This expected fall in the corporate tax means greater profits for the owners of capital. These higher expected profits raise the value of stock today, raise Tobin's q and therefore encourage investment today. Thus, Tobin's q theory of investment emphasizes that investment decisions depend not only on current economic policies, but also on policies expected to prevail in the future.[2]

CASE STUDY

The Stock Market as an Economic Indicator

In a wry comment on the stock market's reliability as an economic indicator, the economist Paul Samuelson once remarked: 'The stock market has predicted nine out of the last five recessions.' The stock market is in fact quite volatile, and it can give false signals about the future of an economy. Yet one should not ignore the link between the stock market and the economy. Figure 19-5 shows that changes in the stock market often reflect changes in real GDP. Whenever the stock market experiences a substantial decline, there is reason to fear that a recession may be around the corner. The 2008–2009 financial crash, and subsequent recession, can clearly be seen.

Why do stock prices and economic activity tend to fluctuate together? One reason is given by Tobin's q theory, together with the model of aggregate demand and aggregate supply. Suppose, for instance, that you observe a fall in stock prices. Because

---

[2] To read more about the relationship between the neoclassical model of investment and q theory, see Fumio Hayashi, 'Tobin's Marginal q and Average q: A Neoclassical Approach', *Econometrica*, January 1982, vol. 50, pp. 213–224; and Lawrence H. Summers, 'Taxation and Corporate Investment: A q-theory Approach', *Brookings Papers on Economic Activity*, 1981, vol. 1, pp. 67–140.

FIGURE 19-5

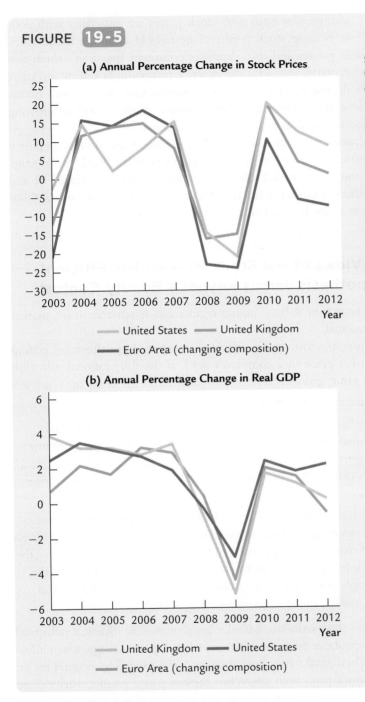

(a) Annual Percentage Change in Stock Prices

United States ▬▬ United Kingdom

Euro Area (changing composition)

(b) Annual Percentage Change in Real GDP

United Kingdom ▬▬ United States

Euro Area (changing composition)

Stock Market Movements and GDP Growth in the UK, the Euro Area and the US This figure shows the association between the stock market and real economic activity. Using annual data from 2003 to 2012, panel (a) presents the annual percentage change from one year earlier in an index of stock prices for the UK, the US and the Euro Area countries as a whole, while panel (b) presents the annual percentage change in GDP for the same years. The figure shows that the stock market and GDP tend to move together, but that the association is far from precise.

Source: Eurostat.

the replacement cost of capital is fairly stable, a fall in the stock market is usually associated with a fall in Tobin's q. A fall in q reflects investors' pessimism about the current or future profitability of capital. This means that the investment function has shifted inward: investment is lower at any given interest rate. As a result, the aggregate demand for goods and services contracts, leading to lower output and employment.

There are two additional reasons why stock prices are associated with economic activity. First, because stock is part of household wealth, a fall in stock prices makes people poorer and thus depresses consumer spending, which also reduces aggregate demand. Second, a fall in stock prices might reflect bad news about technological progress and long-run economic growth. If so, this means that the natural level of output – and thus aggregate supply – will be growing more slowly in the future than was previously expected.

These links between the stock market and the economy are not lost on policy makers, such as those at the European Central Bank or the Bank of England. Indeed, because the stock market often anticipates changes in real GDP, and because data on the stock market are available more quickly than data on GDP, the stock market is a closely watched economic indicator. ■

Alternative Views of the Stock Market: The Efficient Markets Hypothesis versus Keynes's Beauty Contest

One continuing source of debate among economists is whether stock market fluctuations are rational.

Some economists subscribe to the **efficient markets hypothesis**, according to which the market price of a company's stock is the fully rational valuation of the company's value, given current information about the company's business prospects. This hypothesis rests on two foundations:

1. Each company listed on a major stock exchange is followed closely by many professional portfolio managers. Every day, these managers monitor news stories to try to determine the company's value. Their job is to buy a stock when its price falls below its value, and to sell it when its price rises above its value.

2. The price of each stock is set by the equilibrium of supply and demand. At the market price, the number of shares being offered for sale exactly equals the number of shares that people want to buy. That is, at the market price, the number of people who think the stock is overvalued exactly balances the number of people who think it is undervalued. As judged by the typical person in the market, the stock must be fairly valued.

According to this theory, the stock market is *informationally efficient*: it reflects all available information about the value of the asset. Stock prices change when information changes. When good news about the company's prospects becomes public, the value and the stock price both rise. When the company's prospects deteriorate, both the value and price fall. But at any moment in time and using the information available, the market price is the rational best guess of the company's value.

One implication of the efficient markets hypothesis is that stock prices should follow a *random walk*. This means that the changes in stock prices should be impossible to predict from available information. If, based on publicly available information, a person could predict that a stock price would rise by 10 per cent tomorrow, then the stock market must be failing to incorporate that information today. According to this theory, the only thing that can move stock prices is news that changes the market's perception of the company's value. But news must be unpredictable – otherwise, it would not really be news. For the same reason, changes in stock prices should be unpredictable as well.

What is the evidence for the efficient markets hypothesis? Its proponents point out that it is hard to beat the market by buying allegedly undervalued stocks and selling allegedly overvalued stocks. Statistical tests show that stock prices are random walks, or at least approximately so. Moreover, index funds, which buy all companies in a stock market index, outperform most actively managed portfolios run by professional money managers.

Although the efficient markets hypothesis has many proponents, some economists are less convinced that the stock market is so rational. These economists point out that many movements in stock prices are hard to attribute to news. They suggest that when buying and selling, stock investors are less focused on companies' fundamental values and more focused on what they expect other investors will pay later.

John Maynard Keynes proposed a famous analogy to explain stock market speculation. In his day, some newspapers held 'beauty contests', in which the paper printed the pictures of 100 women and invited readers to submit a list of the five most beautiful. A prize went to the reader whose choices most closely matched those of the consensus of the other entrants. A naive entrant would simply have picked the five most beautiful women. But a slightly more sophisticated strategy would have been to guess the five women that other people considered the most beautiful. Other people, however, were likely thinking along the same lines. So an even more sophisticated strategy would have been to try to guess what other people thought other people thought were the most beautiful women. And so on. At the end of the process, judging true beauty would be less important to winning the contest than guessing other people's opinions of other people's opinions.

Similarly, Keynes reasoned that because stock market investors will eventually sell their shares to others, they were more concerned about other people's valuation of a company than the company's true worth. The best stock investors, in his view, were those who were good at outguessing mass psychology. He believed that movements in stock prices often reflect irrational waves of optimism and pessimism, which he called the 'animal spirits' of investors.

The two views of the stock market persist to this day. Some economists see the stock market through the lens of the efficient markets hypothesis. They believe fluctuations in stock prices are a rational reflection of changes in underlying economic fundamentals. Other economists, however, take Keynes's beauty contest as a metaphor for stock speculation. In their view, the stock market often fluctuates for no good reason, and because the stock market influences the aggregate demand for goods and services, these fluctuations are a source of short-run economic fluctuations.[3]

---

[3] A classic reference on the efficient markets hypothesis is Eugene Fama, 'Efficient Capital Markets: A Review of Theory and Empirical Work', *Journal of Finance*, 1970, vol. 25, pp. 383–417. For the alternative view, see Robert J. Shiller, 'From Efficient Markets Theory to Behavioral Finance', *Journal of Economic Perspectives*, winter 2003, vol. 17, pp. 83–104.

Financing Constraints

When a firm wants to invest in new capital, for example by building a new factory, it often raises the necessary funds in financial markets. This financing may take several forms: obtaining loans from banks, selling bonds to the public or selling shares in future profits on the stock market. The neoclassical model assumes that if a firm is willing to pay the cost of capital, the financial markets will make the funds available.

Yet sometimes firms face **financing constraints** – limits on the amount they can raise in financial markets. Financing constraints can prevent firms from undertaking profitable investments. When a firm is unable to raise funds in financial markets, the amount it can spend on new capital goods is limited to the amount it is currently earning. Financing constraints influence the investment behaviour of firms just as borrowing constraints influence the consumption behaviour of households. Borrowing constraints cause households to determine their consumption on the basis of current rather than permanent income; financing constraints cause firms to determine their investment on the basis of their current cash flow rather than expected profitability.

To see the impact of financing constraints, consider the effect of a short recession on investment spending. A recession reduces employment, the rental price of capital and profits. If firms expect the recession to be short-lived, however, they will want to continue investing, knowing that their investments will be profitable in the future. That is, a short recession will have only a small effect on Tobin's q. For firms that can raise funds in financial markets, the recession should have only a small effect on investment.

Quite the opposite is true for firms that face financing constraints. The fall in current profits restricts the amount that these firms can spend on new capital goods and may prevent them from making profitable investments. Thus, financing constraints make investment more sensitive to current economic conditions.[4]

The extent to which financing constraints can impede investment spending can vary over time, depending on the health of the financial system, and this can in turn become a source of short-term fluctuations. As we discussed in Chapter 12, for example, during the Great Depression of the 1930s many banks found themselves insolvent, as the value of their assets fell below the value of their liabilities. These banks were forced to suspend operations, making it more difficult for their previous customers to obtain financing for potential investment projects. Many economists believe that the widespread bank failure during this period helps to explain the Depression's depth and persistence. Similarly, the severe recession of 2008–2009 came on the heels of a widespread financial crisis that began with a downturn in the housing market. Chapter 20 discusses the causes and effects of such financial crises in greater detail.

---

[4] For empirical work supporting the importance of these financing constraints, see Steven M. Fazzari, R. Glenn Hubbard and Bruce C. Petersen, 'Financing Constraints and Corporate Investment', *Brookings Papers on Economic Activity*, 1988, vol. 1, pp. 141–195.

Banking Crises and Credit Crunches

Throughout history, problems in the banking system have often coincided with downturns in economic activity. This was true, for instance, during the Great Depression of the 1930s (which we discussed in Chapter 12), during the 1990s slump in Japan (as we saw in Chapter 12), during the financial crisis in East Asia during the late 1990s (Chapter 13), and during the financial crisis of 2008–2009 (which we shall look at in further detail in Chapter 20).

Why are banking crises so often at the centre of economic crises? Banks have an important role in allocating financial resources: they serve as *intermediaries* between those people who have income they want to save and those people who have profitable investment projects but need to borrow to invest. When banks become insolvent, or nearly so, they are less able to serve this function. Financing constraints become more common, and some investors are forced to forgo potentially profitable investment projects. Such an increase in financing constraints is sometimes called a *credit crunch*.

We can use the *IS-LM* model to interpret the short-run effects of a credit crunch. When some would-be investors are denied credit, the demand for investment goods falls at every interest rate. The result is a contractionary shift in the *IS* curve. This reduces aggregate demand, production and employment.

The long-run effects of a credit crunch are best understood from the perspective of growth theory, with its emphasis on capital accumulation as a source of growth. When a credit crunch prevents some firms from investing, the financial markets fail to allocate national saving to its best use. Less productive investment projects may take the place of more productive projects, reducing the economy's potential for producing goods and services.

Because of these effects, policy makers at central banks and other parts of government are always trying to monitor the health of the nation's banking system. Their goal is to avert banking crises and credit crunches and, when they do occur, to respond quickly to minimize the resulting disruption to the economy. ∎

19-2 Residential Investment

In this section we consider the determinants of residential investment. We begin by presenting a simple model of the housing market. Residential investment includes the purchase of new housing, both by people who plan to live in it themselves and by landlords who plan to rent it to others. Patterns of home ownership differ markedly across developed countries. In particular, families in Continental European countries are much more likely to rent their homes than are families in the UK or the US. A major factor driving residential investment by owner-occupiers is the imputed rent that owners expect to receive from owning their home – that is, the flow of 'housing services' that the home supplies. If residential investment in a particular country is undertaken largely by landlords, we can think of these imputed rents as actual rents that the landlord can charge on his property, so the analysis will be similar.

To keep things simple, however, it is useful to imagine that all housing is owner-occupied.

The Stock Equilibrium and the Flow Supply

There are two parts to the model. First, the market for the existing stock of houses determines the equilibrium housing price. Second, the housing price determines the flow of residential investment.

Panel (a) of Figure 19-6 shows how the relative price of housing P_H/P is determined by the supply and demand for the existing stock of houses. At any point in time, the supply of houses is fixed. We represent this stock with a vertical supply curve. The demand curve for houses slopes downward, because high prices cause people to live in smaller houses, to share residences or sometimes even to become homeless. The price of housing adjusts to equilibrate supply and demand.

Panel (b) of Figure 19-6 shows how the relative price of housing determines the supply of new houses. Construction firms buy materials and hire labour to build houses, and then sell the houses at the market price. Their costs depend on the overall price level P (which reflects the cost of wood, bricks, plaster, etc.), and their revenue depends on the price of houses P_H. The higher the relative price of housing, the greater the incentive to build houses, and the more houses are built. The flow of new houses – residential investment – therefore depends on the equilibrium price set in the market for existing houses.

FIGURE 19-6

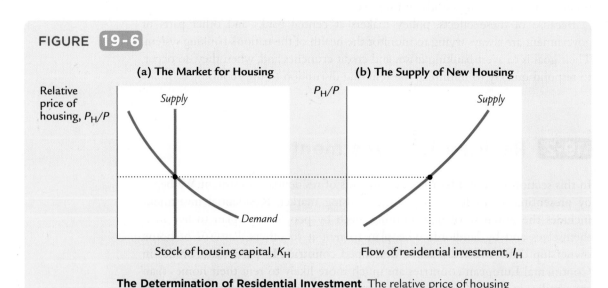

(a) The Market for Housing

Relative price of housing, P_H/P

Supply

Demand

Stock of housing capital, K_H

(b) The Supply of New Housing

P_H/P

Supply

Flow of residential investment, I_H

The Determination of Residential Investment The relative price of housing adjusts to equilibrate supply and demand for the existing stock of housing capital. The relative price then determines residential investment, the flow of new housing that construction firms build.

This model of residential investment is similar to the q theory of business fixed investment. According to the q theory, business fixed investment depends on the market price of installed capital relative to its replacement cost; this relative price, in turn, depends on the expected profits from owning installed capital. According to this model of the housing market, residential investment depends on the relative price of housing. The relative price of housing, in turn, depends on the demand for housing, which depends on the imputed rent that individuals expect to receive from their housing. Hence, the relative price of housing plays much the same role for residential investment as Tobin's q does for business fixed investment.

Changes in Housing Demand

When the demand for housing shifts, the equilibrium price of housing changes, and this change, in turn, affects residential investment. The demand curve for housing can shift for various reasons. An economic boom raises national income and therefore the demand for housing. A large increase in the population, perhaps because of immigration, also raises the demand for housing. Panel (a) of Figure 19-7 shows that an expansionary shift in demand raises the equilibrium price. Panel (b) shows that the increase in the housing price increases residential investment.

One important determinant of housing demand is the real interest rate. Many people take out loans – mortgages – to buy their homes; the interest rate is the cost of the loan. Even the few people who do not have to borrow to purchase

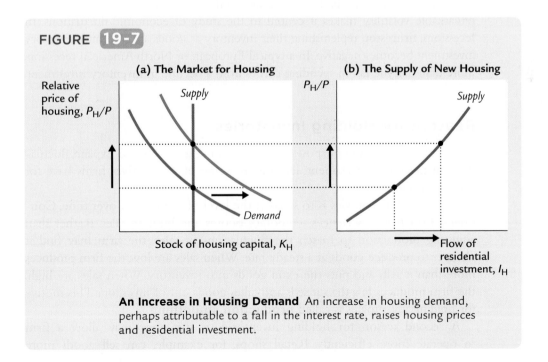

FIGURE 19-7

(a) The Market for Housing

Relative price of housing, P_H/P

Supply

Demand

Stock of housing capital, K_H

(b) The Supply of New Housing

P_H/P

Supply

Flow of residential investment, I_H

An Increase in Housing Demand An increase in housing demand, perhaps attributable to a fall in the interest rate, raises housing prices and residential investment.

a home will respond to the interest rate, because the interest rate is the opportunity cost of holding their wealth in housing rather than putting it in a bank. A reduction in the interest rate therefore raises housing demand, housing prices and residential investment.

Another important determinant of housing demand is credit availability. When it is easy to get a loan, more households buy their own homes, and they buy larger ones than they otherwise might, thus increasing the demand for housing. When credit conditions become tight, fewer people buy their own homes or trade up to larger ones, and the demand for housing falls.

An example of this phenomenon occurred during the first decade of the 2000s. Early in this decade, interest rates were low, and mortgages were easy to come by. Many households with questionable credit histories – often called subprime borrowers – were able to get mortgages with small down payments. Not surprisingly, the housing market boomed. Housing prices rose, and residential investment was strong. However, following the financial crisis of 2008–2009, credit conditions tightened, and so housing demand and housing prices started to fall, construction of new houses fell, which then had a significant negative impact on overall economic activity.

19-3 Inventory Investment

Inventory investment – the goods that businesses put aside in storage – is at the same time negligible and of great significance. It is one of the smallest components of spending, averaging about 1 per cent of GDP in advanced economies. Yet its remarkable volatility makes it central to the study of economic fluctuations. In recessions, firms stop replenishing their inventory as goods are sold, and inventory investment becomes negative. In a typical European or North American recession, more than half the fall in spending comes from a decline in inventory investment.

Reasons for Holding Inventories

Inventories serve many purposes. Before presenting a model to explain fluctuations in inventory investment, let's discuss some of the motives firms have for holding inventories.

One use of inventories is to smooth the level of production over time. Consider a firm that experiences temporary booms and busts in sales. Rather than adjusting production to match the fluctuations in sales, the firm may find it cheaper to produce goods at a steady rate. When sales are low, the firm produces more than it sells and puts the extra goods into inventory. When sales are high, the firm produces less than it sells and takes goods out of inventory. This motive for holding inventories is called **production smoothing**.

A second reason for holding inventories is that they may allow a firm to operate more efficiently. Retail shops, for example, can sell goods more effectively if they have them on hand to show to customers. Manufacturing firms keep inventories of spare parts to reduce the time that the assembly line is shut down when a machine breaks. In some ways, we can view **inventories as a factor of production**: the larger the stock of inventories a firm holds, the more output it can produce.

A third reason for holding inventories is to avoid running out of goods when sales are unexpectedly high. Firms often have to make production decisions before knowing the level of customer demand. For example, a publisher must decide how many copies of a new book to print before knowing whether the book will be popular. If demand exceeds production and there are no inventories, the good will be out of stock for a period, and the firm will lose sales and profit. Inventories can prevent this from happening. This motive for holding inventories is called **stock-out avoidance**.

A fourth explanation of inventories is dictated by the production process. Many goods require a number of steps in production and, therefore, take time to produce. When a product is only partly completed, its components are counted as part of a firm's inventory. These inventories are called **work in progress**.

The Accelerator Model of Inventories

Because there are many motives for holding inventories, there are many models of inventory investment. One simple model that explains the data well, without endorsing a particular motive, is the **accelerator model**. This model was developed around the middle of the 20th century, and it is sometimes applied to all types of investment. Here we apply it to the type for which it works best – inventory investment.

The accelerator model of inventories assumes that firms hold a stock of inventories that is proportional to the firms' level of output. There are various reasons for this assumption. When output is high, manufacturing firms need more materials and supplies on hand, and they have more goods in the process of being completed. When the economy is booming, retail firms want to have more merchandise on the shelves to show customers. Thus, if N is the economy's stock of inventories and Y is output, then

$$N = \beta Y,$$

where β is a parameter reflecting how much inventory firms wish to hold as a proportion of output.

Inventory investment I is the change in the stock of inventories ΔN. Therefore,

$$I = \Delta N = \beta \Delta Y.$$

The accelerator model predicts that inventory investment is proportional to the change in output. When output rises, firms want to hold a larger stock of inventory, so inventory investment is high. When output falls, firms want to hold a smaller stock of inventory, so they allow their inventory to run down, and inventory investment is negative.

Inventories and the Real Interest Rate

Like other components of investment, inventory investment depends on the real interest rate. When a firm holds a good in inventory and sells it tomorrow rather than selling it today, it gives up the interest it could have earned between today and tomorrow. Thus, the real interest rate measures the opportunity cost of holding inventories.

When the real interest rate rises, holding inventories becomes more costly, so rational firms try to reduce their stock. Therefore, an increase in the real interest rate depresses inventory investment. For example, in the 1980s, many European and US firms adopted 'just-in-time' production plans, which were designed to reduce the amount of inventory by producing goods just before sale. The high real interest rates that prevailed during most of this decade are one possible explanation for this change in business strategy.

19-4 Conclusion

The purpose of this chapter has been to examine the determinants of investment in detail. Looking back on the various models of investment, we can identify three themes.

First, all types of investment spending are inversely related to the real interest rate. A higher interest rate raises the cost of capital for firms that invest in plant and equipment, raises the cost of borrowing for home buyers, and raises the cost of holding inventories. Thus, the models of investment developed here justify the investment function we have used throughout this book.

Second, there are various causes of shifts in the investment function. An improvement in the available technology raises the marginal product of capital and raises business fixed investment. An increase in the population raises the demand for housing and raises residential investment. Most importantly, various economic policies, such as changes in investment tax credits and corporation tax, alter the incentives to invest and thus shift the investment function.

Third, it is natural to expect investment to be volatile over the business cycle, because investment spending depends on the output of the economy as well as on the interest rate. In the neoclassical model of business fixed investment, higher employment raises the marginal product of capital and the incentive to invest. Higher output also raises firms' profits and, thereby, relaxes the financing constraints that some firms face. In addition, higher income raises the demand for houses, in turn raising housing prices and residential investment. Higher output raises the stock of inventories that firms wish to hold, stimulating inventory investment. Our models predict that an economic boom should stimulate investment and a recession should depress it. This is exactly what we observe.

Summary

1. The marginal product of capital determines the real rental price of capital. The real interest rate, the depreciation rate and the relative price of capital goods determine the cost of capital. According to the neoclassical model, firms invest if the rental price is greater than the cost of capital, and they disinvest if the rental price is less than the cost of capital.

2. Various parts of a country's tax system influence the incentive to invest. Corporation tax discourages investment and investment tax credits encourage it.

3. An alternative way of expressing the neoclassical model is to state that investment depends on Tobin's q, the ratio of the market value of installed capital to its replacement cost. This ratio reflects the current and expected future profitability of capital. The higher q is, the greater the market value of installed capital relative to its replacement cost, and the greater the incentive to invest.

4. Economists debate whether fluctuations in the stock market are a rational reflection of companies' true value or if they are driven by irrational waves of optimism and pessimism.

5. In contrast to the assumption of the neoclassical model, firms cannot always raise funds to finance investment. Financing constraints make investment sensitive to firms' current cash flow.

6. Residential investment depends on the relative price of housing. Housing prices, in turn, depend on the demand for housing and the current fixed supply. An increase in housing demand, perhaps attributable to a fall in the interest rate, raises housing prices and residential investment.

7. Firms have various motives for holding inventories of goods: smoothing production, using them as a factor of production, avoiding stock-outs and storing work in process. One model of inventory investment that works well, without endorsing a particular motive, is the accelerator model. According to this model, the stock of inventories depends on the level of GDP, and inventory investment depends on the change in GDP.

KEY CONCEPTS

Business fixed investment	Corporation tax	Production smoothing
Residential investment	Investment tax credit	Inventories as a factor of production
Inventory investment	Stock	
Neoclassical model of investment	Stock market	Stock-out avoidance
Depreciation	Tobin's q	Work in progress
Real cost of capital	Efficient markets hypothesis	Accelerator model
Net investment	Financing constraints	

QUESTIONS FOR REVIEW

1. In the neoclassical model of business fixed investment, under what conditions will firms find it profitable to add to their capital stock?

2. What is Tobin's q, and what does it have to do with investment?

3. Explain why an increase in the interest rate reduces the amount of residential investment.

4. List four reasons firms might hold inventories.

PROBLEMS AND APPLICATIONS

1. Use the neoclassical model of investment to explain the impact of each of the following on the rental price of capital, the cost of capital and investment:

   a. Anti-inflationary monetary policy raises the real interest rate.

   b. An earthquake destroys part of the capital stock.

   c. Immigration of foreign workers increases the size of the labour force.

2. Suppose that the government levies a tax on oil companies equal to a proportion of the value of the company's oil reserves. (The government assures the firms that the tax is for one time only.) According to the neoclassical model, what effect will the tax have on business fixed investment by these firms? What if these firms face financing constraints?

3. The *IS-LM* model developed in Chapters 11 and 12 assumes that investment depends only on the interest rate. Yet our theories of investment suggest that investment might also depend on national income: higher income might induce firms to invest more.

   a. Explain why investment might depend on national income.

   b. Suppose that investment is determined by

$$I = \bar{I} + aY,$$

   where a is a constant between zero and one which measures the influence of national income on investment. With investment set

this way, what are the fiscal-policy multipliers in the Keynesian cross model? Explain.

   c. Suppose that investment depends on both income and the interest rate. That is, the investment function is

$$I = \bar{I} + aY - br,$$

   where a is a constant between zero and one which measures the influence of national income on investment, and b is a constant greater than zero which measures the influence of the interest rate on investment. Use the *IS-LM* model to consider the short-run impact of an increase in government purchases on national income Y, the interest rate r, consumption C and investment I. How might this investment function alter the conclusions implied by the basic *IS-LM* model?

4. When the stock market crashes, as it did in many countries in 2008, how should the central bank respond? Why?

5. It is an election year and the economy is in a recession. The opposition party campaigns on a platform of passing an investment tax credit, which would be effective the year after it takes office. What impact does this campaign promise have on economic conditions during the current year?

6. In some countries, the tax laws encourage investment in housing and discourage investment in business capital. What are the long-run effects of this policy? (*Hint:* Think about the labour market.)

CHAPTER 20

The Financial System: Opportunities and Dangers

When written in Chinese the word crisis is composed of two characters. One represents danger, and the other represents opportunity.

– John F. Kennedy

In 2008 and 2009, the US, the UK and many European countries experienced financial crises and a subsequent economic downturn. The origins of these crises can be traced back to the US housing market (but other housing markets, especially the UK, had similar problems). In the early 2000s, loans to buy property began to be extended to households who would not previously have been offered mortgages on such favourable terms – the so-called 'subprime' market. Essentially too much was lent too cheaply to households whose ability to repay their debt would be compromised if their economic circumstances were to worsen, or if the values of the properties which secured their loans were to fall. The problem was compounded by this debt then being parcelled up and sold on within the financial system in ways that obscured how risky that debt really was. The interdependence of the financial system was such that many financial institutions became overexposed to such 'toxic debt'. The inevitable decline in house prices thus led to problems in many financial institutions, which in turn led to the most severe economic downturn since the Great Depression of the 1930s. This event was a vivid reminder of the inexorable links between the financial system and the broader global economy. When America sneezes, the world catches a cold.

In this chapter we examine the links between the economy and the financial system more thoroughly. We discuss what the financial system is and how it works. We also discuss the new challenges that the financial system provides to policy makers charged with promoting short-run economic stability and long-run economic growth.

The financial system has been present in much of the macroeconomic theory we have developed throughout this book. In Chapter 3 we discussed a model of the loanable funds market. There we saw that the interest rate adjusts to balance the supply of loanable funds (derived from the nation's saving) and the demand for loanable funds (for purpose of investment). In Chapters 8 and 9 we used the Solow model to examine the sources of economic growth. In that model, the financial system is in the background, ensuring that the economy's saving is directed into investment and capital accumulation.

The financial system was similarly present in our short-run analysis. In the *IS-LM* model of Chapters 11 and 12, the interest rate is the link between the goods market and the money market. In that model, the interest rate determines both the cost of holding money and the cost of borrowing to fund investment spending. It is therefore the crucial variable through which monetary policy influences the aggregate demand for goods and services.

By studying the financial system in more detail, we can make our analysis of economic growth and fluctuations more nuanced. The financial system is more than a single market for loanable funds, and there are more prices in this system than a single interest rate. Indeed, the complexity of the financial system is sufficiently great that there is an entire subfield of economics, called *finance*, devoted to its study. This chapter focuses on some of the topics within finance that are crucial to a fuller understanding of macroeconomics. In particular, we start by examining the fundamental role of the financial system in the economy. We then examine the causes of financial crises and the policy responses to them.

20-1 What Does the Financial System Do?

John is a rational, forward-looking consumer. He earns a good income of €200,000 a year but does not plan to spend all of it this year. He wants to put some of his income aside, perhaps for retirement, a future vacation, sending his newborn son to college, or just as a precaution to prepare for future uncertainties. The part of John's income that he does not currently spend contributes to the nation's saving.

Anne is an entrepreneur starting a new business. She has an idea for a toy that she believes would enchant young children around the world and therefore be quite profitable. To put her idea into action, she needs to obtain some resources: plastics, moulds, fabric, sewing machines and a building to house her small manufacturing operation. Anne's purchases of these capital goods contribute to the nation's investment.

In short, John has some income he wants to save, and Anne has ideas for investments but may not have to funds to pay for them. The solution is obvious: John can finance Anne's venture. The **financial system** is the broad term for the institutions in the economy that facilitate the flow of funds between savers and investors. That is, the financial system brings people like John and people like Anne together.

Financing Investment

Throughout much of this book, the economy's financial system has been represented as a single market – the market for loanable funds. Those like John, who have some income they don't want to immediately consume, bring their saving to this market so that they can lend these funds to others. Those like Anne, who have investment projects they want to undertake, finance these investments by borrowing in this market. In this simple model, there is a single interest rate that adjusts to bring saving and investment into balance.

The actual financial system is more complicated than this description. As in the simple model, the goal of the system is to channel resources from savers into various forms of investment. But the system includes a large variety of mechanisms to facilitate this transfer of resources.

One piece of the financial system is the set of **financial markets** through which households can directly provide resources for investment. Two important financial markets are the market for **bonds** and the market for **stocks**. A bond represents a loan from the bondholder to the firm; a share of stock represents an ownership claim by the shareholder in the firm. That is, a person who buys a bond from, say, Apple Corporation, becomes a creditor of the company, while a person who buys newly issued stock from Apple becomes a part owner of the company. (A purchase of stock on a stock exchange, however, represents a transfer of ownership shares from one person to another and does not provide new funds for investment projects.) Raising investment funds by issuing bonds is called **debt finance**, and raising funds by issuing stock is called **equity finance**.

Another piece of the financial system is the set of **financial intermediaries** through which households can indirectly provide resources for investment. As the term suggests, a financial intermediary stands between the two sides of the market and helps direct financial resources toward their best use. Banks are the best-known type of financial intermediary. They take deposits from savers and use these deposits to make loans to those who have investments projects they need to finance. Other examples of financial intermediaries include mutual funds, pension funds, and insurance companies. In contrast to buying a stock or bond on a financial market, when a financial intermediary is involved, the saver is often unaware of the investments that his saving is financing.

To continue with our example, John and Anne can take advantage of any of these opportunities. If Anne and John know each other, Anne could borrow money directly from John and pay him interest for the loan. In this case, she would in effect be selling him a bond. Or Anne could, in exchange for John's money, give him an ownership stake in her new business, and John would enjoy a share of the future profits. In this case, she would be selling him some stock. Or he could deposit his saving in a local bank, which in turn lends the funds to Anne. In this last case, John would be financing her new venture indirectly: They might never meet, or even know of each other's existence. In all of these cases, John and Anne engage in a mutually advantageous exchange. John finds a way to earn a return on his saving, and Anne finds a way to finance her investment project.

Sharing Risk

Investment is inherently risky. Anne's new toy might be the next craze, or it might be a flop. Like all entrepreneurs, Anne is starting her venture because she expects it to be profitable, but she cannot be certain of that outcome.

One function of the financial system is to allocate risk. When Anne sells stock to John, she is sharing the risk of her venture with him. If Anne's toy-making business is profitable, John will enjoy some of the gains. If it loses money, he will share in the losses. Anne might be eager to share the risk, rather than bear it all herself, because she is **risk averse**. That is, other things being equal, she dislikes randomness in her economic circumstances. John might be willing to accept some of the risk if the return he expects on this risky venture is higher than he would obtain by putting his saving into safer assets. Thus, equity finance provides a way for entrepreneurs and savers to share the risks and returns associated with the entrepreneur's investment ideas.

In addition, the financial system allows savers to reduce their risk by spreading their wealth across many different businesses. John knows that buying stock in Anne's toy venture is risky, so he would be smart to use only some of his saving to buy stock in her business. He could also buy stock from his friend Steve, who is opening an ice-cream store. And he could buy stock in established companies, such as Vodafone, IBM or BSkyB. Because the success of Anne's toy-making venture is not perfectly correlated with the success of Steve's ice-cream store, or with the profitability of Vodafone, IBM or BSkyB, John reduces the overall risk he faces when he spreads his wealth around. Reducing risk by holding many imperfectly correlated assets is called **diversification**.

Various financial institutions facilitate diversification. Among the most important are mutual funds. **Mutual funds** are financial intermediaries that sell shares to savers and use their funds to buy diversified pools of assets. Even a small saver can put, say, €1000 into a mutual fund and become a part owner of thousands of businesses. Because the fortunes of these many businesses do not rise and fall together, putting the €1000 into a mutual fund is far less risky than using it to buy stock in a single company.

There are limits, however, to how much diversification reduces risk. Some macroeconomic events affect many businesses at the same time. Such risk is called *systematic risk*. In particular, recessions tend to reduce the demand for most products and thus the profitability of most businesses. Diversification cannot reduce this kind of risk. Yet it can largely eliminate the risks associated with individual businesses, called *idiosyncratic risk*, such as whether Anne's toys or Steve's ice cream proves popular. For this reason, it is wise for savers such as John to limit how much of their savings they allocate to the stock of any one company.

Dealing with Asymmetric Information

As John considers financing Anne's business venture, one question is paramount in his mind: will her company succeed? If John offers her equity financing, the fortune of the business will be crucial, because he is being promised a share of future profits. But even if John offers her debt financing, Anne's success is still relevant. If the toy business is a failure, Anne may not be able to repay the loan. That is, Anne might default. Not only might John not get the interest he was promised, but he might lose his principal (the amount of the loan to Anne) as well.

Making matters worse is the fact that Anne knows a lot more than John about herself and her business. Economists use the phrase **asymmetric information** to describe a situation in which one party to an economic transaction knows more information about the transaction than the other. There are two classic types of asymmetric information, both of which are relevant as John ponders whether to finance Anne's venture.

The first type of asymmetric information concerns *hidden knowledge about attributes*. Is Anne's toy design a good one that will have wide appeal? Is the toy market ready for a new product, or is it oversaturated? Is Anne a talented businesswoman? Anne is more likely than John to have reliable answers to these questions. This is generally the case: entrepreneurs have more information about whether their investment projects are good ones than those who provide the financing.

In this situation, John should worry about the problem of **adverse selection**. As we noted in Chapter 7 in a different context, the term 'adverse selection' describes the tendency of people with more information (here, the entrepreneurs) to sort themselves in a way that disadvantages people with less information (those providing the financing). In our example, John may be concerned that he will be offered opportunities to finance only less desirable business ventures. If Anne were truly confident in her idea, she might try harder to finance it herself using more of her own savings. The fact that she is asking John to provide financing and share some of the risk suggests that perhaps she knows something adverse that he does not know. As a result, John has reason to be wary.

The second type of asymmetric information concerns *hidden knowledge about actions*. Once Anne obtains financing from John, she will have many decisions to make. Will she work long hours at the job, or will she go home early to play tennis with friends? Will she spend the money she has raised in the most profitable way, or will she use it to provide herself with a cushy office and a fancy company car? Anne can promise to make decisions in the best interest of the business, but it will be hard for John to verify that she in fact does so, because he won't be at the toy factory every day to observe all the decisions that she makes.

In this case, the problem that arises is **moral hazard**, the risk that an imperfectly monitored agent will act in a dishonest or otherwise inappropriate way. In particular, entrepreneurs investing other peoples' money may not look after the investment projects as carefully as those investing their own. Once Anne has John's money in hand, she may be tempted to choose the easy life. If she succumbs to moral hazard, she will reduce the future profitability of the firm and increase the risk of default on her firm's debts.

The financial system has developed various institutions that mitigate the effects of adverse selection and moral hazard. Banks are among the most important. When a person applies for a bank loan, the application is scrutinized by loan officers who are trained to evaluate businesses and their prospects. Thus, the loan officers stand a good chance of uncovering the hidden attributes that lead to adverse selection. To reduce the problem of moral hazard, bank loans may contain restrictions on how the loan proceeds are spent, and the loan officers may monitor the business after the loan is made. As a result, rather than John making a direct loan to Anne, it may make sense for him to deposit his money in a bank, which in turn will lend it to various entrepreneurs such as Anne. The bank would charge a fee for serving as an intermediary, reflected in the spread between the interest rate it charges on loans and the interest rate it pays on deposits. But the bank earns its fee by reducing the problems associated with asymmetric information.

Fostering Economic Growth

In Chapters 8 and 9 we used the Solow model to examine the forces that govern long-run economic growth. In that model, we saw that a nation's saving determines the steady-state level of capital, which in turn determines the steady-state level of income per person. The more a nation saves, the more capital its labour force has to work with, the more it produces, and the more income its citizens enjoy.

The Solow model makes the simplifying assumption that there is only a single type of capital, but the real world includes many thousands of firms with diverse investment projects competing for the economy's limited resources. John's saving can finance Anne's toy business, but it could instead finance Steve's ice-cream store, an Airbus aircraft factory, or a Lidl retail outlet. The financial system has the job of allocating the economy's scarce saving among the alternative types of investment.

Ideally, to allocate saving to investment, all the financial system needs are market forces and the magic of Adam Smith's invisible hand. Firms with particularly productive and profitable investment opportunities will be willing to pay higher interest rates for loans than those with less desirable projects. Thus, if the interest rate adjusts to balance the supply and demand for loanable funds, the economy's saving will be allocated to the best of the many possible investments.

Yet, as we have seen, because the financial system is full of problems arising from asymmetric information, it can deviate from this simple, classical ideal. Banks mitigate adverse selection and moral hazard to some extent, but they do not completely eliminate them. As a result, some good investment projects may be passed up because entrepreneurs cannot raise the funds to finance them. If the financial system fails to allocate the economy's saving to its best uses, the economy's overall level of productivity is lower than it could be.

Government policy plays a role in helping ensure that the financial system works well. First, it can reduce the problem of moral hazard by prosecuting fraud and similar malpractice. The law cannot ensure that Anne will put John's money to its best use, but if she uses it to pay her personal living expenses, she may well end up in jail. Second, the government can reduce the problem of adverse selection by requiring some kinds of disclosure. If Anne's toy business ever grows large enough to issue stock on a public stock exchange, the government's Securities and Exchange Commission or Financial Services Authority will require that she issue regular reports on her firm's earnings and assets and that these reports be certified by accredited accountants.

Because the quality of legal institutions varies around the world, some countries have better financial systems than others, and this difference is one source of international variation in living standards. Rich nations tend to have larger stock markets and larger banking systems (relative to the size of their economies) than poorer nations. As always, sorting out cause-and-effect is difficult when examining differences across countries. Nonetheless, many economists believe that one reason poor nations remain poor is that their financial systems are unable to direct their saving to the best possible investments. These nations can foster economic growth by reforming their legal institutions with an eye toward improving the performance of their financial systems. If they succeed, entrepreneurs such as Anne with good ideas will find it easier to start their businesses.

CASE STUDY

Microfinance: Professor Yunus's Profound Idea

In the 1970s, Muhammad Yunus was a professor of economics in Bangladesh. Like all economists, he knew that economic prosperity depended on the ability of entrepreneurs to get the financing they need to start their businesses. But he also knew that in his country and in similar developing nations, financing is often hard to find. In the United Kingdom, someone like Anne might well find a bank willing to make her a loan, especially if she had some of her own money she could put into her business. But if she were living in a country with a less developed financial system, such as Bangladesh, and especially if she were poor, she would have a harder time financing her venture, no matter how profitable it might be.

Professor Yunus was not content just to study the problem; he wanted to solve it. In 1976, he founded the Grameen Bank, a non-profit financial institution with the goal of making very small loans primarily to poor women, so they could start working their way out of poverty. In Bangla, the language of Bangladesh, Grameen Bank means 'bank of the villages'.

Here is how the Grameen Bank explains its mission:

> Microfinance is a proven tool for fighting poverty on a large scale. It provides very small loans, or micro-loans, to poor people, mostly women, to start or expand very small, self-sufficient businesses. Through their own ingenuity and drive, and the support of the lending microfinance institution (MFI), poor women are able start their journey out of poverty.
>
> Unlike commercial loans, no collateral is required for a micro-loan and it is usually repaid within six months to a year. Those funds are then recycled as other loans, keeping money working and in the hands of borrowers. For example, a woman could borrow $50 to buy chickens so that she can sell their eggs. As the chickens reproduce, she can sell more eggs and eventually sell the chicks. As a borrower, she receives advice and support from the MFI that issued her loan, and support from other borrowers just like her. Some MFIs also provide social services, such as basic health care for her and her children. As her business grows and diversifies, she begins to earn enough to improve the living conditions for her and her family. Microfinance clients boast very high repayment rates. Averaging between 95 and 98 per cent, the repayment rates are better than that of student loan and credit card debts in the United States.

Professor Yunus's plan has been remarkably successful, and it has been replicated in many other places. In 2006, he and the Grameen Bank won the Nobel Peace Prize for helping foster economic development in some world's poorest nations. Muhammad Yunus is the first economist to win a Nobel Prize in a field other than economics.[1] ∎

20-2 Financial Crises

So far in this chapter we have discussed how the financial system works. We now discuss why the financial system might stop working and the broad macroeconomic ramifications of such a disruption.

When we discussed the theory of the business cycle in Chapters 10 to 14, we saw that many kinds of shocks can lead to short-run fluctuations. A shift in consumer or business confidence, a rise or fall in world oil prices, or a sudden change in monetary or fiscal policy can alter aggregate demand or aggregate supply (or both). When this occurs, output and employment are pushed away from their natural levels, and inflation rises or falls as well.

Here we focus on one particular kind of shock. A **financial crisis** is a major disruption in the financial system that impedes the economy's ability to intermediate between those who want to save and those who want to borrow and invest. Not surprisingly, given the financial system's central role, financial crises have broad macroeconomic impact. Throughout history many of the deepest recessions have followed problems in the financial system. These downturns include the Great Depression of the 1930s and the Great Recession of 2008–2009.

The Anatomy of a Crisis

Financial crises are not all alike, but they share some common features. In a nutshell, here are the six elements that are at the centre of most financial crises. The financial crisis of 2008–2009 provides a good example of each element.

1. Asset-Price Booms and Busts Often, a period of optimism, leading to a large increase in asset prices, precedes a financial crisis. Sometimes people bid up the price of an asset above its fundamental value (that is, the true value based on an objective analysis of the cash flows the asset will generate). In this case, the market for that asset is said to be in the grips of a **speculative bubble**. Later, when sentiment shifts and optimism turns to pessimism, the bubble bursts and prices begin to fall. The decline in asset prices is the catalyst for the financial crisis.

In 2008 and 2009, the crucial asset was residential real estate. The average price of housing, particularly in the United States, Spain, Ireland and the United Kingdom, experienced a boom earlier in the decade. This boom was driven in part by lax

---

[1] The source of the quotation is www.grameenfoundation.org/what-we-do/microfinance-basics. For more on this topic, see Beatriz Armendáriz and Jonathan Morduch, *The Economics of Microfinance*, Cambridge, MA: The MIT Press, 2007.

lending standards; many *subprime* borrowers – those with particularly risky credit profiles – were lent money to buy a house while offering only a very small down payment. In essence, the financial system failed to do its job of dealing with asymmetric information by making loans to many borrowers who, it turned out, would later have trouble making their mortgage payments. The housing boom was also encouraged by government policies that promoted homeownership and was fed by excessive optimism on the part of homebuyers, who thought prices would rise forever. The housing boom, however, proved unsustainable. Over time, the number of homeowners falling behind on their mortgage payments rose, and sentiment among homebuyers shifted. Housing prices in the US, for example, fell by about 30 per cent from 2006 to 2009. The US had not experienced such a large decline in housing prices since the 1930s.

2. Insolvencies at Financial Institutions A large decline in asset prices may cause problems at banks and other financial institutions. To ensure that borrowers repay their loans, banks often require them to post collateral. That is, a borrower has to pledge assets that the bank can seize if the borrower defaults. Yet when assets decline in price, the collateral falls in value, perhaps below the amount of the loan. In this case, if the borrower defaults on the loan, the bank may be unable to recover its money.

As we discussed in Chapter 4, banks rely heavily on **leverage**, the use of borrowed funds for the purposes of investment. Leverage amplifies the positive and negative effect of asset returns on a bank's financial position. A key number is the *leverage ratio*: the ratio of bank assets to bank capital. A leverage ratio of 20, for example, means that for every €1 in capital put into the bank by its owners, the bank has borrowed (via deposits and other loans) €19, which then allows the bank to hold €20 in assets. In this case, if defaults cause the value of the bank's assets to fall by 2 per cent, then the bank's capital will fall by 40 per cent. If the value of bank assets falls by more than 5 per cent, then its assets will fall below its liabilities, and the bank will be insolvent. In this case, the bank will not have the resources to pay off all its depositors and other creditors. Widespread insolvency within the financial system is the second element of a financial crisis.

In 2008 and 2009, many banks and other financial firms had in effect placed bets on real estate prices by holding mortgages backed by that real estate. They assumed that housing prices would keep rising or at least hold steady, so the collateral backing these loans would ensure their repayment. When house prices fell, however, large numbers of homeowners found themselves in negative equity: the value of their homes was below the amount they owed on their mortgages. When many homeowners stopped repaying their loans, the banks could foreclose on or repossess the houses, but they could recover only a fraction of what they were owed. These defaults pushed several financial institutions toward bankruptcy. In the US, these institutions included major investment banks (Bear Stearns and Lehman Brothers), government-sponsored enterprises involved in the mortgage market (Fannie Mae and Freddie Mac), and a large insurance company (AIG). In the UK, the Treasury injected

The TED Spread

A common type of indicator of perceived credit risk is the spread between two interest rates of similar maturity. For example, Financial Shaky Corporation might have to pay 7 per cent for a one-year loan, whereas Safe and Solid Corporation has to pay only 3 per cent. That spread of 4 percentage point occurs because lenders are worried that Financial Shaky might default and so they demand compensation for bearing that risk. If Financial Shaky gets some bad news about its financial position, the interest rate spread might rise to 5 or 6 per cent or even higher. Thus, one way to monitor perceptions of credit risk is to follow interest-rate spreads.

One particularly noteworthy interest-rate spread is the so-called TED spread (and not just because it rhymes). The TED spread is the difference between three-month interbank loans and three-month Treasury Bills. The T in TED stands for T-bills, and ED stands for EuroDollars (because, for regulatory reasons, these interbank loans typically take place in London). The TED spread is measured in basis points, where a basis point is one one-hundredth of a percentage point (0.01 per cent). Normally, the TED spread is about 10 to 50 basis points (0.1 to 0.5 per cent). The spread is small because commercial banks, while a bit riskier than the government, are still very safe. Lenders do not require much extra compensation to accept the debt of banks rather than the government.

In times of financial crisis, however, confidence in the banking system falls. As a result, banks become reluctant to lend to one another, and so the TED spread rises substantially. Figure 20-1 shows the TED spread before, during, and after the financial crisis of 2008–2009. As the crisis unfolded, the TED spread rose substantially, reaching 464 basis points in October 2008, just after the investment bank Lehman Brothers declared bankruptcy. The high level of the TED spread is a direct indicator of how worried people were about the solvency of the banking system.

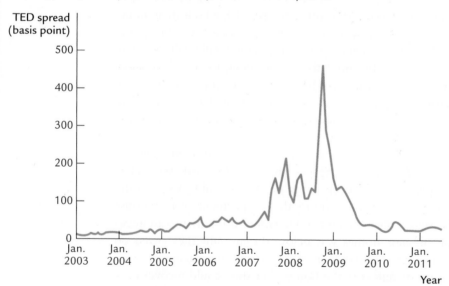

Figure 20-1 The TED Spread The TED spread is the difference between the interest rate on three-month interbank loans and the interest rate on three-month Treasury bills. It rises when lending to banks is considered particularly risky.

Source: Federal Reserve Bank of St Louis.

substantial funds into several UK banks in an attempt to avert a major failure of the banking sector.

3. Falling Confidence The third element of a financial crisis is a decline in confidence in financial institutions. While some deposits in banks are insured by government policies, not all are. As insolvencies mount, every financial institution becomes a possible candidate for the next bankruptcy. Those with uninsured deposits in those institutions pull out their money. In the UK, in 2007 the Northern Rock bank faced such a bank run, with customers queuing to withdraw their funds. Other banks, such as the French bank BNP Paribas, restricted withdrawals. More recently, in March 2013, banks in Cyprus had double the withdrawals they faced in the previous month, despite banks being closed for two weeks due to the banking crisis there. Facing a rash of withdrawals, banks cut back on new lending and started selling off assets to increase their cash reserves.

As banks sell some of the assets they are holding, they depress the market prices of these assets. Because buyers of risky assets are hard to find in the midst of a crisis, the assets' prices can sometimes fall precipitously. Such a phenomenon is called a **fire sale**, similar to the reduced prices that a store might charge to get rid of merchandise quickly after a fire. These fire-sale prices, however, cause problems at other banks. Accountants and regulators may require these banks to revise their balance sheets and reduce the reported value of their own holdings of these assets. In this way, problems in one bank can spread to others.

In 2008 and 2009, the financial system was seized by great uncertainty about where the insolvencies would stop. The collapse of the giants such as Lehman Brothers made people wonder whether other large financial firms such as Morgan Stanley, Goldman Sachs, and Citigroup would meet a similar fate. The problem was exacerbated by the firms' interdependence. Because they had many contracts with one another, the demise of any one of these institutions undermined all the others. Moreover, because of the complexity of the arrangements, depositors could not be sure how vulnerable these firms were. The lack of transparency fed the crisis of confidence.

4. Credit Crunch The fourth element of a financial crisis is a credit crunch. With many financial institutions facing difficulties, would-be borrowers have trouble getting loans, even if they have profitable investment projects. In essence, the financial system has trouble performing its normal function of directing the resources of savers into the hands of borrowers with the best investment opportunities.

The tightening of credit was clear during the 2008–2009 financial crisis. Not surprisingly, as banks realized that housing prices were falling and that previous lending standards had been too lax, they started raising standards for those applying for mortgages. They required larger down payments and scrutinized borrowers' financial information more closely. But the reduction in lending did not just affect homebuyers. Small businesses found it harder to borrow to finance business expansions or to buy inventories. Consumers found it harder to qualify for a credit card or car loan. Thus, banks responded to their own financial problems by becoming more cautious in all kinds of lending.

5. Recession The fifth element of a financial crisis is an economic downturn. With people unable to obtain consumer credit and firms unable to obtain financing for new investment projects, the overall demand for goods and services declines. Within the context of the *IS-LM* model, this event can be interpreted as a contractionary shift in the consumption and investment functions, which in turn leads to similar shifts in the *IS* curve and the aggregate-demand curve. As a result, national income falls and unemployment rises.

Indeed, the recession following the financial crisis of 2008–2009 was a deep one. Unemployment rose to around 10 per cent in the US and in the Euro Area (Eurozone) countries. Worse yet, it lingered at a high level for a long time. Even after the recovery began, growth in GDP was so meagre that unemployment declined only slightly. In 2012, the unemployment rate was still over 11 per cent in the Euro Area and around 8 per cent in the US and UK.

6. A Vicious Circle The sixth and final element of a financial crisis is a vicious circle. The economic downturn reduces the profitability of many companies and the value of many assets. The stock market declines. Some firms go bankrupt and default on their business loans. Many workers become unemployed and default on their personal loans. Thus, we return to steps one (asset price busts) and two (financial institution insolvencies). The problems in the financial system and the economic downturn reinforce each other. Figure 20-2 illustrates the process.

In 2008 and 2009, the vicious circle was apparent. Some feared that the combination of a weakening financial system and a weakening economy would spiral out of control, pushing the economy into another Great Depression.

FIGURE 20-2

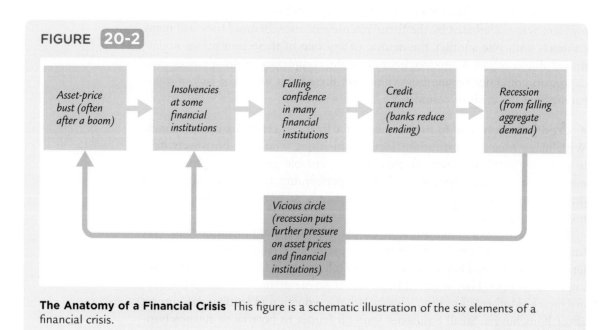

The Anatomy of a Financial Crisis This figure is a schematic illustration of the six elements of a financial crisis.

Fortunately, that did not occur, in part because policy makers were intent on preventing it.

That brings us to the next question: Faced with a financial crisis, what can policy makers do?

Who Should Be Blamed for the Financial Crisis of 2008 and 2009?

'Victory has a thousand fathers, but defeat is an orphan.' This famous quotation from John F. Kennedy contains a perennial truth. Everyone is eager take credit for success, but no one wants to accept blame for failure. In the aftermath of the financial crisis of 2008 and 2009, many people wondered who was to blame. Not surprisingly, no one stepped forward to accept responsibility.

Nonetheless, economic observers have pointed their fingers at many possible culprits. The accused include the following:

- *Central banks.* Central banks, and in particular the US Federal Reserve, kept interest rates low in the early 2000s. These policies help to promote a recovery, but also encourage households to borrow and buy housing. Some economists believe that by keeping interest rates too low for too long, this contributed to the housing bubble that eventually led to the financial crisis.

- *Homebuyers.* Many people were reckless in borrowing more than they could afford to repay. Others bought houses as an investment, hoping that house prices would keep rising at a rapid pace. When house prices fell instead, many of these homeowners defaulted on their debts.

- *Mortgage brokers.* Many providers of home loans encouraged households to borrow excessively. Sometimes they pushed complicated mortgage products with payments that were low initially but exploded later. Some offered what were called Ninja loans (an acronym for 'no income, no job or assets') to households that should not have qualified for a mortgage. The brokers did not hold these risky loans, but instead sold them for a fee after they were issued.

- *Investment banks.* Many of these financial institutions packaged bundles of risky mortgages into mortgage-backed securities and then sold them to buyers (such as pension funds) who were not fully aware of the risks they were taking on.

- *Rating agencies.* The agencies that evaluated the riskiness of debt instruments gave high ratings to various mortgage-backed securities that later turned out to be highly risky. With the benefit of hindsight, it is clear that the models the agencies used to evaluate the risks were based on dubious assumptions.

- *Regulators.* Regulators of banks and other financial institutions are supposed to ensure that these firms do not take undue risk. Yet the regulators failed to appreciate that a substantial decline in house prices might occur and that, if it did, it could have systemic implications for the financial system.

- *Government policy makers.* For many years, political leaders have pursued policies to encourage homeownership. Such policies include the tax deductibility of mortgage interest. Households with shaky finances, however, might have been better off renting.

In the end, it seems that each of these groups (and perhaps a few others as well) bear some of the blame. As *The Economist* magazine once put it, the problem was one of 'layered irresponsibility'.

Finally, keep in mind that this financial crisis was not the first one in history. Such events, though fortunately rare, do occur from time to time. Rather than looking for a culprit to blame for this singular event, perhaps we should view speculative excess and its ramifications as an inherent feature of market economies. Policy makers can respond to financial crises as they happen, and they can take steps to reduce the likelihood and severity of such crises, but preventing them entirely may be too much to ask given our current knowledge.[2] ■

Policy Responses to a Crisis

Because financial crises are both severe and multifaceted, macroeconomic policy makers use various tools, often simultaneously, to try to control the damage. Here we discuss three broad categories of policy responses.

Conventional Monetary and Fiscal Policy As we have seen, financial crises raise unemployment and lower incomes because they lead to a contraction in the aggregate demand for goods and services. Policy makers can mitigate these effects by using the tools of monetary and fiscal policy to expand aggregate demand. The central bank can increase the money supply and lower interest rates. The government can increase government spending and cut taxes. That is, a financial crisis can be seen as a shock to the aggregate-demand curve, which can, to some degree, be offset by appropriate monetary and fiscal policy.

Policy makers in many countries did precisely this during the financial crisis of 2008 and 2009. In the US interest rates were lowered, tax rebates were offered, and there were significant increases in government spending. In the UK, the rate of value-added tax was reduced for a period, and the Bank of England began a programme of quantitative easing while maintaining low interest rates. All these moves were aimed to prop up aggregate demand.

There are limits, however, to how much conventional monetary and fiscal policy can do. A central bank cannot cut its target for the interest rate below zero. (Recall the discussion of the *liquidity trap* in Chapter 12.) Fiscal policy is limited as well. Stimulus packages add to the government budget deficit, which is

---

[2] To read more about the history of financial crises, see Charles P. Kindleberger and Robert Z. Aliber, *Manias, Panics, and Crashes: A History of Financial Crises*, 6th edn, New York: Palgrave Macmillan, 2011; and Carmen M. Reinhart and Kenneth S. Rogoff, *This Time is Different: Eight Centuries of Financial Folly*, Princeton, NJ: Princeton University Press, 2009.

already enlarged because economic downturns automatically increase unemployment insurance payments and decrease tax revenue. Increases in government debt are a concern in themselves, because they place a burden on future generations of taxpayers and they call into question the government's own solvency. In the aftermath of the financial crisis of 2008 and 2009, many European governments' budget deficits reached historic levels. This has led to credit rating agencies reducing their rating on government debt, which makes additional fiscal stimulus more difficult.

The limits of monetary and fiscal policy during a financial crisis naturally lead policy makers to consider other, and sometimes unusual, alternatives. These other types of policy are of a fundamentally different nature. Rather than addressing the symptom of a financial crisis (a decline in aggregate demand), they aim to fix the financial system itself. If the normal process of financial intermediation can be restored, consumers and business will be able to borrow again, and the economy's aggregate demand will recover. The economy can then return to full employment and rising incomes. The next two categories describe the major policies aimed directly at fixing the financial system.

Lender of Last Resort When the public starts to lose confidence in a bank, they withdraw their deposits. In a system of fractional-reserve banking, large and sudden withdrawals can be a problem. Even if the bank is solvent (meaning that the value of its assets exceed the value of its liabilities), it may have trouble satisfying all its depositors' requests. Many of the bank's assets are illiquid – that is, they cannot be easily sold and turned into cash. A business loan to a local restaurant, a car loan to a local family, and a student loan to your roommate, for example, may be valuable assets to the bank, but they cannot be easily used to satisfy depositors who are demanding their money back immediately. A situation in which a solvent bank has insufficient funds to satisfy its depositors' withdrawals is called a **liquidity crisis**.

The central bank can remedy this problem by lending money directly to the bank. As we discussed in Chapter 4, the central bank can create money out of thin air by, in effect, printing it. (Or, more realistically in our electronic era, it creates a bookkeeping entry for itself that represents those monetary units.) It can then lend this newly created money to the bank experiencing withdrawals and accept the bank's illiquid assets as collateral. When a central bank lends to a bank in the midst of a liquidity crisis, it is said to act as a **lender of last resort**.

The goal of such a policy is to allow a bank experiencing withdrawals to weather the storm of reduced confidence. Without such a loan, the bank might be forced to sell its illiquid assets at fire-sale prices. If such a fire sale were to occur, the value of the bank's assets would decline, and a liquidity crisis could then threaten the bank's solvency. By acting as a lender of last resort, the central bank stems the problem of bank insolvency and helps restore the public's confidence in the banking system.

During 2008 and 2009, the Federal Reserve in particular was extraordinarily active as a lender of last resort. During this crisis, the Fed set up a variety of new ways to lend to financial institutions. These programmes have one purpose:

to ensure that the financial system remains liquid. That is, as long as a bank (or **shadow bank** – a financial institution that, although technically not a bank, fulfils similar functions) had assets that could serve as reliable collateral, the central bank stood ready to lend money to the financial institution so that its depositors could make withdrawals.

Injections of Government Funds The third category of policy responses to a financial crisis involves the government using public funds to prop up the financial system.

The most direct action of this sort is a giveaway of public funds to those who have experienced losses. Deposit insurance is one example. The goal is to assure bank depositors that their funds are safe, by the government guaranteeing to make up for losses the depositor would experience if the bank becomes insolvent. The maximum deposits that would be covered by these schemes have increased since the financial crisis to £85,000 in the UK and €100,000 in most European countries.

Giveaways of public funds can also occur on a more discretionary basis. For example, in 1984 a large bank in the US called Continental Illinois found itself on the brink of insolvency. Because Continental Illinois had so many relationships with other banks, regulators feared that allowing it to fail would threaten the entire financial system. As a result, the Federal Deposit Insurance Corporation (FDIC), which makes up for losses (up to a certain insurance limit) that a depositor experiences when a bank becomes insolvent, promised to protect all of its depositors, not just those under the insurance limit. Eventually, it bought the bank from shareholders, added capital, and sold it to Bank of America. This policy operation cost taxpayers about $1 billion. It was during this episode that a congressman coined the phrase 'too big to fail' to describe a firm so central to the financial system that policy makers would not allow it to enter bankruptcy.

Another way for the government to inject public funds is to make risky loans. Normally, when the central bank acts as lender of last resort, it does so by lending to a financial institution that can pledge good collateral. But if the government makes loans that might not be repaid, it is putting public funds at risk. If the loans do indeed default, taxpayers end up losing.

During the financial crisis of 2008–2009, for example, the Federal Reserve in the US engaged in a variety of risky lending. In March 2008, it made a $29 billion loan to JP Morgan Chase to facilitate its purchase of the nearly insolvent Bear Stearns. The only collateral the Fed received was Bear's holdings of mortgage-backed securities, which were of dubious value. Similarly, in September 2008, the Fed lent $85 billion to prop up the insurance giant AIG, which faced large losses from having insured the value of some mortgage-backed securities (through an agreement called a credit default swap). The Fed took these actions to prevent Bear Stearns and AIG from entering a long bankruptcy process, which could have further threatened the financial system.

A final way for the government to use public funds to address a financial crisis is for the government itself to inject capital into financial institutions. In this case, rather than being just a creditor, the government gets an ownership stake in the companies. The UK led the way in October 2008 with a £500 billion rescue package, taken up for the most part by Lloyds and the Royal Bank of Scotland (RBS). This was reinforced early in the following year with a further rescue package, increasing government ownership to 40 per cent of the total share capital of Lloyds Banking Group and 82 per cent of the total share capital of RBS. US and European governments quickly followed suit. Such measures were designed to maintain the banks' solvency and keep the process of financial intermediation intact. They also had welcome positive effects on stock markets in the US and UK.

Not surprisingly, the use of public funds to prop up the financial system, whether done with giveaways, risky lending, or capital injections, is controversial. Critics assert that it is unfair to taxpayers to use their resources to rescue financial-market participants from their own mistakes. Moreover, the prospect of such financial bailouts may increase moral hazard, because when people believe the government will cover their losses, they are more likely to take excessive risks. Financial risk-taking becomes 'heads I win, tails the taxpayers lose'. Advocates of these policies acknowledge these problems but they point out that risky lending and capital injections could actually make money for taxpayers if the economy recovers. More important, they believe that the costs of these policies are more than offset by the benefits of averting a deeper crisis and more severe economic downturn.

Policies to Prevent Crises

In addition to the question of how policy makers should respond once facing a financial crisis, there is another key policy debate: How should policy makers prevent future financial crises? Unfortunately, there is no easy answer. But here are four areas where policy makers have been considering their options and, in some cases, revising their policies.

Focusing on Shadow Banks Traditional commercial banks are heavily regulated. One justification is that the government insures some of their deposits through the FDIC. Policy makers have long understood that deposit insurance produces a moral-hazard problem. Because of deposit insurance, depositors have no incentive to monitor the riskiness of banks in which they make their deposits; as a result, bankers have an incentive to make excessively risky loans, knowing they will reap any gains while the deposit insurance system will cover any losses. In response to this moral-hazard problem, the government regulates the risks that banks take.

Much of the crisis of 2008 and 2009, however, concerned not traditional banks but rather *shadow banks* – financial institutions that (like banks) are at the centre of financial intermediation but (unlike banks) do not take in deposits insured by the FDIC. Bear Sterns and Lehman Brothers, for example, were investment banks and, therefore, as shadow banks, subject to less regulation. Similarly, hedge funds, insurance companies, and private equity firms can be considered shadow banks. These institutions do not suffer from the traditional problem of moral hazard arising from deposit insurance, but the risks they take may nonetheless be a concern of public policy, because their failure can have macroeconomic ramifications.

FYI

CoCo Bonds

One intriguing idea for reforming the financial system is to introduce a new financial instrument called Contingent, Convertible Debt, sometimes simply called *CoCo bonds*. The proposal works as follows: Require banks, or perhaps a broader class of financial institutions, to sell some debt that can be converted into equity when these institutions are deemed to have insufficient capital.

This debt would be a form of preplanned recapitalization in the event of a financial crisis. Unlike the bank rescues in 2008–2009, however, the recapitalization would have the crucial advantage of being done with private, rather than taxpayer, funds. That is, when things go bad and a bank approaches insolvency, it would not need to turn to the government to replenish its capital. Nor would it need to convince private investors to chip in more capital in times of financial stress. Instead, the bank would simply convert the CoCo bonds it had previously issued, wiping out one of its liabilities. The holders of the CoCo bonds would no longer be creditors of the bank; they would be given shares of stock and become part owners. Think of it as crisis insurance.

Some bankers balk at this proposal, because it would raise the cost of doing business. The buyers of these CoCo bonds would need to be compensated for providing this insurance. The compensation would take the form of a higher interest rate than would be earned on standard bonds without the conversion feature.

But this contingent, convertible debt would make it easier for the financial system to weather a future crisis. Moreover, it would give bankers an incentive to limit risk by, say, reducing leverage and maintaining strict lending standards. The safer these financial institutions are, the less likely the contingency would be triggered and the less they would need to pay to issue this debt. By inducing bankers to be more prudent, this reform could reduce the likelihood of financial crises.

CoCo bonds are still a new and untried idea. But they may offer one tool to guard against future financial crises. In 2011, the European Banking Authority established guidelines for the issuance of these bonds. How prevalent they will become in the future remains to be seen.

Many policy makers have suggested that these shadow banks should be limited in how much risk they take. One way to do that would be to require that they hold more capital, which would in turn limit these firms' ability to use leverage. Advocates of this idea say it would enhance financial stability. Critics say it would limit these institutions' ability to do their job of financial intermediation. In Europe, the Basel-based Financial Stability Board (FSB), which coordinates international regulatory activities, is also targeting the shadow banking sector, amid fears that shadow banks may create a future banking crisis. The FSB wishes to bring the regulations for shadow banks more in line with those for mainstream banks.

Another issue concerns what happens when a shadow bank runs into trouble and nears insolvency. Legislation passed in the US in 2010, the so-called Dodd–Frank Act, gave the FDIC *resolution authority* over shadow banks, much as it already had over traditional commercial banks. That is, the FDIC can now take over and close a non-bank financial institution if the institution is having trouble and the FDIC believes it could create systemic risk for the economy. Advocates of this new law believe it will allow a more orderly process when a shadow bank fails and thereby prevent a more general loss of confidence in the financial system. Critics fear it will make bailouts of these institutions with taxpayer funds more common and exacerbate moral hazard.

Restricting Size The financial crisis of 2008–2009 centred on a few very large financial institutions. Some economists have suggested that the problem would have been averted, or at least would have been less severe, if the financial system had been less concentrated. When a small institution fails, bankruptcy law can take over as it usually does, adjudicating the claims of the various stakeholders, without resulting in economy-wide problems. These economists argue that if a financial institution is too big to fail, it is too big.

Various ideas have been proposed to limit the size of financial firms. One would be to restrict mergers among banks. (Over the past half century, the banking industry has become vastly more concentrated, largely through bank mergers.) Another idea is to oblige larger banks to have higher capital requirements. Advocates of these ideas say that a financial system with smaller firms would be more stable. Critics say that such a policy would prevent banks from taking advantage of economies of scale and that the higher costs would eventually be passed on to the banks' customers.

Reducing Excessive Risk Taking The financial firms that failed during the financial crisis of 2008 and 2009 did so because they took risks that ended up losing large sums of money. Some observers believe that one way to reduce the risk of future crises is to limit excessive risk taking. Yet because risk taking is at the heart of what many financial institutions do, there is no easy way to draw the line between excessive and appropriate risks.

Nonetheless, the Dodd–Frank Act in the US included several provisions aimed at limiting risk taking. Perhaps the best known is the so-called Volcker Rule, named after Paul Volcker, the former Federal Reserve chairman who first proposed it. Under the Volcker Rule, commercial banks are restricted from making certain kinds of speculative investments. Advocates say the rule will help protect banks. Critics say that by restricting the banks' trading activities, it will make the market for those speculative financial instruments less liquid. In contrast, the UK's Independent Commission on Banking recommended 'ring fencing' – the separation and protection (by enhanced capital requirements) of essential banking services, such as customer accounts and lending to small and medium businesses, from their more risky investment activities. The UK government plans to pass legislation relating to these recommendations by 2015. A third alternative has been suggested by the Liikanen Review to the European Commission which also involves ring fencing, but the enhanced capital requirements accrue to the riskier investment arms of the banks.

Making Regulation Work Better The financial system is diverse, with many different types of firms performing various functions and having developed at different stages of history. As a result, the regulatory apparatus overseeing these firms is highly fragmented. After the financial crisis of 2008 and 2009, policy makers in the UK and Europe tried to improve the system of regulation. In April 2013, the UK's banking regulator, the Financial Services Authority (FSA), was abolished and replaced with two successor organizations. The Prudential Regulation Authority (PRA), part of the Bank of England, ensures the stability of financial services firms. A separate body, the Financial Conduct Authority (FCA), is responsible for business and market conduct. The Bank of England directly supervises the whole banking system through its powerful Financial Policy Committee (FPC), which can instruct the two new regulators. In December 2012, Euro Area leaders agreed to make the European Central Bank the heart of bank supervision for the 17 member countries. Large banks within the Euro Area will come under the ECB's direct supervision in 2014, monitoring their health and the risks they take, and intervening if any gets into trouble. Only time will tell whether or not these new regulatory structures work better than the old ones.

CASE STUDY

The European Sovereign Debt Crisis

In recent years many European nations have had to struggle to prevent financial crises. The problems stemmed from sovereign debt – that is, debt issued by governments. For many years, banks and bank regulators treated such debt as risk-free. The central governments of Europe, they presumed, would always honour their obligations. This belief meant that these bonds paid a lower interest rate and commanded a higher price than they would if they were perceived as less reliable credit risks.

In 2010, however, financial market participants started to doubt that this optimism about European governments was warranted. The problem began with Greece. In 2010, Greek debt (net financial liabilities) had increased to 148 per cent of its GDP (and still remains high, having subsequently peaked at over 170 per cent), compared with a European average of around 80 per cent. Moreover, it seemed that Greece had for years been misreporting the state of its finances and that it had no plan to rein in its soaring debts. In April 2010, Standard & Poors reduced the rating on Greek debt to junk status, indicating a particularly poor credit risk. Because many feared that default was likely, the prices of Greek debt fell, and the interest rate that Greece had to pay on new borrowing rose markedly. By the summer of 2011, the interest rate on Greek debt was 26 per cent. In November of that year, it rose to over 100 per cent, before falling back in 2012 to an average of just over 20 per cent.

European policy makers were concerned that problems in Greece could have repercussions throughout Europe. Many European banks held Greek debt among their assets. As the value of Greek debt fell, the banks were pushed toward insolvency. A Greek default could push many banks over the edge, leading to a broader crisis in confidence, a credit crunch, and an economic downturn.

As a result, policy makers in healthier European economies, such as Germany and France, helped arrange continuing loans to Greece to prevent an immediate default. Some of these loans were from the European Central Bank. This policy move was not popular. Voters in Germany and France wondered why their tax should help rescue the Greeks from their own fiscal profligacy. Voters in Greece, meanwhile, were also unhappy, because these loans came with the conditions that Greece drastically cut government spending and raise taxes. These austerity measures led to rioting on Greek streets.

Making matters worse was that Greece was not the only country with such problems. Portugal, Ireland, Spain, and Italy had many similar problems, albeit that arguably those faced by Spain and Ireland were very different in origin from those in Greece, being largely due to banks there making bad loans on a large scale. If Greece were allowed to default, rather than being bailed out by its richer neighbours, some feared that Portugal, Ireland, Spain, and Italy would be close behind. A widespread decline in the value of the sovereign debt of all these nations would surely put serious strains on the European banking system. And since the world's banking systems are highly interconnected, it would put strains on the rest of the world as well. In the spring of 2012, a restructuring deal was agreed, whereby the majority of private holders of Greek debt agreed to take a 'haircut' of a little over 50 per cent of the face value of their holdings. Together with continuing austerity measures and structural reforms, including the privatization of state assets, these measures helped to secure further bailouts. Taken together, these measures have gone some way to stabilizing the situation, and the threat of Greek default and possible exit from the euro appears to have receded for now. However, the cost to ordinary Greeks has been very high. The austerity measures have led to almost five years of continual GDP contraction (a little over 5 per cent in the first quarter of 2013 alone). Unemployment has increased, and in early 2013 stands at a little over 25 per cent. This has provided a breeding ground for social unrest, and in particular, widespread dissatisfaction with Germany's role in preserving the value of the euro to its own advantage. It remains to be seen whether the downward spiral and negative multiplier effect of the austerity measures can be sustained in the long term without an unacceptable social cost and increased tensions from widening inequality within the Euro Area. ■

20-3 Conclusion

Throughout history, financial crises have been a major source of economic fluctuations and a main driver of economic policy. In 1873 Walter Bagehot published a celebrated book called *Lombard Street* about how the Bank of England should manage a financial crisis. His recommendation that it should act as a lender of last resort has over time become the conventional wisdom. In 1913, in the aftermath of the banking panic of 1907, the US Congress passed the act establishing the Federal Reserve. Congress wanted the new central bank to oversee the banking system to ensure greater financial and macroeconomic stability.

The Fed has not always been successful in accomplishing this goal. To this day, many economists believe that the Great Depression was so severe because the Fed failed to follow Bagehot's advice and act as lender of last resort. If it had acted more aggressively, the crisis of confidence in the banks and the resulting collapse in the money supply and aggregate demand might have been averted. Mindful of this history, the Fed played a much more active role in trying to mitigate the impact of the financial crisis of 2008–2009, following the lead provided by the UK's response to the financial crisis. In turn, European institutions have likewise followed suit, providing bailouts to a number of Euro Area countries in crisis.

Following a crisis, it is easy to lament the problems caused by the financial system, but we should not lose sight of the great benefits that the system brings. The financial system gives savers the ability to earn the best possible rate of return at the lowest possible risk. It gives entrepreneurs the ability to fund their ideas for new business ventures. By bringing together those who want to save and those who want to invest, the financial system promotes economic growth and overall prosperity.

Summary

1. A central purpose of the financial system is to direct the resources of savers into the hands of borrowers who have investment projects to finance. Sometimes this task is done directly through the stock and bond markets. Sometimes it is done indirectly through financial intermediaries such as banks.

2. Another purpose of the financial system is to allocate risk among market participants. The financial system allows individuals to reduce the risk they face through diversification.

3. Financial arrangements are rife with asymmetric information. Because entrepreneurs know more about the inherent quality of their ventures than do those providing the financing, there is a problem of adverse selection. Because entrepreneurs know more about the decisions they make and actions they take, there is a problem of moral hazard. Financial institutions such as banks mitigate (but do not completely solve) the problems that arise from asymmetric information.

4. Because the accumulation and allocation of capital are a source of economic growth, a well-functioning financial system is a key element of long-run economic prosperity.

5. Crises in the financial system begin when a decline in asset prices, often after a speculative bubble, causes insolvency in some highly leveraged financial institutions. These insolvencies then lead to falling confidence in the overall system, which in turn causes depositors to withdraw funds and induces banks to reduce lending. The ensuing credit crunch reduces aggregate demand and leads to a recession, which, in a vicious circle, exacerbates the problem of rising insolvencies and falling confidence.

6. Policy makers can respond to a financial crisis in three ways. First, they can use conventional monetary and fiscal policy to expand aggregate demand.

Second, the central bank can provide liquidity by acting as a lender of last resort. Third, policy makers can use public funds to prop up the financial system.

7. Preventing financial crises is not easy, but policy makers have tried to reduce the likelihood of future crises by focusing more on regulating shadow banks, by restricting the size of financial firms, by trying to limit excessive risk taking, and by reforming the regulatory agencies that oversee the financial system.

KEY CONCEPTS

Financial system	Risk averse	Speculative bubble
Financial markets	Diversification	Leverage
Bonds	Mutual funds	Fire sale
Stocks	Asymmetric information	Liquidity crisis
Debt finance	Adverse selection	Lender of last resort
Equity finance	Moral hazard	Shadow banks
Financial intermediaries	Financial crisis	

QUESTIONS FOR REVIEW

1. Explain the difference between debt finance and equity finance.

2. What is the main advantage of holding a stock mutual fund over an individual stock?

3. What are adverse selection and moral hazard? How do banks mitigate these problems?

4. How does the leverage ratio influence a financial institution's stability in response to bad economic news?

5. Explain how a financial crisis reduces the aggregate demand for goods and services.

6. What does it mean for a central bank to act as 'lender of last resort'?

7. What are the pros and cons of using public funds to prop up a financial system in crisis?

PROBLEMS AND APPLICATIONS

1. In each case, identify whether the problem is adverse selection or moral hazard, and explain your answer. How might the problem be dealt with?

   a. Rick has secured a large advance to write a textbook. With the money in hand, he prefers spending his time sailing rather than sitting in his office working on the book.

   b. David is trying to get a large advance to write a textbook. He got poor scores for his written skills examinations, but the publishers don't know this.

   c. Brenda is buying a life insurance policy. She knows that members of her family tend to die young.

d. Maria, who has a large life insurance policy, spends her vacation pursuing her favorite hobbies: skydiving, bungee jumping, and bullfighting.

2. Nation A has a well developed financial system, where resources flow to the capital investments with the highest marginal product. Nation B has a less developed financial system from which some would-be investors are excluded.

a. Which nation would you expect to have higher level of total factor productivity? Explain. (*Hint*: See the appendix to Chapter 9 for the definition of total factor productivity.)

b. Suppose that the two nations have the same saving rate, depreciation rate, and rate of technological progress. According to the Solow growth model, how does output per worker, capital per worker, and the capital–output ratio compare in the two countries?

c. Assume the production function is Cobb–Douglas. Compare the real wage and the real rental price of capital in the two countries.

d. Who benefits from having a better developed financial system?

3. Some commentators argue that when a financial firm is rescued by the government in the midst of a financial crisis, the firm's equity holders should be wiped out, but the firm's creditors should be protected. Does this solve the moral hazard problem? Why or why not?

4. In recent years, as described in this chapter, both the United States and Greece have experienced increases in government debt and a significant economic downturn. In what ways were the two situations similar? In what ways were they different? Why did the two nations have different policy options at their disposal?

What We Know, What We Don't

The theory of economics does not furnish a body of settled conclusions immediately applicable to policy. It is a method rather than a doctrine, an apparatus of the mind, which helps its possessor to draw correct conclusions.

— *John Maynard Keynes*

If all economists were laid end to end, they would not reach a conclusion.

— *George Bernard Shaw*

The first chapter of this book states that the purpose of macroeconomics is to understand economic events and to improve economic policy. Now that we have developed and used many of the most important models in the macroeconomist's toolbox, we can assess whether or not macroeconomists have achieved these goals.

Any fair assessment of macroeconomics today must admit that the science is incomplete. There are some principles that almost all macroeconomists accept and on which we can rely when trying to analyse events or formulate policies. Yet there are also many questions about the economy that remain open to debate. In this last chapter we briefly review the central lessons of macroeconomics, and we discuss the most pressing unresolved questions.

The Four Most Important Lessons of Macroeconomics

We begin with four lessons that have recurred throughout this book and that most economists today would endorse. Each lesson tells us how policy can influence a key economic variable – output, inflation or unemployment – either in the long run or in the short run.

Lesson 1: In the Long Run, a Country's Capacity to Produce Goods and Services Determines the Standard of Living of its Residents

Of all the measures of economic performance introduced in Chapter 2 and used throughout this book, the one that best measures economic well-being is GDP. Real GDP measures the economy's total output of goods and services, and, therefore, a country's ability to satisfy the needs and desires of its residents. Nations with higher GDP per person have more of almost everything – bigger homes, more cars, higher literacy, better health care, longer life expectancy and more Internet connections. Perhaps the most important question in macro-economics is what determines the level and the growth of GDP.

The models in Chapters 3, 8 and 9 identify the long-run determinants of GDP. In the long run, GDP depends on the factors of production – capital and labour – and on the technology for turning capital and labour into output. GDP grows when the factors of production increase or when the economy becomes better at turning these inputs into an output of goods and services.

This lesson has an obvious but important corollary: public policy can raise GDP in the long run only by improving the productive capability of the economy. There are many ways in which policy makers can attempt to do this. Policies that raise national saving – either through higher public saving or higher private saving – eventually lead to a larger capital stock. Policies that raise the efficiency of labour – such as those that improve education or increase technological progress – lead to a more productive use of capital and labour. Policies that improve a nation's institutions – such as crackdowns on official corruption – lead to both greater capital accumulation and a more efficient use of the economy's resources. All these policies increase the economy's output of goods and services, and thereby improve the standard of living. It is less clear, however, which of these policies is the best way to raise an economy's productive capability.

'And please let the President of the Central Bank accept the things he cannot change, give him the courage to change the things he can and the wisdom to know the difference.'

Lesson 2: In the Short Run, Aggregate Demand Influences the Amount of Goods and Services that a Country Produces

Although the economy's ability to *supply* goods and services is the sole determinant of GDP in the long run, in the short run GDP depends also on the aggregate *demand* for goods and services. Aggregate demand is of key importance because prices are sticky in the short run. The *IS-LM* model developed in Chapters 11 and 12 shows what causes changes in aggregate demand and, therefore, short-run fluctuations in GDP.

Because aggregate demand influences output in the short run, all the variables that affect aggregate demand can influence economic fluctuations. Monetary policy, fiscal policy and shocks to the money and goods markets are often responsible for year-to-year changes in output and employment. Because changes in aggregate demand are crucial to short-run fluctuations, policy makers monitor the economy closely. Before making any change in monetary or fiscal policy, they want to know whether the economy is booming or heading into a recession.

Lesson 3: In the Long Run, the Rate of Money Growth Determines the Rate of Inflation, But It Does Not Affect the Rate of Unemployment

In addition to GDP, inflation and unemployment are among the most closely watched measures of economic performance. Chapter 2 discussed how these two variables are measured, and subsequent chapters developed models to explain how they are determined.

The long-run analysis of Chapter 5 stresses that growth in the money supply is the ultimate determinant of inflation. That is, in the long run, a currency loses real value over time if, and only if, the central bank prints more and more of it. This lesson can explain the decade-to-decade variation in the inflation rate that we have observed in the advanced Western European and North American economies since the mid-20th century, as well as the far more dramatic hyperinflations that various countries have experienced from time to time.

We have also seen many of the long-run effects of high money growth and high inflation. In Chapter 5 we saw that, according to the Fisher effect, high inflation raises the nominal interest rate (so that the real interest rate remains unaffected). In Chapter 6 we saw that high inflation leads to a depreciation of the currency in the market for foreign exchange.

The long-run determinants of unemployment are very different. According to the classical dichotomy – the irrelevance of nominal variables in the determination of real variables – growth in the money supply does not affect unemployment in the long run. As we saw in Chapter 7, the natural rate of unemployment is determined by the rates of job separation and job finding, which in turn are determined by the process of job search and by the rigidity of the real wage.

Thus we concluded that persistent inflation and persistent unemployment are unrelated problems. To combat inflation in the long run, policy makers have to reduce the growth in the money supply. To combat unemployment, they have to alter the structure of labour markets. In the long run, there is no trade-off between inflation and unemployment.

Lesson 4: In the Short Run, Policy Makers Who Control Monetary and Fiscal Policy Face a Trade-off Between Inflation and Unemployment

Although inflation and unemployment are not related in the long run, in the short run there is a trade-off between these two variables, which is illustrated by the short-run Phillips curve. As we discussed in Chapter 14, policy makers can use monetary and fiscal policies to expand aggregate demand, which lowers unemployment and raises inflation. Or they can use these policies to contract aggregate demand, which raises unemployment and lowers inflation.

Policy makers face a fixed trade-off between inflation and unemployment only in the short run. Over time, the short-run Phillips curve shifts for two reasons. First, supply shocks, such as changes in the price of oil, change the short-run trade-off; an adverse supply shock offers policy makers the difficult choice of higher inflation or higher unemployment. Second, when people change their expectations of inflation, the short-run trade-off between inflation and unemployment changes. The adjustment of expectations ensures that the trade-off exists only in the short run. That is, only in the short run does unemployment deviate from its natural rate, and only in the short run does monetary policy have real effects. In the long run, the classical model of Chapters 3 to 9 describes the world.

The Four Most Important Unresolved Questions of Macroeconomics

So far, we have been discussing some of the broad lessons about which most economists would agree. We now turn to four questions about which there is continuing debate. Some of the disagreements concern the validity of alternative economic theories; others concern how economic theory should be applied to economic policy.

Question 1: How Should Policy Makers Try to Promote Growth in the Economy's Natural Level of Output?

The economy's natural level of output depends on the amount of capital, the amount of labour and the level of technology. Any policy designed to raise output in the long run must aim to increase the amount of capital, improve the use of labour or enhance the available technology. There is, however, no simple and costless way to achieve these goals.

The Solow growth model explored in Chapters 8 and 9 shows that increasing the amount of capital requires raising the economy's rate of saving and investment. Therefore, many economists advocate policies to increase national saving. Yet the Solow model also shows that raising the capital stock requires a period of reduced consumption for current generations. Some argue that policy makers should not encourage current generations to make this sacrifice, because technological progress will ensure that future generations are better off than current generations. (One waggish economist asked, 'What has posterity ever done for me?') Even those who advocate increased saving and investment disagree about how to encourage additional saving and whether the investment should be in privately owned plants and equipment or in public infrastructure, such as roads and schools.

To improve the economy's use of its labour force, most policy makers would like to lower the natural rate of unemployment. As we discussed in Chapter 7, the large differences in unemployment that we observe across countries, and the large changes in unemployment we observe over time within countries, suggest that the natural rate is not an immutable constant but depends on a nation's policies and institutions. Yet reducing unemployment is a task fraught with peril. The natural rate of unemployment could likely be reduced by decreasing unemployment-insurance benefits (and thus increasing the search effort of the unemployed) or by decreasing the minimum wage (and thus bringing wages closer to equilibrium levels). Yet these policies would also hurt some of those members of society most in need, and therefore do not command a consensus among economists. Indeed, in some countries, such as the US after the 2008–2009 financial crisis and subsequent recession, eligibility for unemployment insurance was in fact extended.

In many countries, the natural level of output is depressed by a lack of institutions that people in developed nations take for granted. The citizens of Western European countries, for example, no longer worry about revolutions, coups or civil wars. For the most part, they trust the police and the court system to respect the laws, maintain order, protect property rights and enforce private contracts. In nations without such institutions, however, people face the wrong incentives: if creating something of economic value is a less reliable path to riches than stealing from a neighbour, an economy is unlikely to prosper. All economists agree that setting up the right institutions is a prerequisite for increasing growth in the world's poor nations, but changing a nation's institutions requires overcoming some difficult political hurdles.

Raising the rate of technological progress is, according to some economists, the most important objective for public policy. The Solow growth model shows that persistent growth in living standards requires continuing technological progress. Despite much work on the new theories of endogenous growth, which highlight the societal decisions that determine technological progress, economists cannot offer a reliable recipe to ensure rapid advances in technology. They continue to debate the extent to which the government should take an active role in promoting the development and spread of particular technologies.

Question 2: Should Policy Makers Try to Stabilize the Economy?

The model of aggregate supply and aggregate demand developed in Chapters 10 to 14 shows how various shocks to the economy cause economic fluctuations, and how monetary and fiscal policy can influence these fluctuations. Some economists believe that policy makers should use this analysis in an attempt to stabilize the economy. They believe that monetary and fiscal policy should try to offset shocks in order to keep output and employment close to their natural levels.

Yet, as we discussed in Chapter 15, others are sceptical about our ability to stabilize the economy. These economists cite the long and variable lags inherent in economic policy making, the poor record of economic forecasting, and our still-limited understanding of the economy. They conclude that the best policy is a passive one. In addition, many economists believe that policy makers are all too often opportunistic or follow time-inconsistent policies. They conclude that policy makers should not have discretion over monetary and fiscal policy, but should be committed to following a fixed policy rule. Or, at the very least, their discretion should be somewhat constrained, as is the case when central banks adopt a policy of inflation targeting. There is also debate among economists about which macroeconomic tools are best suited for purposes of economic stabilization. Typically, monetary policy is the first line of defence against the business cycle. However, when interest rates fall close to their lower bound of zero, the focus of macroeconomic discussions turns to fiscal policy. Among economists, there is widespread disagreement about the extent to which fiscal policy should be used to stimulate the economy in downturns and whether tax cuts or spending increases are the preferred policy tool.

A related question is whether the benefits of economic stabilization – assuming stabilization could be achieved – would be large or small. Without any change in the natural rate of unemployment, stabilization policy can only reduce the magnitude of fluctuations around the natural rate. Thus, successful stabilization policy would eliminate booms as well as recessions. Some economists have suggested that the average gain from stabilization would be small.

Finally, in the aftermath of the financial crisis and recession of 2008–2009, economists questioned whether they could stabilize the economy by avoiding such shocks in the future. As we discussed in Chapter 20, problems in the financial system can lead to problems throughout the economy. Indeed, throughout history, financial crises have led to some of the deepest economic downturns. Unfortunately, it is not clear how best to prevent such crises.

One point of debate centres on the response of monetary policy to asset price bubbles. Some economists argue that central banks should monitor these markets and try to prevent large bubbles in asset prices from arising in the first place. This might mean raising interest rates earlier than otherwise to deflate bubbles as they begin to form. Other economists believe that monetary policy makers are no better than market participants at telling when a rise in asset prices is a bubble rather than based on fundamentals. Moreover, they argue, the tools of monetary policy are too crude to prick bubbles, and trying to do so could distract central banks from their primary objectives of stable employment and low inflation.

Another point of debate concerns regulation. Some economists argue that more vigilant regulation of financial institutions can limit the scope of reckless risk-taking and thereby prevent financial crises. Others believe that financial regulation is hard to do well, easy to circumvent, and could give the public a false hope that the financial system is safer than it really is. In addition, they argue that excessive regulation could prevent the financial system from efficiently performing its crucial job of allocating capital and risk, which in turn could impede long-run economic growth.

Question 3: How Costly Is Inflation, and How Costly Is Reducing Inflation?

Whenever prices are rising, policy makers confront the question of whether to pursue policies to reduce the rate of inflation. To make this decision, they must compare the cost of allowing inflation to continue at its current rate to the cost of reducing inflation. Yet economists cannot offer accurate estimates of either of these two costs.

The cost of inflation is a topic on which economists and laymen often disagree. When inflation is high – above 10 per cent per year, as it was in many advanced economies in the late 1970s – opinion polls reveal the public tends to view inflation as a major economic problem. Yet, as we discussed in Chapter 5, when economists try to identify the social costs of inflation, they can point only to shoe-leather costs, menu costs, the costs of a non-indexed tax system, and so on. These costs become large when countries experience hyperinflation, but they seem relatively minor at the moderate rates of inflation experienced in most major economies. Some economists believe that the public confuses inflation with other economic problems that coincide with inflation. For example, growth in productivity and real wages slowed in the 1970s in most advanced economies; some laymen might have viewed inflation as the cause of the slowdown in real wages. Yet it is also possible that economists are mistaken: perhaps inflation is in fact very costly, and we have yet to figure out why.

It is also possible that some amount of inflation is desirable. If workers are highly resistant to cuts in nominal wages, then a positive amount of inflation makes it easier for real wages to fall when necessary to equilibrate the supply and demand for labour. That is, inflation may 'grease the wheels' of labour markets. In addition, higher inflation can raise the nominal interest rate through the Fisher effect. A higher nominal interest rate gives the central bank more room to cut interest rates when necessary to stimulate the economy. In other words, higher inflation may make it less likely that the central bank hits the zero lower bound on nominal interest rates, reducing the risk of the economy falling into a liquidity trap.

The cost of reducing inflation is a topic on which economists often disagree among themselves. As we discussed in Chapter 14, the standard view – as described by the short-run Phillips curve – is that reducing inflation requires a period of low output and high unemployment. According to this view, the cost of reducing inflation is measured by the sacrifice ratio, which is the number of percentage points of a year's GDP that must be forgone to reduce inflation by one percentage point.

Some economists think that the cost of reducing inflation can be much smaller than standard estimates of the sacrifice ratio indicate. According to the rational-expectations approach, discussed in Chapter 14, if a disinflationary policy is announced in advance and is credible, people will adjust their expectations quickly, so the disinflation need not cause a recession.

Other economists believe that the cost of reducing inflation is much larger than standard estimates of the sacrifice ratio indicate. The theories of hysteresis discussed in Chapter 14 suggest that a recession caused by disinflationary policy could raise the natural rate of unemployment. If so, the cost of reducing inflation is not merely a temporary recession, but a persistently higher level of unemployment.

Because the costs of inflation and disinflation remain open to debate, economists sometimes offer conflicting advice to policy makers. Perhaps, with further research, we can reach a consensus on the benefits of low inflation and the best way to achieve it.

Question 4: How Big a Problem Are Government Budget Deficits?

Most models in this book, and most economists, take the traditional view of government debt. According to this view, when the government runs a budget deficit and issues debt, it reduces national saving, which in turn leads to lower investment and a trade deficit. In the long run, it leads to a smaller steady-state capital stock and a larger foreign debt. Those who hold the traditional view conclude that government debt places a burden on future generations.

Yet, as we discussed in Chapter 16, some economists are sceptical of this assessment. Advocates of the Ricardian view of government debt stress that a budget deficit merely represents a substitution of future taxes for current taxes. As long as consumers are forward-looking, as the theories of consumption presented in Chapter 18 assume, they will save today to meet their or their children's future tax liability. These economists believe that the level of government debt has only a minor effect on the economy. They believe that the government's spending decisions matter, but whether that spending is financed by taxation or by selling government bonds is of secondary importance.

Still other economists believe that standard measures of fiscal policy are too flawed to be of much use. Although the government's choices regarding taxes and spending have great influence on the welfare of different generations, many of these choices are not reflected in the size of the government debt. The level of welfare benefits and taxes, for instance, determines the welfare of the elder beneficiaries versus the working-age taxpayers, but measures of the budget deficit do not reflect this policy choice. According to some economists, we should stop focusing on the government's current budget deficit and concentrate instead on the longer-term generational impacts of fiscal policy.

Recent events have focused renewed attention on the possibility of government default. It looked possible that Greece, and perhaps other countries, could default if they were not granted substantial bailouts. Even the US and UK have had their credit ratings downgraded. As the European political system struggled with large budget deficits, economists as well as the general public were divided about what should be done to put the government back on a sustainable path. In particular, they were divided over how much of the fiscal adjustment should come from higher tax revenue and how much should come from reduced government spending.

Conclusion

Economists and policy makers must deal with ambiguity. The current state of macroeconomics offers many insights, but it also leaves open many questions. The challenge for economists is to find answers to these questions and to expand our knowledge. The challenge for policy makers is to use the knowledge we now have to improve economic performance. Both challenges are formidable, but neither is insuperable.

glossary

100 per cent reserve banking: A system in which banks keep all deposits on reserve. (Cf. fractional-reserve banking.)

Accommodating policy: A policy that yields to the effect of a shock and thereby prevents the shock from being disruptive; for example, a policy that raises aggregate demand in response to an adverse supply shock, sustaining the effect of the shock on prices and keeping output at its natural level.

Accounting profit: The amount of revenue remaining for the owners of a firm after all the factors of production except capital have been compensated. (Cf. economic profit, profit.)

Acyclical: Moving in no consistent direction over the business cycle. (Cf. counter-cyclical, pro-cyclical)

Adaptive expectations: An approach that assumes that people form their expectation of a variable based on recently observed values of the variable. (Cf. rational expectations.)

Adverse selection: An unfavourable sorting of individuals by their own choices; for example, in efficiency-wage theory, when a wage cut induces good workers to quit and bad workers to remain with the firm.

Aggregate: Total for the whole economy.

Aggregate demand curve: The negative relationship between the price level and the aggregate quantity of output demanded that arises from the interaction between the goods market and the money market.

Aggregate supply curve: The relationship between the price level and the aggregate quantity of output firms produce.

Animal spirits: Exogenous and perhaps self-fulfilling waves of optimism and pessimism about the state of the economy that, according to some economists, influence the level of investment.

Appreciation: A rise in the value of a currency relative to other currencies in the market for foreign exchange. (Cf. depreciation.)

Arbitrage: The act of buying an item in one market and selling it at a higher price in another market in order to profit from the price differential in the two markets.

Asymmetric information: A situation in which one party in an economic transaction has some relevant information not available to the other party.

Automatic stabilizer: A policy that reduces the amplitude of economic fluctuations without regular and deliberate changes in economic policy; for example, an income tax system that automatically reduces taxes when income falls.

Average propensity to consume (*APC*): The ratio of consumption to income (C/Y).

Bail-out agreement: A rescue package given to countries facing difficulties, for example, when debt levels become unsustainable, to prevent contagion, often with strings attached, for example agreements to substantial cuts in public spending.

Balance sheet: An accounting statement that shows assets and liabilities.

Balanced budget: A budget in which receipts equal expenditures.

Balanced growth: The condition under which many economic variables, such as income per person, capital per person and the real wage, all grow at the same rate.

Balanced trade: A situation in which the value of imports equals the value of exports, so net exports equal zero.

Bank capital: The resources the bank owners have put into the institution.

Bond: A document representing an interest-bearing debt of the issuer, usually a corporation or the government.

Borrowing constraint: A restriction on the amount a person can borrow from financial institutions, limiting that person's ability to spend his or her future income today; also called a liquidity constraint.

Budget constraint: The limit that income places on expenditure. (Cf. intertemporal budget constraint.)

Budget deficit: A shortfall of receipts from expenditure.

Budget surplus: An excess of receipts over expenditure.

Business cycle: Economy-wide fluctuations in output, incomes, and employment.

Business fixed investment: Equipment and structures that businesses buy for use in future production.

Capital: 1. The stock of equipment and structures used in production. 2. The funds to finance the accumulation of equipment and structures.

Capital budgeting: An accounting procedure that measures both assets and liabilities.

Capital requirement: A minimum amount of bank capital mandated by regulators.

Central bank: The institution responsible for the conduct of monetary policy, such as the Federal Reserve in the United States or the European Central Bank in Europe.

Classical dichotomy: The theoretical separation of real and nominal variables in the classical model, which implies that nominal variables do not influence real variables. (Cf. neutrality of money.)

Classical model: A model of the economy derived from the ideas of the classical, or pre-Keynesian, economists; a model based on the assumptions that wages and prices adjust to clear markets and that monetary policy does not influence real variables. (Cf. Keynesian model.)

Closed economy: An economy that does not engage in international trade. (Cf. open economy.)

Cobb–Douglas production function: A production function of the form $F(K, L) = AK^{\alpha}L^{1-\alpha}$, where K is capital, L is labour, and A and α are parameters.

Commodity money: Money that is intrinsically useful and would be valued even if it did not serve as money. (Cf. fiat money, money.)

Common currency area: A geographical area through which one currency circulates and is accepted as the medium of exchange. (Cf. currency union, monetary union.)

Competition: A situation in which there are many individuals or firms, so that the actions of any one of them do not influence market prices.

Conditional convergence: The tendency of economies with different initial levels of income, but similar economic policies and institutions, to become more similar in income over time.

Constant returns to scale: A property of a production function whereby a proportionate increase in all factors of production leads to an increase in output of the same proportion.

Consumer price index (CPI): A measure of the overall level of prices that shows the cost of a fixed basket of consumer goods relative to the cost of the same basket in a base year.

Consumption: Goods and services purchased by consumers.

Consumption function: A relationship showing the determinants of consumption; for example, a relationship between consumption and disposable income, $C = C(Y - T)$.

Contagion: The likelihood that economic conditions can spread from one country to another, for example a banking crisis in one country spreading to another through globally interconnected financial markets.

Contractionary policy: Policy that reduces aggregate demand, real income and employment. (Cf. expansionary policy.)

Convergence: The tendency of economies with different initial levels of income to become more similar in income over time.

Corporate income tax: The tax levied on the accounting profit of corporations.

Cost of capital: The amount forgone by holding a unit of capital for one period, including interest, depreciation and the gain or loss from the change in the price of capital.

Cost-push inflation: Inflation resulting from shocks to aggregate supply. (Cf. demand-pull inflation.)

Counter-cyclical: Moving in the opposite direction from output, incomes and employment over the business cycle; rising during recessions and falling during recoveries. (Cf. acyclical, pro-cyclical.)

CPI: *See* consumer price index.

Creative destruction: The process whereby entrepreneurs introduce innovations that render some incumbent producers unprofitable while promoting overall economic growth.

Credit crunch: A change in conditions at financial institutions that makes it hard for potential borrowers to obtain loans.

Crowding out: The reduction in investment that results when expansionary fiscal policy raises the interest rate.

Currency: The sum of outstanding paper money and coins.

Currency board: A fixed exchange rate system under which a central bank backs all of the nation's currency with the currency of another country.

Currency-deposit ratio: The ratio of the amount of currency that people choose to hold to the amount of demand deposits they hold at banks.

Currency union: A geographical area through which one currency circulates and is accepted as the medium of exchange. (Cf. common currency area, monetary union.)

Cyclical unemployment: The unemployment associated with short-run economic fluctuations;

the deviation of the unemployment rate from the natural rate.

Cyclically adjusted budget deficit: The budget deficit adjusted for the influence of the business cycle on government spending and tax revenue; the budget deficit that would occur if the economy's production and employment were at their natural levels. Also called full-employment budget deficit.

Debt–deflation: A theory according to which an unexpected fall in the price level redistributes real wealth from debtors to creditors and therefore reduces total spending in the economy.

Debt finance: Obtaining funds for a business by borrowing, such as through the bond market.

Deflation: A decrease in the overall level of prices. (Cf. disinflation, inflation.)

Deflator: *See* GDP deflator.

Demand deposits: Assets that are held in banks and can be used on demand to make transactions, such as checking accounts.

Demand-pull inflation: Inflation resulting from shocks to aggregate demand. (Cf. cost-push inflation.)

Demand shocks: Exogenous events that shift the aggregate demand curve.

Depreciation: 1. The reduction in the capital stock that occurs over time because of aging and use. 2. A fall in the value of a currency relative to other currencies in the market for foreign exchange. (Cf. appreciation.)

Depression: A very severe recession.

Devaluation: An action by the central bank to decrease the value of a currency under a system of fixed exchange rates. (Cf. revaluation.)

Diminishing marginal product: A characteristic of a production function whereby the marginal product of a factor falls as the amount of the factor increases while all other factors are held constant.

Discount rate: The interest rate that the central bank charges when it makes loans to banks.

Discounting: The reduction in value of future expenditure and receipts, compared to current expenditure and receipts, resulting from the presence of a positive interest rate.

Discouraged workers: Individuals who have left the labour force because they believe that there is little hope of finding a job.

Disinflation: A reduction in the rate at which prices are rising. (Cf. deflation, inflation.)

Disposable income: Income remaining after the payment of taxes.

Diversification: Reduction of risk by holding assets with imperfectly correlated returns.

Dollarization: The adoption of the US dollar as the currency in another country.

Double coincidence of wants: A situation in which two individuals each have precisely the good that the other wants.

Economic profit: The amount of revenue remaining for the owners of a firm after all the factors of production have been compensated. (Cf. accounting profit, profit.)

Efficiency of labour: A variable in the Solow growth model that measures the health, education, skills and knowledge of the labour force.

Efficiency units of labour: A measure of the labour force that incorporates both the number of workers and the efficiency of each worker.

Efficiency-wage theories: Theories of real-wage rigidity and unemployment according to which firms raise labour productivity and profits by keeping real wages above the equilibrium level.

Efficient markets hypothesis: The theory that asset prices reflect all publicly available information about the value of an asset.

Elasticity: The percentage change in a variable caused by a 1 per cent change in another variable.

EMU: The common currency area formed by the European countries that use the euro as their common currency. (Cf. European Economic and Monetary Union, Euro Area.)

Endogenous growth theory: Models of economic growth that try to explain the rate of technological change.

Endogenous variable: A variable that is explained by a particular model; a variable whose value is determined by the model's solution. (Cf. exogenous variable.)

Equilibrium: A state of balance between opposing forces, such as the balance of supply and demand in a market.

Equity finance: Obtaining funds for a business by issuing ownership shares, such as through the stock market.

Euler's theorem: The mathematical result economists use to show that economic profit must be zero if the production function has constant returns to scale and if factors are paid their marginal products.

Euro: The common currency which is used within the European Economic and Monetary Union, or EMU.

Euro Area: The common currency area formed by the European countries that use the euro as their common currency. (Cf. EMU, European Economic and Monetary Union.)

Euro Crisis: A crisis of confidence following the financial crash of 2008 as to whether the euro offers sufficient flexibility for member countries to withstand and mitigate the effects of financial crisis and recession.

Euroization: The adoption of the euro as the currency in another country.

European Economic and Monetary Union: The common currency area formed by the European countries that use the euro as their common currency. (Cf. EMU, Euro Area.)

European Central Bank (ECB): The central bank, based in Frankfurt, which formulates and implements the monetary policies of the Euro Area.

Ex ante real interest rate: The real interest rate anticipated when a loan is made; the nominal interest rate minus expected inflation. (Cf. *ex post* real interest rate.)

Ex post real interest rate: The real interest rate actually realized; the nominal interest rate minus actual inflation. (Cf. *ex ante* real interest rate.)

Excess reserves: Reserves held by banks above the amount mandated by reserve requirements.

Exchange rate: The rate at which a country makes exchanges in world markets. (Cf. nominal exchange rate, real exchange rate.)

Exogenous variable: A variable that a particular model takes as given; a variable whose value is independent of the model's solution. (Cf. endogenous variable.)

Expansionary policy: Policy that raises aggregate demand, real income and employment. (Cf. contractionary policy.)

Exports: Goods and services sold to other countries.

Factor of production: An input used to produce goods and services; for example, capital or labour.

Factor price: The amount paid for one unit of a factor of production.

Factor share: The proportion of total income being paid to a factor of production.

Federal funds rate: The overnight interest rate at which banks lend to one another.

Federal Reserve (the Fed): The central bank of the United States.

Fiat money: Money that is not intrinsically useful and is valued only because it is used as money. (Cf. commodity money, money.)

Financial crisis: A major disruption in the financial system that impedes the economy's ability to intermediate between those who want to save and those who want to borrow and invest.

Financial intermediaries: Institutions that facilitate the matching of savers and borrowers, such as banks.

Financial intermediation: The process by which resources are allocated from those individuals who wish to save some of their income for future consumption to those individuals and firms who wish to borrow to buy investment goods for future production.

Financial markets: Markets through which savers can directly provide resources to borrowers, such as the stock market and bond market.

Financial system: The set of institutions through which the resources of those who want to save are allocated to those who want to borrow.

Financing constraint: A limit on the quantity of funds a firm can raise – such as through borrowing – in order to buy capital.

Fire sale: The precipitous fall in the price of assets that takes place when financial institutions must sell their assets quickly in the midst of a crisis.

Fiscal federalism: A fiscal system for a group of countries involving a common fiscal budget and a system of taxes and fiscal transfers across countries.

Fiscal policy: The government's choices regarding levels of spending and taxation.

Fisher effect: The one-for-one influence of expected inflation on the nominal interest rate.

Fisher equation: The equation stating that the nominal interest rate is the sum of the real interest rate and expected inflation ($i = r + \pi^2$).

Fixed exchange rate: An exchange rate that is set by the central bank's willingness to buy and sell the domestic currency for foreign currencies at a predetermined price. (Cf. floating exchange rate.)

Flexible prices: Prices that adjust quickly to equilibrate supply and demand. (Cf. sticky prices.)

Floating exchange rate: An exchange rate that the central bank allows to change in response to changing economic conditions and economic policies. (Cf. fixed exchange rate.)

Flow: A variable measured as a quantity per unit of time. (Cf. stock.)

Fractional reserve banking: A system in which banks keep only some of their deposits on reserve. (Cf. 100 per cent reserve banking.)

Frictional unemployment: The unemployment that results because it takes time for workers to search for the jobs that best suit their skills and tastes. (Cf. structural unemployment.)

Full-employment budget deficit: *See* cyclically adjusted budget deficit.

GDP: *See* gross domestic product.

GDP deflator: The ratio of nominal GDP to real GDP; a measure of the overall level of prices that shows the cost of the currently produced basket of goods relative to the cost of that basket in a base year.

General equilibrium: The simultaneous equilibrium of all the markets in the economy.

GNP: *See* gross national product.

Gold standard: A monetary system in which gold serves as money or in which all money is convertible into gold at a fixed rate.

Golden rule: The saving rate in the Solow growth model that leads to the steady state in which consumption per worker (or consumption per efficiency unit of labour) is maximized.

Government purchases: Goods and services bought by the government. (Cf. transfer payments.)

Government-purchases multiplier: The change in aggregate income resulting from a one-euro change in government purchases.

Gross domestic product (GDP): The total income earned domestically, including the income earned by foreign-owned factors of production; the total expenditure on domestically produced goods and services.

Gross national product (GNP): The total income of all residents of a nation, including the income from factors of production used abroad; the total expenditure on the nation's output of goods and services.

Haircut: The percentage reduction of the market value of an asset that will be repaid to creditors.

High-powered money: The sum of currency and bank reserves; also called the monetary base.

Human capital: The accumulation of investments in people, such as education.

Hyperinflation: Extremely high inflation.

Hysteresis: The long-lasting influence of history, for example on the natural rate of unemployment.

Imperfect-information model: The model of aggregate supply emphasizing that individuals do not always know the overall price level because they cannot observe the prices of all goods and services in the economy.

Import quota: A legal limit on the amount of a good that can be imported.

Imports: Goods and services bought from other countries.

Impossible trinity: The fact that a nation cannot simultaneously have free capital flows, a fixed exchange rate and independent monetary policy. Sometimes called the trilemma of international finance.

Imputed value: An estimate of the value of a good or service that is not sold in the marketplace and therefore does not have a market price.

Income effect: The change in consumption of a good resulting from a movement to a higher or lower indifference curve, holding the relative price constant. (Cf. substitution effect.)

Income velocity of money: The ratio of national income, as measured by GDP, to the money supply.

Index of leading indicators: *See* leading indicators.

Indifference curves: A graphical representation of preferences that shows different combinations of goods producing the same level of satisfaction.

Inflation: An increase in the overall level of prices. (Cf. deflation, disinflation.)

Inflation targeting: A monetary policy under which the central bank announces a specific target, or target range, for the inflation rate.

Inflation tax: The revenue raised by the government through the creation of money; also called seigniorage.

Inside lag: The time between a shock hitting the economy and the policy action taken to respond to the shock. (Cf. outside lag.)

Insiders: Workers who are already employed and therefore have an influence on wage bargaining. (Cf. outsiders.)

Interest on reserves: The central bank's policy of paying banks an interest rate for the deposits that they hold as reserves.

Interest rate: The market price at which resources are transferred between the present and the future; the return to saving and the cost of borrowing.

Intermediation: *See* financial intermediation.

Intertemporal budget constraint: The budget constraint applying to expenditure and income in more than one period of time. (Cf. budget constraint.)

Inventories as a factor of production: Inventories that a firm holds because a larger stock of inventories increases the firm's production of goods and services.

Inventory investment: The change in the quantity of goods that firms hold in storage, including materials and supplies, work in process and finished goods.

Investment: Goods purchased by individuals and firms to add to their stock of capital.

Investment tax credit: A provision of the corporate income tax that reduces a firm's tax when it buys new capital goods.

IS curve: The negative relationship between the interest rate and the level of income that arises in the market for goods and services. (Cf. *IS–LM* model, *LM* curve.)

IS–LM model: A model of aggregate demand that shows what determines aggregate income for a given price level by analyzing the interaction between the goods market and the money market. (Cf. *IS* curve, *LM* curve.)

Keynesian cross: A simple model of income determination, based on the ideas in Keynes's *General Theory,* which shows how changes in spending can have a multiplied effect on aggregate income.

Keynesian model: A model derived from the ideas of Keynes's *General Theory;* a model based on the assumptions that wages and prices do not adjust to clear markets and that aggregate demand determines the economy's output and employment. (Cf. classical model.)

Labour-augmenting technological progress: Advances in productive capability that raise the efficiency of labour.

Labour force: Those in the population who have a job or are looking for a job.

Labour-force participation rate: The percentage of the adult population in the labour force.

Labour hoarding: The phenomenon of firms employing workers whom they do not need when the demand for their products is low, so that they will still have these workers when demand recovers.

Large open economy: An open economy that can influence its domestic interest rate; an economy that, by virtue of its size, can have a substantial impact on world markets and, in particular, on the world interest rate. (Cf. small open economy.)

Laspeyres price index: A measure of the level of prices based on a fixed basket of goods. (Cf. Paasche price index.)

Leading indicators: Economic variables that fluctuate in advance of the economy's output and thus signal the direction of economic fluctuations.

Lender of last resort: The role a central bank plays when it lends to financial institutions in the midst of a liquidity crisis.

Leverage: The use of borrowed money to supplement existing funds for purposes of investment.

Life-cycle hypothesis: The theory of consumption that emphasizes the role of saving and borrowing as transferring resources from those times in life when income is high to those times in life when income is low, such as from working years to retirement.

Liquid: Readily convertible into the medium of exchange; easily used to make transactions.

Liquidity constraint: A restriction on the amount a person can borrow from a financial institution, which limits the person's ability to spend his future income today; also called a borrowing constraint.

Liquidity crisis: A situation in which a solvent bank does not have sufficient cash on hand to satisfy the withdrawal demands of depositors.

Liquidity-preference theory: A simple model of the interest rate, based on the ideas in Keynes's *General Theory,* which says that the interest rate adjusts to equilibrate the supply and demand for real money balances.

LM curve: The positive relationship between the interest rate and the level of income (while holding the price level fixed) that arises in the market for real money balances. (Cf. *IS–LM* model, *IS* curve.)

Loanable funds: The flow of resources available to finance capital accumulation.

Lucas critique: The argument that traditional policy analysis does not adequately take into account the impact of policy changes on people's expectations.

M_1, M_2, M_3: Various measures of the stock of money, where larger numbers signify a broader definition of money.

Macroeconometric model: A model that uses data and statistical techniques to describe the economy quantitatively, rather than just qualitatively.

Macroeconomics: The study of the economy as a whole. (Cf. microeconomics.)

Marginal product of capital (*MPK*): The amount of extra output produced when the capital input is increased by one unit.

Marginal product of labour (*MPL*): The amount of extra output produced when the labour input is increased by one unit.

Marginal propensity to consume (*MPC*): The increase in consumption resulting from a one-euro increase in disposable income.

Marginal rate of substitution (*MRS*): The rate at which a consumer is willing to give up some of one good in exchange for more of another; the slope of the indifference curve.

Market-clearing model: A model that assumes that prices freely adjust to equilibrate supply and demand.

Medium of exchange: The item widely accepted in transactions for goods and services; one of the functions of money. (Cf. store of value, unit of account.)

Menu cost: The cost of changing a price.

Microeconomics: The study of individual markets and decision makers. (Cf. macroeconomics.)

Model: A simplified representation of reality, often using diagrams or equations, that shows how variables interact.

Monetarism: The doctrine according to which changes in the money supply are the primary cause of economic fluctuations, implying that a stable money supply would lead to a stable economy.

Monetary base: The sum of currency and bank reserves; also called high-powered money.

Monetary neutrality: *See* neutrality of money.

Monetary policy: The central bank's choice regarding the supply of money.

Monetary transmission mechanism: The process by which changes in the money supply influence the amount that households and firms wish to spend on goods and services.

Monetary union: A group of economies that have decided to share a common currency and thus a common monetary policy. (Cf. common currency area, currency union.)

Money: The stock of assets used for transactions. (Cf. commodity money, fiat money.)

Money demand function: A function showing the determinants of the demand for real money balances; for example $(M/P)^d = L(i, Y)$.

Money multiplier: The increase in the money supply resulting from a one-euro increase in the monetary base.

Money supply: The amount of money available, usually as determined by the central bank and the banking system.

Moral hazard: The possibility of dishonest behaviour in situations in which behaviour is imperfectly monitored; for example, in efficiency-wage theory, the possibility that low-wage workers may shirk their responsibilities and risk getting caught and fired.

Multiplier: *See* government-purchases multiplier, money multiplier, or tax multiplier.

Mundell–Fleming model: The *IS–LM* model for a small open economy.

Mundell–Tobin effect: The fall in the real interest rate that results when an increase in expected inflation raises the nominal interest rate, lowers real money balances and real wealth and thereby reduces consumption and raises saving.

Mutual fund: A financial intermediary that holds a diversified portfolio of stock or bonds.

NAIRU: Non-accelerating inflation rate of unemployment.

National income accounting: The accounting system that measures GDP and many other related statistics.

National income accounts identity: The equation showing that GDP is the sum of consumption, investment, government purchases and net exports.

National saving: A nation's income minus consumption and government purchases; the sum of private and public saving.

Natural rate of unemployment: The steady-state rate of unemployment; the rate of unemployment toward which the economy gravitates in the long run.

Natural-rate hypothesis: The premise that fluctuations in aggregate demand influence output, employment and unemployment only in the short run, and that in the long run these variables return to the levels implied by the classical model.

Neoclassical model of investment: The theory according to which investment depends on the deviation of the marginal product of capital from the cost of capital.

Net capital outflow: The net flow of funds being invested abroad; domestic saving minus domestic investment; also called net foreign investment.

Net exports: Exports minus imports.

Net foreign investment: *See* net capital outflow.

Net investment: The amount of investment after the replacement of depreciated capital; the change in the capital stock.

Neutrality of money: The property that a change in the money supply does not influence real variables. (Cf. classical dichotomy.)

Nominal: Measured in current euros; not adjusted for inflation. (Cf. real.)

Nominal exchange rate: The rate at which one country's currency trades for another country's currency. (Cf. exchange rate, real exchange rate.)

Nominal interest rate: The return to saving and the cost of borrowing without adjustment for inflation. (Cf. real interest rate.)

Normal good: A good that a consumer demands in greater quantity when his or her income rises.

Okun's law: The negative relationship between unemployment and real GDP, according to which a decrease in unemployment of 1 percentage point is associated with additional growth in real GDP of approximately 2 per cent.

Open economy: An economy in which people can freely engage in international trade in goods and capital. (Cf. closed economy.)

Open-market operations: The purchase or sale of government bonds by the central bank for the purpose of increasing or decreasing the money supply.

Optimize: To achieve the best possible outcome subject to a set of constraints.

Optimum currency area: A group of countries for which the benefits of adopting a single currency heavily outweigh the costs.

Outside lag: The time between a policy action and its influence on the economy. (Cf. inside lag.)

Outsiders: Workers who are not employed and therefore have no influence on wage bargaining. (Cf. insiders.)

Paasche price index: A measure of the level of prices based on a changing basket of goods. (Cf. Laspeyres price index.)

Permanent income: Income that people expect to persist into the future; normal income. (Cf. transitory income.)

Permanent-income hypothesis: The theory of consumption according to which people choose consumption according to their permanent income, and use saving and borrowing to smooth consumption in response to transitory variations in income.

Phillips curve: A negative relationship between inflation and unemployment; in its modern form, a relationship among inflation, cyclical unemployment, expected inflation and supply shocks, derived from the short-run aggregate supply curve.

Pigou effect: The increase in consumer spending that results when a fall in the price level raises real money balances and, thereby, consumers' wealth.

Political business cycle: The fluctuations in output and employment resulting from the manipulation of the economy for electoral gain.

Precautionary saving: The extra saving that results from uncertainty regarding, for example, longevity or future income.

Predetermined variable: A variable whose value was fixed in a previous period of time.

Present value: The amount today that is equivalent to an amount to be received in the future, taking into account the interest that could be earned over the interval of time.

Private saving: Disposable income minus consumption.

Pro-cyclical: Moving in the same direction as output, incomes and employment over the business cycle; falling during recessions and rising during recoveries. (Cf. acyclical, counter-cyclical.)

Production function: The mathematical relationship showing how the quantities of the factors of production determine the quantity of goods and services produced; for example, $Y = F(K, L)$.

Production smoothing: The motive for holding inventories according to which a firm can reduce its costs by keeping the amount of output it produces steady and allowing its stock of inventories to respond to fluctuating sales.

Profit: The income of firm owners; firm revenue minus firm costs. (Cf. accounting profit, economic profit.)

Public saving: Government receipts minus government spending; the budget surplus.

Purchasing power parity: The doctrine according to which goods must sell for the same price in every country, implying that the nominal exchange rate reflects differences in price levels.

q theory of investment: The theory according to which expenditure on capital goods depends on the ratio of the market value of installed capital to its replacement cost.

Quantity equation: The identity stating that the product of the money supply and the velocity of money equals nominal expenditure ($MV = PY$); coupled with the assumption of stable velocity, an explanation of nominal expenditure called the quantity theory of money.

Quantity theory of money: The doctrine emphasizing that changes in the quantity of money lead to changes in nominal expenditure.

Quota: *See* import quota.

Random variable: A variable whose value is determined by chance.

Random walk: The path followed by a variable whose changes over time are unpredictable.

Rational expectations: An approach that assumes that people optimally use all available information – including information about current and prospective policies – to forecast the future. (Cf. adaptive expectations.)

Real: Measured in constant euros; adjusted for inflation. (Cf. nominal.)

Real business cycle theory: The theory according to which economic fluctuations can be explained by real changes in the economy (such as changes in technology) and without any role for nominal variables (such as the money supply).

Real cost of capital: The cost of capital adjusted for the overall price level.

Real exchange rate: The rate at which one country's goods trade for another country's goods. (Cf. exchange rate, nominal exchange rate.)

Real interest rate: The return to saving and the cost of borrowing after adjustment for inflation. (Cf. nominal interest rate.)

Real money balances: The quantity of money expressed in terms of the quantity of goods and services it can buy; the quantity of money divided by the price level (M/P).

Recession: A sustained period of falling real income.

Rental price of capital: The amount paid to rent one unit of capital.

Reserve-deposit ratio: The ratio of the amount of reserves banks choose to hold to the amount of demand deposits they have.

Reserve requirements: Regulations imposed on banks by the central bank that specify a minimum reserve–deposit ratio.

Reserves: The money that banks have received from depositors but have not used to make loans.

Residential investment: New housing bought by people to live in and by landlords to rent out.

Revaluation: An action undertaken by the central bank to raise the value of a currency under a system of fixed exchange rates. (Cf. devaluation.)

Ricardian equivalence: The theory according to which forward-looking consumers fully anticipate the future taxes implied by government debt, so that government borrowing today coupled with a tax increase in the future to repay the debt has the same effect on the economy as a tax increase today.

Ring fencing: The separation and protection (by enhanced capital requirements) of essential banking services, such as customer accounts and lending to small and medium businesses, from their more risky investment activities.

Risk averse: A dislike of uncertainty.

Sacrifice ratio: The number of percentage points of a year's real GDP that must be forgone to reduce inflation by 1 percentage point.

Saving: *See* national saving, private saving and public saving.

Seasonal adjustment: The removal of the regular fluctuations in an economic variable that occur as a function of the time of year.

Sectoral shift: A change in the composition of demand among industries or regions.

Seigniorage: The revenue raised by the government through the creation of money; also called the inflation tax.

Shadow banks: Financial institutions that (like banks) are at the centre of financial intermediation but (unlike banks) do not take in deposits insured by the FDIC.

Shock: An exogenous change in an economic relationship, such as the aggregate demand or aggregate supply curve.

Shoeleather cost: The cost of inflation from reducing real money balances, such as the inconvenience of needing to make more frequent trips to the bank.

Small open economy: An open economy that takes its interest rate as given by world financial markets; an economy that, by virtue of its size, has a negligible impact on world markets and, in particular, on the world interest rate. (Cf. large open economy.)

Solow growth model: A model showing how saving, population growth and technological progress determine the level of and growth in the standard of living.

Solow residual: The growth in total factor productivity, measured as the percentage change in output minus the percentage change in inputs, where the inputs are weighted by their factor shares. (Cf. total factor productivity.)

Speculative attack: The massive selling of a country's currency, often because of a change in investors' perceptions, that renders a fixed exchange rate untenable.

Speculative bubble: A rise in the price of an asset above its fundamental value.

Stabilization policy: Public policy aimed at reducing the severity of short-run economic fluctuations.

Stagflation: A situation of falling output and rising prices; combination of stagnation and inflation.

Steady state: A condition in which key variables are not changing.

Sticky prices: Prices that adjust sluggishly and therefore do not always equilibrate supply and demand. (Cf. flexible prices.)

Sticky-price model: The model of aggregate supply emphasizing the slow adjustment of the prices of goods and services.

Sticky-wage model: The model of aggregate supply emphasizing the slow adjustment of nominal wages.

Stock: 1. A variable measured as a quantity at a point in time. (Cf. flow.) 2. Shares of ownership in a corporation.

Stock market: A market in which shares of ownership in corporations are bought and sold.

Stock-out avoidance: The motive for holding inventories according to which firms keep extra goods on hand to prevent running out if sales are unexpectedly high.

Store of value: A way of transferring purchasing power from the present to the future; one of the functions of money. (Cf. medium of exchange, unit of account.)

Structural unemployment: The unemployment resulting from wage rigidity and job rationing. (Cf. frictional unemployment.)

Sub-prime borrower: A borrower with lower income and assets and thus higher risk of default.

Substitution effect: The change in consumption of a good resulting from a movement along an indifference curve because of a change in the relative price. (Cf. income effect.)

Supply shocks: Exogenous events that shift the aggregate supply curve.

Tariff: A tax on imported goods.

Tax multiplier: The change in aggregate income resulting from a one-euro change in taxes.

Taylor principle: The proposition that a central bank should respond to an increase in inflation with an even greater increase in the nominal interest rate.

Taylor rule: A rule for monetary policy according to which the central bank sets the interest rate as a positive function of inflation and a negative function of the shortfall of output from its natural level.

Time inconsistency: The tendency of policy makers to announce policies in advance of implementation in order to influence the expectations of private decision makers, and then to follow different policies after those expectations have been formed and acted upon.

Tobin's _q_: The ratio of the market value of installed capital to its replacement cost.

Total factor productivity: A measure of the level of technology; the amount of output per unit of input, where different inputs are combined on the basis of their factor shares. (Cf. Solow residual.)

Trade balance: The receipts from exports minus the payments for imports.

Trade deficit: An excess of imports over exports.

Trade surplus: An excess of exports over imports.

Transactions theories of money demand: Theories that explain how much money people choose to hold and that stress the role of money as a medium of exchange. (Cf. portfolio theories of money demand.)

Transactions velocity of money: The ratio of the dollar value of all transactions to the money supply.

Transfer payments: Payments from the government to individuals that are not in exchange for goods and services, such as Social Security payments. (Cf. government purchases.)

Transitory income: Income that people do not expect to persist into the future; current income minus normal income. (Cf. permanent income.)

Underground economy: Economic transactions that are hidden in order to evade taxes or conceal illegal activity.

Unemployment insurance: A government program under which unemployed workers can collect benefits for a certain period of time after losing their jobs.

Unemployment rate: The percentage of those in the labour force who do not have jobs.

Unit of account: The measure in which prices and other accounting records are recorded; one of the functions of money. (Cf. medium of exchange, store of value.)

Utility: A measure of household satisfaction.

Value added: The value of a firm's output minus the value of the intermediate goods the firm purchased.

Velocity of money: The ratio of nominal expenditure to the money supply; the rate at which money changes hands.

Wage: The amount paid for one unit of labour.

Wage rigidity: The failure of wages to adjust to equilibrate labour supply and labour demand.

Work in process: Goods in inventory that are in the process of being completed.

World interest rate: The interest rate prevailing in world financial markets.

index

Page numbers in *italics* indicate figures and tables

accelerator model 619
accounting profit 71
Acemoglu, Daron 279
actual expenditure 333
added value 28
adverse selection 213, 627
aggregate demand (AD)
  basic model *see* Keynesian cross
  comprehensive model 466–468
  curve 368–371
  IS-LM model 368–373, 388–392
  long-run equilibrium 371–373
  shocks 323–324, 365–366
  short-run equilibrium 355–356,
    360–363, 371–373
aggregate supply (AS)
  comprehensive model 466–468
  imperfect information model 444–447
  international differences 446–447
  Phillips curve 449–462
  shocks 324–325, *326*
  sticky price model 439–440
  sticky wage model 440–444
Akerlof, George 18, 437
Ando, Albert 584
assets
  diversification of 626
  measurement problem 504–505
  price booms and busts 630–631
asymmetric demand shocks 537–541
asymmetric information 626–628
asymmetric supply shocks 541
Austria 534, 552–553, 608
automatic stabilizers 474
average propensity to consume 568

Bageholt, Walter 643
bailout loans, Euro Area 473, 556,
  642–643
balanced growth 269–270
Ball, Laurence 457, 461
Bangladesh, Grameen Bank 629–630
Bank of England 490–491
  asymmetric supply shocks 541
  and ERM 421–422
  and financial crisis 636, 643
  Financial Policy Committee (FPC) 642
  inflation and CPI 47, 490–491
  inflation targeting 490–491
  international gold standard 406
  Monetary Policy Committee (MPC)
    101, 367, 382, 490, 491
  regulation 642
  repurchase/repo rate 112, 368
  reserve requirements 113
  and stock market 612

Bank of England Act 1998 487
Bank of Japan 381
banks/banking system
  100 per cent reserve 105–106
  capital, leverage, and capital
    requirements 108–109
  crises and credit crunches 615
  see also financial crises; Great
    Depression
  fractional reserve 106–108, 637
  money supply role 105–109
  shadow 638, 639–641
  see also central banks
Barro, Robert 515, 516
Bear Sterns 631, 639
Becker, Gary 343
behavioural economics 594–596
Belgium 153, 211, 273, 457, 501–502
  corporation tax 608
  EMU/Euro Area membership 534,
    549, 552
  GDP 552–553
bilateral trade balances 161
Black Death 72
black economy 29
  size, international estimates 30–31
'Black Wednesday' 421–422
bond markets 625
bond prices 132
booms and busts 630–631
borrowing, government 81, 87–88, 89
borrowing constraints 581, *582*, 614
Brazil 522
break-even investment 254, 268, *269*
Brumberg, Richard 584
budget
  capital 504–505
  deficit 81, 275
  intertemporal budget constraint 572–574
  suplus 81, 276
  see also government debt
Bush, George W. 171, 394, 424–425
business cycle 303, 305–311
  debt measurement 505
  GDP and components 305–307
  leading economic indicators 310–311
  political 481
  unemployment and Okun's Law
    307–310
business fixed investment 601, 602–615
  banking system 615
  cost of capital 604–606
  determinants of 606–608
  financing constraints 614
  rental price of capital 603–604
  stock market and 609–613
  taxes and 608–609

Tobin's *q* 609–612, 614, 617

Cagan model 150–152
Canada 279, 283, 394, 485
  NAFTA 414
capital
  accumulation 235–246
  assets 504–505
  bank 108–109
  budgeting 504–505
  cost of 604–606
  demand 69–70
  flows *see* open economies
  Golden Rule level of 246–253
  Golden Rule steady state 249–253
  gross capital formation 35
  human 276–277
  investment and depreciation 237–240
  knowledge as 286–287
  and labour 63–64, 65–77
  marginal product of (MPC) 69–70
  mobility 164–165, 395, 399,
    545–547, 551–552
  physical 276, 546
  private 276, 278
  public 276, 278
  real rental price of 70
  rental price of 603–604
  requirement 109
capital gains tax 138
Carlyle, Thomas 201
cash management 141
Casio 289–290
casual observations 23, 568
central banks 101–102
  financial crisis (2008–9) 635
  independence 487–488
  inflation targeting 489–492
  IS-LM model 367–368
  lender of last resort 637–638
  money supply model 109–110
  money supply problems 115–117
  open-market operations 111–113
  quantity theory of money 126
  reserve requirements 113
  see also specific central banks
chained-volume measures 32–34
Chile 522
China 280
  Big Mac PPP 186
  currency controversy 424–425
  intellectual property rights 280
  oil demand 328
  population policy 258
  standard of living, international
    comparison *234*

Chirac, Jacques 227
Churchill, Winston 322
Cicero, Quintus Tullius 499
cigarette money (POW camps) 99–100
circular flow 24–25, *62*
Citigroup 633
civil law systems 278
claimant count method 52
classical dichotomy 147
classical model 20, 62, 83
closed economies 77–83, 467
    vs open economies 156, 165–166,
        192–193, 273
Cobb, Charles 72
Cobb–Douglas production function
    72–75, 76, 604
    capital flow to poor countries 172, 173
    steady state and 240
CoCo bonds 640
cold-turkey solution 458, 461
collective bargaining 211–212
colonial origins of modern institutions
    279–280
Columbia 522
commodity money 99, 100
common currency areas 533–534
    benefits of 535–537
    costs of 537–543
    fiscal federalism 554–555
    fiscal policy 554–560
    free-rider problem 555–556
    optimum 548–553
    theory 543–548
    see also Euro Area
common law systems 278
competitive firms
    decisions facing 65–67
    demand for factors 67–70
    division of national income 70–71
computer and information technology
    284–285
Conference Board Index, US 310–311
constant returns to scale 64, 71, 73
constant velocity of money 125, 126,
    354
consumer price index (CPI) 45–51
    and inflation 47–48, 490–491
    price of basket of goods 45–46
    and RPI 48–51
    vs GDP deflator 46–47
consumer(s)
    current and future 253
    expectations, index of 311
    and future taxes 514–515
    preferences 576–577
consumption 77–78
    borrowing constraint 581, *582*
    elderly savings and 587–588
    final consumption expenditure 34–35
    of fixed capital 42
    function 78, 568–572
    government 35
    see also government purchases

household 34–35, 36
income changes, effect of 578–579,
    593–594
intertemporal budget constraint
    572–574
intertemporal choice 572–584
Japanese saving rate and 583–584
Keynes's conjectures 568–569
life-cycle hypothesis 584–588
NPISH 35, 36
optimization 577, *578*
permanent income hypothesis
    589–591
pull of instant gratification 594–596
puzzle 571–572, 586
random-walk hypothesis 592–594
real interest rate changes, effect of
    579–581
secular-stagnation hypothesis
    570–571
steady-state 246–248
supply and demand for goods/
    services 83–92, 236–237
tax changes, effects of 591
wealth-shift, effects of 586–587
Contingent, Convertible (CoCo)
    bonds 640
convergence 270–271
corporation tax 608–609
cost of capital 604–606
cost of holding money 134
cost of living *see* consumer price index
    (CPI)
cost-push inflation 452
costs of inflation
    expected 138–139
    and inflation reduction 653–654
    unexpected 139–140
CPE (First Employment Contract),
    France 227
CPI *see* consumer price index
creative destruction thesis 289–290
credit cards 102, 323
credit crunches 615, 633–634
crowd out investment 87–88, 90
currency 99, 102
    Chinese controversy 424–425
    devaluation and revaluation 409
    Euro Area crisis 559–560
    see also common currency areas;
        exchange rates
currency boards 420
currency-deposit ratio 109–110
current account balance 162
    European countries 163–164
    and trade balance 160–164
current accounts 103
cyclically adjusted budget deficit 507
Cyprus 473, 502
    bailout loans 556
    EMU membership 534
    Euro Area crisis 560, 633
Czech Republic 550, 609

de Villepin, Dominique 277
debit cards 103
debt *see* government debt
debt crises *see* financial crises
debt-deflation theory 377
debt-to-GDP ratio 524–525
deflation 10–11
    destabilizing effects of 377–379
    expected: *IS-LM* model 378–379
    stabilizing effects of 377
    see also Great Depression
demand
    deposits 103
    for goods/services 83–92, 236–237
    see also aggregate demand (AD)
demand shocks
    aggregate 323–324, 365–366
    asymmetric 537–541
    symmetric 552–553
demand-pull inflation 452
demographics
    Europe unemployment 224–225
    UK unemployment 216–217, 218
Denmark 83, 187, 221, 409
    corporation tax 608
    ERM 421
    European Social Model 226
    GDP 38, *39*, 83
    sacrifice ratio 457
    trade integration 550
depreciation 42, 605
    exchange rates 174, 182–183
    and investment: steady state 237–240
depressions 10
    see also Great Depression
devaluation 409
developing and developed countries,
    compared 172–173, 255–256,
    270–271, 279–280
differentials *see* interest rate differentials
diminishing marginal product 68
discount rate 112
discouraged worker effect 217, 221
discretionary policy 480–485
    constrained 485–487
disinflation
    rational expectations and 458–460
    and sacrifice ratio 456–458, 460–461
disposable income 78
distribution
    intergenerational 518–519
    neoclassical theory of distribution 65–77
diversification of assets 626
Dodd–Frank Act 2010, US 640–641
dollarization 420
double coincidence of wants 98
Douglas, Paul 72

East Asia
    financial crisis 415–416
    Tigers 298–299
    see also China; Japan

ECB *see* European Central Bank
economic fluctuations 303–305
  aggregate demand (AD) 314–317
  aggregate supply (AS) 317–322
  business cycle and 305–311
  OPEC embargo 326–328
  short-run and long-run, compared
    312–313, 320–322
  stabilization policy 323–328
  supply and demand model 313–314
  time horizons 312–314
economic forecasting 474–477
economic growth
  balanced growth 269–270
  capital stock 237–246
  convergence 270–271
  creative destruction thesis 289–290
  East Asian Tigers 298–299
  factor accumulation *vs* production
    efficiency 271–272
  factors of production 294–296
  financial system role 628–629
  free trade and 272–273
  Germany 242–244
  international comparison 283–285
  Japan 242–244
  measurement problems 281–282
  model *see* Solow model
  output per person *281*
  policies promoting 273–285
  savings and 243–246, 274–276
  sources of 298, *299*
  technological progress 267–269,
    284–285, 296–297
  theory development 269–273
  world slowdown (1972–2011)
    281–283
economic indicators 310–311
economic policies 273–285
  frictional unemployment and 205–207
  investment allocation 276–278
  rate of saving 274–276
  role of institutions 278–280
  technological progress 280
  see also fiscal policies; monetary
    policies; stabilization policy
economic profit 71
economies
  fine-tuning 341–342
  manipulation of 481
  natural level of output 371, *372*
  see also closed economies; open
    economies
economists
  Nobel Prize winners 18–19
  thinking processes 12–20
  vs lay perspectives on inflation 137
Edward III (England) 520
efficiency-wage theories 212–214
efficient markets hypothesis 612–613
elderly, savings of 587–588
employment *see* job finding rate;
  unemployment

EMU *see* European Economic and
  Monetary Union (EMU)
endogenous growth theory 285–290
  basic model 286–287
  creative destruction thesis 289–290
  research and development 288–289
  two-sector model 287–288
endogenous variables 13
equilibrium
  financial markets 84–86
  general model *see* circular flow
  interest rate 84–86, 91
  Keynesian cross 335–337
  long-run 371–373
  short-run 355–356, 360–363,
    371–373
  supply and demand for goods and
    services 83–92
equity finance 625
Estonia 534, 549
Euler's theorum 71
Euro Area 534
  bailout loans 473, 556, 642–643
  Big Mac PPP 186
  costs and benefits of monetary union
    418–419
  crisis 419, 559–560, 642–643
  crisis management mechanisms 473
  exchange rate 22, 197
  government deficits 500
  indexed bonds 521
  interest rates/investment 191, 193,
    196, 197, 198
  large open economy model 187,
    191, 193
  map *535*
  real GDP growth 552–553
  trade integration 548–550
  and UK, measurement of money
    supply 103, *104*
  unemployment 6–8
  wage flexibility 551
  see also common currency areas;
    European Monetary Union
    (EMU)
Euro exchange rate debate 417–419
Euro-Barometer happiness survey 210
euroization 420
European Central Bank (ECB) 101,
  418, 489–490
  Governing Council 101
  price stability objective 487, 489–490
  refinancing rate 112
  supervisory role 642
European Commission: Liikanen
  Review 641
European countries/EU
  consumption, investment and
    government purchases 81–83
  CPI and RPI 48–51
  current account balance 163–164
  decline in GDP growth 366–367
  indexed bonds 521

inflation rates 6–9
inflation and unemployment 6–9
lottery prizes 575
minimum wage 208–209
real GDP per person across 42–44
recovery from Great Depression 409
seigniorage as percentage of national
  output 128–129
unemployment trends *202*, 221–227
European Exchange Rate Mechanism
  (ERM) 420–422
European Financial Stability
  Mechanism (EFSM) 560
European Monetary Union (EMU) 533
  policy trilemma 423–424
  Stability and Growth Pact (SGP)
    526–527, 557–559
European Social Model 226
European Stability Mechanism (ESM)
  473
ex ante real interest rate 132–133
ex post real interest rate 132–133
excess reserves 115
exchange, medium of 98
exchange rates 173–186
  capital flow 194, *195*
  country risk and 411–412
  and purchasing power parity (PPP)
    183–186
  trade policies, effects of 180–181
  see also fixed exchange rates; floating
    exchange rates; nominal
    exchange rates; real exchange
    rates
exogenous variables 13
expected deflation 378–379
expected inflation 138–139
expenditure
  actual 333
  components of 34–41
  in computing GDP 25, 26–31
  income and circular flow 24–25
  planned 333–334
  see also consumption; government
    purchases; investment; net
    exports
exports *see* net exports; *entries beginning*
  trade
extractive institutions 279–280

factor prices 65
  Black Death 72
  Solow model 270
factors of production 63
  economic growth 294–296
  inventories as 619
  national income distributed to 65–77
  and production function 63–64, 84,
    126
falling confidence 633
Federal Deposit Insurance Corporation
  (FDIC), US 638, 639, 640

Federal Open Market Committee (FOMC) 101
fiat money 99, 100
final consumption expenditure 34–35
financial capital 547
    mobility 551–552
Financial Conduct Authority (FCA), UK 642
financial crises 630–643
    anatomy (2008–9) 630–635
    asset-price booms and busts 630–631
    blame for 635–636
    CoCo bonds 640
    conventional monetary and fiscal policy 636–637
    credit crunch 615, 633–634
    East Asia (1997–98) 415–416
    and economic downturn 381–384
    Euro Area 559–560, 642–643
    falling confidence 633
    implications for government funds 638–639
    insolvency of financial institutions 631–633
    lender of last resort 637–638
    markets and intermediaries 87
    Mexico (1994–95) 414–415
    mortgage-backed securities 87, 381–383, 631–634, 635
    policy responses 636–639
    policy to prevent 639–643
    recession 634
    regulation 641–642
    shadow banks 638, 639–641
    size restriction of financial institutions 641
    TED spread 632
    unemployment, Europe 223–224
    vicious circle 634–635
    see also Great Depression
financial institutions *see* banks/banking system; central banks; financial crises
financial intermediation 87, 107–108, 625
financial markets 625
    equilibrium 84–86
Financial Stability Board (FSB) 640
financial system, roles of 624–630
    dealing with asymmetric information 626–628
    financial crisis (2008–9) 87
    financing investment 624–625
    fostering economic growth 628–629
    microfinance 629–630
    risk sharing 625–626
financing constraints 614
Finland 211, 409, 549
    EMU membership 534
    GDP 38, *40*
fire sales 633, 637
firms

price level rises 138
research and development 287–289
taxes 608–609
see also competitive firms
First Employment Contract, France 227
fiscal federalism 554–555
fiscal policies
    common currency areas 554–560
    conventional, in financial crises 636–637
    fixed exchange rates 407–408
    floating exchange rates 400–401
    government debt 518–519
    government purchases 337–339, 360, *361*
    IS curve shifts 345, *346*, 360–361, *364*
    large open economies 195–196, *197*
    and monetary policy interaction: *IS-LM* model 363–365, 391–392
    multipliers 337–339, *339*, *340*
    popularity of 340–342
    real exchange rate 177–178, *179*
    savings 86–92
    taxes 339, *340*, 360–361, *364*
    trade balance 166–168
fiscal sustainability 523–529
Fisher, Irving 130, 133, 475, 572, 589, 594
    intertemporal choice 572–584
Fisher equation/effect 130–132, 133, 134, 135–136, 350, 351
fixed exchange rates
    devaluation and European recovery from Great Depression 409
    fiscal policy 407–408
    and floating exchange rates, compared 416–425
    international gold standard 406–407
    mechanism 404–406
    monetary policy 408–409
    small open economies 404–411
    trade policy 409–410
    trilemma of international finance 422, *423*
fixed-rate mortgages 139
flexibility
    price 17, 312–313, 314
    wage 544–545, 551
Flinders Island 260
floating exchange rates
    fiscal policy 400–401
    and fixed exchange rates, compared 416–425
    monetary policy 401–402
    small open economies 399–404
    trade policy 402–404
flow
    circular 24–25, *62*
    and stock 26
FOMC *see* Federal Open Market Committee

Ford, Henry 214
Ford Motor Company, US 214–215
forecasting 474–477
forward-looking Taylor rule 486–487
fractional reserve banking 109–110
France
    black economy 30–31
    consumption growth *306*
    corporation tax 608
    economic growth 305, *306*, *307*
    EMU membership 534
    European debt crisis 642–643
    First Employment Contract (CPE) 227
    GDP *41*, 305, 478–479, 552–553
    and Germany: costs of single currency 537–542
    and Germany: exchange rate 418, 424
    and Germany: fiscal federalism 554–555
    government debt 501–502
    and Great Depression 373–374, 409
    indexed bonds 521
    investment growth *307*
    labour market reform 226–227
    labour mobility 545
    OPEC-induced fluctuations *326*, *327*
    recessions 303–304
    SGP 559
    trade integration 549
    and UK: business cycle 303–308
    unemployment rates 308
    wages 544, 551
    youth unemployment 226–227
Frankel, Jeffrey 273
free trade 272–273
free-rider problem 555–556
frictional unemployment
    government policy and 205–207
    job search and 204–207
Friedman, Ben 520
Friedman, Milton
    consumption puzzle 572
    inflation and money growth 126–127
    inflation/unemployment trade-off 437, 438
    monetary policy 471, 483
    money hypothesis: Great Depression 376
    Nobel Prize 19
    permanent-income hypothesis 589–591
    and Phillips curve 451
full-employment budget deficit *see* cyclically adjusted budget deficit
functions, use of mathematical concept of 16

GDP *see* gross domestic product
GDP deflator 32, 126
    vs consumer price index (CPI) 46–47

general government consumption 36
Germany
  black economy 30–31
  current account 163
  economic growth 242–243, 244
  EMU membership 534
  European debt crisis 642–643
  and France: costs of single currency
    537–542
  and France: exchange rate 418, 424
  and France: fiscal federalism 554–555
  and free-rider problem 555–556
  GDP 38, *39*, 41
  and Great Depression 373–374, 409
  indexed bonds 521
  interwar hyperinflation 144–145
  labour market 224
  labour mobility 545
  macroeconomic history 4–6
  seigniorage 129
  SGP 559
  trade integration 550
  and UK: macroeconomic history 4–6
  unemployment rates 8
  wages 544
globalization 155–156
GNP *see* gross national product
gold standard 99, 100
  and fixed exchange rates 406–407
  UK (1920s) 321–322
Golden Rule level of capital 246–253,
    256, 269
Golden Rule steady state 249–253
  numerical example 249–252
  transition to 251–253
Golden Rule of UK public finance
    527–529
Goldman Sachs 633
goods and services
  AD and 648–649
  computing GDP 26–31
  consumption and 83–92
  demand, determinants of 77–83
  equilibrium 83–92, 335–337
  intermediate 28
  IS curve 333–348
  Keynesian cross 333–340
  long-run capacity 648
  Mundell–Fleming model 395–399
  short-run production 648–649
  standard of living 648
  supply of 64
  total production 63–64
  used 27
Governing Council, ECB 101
government, role of 279
government bonds 101–102
  consoles 89
  indexed 520–522
government borrowing 81, 87–88, 89
government consumption 35
government debt 499–500
  balanced budget view 518–519

budget deficits 523–529
business cycle 505
capital assets 504–505
cyclically adjusted budget deficit 507
debt-to-GDP ratio 523–529
future generations 514–515
Golden Rule of UK public finance
    527–529
gross debt *vs* public sector net debt
    506–507
indexed bonds 520–522
inflation 503–504
international dimensions 520
Laffer curve and supply-side
    economics 509–512
measurement problems 503–507
monetary policy 519
optimal fiscal policy view 518–519
Ponzi finance 528
Ricardian view 512–517
size of 501–503
Stability and Growth Pact 526–527
tax and incentives 510
traditional view 508–512
uncounted liabilities 505
government funds, implications of
    financial crises 638–639
government purchases 36–37, 81
  European countries, compared 81–83
  increase in 86–90
  IS-LM model 337–339, 360, *361*
Grameen Bank, Bangladesh 629–630
Great Depression 373–380
  bank failures 116–117
  deflation effects 377–379
  European recovery from 409
  and financial crisis (2008–9) 381
  IS-LM analysis 373–380
  and Japanese slump (1990s) 380–381
  money hypothesis 376, 377–379
  repetition of 379–380
  spending hypothesis 374–376
Greece
  bailout loans 473, 556, 560
  black economy 30–31
  debt crisis (2008–9) 419, 559–560,
    642–643
  GDP 41, 43, 552–553
  indexed bonds 521
  size of government debt 501
  trade integration 549–550
gross capital formation 35
gross domestic product (GDP) 24–45
  added value 28
  arithmetic trick 33
  business cycle 305–307
  circular flow 24–25
  components 37–41, 77–83
  current account balance 160–164
  deflator *see* GDP deflator
  Euro Area 552–553
  expenditure and 24–25, 26–31,
    34–41

government debt-to-GDP ratio
    524–525
housing services 28–29
imputations 28–31
intermediate goods 28
international decline in growth
    (2001) 366–367
inventories 27–28
national income accounts 34–41
percentage changes 33
real and nominal 31–32, 126
rules for computing 26–31
seasonal adjustment 44–45
stocks and flows 26
trade balance 160–164
used goods 27
see also real gross domestic product
    (GDP)
gross national product (GNP) 42
  trade balance 160–164

Hall, Robert 592, 594
happiness: European survey 210
Harmonized Indices of Consumer
    Prices (HICPs) 50
Hayek, Nicolas 290
high-powered money *see* monetary base
Hong Kong 298, 422
household consumption 34–35, 36
housing market
  financial crisis (2008–9) 87, 381–383,
    630–631, 635–636
  see also mortgages; residential
    investment
housing services 28–29
human capital 276–277
Hume, David 122
Hungary 50, 522, 550, 609
hyperinflation 141–146
  causes of 143–146
  costs of 141–143
hysteresis 461–462

Iceland 9, 521, 522
ideas, depletion of 282–283
ILO *see* International Labour
    Organization (ILO)
IMF *see* International Monetary Fund
imperfect information model 444–447
implicit price deflator for GDP *see*
    GDP deflator
imports *see entries beginning* trade
impossible trinity 422, *423*
income
  changes 578–579, 593–594
  circular flow 24–25
  consumption and 578–579, 589–591,
    593–594
  disposable 78
  effect 580
  national *see* national income

income *(Continued)*
permanent-income hypothesis 589–591
quantity theory of money 124
theory of liquid preference 352–353
income per person
and investment rate 244–246
and population growth 257–258
income velocity of money 124
Independent Commission on Banking, UK 641
indexed bonds 520–522
indifference curves 576–577
industrial policy 277, 280
inflation 121–122
benefit of 140–141
Cagan model 150–152
causes of 452
classical response 136–137
cold-turkey solution 458, 461
cost-push 452
costs of 136–141
and CPI 47–48, 490–491
demand-pull 452
expected 138–139
government debt 503–504
inertia 451–452
and interest rates 130–133, 134–136
layman's view 137
life satisfaction 210
and money growth 126–127, 129–130, 649
and nominal exchange rates 182–183
and nominal interest rates 131–132, 134–136
Phillips curve 449–456
and prices 126–127, 134–136
rate: Europe and US 6–9
reduction 653–654
tax/tax laws and 128–130, 138
and unemployment trade-offs 455–456, 496–499, 650
unexpected 139–140
see also hyperinflation
inflation targeting
central bank independence and 489–492
rule *vs* discretion 483–484, 485–487
Taylor rule 484–485, 486–487
infrastructure 276, 278
inside lag 473
insolvency of financial institutions 631–633
instant gratification, pull of 594–596
institutions
establishing 278–279
modern, colonial origins of 279–280
intellectual property rights 280
interest rate differentials 411–416
country risk 411–412
East Asian financial crisis (1997–98) 415–416
exchange rate expectations 411–412

Mexican financial crisis (1994–95) 414–415
Mundell–Fleming model 412–414
interest rates 79–80
Euro Area 191, 193, 196, 197, 198
and financial markets equilibrium 84–86, 91
and inflation 130–133, 134–136
IS-LM model 343–345, 350–351, 367–368
nominal *see* nominal interest rates
real *see* real interest rates
TED spread 632
and wars, UK (1730–1920) 88–90
world 164–165
intergenerational distribution 518–519
international flows of capital and goods 156–164
capital mobility 164–165
current account balance 160–164
example 159–160
net exports, role of 156–157
poor countries 172–173
trade balance 157–159
International Labour Organization (ILO) 52–53
International Monetary Fund (IMF) 415, 416, 473
intertemporal budget constraint 572–574
borrowing constraint 581, *582*
consumer preferences 576–577
income 578–579
Japanese savings rate 583–584
lottery prize values: Europe and US 575
optimization 577, *578*
real interest rate 579–581
inventories
as factor of production 619
GDP 27–28
inventory investment 601, 618–620
accelerator model 619
and real interest rate 620
reasons for holding 618–619
investment 36–37, 79–80
allocation, government policy 276–278
break-even 254, 268, *269*
business fixed *see* business fixed investment
components 601–602
crowd out 87–88, 90
definition 37
depreciation 237–240
Euro Area 191, 193, 196, 197, 198
European countries 81–83
financing 624–625
gross capital formation 35
impact of increased government purchases 86–90
international capital flows and trade balance 157–159
international comparison 244–246

inventory *see* inventory investment
IS-LM model 343–345
neoclassical model 602
rate and income per person 244–246
and real interest rate 178–179, 620
residential *see* residential investment
small open economies 164–173
tax credit 609
investment banks 635
investment demand shifts 90–92, 196, *198*
and real interest rate 178–179
and trade balance 168–169
Ireland
bailout loans 473, 556, 560
corporation tax 608
current account/trade balance 163–164
EMU membership 534
Euro Area crisis 560, 643
financial crisis (2008–9) 630–631
GDP 38, *40*, 153, 552–553
government debt 501
inflation rate 50
minumum wage 209
sacrifice ratio 457
trade integration 550
unemployment 8, 462
IS curve 332–333
AD 388–389
goods and services 333–348
Great Depression 374–376
loanable funds 345–348
and Mundell–Fleming model 395–396, *397*
shifts: fiscal policies 345, *346*, 360–361, *364*
IS-LM model 332–333
aggregate demand (AD) 368–373, 388–392
central bank policy instrument 367–368
expected deflation 378–379
explaining fluctuations 360–368
fiscal and monetary policies interaction 363–365, 391–392
government purchases 337–339, 360, *361*
Great Depression analysis 373–380
interest rates 343–345, 350–351, 367–368
investment 343–345
long-run equilibrium 371–373
monetary policy 350–351, 353–354, 361–365, 391–392
Mundell–Fleming model and 393–394, *399*, 431–433, 437
short-run equilibrium 355–356, 360–363, 371–373
short-run fluctuations 360–363
special case 467
Israel 485, 522

Italy
 EMU membership 534
 Euro Area crisis 560, 643
 GDP *41*, 552–553
 government debt 501
 unemployment 462

Japan
 Bank of Japan 381
 black economy 31
 corporation tax 608
 economic growth 242–243, 244
 economic slump 283, 284, 380–381
 savings rate 583–584
 watch industry 289–290
job finding rate 203, 204
 unemployment benefit and 206–207
job rationing 207–208
job search and frictional unemployment
  204–207
job separation rate 203, 204
Jobseekers Allowance (JSA), UK 220
Johnson, Lyndon 591
Johnson, Simon 279
JP Morgan Chase 638

Keynes, John Maynard
 consumption function 568–572, 596
 economics 647
 General Theory 331
 gold standard 322
 inflation 121, 122
 inflation as taxation 129
 interest rate determination 348
 investment 601
 IS-LM model 332
 liquidity trap 284
 real wages, cyclical behaviour of 443
 role of policy makers 493
 stock markets 613
Keynesian cross 333–340, 396, *397*
 dwindling popularity of fiscal policy
  340–342
 economy in equilibrium 335–337
 government purchases 337–339,
  342–343, 360
 planned expenditure 333–334
 taxes 339, *340*, 361
knowledge production 287
knowledge spillover 277
Kremer, Michael 259
Kremerian model 259–260
Kuznets, Simon 19, 571

labour
 capital and 63–64, 65–77
 demand 68–69
 efficiency of 266–267
 marginal product of (MPL) 67–68, *70*
 mobility 545, 551

 productivity and real wages 76–77
 quality of 282
labour force
 definition 53
 participation rate 53–55
 transition in and out of 220–221
 women's participation 55, 217, 225
Labour Force Survey 53
labour markets
 effect of inflation 140–141
 Europe 221–227
 French reform 226–227
 Germany 224
 see also unemployment
labour unions *see* unions
labour-augmenting technological
  progress 267, *268*
Laffer curve 509–512
large open economies 191–200
 Euro Area 187, 191, 193
 influence of policies 195–199
 model 193–195
 net capital outflow 191–193, *200*
 short run model 431–436
Laspeyres index 46–47
law of one price 183–184
learning by doing 277
legal systems 278
Lehman Brothers 631, 633, 639
lender of last resort 637–638
Lenin, Vladimir 121
leverage 108–109, 631
liabilities, uncounted 505
life-cycle hypothesis 584–588
Liikanen Review 641
liquid preference theory 348–350
 income, money demand and 352–353
 and monetary policy 350–351,
  353–354
liquidity 98
 constraints *see* borrowing constraints
 crisis 637
 trap 382–383
Lithuania 50
Lloyds Banking Group 639
LM curve 332–333
 AD 389–391
 Great Depression 376
 money demand 352–353
 money markets 348–355
 and Mundell–Fleming model
  396–398, 409
 quantity equation 354–355
 shifts: monetary policy 361–363
loanable funds
 IS curve interpretation 345–348
 market for 84–86, 193–194
 supply and demand equilibrium
  84–86
loans, bailout 473, 556, 642–643
long-run equilibrium 371–373
long-run fluctuations
 AS vertical curve 317–318

Mundell–Fleming model 425–428
 and short-run fluctuations, compared
  312–313, 320–322
lottery prizes, US and EU comparison
  575
Lucas, Robert E., Jr. 18, 265, 447
Lucas critique 477–478
Luddites 289, 290
Luxembourg 43–44, 221

Maastricht criteria 283, 543
Maastricht Treaty 526–527, 557
MacDonald's Big Mac purchasing
  power parity (PPP) 185–186
macroeconomics
 function of data 23
 important lessons 647–650
 important unsolved questions
  650–655
 study of 3–6
Malta 534, 549
Malthus, Thomas Robert 258–259
marginal product of capital (MPK) 71
 and capital demand 69–70
 Cobb–Douglas production function
  72–73, 74
 net 274–275
marginal product of labour (MPL)
  67–68, *70*
 Cobb–Douglas production function
  72–74
 and labour demand 68–69
marginal propensity to consume (MPC)
  78, 90, 568
 Keynesian cross 334, 338–339
marginal rate of substitution 576–577
market clearing 17
medium of exchange 98
menu costs
 of expected inflation 138
 of hyperinflation 141
Mexico
 Big Mac purchasing power parity
  (PPP) 186
 financial crisis (1994–95) 414–415
microeconomics 19–20
microfinance 629–630
military spending 88, *89*
minimum-wage laws 208–210
models
 function of 12–16
 microeconomics 19–20
 multitude of 16–17
 see also specific models
Modigliani, Franco 18, 572
 life-cycle hypothesis 584–588
monetarists 483
monetary base 109–110
 changes (open-market operations)
  111–113
 US quantitative easing and 113–115
monetary neutrality 147

monetary policy 101
    conventional, in financial crises
        636–637
    effect on interest rates 350–351
    and fiscal policy interaction 363–365,
        391–392
    fixed exchange rates 408–409
    floating exchange rates 401–402
    government debt 519
    instruments of 111–115
    IS-LM model 350–351, 353–354,
        361–365, 391–392
    and liquid preference theory
        350–351, 353–354
    rules of 483–484
    Taylor rule 484–485
Monetary Policy Committee (MPC),
    UK 101, 367, 382, 490, 491
monetary transmission mechanism
    362–363
monetary union *see* common currency
    areas; Euro Area; European
    Monetary Union (EMU)
money
    circular flow of 24–25, *62*
    constant velocity of 125, 126, 354
    cost of holding 134
    demand function 124–125
    demand *LM* curve 352–353
    functions of 98
    future 134–136
    income velocity of 124
    and prices 126–127, 134–136,
        377–379
    seigniorage 128–130
    transaction velocity of 123
    types of 99–101
    see also quantity theory of money
money demand
    liquid preference theory 352–353
    nominal interest rate and 134–136
money growth
    and inflation 126–127, 649
    and inflation tax, Island of Yap
        129–130
money hypothesis, Great Depression
    377–379
    destabilizing effects of deflation
        377–379
    shock to *LM* curve 376
    stabilizing effects of deflation 377
money markets
    and *LM* curve 348–355
    Mundell–Fleming model 396–398
money multiplier 110
money supply
    Cagan model 150–152
    control of 101–102
    measurement 102–104
    model 109–110
    role of banks 105–109
    role of central banks 109–117
    theory of liquid preference 348–350
    vs interest rate 367–368

Moore's law 284, 285
moral hazards 214, 627
Morgan Stanley 633
mortgage-backed securities: financial
    crisis (2008–9) 87, 381–383,
        631–634, 635
mortgages 79, 87
    fixed *vs* variable rates 139
    and real interest rate 617–618
    subprime borrowers 381–383, 618,
        623, 630–631
MPC *see* marginal propensity to
    consume; Monetary Policy
    Committee, UK
MPK *see* marginal product of capital
MPL *see* marginal product of labour
multipliers
    government purchases 337–339
    money 110
    taxes 339, *340*
Mundell, Robert 18, 393, 533–534
Mundell–Fleming model 395–399
    changing price level 425–428
    devaluation 409
    differentials 412–414
    fixed exchange rate 467
    fixed prices 406
    floating exchange rate 467
    goods market 395–396, *397*
    government debt 508
    IS curve 395–396, *397*
    and *IS-LM* model 393–394, *399*,
        431–433, 437
    LM curve 396–398, 409
    money market 396–398
    policy effects 400, 404, 410–411
    small open economy with perfect
        capital mobility 395, 399
mutual funds 626

NAFTA 414
NAIRU *see* non-accelerating inflation
    rate of unemployment
national income 61–63
    accounts 34–41
    accounts identity 36–37, 84–85,
        157–159
    distributed to factors of production
        65–77
    division of 70–71
national savings 84–85
natural level of output 371, *372*
    growth promotion in 650–651
natural rate of unemployment 202–204
natural-rate hypothesis 461–462
neoclassical model of investment 602
net capital outflow 158, 191–195
    shifts 197–198, *200*
net exports 36–37
    role of 156–157
    schedule 396, *397*
net factor income from abroad (NFIA)
    161–162

net marginal production of capital
    274–275
net national product (NNP) 42
Netherlands
    consumption 83
    corporation tax 608
    current account 163
    EMU membership 534
    GDP 38, *39*
    intra-EU trade 549
    sacrifice ratio 457
    unemployment 8, 221
Nevins, Alan 215
Newton, Isaac 288
Nickell, Stephen 217–218
NNP *see* net national product
Nobel Prize winners 18–19
nominal exchange rates 173–174
    determinants of 181–183
    inflation and 182–183
    and real exchange rates 173–175
    see also purchasing power parity
        (PPP)
nominal gross domestic product (GDP)
    31–32, 126
nominal interest rates 79, 133
    19th century 133
    cost of holding money 134
    Fisher equation 130–132
    future money and current prices
        134–136
    and inflation 131–132, 134–136
    and money demand 134–136
nominal variables 147
non-accelerating inflation rate of
    unemployment (NAIRU) 213,
        452, 457
non-profit institutions serving
    households (NPISH) 35, 36
Norges Bank 492
normal good 578–579
North Atlantic Free Trade Treaty
    Agreement (NAFTA) 414
Northern Rock 633
Norway 83
    ERM 421, 422
    GDP 38, *40*
    income per person 233
    independent monetary policy 422
    Norges Bank 492
    unemployment insurance system
        206–207
    unemployment rate 8
NPISH *see* non-profit institutions
    serving households

Obama, Barack 394, 425, 518
    spending plan 342–343
Office for National Statistics (ONS),
    UK 33–34, 50
oil prices 218, 282, 326–328, 451,
    453–454
O'Keefe, David 129

Okun, Arthur 308
Okun's Law 307–310
open economies 153–155
  globalization 155–156
  international flows of capital and
    goods 156–164
  large *see* large open economies
  model *see* Mundell-Fleming model
  net capital outflow 191–193
  small *see* small open economies
open-market operations 101–102,
  111–113
Organization of Petroleum Exporting
  Countries (OPEC) 218, 282,
  326–328, 453–454
  Phillips curve 451
outside lag 473

Paasche index 46–47
parental bequests 516
pensions 140, 276
permanent-income hypothesis 589–591
Phelps, Edmund 18, 451
Phillips curve 449–463
  adaptive expectations 451–452
  AS curve and 449–451
  causes of rising and falling inflation
    452
  disinflation 456–461
  history 451
  hysteresis and challenge to natural
    rate hypothesis 461–462
  inflation inertia 451–452
  rational expectations 458–460
  sacrifice ratio 456–458, 460–461
  trade-off between inflation and
    unemployment 455–456, 650
physical capital 276, 546
Pigou effect 377
planned expenditure 333–334
Poland 522, 609
policy makers
  distrust of 480–481
  and financial crisis (2008–9) 636
  role of 493
policy trilemma 422, *423*
  EMU 423–424
political business cycle 481
Ponzi, Charles 528
Ponzi finance 528
population growth 253–260
  effects of 255–256
  international comparison 257–258
  Kremerian model 259–260
  Malthusian model 258–259
  steady state with 254–255
Portugal
  bailout loans 473, 556, 560
  Euro Area crisis 560, 643
  government debt 501
pound sterling 321–322
precautionary saving 587–588

Prescott, Edward 18
price(s)
  Big Mac 185–186
  current 134–136
  discrimination 536
  falling *see* deflation
  and inflation 126–127, 134–136
  levels 126, 138, 425–428
  and money 126–127, 134–136,
    377–379
  and real GDP 17, 33
  shocks 324
  stickiness 313, 439–440
  stickiness *vs* flexibility 17, 312–313,
    314
  see also hyperinflation
primary budget deficit 523–524
private capital 276, 278
private saving 85, 276
production
  just-in-time 620
  smoothing 618
  total 63–64
  see also factors of production
production function
  and factors of production 63–64, 84,
    126
  total factor productivity (TFP) 281,
    296–297, 298, *299*
  universities and firms 287–289
  see also Cobb–Douglas production
    function
productivity
  total factor (TFP) 281, 296–297,
    298, *299*
  UK trends 218–219
  as wage determinant 76–77
profit(s) 67
  accounting 71
  economic 71
property rights 173, 279, 280
  intellectual 280
protectionist trade policies 180–181
Prudential Regulation Authority, UK
  642
public capital 276, 278
public saving 85, 275–276
public sector net debt 506–507
pull of instant gratification 594–596
purchasing power parity (PPP)
  183–186

quantitative easing and exploding
  monetary base, US 113–115
quantity equation
  as AD 315
  LM curve interpretation 354–355
  money demand function and
    124–125
  transactions and 123
quantity theory of money 122–127
  central bank role 126

  demand function 124–125
  income 124
  and nominal interest rate 134–136
  prices and inflation 126–127
  transactions 123, 124

random-walk hypothesis 592–594
  stock markets and 612–613
rational expectations 458–460
RBS *see* Royal Bank of Scotland
Reagan, Ronald 511, 512
real exchange rates 174–175, 194, *195*
  determinants of 176–177
  influence of policy 177–179
  and nominal exchange rates 173–175
  and purchasing power parity (PPP)
    184–185
  and trade balance 175–176
real gross domestic product (GDP)
  chained-volume measures of 32–34
  Euro Area 552–553
  and nominal GDP 31–32, 126
  per person, EU 42–44
  per person, UK 9–10
  policy implications 648
  and prices 17, 33
  seasonal adjustment 44–45
  stock market changes 610–611, 612
real interest rates 79
  and consumption 579–581
  ex ante 132–133
  ex post 132–133
  Fisher equation 130–132
  housing demand and 617–618
  and investment 178–179, 620
real money balances 124–125
real rental price of capital 70
real variables 147
real wage 69
  cyclical behaviour of 443–444
  flexibility 544–545, 551
  labour productivity as determinant
    of 76–77
real wage rigidity
  efficiency-wage theories 212–214
  minimum-wage laws 208–210
  structural unemployment and
    207–215
  unions and collective bargaining
    211–212
recessions 634
  business cycle and 303–308
  'double-dip' 384
  Japan (1990s) 380–381
Red Cross 99
refinancing rate 111–113
regulation of financial institutions
  641–642
  failure 635–636
rental price of capital 603–604
repurchasing agreement/repo 111, 112
research and development 288–289

reserve ratio 111–112
reserve requirements 113
reserve-deposit ratio 109–110
reserves 105–106
residential investment 601, 615–618
    changes in demand 617–618
    flow supply 616–617
    stock equilibrium 616–617
    see also housing market; mortgages
retail price index (RPI) 48–51
revaluation 409
Revenue Act 1932, US 375–376
Ricardian equivalence 512–517
    basic logic 513
    borrowing constraints 514
    consumers 514–515
    future generations 414–415
    myopia 514
    parental bequests 516
    taxes 514–515, 517
    traditional view and 516–517
Ricardo, David 272, 513, 517
Riksbank 491–492
risk aversion 626
risk sharing 625–626
Robinson, James 279
Rogers, Will 97
Romania 9, 50, 522
Romer, David 273
Royal Bank of Scotland (RBS) 639
RPI *see* retail price index

Sachs, Jeffrey 273
sacrifice ratio 456–458, 460–461
Samuelson, Paul 359, 610
Sargent, Thomas 459
savings/savings rate
    economic growth and 243–246,
        274–276
    elderly 587–588
    encouraging 595–596
    fiscal policy effects 86–92, 195–196
    international capital flows and trade
        balance 157–159
    international comparison 244–246
    Japanese 583–584
    large open economies 195–196, *197*
    market for loanable funds 84–86,
        193–194
    national 84–85
    private 85, 276
    public 85, 275–276
    small open economies 164–173
    steady state 243–246, 248, *249*,
        251–253, 274, 275
    tax effects 90
Schumpeter, Joseph 289, 290
Schwartz, Anna 376
seasonal adjustment, GDP 44–45
sectoral shifts 205, 218
secular stagnation and consumption
    puzzle 570–572

seigniorage 128–130
services *see* goods and services
shadow banks 638, 639–641
Shaw, George Bernard 647
Shiller, Robert 137
shocks
    AD 323–324, 365–366
    AS 324–325, *326*
    asymmetric demand 537–541
    asymmetric supply 541
    definition 323
    money hypothesis: *LM* curve 376
    oil prices 218, 282, 326–328, 451
    price 324
    spending hypothesis: *IS* curve
        374–376
    symmetric demand 552–553
    symmetric macroeconomic 547
    technology-driven 222
shoe-leather cost of inflation 138
short-run equilibrium 371–373
short-run fluctuations 318–320
    AS horizontal curve 318–320
    IS-LM model 360–363
    large open economies 431–436
    and long-run fluctuations, compared
        312–313, 320–322
    Mundell–Fleming model 425–428
Singapore 298
single currency *see* common currency
        areas; Euro Area
size
    of government debt 501–503
    of international black economy
        30–31
    restriction of financial institutions 641
skilled *vs* unskilled workers 223
Slovakia 534, 549
Slovenia 534, 549, 609
small open economies
    capital mobility 164–165, 395, 399
    fixed exchange rates 404–411
    floating exchange rates 399–404
    model 165–166
    policy 166–169
    policy evaluation 169–173
    saving and investment 164–173
    special case 192–193, 467
    trade balance 166–169
    world interest rate 164–165
    see also Mundell–Fleming model
Smith, Adam 153, 272, 273, 279,
        567, 628
social conventions 100–101
social costs of inflation 138–140
Solow, Robert 18, 284
Solow growth model
    balanced growth 269–270
    capital accumulation 235–246
    convergence 270–271
    factor accumulation *vs* production
        efficiency 271–272
    Golden Rule level of capital 246–253

population growth 253–258
savings rate 274–276, 583, 595
technological progress in 266–269
Soros, George 421, 422
South Korea 298
Soviet Union, break-up of 143
Spain
    EMU membership 534
    Euro Area crisis 560, 643
    GDP *41*
    sacrifice ratio 457
    unemployment 462
speculative attacks 419–422
    European exchange rate mechanism
        (1992) 420–422
speculative bubble 630
spending hypothesis, Great Depression
        374–376
SPG *see* Stability and Growth Pact
Stability and Growth Pact (SGP)
        526–527, 557–559
stabilization 518
stabilization policy
    active *vs* passive 472–480
    central bank independence 487–488
    forecasting 474–477
    historical record 478
    implementation lags 472–474
    inflation targeting 485–487, 489–492
    Lucas critique 477–478
    monetary policy 483–484
    policy makers 480–481
    rule *vs* discretion debate 480–487
    time inconsistency 481–483
    uncertainty 493
stagflation (1970s) 326–328
stagnation and consumption puzzle
        570–572
standards of living
    convergence 270–271
    goods and services 648
    international comparison *234*
'standing on shoulders' effect 288–289
steady states
    capital stock and 237–246
    numerical example 240–242
    population growth 254–255
    savings rate 243–246, 248, *249*,
        251–253, 274, 275
    technological progress 267, 268–269
    see also Golden Rule steady state
'stepping on toes' effect 288–289
sticky prices 313
    model 439–440
    vs flexible prices 17, 312–313, 314
sticky wage model 440–444
stock markets 609–613, 625
    as economic indicator 610–612
    efficient markets hypothesis 612–613
    and financial crisis (2008–9) 384
    Keynesian 'beauty contest' 613
    US crash (1929) 374–375, 475
stock-out avoidance 619

stocks, defined 625
store of value, money as 98
strategic bequest motive 516
structural unemployment *see* real wage rigidity
subprime borrowers 381–383, 618, 623, 630–631
substitution effect 580
supply
  goods and services 64
  see also aggregate supply (AS); money supply
supply and demand
  capital accumulation 235–237
  loanable funds 84–86
  model 313–314
Sustainable Investment Rule 527–528
SWATCH 290
Sweden 83
  ERM 421, 422
  GDP *40*
  independent monetary policy 422
  inflation targeting 491
  intra-EU trade 550
  Riksbank 491–492
  sacrifice ratio 457
  tax rate 512
Switzerland
  GDP *39*
  watch industry 290
symmetric demand shocks 552–553
symmetric macroeconomic shocks 547

Taiwan 298
tax
  business fixed investment 608–609
  changes 360–361, *364*
  changes, permanent *vs* temporary 591
  consumption and 514–515, 591
  fiscal federalism 554–555
  fiscal policies 339, *340*, 360–361, *364*
  and incentives 510
  income *vs* consumption 276
  and inflation 128–130, 138
  intergenerational redistribution 514–515
  laws 138
  multipliers 339, *340*, 361
  Ricardian equivalence 514–515, 517
  and savings 90
  seigniorage 128–130
  smoothing 518
Taylor rule 484–485, 486–487
technological externality 277
technological progress 266–269, 270
  computer and information technology 284–285
  creative destruction 289–290
  economic growth and 267–269, 284–285, 296–297
  efficiency of labour 266–267
  labour-augmenting 267, *268*

policies to promote 280
  and population growth 259–260
  research and development 288–289
  shocks 222
  steady state with 267, 268–269
TED spread 632
terms of trade 22
Thaler, Richard 595
Thatcher, Margaret 5, 219, 220, 454
  disinflation 460–461
  income tax rate 511–512
  inflation rate 351
time inconsistency 481–483
  inflation and unemployment trade-off 496–499
Tobin, James 18–19, 233, 609
Tobin's *q* 609–612, 614, 617
total factor productivity (TFP) 281, 296–297, 298, *299*
trade
  deficit 158–159, 169–172
  free 272–273
  surplus 158–159
  terms of 22
trade balance
  bilateral 161
  current account balance and 160–164
  fiscal policies 166–168
  investment demand shifts 168–169
  investment and savings 157–159
  real exchange rates 175–176
  small open economies 166–169
trade integration 547–548
  Europe 548–550
trade policies
  and exchange rates 180–181
  and fixed exchange rates 409–410
  and floating exchange rates 402–404
  import restriction 196–197, *199*
  protectionist 180–181
transaction velocity of money 123
transfer payments 35, 81
transitory income 589–590, 591

uncounted liabilities 505
unemployment 202–204
  benefit systems 205–207, 220, 223, 226
  business cycle and 307–310
  demographic variation 216–217, 218
  discouraged worker effect 217, 221
  duration 215–216
  European Social Model 226
  European trends *202*, 221–227
  frictional 204–207
  and inflation, Europe 6–9
  and inflation trade-offs 455–456, 496–499, 650
  insurance 205–206
  life satisfaction 210
  measurement of rate 52–55
  natural rate of 202–204

non-accelerating inflation rate of (NAIRU) 213
  productivity 218–219
  sectoral shifts 218
  structural *see* real wage rigidity
  Thatcher disinflation 460–461
  transition in and out of labour force 220–221
  UK trends 11–12, 217–221, *309*
unexpected inflation 139–140
unilateral transfers 161–162
unions 211–212, 223
  decline, UK 219–220
unit of account, money as 98
United Kingdom (UK)
  black economy 31
  consumption growth *306*
  contraction (1920s) 321–322
  corporation tax 608
  current account/trade deficits 163
  economic growth 305
  economic history 4–6, 9–12
  ERM participation 421–422
  financial crisis (2008–9) 630–631, 638–639
  GDP 37–38
  government debt 501–502
  income tax rates 511–512
  Independent Commission on Banking 641
  independent monetary policy 422
  inflation rate (1970s) 351
  inflation and unemployment 453–455
  investment growth *307*
  labour-force participation rate 54–55
  OPEC-induced fluctuations *326, 327*
  real wage determinant 76–77
  recessions 303–304, 307
  Thatcher disinflation 460–461
  unemployment trends 11–12, 217–221, *309*
  unions, decline of 219–220
  wars and interest rates (1730–1920) 88–90
  youth unemployment 209, 216, 217
  see also Bank of England
United States (US)
  black economy 31
  Conference Board Index 310–311
  corporation tax 608
  decline in GDP growth 366–367
  Dodd–Frank Act 2010 640-1
  Federal Deposit Insurance Corporation (FDIC) 638, 639, 640
  financial crisis (2008–9) 113–115, 381–384, 630–631
  Ford Motor Company 214–215
  government purchases: Obama spending plan 342–343
  growing wealth gap 75
  income tax rates 511–512
  inflation and unemployment 6–9

United States (US) *(Continued)*
  lottery prizes 575
  minimum wage 208–209
  quantitative easing and exploding
    monetary base 113–115
  Revenue Act 1932 375–376
  stock market crash (1929) 374–375,
    475
  see also Great Depression
  trade deficit 169–172
  Vietnam War 591
  yuan controversy 424–425
United States (US) Federal Reserve 101
  financial crisis (2008–9) 113–115,
    381, 384, 635, 638
  founding of 643
  inflation targeting 492
  as lender of last resort 637–638
universities: research and development
  287–289
used goods 27

value of economy *see* gross domestic
  product (GDP)
variable-rate mortgages 139

variables
  endogenous 13
  exogenous 13
  nominal 147
  real 147
  using functions to express 16
velocity of money
  constant 125, 126, 354
  income 124
  transaction 123
Volker Rule 641

wages
  Ford Motor Company 214–215
  sticky wage model 440–444
  see also real wage; real wage rigidity
Warner, Andrew 273
wars
  economic disruption and
    hyperinflation 142–143
  interest rates (1730–1920) 88–90
  tax surcharge, US 591
watch technology 289–290
wealth-shift, consumption effects of
  586–587

Williams, Geraldine 575
women's labour participation 55, 217,
  225
work in progress inventories 619
World Bank 258
world interest rate 164–166

Yap, Island of 129–130
youth unemployment
  Europe 224
  France 226–227
  UK 209, 216, 217
yuan controversy 424–425
Yunus, Muhammad 629–630

Zimbabwe, hyperinflation in 146